RAILROADS
TRIUMPHANT

RAILROADS TRIUMPHANT

The Growth, Rejection, and Rebirth of a Vital American Force

ALBRO MARTIN

New York   Oxford
OXFORD UNIVERSITY PRESS
1992

Oxford University Press

Oxford   New York   Toronto
Delhi   Bombay   Calcutta   Madras   Karachi
Petaling Jaya   Singapore   Hong Kong   Tokyo
Nairobi   Dar es Salaam   Cape Town
Melbourne   Auckland

and associated companies in
Berlin   Ibadan

Library of Congress Cataloging-in-Publication Data
Martin, Albro.
Railroads triumphant: the growth, rejection, and rebirth
of a vital American force / Albro Martin.
p.   cm.
Includes index.
ISBN 0-19-503853-3
1. Railroads—United States—History.   I. Title.
HE2751.M35   1992
385′.0973—dc20   90-7845   CIP

9 8 7 6 5 4 3 2 1

Printed in the United States of America

In Memory of
John M. Budd
1907–1979

and to the honor
of countless others,
living and dead,
who kept the faith,
this book is dedicated.

Preface

This book is an effort to resolve what I have come to think of as the Grand Paradox in the history of American material civilization. How was it that an innovation as clearly revolutionary as the steam railway in its potential to do so many things better and to do so many other things that could not be done at all without railroads came to be "despised and rejected" by a politically contentious people who made it the chief scapegoat of their discontents? Why did the making of basic business decisions become a matter for political rather than economic resolution on the railroads and few other places in American society? Why did a great people, watching the cost of transportation rise ever higher in real economic terms, fail to see that less efficient modes and methods of hauling goods and people were flourishing under laws repressive of the railroads' efforts to adjust to new conditions? Why did we fail to heed the warnings of two generations of railroad leaders and, finally, another generation of transportation experts who were beginning to adjust to the new realities, until disaster was on the doorstep of Congress? What did it take to revive the faithful old servant, how complete has been his convalescence, and how well prepared is he for a future that depends upon his vigorous rebirth?

I do not pretend that these questions are answered adequately in this book, nor even that there *are* answers that will satisfy everyone. "It all depends upon whose ox is gored," and, as the railroads found out from their beginnings, no big change in the ordering of human affairs takes place without a lot of oxen being gored. I have tried, however, to perform the historian's most delicate task—selection of the main topics—and his second most difficult—attribution of cause and effect—as sincerely as I know how. After all, I am as anxious as anyone to know just what happened. I have never had any material or family interest in railroading and have never worked for one. I do not consider myself a "railroad historian," but rather one who believes that history can be made coherent only with a rich fund of examples from the past, and that the railroads have contributed more, over a longer period, to such a fund than any other social institution, with the possible exception of politics itself.

Academic historians may frown at the absence of foot- or endnotes to this book. I have not the years left that it would take to document in the traditional manner a work that ranges so widely, nor my publisher the time, patience, or money to include it in the book if I did. Only trains like the *Twentieth Century Limited* and books like Robert W. Fogel's on slavery have the opportunity to come out in two sections! My Comments on the Sources should prove a manageable reading list for anyone who wishes to find out for himself. If much of my material is anecdotal, which seems to bother academic historians, I would reply that since events that really happened, especially to the narrator, are what make some of our best novels, short stories, plays, and films live, it just might be that anecdotes can contribute zest to the reading of otherwise unappealing subjects, just as the lack of them can make soporifics of the most engaging topics. History has fared poorly since somebody decided that its chief thrust was as "social science" rather than as literature. Wit and passion are what make things happen and they are what make the story of those happenings history.

The time has finally passed when an author had to apologize in his preface for having any kind words to say about railroads. Whereas some may dismiss this book as mere "polemic," I insist that it is no such thing. The pudding of American railroad policy has been stirred, steamed, sauced, eaten, and found inedible. The subject is, or should be, no longer controversial. I have nothing to ask of the powers that be save that the spirit of enterprise which the steam railway has traditionally called forth in men and women should be allowed to continue its good work, and I have no doubt we shall be the better for it, in body as well as in spirit. "Railroad history" has been bowdlerized, prostituted, and—worst of all—ignored for the most part, during my lifetime. Rarely has more than a weak "yes, but . . ." been the substance of serious efforts to untie the Grand Paradox, and I think the reason for that is very simply the scholar's adjuration to "treat both sides of the subject." (Woodrow Wilson is said to have remarked, when reminded of this duty, "Yes, there *are* two sides to every question: the *right side,* and the *wrong side.*") I was reminded of this old imperative when one of our most prominent business historians, who made a good thing of my findings in my first book, *Enterprise Denied* (1971), recently referred to it as "biased." Now, I take it that "biased" is not so bad as "prejudiced" and that a proper bias can make for a more effective work. I hope he meant it that way, but I fear he did not. Well, we cannot expect others to fight our battles for us. That book is still selling nineteen years after publication, and its author was once introduced at a historians' conference somewhat excessively as "the man who made deregulation academically respectable." If this present book does half as well, I shall have been well rewarded.

Great Maple   A. M.
Bethel, Connecticut
April 27, 1990

Acknowledgments

Financial assistance in researching and writing this book were generously provided by the Harvard University Graduate School of Business Administration, in the form of faculty research grants, and by Bradley University, as part of the research funds assigned to the Oglesby Professor of the American Heritage, of which chair I had the honor to be the first occupant. At Harvard I benefited from my close association with Alfred D. Chandler, Jr., and Thomas K. McCraw (to whom I still owe an explanation of the long-short-haul controversy). At Bradley my work was enthusiastically supported by John Hitt, then the provost, and by Max H. Kele, dean of the College of Liberal Arts and Sciences, for all of which I am most grateful. The Baker Library of the Harvard Business School, one of the finest collections of American economic and business history anywhere, is sadly underutilized but a pleasure to work in, and the staff were very accommodating. I was also granted full library privileges at Yale University during the writing of the last several chapters, and again encountered every kindness. As the shadows lengthen, one comes to appreciate the efficient paging service of Sterling Library as a substitute for prowling in the stacks. The reference collections of the libraries of Columbia University, Bradley University, Western Connecticut University, and the public libraries of New York City and Danbury and Bethel, Connecticut, also welcomed me regularly.

There are so many people with whom I have discussed my topic over the decades that I could not possibly list all of them. To the resourcefulness of Don Hofsommer, longtime secretary of the Lexington Group of Transportation Historians, who has arranged annual visits to various railroad operations and related institutions, I owe much of what I have learned about American railroads in the modern age. To all of the officers and men and women of those railroads whom I have had the pleasure of meeting over the years, I express my appreciation and renew my best wishes for the bright future of American railroads and those responsible for them. I especially thank Frank N. Wilner, of the Association of American Railroads, who allowed me to read the text of his then forthcoming article on railroad labor legislation. I am grateful to my valued friend, Professor Maury Klein, a foremost railroad historian, for reading and commenting copiously on the entire manuscript.

I received enthusiastic cooperation from several persons in assembling the illustrations for this book, among them Don Snoddy, of the Union Pacific Museum; John Hankey, archivist, and Anne Calhoun, assistant archivist, of the B. & O. Railroad Museum; Richard Bressler, chairman, and Allan R. Boyce, senior vice president, Burlington Resources, Inc.; Kim Forman, Burlington Northern; G. William Schafer III, Norfolk Southern Corp.; and John Stine, archivist, Smithsonian Institution (retired). For this valuable service, much thanks. Only a longtime, very good friend could be prevailed upon to give an author's galley proofs a second reading, and I was fortunate to have one in James H. McKendrick, who made many useful suggestions.

"Every author needs an editor," as I used to say to contributors to the *Business History Review* when I was editing it, and I have certainly had one in Sheldon Meyer of Oxford University Press. He has patiently waited, longer than I will admit and longer, I suspect, than he can remember, for this work to be finished, and read and commented on all the chapters as I finished them. Whatever the merits of this book, they would have been the less without Sheldon. I also had the pleasure of working with Karen Wolny, Susan Meigs, and Scott Lenz at Oxford, who helped to turn the manuscript into a book.

I am responsible for all of the factual material in this book. As far as I can tell, everything cited as an event actually happened, at one time and in one place or another. If it did not, I am sure that "It *could* have happened." *Se non è vero, è ben trovato.*

Contents

Illustrations and Maps

Railroads
Triumphant

CHAPTER 1

Nerves of Copper, Arteries of Iron

> They build not merely roads of earth and stone, as of old, but they build iron roads; and, not content with horses of flesh, they are building horses of iron, such as never faint nor lose their breath.
>
> Anon., ca. 1840

In the Beginning

He was an old man, and very tired. The babble of the crowd annoyed him, and the long-winded speeches seemed foolish to one who had heard the budding American talent for oratory exercised in much more important causes. It was July 4, 1828, and it was hot. It was *always* hot in Baltimore on the Fourth of July, at least by midday. The place for him was the cool shade of his veranda at Carrollton. But he could not disappoint them, these men and women who were celebrating what everybody said would turn out to be a historic day, not only for Baltimore and for Maryland, but for the whole United States. After all, it was not nearly so hot as that July day in Philadelphia fifty-two years ago. And to tell the truth, he rather enjoyed playing the role of Baltimore's most famous citizen, although he sometimes suspected that he was more of a curiosity than a celebrity.

A curiosity he certainly was, and a national one. He was the very last of that celebrated group of men who had voted to declare the thirteen British colonies in America free and independent states. Yes, they were all gone but him: from the noble Washington to the pompous John Hancock to Button Gwinett (what's in a name, indeed!) to that odd pair who had become the second and third presidents of the United States. Strange how time and the arrival of old age can bring former adversaries together. John Adams and Thomas Jefferson, so at odds in their interpretation of the Constitution, had ended their lives in firm agreement that nothing was more important than strengthening the great union against all dangers. But how dramatically *their* lives had ended! Within hours of each other, on July 4, 1826, exactly fifty years to the day since the adoption of the Declaration of Independence! Old Tom

3

had always had a good eye for the galleries—but *Adams?* Speaking of
Adams, where was that son of his, John Quincy, President of the United
States, at least until the next fourth of March? Why, doing something
more important than breaking ground for anything as risky as a "railway." He was at Georgetown, in the District of Columbia, turning the
first earth for the new Chesapeake & Ohio Canal which, like Baltimore's new railroad, was to join the navigable waters of Chesapeake
Bay with those of the Ohio River at some mangy frontier settlement
called Wheeling. That ought to show the citizens of Baltimore just
where their railroad project stood in the grand national plan.

His companion in the barouche in which he was riding was saying
something to him. Yes, General, he replied to General Sam Smith, one
of Maryland's two senators. Yes, he understood that when they arrived
at the spot where the first stone of the Baltimore & Ohio Railroad was
to be laid, they would stand and wait until the long procession following
them had passed and taken up their positions. There were forty-seven
groups in the procession, the old man reflected wearily: every trade
and craft in Baltimore still carrying out the old medieval guild custom
of showing itself off at any opportunity. The Masons, hogging most of
the attention as usual, would do the actual laying of the stone, after
much mumbo jumbo with their instruments to ascertain that the stone
was "well-formed, true and trusty." But the blacksmiths had written a
good part for themselves, too. They had hammered out the pick, spade,
stone-hammer, and trowel with which the stone was to be laid. The
blacksmiths' delegation would present him with these tools (only the
spade, actually), and he, Charles Carroll of Carrollton, last surviving
signer of the Declaration of Independence, would turn the first spade
of earth to begin the construction of Baltimore's daring (some said desperate) effort to establish a practical trade route to the interior of the
United States.

He was glad for the pavilion they had erected at the site, for the
sun was beating down by ten o'clock when the last of the marchers
arrived. Pity they had not adopted clever Ben Franklin's idea of setting
the clock ahead one hour in the summer. Many people might say that
what they were about to do was far more foolish than daylight saving
time. But they *had* to do something. Baltimore, which had been little
more than a village in 1776, had prospered mightily since, especially
at times during the Napoleonic wars. (Piracy, like printing money, can
be extremely profitable when legalized by letters of marque or bank
charters!) But that was all changing rapidly. New York City had been
the first to see that the future of the United States lay to the West, in
the vast interior where so many of her people yearned to go, and not
on the seas. And so New York had built her Erie Canal, which the well-
heeled burghers of Philadelphia had recently decided to imitate.

Well, Baltimore could afford no canal—certainly not one across
the Alleghenies!—that much was certain. Perhaps wagons with flanged

wheels, running on iron rails, could succeed in trade across the mountains, where all else had failed. Such wagons, pulled by horses, were able to carry much heavier loads than conventional wagons running on ordinary roads. And from England had recently come the stirring news that men were planning "trials" of steam engines on wheels that could move themselves and a cargo. They had been doing some amazing things with steam in his declining years. Men who had laughed at Robert Fulton had subsequently spent a fortune to break the monopoly of steam navigation on the Hudson River that Fulton and his backers had won. Maybe his daring fellow citizens of Baltimore were not so crazy, after all.

The old man's musings were interrupted by a handshake from John B. Morris, a director of the new railroad company and a member of the committee of arrangements, who was welcoming him to the place of honor under the pavilion. Soon the great crowd (the newspapers would claim fifty thousand) was whipping off its hats and caps as the Masonic chaplain offered the prayer. Then Morris, as the old man had feared, launched into a speech that threatened to be a long one. Meanwhile he, the curiosity, stood by, as he had on so many previous occasions, quaint as ever in the old-fashioned knee breeches that he still refused to give up for the voluminous trousers that had long since replaced the costume of his day. He enjoyed what Morris had to say about him, although he had heard it so many times before. Today there seemed to be a real connection between the ritual praise of an old man and the event that was about to take place. Perhaps there was. Not a soul that day in Independence Hall could have guessed where their actions would lead. And now here he was, fifty-two years later, helping to start a revolution in human affairs that might well prove as profound as the adoption of the Declaration of Independence. Was not this thing he was about to do with the spade just as important, after all, to the new generation as that business with the pen had been to his?

And now, Morris was handing him the spade and taking his arm to lead him to the spot where ground was to be broken. He pushed his old-fashioned buckled shoe down on the spade with all his might, and smiled broadly at the ovation that greeted the clump of sod he turned up. It was a time for him to say something memorable, if he was ever to do so. He looked at the thousands of eyes turned upon him, most of which would see—as he almost certainly would not—this new undertaking in the moment of its triumph. Momentous events, he sensed, are *always* the most momentous in history at the time they are happening, for the past has had its day and the present is what the future is made of. Clearly and firmly, in a voice that had stood up well through ninety-one North American winters, he told them what he now believed so deeply: "I consider what I have just now done to be among the most important acts of my life, second only to my signing the Declaration of Independence, if indeed, it be even second to that."

Figure 1.1   Charles Carroll of Carrollton about to dig the first shovelful of earth as the leading citizens of Baltimore prepare to lay the first stone of the Baltimore & Ohio Railroad, July 4, 1828. From a painting by Stanley M. Arthurs for the Fair of the Iron Horse, produced by the B. & O. in Baltimore in the summer of 1928 to celebrate the completion of its first century as the first American common-carrier railroad. *(Courtesy of Baltimore & Ohio Railroad Museum)*

Before the Land Was Ours

When the members of the First Congress traveled to the capital at New York in the spring of 1789 to begin the government under the new Constitution, they went by means that were no faster and no more comfortable than those by which the Roman senators had journeyed from their villas to Rome almost two thousand years before. Not until April 6, more than a month late, had a quorum assembled to count the ballots of the Electoral College and declare General George Washington the duly elected President of the United States. That gentleman, traveling by coach as befitted his new rank, found the going slow over the muddy roads, and it was April 30 before he was on hand and ready to take the oath of office.

If the art of shipbuilding and the science of navigation had greatly improved the quality of travel on the open seas since Roman times, inland travel was still caught in the vicious circle that had always plagued it. As long as travel was limited to the expensive, five- to seven-mile-an-hour progress of the saddle horse or the coach, and as long as goods had to be hauled by the even slower and more expensive team and wagon, there would be as little traveling and hauling as the people could get by with. Under these circumstances, there would be little interest in building better roads except on a few heavily traveled routes and, therefore, little travel at all outside the cities. In overwhelmingly agricultural America, this meant that all but a very few of the people were nearly rooted to the spot where they lived.

The United States of America in 1790 consisted of the original thirteen colonies, now "sovereign" states, lining the Atlantic seaboard from what would one day be Maine down to Georgia, and the Northwest Territory, the public domain towards which would-be settlers looked longingly. North of Boston and south of Richmond the population was so thinly distributed that the arrival of "civilization" could barely be said to have occurred at all. Although there were four million people living in the 888,000 square miles that comprised the thirteen United States in 1790, the nation was in reality a "shoestring republic," with few people living as much as a hundred miles from the coast.

There were several good reasons why the land was not yet ours. The Indians were still a fearsome obstacle to westward expansion. The British, who had discouraged westward expansion during the colonial era, still occupied strategic forts. Other nations still claimed large sections of the interior. But the chief obstacle was Nature herself. The thriving cities of Boston, New York, Philadelphia, and Baltimore had all grown up, not through trade with the interior but with their faces set across the Atlantic. Not many miles in from the coast the rolling farmland gives way to one of the most important geographic features of our planet: the Appalachian Mountain chain. With one important exception, not a single "gap" cleaves it, and beyond it, in 1790, lived barely one hundred thousand Americans.

But in the next two generations the great, flat, fertile Mississippi Valley would become a vital part of the national and the world economy. Before Charles Carroll died it would successfully challenge the conservative East for political control of the nation. In another generation, by an intricate series of imitative and innovative "internal improvements," founded on both public and private resources, the United States achieved the general outlines of a practical system of inland transporation: cheap, dependable, fast, able to serve virtually any point in the country without regard to its disadvantages of location, and available the year around.

Unsuccessful Imitation: The Turnpikes

Albert Gallatin, Thomas Jefferson's Secretary of the Treasury, was an island of support for federally sponsored "internal improvements" in an administration that took a narrow view of the central government's powers. In 1808, Gallatin reported to Congress that the nation sorely needed to create a link across the Appalachians with the major navigable bodies of water on their western side: the Ohio and Mississippi rivers and the Great Lakes.

Gallatin felt that the only solution lay in "artificial roads," by which he meant roads that were surveyed to have no more than a 5 percent grade (a rise of about 250 feet in a distance of 1 mile), that were ditched on the sides and crowned in the center for drainage purposes, and finished with crushed rock or gravel. Experience with turnpikes, as such toll-financed roads were called, gave Gallatin little room for enthusiasm, but he could see no other practical way of getting across the mountains.

Turnpike construction was on the increase at the time Gallatin wrote, although well-made roads were limited to those radiating from Boston, New York, and Philadelphia, and linking the more important populated places in New England. The South had few improved roads, and almost none that measured up to what Gallatin had in mind. Looking back, it is clear that turnpike promoters had had the good sense to select in 1792 the most promising route for their first venture: the heavily traveled route between the rich farming area around Lancaster, Pennsylvania and Philadelphia.

More road building followed in the next two decades, and after long arguments over which city should be favored by selection as the eastern terminal of a federally financed turnpike, the government finally decided in 1811 to build the National Road, popularly called the Cumberland Road, from Cumberland, Maryland, on the Potomac River, to Wheeling, on the Ohio. From that point the eager crowds of immigrants could float all the way to New Orleans, if they chose, and some of the earliest settlements in the Old Northwest (Ohio, Indiana, Illinois, and Missouri) were encouraged by the building of the National Road.

But if turnpikes made transporation *possible*, they did not make it *cheap*, and that was the reason for their failure. Even the Lancaster-Philadelphia turnpike, after taking longer and costing much more to build than anyone had expected, did not develop the volume of traffic that would have made it highly profitable. The reason was simple. Nearly all that the interior settlements had to ship east were bulky commodities of little value per unit of weight or volume, such as wheat and other food grains, corn, and pork. (Live cattle could make it on their own legs, but they lost much of their weight on the way despite the drovers' efforts to graze them on whatever farmer's meadows they passed.) Road haulage could only be had at rates per ton that exceeded by several times the market value of such commodities at eastern points.

So the settlers sent their high-value produce, consisting mostly of whiskey (concentrated grain!) and fur pelts, east by the National Road until it wore out, which, as with modern highways, happened far sooner than anyone had expected. And even before cheap transportation was available, high-value goods, like cutlery and firearms, were rumbling westward across the mountains by wagon. But farmers shipped their main produce down the Ohio and the Mississippi on flatboats and keelboats to New Orleans, and thence east by sailing vessel. This was the famous counterclockwise transportation pattern, which was grossly inefficient and made the South more important in the national trade pattern than was justified. The system was considerably moderated by the coming of the steamboat, but it remained for the railroad to replace it completely.

Partially Successful Innovation: The Steamboat

There was one river in the East that had been an important artery of commerce almost from the day in 1609 when Henry Hudson sailed up it as far as present-day Albany. By 1807 New York City was forging ahead in the cotton trade and in coastal shipping, pressing Philadelphia for first place among American cities. The Hudson River was a superb avenue into the hinterland, but better shipping was urgently needed, and the state legislature offered a monopoly of steam navigation on the river to anyone who would prove his ability to do so with a steamboat of certain minimum specifications. As history repeatedly demonstrates, it was the entrepreneur and not the inventor who made things happen. Robert Fulton did not invent the steamboat (the boiler and engine of the *Clermont,* in fact were imported from England), but he secured the support of the wealthy and influential Robert Livingston, had a boat built, and made it work. The short, romantic career of the steamboat in America began.

In the long run the steam-powered vessel made its greatest contribution to shipping on the open seas, once the problem of hauling enough fuel across the oceans was solved. But for almost fifty years, in those places that were favored with navigable rivers, it was the chief instrument for the development of the interior. Where the rivers petered out only a few miles inland, the steamboat was never very satisfactory. Charles Dickens, touring America, sourly described a little craft that struggled remarkably far up one stream as "a warm sandwich about three feet thick." On the northern Great Plains, men wryly remarked that the chief requirement for a steamboat was its ability "to navigate on a heavy dew."

But it was in the Old Northwest, with its Ohio, Mississippi, and Missouri rivers and its Great Lakes, that the steamboat truly dominated transportation during its short ascendancy. In 1811, Nicholas J. Roosevelt launched the *New Orleans* at Pittsburgh, on the Ohio, and about two months later she steamed into her namesake city, which thereupon entered its golden age as the most important port in North America beyond the northeastern seaboard. Steamboats not only make the trip downstream much faster than unpowered boats, but they could churn their way upstream, too. Now men who had floated down river on flatboats could sail home in comfort, although such were the temptations aboard these floating hotels that they did not always arrive with the proceeds of their trip intact. On the Great Lakes, sailing vessels had always fared badly during the sudden violent storms, since they lacked the space to ride out the gale as they would have done on the ocean and frequently ended up on the desolate, rocky shores. Only nine years after Fulton's *Clermont* showed the way, therefore, steamboats inaugurated a service on the Lakes that remains today one of the busiest in the world. Then, in 1823 the *Virginia*, loaded with supplies for the U.S. Army Post at Fort Snelling, tied up at the mouth of the St. Peter (now the Minnesota) River near the head of navigation on the Mississippi River near the present site of St. Paul. Soon boats were picking their way farther and farther up the tortuous, treacherous Missouri River, as well.

But the steamboat was not, after all, the dependable, ubiquitous form of inland transporation for which Americans yearned. Cheap, it surely was, for those who were in the right location, and if you did not count the cost of insurance on cargoes that might be burned to the water's edge or blown to bits when the captain, racing another line's boat, kept the safety valve tied down too long. Dependable, it often was not. Steamboating on the rivers was open to anyone who could meet the rudimentary navigation requirements, and a captain could accept or decline any cargo or passenger as he chose, naming his own rate, and set them down wherever he chose, while bearing no responsibility for their safekeeping. Many a disgruntled passenger, having boarded, say, at Dunleith, Illinois, with a ticket for St. Paul, found himself stranded in Prairie du Chien, Wisconsin, because the captain decided not to complete the trip as advertised.

Above a certain latitude in winter the steamboats did not move at all, as Americans, their fuel supplies running low, would periodically rediscover in winters like the record-breaking one of 1976–1977. Most frustrating of all, however, was the fact that navigation on the Hudson, the western rivers, and the Great Lakes could never achieve its true potential until something cheaper than wagon haulage was found for the overland segments between the seaboard and the western waters. Thus, the success of the steamboat led to the digging of one of the world's most famous canals.

After 1865, as the railroad frontier advanced, the intrepid steamboat men moved their craft farther and farther west, to the upper Missouri, the Red River of the North, even the Assiniboine in the wilds of western Canada. But by 1885 it was all over.

Partially Successful Imitation: The Canals

Men may have yearned longer for the Northwest passage, but they never yearned any harder for it than they did for a practical link between the headwaters of eastern rivers like the Hudson, the Delaware, and the Potomac, on the one hand, and the upper reaches of the Ohio River or the easternmost shores of the Great Lakes. By 1816 it was clear that New York City's past growth was nothing compared to what it could achieve with better access to the interior, and DeWitt Clinton, the Empire State's most famous citizen after Alexander Hamilton and Franklin D. Roosevelt, was determined to do something about it. At the head of a group of remarkably enterprising men, he persuaded the legislature to charter a company to dig the longest canal in the world, from Albany up the Mohawk River valley (the only water-level break in the Appalachians) to Lake Erie at Buffalo.

It is tempting to speculate that if the westward surge in America had been delayed ten or fifteen years almost no canals would have been dug. It may be more accurate to say that without canals and the great stimulus they gave to settlement, the demand for something better still—that is, railroads—would have languished. In 1816 an artificial waterway was the only alternative to the prohibitively high costs of turnpike transportation. Late in the eighteenth century the demands of the industrial revolution had led England to build many miles of canals that served her needs admirably. It was only a matter of having a good supply of water; a location that would not require too many rises and falls and, therefore, not too many expensive locks that would slow down the passage of the boats; and, of course, a heavy potential traffic.

The Erie Canal met all of the requirements for a successful canal, and it paid for itself several times over during the sixty or seventy years that it was an important factor in east-west transportation. No other internal improvement of the pre-railroad era, whether publicly or privately financed, was a bigger success, and none earned a more permanent place in American history. Today's folksingers keep alive the song of the patient, thirsty boatmen:

> And I scarcely think
>   We'll git a drink
> Till we git to Buffalo.

Alas, the Erie Canal was virtually unique. With a few exceptions, no other canals built during the "mania" that held sway for the next ten years came anywhere near the Erie's record, and most were dismal failures. In the key states of Ohio and Indiana half a dozen canals were built to link Lake Erie with the Ohio River, and all were financial failures that blighted the credit of the states that built and operated them for almost a generation. The South undertook to build the Chesapeake & Ohio Canal to the Ohio River, but it never got any farther than Cumberland, Maryland, by which time it had been upstaged by the Baltimore & Ohio Railroad.

The most spectacular miscalculation of all was the so-called Main Line works in Pennsylvania. The merchants of Philadelphia, watching the success of the Erie Canal and desperate to retain their valuable commerce with the interior, agonized over how to do it and decided upon imitation instead of innovation. Today the idea of a canal built over the most rugged section of the Appalachians appears ludicrous, but Philadelphia thought that "portage railways," consisting of a stationary engine and winch at the head of an inclined plane, could economically drag the boats, mounted on railway cars, over the toughest spots. They were wrong, and in a dozen years one of the country's most unsuccessful internal improvements was succeeded by one of the world's most notable business enterprises, the Pennsylvania Railroad.

There were other exceptions, besides the Erie, to these tales of failure. A few canals, some of which are still in use, were built around falls and rapids and to connect one Great Lake with another. Others, almost forgotten today, were of vital importance in the earliest stages of America's industrial revolution. These were the canals of eastern Pennsylvania and New Jersey that were built to bring anthracite coal to tidewater. This superb fuel hastened the arrival of the age of steam in manufacturing, and the canals that were built to get it to market—the Delaware & Hudson, the Morris, the Delaware & Raritan, and the Lehigh, to name four—were abundantly successful. So effective were they in demonstrating the value of anthracite coal, in fact, that some of the earliest and most important railroads were built to replace the canals in the coal trade.

The best of the canals suffered shortcomings that assured their demise as the railroad era began in earnest. Sometimes there was too much water in the ditches; more frequently, not enough. The most important ones were unusable during the winter months, and maintenance of embankments and locks turned out to be far more expensive than anyone had counted on. Most important, however, was the fact that they were not much more versatile than the rivers when it came to furnishing every inhabited place with vital transportation without regard to its natural disadvantages of location. By the 1880s the railroad ruled supreme, and even the Erie Canal was crumbling into ruin.

In the long view of history, the greatest achievement of the Erie and the Ohio canals was to fill the old Northwest with energetic, ambitious settlers who were determined to find a way to carry the huge yields of these rich lands to market at a profit. For this they would need something better than turnpikes, steamboats, or canals.

An Idea Whose Time Had Come: The Steam Railroad

There has never been any sustained attack on the idea that the steam railroad was the most significant invention or innovation in the rise of an industrial society. Indeed, it has served as the centerpiece of the most highly developed theory of economic growth that modern economic thought has produced. It would be dramatic indeed, therefore, to be able to point to one brilliant act of creation as the point at which the railroad was "invented." In fact, both of the key elements of the steam railroad had been in common use for many years before the first definitive demonstration of a practical steam railroad in 1829.

As early as the sixteenth century in primitive coal mines in Alsace, and later, on a fairly large scale in England, the heavy product of mines had been trundled short distances in wagons running on some kind of rails and guided by flanges on the wheels. Early in the nineteenth century the stone for the Bunker Hill Monument was carted from the quarry at Quincy, Massachusetts, to the boats by such a "railway." As for steam power, men had been trying to harness it to a wheeled vehicle since the latter part of the eighteenth century. But the only kind of vehicle people had ever known had run on roads, which could not even support a heavy steam car. It was not until the rising demands of the industrial revolution made improved transportation a necessity that the bright idea of joining the two principles in a single system gave birth to the modern railroad.

It happened, of course, in England, where both the need and the know-how were about a generation ahead of the rest of the world. The problem turned on making the steam engine more compact, lighter, and more efficient than the clumsy stationary engines of the previous generation. George Stephenson, who conceived the brilliant idea of using a tubular boiler, built his "Rocket," entered it in the Rainhill trials sponsored by the embryonic Liverpool & Manchester Railway, won a prize of £500, and gained immortality as the inventor of the steam locomotive. (It is also claimed that, in trying to decide how far apart to space the "Rocket's" wheels, he settled for the distance between the wheels of a manure cart and thus fastened upon the world the too-narrow standard gauge of four feet eight-and-one-half inches.)

Once the problem of motive power had been solved, little stood in the way of the rapid displacement of earlier forms of transportation by the railroad. As the sweating quarrymen of Quincy and many a British coal miner knew well, its basic virtue lay in the fact that the flanged wheel running on a flat-laid rail encounters less friction than any other type of wheeled conveyance. And the earliest forms of the railroad proved to be only the beginning of what seemed like unlimited possibilities for improvement. A modern comparison makes this very clear. Today, a forty-ton boxcar of freight, set in motion at sixty miles an hour on a level track, will coast by itself for over five miles. A locomotive of five thousand horsepower can haul, over a route of *average* gradient, a train of a gross weight of five thousand tons, or about seventy loaded boxcars. In contrast, a modern semitrailer truck rig requires ten times as much power per ton, and ten times as much energy to haul a ton of freight one mile. If we make the same kind of comparison between the primitive railroad train and a typical horse- or ox-drawn wagon on the

National Road, we must conclude that the superiority of the very earliest railroads, where no water route was available, was almost beyond calculating.

The railroad idea took hold in America with remarkable speed. Just about the earliest corporation chartered in America for the purpose of hauling passengers was in what one would think the unlikeliest of places: paralleling the Erie Canal. Erastus Corning, an upstate New York merchant of singular vision, realized that the hordes of "westering" Americans who sent their household effects via the canal would themselves pay a premium to travel by a more comfortable and speedier mode. In 1827 Corning chartered the Mohawk & Hudson Railroad, and it was such an instantaneous success, despite the punitive tax he had to pay the State of New York for taking customers away from its vaunted canal, that in a few years there was a continuous rail line, consisting originally of nearly a dozen separate corporate entities, all the way to Buffalo. It was the beginning of the mighty New York Central Railroad and of the end of the Erie Canal. The citizens of Baltimore, meanwhile, had wasted no time in deciding in 1828 that a railroad was their only hope to stay in the game of trading with the rapidly expanding interior, now that both New York and Philadelphia had, or soon would have, western canals. They had no sure idea of what kind of motive power they would use—they experimented with sails, and settled for a short time for real horsepower—but their faith in the new system was reaffirmed when news came that Stephenson had removed all doubt at Rainhill that steam could do the job. The Baltimore & Ohio became the first American railroad to haul both freight and passengers by steam on a regular schedule.

But the B. & O. locomotive was not quite the first to haul passengers by steam on a regular schedule. That distinction belongs to the aptly named "Best Friend of Charleston," operated by the Charleston & Hamburg Railroad. This railroad may serve as a symbol of the South's shortcomings in the industrial revolution, and a monument to one of the most tragic figures in its economic development, Robert Y. Hayne. Remembered today, if at all, as the South Carolina Senator whose flaming speech on states' rights provided the occasion for one of Daniel Webster's most famous orations, Hayne began early his effort to propel the South into the industrial age. He envisioned a railroad that would run all the way from Charleston, the South's best port, to Memphis and, for a few years, the Charleston & Hamburg was the longest railroad in the country.

But nothing could make up for the inferiority of the South's ports, the lack of adequate markets for imports and diversity of exports, and a slave-labor system that immobilized her capital resources. With the sudden, early death of Hayne, what entrepreneurial spirit there was in the southern railroad-building program declined, and on the eve of the Civil War she had barely begun to evolve a true system.

As those who had turned to railroad building in desperation discovered that they had made the best of all possible choices, the 1830s
became the "demonstration decade" of the railroad age. Like Baltimore, another important seacoast city, Boston, observed developments
in England and decided that only a railroad could carry its commerce
across the Berkshires to Albany and a connection with the Erie Canal
and the railroads that quickly paralleled it. Efforts to make Massachusetts railroads a public works project failed, but private capital, in part
with state-guaranteed bonds, got behind three of the most important
early railroads in America: the Boston & Worcester, which soon joined
with the Western Railroad of Massachusetts and enabled New England
to "horn in" on New York's rich western trade; the Boston & Lowell,
running northward to serve the booming textile industry and soon putting the Middlesex Canal out of business; and the Boston & Providence,
traversing a route that for years had carried a heavy turnpike traffic.

To the south, it was in Pennsylvania that railroads had their most
significant beginnings, but not along the "Main Line" between Philadelphia and Pittsburgh, where the great false start, of the rail/canal/
inclined-plane system, was underway. It was the anthracite coal producers of eastern Pennsylvania, anxious to ship their coveted fuel to
domestic and commercial users in New York and New England, who
undertook some of the most successful railroads in American history:
the Philadelphia & Reading, the Delaware & Hudson, the Delaware &
Lackawanna, and the Lehigh Valley. These railroads soon made
antiques of the canals that had created the market for anthracite coal in
the preceding two decades.

Meanwhile, the railroad solved the ancient problem of how to haul
the great number of travelers between New York and Philadelphia in
speed and comfort. The venerable stagecoach line was quickly replaced
by the Camden & Amboy Railroad, operating between the New Jersey
steamboat pier on lower New York Bay and the thriving town just
across the Delaware River from Philadelphia. Its earliest cars, quaint
copies of the stagecoaches, provided a grueling ride, and the monopolistic grasp that the railroad had on business irked most travelers, but it
was a vast improvement over what had been available. Shortly thereafter (1838) it was, in effect, extended to the nation's capital via the
Philadelphia, Wilmington & Baltimore Railroad, a ferry across the Susquehanna, and the B. & O.'s branch from Baltimore to Washington.
Whether in primitive coaches or modern Metroliners, this New-York-
to-Washington corridor has carried for nearly 150 years one of the largest and most important streams of travelers in the world.

Railroad building in New York, meanwhile, gathered momentum
despite the success of the Erie Canal and the repressive limitations on
railroads adopted by canal-biased state legislators. In the valley of the
Mohawk River between Albany and Buffalo (the only "water level"
route west), a group of short railroads were built by such intensely com-

petitive towns as Troy, Schenectady, Rome, Rochester, and Syracuse to haul the passenger traffic that the Canal had engendered but for whom the Canal was too slow. Soon, travelers arriving by steamboat at Albany were able to transfer to the first of eight railroads that would carry them with comparative speed to Buffalo, and shippers were beginning to discover that even at the high rates the railroads charged, it was advantageous to dispatch their more valuable freight that way, too. By 1840 there were as many miles of railroads in the United States as there were miles of canals.

General Acceptance of the Railroads: The 1840s

In the decade of the 1840s the shift to railroads became a near riot. In New York State the residents of the southern tier of counties, disgruntled at the advantages the Erie Canal gave their upstate neighbors, clamored for and got a railroad through their region between the Hudson River and Lake Erie. The Erie Railroad was the most poorly planned of the antebellum lines. It began in the wrong place (Piermont, New York, on the west bank of the Hudson opposite Tarrytown, instead of across the river from Manhattan) and ended in an even wronger place (the Lake Erie village of Dunkirk, instead of Buffalo). As if to top those mistakes it selected a broad gauge in the mistaken notion that it would not have to share its traffic with standard gauge roads. Nevertheless, by 1851, when it reached the lake, it was the longest railroad in the country under one management and an important east-west through route.

By the mid-1840s it was obvious that the Erie Canal and the Lakes could not compete with the kind of transporation that the railroads could provide. Lines that eventually became some of the most important in the nation suddenly burst westward from Buffalo towards the raw new cities of Cleveland and Toledo, while west of Detroit the state of Michigan began a blundering effort to build the Michigan Central ("Democracy's railroad," as one historian has called it) towards infant Chicago.

The merchants of New York City, alarmed by the ease with which Boston was exchanging east-west trade at Albany via its new railroad, overcame their smugness at the success of their wonderful canal. They privately financed a railroad up the east bank of the Hudson to Albany, where passengers (and more and more freight) could be transferred to the lines that continued west. It remained for Commodore Vanderbilt to recognize the true potential of the Hudson River Railroad after the Civil War, but without it New York City would have declined steadily from the mid-1840s on.

And what of Philadelphia, which on the eve of the Revolution had been the second largest city in the British Empire? By the mid-1840s not even its most obscurantist citizen could ignore any longer the fact that its system of canals and inclined planes was a miserable failure. In 1846 a group of private businessmen, suspecting correctly that they would later be able to buy at a bargain price the usable rail sections of the Main Line works, secured a charter for what came to be called the Pennsylvania Railroad and tackled the awesome task of building a railroad over the Alleghenies to Pittsburgh. They were spurred on by an act of their state legislature that granted the B. & O. Railroad a charter to build a branch to Pittsburgh if the Pennsylvania Railroad had not reached Pittsburgh within ten years: a fate too horrible for the merchants to contemplate. They made it with two years to spare, and the remarkable enterprise that they created made them, and three succeeding generations, prosperous almost beyond measure.

The First Great Wave of Railroad Building: The 1850s

Historians who prefer to make the Civil War the great watershed in American economic development would do well to reflect upon the great wave of optimism that swept over the United States with the adoption of the Compromise of 1850. For a few years it would appear that the grave constitutional issues posed by slavery and complicated by the acquisition of vast new territories had been permanently solved. Thus the 1850s became the "miraculous decade" in the development of the American railroad system. Daniel Webster, supposedly ostracized by Bostonians for his support of a fugitive slave law as part of the Compromise, was in fact one of the city's honored guests the following year when the city held its Great Railroad Jubilee. (Boston's elite denied him the use of Faneuil Hall, so he spoke in the open air to a great crowd who cheered his enthusiastic description of the prosperous, united America that the railroad would bring.) The 1850s were a period not only of railroad building on an unprecedented scale, but also of the beginnings, formal and informal, of the consolidation of individual lines into a national system. By 1850 it was clear that the railroad's role was to be far greater than that of a connecting link between navigable bodies of water: the trains were becoming, in fact, the basic means of transportation regardless of the distances involved, the difficulty of the terrain, and the existence of water routes.

In 1853 Erastus Corning, whose efficiency in providing upstate New York with railroads had been spurred by an exclusive contract to sell them iron rails, engineered the merger of fourteen short lines into one continuous line between Albany and Buffalo. Christened the New York Central, it may rank as the first great corporate merger in our history. At almost the same moment, the Lake Shore Railroad and the

Michigan Southern Railroad, destined to be joined into one of the world's great profit machines, were completed and through service from New York City to Chicago began. The axis thus created was the chief one around which the commerce of North America would revolve for the next 150 years.

The approach of the Pennsylvania Railroad towards Pittsburgh stimulated the construction of extensions towards Chicago and St. Louis, and by 1860 the east-west railroad system had assumed the general form that it has had ever since. But the expansion of railroads in the Old Northwest in the 1850s—from thirteen hundred miles in 1850 to eleven thousand in 1860—was truly remarkable, especially in view of the disgraceful defaults and outright repudiations of state bonds issued in the 1840s to build railroads. The ironmasters of England and Wales would not have sold these states a single fishplate on credit after that doleful period, but by 1850 private capital had rushed in to fill the vacuum. Important north-south lines were also built to do the work of the forlorn, forgotten canals.

At this point a major shift in federal public improvements policy occurred. Nationalistic Democrats like Stephen A. Douglas, convinced that an America preoccupied with the great work of filling up a continent would forget its sectional differences and even the ugliness of slavery, pushed through Congress the first railroad land grant law. The railroad it helped make possible, the Illinois Central, lived up to its every expectation. Thrusting downward into southern Illinois, it siphoned off the rapidly growing commerce of the lower Mississippi and sent it east over the new railroads. No other factor, save the repugnance of slavery itself, was so important a factor in persuading the Northwest to cast its lot with the Northeast when war finally came.

Reenforcing this development was the rapid extension of railroads westward from Chicago. In 1856 the Rock Island Railroad had built the first bridge across the Mississippi at Rock Island, Illinois, after its brilliant attorney, Abraham Lincoln, had defeated the efforts of river boatmen to prevent it, and was heading across the prairies of Iowa. Railroads had reached the east bank of the Mississippi at seven other places, from LaCrosse, Wisconsin, to St. Louis, and one, a predecessor of the Burlington Railroad, stretched all the way across Missouri to St. Joseph. The impact of the railroads of the North was felt almost immediately on patterns of interregional trade. No one put it better than New York politician Thurlow Weed, on a trip out West in 1854, who said in a letter to the New York *Tribune*:

> Time is working a phenomenon upon the Mississippi River. In a business point of view this river is beginning to run up stream! A large share of the products of the Valley of the Mississippi are soon to find a market up instead of down the river. There is a West growing with a rapidity that has no parallel [and] the railroads that are being constructed . . . are to take the corn, pork, beef, &c, &c, to a northern instead of southern markets.

The Antediluvian Railroad

American railroads in 1860 were primitive even by the standards of the next generation. Although contemporary maps appear to show a smooth, integrated system, many of the routes were in fact broken at numerous points. The science of bridge building was still in its infancy, and most major river crossings required travelers to take a ferry, although boats that carried passenger and freight cars intact from one bank to the other were widely used. Thus, trains were ferried across the Susquehanna at Havre de Grace on the important Philadelphia-Baltimore line and across the broad Ohio at Cairo, Illinois, between the Illinois Central and its southern connection.

The city of St. Louis, its golden age as the most important steamboat town on the Mississippi at zenith, did not bestir itself to build a bridge across the river at that point until the 1870s; but Chicago, with its superb location at the foot of Lake Michigan, would have eclipsed it anyway. There was no bridge on the Thames River at New London, Connecticut, until the 1880s, so through traffic between Boston and New York moved by an inland route, and the famous "Shore Line" did not come into its own until the twentieth century. Until low-cost, high-tensile-strength steel became available late in the century, the cost of bridges and trestles remained a major obstacle to the full integration of the railroad system. Most serious of all was the variation in track gauges, especially in the South, which was not fully corrected until the 1880s.

The roadbeds and rails of antebellum lines were almost toylike. Even the best-engineered lines ran on iron rails that weighed barely a third as much, per yard, as those on the best railroads today, reflecting the fact that rails were more expensive in the United States than in England until after the introduction of the Bessemer steel process in the 1870s. Most lines were poorly built, and some had no rails at all, relying on iron straps bolted to wooden stringers. The straps could pop up, pierce the car floor, and impale the passengers. Speeds of ten to fifteen miles an hour were typical, and speeds of more than thirty miles an hour virtually unknown. Even so, derailments were frequent, and did not so much crush the passengers as cremate them when the pot-bellied stoves (the only source of heat in winter) set the wooden cars afire. Collisions, front-end and rear-end, produced appalling results, even after the telegraph began to be used to dispatch trains in lieu of "running by the book."

Travelers found few amenities on antebellum railroads, either in the railroad stations or on the trains. Sleeping cars did not come into general use until after the Civil War, and meals for the traveler who did not prudently carry his own food meant a mad scramble for "refreshments" at railroad lunch rooms en route. In the years before the dining car became widely used, the railroad eating house became synonymous with unappetizing and indigestible food dispensed ungraciously and expensively. Like the airliner of today, the train was boring and uncomfortable, but far, far faster than any alternative.

As an occupation, railroad work was grueling and dangerous. The automatic air brake, applied simultaneously throughout the entire train by the engineer, would not make its appearance until the last quarter of the century. Meanwhile men scrambled down the catwalks atop boxcars, in all kinds of weather, to twist the handbrake wheels when the engineer whistled, "down brakes!" In the yards brakemen stood between cars to couple them by means of links and pins before the automatic coupler was finally invented late in the century. The outcome was frequently unpleasant in the extreme. We would have considered it a hell of a way to run a railroad. So did our ancestors, and they labored almost incessantly to improve things as fast as the slender resources of the American commonwealth would permit.

Primitive as it was, the antebellum railroad was a thing of wonder to a people whose ideas of what it cost and how long it took to move goods and people had been formed in the age of the turnpike, the steamboat, and the canal. It is often overlooked that railroad rates, *from the beginning,* were significantly cheaper than wagon rates. The criticism of "high rates" that swelled up in the post-Civil War era reflected farmers' expectations that they could settle virgin lands hundreds and even thousands of miles from markets, raise great surpluses of heavy, bulky, low-value commodities, and *still* ship them to market at a profit. But the real story lies in the fact that what Americans had already achieved with their railroads by 1865 was as nothing compared with what they would accomplish with them thereafter. If it were not so, the story would hardly be worth the telling.

Writing with "Lightning"

Not long after Daniel Webster, Henry Clay, and a few other compromise-minded statesmen had stitched the union back together in 1850, a gentleman in Boston married a lady in New York without either leaving home. It was not a typical use of the telegraph wires that a dozen or more groups of businessmen were feverishly stringing throughout the country, but it was symbolic of what was about to happen to this revolutionary use of "lightning," as many still called the mysterious new force, electricity. The era of consolidation of the poorly integrated telegraph "system" was at hand, and in the last five or six years before the Civil War a series of startling mergers brought into existence America's first "natural monopoly."

If the use of steam to propel vehicles on land was a relatively new art, the use of electricity in any constructive or economically valuable way was unheard of in 1844 when Samuel F. B. Morse sent his first message, "What hath God wrought," over the experimental line between Washington and Baltimore. After 1800 a series of remarkable scientific discoveries had greatly stimulated interest in the practical use of electricity. Volta's invention of the chemical battery, which produced a continuous current instead of a static jolt of electricity; G. S. Ohm's laws of electrical circuits; and Oersted and Faraday's discovery of electromagnetism, opened the way for tinkerers like Morse to devise a way of signaling over long distances by means of a simple electric circuit. All that came out of Morse's device at the receiving end was a crude paper recording of dots and dashes—short and long bursts of current—but a code was quickly worked out that expressed the letters of the alphabet and the numbers from zero to nine in the simple new language. So adaptable are the human powers of conditioned reflexes that before long operators were able to "read" messages solely from the clicking sound of the receiving instrument. Eventually the clumsy devices for recording dots and dashes, or the letters and numbers themselves, fell by the wayside and the telegraph key, in the hands of an expert operator, became the standard device for long-distance communication for the next hundred years.

By 1850 it was obvious to the numerous contenders in the telegraph industry that they were failing to provide the public with a dependable, cheap system of instantaneous, long-distance communication—which, after all, was what the telegraph was all about. What was needed was not better equipment, primitive as these men's gadgets were, or even more miles of line (a higher standard of construction would have helped) but coordination and discipline. From that fateful day when the Congress of the United States rejected the idea that the telegraph was a logical extension of the postal service, the growth of the industry had been chaotic. Strong as the Morse patents were, and as determined as his chief business associate, Amos Kendall, was to assign them in an orderly and efficient manner, the classic American principle of individualism overrode all efforts at rational development until the times and the man who could do it finally coincided to produce a consolidated telegraph system.

Kendall, who had been the most influential member of Andrew Jackson's "kitchen cabinet," had superb political connections and valuable experience as postmaster general, but these were of little use in building a telegraph industry. What was required was capital, which was chronically short in young, poor America at mid-century, and entrepreneurship, which is scarce in all times and places. Men who possessed outstanding business vision in combination with a talent for leadership would appear even later in the railroad industry than in communications. Kendall parceled out exclusive territorial rights to exploit the Morse patents, and trouble began almost immediately. Rugged individualists like F.O.J. Smith, in the Northeast, and Ezra Cornell, in upstate New York, to name the most important, behaved from the beginning as though they expected their systems to become the center of the telegraphic universe. Henry O'Rielly, whose individualism extended even to changing the spelling of the family name, secured rights to build a line from the seaboard to the Great Lakes and the Mississippi River and proceeded to ride off in all directions. He recognized the need to coordinate the lines he controlled or influenced, but his fatuous notion of a "democratic" confederation of independent companies never had a chance. Meanwhile various devices for printing messages at the receiving end, which got around Morse's patents easily, further weakened Kendall's control and ended any chance that the "magnetic telegraph" interests could ever bring into being a viable telegraph system.

What was the chief problem with the telegraph in the early 1850s, and why did it call not merely for consolidation but for ruthless monopolization? As everyone knows who has ever played the children's parlor game, "gossip," a statement relayed repeatedly from one person to another will have undergone strange transformations by the end of its journey, if it arrives at all. So it was with telegraphic messages. Geographic division of rights to the telegraph, in short, never had made any sense. If there was to be competition, it would have to be between companies operating nationally, at least in the populated parts of the United States. (Such parallel competition did actually emerge here and there, but, being even more wasteful and irrational than similar competition in the railroad business, soon faded.) But a system composed of independent companies linked end-to-end by voluntary agreements to relay messages was consistently unreliable, and over the longer distances— notably between the eastern seaboard cities and the deep South—a bad joke. What was required was an organizer and a leader, a man who could see that the future of the telegraph industry was limited not so much by its *potential* usefulness (at which one could only guess) but by the quality of the service it could actually deliver, and who could convince others of that fact as well. A leader, in short, who could convince lesser men that, as in most human endeavors, the telegraphic whole would be vastly greater than the sum of its numerous parts. Such a leader finally emerged in the mid-1850s in the person of Hiram Sibley of Rochester. He and his associates built Western Union, around which the entire American telegraphic system would coalesce in the next ten years.

They built Western Union upon the foundation of the New York & Mississippi Valley Printing Telegraph Co., which had been established to exploit a patent issued to one Royal E. House in 1848. The company operated in that fabulous corridor between Buffalo and Chicago, over which American industry, commerce, and agriculture surged westward with the coming of the railroad, and it was the irresistible rate of economic growth in this region that made the risks Sibley constantly took such good ones. Never letting up, always on the offensive, and unblushingly determined to be number one in the succession of telegraph company associations that came and went in the 1850s, Sibley made Western Union, as the company was renamed in 1856, the dominant factor west of Buffalo. And "west" soon meant all the way to the Pacific coast, for it was Sibley and his associates who won the government contract to string a wire across the great American desert and into San Francisco on the eve of the Civil War. The prestige, not to mention the flood of business, which this extension brought Western Union was, in the end, the deciding factor in its absorption of all the remaining companies.

Only one other group had emerged in the 1850s that might have challenged the leadership of the Western Union men. Cyrus W. Field, a New York merchant whose early success left him wealthy yet restless for new worlds to conquer, built a new telegraph company on the basis of the vast domestic business that it expected to enjoy once Field's great dream, a cable beneath the Atlantic Ocean, became a reality. Enjoying the support of some of New York's richest men, Field's American Telegraph Company might have given Western Union a run for its money if the cable project had succeeded by 1860, instead of being delayed until 1866, and if the Civil War had not thrown much of its wire mileage into Confederate hands.

The war, however, brought great prosperity to Western Union; although by 1865 the company's finances manifested all of the daredevil practices that underlie the "Robber Baron" interpretation of American business history, both American Telegraph and United States Telegraph (a lesser, independent company that had attempted parallel competition) were glad to be absorbed into Western Union. This event marked the end of the Sibley era, for that remarkable man, exhausted by labors that had done so much to create modern America, soon departed from the scene. In another few years Western Union would become the most highly valued property of a man—Jay Gould—who is as famous as Hiram Sibley is forgotten.

Of all the innovations which entrepreneurs, great and small, brought to the development of the telegraph industry, none is more important nor more dramatic than the discovery of the symbiotic relationship between the telegraph and the railroad. From the Civil War to the day when Americans began to use the long-distance telephone instead of the telegraph, nothing was more taken for granted than the fact that at a railroad depot one could send a telegram or cable to the ends of the earth at any time of the day or night.

Looking back, the advantages of locating a telegraph line along a railroad ought to have become obvious sooner than they did. Although the railroad seldom traversed the *shortest* distance between two points, it did usually follow the easiest route. Its builders cleared the trees back from the right of way at least far enough to leave room for telegraph poles, and the traffic on the line meant that every point along it would be observed several times a day and breaks could be quickly located and repaired. The value of the telegraph to the railroad, however, was not so obvious. After all, trains had been running on thousands of miles of track for nearly twenty years when the telegraph appeared. But traffic had grown on many lines to the point that operating trains in two directions on a single track had become a problem. One day in June 1851, Charles Minot, superintendent of the Erie Railroad, grew impatient as his westbound train waited at a siding for an eastbound train to arrive and pass. He asked the station agent, who was also the telegraph operator, to inquire of the next station down the line whether the eastbound train had cleared the passing track at that point. Finding that it had not, Minot ordered the agent to telegraph the station to hold it there and then wrote out an order to his engineer to proceed. The engineer flatly refused to trust to writing by lightning, so Minot took the throttle himself while the worried engineer retreated to the last seat of the last car on the train. At the next station, finding that the eastbound had not even arrived at the station still farther down the line, Minot repeated the process at two more way stations en route, for the eastbound was late indeed. Another few years had to pass before telegraphic dispatching of trains was common (trains on the busy Boston & Lowell Railroad were still being run by the book instead of the telegraph at the time of a disastrous wreck in the 1870s), but eventually the practice became universal.

If the telegraph was a great boon to the railroad, the telegraph companies soon came to wonder how they had ever managed without making common cause with the railroads. Hiram Sibley's early recognition of the synergistic nature of collaboration with the railroad companies, and his skill in working out mutually beneficial contracts, did much to make Western Union so formidable by 1860. While arrangements differed from place to place, the railroad had free use of the telegraph for its own business; in the case of the actual operation of the trains, its messages took precedence over private messages. The railroad maintained the office and its agent manned the key (an expert knowledge of telegraphy soon became a prerequisite for employment as station agent), with all receipts going to the telegraph company. Train crews were required to keep a sharp eye out for breaks, acts of vandalism, and any other problems and either to fix them on the spot or report them at the next station.

For over a century the metal sign of Western Union swung in the sunshine and rain outside railroad depots across America, alongside the symbols of the railroad and the express company and the name of the town itself. Natural history offers no better example of constructive cooperation between God's creatures.

Iron Horse Rampant: 1865–1897

What the telegraph industry achieved in barely a decade from 1856 to 1866, the railroads would require another generation and the rest of

Figure 1.2 Hiram Sibley (1807–1888), was the main force in the combination of leading telegraph companies in 1865 into a national network under the corporate name of Western Union. *(Smithsonian Institution)*

the century to accomplish. It was not merely that the need for rational consolidation in the telegraph industry had become critical by mid-century. Nor was it for a lack of railroad leadership, for the railroads had claimed by far the greater part of the not inconsiderable business talent that had come to the fore since 1850. The fact is that in 1865, after thirty-five years of steady, cautious development confined, for the most part, to the Northeast and Midwest, the American railroad system was far from complete. The twenty-five years following the Civil War belong to the iron horse, if any period in history does, for this was the great era of railroad building. From about 35,000 miles in 1865, the American railroad network grew to embrace nearly 200,000 miles by 1897, with many more thousands in multiple mainline tracks, sidings, and yards. In one year during the remarkable decade of the 1880s more miles of track were built than had existed in the entire United States as late as the mid-1850s. It was a hectic, madcap era that left its mark on every aspect of American life and produced a case of economic and political indigestion that persisted well into the twentieth century. Not until the last decade of the century would the need for rational consolidation have to be faced. By then the problem would be acute, indeed.

The history of railroad building in the United States after the Civil War is a grand *accelerando* down to the year 1893, marked by only two pauses: a rather long one during the depression of 1873–1876, and a much shorter one during the panic of 1884. Throughout the nineteenth century, railroad affairs crowded the front pages of every newspaper in the country, while business deals great and small hinged on what railroad promoters, often sitting in offices many miles from the scene, might decide. The historian, immersing himself at any given point in this flood tide of railroad building, is hard put to find a pattern. But the heart of the story, it seems clear, lies in four major accomplishments. First, the superb system of railroads dubbed the "trunk lines," linking the eastern seaboard with the key Mississippi valley cities of Chicago and St. Louis, was completed and assumed its permanent form. Second, a truly amazing network of main and branch lines sprang forth in the rich farming areas of middle America. Taking their general name from their chief mission, which was to gather up the vast surplus produce of this breadbasket of the world and deliver it to the trunk line railroads, these lines quickly came to be called "granger roads." As their name indicates, they would play a basic role in the social and political history of the nation. Then there was the phase of railroad building that has excited the American imagination more than any other: the building of the transcontinental railroads to the Pacific coast. Finally, there was the slow and stumbling effort to rehabilitate the few railroads the South had built before the war, to extend them, and to weld them into an efficient, rational system.

Taken together, the trunk line railroads of the Northeast may rank as the most impressive aggregation of physical capital upon which any society ever founded its subsequent industrial and commerical development. Two of these four lines were striking successes from the start: the New York Central Railroad and the Pennsylvania Railroad. The Central showed its impressive potential first. As a consolidation of numerous small lines between New York, Albany, and Buffalo, it burst upon the commerical scene with all of the impact of the Erie Canal twenty-five years before, and for much the same reasons. The Central brought to its territory, which had already become one of the most important avenues of commerce in the world, a reduction in shipping and travel costs, an increase in speed, and a year-round dependability that overshadowed even DiWitt Clinton's remarkable ditch. Before the decade of the 1850s was well under way, the Central inspired the building of lines further west of Buffalo which, even in their original corporate dress (the Lake Shore and the Michigan Southern, for example), came to be considered part of a single through route from New York to Chicago long before William H. Vanderbilt, in a reluctant defensive move against Jay Gould, gained absolute control of them. By the 1880s the Central had also consolidated its lines from Cleveland to the southern Midwest and to St. Louis, while at the same time continually fleshing out its system throughout the Northeast. By the late 1870s the Central, under the conservative but clearheaded leadership of this son of Commodore Vanderbilt, was busily improving the physical condition of the line at almost all points (it was the first to have a four-track mainline throughout its major territory) in anticipation of the time, by then rapidly approaching, when the railroads would be called upon to carry a far heavier burden, at much lower rates, than had ever been envisioned for them.

It was the creation of the American steel industry in a few short years, beginning about 1870, that by the 1890s made the Pennsylvania Railroad into the most important enterprise in the nation and the world. This "standard railway of the world," as it proclaimed itself to the hosts of eager men who came to study its methods, continually rebuilt its original mainline between Philadelphia and Pittsburgh to accommodate the vast tonnages of coal, coke, and finished iron and steel that were the kingpins of the industrial revolution. In the 1870s, well before the Vanderbilts had realized that the New York Central would have to play a major role in consolidating railroad service between the seaboard and the major cities of the Midwest, the Pennsylvania's pioneer leader, J. Edgar Thomson, moved to acquire control of lines west of Pittsburgh to Chicago and St. Louis. At the same time it confirmed its control of the lines from Philadelphia to Jersey City (the Pennsylvania would not roll a wheel onto Manhattan Island until the completion of Pennsylvania Station in 1910). These lines, whose importance to the development of America can hardly be overestimated, in combination with the Philadelphia, Wilmington & Baltimore (wrested from the B. & O. in the early 1880s), formed the great through route from New York to Washington, D.C.

The domination of international trade by the port of New York confirmed the New York Central as the preferred route for passengers, high-class freight (merchandise), and high-volume tonnages such as grain and petroleum for export, between the seaboard and the Midwest. The flowering of American heavy industry assured the eminence of the Pennsylvania Railroad. But the B. & O. was preeminent in neither of these kinds of traffic (although it played a major role in opening up soft coal fields) and despite the stubborn efforts of its highly individualistic leader, John Garrett, it declined in importance as the century progressed. Rapid growth in rail traffic, however, assured it of a place as an integrated route to Chicago and St. Louis. It had established very early a natural end-to-end relationship with railroads running west of Marietta, Ohio (once so important in the heyday of the steamboat) to Cincinnati and St. Louis; and it had doggedly completed a line from Cumberland, Maryland to Pittsburgh and on to Chicago the hard way: by building it on its own account. It lost out to the Pennsylvania as the carrier of large numbers of important people between Washington and New York (although it stubbornly refused to admit the fact even down to recent times); and its mainline route, inferior as it was to that of the Pennsylvania and especially the New York Central, inevitably condemned the company to second-class status as the fierce rate competition of the 1870s and 1880s raged. Still, it was an important link in the new coal, iron, and steel economy, and it might have ended the century as an independent factor in the consolidation movement but for John Garrett's excessive willingness to take risks.

A distinctly minor-league factor in the trunk line picture was the Erie Railroad. Built through difficult terrain primarily to serve local needs, and with no entrée to Manhattan, it was never a match for the Central in carrying either freight or passengers. It also lacked the concentration of industry that spelled success for the Pennsylvania Railroad and survival for the B. & O. Its early technical backwardness (that foolish choice of a broad gauge) meant the expenditure of large sums when its mistakes had to be rectified in the 1870s. The Erie built an extension to Buffalo when it became apparent, very early, that almost nobody wanted to ship or travel to Dunkirk, New York, and made an end-to-end alliance into the Midwest with a good line west of Meadville, Pennsylvania. But, like the B. & O., it found no partner to carry it into Chicago and, to the disgust of men like William H. Vanderbilt, who thought three trunk lines were already one too many, built its own. This temporary excess of trunk line capacity, with its downward pressure on rates, its temptation to the practice of rebating, and its role in the long-and-short-haul controversy, is one of the most significant features of nineteenth-century American railroad history.

Meanwhile, important new roads, radiating westward primarily from Chicago and secondarily from St. Louis, were well established by the 1870s and flourished in the ensuing years as Europe's demand for American agricultural products assured them a dependable and growing traffic. Among the most important of these railroads were the Chicago, Burlington & Quincy, which benefited immensely from the shrewd, conservative Boston management that created it; the Chicago, Milwaukee & St. Paul (which would add "& Pacific" to its name in the twentieth century), which was well run in its formative years; the Chicago & North Western, which duplicated the Milwaukee's lines to a considerable extent but which became one of the strongest Midwestern railroads in the nineteenth century; and the Chicago, Rock Island & Pacific, the first railroad to reach and cross the Mississippi and a major factor in American railroading until the dynamics of American transportation sadly passed it by.

Of these important midwestern railroads, only the Burlington grasped what men like James J. Hill, who was busy creating a new railroad empire out of a small but strategically important line in Minnesota, learned very early in their railroad careers: the vital need to control a through route all the way to the Pacific coast. The Burlington, its Boston management unequal to the task of either building or taking over such a route, sensibly decided to sell out at a premium price to Hill, who was more than equal to the task. Neither the North Western nor the Rock Island seemed to recognize the importance of a controlled route to the coast, and when the Milwaukee did, in the twentieth century, it was too late in the game to succeed. As a result these granger roads continued to get the shorter end of the stick in the division of through rates with other railroads and the exchange of through freight with their connections. Thus it was not these roads, which had been first upon the scene, but Hill himself—a virtual newcomer—who would lead the Midwestern consolidation movement.

For all the fanfare that accompanied the building of the first transcontinental railroad in the 1860s, and for all the romantic nonsense that has been written about it since, the importance of this accomplishment for many years was mainly psychological. Asa Whitney, who would live to see a transcontinental railroad a reality, spent much of his own time and money crusading for a road to the Pacific coast in the 1840s. Statesmen in the 1850s argued inconclusively the question of what route it should take, with much talk in favor of a southern or southwestern route. As the Civil War approached, the isolation of California began to worry many people and finally, in 1862, with the southerners conveniently absent from its halls, Congress passed and President Lincoln signed a bill to provide assistance (land grants and loans) to companies that would build lines from Council Bluffs, Iowa, to San Francisco. From this shaky beginning a pair of shaky railroads emerged by 1869: the Union Pacific and the Central Pacific—constituting, together, a route all the way to the Coast.

There was no shortage of railroad schemes with "& Pacific" in their corporate titles, but there was so little need for another transcontinental in these years that the second was not completed until 1883, when Collis P. Huntington, leader of the Southern Pacific, sent a tentacle of his road eastward to Needles, Arizona, to head off the Santa Fe which was about to invade "his" territory. A year later the Northern Pacific, one of the most poorly led railroads in American history, finally spliced together a line between the twin cities of Minneapolis and St. Paul in the East and Portland, Oregon, in the West. The Santa Fe, eventually to become one of America's strongest and best run railroads, completed a line to the Pacific during the 1880s. At a cost that led eventually to bankruptcy, it built its own line from Kansas City into Chicago, and remained for many years the only transcontinental with its own rails all the way from Chicago to the Pacific. The Chicago-Kansas City line of the Santa Fe is today one of the busiest and most vital in America.

Huntington, meanwhile, strengthened his near-monopoly grasp of golden California by building or buying up lines that extended his Southern Pacific all the way to New Orleans. In the process he shut out Tom Scott of the Pennsylvania Railroad who, on his own hook, was trying to line up or build links in a Pacific route, the eastern end of which his own mighty corporation would dominate. The last of the transcon-

tinentals to be built in the nineteenth century was James J. Hill's Great
Northern. Its superb route and rock-bottom operating costs made it the
strongest transcontinental of them all in the dark days that set in in
1893, and by 1901 Hill controlled the Northern Pacific, the Burlington,
and the Great Northern, which, taken together, constituted one of the
best-conceived regional consolidations in the nation.

Attempts to generalize about the progress of railroading in the
South in these years are likely to bog down in detail. One significant
fact, however, towers over all others: poverty. The South was poor in
capital, in managerial talent, in the kind of traffic on which the eastern
and granger roads thrived, and—as the war itself had shown—poor in
the genius for combination and subordination of individual egos which
a rational railroad system demanded.

The southern economy, whose foundations had never been very
deep, was shattered by the war. Not until the mid-1880s did cotton
production climb back to antebellum levels. What railroad building
there was, and what physical improvement southerners were able to
accomplish in their existing railroads, had to be paid for with first-mortgage gold bonds sold at staggering discounts; when they came due—or
even before, since they were forecloseable upon default of payment of
interest—confusion, contention, and reorganization followed. Thoroughly venal state legislators took their pound of flesh from these anemic corporations. And as long as the southern railroad "system"
remained fractured into many small independent lines, headed by
obtuse and often corrupt managers, the efficiencies of integration and
consolidation that produced such dramatic results elsewhere were
unattainable.

By 1883 a rickety consolidation, based upon a number of railroads
in the Southeast, had been assembled under the corporate umbrella of
the Richmond Terminal Company. This group, along with the conservative and well-run Louisville & Nashville Railroad and the north-dom-
inated Illinois Central, made up the most important segments of southern railroading. When panic and depression came in 1893, the
Richmond Terminal combine would collapse and the time would be at
hand for northern men and northern money to reorganize and rebuild
the southern railroad system along modern lines. Meanwhile the South,
in railroading as in most things, was a land of promise but a promise
long deferred.

The Place of the Railroad and the Telegraph
in 1890s America

By the end of the century Americans took it for granted that if they had
need of instantaneous information from afar, or if they had to travel or
ship goods more than a few miles anywhere in their vast country, the
telegraph and the steam railroad would be their only servitors, and, as

far as they could see, they would require no others. Such simplicity of generalization is almost breathtaking to the historian, and it leads him to a more fundamental question. Were the railroad and its handmaiden, the telegraph, merely refinements of innovations that had gone before? Or were they true discontinuities in the story of man's struggle to survive and multiply on earth? Not that historical discontinuities are all *that* rare, if one grants that they exist at all. The discovery of fire; the domestication of animals; the invention of the wheel; the harnessing of the winds and the triumphs of the early navigators that permitted movement of ships out of sight of land; the discovery of America and the population explosion in Europe after 1600—all of these events created new epochs, and can best be studied as fundamental breaks with the past record of material civilization.

The railroad and the telegraph, likewise, were true breaks with the past. Almost miraculous was the telegraph, which in a few short years made men thousands of miles apart privy to the same intelligence at almost the same moment. Modern man's grasp of electricity almost makes Prometheus' firebrand look antique by comparison. The instantaneous nature of the telegraph distinguished it from the postal service in concept, which is probably why Congress voted not to attach the new service to the postmaster general's office. The railroad's claim to uniqueness is not so obvious. Was it not merely faster, cheaper, and more dependable than earlier forms of land transportation? Many would answer, "yes," and because they have lost sight of the most fundamental difference between the railroad and earlier forms, they would place the trains on the continuum that begins with the ox-cart.

But the railroad brought a difference in kind as well: it could go virtually anywhere, given the careful planning and skillful construction that so quickly occurred as soon as the true potential of the railroad became apparent. And that one fact—the railroad's geographic universality—is the key to understanding its profound impact upon society. As sail power and the sextant converted the world's oceans from obstacles to movement to highways of commerce, so the railroad came near to converting the rugged and almost limitless land masses of North America into a broad limpid sea from no part of which man was excluded.

All this was as true of the rest of the world as of America. But it was in America that the railroad's awesome potential for minimizing the constraints of space and time was exploited to the fullest. For here we have the largest land mass on earth that is entirely included within those boundaries of latitude in which humans are at their most energetic. That land mass, furthermore, is ruled by a single sovereignty which has thrust aside traditional efforts of men to "withhold the world from men," assuring the full working-out of all the benefits of geographic specialization of industry, commerce, and agriculture.

In less portentous words: the railroad, by 1897, went virtually everywhere, and it, alone, carried people and their goods wherever they wanted to go. The revolution in travel and communication changed forever the concept of social relations, while the impressive transformation of the way business was carried on destroyed the old concept of the commonwealth and replaced it with one whose implications we are still struggling to work out. The learned professions, notably law, science, and engineering, received the stimuli that brought them and the ivied walls behind which they thrived to a prominence in national affairs they had never known before. American agriculture in its commercial form began with the railroad, and our political system continues to struggle to adapt itself to the new paths from which there was no turning back, despite a nostalgic urge to do so that has never died. And so on.

If Americans have not yet grasped the deeper significance of the railroad and the telegraph in American development it is almost certainly because only recently have they ceased to take them for granted. This is the paradox with which the cultural historian must always contend: forces that have changed society can not be studied systematically so long as they are compared solely to the wonders they made possible, that is, considered in terms of the present rather than the past, wherein they made the present possible. The foregoing is only to say that while the architectural embellishments of a new building may be more interesting to more people than the design and construction of the foundation, it is the latter that made the whole possible, and continues to support it. The automobile, truck, and airplane would decay and disappear if the railroads that made them possible and continue to support them were for any reason precluded from continuing to play their superior role in inland transportation. Just as any good architect—especially one practicing anywhere near the San Andreas fault—always asks about a striking building, "What holds it up?" we need to know this about American economic life. We need to study what the editor of the *Commercial & Financial Chronicle* meant when he commented more than a hundred years ago, "The fact is that the railroad has revolutionized everything."

CHAPTER 2

A Nation on Wheels:
The Formative Years of
the American Passenger
Train, 1830–1870

We hear no more of the clanging hoof,
    And the stage-coach rattling by,
For the steam-king rules the traveled world,
    And the old pike's left to die.

We have circled the earth with an iron rail,
    And the steam-king rules us now.

Rev. John Pierpont, 1859°

There are a briskness of step and a precision of speech about the
people of a railway creation that you never find in a town that is
only accessible to a stage-driver. . . . The locomotive is an
accomplished educator. It teaches everybody that virtue of
princes we call punctuality. It waits for nobody. It demonstrates
what a useful creature a minute is in the economy of things.

Benjamin F. Taylor, The World on Wheels, 1874

Prelude: Ben Franklin Goes to Philadelphia

Benjamin Franklin found out very early in life how far the English colonies in North America were from possessing even the rudiments of
nationhood. This remarkable man, who spent his life helping prepare
the young nation-to-be for its destiny, was only seventeen years old in
1723 when he set out from New York for Philadelphia, which was to
be his home for the next sixty-seven years. He would proceed southward from New York by sailing ship as far as Amboy, on the north Jersey coast, and then by stagecoach across New Jersey to the Delaware
River, down which he would float to Philadelphia.

Although the first English settlements in North America had been
planted over one hundred years before, little trade and even less social

°Grandfather of J. P. Morgan

33

intercourse went on between the colonies. Problems of transportation were one major reason. Even on the New York-Philadelphia corridor, there was not enough traffic to justify much more than the rude trails that passed for roads, and these were unusable much of the year. It is generally supposed that in that age of intrepid sailors, the broad ocean highway along the seaboard served just as well. Indeed, long-distance travel between the cities of the original colonies would be primarily by water well into the nineteenth century, but the peninsulas that created great bays like the Delaware and Chesapeake lengthened all-water journeys intolerably. We have forgotten, perhaps, what an unreliable thing a sailing ship can be, lacking its own source of power, especially in the tricky and dangerous business of navigating coastal waters. Young Franklin found out that there was *no* dependable way of traversing the ninety-odd miles between New York and Philadelphia.

On the first day of his trip, his ship was driven by adverse winds perilously close to the shores of Long Island, which were bordered by the submerged hulks of vessels that had met the same fate. After some thirty hours, the captain managed to maneuver his craft to Amboy. From there, Franklin took the stagecoach across country, still pursued by the storm which kept him thoroughly soaked all the way to the shores of the Delaware River. Missing the Philadelphia boat, he found that a two-week wait faced him before there would be another, and in disgust he rented a rowboat and rowed himself the rest of the way. The route he had followed became one of the most heavily traveled corridors in the world. It did not wait for the railroad to demonstrate its importance, however, for that technological miracle was still a century off when young Franklin began his long journey towards immortality in Philadelphia. A hundred years later, getting between New York and Philadelphia was a bigger problem than ever, but it was finally solved by the ensuing generation.

Travel in America: The Broad View

In a sense, Americans are "born" travelers, having descended for the most part from immigrants who, before the development of the ocean liner or jet airplane, had to face that most terrifying of experiences, a voyage across the wide ocean. As a result of their intrepidity most of us can spend our lives safely, comfortably, even luxuriously by our ancestors' standards, touring the world on budget tours, or never venturing more than fifty miles from the place where we were born. Many of us, in fact, almost never leave home, but travel remains a significant human activity in a nation that embraces an entire continent. There is more "intercity" travel (at least a hundred miles one-way) today than ever before in our history, and most of it is undertaken by clearly discernible groups within our total population. The role of travel in human society before the coming of the modern railroad passenger train was much less important than it is today, but by the time the automobile and the airliner came on the scene, the railroad passenger train had thoroughly revolutionized our views of personal mobility.

Anyone who would place travel in the proper context of social history, needs to bear in mind three fundamental facts. First, travel is highly concentrated among specific social-economic-occupational groups: mainly business travelers; the rich; students and the military; and vacationers in an astonishingly broad economic range. Large families with small incomes, however, hardly travel at all. Second, while innovations in transportation have usually been made in response to specific needs, new methods of travel have always created much of their traffic rather than merely taking it over from the previous technology. In other words, transportation innovations have changed the very economic and psychological environment in which travel takes place. The airliner, especially in transcontinental and transoceanic service, illustrates this dramatically, but so does the private car operating on the modern limited-access highway. Third, the place of the railroad in the history of travel is unique, for the railroad has not merely changed attitudes towards the feasibility of moving around, but it sustains such latter-day innovations as air and automobile travel that have largely replaced rail travel. Without the heavy industry that the railroads made possible, the automobile industry could never have come into being and would soon collapse. A Boeing 747 jetliner moves by rail long before it ever lifts into the air, as subassemblies ride across the continent to their final assembly point in Seattle. The world of 1830 yearned desperately for a better way to embrace the continent and to go about its burgeoning business. The world of 2000, intergalactic though it may be, will still look back to the railroad for reassurance and support.

"A Continuance of Miracles"

Lewis Cass is remembered today, if at all, as one of only two Democratic candidates for president of the United States who got beaten by a Whig. Cass, whose perpetual optimism about the American future seemed, to some, to border on the pompous, took his defeat in 1848 in stride, however, and continued to cheer on the westward march of Americans. In a speech at a celebration of the arrival of the first railroad on the banks of the Mississippi, at Rock Island, Illinois, he floridly declared, "The iron horse will take his morning draft from Lake Michigan, and slake his evening thirst from the waters of the Mississippi." Perhaps he was thinking of that day, more than a half century before, when he had set out for the West from his ancestral home in New England, in the first year of the nineteenth century. Cass's mode of transportation then was the oldest known to man: "shank's mare," or the "ankle wagon," as it was called in the folksy speech of the era. He walked.

We have all but forgotten today how much people depended upon walking to get from one place to another, sometimes considerable distances apart. Saddle horses were not for everyone's purse and, like sports cars, they were rather impractical, being long on engine and short on cargo space and demanding of constant maintenance. Wagons, of course, were the only possibility for families or the surprisingly large number of lone bachelors who were heading into the sunset for a new life and their own farm somewhere—they seldom had much idea just where—in the beckoning public domain. But wagons required at least some kind of roads, and of all the changes that the hand of man was to make in the face of the land during the half century following the Revolution, none would be harder to achieve in the dense, virgin forests that covered the rough terrain of northeastern North America than passable roads.

A miracle would be needed to get families and their household goods over what passed for roads as the westward urge swelled after the War of 1812. A miracle—or nearly so—there was, then, for what had been a trickle when Daniel Boone and his historic party first showed the way was soon a flood. Watching a single wagon desperately and dangerously negotiating the obstacles that stood in its way at any given point along the route over the Appalachians, a miracle seemed indeed to unfold as the heaving, panting horses dragged their burden on. One traveler, resting his horse at a point along the ascent, was profoundly moved by the seemingly endless line of wagons stretching out before his eyes. "A continuance of miracles," he called it, which in its very reality told the perceptive observer of the great nation that was being born.

On the eve of the railroad era, the beginning of a national road system languished as the nation debated the constitutionality of devoting federal aid to "internal improvements." The National Road, starting from Cumberland, Maryland, before 1815, reached Wheeling on the Ohio in 1818 and eventually Vandalia, Illinois, by the late 1840s. But it had never been very feasible to travel by road in this rugged land of such great distances. Westward travelers, especially those with impedimenta, quit the rough, rutty "thoroughfares" for water travel at the slightest opportunity. Remarkable indeed were the inland streams, many of them no more than creeks even during the spring rainy season, that were labeled "navigable." All the ancient arts of unpowered navigation were brought into play: flatboats, barges, keelboats, "arks," which provided some shelter, were knocked together by local entrepreneurs at strategic points, such as Marietta, Ohio, or Wheeling, Virginia, and sold to the pioneers, who would sell them for the lumber at some point farther on. But the road, the most ancient thoroughfare of them all, would not come into its own until the advent of the internal combustion engine.

It should be apparent by now that these westering hordes were not "traveling," in the modern meaning of the word. They were *moving,* going to a new place of habitation, and that was quite a different thing. They might keep going west—many of them did, finding that the pioneer spirit beat more vigorously in their breasts than that of the simple yeoman farmer who knows when he is well off—but few would have need to go east again. Their produce—well, that was quite another matter. The rivers, as we have been told in school, all ran the wrong way, unless somebody could think up a way to breast the current and go upstream. The politics of the Old Northwest bid fair to be molded by economic realities, and until the eve of the Civil War the area would lean noticeably in the direction of the Deep South as the market upon which it had to depend.

Crossing the mountains by means of lightly built, poorly suspended wagons (which have so frequently been turned into heavy eastern Conestoga wagons by ignorant painters and storytellers) was hardly better than walking. In fact, it was worse, in the opinion of many travelers. Still, even the inveterate walker found that if riding in the wagon bruised certain parts of his body, they were different parts from those employed in walking, and everybody rode a mile or two, now and then. It was the children who made the most intensive use of these early "Pullmans." Their very numbers startled one observer, who noted that a party of three wagons contained no less than forty children.

If the mountains were the all but insurmountable obstacle to westward travel, it may be supposed that travel in the tidal plains of the East, especially between the cities of Boston, New York, Philadelphia, Baltimore, and Washington, was fast, comfortable, and cheap by comparison. Geography, and the existence of a much bigger and more demanding traffic did make such key routes as New York-Philadelphia somewhat more civilized, but only gradually as the nineteenth century unfolded. As late as Albert Gallatin's years in Jefferson's cabinet, in the first decade of the new century, conditions remained quite primitive. Fine stone-arch bridges, such as the one across the Schulkyll at Philadelphia, or even the impressive wooden arch spans over the Delaware at Trenton, were a decade in the future, although suspension bridges were making their appearance. The number and breadth of the estuarial rivers—not to mention the bays—was a serious problem. At the turn of the century many bridges encountered on what would become U.S. Highway No. 1 were merely planks laid loose on a rude wooden structure, threatening to part as the carriage wheels jostled them. Leaving Philadelphia for Baltimore, one traveler was disgusted at the attempt primitive engineers had made at building a floating bridge. It floated all right, but the floor, which was a few inches above the water, sank a few inches below when a carriage crossed. The poor horses must have wondered what they had got themselves into.

Further south, ferryboat crossings and nearly vestigial roads were encountered. A trip from Baltimore to the raw, new capital city on the Potomac began with a ferryboat ride across the Patapsco—carriage and all—and ended with a madcap dash in which disaster was constantly averted by the driver's skill in maneuvering between the tree stumps dotting the roadway like so many pylons. Meals and overnight accommodations along the roads of young America are generally said to have been ample, which probably only goes to show how little travelers expected in the first place. On western routes, the "taverns" were little more than huts, and neither comfort, privacy, nor good food and drink were abundant. Pioneers were advised to live in their wagons. The problem of eating and sleeping along the way was solved by the railroads, not long after their introduction, simply by making the taverns part of the trains. In the age of the automobile, vast sums invested in motels provide first-class, if expensive, accommodations. The airlines have never solved the problem, as anyone so unfortunate as to be stuck overnight in a big city airport can testify.

Watery Interlude

The era of the road was still a hundred years in the future early in the nineteenth century, by which time the need for a better way was imperative. A better way was at hand, and the agent of nature that would rule advancing material civilization thereafter was invisible. Live steam embodied a remarkable power to do work, if applied to an appropriate mechanical contrivance by a clever mechanic. The stationary steam engine had been under constant, if painfully slow, improvement since early in the previous century. In 1806 Robert Fulton had put one on a modified keelboat, attached paddle wheels, and demonstrated that the resultant arrangement could make headway upstream against the current of the mighty Hudson River. Though far from obvious at the time, it was one of those milestones beyond which nothing would ever be the same again.

The river steamboats might have created the modern concept of travel as we know it today, but they did not. In the first place, they never constituted a comprehensive system; indeed, only the Hudson, in the East, and the Mississippi system, in the West, ran very far inland, and the western rivers were navigable only as far east as Pittsburgh, roughly speaking. Second, the steamboats were not common carriers, and whether the traveler would succeed in completing a journey as agreed upon when he bought his ticket was often problematical. And, third, while the boats were at least potentially comfortable, private, and well appointed, with plenty of often really good food, they were managed miserably. Just about everybody on the dock at the hour of sailing who wanted to take passage came on board, regardless of whether they had tickets, much less cabin space. Decks were often crowded with such passengers, who bedded down there for the night; the pressure on the dining room was great, and on the sanitary facilities, probably unmentionable.

Safety standards on steamboats were often disregarded in a competitive drive for speed—boatmen, meeting in convention in Cincinnati in 1838, blamed this on the demands of the passengers, but childish pride had a great deal to do with it. In the twenty-five years from 1825 to 1850, there were 150 major explosions on western river boats. The loss of life could be staggering even by the standards of the wide-body-jet age: in 1838, Captain Perrin of the fine boat *Moselle* got in a race and, with the safety valve tied down and pine knots feeding almost pure rosin into the boilers, the rivets gave way and soon 150 people lay dead—scalded, drowned, or trampled in the melée.

The indefatigable Englishwoman Harriet Martineau, whose books narrating her travels in America in those years sold hugely to stay-at-home Englishmen and Americans, said that an experienced traveler on board the *Henry Clay*, a popular boat bound from New Orleans to Louisville, on the Ohio, strongly advised her party to sleep in the daytime and to sit up at night, near the lifeboats. The gamblers, he had explained, who were up all night, would commandeer the lifeboats at the first alarm and quickly row away from the boat, leaving most of the passengers to perish in their nightclothes.

Life aboard the *Henry Clay* could be stimulating or painfully boring by turns, depending upon one's companions on deck or at meals. Miss Martineau found "good company" on board, generally. "Long trains of young men were present," and the lady obviously had an eye for them. One thing she could not understand was that while breakfast was at the normal hour of seven, luncheon and dinner were only two and a half hours apart, at eleven and one-thirty. She does not mention a tradition that Louis Hunter found so amusing in his study, *Steamboats on the Western Rivers*. Meals were anarchic. When the doors were opened, everybody rushed to the tables, upon which had been placed all the dishes that comprised the meal, from soup to dessert. Whatever one found before him, whether first course or last, he devoured, hoping that he would be able to seize something resembling a balanced meal before all the platters were licked clean.

The vaunted American canal system, which reigned briefly as the most important, and certainly the most expensive, internal improvement of the pre-railroad era, was intended to bridge those extensive distances between the eastern limits of river or lake navigation and the seaboard. In a few cases, and in the spectacular case of the Erie Canal, they succeeded in doing so quite well as far as freight was concerned. As an answer to the eastern extension of riverboat travel, they were a flop. To be sure, a timid traveler, such as the unfortunate woman who had to travel alone or a very poor wayfarer, would find the canal boat preferable to proceeding by expensive stagecoach or on horseback. Where the riverboat crawled, especially upstream, the canal boat, which depended upon the primitive technique of being pulled by a team of mules that ambled along a towpath under the direction of the original barefoot boy, must hardly have seemed to move at all. Even so, it was a stately, elegant way to travel, was it not? Listen to Miss Martineau, who had begun her trip west in New York State and decided to give up her seat in the "exclusive extra" coach her party had chartered, to try a night on the Empire State's pride and joy, the Erie Canal:

> I would never advise ladies to travel by canal, unless the boats are quite new and clean . . . On fine days it is pleasant enough sitting outside (except for having to duck under the bridges every quarter of an hour . . .) but the horrors of night and of wet days more than compensate . . . The heat and noise, the known vicinity of a compressed crowd, lying packed like herrings in a barrel, the bumping against the sides of the locks, and the hissing of water therein like an inundation, startling one from sleep; these things are very disagreeable . . . The appearance of the berths in the ladies' cabin was so repulsive that we were seriously contemplating sitting out all night, when it began to rain. . . .

In twenty-four hours' travel by canal boat, Miss Martineau could have covered about a hundred miles in 1838. A child of five, traveling with her on the same boat, might have lived to speed all the way from New York to Chicago in twenty-one hours, during which she would have unknowingly traversed almost the same route, sound asleep in a luxurious Pullman berth.

The young nation would not remain tied much longer to the few navigable streams of the nation, although the first cities of the Mississippi Valley were laid out on the assumption that the river steamboat was the wave of the future. Like the canal, it was transitional and transitory. American rivers were few indeed, and they never, by themselves, would constitute a complete trunk line system between tidewater and that vital center of the Old Northwest, the Great Lakes. Men had already begun to experiment with the application of steam to land vehicles, and sooner or later the light was to dawn effulgent: a steam-powered land vehicle did not have to run on a conventional road but, in fact, would do much better, in view of its concentrated weight, if run on rails. Beyond that, all that was required was a markedly more efficient steam-producing device, and once George Stephenson's tubular boiler had provided that, the railroad era was ready to begin.

The Long Gestation of the Passenger System: 1830–1870

Morning dawned bright but cold on January 6, 1853, reminding New Englanders of the long, hard days of winter that lay ahead. A carriage belonging to one of Boston's leading citizens, Amos A. Lawrence, textile magnate and a leader of the Whig party that had been so badly defeated—some said destroyed—in the presidential election the previous November, drew up before the modest depot of the Boston &

Figure 2.1 United States canal system at its peak, ca. 1860.

Lowell Railroad in Boston's North End. Only the quickness with which the coachman and baggage handler sprang to their tasks of helping the three passengers with their luggage would have seemed even a bit unusual to an onlooker. The travelers were ordinary–looking enough. The man, rather tall and perhaps a bit more than usually good-looking, shepherded the slight, rather dowdy woman, who was obviously his wife, and a little boy towards the train that was preparing to depart for points north of Boston. The man was perhaps fifty, his wife several years younger, although her face suggested great sadness. Their son, about eight years old, was excitedly anticipating a train ride. Hardly anybody took any notice of the three as they boarded one of the coaches, though in less than two months the man was to be inaugurated as the fourteenth president of the United States.

President-elect Franklin Pierce, his wife, and their son, Bennie, had come to Boston a few days before to attend the funeral of the elder Mr. Lawrence who, despite his ardent Whig politics, had been very fond of Pierce. The unexpected visit made it doubly important that they get back to their home in Concord, New Hampshire, to make preparations for the move to Washington. It was a task the pallid Mrs. Pierce dreaded. She longed for the peace and quiet of the granite hills of New England, but her husband's political career had unexpectedly received the big boost that could come from emerging as the "dark horse" compromise candidate for president. She had borne Pierce several children, and watched them flourish and then sicken and die as children so frequently did in that day. Bennie was all that was left to them, and the White House was the last place she would have chosen to rear a little boy. Her spirits sagged as they climbed aboard the coach.

There was little about the railroad coach to minister to their physical comfort, much less their spirits. Railroad car design had not advanced very far in the twenty years or so since the "steam cars" first began to replace the stagecoach for inland travel. It was hardly more than a very large wooden box, employing no metal components save the nails and a few brackets for bracing, here and there. Such warmth as there was came from a smelly, potbellied coal stove at the end of the car, cherry-red against the likelihood that the crew would pay it little attention during the run. Two "bogie" trucks were the running gear— metal and wood assemblies consisting of four flanged wheels and pivoted in the center, one bogie at each end. (The British, who were still using carriages with four rigid wheels at that time, jeered that American railroads were flimsily built and the rails, bridges, and trestles could not support the weight of a car on four wheels, but needed eight!) The straight-backed seats were a considerable improvement over the wooden benches of the earliest passenger coaches, being well-cushioned and reversible so that passengers could sit facing each other. Bennie immediately occupied the one facing his parents. Three or four of the coaches were about all the locomotive, an early wood-burning version of the eight-wheeled locomotive that would dominate American passenger trains to the end of the century, could pull. The train was held together by simple link-and-pin couplers of wrought iron, and each car was stopped individually by a brake wheel mounted on the open platform at each end of the cars.

At the appointed time the little train slowly clanked out of the station and across the low bridge that spanned the Charles River at that point. Along a long earthen embankment, the train had moved about a mile through the open countryside, when suddenly the train lurched, the primitive coupling on the Pierce's coach snapped, and the car ran off the rails, toppling down the embankment. Mr. and Mrs. Pierce were miraculously unscathed, but a shriek from the suddenly stricken Mrs. Pierce chilled the blood of everybody in the car. Beneath the seat on which he had been sitting, Mrs. Pierce saw her little boy, his head crushed by the collapsed seat.

Mrs. Pierce never recovered from her loss, convinced that God had taken Bennie from them so that her husband could give all his attention to the cares of office. But Franklin Pierce could only have found comfort in Bennie's presence in the White House during the unpleasant, frustrating four years that he was to preside over the progressive decay of the Union. As it was, he entered office under grievous psychological handicaps unique among American presidents.

This tragic story of the first and only railroad wreck in which a president or president-elect ever was involved serves to dramatize the primitive nature of American railroads after twenty years of development. The marshaling of capital in the new nation was a slow process. Besides, two decades is a short time in the technological development of a new transportation mode, and the steam railroad was newer than anything else in the western world at that time. The development of the practical, comfortable, safe, and speedy passenger train, which did not require a change of cars between major cities and ran on convenient schedules, was to take place over the three decades following the Civil War. Just getting some kind of rail system in place where it was needed most would occupy Americans well into the post-Civil War period. In 1852 the process was just getting up to full speed.

Primitive as were the Boston & Lowell Railroad's trains, this pioneer railroad and its many New England imitators were more advanced than railroads elsewhere in the Union. For one thing, New England railroad promoters had recognized that their railroads would depend upon interregional trade for a large part of their business, so they made sure that they could interchange freight with each other, by choosing the same track gauge. They could not influence promoters in other regions, of course, notably in Canada, where the broad gauge of five feet six inches was adopted, but they could place their bets prudently on the wisdom of the man who had built and demonstrated the first successful locomotive. George Stephenson's choice of four feet eight-and-one-half inches was good enough for them. It was a smart choice, and saved hundreds of thousands of dollars when the inevitable day came when a uniform American gauge had to be settled on.

The decade of the 1850s was to see a remarkable acceleration in the development of American railroads, hand in hand with the new American industrial system, even as it saw the political decay of Unionism. Not only was total mileage increased severalfold, but combinations of originally independent lines were undertaken in the first halting steps towards the organization of a system of through lines. Only a little more than a year before the Pierce's sad journey from Boston to Concord, Bostonians had put on a boisterous three-day Great Railroad Jubilee, marking the completion of a through railroad line to Montreal, with which Boston expected to have a flourishing inland trade. (The accomplishment was all the more important inasmuch as Portland, Boston's arch rival, was building her own line to Montreal in what would be her last bid to remain a major Atlantic port.) Even more significant, as it turned out, was the completion of the Western Railroad of Massachusetts, which extended the Boston & Worcester's Boston-Pittsfield line to Albany and a connection with the Erie Canal. Eventually to be merged as the Boston & Albany, this through line would remain Boston's chief rail link with the West down to the present day.

New England's railroads, however, would remain largely local or intraregional affairs until after the Civil War. To be sure, all-rail lines extended south to New York and beyond, as well as north to Portland, but service was very slow and was interrupted at numerous points. Consequently, most travelers going any distance up or down the northeast coast still saw the railroads in the role in which they had been cast: as convenient means of getting to ports such as Fall River and New Bedford, from which they could take steamers to New York without having to sail precariously around the tip of Cape Cod. This role was very common along the east coast, broken up as it was by tidal rivers and bays. The little line that western Connecticut residents built in the early 1850s to keep the major inland town of Danbury prosperous, the Danbury & Norwalk, terminated at tidewater at Wilson's landing, where steamers plying to and from New York City via Long Island Sound tied up. Such early railroads were a godsend to towns like Worcester, Massachusetts, barely thirty miles from Boston; from the moment the Boston & Worcester began passenger service in the early 1830s, what had been a tiring overnight trip by coach or wagon became an easy day trip. Businessmen, farmers, and professional men from each city could take the early morning train, spend a full day doing what came so naturally to Yankees—"trading"—and return home in time for supper.

It was in the New York—Philadelphia corridor, where, for at least 125 years, travellers between America's two major cities had endured hardship and frustration, that the early passenger railroad had its most dramatic impact. Among the half-dozen or so pioneer railroads of the period 1827 to 1830 claiming to have been the first to provide rail passenger service was the Camden & Amboy Railroad. Its chief promoter was a superb civil engineer, George Stevens, who had followed George Stephenson's successes in England closely. Stevens knew just what he was doing when he organized a group of men to finance a railroad line from South Amboy, on the Jersey side of New York harbor just below the tip of Manhattan Island, to Bordentown, New Jersey, the nearest point on the Delaware River that a line of railroad could reach. Sure enough, Stevens believed that water transportation should be used where available, employing the steam cars only to fill in the inevitable gaps. Down the Hudson, from a convenient ferry slip in what today we would call lower Manhattan, Philadelphia-bound passengers would float on a pleasant ferry trip to South Amboy. There they would take passage in a line of "stagecoaches" that had neither horses nor drivers. They were the passenger coaches of the Camden & Amboy Railroad, and standing at the head of the line, steam up and ready to haul them to Bordentown (the line was later extended to Camden, thus cutting a couple of hours off the running time) was the *John Bull,* one of Stephenson's earliest locomotives; Stevens had bought it on a trip to England, where it was disassembled, carefully packed, and shipped. Arriving in New Jersey, it was painstakingly reassembled by a man who had never laid eyes on a locomotive before.

The Camden & Amboy Railroad was organized to make a profit, and at that occupation it would have drawn the envy of Midas. True to form, it jealously guarded its monopoly of rail service between New York and Philadelphia for a remarkably long time. A parallel route appeared, beginning at Jersey City, right across the Hudson from Manhattan, then crossing the Delaware on Trenton's historic vehicular bridge and terminating in Philadelphia, thus avoiding the ferry ride across the Delaware. Equally true to form, the two were soon joined in one. Rates were kept high in this antediluvian, competition-free era, and, while passengers complained bitterly, they knew that the Camden & Amboy, at almost any price, was a vast improvement over the stagecoaches of yore. Even so, the C. & A. and links to the south were slow to provide through service; five different lines made up the New York–Washington service, a real annoyance during the Civil War. Among those annoyed were some of the nation's most important political figures, but it was not until 1863 that through service between the two great cities without a change became possible.

To open the Great West, however—that was the destiny of American railroads, was it not? Little more than a start in this direction was made before the Civil War. Fairly dependable transportation was available to the Mississippi and a short distance beyond. Even the South, if you take railroad maps of the period at face value, had rail service from Charleston to Memphis, from Chicago to New Orleans, and along the east coast as far south as Savannah. But if the routes in the North were slow and inconvenient, requiring numerous changes of trains and offering primitive accommodations (early efforts to provide sleeping cars were almost worse than none at all, and most passengers sat up all night), those in the South were beneath contempt. Viewed from the standpoint of the needs of an industrial civilization, the American South did not achieve even minimal travel facilities until late in the century. Indeed, the South's five-foot track gauge was not finally converted to standard gauge until a memorable Monday and Tuesday in 1886, when, in the words of George R. Taylor and Irene D. Neu, "the South joined the Union."

The story of the obstacles to a unified railroad system that were encountered in the first generation of the new technology, and how they were overcome, is a vital chapter in the story of the unification of the American nation. These obstacles were by no means all or even chiefly technological, as modern Americans might assume. Most of them were man-made. The fact is that while the ultimate potentialities of the railroad were apparent to a remarkable number of farsighted men, most Americans viewed them as a means of accomplishing more cheaply and conveniently their own immediate, limited, parochial objectives. Insofar as the railroad threatened to wipe out the traditional advantages of geographical location—as it did almost everywhere, in one way or another—the railroad to many was a force to be carefully reined in. The success with which local interests managed to hobble this lusty steed for over thirty years is a testament to the vigor of state and local rights in an age in which the powers of federalism were hardly realized.

In the beginning, a profound distaste for betting on the future held back the development of railroad systems. Prudent Philadelphians were loath to bet on the steam railroad when, at the end of the 1820s, they decided they had to do something to blunt the power of New York's Erie Canal to preempt interior trade. The Pennyslvania Main Line works, the hybrid system of a steam railroad and canals interspersed with inclined planes powered by stationary engines, amused Charles Dickens during his travels in America because of the emphasis it placed upon leisurely travel:

> The canal has run . . . by the side of the Susquehanna and Juniata rivers, and has been carried through tremendous obstacles. Yesterday we crossed the mountains. This is done by *railroad* [inclined planes hauling up flat cars on which the canal boats have been placed]. You dine at an inn upon the mountain . . . and are rather more than five hours performing this strange part of the journey. The people have terrible legends of its dangers; . . . there are some queer precipices . . . but every precaution is taken.

It is an oft-told tale of how the Philadelphians, upstaged by their neighbor to the south, Baltimore—whose merchants had less capital but more courage—shortly had to abandon their state-owned facility

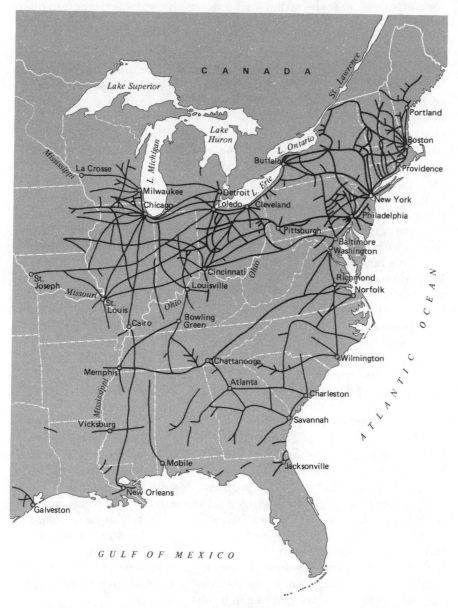

Figure 2.2 The pattern of American rail transportation emerges: the system on the eve of the Civil War.

for a privately built all-rail system across the mountains. It is often overlooked, however, that few Marylanders had all that much faith in the
B. & O.; even as Charles Carroll of Carrollton turned the first spade of
earth, President John Quincy Adams was doing the same for the Chesapeake & Ohio Canal, which had been undertaken to connect the bay
with the Ohio River at Wheeling. The two soon came into conflict over
constricted rights of way through the mountains. As late as 1873, oppo-
nents of the railroad "monopoly" praised waterways as "the natural
channels which seem to be so plainly indicated by the hand of the Great
Architect of the continent," and the Windom Committee of the U.S.
Congress recommended building more canals.

It is remarkable with what confidence Americans in those days conferred absolute priority to the existing state of affairs over new ideas.
Interest in canals and river waterways continued strong to the end of
the century, probably because of their great success in Great Britain.
(The "pork barrel" aspects of government aid to rivers and harbors,
became a factor only in the next century.) To be sure, by 1850, steamboat companies had had it all their own way, where inland commerce
and travel were concerned, for thirty years, and they continued to
wield great power during the vital decade of the 1850s. When the first
bridge across the Mississippi, completed by the Rock Island Railroad in
1856, was declared by the U.S. Supreme Court not to be a hazard to
navigation, it was soon thereafter destroyed by a fire, of which one did
not have to be much of a cynic to fathom the cause. To be sure, bridges
were costly undertakings and few appeared across the Mississippi or,
for that matter, the Ohio and the Missouri, until after 1865.

Most attention is rightfully given to the incompatibility of the non-
standard gauges as the chief reason for the slow unification process,
and, indeed, most sections of the country suffered from this form of
myopia until well after the Civil War. To some extent railroad builders
themselves contributed to the problem, for many adamantly insisted
that the four foot eight inch gauge was too narrow, and today many of
their descendants wish that they had won the fight. The early adoption
of this "standard" gauge by northeastern railroads, where most of the
traffic was, eventually settled the matter. But he who would stick to
technological factors does not know the bulldog tenacity with which
local American businessmen guarded the trade that they had carefully
nurtured before the railroad began to change things.

The railroad became a clear and present danger to local trade once
through travelers and shippers began to complain that railroads were
not joined together within the cities in which they originated or terminated. Most of the complaints came from shippers, enterprising businessmen, and budding manufacturers who were casting their sales nets
farther and farther afield. It was a costly matter to transfer freight by
wagon from one terminal to another. After all, passengers could get

themselves to their transfer station, but someone had to be paid to see that goods were transferred safely and promptly. And one man's cost is another man's revenue! A city like Richmond, Virginia, for example, might appear on maps to have been a junction point for four different railroads in 1861, but a large-scale city map, like the one in Taylor and Neu's *American Railroad Network, 1861–1890,* reveals that no local belt line, much less a union station, made it possible for a train or even a single freight or passenger car entering on one line to depart by another. Every ploy known to shrewd local lawyers was used to keep things nice and cozy for local carting companies, freight forwarders, hack drivers, hotel and restaurant owners, local wholesale merchants, and anyone else who found a foothold in an environment of what we might call "enlightened backwardness."

Differences in gauge were convenient excuses for refusing to run freight or passenger cars through, but they were not necessary. They were just as frequently the result, not the cause, of interruptions in through traffic systems. Local sovereignty was all that was necessary to preserve the *status quo ante* at first, but when the price in terms of money, inconvenience, and compromised military plans eventually became too great, local sovereignty would bite the dust. Philadelphia is the leading case. Four railroads, their traffic booming under Civil War conditions, entered the city (two from the north, one from the west, and one from the south) and not one made connection with another. Recalling the violent revolt of the businessmen of Erie, Pennsylvania, against allowing trains to pass through without paying tribute in the 1850s, the *New York Times* grumbled in 1863 that "Philadelphia . . . has not entirely outgrown the village peevishness manifested at Erie." It was a situation that denied the inevitable promise of the railroads, and later that year, for the first time, it became possible to ride all the way from Jersey City to Washington, D.C., without changing trains. Largely as a result of wartime experience in through freight shipment, Congress in 1866 passed a law requiring all railroads freely to exchange freight in interstate commerce.

Not until 1870, however, did the four railroads—Camden & Amboy, Philadelphia & Trenton, Philadelphia, Wilmington & Baltimore, and Baltimore & Ohio—finally announce through service which would make the New York-Washington run, for all practical purposes, the service of a single railroad as it was destined to become in the next fifteen years. Three conveniently scheduled trains, two day trains and one overnight, made the run in about nine and a half hours, a figure which has been consistently lowered over the last 115 years to as little as two and a half hours, city-center to city-center. Two years later the bridge over the Missouri River from Council Bluffs to Omaha was completed, giving America its first unbroken rail route from sea to sea. At the same time, if less spectacularly, the eastern trunk line railroads were tightening their holds on the lines west of Buffalo, Pittsburgh, and Cincinnati, which would soon be integral links in the most important avenues of travel in the world.

In the 1850s, however, when so many European travelers took the time that Americans could seldom spare to write about the problems of getting around in this huge new land, it seemed a hopeless dream that a comprehensive, coordinated system might ever develop. The young Englishman Henry Arthur Bright journeyed south from New York to Richmond, west to St. Louis, and north to St. Paul, then east to Montreal and Quebec, and back through Boston to New York. He avoided the railroads wherever water transportation was satisfactory, which was possible for much of his trip. Going south from New York, he was amused at the "charming variety of coveyances, ferry, railroad and steamer, that were necessary to get him to Philadelphia. "The railway carriages resemble the Belgian second class," he noted, "and here there is but one class." Clearly, something more than the wooden box that Bennie Pierce died in would have been welcome. Bright thought that one and a half hours to go from Baltimore to Washington was pretty good time, and he was right, in a day when few trains made an average speed of twenty-five to thirty miles an hour between terminals.

South of Washington, on the Orange & Alexandria Railroad, Bright had his first and last experience with southern railroads. Leaving Washington at 6:30 a.m. (by ferry across the Potomac), he did not arrive in Charlottesville until 1:30 that afternoon. "Not a hundred miles to go, and such a time about it," he complained, noting that the cars were hot and dusty. He was content to retrace his steps, make for the Ohio River, and ease downstream for the genteel old city of St. Louis. From there he joined the growing throngs that were headed for the upper Mississippi country and the rapidly growing community at the head of navigation, St. Paul. Minnesota's first railroad, between St. Paul and St. Anthony (later Minneapolis), would not turn a wheel for another ten years, but the route up the river was well developed, and on the boat Bright would have met many people eager to talk about the plans they hoped to mature in the empire opening up to the north.

Bright's trip back east is interesting for what it tells us about the ruggedness of travel on the route south of the Great Lakes, so soon to become a major artery of commerce. Jolting overland from Galena (where he got a look, no doubt, at the lead mines that caused Illinois's pioneer railroad to be built in that direction), he caught a Chicago-bound train at Rockford. Leaving at 5 a.m., it seemed that he would certainly be in Chicago by 10 p.m. for a good night's sleep. Many were the hazards of antebellum railroading, however, and the purpose of the "cow cradle," as Bright called the cowcatcher, was soon made clear to him. Somewhere along the line a hapless calf was caught in the device (the trouble with bovines was that they seldom had enough sense, at any age, to move off the track when a train approached) and the catcher, being devised for larger beasts, was helpless to prevent the inevitable derailment. A delay of six hours ensued.

Continuing east, Bright left Chicago at 8:30 a.m. on the Michigan Southern & Northern Indiana Railroad (later part of the Lake Shore segment of the New York Central System), bound for Toledo. Someone had told him that the scenery was "better" than on the "other Central route to Detroit," and the lake boats from Toledo were finer. After taking thirteen hours to go 250 miles, they arrived in Toledo at about 10 p.m. and took the overnight boat for Cleveland. There they arrived the next evening at 7 p.m., but instead of continuing on shortly for points east, the boat lay at the dock until 1 a.m., waiting for a connecting train to arrive from southern Ohio. "The cars from Cincinnati had run off the line, and then run into another train," Bright explained, as if it were an everyday occurrence.

The worst trains were encountered in the South. Frederick Law Olmsted, the architect of Central Park and other notable landscaping marvels in later years, traveled extensively in the antebellum south and was enraged by southerners' contempt for the importance Yankees attached to having a fresh, clean bed to themselves, digestible food, trains that made their advertised connections at least half the time, and crews that had enough sense to keep lubricants on hand for the axles when they developed "hot boxes." Olmsted's parting assessment of the South's prospects owed much to the travel conditions he had encountered: "There is nothing that is more closely connected, both as cause and effect, with the prosperity and wealth of a country than its means and modes of traveling, and of transportation of the necessities and luxuries of life."

America, as befitted a new land, was a land of contrasts. English travelers commented on the best and the worst with equal vigor. None other than the editor of the foremost travel guide, the British edition of *Baedeker*, approved vigorously of America's open passenger car design, which he considered superior in all ways to the British compartments. But our Pullman sleeping cars repelled him. He disapproved of the skimpy dressing rooms that were provided for women (the traditional open-section Pullman continued until its demise to allocate about twice as much room for men to smoke, dress, and make their toilets as for women, the company pleading that there were far more male passengers to accommodate), and the fact that their berths were not segregated from those of the men. "It is considered tolerable that they should lie with the legs of a strange, disrobing man dangling within a foot of their noses," he snorted. The accident rate was high, and the slowness of branch-line travel intolerable. Steamboats were "floating palaces," and he admired the flat, clumsy, but very efficient ferries he encountered at river crossings. But the mail and telegraph services in America, he thought, were less reliable than in Britain. Another observer noted the heavy dependence, especially in the South, upon shaky wooden trestles to carry railroads through swampy and marshy areas. Curiously, passengers were uniformly terrified at the thought of being delayed at night while sitting on a trestle, but it was not so much the fear of toppling off as the fear of taking a chill from the "bad air."

Everybody seemed to like Cincinnati, where food and lodging were several notches above that found in most western cities. Louisville was another bright spot. Both the Burnet House in Cincinnati and the Galt House in Louisville, one traveler exclaimed, "amazed even the European travelers." American hotels were lively places, not the hushed retreats of Europe. "If motion be life, there is no central point in the world where more vital energy is consumed in 24 hours than in the hotels of the U.S.," said an American travel writer, Marie Grandfort. But it did not pay to inspect one's room too closely. Reflecting the shortage of domestic labor in America, the care of rooms even at the three-hundred-room Burnet House was poor, and the linen was changed infrequently.

Fried foods were characteristic of eateries grand and humble, but travelers discovered there was a great difference between one technique of frying and other. Little variety was offered the traveler. En route, the antebellum visitor would have found few on-board comforts. Stops at lunch rooms soon became the subject of jokes about the inevitable dyspepsia they produced, but in actuality travelers seemed determined to bolt their food in a fraction of the time allotted and climb back aboard quickly in fear of losing their seats or missing the departure altogether. Americans soon became famous for crowding through the gates as soon as a train was ready for boarding, and for standing impatiently in the aisles, luggage in hand, as the train entered the yards at the end of its journey.

The End of the Beginning: The Era of
the Modern Passenger Trains Begins, 1870

By 1870 the era of the modern, high-speed, comfortable, through passenger train was ready to begin. Countless innovations in American life, large and small, had brought American railroads to the point where no journey within the commonwealth would be considered too long to be comfortable. Travel even began to be looked upon less and less as a hardship and more and more as a pleasurable way of seeing a young giant of a country unmistakably passing from adolescence to young manhood.

After 1870, resistance to the establishment of through routes, even where two or more independent railroads were involved, would diminish almost to the vanishing point. The eastern trunk lines, or at least the greatest of the four, the New York Central and the Pennsylvania, were becoming powerful combinations of railroads over which effective central control was exercised. The western connections of these roads—

the Lake Shore, the Michigan Central, and the Pittsburgh, Fort Wayne & Chicago—welcomed the security that came from being acquired by strong eastern railroads. The old Commodore and his cautious son, William, might tremble at the thought of managing a 900-mile-long enterprise, and even J. Edgar Thomson, the genius who put Philadelphia back in the railroad stakes by engineering the Pennsylvania across the Alleghenies, may have had his doubts, but there was to be no turning back. One ghastly scare that control of these vital western extensions might pass into hostile hands was all that was necessary to convert conservative eastern businessmen to the new philosophy of expansion, and Jay Gould provided that scare as the 1860s came to a close. Railroad grand strategy would henceforth dispense with old-fashioned ideas as thoroughly as fashion abandoned the hoop skirt.

By 1870 the New York Central could offer through train service, including sleeping cars, via either the suspension bridge at Niagara Falls and the Michigan Central ("the Great Central Route"), or the Lake Shore at Buffalo. Neither the leading Unionist, Daniel Webster, nor that apostle of western expansion, Henry Clay, would live to see the rail link between the Atlantic seaboard and Chicago joined, first at Niagara Falls and shortly thereafter at Pittsburgh, but they died knowing that the union was imminent. Two more decades had been required to realize the potential of this junction, but by the early 1870s it was accomplished, and that event, in turn, only marked another beginning.

Another young Englishman, W. F. Rae, stepped off the boat from England in 1870, eager for materials for a travel book he had in mind. From the New York Central's shabby depot at 31st and 10th Avenue, soon to be replaced by the huge new Grand Central Depot at 42nd Street and Fourth Avenue in New York City, he departed on the first leg of a trip all the way to the west coast. Rae speaks of the Pullmans being put on at Rochester the next morning. (Perhaps he slept in a Wagner Palace car; W. J. Vanderbilt's daughter had married Pullman's chief competitor, and Pullman cars would not be welcome on the Central for another twenty years.) After the inevitable thrill of passing over the raging Niagara River on John Roebling's delicately suspended bridge, the travelers passed onto the tracks of the Great Western Railroad of Canada, which would carry them to Detroit. Bearing in mind the hundreds of Englishmen who owned Canadian railroad stock, Rae commented that the Great Western was more efficiently operated than the Grand Trunk, because the latter had received government subsidies and was therefore subservient to politicians. At Detroit they passed onto the Michigan Central. Next morning, after two nights and one full day of travel, the train arrived in Chicago, nine hundred miles from New York.

The trip must have been pure pleasure compared to the same trip just a few years earlier. One of the three Pullman cars was a "hotel car," consisting of private rooms and a small kitchen as well as open sections. Following a European custom that American railroads unfortunately dropped later on, the conductor came through to take reservations for meals, which sound adequate in every way to produce the proper Victorian postprandial torpor: five breads, four cold meats, six hot dishes, and eggs cooked seven different ways, in addition to several vegetables and fruits, served on removable tables.

Eastern railroads were already finding the competition for the passenger's dollar heating up, and they were making it as easy as possible for the traveler. In New York, Rae had bought his ticket and checked his baggage right in his hotel, whose porter sent it on ahead to the depot. Entering Chicago, Rae was delighted to find a representative of the omnibus coming through selling tickets for transfer, with baggage, to one's hotel. The best ones in Chicago, Rae noted, were the Sherman and the Tremont. Very soon, someone might have told him, these would be in the shadow of the elegant new Palmer House and that magnificent Victorian pile that spelled Chicago to two generations of travelers, the Grand Pacific Hotel. Most Englishmen, it seems, liked Chicago for "its good hotels, fine buildings, well-stocked shops, and well-kept streets." "Compared with the bustle of Chicago," another traveler remarked, "the bustle of New York seems stagnation."

Chicago was the best place to take trains for the west coast, and the scene at the railroad station was one of great bustle and confusion. In 1870 the bridge at Council Bluffs had not yet been finished, so the train that carried Rae across Iowa did not go through. Here, he noted, there was much room for improvement. Passengers had to crowd into an omnibus to be taken down to the ferry, then board another on the opposite bank to be delivered to a waiting Union Pacific train. Apparently it had not been possible to make advance sleeping car reservations, for at this point a demeaning struggle ensued for one of the few Pullman berths. It was a long, arduous journey they faced, and the traveler who ended up with only a seat in one of the coaches was much to be pitied. The fare in coaches was $33.20 from Omaha to San Francisco, and the small additional sleeping car charge was well worth it, especially after the bridge was finished in 1872, for then Pullmans with drawing rooms were available. Susan Coolidge, writing about her experiences in *Scribner's Monthly,* said the new cars were truly luxurious. Dining car service was good, too, she reported, but the lunch rooms along the way offered little variety.

George Pullman had not yet got his sleeping cars porters well trained in the early 1870s, it seems, for one traveler exclaimed that "there is no one who surpasses in effective malignity the sleeping-car porter." The big complaint, however, was boredom, according to another chronicler, Samuel Storey. The trains went very slowly, and they stopped wherever a station agent flagged them down. "I wish you would put on some steam," remarked a disgruntled traveler to the conductor, "for I'd like to see where my wife is buried before the tombstone is crumbled to pieces."

Very soon after transcontinental service started, the inevitable guidebooks appeared. The best of the early ones was *Crofutts's,* whose publisher claimed in 1882 to have sold half a million copies despite no less than thirty-one imitators. For the nation as a whole, Appleton, a pioneer publisher, put out an early compendium of timetables. Overland travel, however, did not mean that passengers could peer at life in the wild West while insulated from its excesses. Many broke up their journey—perhaps those who failed to get a Pullman berth—and saw the frontier up close at some point along the way. Crofutt was paid to sing the praises of specific western towns, like Cheyenne, and to paint them as solid communities, but travelers often found that the bourgeois ethic was not yet well rooted that far west. Nor were they always entirely safe on the trains. "Cowboy jollification" gave folks something to write home about when parties of liquored-up cowboys, looking for a good time on Saturday night, would commandeer a train and ride along for fifty miles or so while making bets about each other's marksmanship and using the kerosene lamps as targets.

Rail travel was not only faster, but also far safer than any other mode, even steamship, from the beginning, and it would constantly improve. The fastest growth in travel, of course, was in the more populous East. Travel to the west coast grew slowly at first, but took wings after 1880: arrivals and departures on the Southern Pacific at San Francisco averaged only twenty-five thousand a year during the first seven years, but were five times that number by the mid-eighties.

The next sixty years of American travel would belong to the railroad train, for 1870 was only the close of a long opening chapter. Writing of his impressions after a trip all the way to San Francisco and back by rail, the Englishman, Samuel Bowles, was eloquent. "It is the unrolling of a new map," he said; "a revelation of new empire, the creation of a new civilization."

CHAPTER 3

Mobile, Hard-Working, and Hard-Playing: Rail Travel and the Transformation of American Society, 1870–1900

> The closest the average man ever gets to true luxury in America is in a Pullman sleeping car.
>
> Franklin D. Roosevelt (attributed)

An Era of Expanding Dreams and Expectations

Ticket-sellers, conductors, porters, and not a few of the passengers who were waiting for their trains in New York's new Grand Central Depot that cold morning in January 1877, had plenty to talk about. It hardly seemed possible, but the old man was really dead. For far longer than most of them could remember, Commodore Vanderbilt had been calling the tune in transportation, first on the waters around New York, then on the broad Atlantic, until greater opportunities offered themselves in railroading and, in the last decade of his colorful career, on the national transportation scene. To be sure, not many of them quite yet recognized that passenger traffic had become a national phenomenon, but it had. The Commodore, along with men like J. Edgar Thomson of the Pennsylvania and John W. Garrett of the Baltimore & Ohio, had done much to creat it, for they had done the most to weld together through routes under a single owner's control following the Civil War.

Some said it was news of the horrible accident on the Lake Shore & Michigan Southern Railroad at Ashtabula, Ohio, only a few weeks earlier, which took ninety-two lives, that had sapped the ailing old man's will to live. There were many who blamed Vanderbilt's famous stinginess for the defective trestle, through which the Lake Shore's crack train, the *Pacific Express*, had crashed in a fiery heap on the ice far below, killing so many people. Certainly the tragedy had done nothing to raise the Commodore's spirits as he lay dying. (To his doctors, who had been trying to relieve his acidosis with champagne, he

groused, "Won't sody water do jes' as well? It's a deal cheaper.") The
Lake Shore, snatched from Jay Gould's grasp only eight years before,
was his pride and joy. It had made his New York Central & Hudson
River Railroad into a through line to Chicago. He had his doubts that
any one man could oversee such a stupendous property, but he reveled
in the stability and rich profits that owning his own through line
brought. (He would have taken over the troublesome Erie, too, if those
bandits, Gould and Jim Fisk, had not beaten him to it!)

The Commodore had got into the railroad business right after the
Civil War, when he saw that for a long time to come the seas would
belong to naturally seafaring nations like England. It was a transfer of
capital from a less attractive industry to one with a brighter future, in
the classic style that only a free society can tolerate, and whose long-
term benefits only free men and women can reap. First he had acquired
the Hudson River Railroad, which New York merchants had built
rather belatedly up the west side of Manhattan and the east bank of the
river to Albany, once they realized that Mr. Fulton's steamboat was not
to be the last word in trading with the interior. Next came the New
York Central, which Erastus Corning and other upstate businessmen
formed from a dozen small lines that made a through route from Albany
to Buffalo on Lake Erie.

In the process the Commodore had acquired New York's pioneer
railroad line, the New York & Harlem, which had provided Gotham's
first "rapid transit" line, from Park Row downtown up Fourth (later
Park) Avenue to the Harlem River. It had been extended all the way up
into the rich farm lands of Westchester, Putnam, Dutchess, and Columbia counties, which grasped renewed prosperity in supplying New York
with the milk, meat, fruit, and vegetables without which she never
could have grown into a great city. ("Milk run", meaning a train that
stopped at every way station to pick up the milk, eventually became a
railroader's insult, but fresh milk, produced in the country and brought
to the city the same morning by rail, was vital in the lifeblood of urban
history.)

The Harlem line owned what soon became some of the most valuable urban property in the world, the Harlem line's wooding-up yard
at 42nd Street and Fourth Avenue, where the first generation of locomotives had been refueled. Here, the Commodore built what would
become New York's most famous tourist attraction in the nineteenth
century: the Grand Central Depot.* Under one monumental train shed
he combined the arrivals and departures of the New York Central &
Hudson River; the New York & Harlem; and, after a brief misunderstanding was straightened out, the New York, New Haven & Hartford
railroads. No structure better symbolized the beginning of the age of

---

*Considerably remodeled and enlarged in the 1890s, then torn down to make way for
the present Grand Central Station, which was completed in 1913.

modern railroad travel. By 1877, as the Commodore breathed his last, Grand Central Depot was already bursting at the seams. From 1871 until rail travel withered away after World War II, these few acres were the spot where, it seemed, all train travelers dreamed of heading.

"Synergy" is the word for the remarkable interaction between the myriad agencies of growth that transformed Western material civilization in the late nineteenth and early twentieth century. "Two plus two equals five" was the synergistic sum of these nominally independent agencies, of which the most familiar are iron and steel; the steam engine, the steam railroad; the steam ocean liner (which stimulated the mass movement of millions of Europe's surplus population to the western hemisphere); the growth of science and its handmaiden, technology, bringing modern chemistry, electricity, and communication; and the modern financial, legal, and political institutions that tied these forces together.

It was the growth of the American nation that made the steam passenger train necessary, and the ever-modernizing passenger train that made that growth possible: The two are inextricably intertwined. The growth of the population and the economy, and its spread to that most hospitable segment of North America, the United States and southern Canada, is a familiar subject. How the railroads managed it, and with what profound social results, is a story that has seldom gone much beyond the traditional "romance of the rails" approach that has become too superficial for modern historians.

The early post-Civil-War period, concerned largely with the political reconstruction of the Union, quickly matured into the hectic growth era of the "Gilded Age" (which Vernon Louis Parrington called, rather fatuously, the "Great Barbecue"). Then, at the very end of the old century, the nation began a thirty-year period of truly synergistic growth and almost unbroken prosperity. It was in this period that the fast, safe, and—as Franklin D. Roosevelt said, luxurious— American passenger train came into its own. The volume of business transactions and social concerns requiring travel swelled, and more and more travelers wanted to travel longer and longer distances. Something far better than the uncomfortable, poorly lit and dangerously heated wooden coaches of the mid-Victorian era was required, and railroading responded with a range of amenities approaching and often exceeding those of a first-class hotel. Along with comfort went a constant call for faster trains, but also greater safety and dependability. Greater coordination of connecting lines was a *sine qua non* of improved through travel, and this was to spell such a revolution in the leadership structure of American railroads that by 1906 it could be confidently said that most of the hundreds of thousands of miles of railroads, which went just about everywhere, were controlled as integrated systems under the aegis of no more than half a dozen leadership groups.

Out of the host of factors that made modern passenger travel possible, and thereby transformed American life between 1870 and 1930, four stand out. There were the two great depressions—the first and second of the industrial age—which, occurring in the periods 1873–1877 and 1893–1897, literally reformed railroad organization, management, and finance and brought the stability of interroad relations that so many believed could only be attained through the most repressive uses of the government's regulatory powers. More obvious was the striking surge of railroad building that occurred between 1879 and 1893. Meanwhile the "first American big business" began early to benefit from the technological revolution which produced, among many wonders, cheap steel, the most fundamental improvement in industrial raw material since the replacement of charcoal by coal for smelting and refining iron. And from the brilliant wave of entrepreneurial innovation came the modern sleeping car, which made travel comfortable for the first time in history.

Sixty years was less than the average lifespan of a healthy American even in the years from 1870 to 1930. Thus there were many in 1930 who could remember what life in America was like in 1870. Few people anywhere, before or since, experienced such sweeping changes in where and how they lived and, indeed, the very purpose of daily life itself. The reader who believes that the economic and social climate changed only slowly, and always for the better, had better reread history. The years from 1870 to 1897 produced something few Americans today have *ever* experienced: a period of consistently declining prices. Even stranger to relate, the situation caused perhaps even more resentment than the inflation of our day. The great majority of Americans were farmers or merchants, who often saw the "appreciating dollar" as hostile to their prosperity as people who sold things in a "free" market, and, to make matters worse, the refusal of the dollar to "stay put" in purchasing power was a *solid gold dollar*, which seemed to late Victorians downright perverse. The temptation to resort to conspiracy theories by way of explanation was very great; indeed, they are a major theme of the politics of the era, and the railroads, long before other forms of big business, were tagged as the scapegoat.

Even more disturbing, after twenty-five years of declining prices, was the abrupt turnaround in 1898 which during the next thirty-two years would result in a steady increase in prices and even double-digit inflation in some years—again, all on a good, solid gold dollar standard! Almost as disturbing was an abrupt change in the character of immigration to the United States. Priding themselves on their origin as "a nation of immigrants," Americans found themselves making room for millions of eastern and southern Europeans. These new residents included large numbers of illiterate young men whose only ambition was to save enough from their factory wages to return to the old country for a life of indolence. They threatened to upset the process of assimilation that had accommodated millions of immigrants on western farms and in the rising cities of the East and Midwest.

In no other nation of the world was internal movement so important as in the United States. Passengers, therefore, were from the beginning good customers of the railroads. They were less susceptible to cut rates on less desirable routes, and most passenger traffic eventually become profitable, although bitter rate wars were not unknown. Meanwhile, the late nineteenth century saw the bitterest competition for freight traffic railroads ever experienced, resulting in the virtual disappearance of profits on what was ultimately to become the primary business of the railroads. Some railroads found by the 1880s that most if not all of their net profits came from passenger business. "The laborer is worthy of his hire," and the railroads responded enthusiastically to the need for ever more and better trains than the ones they had done so much to create.

Triumph of the Through-Route Concept of Passenger Service: 1873–1893

"The public be damned," expostulated a harried and weary William H. Vanderbilt in 1882, and at that moment the public relations gaffe of the century was born. The famous remark (sometimes attributed to his more colorful father, the Commodore) has been generalized to represent the callous, profit-mad attitute of all American industrialists of the late nineteenth century, by three generations of American historians, who have seldom had any idea of the context in which the remark was uttered. Vanderbilt was in the midst of a tour of his expanding railroad properties. (He had only recently acquired control of the Nickel Plate and could already see ultimate responsibility for that much unneeded line, the West Shore, falling on his shoulders). His doctors had strongly advised against the trip. Indeed, Vanderbilt suffered from a blood pressure so high it would kill him in three more years, although he was still in his sixties. Arriving in Chicago in late afternoon, his private car was parked in the railroad yards and he was looking forward to a good meal, prepared by his own chef and served by his own steward, and then a good night's sleep without the vibrations of rail travel.

But Vanderbilt was news, and newspaper reporters, then no less than now, often ignored even the most common courtesies when they sensed an opportunity to "scoop" the competition. The Pennsylvania Railroad, arch rival of Vanderbilt's New York Central–Lake Shore system for the fast-growing passenger business between the seaboard and Chicago, had recently introduced a fast, luxurious "limited" train on its mountainous mainline, which up to that time had never been as popular a line west as the Central's "water level" route. A "limited" train meant just that: instead of stopping at any way station that lowered its semaphore when someone wanted to climb aboard, the train would stop only at stations explicitly listed in the timetable, and tickets for destinations not so listed would not be good on the limited. After all, by the mid-1880s a train could easily maintain a speed of sixty miles an hour on a good, straight track, which was what both the Lake Shore and the Fort Wayne Line (Pittsburg, Fort Wayne & Chicago), the rivals' midwestern segments, consisted of. But since the railroad passenger business had always been based on the idea of taking the business where one could find it, average running speeds between major terminals seldom exceeded forty miles an hour, and usually were much less.

The Pennsylvania's showpiece train (for that is what it really was) could not hope to make money with mid-1880s equipment and operating procedures. The chief limiting factor was the locomotive, which was only an advanced model of the same "American type" (four driving wheels preceded by four pilot wheels), light, speedy, but not very powerful, that had reigned supreme for a generation. The train was therefore limited to a few cars, the heaviest and most luxurious Pullman Palace cars that George Pullman's booming car factory could produce: two or three sleepers with plenty of private rooms (compartments, drawing rooms, and staterooms), a dining car, a combination sleeper-lounge-observation (Pullman, who was mobile hotelier to the nation, did not like cars that did not have some rentable space in them), and a combination baggage-smoker. No mail, no express, and no coaches into which dozens of profitable "trippers" could be packed. But the train, christened the *Pennsylvania Limited,* was an instant *succes d'estime* and drew much favorable attention; in that age, what happened on the railroads was front-page news even to people who seldom went anywhere and could not have afforded the extra fare. This first "name train" of any distinction made the New York-Chicago run in a breathtaking twenty-five hours, and was the forerunner of the Pennsylvania's famous *Broadway Limited,* which, in the 1960s, the last decade of its life under the Pennsylvania's management, was dashing between Pennsylvania Station, New York, and Union Station, Chicago, in fifteen hours.

Was the Central going to follow suit? Learning that the man who knew the answer to that question was in Chicago at that very moment, sitting in a railroad car parked in the Lake Shore's coach yards, two enterprising reporters rushed to the scene and brazened their way into the very car in which Vanderbilt had just sat down to dinner. Will not the Central follow the Pennsylvania's lead in thus serving the public's need for better passenger service? It may or may not have been a loaded question, but Vanderbilt, like business executives now, did not suffer fools gladly, and Vanderbilt resented the idea that he was motivated by anything but basic principles of good business. "The public be damned," he sputtered, or so legend has it; "we will run limited trains because the Pennsylvania runs limited trains."* It would have been enough to make a modern public relations man collapse in tears.

This memorable episode tells us something about both Victorian social consciousness and the honesty of freelance newspaper men, both of which were lacking. But it tells us much more about the rapid transformation that was taking place in travel as the epochal nineteenth century entered its last years. Social historians, who disagree on so much about these transforming years, are agreed that it was a period of integration and unification of America into one great national economy. The railroad was the chief agent by which this was being accomplished, and the transporation of passengers is its most conspicuous example. The limited trains, soon to be imitated in some degree throughout the nation, met a demand for fast, comfortable, and reasonably safe transporation between major cities, even those separated by half a continent. At the very end of the century, the process would be hastened and virtually completed by the expedient of widespread corporate consolidation of railroads, but even before then, in a trend that was already apparent by the 1870s, a remarkable degree of cooperation between independent railroad companies to create "through" routes brought the new age of travel to America with breathtaking quickness.

The through-route system unified the nation, however, not merely by joining distant terminals, like New York and Chicago, or St. Louis and Washington, or Boston and Montreal, in the way that the airlines have virtually eliminated the time-factor in long-distance travel. The airlines do best with hops of eight hundred to a thousand miles or more and avoid intermediate stops by using a "radial" or "spoke" system of routes: all the flights of a carrier proceed, nonstop, to a single terminal, such as Dallas-Fort Worth, for example, where the passenger must change to an outbound plane for some destination at the end of another spoke on the wheel. The railroads' through routes, by contrast, were like mighty steel clotheslines, along which were pinned the dozens of intermediate points, including good-size cities as well as towns that were so important in the America of that day, and which are increasingly neglected by all forms of public transporation in our own.

The railroads achieved a remarkably comprehensive service throughout the nation by a combination of careful scheduling and the flexibility the detachable Pullman car provided. (How many airline traffic executives have daydreamed about a new kind of airplane with detachable segments that could be dropped down—gently and according to plan!—en route between major cities?) Trains would start their run from a major terminal and throughout the day and night would periodically couple to, or drop off, sleeping cars, diners, and other cars as the need arose. By scheduling at least two daily runs each way over

*Whether he said it or not is open to doubt. Reports differed at the time. That everybody believed he said it, however, is all that matters.

a through route, railroads could offer reasonably civilized sleeper hops between almost any pair of cities even the most sophisticated commerical traveler could think of. To be sure, travelers would sometimes find themselves set down at 4 a.m. on the cold station platform at, for example, Mansfield, Ohio, or Coffeyville, Kansas, but the perfect system still remains to be invented.

On runs of 300 to 400 miles, the Pullman car saved the entire day for work, while respecting the traveler's need for a full night's sleep. Many a traveler would spend almost as much time asleep in his berth with the car at a standstill as with it moving. The famous *Alton Midnight,* in the twentieth century, opened its Pullmans (it carried no coaches) in St. Louis Union Station at 9:30 or 10:00 p.m., pulled out at midnight, and completed the 283-mile trip to Chicago by about sunrise, but passengers could remain in the cars until they had made their toilets and downtown business offices were opening. Go to sleep peacefully, and shave next morning without danger of cutting your throat! Many a "sleeper hop" of barely a hundred miles existed on the timetables of the railroads in the days when they had full responsibility for travel in America.

Regardless of what point one picks to examine the structure of the American railroad passenger system minutely, what he finds is bound to make the system of just a few years earlier seem puny by comparison, so great was the rate of change in this and everything else touched by the railroad. As we shall see, many factors emerged between 1873 and 1893 to transform the primitive conveyances of the earlier years into the glamorous trains that took thousands to the World's Columbian Exposition in Chicago in 1893. Most striking was the evolution of the through routes, which were rapidly assuming the forms that they would hold for the next half century. What the traveler faced in 1893 deserves our close attention.

Spinal Column of 1890s America: The Northeast Corridor

The most heavily traveled route, as it had been since before the Revolution, lay between Boston, New York, Philadelphia, Baltimore, and Washington. In New England, the New York, New Haven & Hartford Railroad had recently embarked, under the stimulation of J. P. Morgan (Hartford was his "hometown"), on a course of consolidation with other railroads in the area. The wide, treacherous Thames River had finally been bridged at New London, Connecticut, where it empties into Long Island Sound, in the late 1880s, producing a "shore line" that quickly became the preferred route from New Haven to Boston and eventually displaced the inland route via Hartford. The Pennsylvania Railroad, growing mightier every year, dominated the service from New York to Philadelphia, offering no less than twenty-six trains a day

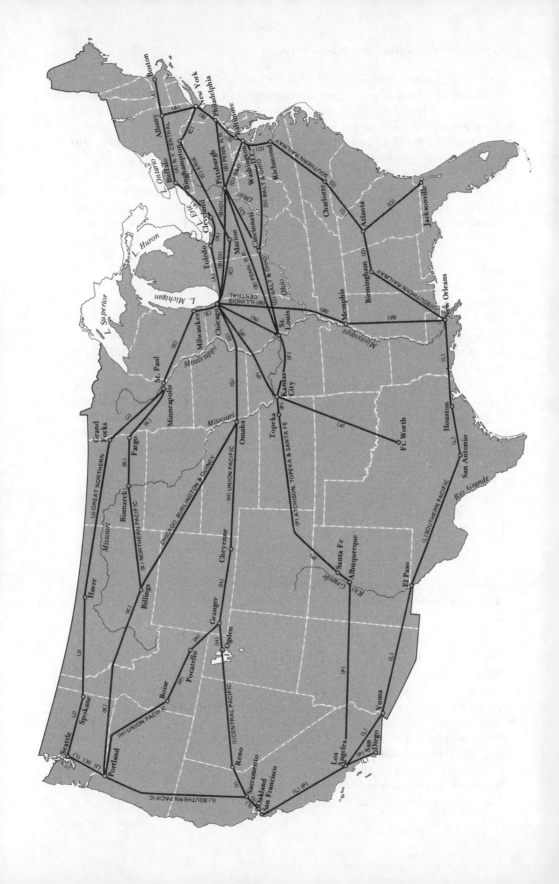

Figure 3.1 Simplified map of major through passenger routes early in the 20th century

A New York Central: New York–Albany–Buffalo–Cleveland–Toledo–Chicago

B Pennsylvania Railroad: New York–Philadelphia–Pittsburgh–Chicago; *and* Pittsburgh–St. Louis

C Erie: New York–Binghamton (N.Y.)–Marion (Ohio)–Chicago

D Baltimore & Ohio: Philadelphia–Baltimore–Washington–Pittsburgh–Chicago; *and* Pittsburgh–Cincinnati–St. Louis, or Washington–Cincinnati–St. Louis

E Chicago to Twin Cities (St. Paul & Minneapolis): Chicago, Milwaukee & St. Paul (later & Pacific), North Western, Burlington, and several lesser routes—through to Pacific Northwest via Great Northern and Northern Pacific

F St. Louis to Kansas City and western connections: Missouri Pacific, Wabash

G Chicago to Omaha and connection with Union Pacific and Northern Pacific (via Chicago, Burlington & Quincy): Chicago, Milwaukee & St. Paul, North Western, Rock Island, Burlington

H Union Pacific ("Overland Route"): Omaha to Ogden and connection with Central Pacific (Southern Pacific) to San Francisco; or, to Granger (Wyoming) northwest to Pocatello (Idaho) and on to Portland (Oregon)

I Central Pacific: Ogden to Oakland (San Francisco), continuously controlled by Southern Pacific

J Great Northern: most northerly transcontinental, Twin Cities–Havre (Montana)–Seattle–Portland

K Northern Pacific: Twin Cities–Bismarck (North Dakota)–Billings–Portland–Seattle

L Southern Pacific: New Orleans–Houston–San Antonio–El Paso–Los Angeles (San Diego)–San Francisco–Portland, Seattle

M Illinois Central: First land-grant railroad; Chicago–Memphis–New Orleans

N St. Louis to Chicago: Chicago & Alton, Illinois Central, Wabash, Chicago & Eastern Illinois—most heavily traveled route in Midwest.

O Southern Railway: 1890s merger of many lines; principally Washington (D.C.)–Richmond–Atlanta–Birmingham–New Orleans–and controlled connection Atlanta–Jacksonville, principal jumping-off point for Florida in 19th century

P Atchison, Topeka & Santa Fe: Chicago (only transcontinental with own line into Chicago)–Kansas City–Topeka–Albuquerque–Los Angeles–San Francisco–San Diego and important connections Kansas City to Texas.

each way, on weekdays, making the ninety-mile run in two hours and twenty minutes. The Philadelphia & Reading offered another nineteen trains and a running time only ten minutes longer, its trains hauled by the Central of New Jersey between Bound Brook and New York. Both lines terminated at Jersey City ferry terminals, from which passengers had a choice of boats to both lower and midtown Manhattan and, on the Pennsylvania, around the tip of Manhattan to the still-independent city of Brooklyn. In Philadelphia, both lines had terminals on expensive real estate in the heart of the city. The Pennsylvania's famous Broad Street Station, approached by trains via its domineering "Chinese Wall," exemplified the penalties that could result from a pioneer line's failure to guess the future development pattern of a great city. The Pennsylvania, originally an east-west line, came into the city on the west side of the Schuylkill River. A station there proved unsatisfactory in the days of poor intra-urban transportation, so the huge Broad Street station was built on the east side of the river, where downtown Philadelphia was concentrated. The railroad built the "Chinese Wall," as three generations of discommoded Philadelphians called it, to elevate the tracks into the station above street level, but the Wall remained an eyesore and obstacle to traffic until it was torn down after World War II. By then good city transportation made a new station, at 30th Street, satisfactory, and today it has become the only station operated by Amtrak, the Pennsylvania's successor in the passenger business, in Philadelphia.

South of Philadelphia to Baltimore and Washington, the Pennsylvania's main competitor was the Baltimore & Ohio. The key link for many years had been the Philadelphia, Wilmington & Baltimore Railroad; both lines had used it for through service as long as it was independent, but the Pennsylvania snatched it from under the nose of the B. & O.'s John W. Garrett in the early 1880s. The B. & O. thought it had a card left in its hand—its own line from Baltimore to Washington, which the Pennsylvania had shared—but when it shut the Pennsylvania out, that line's clever lawyers found a loophole in the corporate charter that enabled the Pennsylvania to build its own line from Baltimore to Washington. By 1893 it ran twelve daily trains each way between Jersey City and Washington, making the run in as little as five and a half hours. The B. & O., meanwhile, had had to decide whether to abandon the prestigious and profitable New York-Washington service, or build its own line from Baltimore to Philadelphia. It boldly chose the latter course in 1885, linking up with the Reading and the Central of New Jersey at Philadelphia and Bound Brook. The "Royal Blue Line" service, including the 5-hour New York-Washington "Royal Blue," was very popular, with seven trains a day, until the Pennsylvania completed its tunnel under the Hudson and into Pennsylvania Station. In fact, the B. & O. was never truly independent after taking receivership in the 1890s depression, having entered the era of hard times already financially weakened by its push to Philadelphia.

From New York to Boston, the traveler might take either one of the seven trains on the shore line, or one of the nine still running on the old inland line via Hartford. Both offered running times as short as five hours and forty minutes. Wisely, or luckily, in the 1840s the New Haven had accepted the New York & Harlem Railroad's offer to share its line into New York City south of Woodlawn Cemetery, and after 1871 these Boston-New York trains had the permanent use, for a very modest rental, of the Grand Central Depot.

The Boston service was very lucrative (no bluer chip stock existed in those days than New Haven Railroad), and it naturally attracted a competitor. The New York & New England Railroad paralleled many New Haven lines south of Boston, but it never got to New York on its own lines. The New Haven—for a price, of course—gave it limited running rights into New York for the only two New York & New England Railroad trains that are remembered today, the *White Train* and the *Mid-day Express.* The former offered luxury and showmanship, since it had nothing else to offer, and decked itself out all in white, from locomotive to observation car. Even the coal in the tender was sprayed with whitewash. It was a popular train, and its sister did well, too, but when hard times came in 1893, A. A. McLeod, head of the New York & New England, made the mistake of resorting to rate-cutting on anthracite coal from eastern Pennsylvania to Boston via the New England's only real asset, a direct, all-rail route to New England via the bridge across the Hudson River at Poughkeepsie. When J. P. Morgan, who had undertaken to stabilize eastern coal roads in those hard times, admonished him, McLeod is supposed to have said that he would rather run a peanut stand than take his orders from Morgan. Apparently he got his wish, because the New England went into receivership, the New Haven took over the New England's lines, and McLeod's career was finished.

These were the years in which it was becoming apparent that a far better all-rail through route from New England to Washington and points south was necessary. Neither the New Haven nor the Pennsylvania, mighty as they were, could provide it until the Hell Gate Bridge route (employing the Hudson and East River tunnels of the Pennsylvania Station development) opened just before World War I. A Boston to Washington traveler had just about an hour and fifteen minutes to dash out of Grand Central Depot, hail a cab for the Pennsylvania's Hudson River ferry slip, cross the river, and climb aboard the express to Washington. But the Reading, the New York & New England, and the Baltimore & Ohio, fighting the "good fight" against the growing domination of the Pennsylvania, had a trump card. The New York & New England (McLeod the peanut vendor's railroad) had a great asset in its Poughkeepsie River bridge, on what began life as the Boston & Erie, a line from Hartford westward through Danbury to the bridge, the only railroad crossing of the Hudson south of Albany until the completion of

the Pennsylvania's Hudson River tunnels about 1910. The route continued west of the river via a small line, the Lehigh & Hudson River, to
Belvidere, in pleasant, rural western New Jersey. There it connected
with the Reading, which delivered it to the Baltimore & Ohio at Philadelphia. The run of only 450 miles, however, took twenty hours (leaving at 3:30 p.m. and arriving at 11:26 a.m. in Washington), and as usual,
the Pennsylvania and New Haven had an answer.

When the Philadelphia, Wilmington & Baltimore opened for business in the 1840s, it faced a formidable obstacle in the broad Susquehanna River. At that early date a bridge was out of the question (the
tides there are forbidding, and money was scarce) so a steam car-ferry,
the *Maryland,* was built which successfully floated the light wooden
cars of antebellum trains across the river for the next twenty years. It
was still going strong elsewhere when the Pennsylvania pressed it into
service in the 1870s to provide through Pullman service overnight
between Boston and Washington. The New Haven had its own line to
the edge of the water on the Harlem River in the south Bronx (today a
scene of urban decay, but in those days a busy produce and freight terminal). Here, the gallant old *Maryland* tied up twice daily to await the
arrival of the express from Boston, take on its cars, and wheeze down
the East River and up the Hudson with them to the Pennsylvania's Jersey City terminal. The tough old boat burned to the water's edge in the
1880s, but, rebuilt, she remained the key link in this fifteen-hour overnight service. As the century neared its end, she was still showing that
it was necessary, sometimes, to resort to water transportation, even this
late in the railroad age.

Victorian Speedway: The Trunk Line Limiteds

As important as the east coast corridors were, it was the flourishing passenger service on the trunk line routes between the seaboard cities of
Boston, New York, and Philadelphia, and the mushrooming cities of the
Midwest that captured the public imagination. Fully a dozen different
through routes existed, some of them frankly trying only for the intermediate cities' traffic for they were too slow, or too circuitous, or too
poorly supplied with terminals and equipment seriously to compete
with the leaders. And the leader, notwithstanding the Pennsylvania's
pioneering efforts to establish limited trains in the 1880s, was the New
York Central system. In the timetables, the "Vanderbilt roads," as they
were colloquially known, maintained a chaste separateness, but this
fooled no one. The leader in the New York Central system was the New
York Central & Hudson River Railroad, Commodore Vanderbilt's original New York-Buffalo system that gloried in its superb, low-gradient
"water-level" route through the valley of the Mohawk River. The real
value of this route, actually not much shorter than the Pennsylvania's
through the mountains, was the incredibly low cost of hauling freight
over it, but it was an excellent selling point for passenger business, too.

Moreover, the entire route from New York to Buffalo had been quadruple-tracked during the late 1870s, permitting separation of two-way freight and passenger service. This facilitated both speed and safety, an improvement that vastly increased the traffic capacity and was quickly imitated by the Pennsylvania.

West of Buffalo, the Vanderbilt roads consisted of two trunk lines into Chicago and one into St. Louis via Cleveland, Columbus, and Indianapolis, the "Big Four" route. The oldest, the Michigan Central, crossed the Niagara River on one of the world's famous pioneer structures, John Roebling's suspension bridge, which was the dress rehearsal for his greatest life work, the Brooklyn Bridge. The Michigan Central continued west on a fine, direct route across southern Ontario and into Detroit, an important Great Lakes city even before the dawn of the automobile age. Jackson and Kalamazoo, plus dozens of up-and-coming midwestern cities lay ahead and after them the commodious terminal right on Lake Michigan in Chicago, which it shared with the Illinois Central. Four of the eight New York City expresses took this route each day, including the pride of the fleet, the *North Shore Limited*, whose twenty-five hour schedule matched that of the *Pennsylvania Limited*. (Actually, Michigan Central train No. 1, the *New York and Chicago Limited*, beat its running time by fifteen minutes.) These trains were the last word in luxury, even though they did not carry Pullmans.

Just as fast was the *Exposition Flyer*, which the Central put on in its bid to take easterners to the World's Columbian Exposition in Chicago in 1893, via that fabulous money-making machine, the Lake Shore route. Hugging the shore of Lake Erie from Buffalo, this route included the important manufacturing cities of Toledo and Cleveland and many others in the very heartland of America's burgeoning new industrial might. Millions of copies of Currier & Ives' famous lithograph "The Fast Mail" celebrated this superb steel highway from the 1870s on, and at the end of the century train No. 13, the *Fast Mail*, with both Lake Shore and Michigan Central sections, continued the tradition.

In all, the Central offered eight through expresses between east coast cities and Chicago. The ones we have mentioned were the best of the lot; most of them charged an extra fare and picked up Boston sleepers at Albany, from the Boston & Albany. One of the oldest railroads in America, and since the Civil War securely in the Vanderbilt fold, the Boston & Albany's trains traversed the ravishingly beautiful scenery of the Berkshire mountains. But these statistics hardly hint at the remarkable job of hauling growing hordes of travelers between most of the cities and towns of the northeastern United States.

Serving the Grass Roots

Businessmen, who a hundred years ago, as now, were the bread-and-butter of the travel business, wanted to arrive at their destination in the morning, and generally the blue-ribbon limiteds of the Central obliged with morning departures from Grand Central Depot. Not everybody was going to Chicago, by a long shot, however, and they wanted convenient arrival times at *their* destinations. Let's follow a typical Central intermediate-point train, No. 5-25, the *Fast Western Express*, and see what it was up to during the long night. At 4:20 in the afternoon, No. 25 pulled out of the old Boston & Albany station in Boston, carrying a Chicago sleeping car in a train that would run as No. 25 west of Albany on the Lake Shore. At 6:00 p.m., No. 5 would leave Grand Central Depot, with a consist of sleeping cars that would keep dispatchers shuffling train orders carefully right to the end of the 900-mile line.

Arriving at Albany about 10 p.m., the Boston sleeping car (not always just one, by any means) was cut in the main section, and the train ran thence westward in two sections, Michigan Central and Lake Shore. First, the diner that had served dinner on the scenic run up the Hudson from New York was cut out, along with the Pullman drawing room (provided, one may speculate, for the hatching of political schemes on the way to the capital of the Empire State). At Buffalo early the next morning a sleepy-eyed dining-car crew climbed aboard two steaming diners in the station, and by the time one was coupled to the Michigan Central section at 5:45, it was ready to serve breakfast. At 9:50 a.m., 139 miles into the province of Ontario, the same diner was uncoupled at St. Thomas and made ready to serve lunch to an eastbound train due shortly.

The Lake Shore section, not forgetting that it, too, would shortly have a horde of passengers demanding a big Victorian breakfast, cut in the other diner at Buffalo at the same time, dropping it about three hours later at 9:01 a.m. in Ashtabula, Ohio. Barely an hour and a half later, at 10:30, the diner that would serve "dinner" and "supper," as the unpretentious Lake Shore designated the noon and evening meals, was cut in. At 1:05 p.m. the Michigan Central section cut in a diner at Detroit for noon and evening meals. While the Lake Shore was getting its diner at Cleveland, it also got a drawing-room car for day passengers to Chicago. At 1:45 p.m. the Lake Shore section, arriving in Toledo, cut out a sleeper bound for St. Louis on the Wabash Railroad; its weary passengers faced another full night on the train before arriving at 7:35 next morning. At 9:00 and 9:10 that evening, tired but presumably very well fed, the passengers in the two versatile trains arrived in the Lake Shore and Michigan Central stations.

This odyssey merely samples, but nowhere near exhausts, the diversity of railroad passenger scheduling as the industry approached maturity. The *Chicago Night Express*, No. 9, departing New York at 9:15 p.m., shows even more diversity, with cars for such branch-line points as Cape Vincent, at the head of the St. Lawrence River, reached from Syracuse on the affiliate, Rome, Watertown & Ogdensburg; or Grand Rapids, furniture manufacturing center of the nation, on a branch of the Michigan Central. The peripatetic Pullman sleeper played a role in the development of American society that no one could possibly put in quantitative terms. Even the most casual observer of human nature, however, can see the implications of placing thousands of industrious, ambitious people in close proximity for many hours at a time. The table shared in the dining car, the midnight conversations in the Pullman smoking room between business travelers, who would not or could not sleep, the running commentary on the mines and mills that flashed past the windows of the observation car, all intensified the exchange of ideas and the making of deals that went on in cities and towns, great and small, throughout an America on the move.

The New York Central, wits never grew tired of saying, went west from New York by striking out due north for 143 miles! Yes, rejoined others, and the Pennsylvania went west by strking out due south (more or less) for 91 miles! And so they did, and for the best of reasons. The Appalachian Mountains were a problem to be overcome, and a frontal attack, as the Erie Railroad discovered early in the game, was not always the best way. The Central went due north until it could enter the valley of the Mohawk River, thus securing what a railroad wants more than anything else: a good, flat route with only gentle rises and falls of terrain, and not many of those. The Pennsylvania did not go south, at all, but went north by way of extending its original main terminal, Philadelphia, to what was undeniably becoming America and the world's greatest city, New York. By 1893 the Pennsylvania was as much a New York–Midwest trunk line as the Central, and if it did not have the natural advantages of location, it had the finest and most devoted group of leaders and engineers any American enterprise has ever boasted. It had, moreover, the industrial heart of America, the coal, iron, and steel industry of the mighty state of Pennsylvania, which for a century would feed it millions of tons of freight and make it the world's greatest private enterprise.

In the pivotal year of 1893, however, the Pennsylvania still suffered the handicap of having no direct entry into New York City, and it would have none until 1910. Even so, it offered excellent through service between its New York and Brooklyn ferry terminals to its mammoth wooden maritime terminal on the Hudson shore at Jersey City. This strip of shore, in fact, became something of a wonder of the world, for the huge traffic, human and freight, between the mainland, Manhattan, and Long Island was brought by a congeries of railroads, of which the Pennsylvania, the Delaware, Lackawanna & Western, the Erie, the Lehigh Valley, and the Central of New Jersey, were only the most prominent. The shore was almost one continuous line of ferry slips, and these doughty little boats had been puffing (and before that, sailing) across and up and down the North (Hudson) and East Rivers and around the island of Manhattan for at least two hundred years. Behind the ships were hundreds of acres of railroad yards for the thousands of freight and passenger cars that congregated there daily.

From its Jersey City terminal, in addition to the eastern corridor trains we have already discussed, the Pennsylvania dispatched daily five trains for Chicago. Its pride, No. 5, the *Pennsylvania Limited,* left Jersey City at noon every day and arrived at noon (Chicago time, twenty-five hours later) the next day. Number 25, the *Columbian Express,* was the Pennsylvania's answer to the New York Central's *Exposition Flyer,* offering fast service (twenty-six hours) without extra fare. At Philadelphia, however, the Pennsylvania's long-distance train service fattened considerably, because this "capital of the Middle Atlantic States" generated an enormous traffic.

The Lesser Trunk Line Through Routes

But how about the "weak sisters" among the trunk lines? The Erie, which threatened to expire repeatedly in its first one hundred years of life, finally built, in the 1880s, its own line into Chicago (well, into Hammond, Indiana, where friendly roads were delighted to rent it the last few miles required to put it in Chicago's flamboyantly gothic Dearborn Street Station). Since the Lake Shore and the Pennsylvania (the former Fort Wayne line) had co-opted the direct route between Buffalo and Chicago years before, the Erie "drooped" down between the two like a slack rope to encounter the many smaller cities and towns that yearned for direct east-west connections. (The largest city on this route is Marion, Ohio; in our day, with the Erie part of Conrail and the emphasis on direct, low-cost through-freight lines, this once excellent double-track line, much of which ultimately had centralized traffic control, has been abandoned and the rails removed.) But in the heyday of the passenger train, the Erie bravely operated four through trains a day to Chicago, although the fastest required thirty hours for the run. The Baltimore & Ohio made some show of originating its long-distance trains at the C.N.J.'s Hoboken terminal, but the east coast passengers it carried into Chicago's elegant little Grand Central Depot almost all got on in Baltimore or Washington.

One of the Erie's Chicago runs went via the Grand Trunk Railway of Canada from Buffalo to Detroit, and into Chicago via its American subsidiary. And thereby hangs a tale too complicated to tell here. It is enough to say that the American trunk lines were not vying only with each other in the ruinous competition that tormented them to the end of the century, for they were paralleled by Canadian lines that would have starved to death on the sparse freight and passenger traffic that Canada's slight population generated. The Canadian lines were part of the American trunk line system, and the fact that they were not subject to American laws only complicated the situation. West of Buffalo, the Grand Trunk made the long-distance-carrier pretensions of the Lackawanna and the West Shore railroads a reality. Indeed, the New York, Chicago & St. Louis, better known as the "Nickel Plate" (a Wall Street wag had commented that if the par value of its stock had really represented moneys invested in the road, the rails would have been nickel-plated) was built to muscle in on the New York Central's lucrative through business. Vanderbilt ultimately bought the Nickel Plate at an inflated price (it was truly a "blackmail road") and neutralized it. He was persuaded by J. P. Morgan to do the same for the West Shore, but the Grand Trunk of Canada was not for sale. Three generations of historians, if they had mulled these hard truths over, would have written far better history of these wheeling-and-dealing years in American development.

As Chicago, one of America's youngest cities, thundered on towards greatness as the world's largest railroad center, venerable St. Louis almost languished at the end of a much longer and less impressive rail-link to the seaboard. By the 1880s, St. Louisans bitterly resented what they considered discrimination by the trunk line railroads in favor of Chicago, but in truth St. Louis was never destined to become the "city of broad shoulders" that Carl Sandburg saw in Chicago. Its link to the seaboard depended, east of Cleveland (in the case of the New York Central) and Pittsburgh (for the Pennsylvania) upon the same lines that served Chicago. Its most direct first-class route was the Baltimore & Ohio, which had acquired control of the Ohio & Mississippi (Cincinnati to St. Louis) in the 1870s, but its latitude was too southerly, bringing it to tidewater at Baltimore. Over this route it operated two of America's favorite trains: No. 1, an all-vestibule-car train, which left Washington at 3:30 p.m. to arrive in St. Louis at 6:20 p.m. the next day, and No. 3, leaving Washington at 12:35 a.m. and arriving in St. Louis at 7:15 a.m. the second morning. Twenty-eight hours and thirty-two hours made for a long, wearying haul (as long as big-league baseball teams traveled by rail, they dreaded their trips to St. Louis), but the B. & O. tried to make up for it with some of the most elegant service and fine dining-car cuisine on America's railroads. These two trains, long since named the *National Limited* and the *Diplomat*, appeared on timetables well into the postwar period after 1945 and were among the first eastern limiteds to be dieselized.

The B. & O., we must not forget, also offered the best service between the nation's capital and Chicago, with Pittsburgh along the way. Number 5 (eventually the all-Pullman *Capitol Limited*) made the run in twenty-five and a half hours via Pittsburgh, and at the end of the century the company still operated a Washington-Chicago train via the old mainline to Wheeling, West Virginia, but the run was several hours longer. Notwithstanding the overweening importance of the trunk line route to Chicago, the unique importance of the Midwest in national politics from the end of the Civil War to the 1920s meant that the stately B. & O. would carry a larger percentage of important people than perhaps any other line in America.

St. Louis was linked to the bustling Northeast, however, by the

Central and the Pennsylvania systems, each of which offered two trains a day. Taking, respectively, a minimum of thirty-one and a half hours, the trip on the Central and the Pennsylvania wore out many a baseball player and traveling salesman, not to mention countless decks of cards for the poker games that made the run bearable. The Central's route was patched out of the Central and Lake Shore to Cleveland, and the "Big Four" (Cleveland, Cincinnati, Chicago, & St. Louis Railroad) which it had leased for 999 years during the years of system building. With three basic routes in the heart of this Midwest system, between Galion, Ohio, and Indianapolis, Indiana, the Big Four busied itself night and day picking up or setting out sleepers at such booming industrial centers as Columbus, Dayton, Springfield, Cincinnati, and Indianapolis.

The Pennsylvania, in like manner, had acquired very early the Pittsburgh, Cincinnati & St. Louis Railroad, which, with the Vandalia Line at Indianapolis, put it into vigorous competition with the New York Central for the business of America's heartland.

Notwithstanding their bitter competition during the previous generation for leadership of the Midwest, St. Louis and Chicago carried on an impressive travel relationship. The Chicago & Alton, the Wabash, and the Illinois Central, all with fine, direct lines across the Illinois prairie into Chicago, offered a total of ten trains a day in each direction. Next to the traffic between Chicago and Minneapolis/St. Paul, that between Chicago and St. Louis was the most intensely fought-over travel market outside the Northeast.

The Great American West:
A Promise Unfulfilled in 1900

With all the fanfare that attended the completion of the first "transcontinental" railroad at Promontory Point, Utah in 1869, and all that historians have made of the event since, one might suppose that the far west was off to a booming start. Not at all; the phenomena of golden California and wheeling-dealing Texas do not appear until well into the twentienth century for reasons that we shall deal with later. An exception to this broad generalization may be made in the case of the Pacific Northwest, the most promising part of the far West as the century neared its end. Here, awe-inspiring forests of fir and spruce offered a new lease on life for the booming American lumber business, which was rapidly denuding the pineries of the upper Midwest to build countless Victorian homesteads for prospering merchants, farmers, and professional men in the new towns and cities of the plain.

Once the Union Pacific, from the East, and the Central Pacific were linked together just north of the Great Salt Lake, another twelve years would pass before the second American transcontinental was formed, when the Atchison, Topeka & Santa Fe and C. P. Huntington's Southern Pacific met at Deming, New Mexico just west of El Paso,

Texas in 1881. Heaven knows, it was not from lack of trying that the number of transcontinentals increased so slowly; witness the Northern Pacific which, two years later, in 1883, after creeping across the northern tier of states for nearly fifteen years, joined up with Henry Villard's Oregon Railway & Navigation Co. in the valley of the Columbia River, which carried its trains the last hundred miles or so to Portland, Oregon.

Almost immediately thereafter, the Southern Pacific rushed construction eastward, to El Paso, beating Tom Scott, ebullient former president of the Pennsylvania Railroad, who had resigned to build a southwestern trunk line from St. Louis across Texas. The unwise plan of the 1860s, whereby the first transcontinental was divided between Union Pacific and Southern Pacific, led Huntington to shut Union Pacific out at Ogden, Utah, by means of an illiberal through-rate policy. Huntington saw no reason to exchange transcontinental freight with the U.P. when he might have the haulage all the way to the Mississippi by building an all Southern Pacific line in the southernmost part of the nation. The combination of S.P.-built and acquired lines through Yuma, El Paso, San Antonio, and Houston into New Orleans was nicknamed the "Sunset Route" and eventually became the most heavily used single-track freight route in the world.

Los Angeles was still a sleepy Mexicanesque town in 1887 when the railroad that would place its main bets on it—the Santa Fe—began to push its own line in that direction. Arriving, in 1887, the Santa Fe found something of a boom under way, but the population counted in the next census, in 1890, would barely fill half of the modern city's Coliseum: fifty thousand people! The Santa Fe shortly thereafter made arrangements to enter San Francisco—a relatively old and well-established city by then—and San Diego, and it served all three with two trains a day out of Chicago's picturesque Dearborn Street Station. At about the same time the Santa Fe, unable to persuade the Chicago & Alton of the mutual advantages of a merger, overloaded its debt structure by building its own line from Kansas City to Chicago.

Few could look forward to spending the five days required to reach Los Angeles from Chicago in one of the Santa Fe's "free reclining chair cars," no matter how proud the line was of them. An ordinary Pullman would be strenuous enough, and the "family apartment" accommodations advertised in the company's publicity were eagerly sought after. It was a slow route, built cheaply with light rail, even if it was the only transcontinental with its own track from Chicago! It was on the edge of insolvency and receivership, which it slid into in 1893. It had plenty of company, from the Union Pacific and Northern Pacific and a host of eastern railroads. American railroads would work many seeming miracles in the first decade of the twentieth century, but the transformation of the Santa Fe into a first-class railroad would be one of the most striking.

One strong string that the Santa Fe had to its bow was its exemplary dining-car service, and it was the choice of thousands of passengers over the years who knew nothing about the line except that Fred Harvey operated the diners. The enterprising Mr. Harvey, recognizing that the slop served in the typical western railroad eating house simply would not do, contracted with the Santa Fe for the right to operate a restaurant chain along its route. He replaced the fat Mexican in the dirty apron with neat, polite, and not unattractive young women whom he recruited for the occasion. Fred Harvey's "Harvey Girls" were an echo of the wholesome young New England farm women whom Francis Cabot Lowell recruited early in the century to run his cotton mills, and Harvey looked after the life-style of his girls just as scrupulously as Mr. Lowell did. When the next change—dining cars—came, the girls disappeared from the restaurants and were replaced with genial black waiters aboard trains that sped faster and faster. Where did the girls go? Many, no doubt (or their daughters), reappeared behind the counters of Fred Harvey Restaurants in the handsome terminals that graced the new union stations in Chicago, St. Louis, Kansas City, and Los Angeles.

The trip to the west coast was slow on any of the transcontinental lines until well into the twentieth century. The Union Pacific operated the most popular train in the days when San Francisco was the main goal of western travelers. The *Overland Flyer* (later the *Overland Limited*) offered the traveler, who was always something of a tourist no matter how serious his business, a view of the West that had been so wild just a few years before. He left Chicago on the Chicago North Western Railroad at 10:15 p.m. and sped across Illinois and Iowa to Council Bluffs, where he transferred to the U.P. train, at 1:22 p.m. next day. At 10:45 in the morning of the fourth day out of Chicago he was due in San Francisco. If he transferred to the U.P.'s "Oregon Short Line" to the Pacific Northwest at Granger, Wyoming, he expected to be in Portland early in the morning of the fifth day.

This "Oregon Short Line" was to the U.P. what the Kansas City-Chicago line was to the Santa Fe: an expensive expedient adopted in the days of rugged individualism among railroad men, which distorted its debt structure and would put it in receivership along with the Santa Fe in 1893. The U.P. enjoyed the California traffic only as far as Ogden, Utah, where the cars passed into the reluctant arms of Huntington's C.P., who saw to it that the U.P. made little or nothing on the run. The U.P., without important terminuses at either end, seemed to its builder, Sidney Dillon, little more than "an apple tree without a limb." The U.P. took the initiative in promoting the train, but Huntington's S.P., which owned the C.P., made nothing of its existence in its section in the *Official Railway Guide,* and even listed all but four of the seventy-three way stations on the C.P. portion of the *Overland Flyer* timetable as scheduled stops! It would remain for one of America's greatest railroad leaders, Edward H. Harriman, to change all that nonsense.

The Southern Pacific in fact did its best to ignore both the central route and the mighty metropolis on Lake Michigan, offering a 5:30 p.m. departure from San Francisco and a 10:55 a.m. arrival in New Orleans on the fifth day. Of course, there was the *Overland Flyer,* but why endure the snows of the Sierras and the central Rockies, which could still be dangerous to snowbound trains and their passengers? The Sunset Route offered a good look at picturesque New Orleans along the way. (If you continued east beyond New Orleans, it also offered a good lesson in the backwardness of southern railroads as late as 1900; during the South's six-month summers it offered a total of nearly three thousand miles of unbelievable discomfort.) The Sunset Route was never America's favorite, except perhaps during the Mardi Gras season.

There were yet other routes to the West coast. Lines like the Burlington, Missouri Pacific, Alton, and Rio Grande, combined with lines both east and west of themselves to provide transcontinental service. Most noteworthy was the Burlington Railroad, which offered through service via both Omaha and Kansas City over the Denver & Rio Grande at Denver and the Southern Pacific at Ogden. After the Western Pacific was built from Ogden to San Francisco in this century, it replaced the Southern Pacific to constitute, with Rio Grande and Burlington, one of the favorite scenic routes west, which ended its days as the *California Zephyr.* Meanwhile, the stodgy Chicago & Alton touted the "True Southern Route," taking Chicago departures as far as St. Louis, over the best line between the two metropolises, whence the St. Louis, Iron Mountain & Southern (to revert to the name of the Missouri Pacific's subsidiary that linked it to Texas across Arkansas) took it to Texarkana, and the Texas & Pacific (another subsidiary) then handed it off to the S.P. at El Paso. In later years the Rock Island, with its own tracks from Chicago as far as Tucumcari, New Mexico, would link up with the S.P. to the coast to form the "Golden State Route," but in 1893 the Rock Island advertised no west coast service.

Some of the most spectacular scenery—and some of the most boring—on the way west could be found on the northern routes, which trudged across the endless Great Plains of the Dakotas and Montana, helping along some of the last western colonization that took place in the United States, before heading into the rugged Rockies and even more striking Cascade range. Between these two stern sentinels lay the "Inland Empire" devoted to grain and horticulture, whose capital was Spokane, and beyond the Cascades, three cities striving to be the capital of the Pacific Northwest: Portland, Seattle, and Tacoma. The Northern Pacific, in cooperation with the Oregon Railway & Navigation Co., had been providing through service to Portland for ten years by 1893, and in the mid-1880s had completed its own line across the state of Washington, through the Cascades via the Stampede Tunnel, and into Tacoma. In June 1893 a second and much more vigorous northern route—James J. Hill's Great Northern—began service as far as Spokane, and soon after that to Seattle, via its own tunnel through the Cascades. Hill's tenacity in finding the best route would soon be justified in lower operating costs and higher profits than the Northern Pacific, which was headed for receivership in the fateful crash of 1893. All this made the "Empire Builder," as Hill came be to be called, the boss of both G.N. and N.P. and the worthy opponent of Edward H. Harriman for control of all western railroads.

The N.P. had led in providing comfortable, reasonable passenger service all the weary way from the cities of Chicago and Milwaukee, from which thousands of "westering" Americans (both old and new) were hopping off for new lands on the Great Plains. After losing control in the 1884 panic, Henry Villard had retaken command of the N.P. in 1889 and would shortly ride it to its second disaster. He—or more properly, the local managerial mice, who played while the cat was away tending to other big deals back East—had acquired a second-rate Chicago/Twin Cities line, the Wisconsin Central, and over this they offered through-car service via St. Paul and Minneapolis to Portland and Puget Sound. It was a six-day trip, but a scenic treat, with Glacier National Park an extra feature that Hill's son, Louis, succeeded in getting the government to establish after the turn of the century. In summer it was the only comfortable line, but even in the North, where thirty-below temperatures savaged the land each winter, it could be pretty warm for a week or two in July.

Unquestionably, it was the ghastly heat of the deserts that discouraged transcontinental travel until the 1930s, especially as Los Angeles and Southern California became the most popular destination. Actress Ruth Gordon, recalling the grueling trip across the Mojave Desert in the earily 1930s, remembered the elegant Pullman passengers, including many a star of stage and screen, gasping for breath under moistened linen handkerchiefs or towels draped across their reddened faces. But civilizing the inside temperatures of crack transcontinental trains was not the most important unfinished business for the American railroad passenger train at the end of the century. The winter playgrounds of Florida—almost totally undeveloped south of Jacksonville in 1893—and the Gulf coast beckoned northerners while the Southland quickened, if imperceptibly, the long process of recovering from the Civil War. The Southeast promised much but delivered little to the American traveler of the 1890s.

Slow Train Through Dixie:
Southern Railroads at the Turn of the Century

When Henry Adams made his famous remark that the nineteenth century was mortgaged to the railroads, he might well have had the Southland especially in mind. On the eve of the Civil War the cotton South had seemed to promise a permanent affluence. It was a triumph of agricultural capitalism, accounting for by far the larger part of American export credits, and the textile mills of England, Belgium, France, and New England eagerly sought its staple product. But the South had hardly made a start towards industrialization. Less than one-third of the total railroad mileage in 1860 was in the South, and what there was was poorly integrated. In fact, except for a line that continued the northeastern "spinal cord" south of Washington to Richmond; a long, spindly line of track from Charleston to Memphis; and the route of the Louisville & Nashville southward from Cincinnati and St. Louis to the Gulf; there was no system worthy of the name at all.

After the war, the South's great need was for capital to rebuild its prewar railroads and to construct a truly efficient system that would reflect its new and frankly subordinate economic relationship to the North. In truth, however, it was neither financial nor physical capital that was most grievously lacking, but leadership: "human capital," as we might say today. The petty independence of numerous railroad enterprises that marked the antebellum period flourished anew as new lines, financed at exorbitant rates of interest on bonds that crooked state legislators took a slice of, sprouted in every direction. Efforts to weld dozens of smaller railroads into systems were hampered by the ambitions of local communities. As the judgment day of 1893 approached, the "systems" consisted of the Louisville & Nashville, which fared best as far as leadership was concerned; the Richmond, Fredericksburg & Potomac (a very early line) that linked the thriving northeastern railroads north of Washington with a welter of lines that formed, south of Richmond, a "Florida Fast Line" along the southeastern coast; a line from western Viriginia through the Appalachians and down into the Old Southwest, to Memphis, New Orleans, and Mobile, Alabama, which was based on the East Tennessee, Viriginia & Georgia Railroad, and half a dozen other southern lines to form the "Queen and Crescent" Route (from the Queen City of the West, Cincinnati, to the Crescent City of New Orleans); and the east-west coal-carrying roads, the Chesapeake & Ohio and Norfolk & Western, which were already staggering under the blows of bitter rate competition. The most promising of the loose combines was the holding company that had been formed on the Richmond Terminal Company. Looking at a map of this system as it existed at its receivership in 1893, one can see the general outline of the Southern Railway that succeeded it after one of the most complicated corporate reorganizations up to that time. Its main component was the Richmond & Danville, a very old antebellum road, but it came closest to serving the Southeast comprehensively.

It was the populous Northeast, of course, that accounted for most of the through railroad travel in the South, but southerners flocked north in droves, too, to run their businesses, attend the fine colleges and universities, and tour the growing attractions of the big new cities. The Richmond & Danville connected the Northeast at Washington with Atlanta, fastest growing city in the South; raw, new Birmingham, the "Pittsburgh of the South"; New Orleans; and the budding Florida centers of Jacksonville and Tampa. Leaving Boston at 7:30 p.m., the traveler could sleep the night away as the steamer *Maryland* urged his train down the East River, around the tip of Manhattan, and into the Pennsylvania Railroad's terminal at Jersey City from which, without delay, he would continue on his way to Washington. Arriving there at 10:42 a.m., he would soon be on his way at 11:10 a.m. on the Richmond & Danville. Next morning at 6:00 he was due in Atlanta, and if New Orleans was his destination, his journey would end on the third morning at 7:35, sixty-one hours out of Boston. If he was on his way to Florida, he would be in Jacksonville at 8:30 that night. Tampa, on the west coast, and the village of Rock Ledge, on the east coast, were as far south as railroads extended into Florida in those days. Steamboats served the lower portion of the state. Clearly, Florida awaited the enterprising spirit of men like Henry M. Flagler to build railroads farther south, but his enterprise and his capital would not be long in coming.

The railroads of the Southeast and Southwest exploited the "detachable Pullman" to the limit in the late nineteenth century. No such thing as a "solid" train between Washington or Cincinnati or St. Louis or Memphis and the South existed. Harried conductors were kept busy all night seeing to it that the right sleeper was dropped off at the right place along the route, and that no cars scheduled to be coupled at other points were forgotten. Apparently few mistakes were made, but doubtless now and then a Florida passenger would peer sleepily from his window at dawn, wondering why the train should just be entering the Birmingham, Alabama station!

The Passenger Train at the End of the Century

By 1900 the American passenger train served beautifully, in a passionately bourgeois society, to symbolize the enthusiasm for youth of poets from Wordsworth to Whitman to James Whitcomb Riley. Its early promise as a unifier and developer of the American nation had been fulfilled beyond the dreams of the wildest optimist of 1865, but they were nothing compared to what railroad men and their travelers looked foward to in 1900. Yet one more generation would have the opportunity to take this miracle of speed, comfort, and convenience to new heights. The passenger train's role in American society began to change markedly by the 1920s. By that time the classic concept of the long-distance, through express train would be in sight of the end of its spectacular run in history. In the first thirty years of the Brave New Century, however, it would leave its mark more indelibly than ever on the social fabric. The stunning improvements in passenger travel after 1900, the technology that made them possible, and the vibrant second industrial revolution that made them necessary, deserve a chapter to themselves.

CHAPTER 4

The Passenger Train Creates Modern America

Thine alabaster cities gleam,
Undimmed by human tears
Katherine Lee Bates, "America the Beautiful" (1893)

Drive slow and watch us grow.
City limits sign in thousands of American small towns

Small or Large, but Cities Nonetheless!

The depopulation of the countryside by the industrial revolution, which so troubled the English, did not take place in the United States, although the character of the population changed dramatically. A growing tendency for farm boys (and more and more girls) to forsake the land for the rising urban centers was apparent by the turn of the century, and it alarmed a few old-timers like James J. Hill, who saw in it a fatuous belief on the part of young people that they could "live without working." But most Americans were proud of the transformation of villages into towns and towns into ambitious cities—a trend that would last as long as the railroad train was the chief mode of intercity transportation. Most people saw in such trends nothing less than the march of progress across what had been, within the memory of many still living in 1920, an empty, inviting landscape. The passenger train, which so many historians have seen as "knitting together" localities into a national whole, did no such thing. It rather *created* those local and regional centers, in the process of creating a highly vertebrate nation that by the early twentieth century had achieved an efficiency and trustworthiness of travel, transport, and communication that would not survive the emergence of the automobile and its suburbs. Reflecting upon the fact that it was the railroads that created the heavy industry that made universal ownership of cars possible, we can see how the passenger train contained the seeds of its own destruction. In its day, however, which lasted almost a century, the train was as totally in command of national mobility as the car has been since.

It is doubtful if many towns' futures ever depended so completely upon becoming an important railroad center as the city fathers anxiously warned, but no one doubted that it was the railroads, with their power to determine how easy or difficult, how cheap or how expensive, it would be for a townspeople to travel and trade in the new era, that held the key to its future. The value of the steam railroad in the development of American towns and cities is usually stated in terms of freight transportation. But "getting there" was more important, in the first instance, than "being there." Making the land accessible—both by train and, first, by mail, and, later, by telegraph, which followed the new railroad lines—was the achievement of the passenger train. By dramatically opening up the most unlikely places for settlement, and by doing so with speed, dependability, and relative comfort and safety, the passenger train brought everything else in its wake. In a more practical sense, of course, the significance—social, economic, and cultural—of both passenger and freight trains is but a single, interdependent subject. The traveling salesman's smoky daycoach that brought him to River City was followed, if his visit was successful, in a few weeks by the local that paused at the freight depot long enough to disgorge the goods the local merchants had ordered from him. And the local produce that would be sold in distant markets for the money that would move those goods off their shelves went out, sometimes by the same freight train.

Until the automobile began to make inroads, first on local travel and then on increasingly longer hops between cities, the passenger train hauled virtually everybody who had any reason to go someplace distant from their homes. The steady improvement of the American passenger train after about 1890 encouraged business travel, just as the airplane has done in our time, leading to the gradual extinction of the leisurely, well-thought-out, and permanently recorded letter of earlier days, which is the historian's and biographer's delight. Thousands of salesmen traveled up and down the main rail lines, the branches, and, when necessary, into the hinterland in a rig rented from the local livery stable. The cities, large and small, catered to them in their working and playtime hours, day and night, but even in the countryside it was a mean little burg indeed that could not offer them at least a comfortable lodging, a digestible (and sometimes remarkably good) meal, and an evening's diversion at the local "opera house," with perhaps a drop-in at the saloon or hotel bar (which the rising Prohibition movement was making less common). Many chose just to sit in the hotel lobby in the mammoth tufted leather chairs, taking in the regional political news and local gossip, while adding to their stock of droll stories suitable for all occasions.

The railroads made small-town America. Not even the haughtiest river city during the steamboat era had quite the easy intercourse with the world around the bend or beyond the vanishing point on the straightaway that the railroad brought to the "small" town. James Whitcomb Riley regretted that the railroad trestle had robbed the old swimming hole of his youth of its privacy and sylvan serenity, but by the turn of the century folksy poets were writing on such themes as "Go Home for Christmas, My Boy—Go Home!" or that old tearjerker, "Down at the Station When the Train Comes In." And in summer, bands of naked small boys waved gleefully from many a creek bank to the amused or scandalized passengers on the passing express.

Transformation of the Passenger Train after 1880

Working for Jim Hill was about as demanding as a railroad job could get, and for Allen Manvel, in whom the Protestant work ethic amounted to a disease, being general manager of Hill's St. Paul, Minneapolis & Manitoba Railroad (predecessor of the transcontinental Great Northern) was leading straight to a physical breakdown by 1886. Hill ordered him to "get away from it all" for at least a month, which in those days meant a trip to Europe. Once there, Manvel spent much of his time inspecting western Europe's vaunted railways, and he could hardly express his contempt for their passenger cars. "No heat except a foot warmer, which is a fraud," he said. "No light more than a good candle would give. No water, no urinal, no arsenal. All passengers on continental railways ought to be tested for pressure before starting out!"

By the early years of the new century, the superiority of American passenger travel to any in the rest of the world was beginning to be taken for granted. To be sure, the average intercity train trip was much longer here than in Europe. In the 1890s, for example, train No. 7 on the "Big Four" left Cleveland at noon, and when it pulled into Cincinnati seven and a half hours later, it had traveled almost 250 miles, without ever leaving the state of Ohio. It was an ordinary day trip in the expansive Midwest, but accommodations befitted the time and distance traveled. For a small surcharge, the traveler could sit in a plush parlor car seat and be served by a white-uniformed waiter; otherwise, he could sit on a not much harder seat in the daycoach, replete with the odor of orange peel and banana skins, supplied by "candy butchers" who worked the train from one end to the other, or have lunch in the diner (as much a treat as a necessity for the infrequent traveler). All of the cars were well equipped with "water, urinal, and arsenal," whereas a century later American travelers in "first" class on the German railways were still being told, with a perfectly straight face, that it was not possible to provide potable drinking water on tap.

Evolution of the modern American railroad passenger car is a far more complex story than what the layman sees at the grade crossing might suggest. Because car building was a labor-intensive industry, for a long time making major use of woods in the hands of carpenters and cabinetmakers, and dealing with only a relatively few units in each order, there tended to be many car manufacturers, only a few of whom

Figure 4.1 "Go Home for Christmas, My Boy—Go Home!" was the line that closed each stanza of an old platform favorite of long ago. Here, *Harper's Weekly* for Jan. 2, 1869, records what had already become an American institution: arrival of friends and relatives for the holidays. (Probably more than half of the people on the platform were greeters, habitual train-meeters, or just gawkers, like the lad sitting on the trunk.)

were ever prominent enough or profitable long enough to be generally remembered today. A large, varied industry grew up to supply the car builders with design and operating details, fixtures, and furnishings. As steel came to be used widely and eventually exclusively in car building, the number of builders naturally declined. By the 1970s, when the contribution that rail passenger service could make to American life under certain circumstances began to be recalled, we had lost our traditional leadership in this once-great industry. Today Europeans (especially Germans and Scandinavians), Canadians, and others are building a large percentage of our rail passenger cars because, as we frankly admit, we forgot how. To the aficionado of railroad rolling stock, there can be no more fascinating book than John W. White, Jr.'s *The American Railroad Passenger Car* (1978), especially the chapters on fixtures and running gear and the excellent essay—the best source we have—on George Pullman's contribution to safe, comfortable rail travel.

Probably the most striking departure from earlier nineteenth-century rail passenger-car design, which tended to confine the passengers—at least, the prudent ones—in the same car for the duration of their journey, was the development of the vestibule car. Even the most luxurious sleeping cars and private conveyances until the 1880s had a platform on each end, to which one ascended by the car steps. It was ringed with an iron railing, and a brake wheel, for the manual application of the car brakes even after the application of air brakes operated from the locomotive, stood prominently on one or both ends. Movement from one car to another was an unpleasant and distinctly dangerous undertaking, and for a woman in the tight garments of the 1880s and carrying or leading a small child, it was not to be considered. Of course it was possible—the crew had to get from one car to another— but the wise traveler, and probably more than one middle-aged conductor, at least waited until the train was pausing at a station. The vestibule car changed all that. The ends of the cars were equipped with expandable, fabric-covered canopies, framed in iron and later steel— literally, "bellows"—which pressed tightly against each other as two car ends came together in switching. Continual improvement made the passage from one car to another almost routine, if we overlook the natural swaying of cars on curves. More than one little boy or girl, even so, anxiously pointed out to their mothers the glimpse of railroad ties rushing by below. As for the vestibule, it was expanded laterally; that is, it came to occupy the entire end of the car, not just the passageway, and there was no longer any open area on the end platform. The entire train took on a uniform, sleeker, finished appearance, and vestibule cars replaced the old cars as quickly as corporate treasurers would approve, if not more quickly. Soon the key word in rail passenger train advertising, in places like the *Official Guide*, became "solid." "Solid vestibuled trains from all major cities in the Midwest to the World's Columbian Exposition in Chicago," proclaimed many of the myriad railroad companies hoping to cash in on profitable passenger travel in 1893.

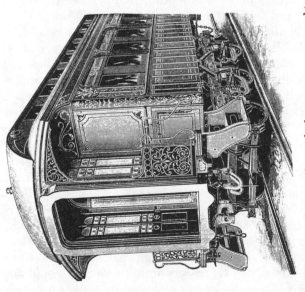

Figure 4.2 Early (1880) vestibule passenger car and interior of Pullman car of the same era, revealing the taste for plush surroundings and the abundant artisanry, especially in marquetry and fine wood paneling, that supported it.

The Pullman sleeping car became the standard overnight conveyance on American railroads long before the old century was over. It made overnight travel comfortable and inexpensive, particularly on the well-traveled "hops" between major cities. How George Pullman maintained the standards of a first-class hotel at the low fares of that day for a remarkably democratic range of sleeping-car patrons would stump any hotel manager nowadays. Only the very poor or the very stingy found it necessary to sit up all night, except on those unfortunate occasions when the sleeping cars were sold out. Black travelers in the South—those few who traveled more than a few miles and had the small extra fare to spend—were routinely assigned "Lower 13," which was Jim Crow code for the private "drawing room" at the end of the twelve open sections, a private room that normally accommodated three persons but was seldom taken. The black patron paid only the lower berth fare, and the porter (himself black) served his meals, if required, in the room. Such were the forgotten "advantages" of discrimination. As for the porter, he found himself among the patricians of his race when he was at home between assignments. His pay was low, and based almost entirely on tips, but considering the deprived circumstances from which he had thus escaped, his cheerful demeanor was probably genuine.

The economical sleeping car accommodations began to die long before the automobile and airliner had a chance to kill them. By 1917 operating costs had risen far faster than fares, which came under regulation in 1906. Meanwhile, the cars had grown into steel behemoths that were expensive to drag back and forth across a continent. When World War I came to America, one of the first acts of the railroad administrator was to place a steep surcharge on railroad tickets that would be honored in Pullmans—with, of course, the space charge additional. Thus the "first-class fare" was born, and sleeper travel for the masses ended. The Depression finished off the hotel concept of railroad travel: the Missouri Pacific, for example, dragged a standard twelve-section/drawing-room Pullman back and forth through the small-town depots between Little Rock and Kansas City throughout the 1930s, and during many a summer's twilight the idlers who met all the trains would see only a single face, the porter's, staring morosely out of the Pullman windows. When the railroads were returned to private control in 1920 they had begged to be allowed to keep the first-class surcharge and, like so many "wartime" measures, it proved to be permanent. In World War II the national fleet of sleepers had one last fling, and then it was all over; sleeping accommodations on Amtrak's long-distance trains nowadays are almost as scarce as the trains themselves.

It had been a totally different story in the fat years of what the French call "La Belle Epoque," from the Gay Nineties to the eve of World War I. By 1900, with the railroads that accounted for the great bulk of railroad business neatly tucked into a half a dozen or so "communities of interest," and cutthroat competition with its attendant financial disaster forestalled by almost unbelievable prosperity, the highly profitable passenger business flourished, and improvements in comfort and safety came thick and fast. The passenger cars running on through routes by 1917 put the passenger car of a generation before to shame, for air brakes, central heat, electric light, and flush toilets made travel more pleasant, while all-steel cars, multiple tracking, reduced curvature and grades, heavier and higher quality rail, and increasingly automatic "block" signals, made travel easier. Dining cars, seldom profitable, rounded out the hotel-on-wheels idea. First- and second-generation railroad stations were swept away in city after city and replaced with more or less monumental structures that more often than not became the keystone of the "city beautiful" plans of a new breed of urban planner.

Countless nineteenth-century inventors, few of whom are remembered today, had dreamed of solving the many technological problems of moving people swiftly, comfortably, and safely from one place to another. The evolution of the modern, all-steel, centrally steam-heated and electrically lighted and air-conditioned passenger car was long and full of false starts. As late as the 1880s, when rail travel had virtually replaced all earlier forms of land travel, boarding even a first-class car seemed perilous. Cars were still made almost entirely of wood, for steel would become a cheap industrial material only towards the end of the century. The most common form of collision was the "rear-ender," in which a locomotive would plow into the rear of a train pausing on the same track up ahead. Almost invariably, the rear car of the train ahead would be telescoped into its next-to-last mate, with the errant locomotive perhaps ending up astride the wreckage. Derailments were appallingly frequent, for the new Bessemer steel rails, superior though they were to the old wrought-iron rails in toughness, were brittle and far from uniform in crystalline structure; when they broke, often after only a few years in service, the consequences were frequently lamentable. Indeed, politicians lamented over this issue at the drop of a proposed rate increase by the railroads, which meanwhile struggled to carry record-breaking volumes of traffic. But, as the leading authority on the rail passenger car says, the biggest news of 1904 in the railroad business was the introduction of the first all-steel cars on the New York subway and the Long Island commuter railroad. Intercity trains quickly followed suit, and within a decade locomotives were struggling to haul longer and longer coaches that weighed far more than the old wooden ones.

At the same time, the classic *bête noire* of the nineteenth century railway coach, the potbellied stove, was finally made obsolete. After much fooling around with central-heating methods based on some kind of furnace located within the car, inventors finally turned to heating the cars with steam from the larger locomotives that were replacing small early-century models. Steam had been shown in large buildings to be the only practical and effective way of warming large interiors. Now there remained only one source of the deadly fire that often destroyed cars and passengers: the lamps that lighted the conveyances. By the 1890s the Pintsch gas lamp, making use of the Welsbach mantle to produce a brilliant white flame, and supplied with gas from a tank beneath the car body, had become the standard form of railroad car lighting. It was a welcome improvement over the old yellow-flame kerosene lamps, but electric lamps were not to be delayed much longer. More and more railroads, during the first decade of the new century, began to advertise that their name trains used electric lighting, the "juice" being provided by generators turned by midget steam engines that chugged away in the baggage car. But baggage cars with smoke stacks did not last long, and the lights were soon taking their energy from storage batteries (itself a marvelous if prosaic invention) that were constantly recharged by generators connected by belts to the car wheels.

The last major improvement was air conditioning, which did not begin to appear until the 1930s, and then only haltingly. By the late 1930s it was to be found in the standard equipment of most of the "name" trains, but woe unto him who found himself assigned to back-up equipment during the summer, especially in the South and South-west. Idlers on the crosswalk over the tracks of the Missouri Pacific depot in Little Rock, Arkansas, remember the huge blocks of ice that husky black men, sweating profusely, manhandled into the bunkers of the *Sunshine Special* in the one-hundred-degree heat. The *Special* disappeared in the mid-1940s when it was replaced by the *Eagle*, a brand new diesel-electric streamliner. The *Eagle* typified the American railroads' last desperate effort to keep their passenger business, sporting air conditioning that was based on fully mechanical refrigeration machinery. There were no blocks of ice to melt away if the train was delayed on a siding in, say, Longview, Texas, but if the machinery failed (which it did more and more frequently as the passenger business fell into desuetude) the effect was the same.

The modern railroad passenger car, like all basic improvements in human life, was the work of many, but if one man must be singled out for his contribution to the distinctly American way of doing things, it is George Pullman. When he died in 1897 he was one of the richest men in America and, mainly because of his intransigence in the Pullman strike of 1894, one of the most hated. Beginning in 1864 with a prototype car that was convertible from day coach to sleeping berths at night, he built manufacturing facilities that no one else could begin to match for efficiency and perfection of workmanship, and he soon convinced most of the railroads of the country that they could best serve their patrons' needs for overnight travel by hauling his cars staffed with his own people and operating out of his own commissaries in major terminals. The familiar process of mergers and acquisitions took its course, and, well before Pullman died, his name had become synonymous with sleeping cars, and his standards of service equal to those of the best hotels.

It was Pullman's firm belief in the importance of giving travelers the kind of comfort and service that most were not accustomed to getting at home that accounted for his preeminence. He knew that American travelers, most of whom were businessmen, would pay for comfort, and in an era when an overnight journey of several hundred miles might otherwise take a day to recover from—much like the "jet lag" of today's air travel—Pullman travel was a godsend to the peripatetic American. Pullman sought to make his cars quieter, freer from vibration, more elegant, and generally more suited to the needs of the long-distance traveler. One example was his famous paper wheel, an incredibly long roll of ordinary paper that formed the core of the steel car wheels. No one has ever found a better shock absorber, and with its eleven mates on a big, heavy steel Pullman it was the standard for years.

Most striking of all was Pullman's innovative configurations of day and night spaces, which endeared him to the traveler whose greatest enemy was boredom. After returning from a trip to Europe in the 1880s, he immediately introduced an idea he had got from the Wagon-Lit on which he had ridden across the continent. At one end of his standard open-section-plus-drawing-room car layout, he installed a small galley in which the porter could prepare light meals for his passengers. This "buffet car" made him independent of the railroad management, which often found it inconvenient to cut dining cars in and out of trains or, on some lightly traveled routes, to run them at all. George Pullman himself hated railroad cars that produced no revenue from the sale of space (like the dining cars, lounge cars, and other special amenities that the railroads offered on their best trains). He began to combine open lounge sections with sleeping accommodations in the same car and successfully introduced several private-room layouts.

It was all fearfully demanding of capital, of course, but the rapid growth in the cost per railroad passenger car was more than offset for a generation by higher traffic volume and, to a lesser extent, by fare increases. The wooden coach in which the Franklin Pierce family suffered its grievous loss had cost, in 1850, about $2000, whereas Pullman's earliest sleeping car cost $6500 in 1863. Early in the new century, coach and sleeper price tags had soared to $12,500 and $22,000, but such figures had been eclipsed by the end of the passenger era: the average coach cost $235,934 and the average sleeping car, $307,497 in 1958. Such equipment in the Amtrak era is touching a million dollars a copy.

Railroads and the Pullman Company aggressively embraced improvements in the safety and comfort of their rolling stock, and, until the automobile and tourist-class airplane took over intercity travel, American passenger trains set the standard for the world. By the time

George Pullman died, a trip by train with Pullman accommodations was something to look forward to with pleasure and not a little pride, for travel has always had its status-symbol function. Touring by car under incredibly rugged and often dangerous conditions began to appeal to a certain type of personality by the second decade of this century; such people were loudly vocal in the scorn they heaped upon rail travelers who, they said, saw nothing of America but factories, warehouses, and railroad yards—as if that was not what the country was really all about. But it would be a long time before any halfway decent roads went into such areas of spectacular scenery as the western railroads offered or brought people to the national parks with such efficiency. In any case, the smart young thing of the 1920s who looked forward to a week in the big city, with all the excitement and posh of downtown and life in a big, modern hotel, could hardly see the allure of roughing it on a camping trip in a touring car. No better explanation of the enthusiasm with which Americans flocked onto their trains after 1900 can be found than prosperity and the aching desire to see something of the world, in the fulfillment of which the modern passenger train stood ready. For almost two marvelous decades, passenger travel joined the strong upward trend in freight business that had begun years before.

Dependability, Economy, Convenience

Among the innumerable stories about the uncertainties of air travel in its first great growth period in the 1950s is one about a group of travelers who were proceeding arduously northward on old U.S. Route One between Washington and New York. "If you had taken Eastern Airlines to New York, you'd be home now," sneered a roadside sign somewhere between Baltimore and Wilmington. It was all too ironic, for our friends had already flown to New York that day but, unable to land in the fog that enveloped the entire metropolitan area, they had returned to National Airport in Washington, rented a car, and set out anew. As if to throw salt in their wounds, just as the highway paralleled the four-track mainline of the Pennsylvania Railroad, the *Congressional*—the three-and-one-half-hour train to New York—flashed by and disappeared into the dreary gray mist. It would be in New York's Pennsylvania Station hours before they would emerge from the Lincoln Tunnel.

No mode of transportation has ever been 100 percent dependable, nor will any ever be. "We live in a world of space and time," goes the cliché, and there is space enough and time for almost anything to happen. By the turn of the century, however, Americans had come to expect from their passenger trains great regularity of departure and reliability of arrival, and the energetic society that had poured so much of the old century's sweat and treasure into building the railroads had learned to use them as the chief tool of an expansive material civiliza-

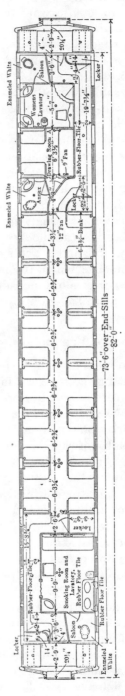

Figure 4.3 The first all-steel Pullman car, *Carnegie*, outshopped 1910, and its floor plan, which was the classic twelve-section drawing-room configuration that flashed daily (and nightly) through thousands of American cities and towns until the coming of the all-room Pullmans in the dying days of Pullman travel.

tion. Few Americans lived more than a short buggy or hack ride from a depot where a through train paused, at least on flag signal. Air travel has never matched such convenience at either end of the journey, while the car has proved remarkably wanting as a universal means of transportation to a people that have unthinkingly done away with the old and faithful servant.

A well-disciplined world of affairs was built on the trains' regular and almost universal comings and goings. Salesmen, vaudeville performers, commercial travelers in general, set their itineraries a month or even a season in advance. Businessmen arranged their appointments to avoid interfering with the regular twice-a-day mail delivery that made it possible, for example, to mail a letter from Boston to New York at the end of the day and be handed a reply before 10 a.m. two mornings later. (Try it nowadays.) Farmers paused in their fields to set their pocket watches as the express roared through the waving wheat or ripening corn. Pearl White traveled from one silent movie theater to the next, snug in her film cans, to be delivered by the expressman only hours before she was to reenact the latest "Perils of Pauline" for local moviegoers. Bicycles, velocipedes, live billy goats (the goat-drawn wagon had a brief vogue among upper middle-class children), and countless other treasures, destined for birthday parties or Christmas trees, were deftly offloaded from the express cars along with more prosaic but valuable shipments as the *Flyer* paused briefly alongside the station platform in its rush toward the big city.

Passengers detraining a few cars behind confidently expected that the baggage men, meanwhile, would slide their substantial impedimenta off the train onto handtrucks (they were sometimes disappointed), while entraining passengers assumed that their own stuff was being loaded. Now and then a hush descended upon the throng of train-meeters as a big oblong pine box with bronze handles was gingerly handed out to the waiting funeral director and his assistants: someone was coming home for the last time. Outgoing mailbags were quickly grasped by railway mail clerks who tossed the incoming bags onto the handtruck. A few feet away a little girl in a pink dress giggled as her father held her up to the side of the railway post-office car so that she could mail her letter to Grandma through the slot provided.

In our age of direct-dial telephones, any discussion of the U.S. mails is likely to produce a barely muffled yawn. It was not always so. Humans are never so much at loose ends as when they are deprived of news of loved ones far away, or the outcome of business and personal affairs so long nurtured. The story of how even the most isolated pioneers managed to be reached by these precious pieces of paper is long and complicated and need not detain us here, for we are interested only in demonstrating that it was the railroads that created cheap, dependable, high-volume mail service—indeed, the postal service as we have known it since the mid-nineteenth century. It was the universal passenger train that made it possible. The passenger trains went everywhere, and they took over the carrying of the mail as a matter of course. The explosion in the volume of mail that ensued is one of the most astounding social statistics of modern peoples. Useful statistics on the volume of mail carried only begin with the arrival of the steam railroads at adolescence; that is, with data on the number of postage stamps sold by U.S. post offices. That year is 1853. Why did the post offices keep no such records for earlier years? Because they did not sell stamps. It made little sense to sell stamps before a coherent mail-routing system arose. Only God could know what the poor little sheet of tissue paper that was a lettter in the dark ages of communication would have to go through before reaching its destination, or what the charges due on delivery would be.

The first U.S. postal stamps went on sale in the New York Post Office on July 1, 1847. In 1853 (by no coincidence, the year when direct rail links between the east coast and Chicago were being completed) some sixty-one million stamps and stamped envelopes were sold in the country. Sounds like a lot? In 1886, as the railroads hit their stride after bringing the entire west coast into their net, the first data on total number of pieces of matter handled became available: 3.7 billion! And yet it was only the beginning. In the fifteen years to the end of the century, the total doubled to 7.4 billion, but in the next thirteen years, down to the eve of World War I in 1913, mail volume grew by two-and-one-half times. Onward and upward has always been the rule, give or take a temporary lull in depression and wartime. By 1970, on the eve of a shameful explosion of "junk mail" that threatens to sink the entire system, the mailmen sweated under a volume of not quite eighty-five billion pieces, including a pox of Christmas cards some of which ended up in storm sewers, although that is another story.

No aspect of American life was untouched by the revolution that the trains wrought in bringing mail service almost to the level of a free good. (For many years—ironically enough, until the depression called for an *increase* in the cost of a first class letter to three cents—an ordinary first-class letter went for two cents.) It went fast, and it went dependably, too, for in an era when semiliteracy was common, post offices rose to the challenge of delivering virtually everything, despite creative spelling or even the cutesy use of rebuses instead of names. Special low rates for printed matter, especially periodicals, encouraged reading, although of *what* is not so clear. To Congress, *Scientific American* and the *Atlantic Monthly* counted for no more nor less than the *Police Gazette*, and books, good and bad, newly published and old, circulated in a degree that no one had ever imagined possible before. In conjunction with the telegraph and R. Hoe's web-fed rotary press, the railroad brought the modern newspaper to nearly every doorstep along with the morning's milk delivery. It was no matter of enterprising twelve-year-olds delivering a folksy local paper. In towns located at a distance from the big cities, the morning paper, loaded in neat bundles, arrived in the express car of the *Flyer*, and whether the train stopped in Bug Tussle, Texas, or not, a bundle of papers would hit the platform with a loud plop anywhere from 3 a.m. to 6 p.m. on. Moviemakers knew it: many a film moved the story along by a brief scene in which the expressman pushes a bundle of newspapers onto a platform and the camera comes down tight on the big black headline: WAR DECLARED! Until the coming of radio, not another soul in the town already knew the news save for the telegraph operator and perhaps the tough little woman who manned the town's telephone switchboard through the long silent night.

It all sounds like something the American people must regularly have thanked their lucky stars for, but in fact the way we treated the railroads in return for their making it all possible was a national disgrace. When one deals with the government, it tells him what he must furnish and what he may charge for it, and it usually gets its way, at least when the contractor is as vulnerable as American railroads were in the Populist-Progressive era. Sock it to the railroads: they have ruled our destinies long enough, and, besides, they have more money than they know what to do with. The mail service, virtually all of which the railroads provided, was paid for at rates determined by a sample-period weighing of mail sacks, which was done every four years. One look at the annual rate of growth from 1900 to World War I would convince any fair-minded person that the provider would be chronically underpaid by such a system. So the railroads claimed. But who was being fair-minded? The postmaster general was invariably a political figure, first, last, and always. He gleefully held the administration up as a fighter for getting the people's last penny's worth and their protector from the depredations of the railroad barons, who were so busy marrying off their daughters to English dukes!

Well, a bad contract is nevertheless a valid one, to be sure. But what happened next removes any doubt that, at the very least, any move that could be considered an act of generosity or even fair-mindedness towards the railroads would have been political poison. From the beginning of the railroad era, the trains had hauled in their baggage cars a special class of valuable package freight, called "express," through the agency of such private enterprises as Adams Express, U.S. Express, Wells Fargo, and in some cases subsidiaries of the railroads. The carriers split the charge (which was substantial but reasonable enough to assure a high volume) fifty-fifty with the express companies. The largest users of the service by 1913 were the big retail stores that had gone into the mail order business heavily in the previous century. They then demanded that, along with rural free delivery of letters, the government provide a cheap parcel post service, and they got their way. Well, at least the railroads got the parcel post fee, you may think. Not at all. That was postal service revenue, and went directly into its receipts. The railroads would carry the parcels in the regular mail. It would all be adjusted in the next sample weighing period—three years in the future. Parcel post remains one of the great domestic blessings of the Progressive Movement in the dozens of uncritical histories of that era, and virtually no one knows, or apparently cared to know, this classic example of the failure of democratic government. Most people enjoyed the cheap new service, did not care who subsidized the difference between the fee and the real cost, and if told would probably have said that if the railroads did not deserve ill treatment for one thing, they almost certainly deserved it for another!

We cannot leave this story of the origins of our still-vital mail service without commenting that the success of the U.S. Post Office in materializing, out of what seemed like thin air, a national mail-hauling system to replace the passenger trains and their railway post offices, is something of a bureaucratic miracle. Of course the cost is far greater today, and the service not nearly so good, but such is progress. On the horizon is a national system of privately operated mail and express service, using the post office's one undoubted asset: its thousands of offices throughout the land. And how we shall miss the comings and goings of the passenger trains then!

The Value of Safety, the Price of Speed

People did not flock to the trains just because they were there, nor even because they were the generations that had been "chosen" to populate and exploit this largest and last of the favorably situated major land masses of the world. The many refinements in the design and operation of railroad passenger facilities that we have been describing made a direct and measurable contribution to the attractiveness of faraway places. The railroad fundamentally altered not only the meaning of "getting there" and the meaningfulness of "being there," but it relieved that devastating feeling of separation suffered by migrants presumably since the dawn of time. What only the jet airliner could eventually do for the transoceanic immigrant in ameliorating the sense of final and complete separation from the scenes of childhood, the American railroads had begun to do a century before for citizens of our vast land mass. And this melting of distance was not merely objective, in terms of time, money, and physical comfort, but decidedly subjective, in terms of the traveler's faith in his ability to arrive at his destination in good shape, or at all. When the system failed, it made headlines all across the nation.

Spring is always a welcome visitor to upstate New York, and it was especially so in April 1940, after a long and unusually hard winter. But, as the Yankee farmer said to the tourists who asked if spring was as lovely as fall in the Northeast, "Spring ain't our best season." By late April the Mohawk River, through whose rocky valley the famous water-level route of the New York Central ran, was swollen with melting snow

Figure 4.4 Sorting the mail, in-transit on the New York Central's *Fast Mail* from New York to Chicago in 1888. Learning "by heart" all of the depots (whether the train stopped or not) on the route was a prerequisite for assignment to this plum of Railway Post Office jobs.

and the ground everywhere was soggy as the thawing earth struggled to soak up the excess moisture. But the trains were running as usual, and their steady procession around the "Gulf Curve"—sharpest on the entire mainline—at Little Falls, New York, seventy-three miles west of Albany, was reassuring.

The 1930s had been hard on the New York Central, which for nearly a hundred years had been one of the most intensively operated and profitable railroads in the world. The Central, unlike its coal- and steel-carrying competitor to the south, the Pennsylvania Railroad, was a specialist in the lucrative business of whisking passengers from Boston, New York, and major cities along the way, to the Chicago and St. Louis gateways, while its freight consisted heavily of merchandise— the manufactured products of a thousand vigorous industries on its route. The Great Depression had reduced this flow to all but a trickle.

To make matters worse, it was then, in the early thirties, that trucks had begun to take the cream of what remained of this business away from the railroads, and as obliging states and the federal government poured money into building fine, hard-surface highways, bridges, and under-river tunnels, this bloodletting became a hemorrhage. A measure of prosperity had returned by 1936, but that Christmas businessmen had been appalled by the impunity with which sit-down strikers had taken over the property of General Motors in Detroit and forced the giant automaker to recognize their union as sole bargaining agent for the men. Reelected by a landslide, F.D.R. rekindled the fires under the antitrust torture the next summer. Whether out of pique or real fear, business withdrew into its shell in 1937, and by that fall the decline in new orders for investment in plant and machinery, and a creeping mood of pessimism, had precipitated the "recession" of 1938, one of the sharpest short-term economic downtrends in our history.

The Central turned in a record net loss in 1938. Then came the 1939 New York World's Fair—the World of Tomorrow—and with it high hopes for a return to prosperity for the eastern trunk line railroads. With whatever resources they could scrape up, these lines spruced up their name trains, put new and faster schedules into service, and hoped for the best. But the man who would pull the railroads' chestnuts—and everybody else's, too, for that matter—out of the fire was not the genial president in Washington, but the unpleasant little man with the Charlie Chaplin moustache in Berlin. Adolf Hitler would soon give Americans a chance to show what their huge unemployed resources of men and women, farms and factories, were really capable of. By the spring of 1940 misery was spreading over western Europe, but in America prosperity was returning after ten long years of depression.

The New York Central had made a few feeble attempts to adapt to automobile competition and the Depression after 1929. For many years it had operated eight limited trains between New York's Grand Central Terminal and La Salle Street Station in the heart of Chicago. They were among the best in the nation, sometimes running two, five, or more sections. As the thirties wore on, management shortened the running time of these trains: the trip had taken twenty leisurely hours, for example, on the famous *Twentieth Century Limited* in 1929, but by the late thirties it had been cut to seventeen hours; the train boasted some of Pullman's most modern equipment, notably the new roomette and double bedroom cars, and called itself an "all-room" train. The *Lake Shore Limited*, a name originally given to William H. Vanderbilt's grudging response to the Pennsylvania Railroad's pioneering limited train ("The public be damned!"), had lost most of the glamour, but it was still a good, no-nonsense, fast all-Pullman train that had been speeded up from a pokey twenty-three hours in 1929 to nineteen hours by 1940.

(These 1929 running times testify to the railroad's tardy response to the public's demand for speed as well as comfort and safety, for they were not much speedier than the Central had been capable of early in the century. Even so, the *Lake Shore* and other limited trains still demanded an extra fare in 1929, but except for the *Century* this practice soon disappeared with hard times.) The Central and the Pennsylvania vigorously promoted rail travel, with special appeals to the young, who had discovered the economy of buses, the thrills and speed of flying, and of course the adventure of cross-country automobile travel. (The fledgling airlines, meanwhile, courted the older traveler who was still loyal to Pullman comforts, reliability, and safety; you didn't have to be in a big hurry to fly, they implied, but it did help to have a fat pocketbook.)

Friday, April 19, 1940, was damp and gloomy in New York City and upstate, but in Grand Central Terminal the *Lake Shore Limited* was warm and cheerful in its wreath of steam as it stood poised for its 6:50 p.m. departure to Chicago. Fourteen big, heavy, twelve-wheel, all-steel cars comprised the train, including nine Pullmans, a diner, three daycoaches, and a baggage car, a great bulk but no particular challenge to the big, nearly new Hudson-type locomotive that waited to take over the consist at Harmon, a few miles up the Hudson River at the end of the electrified district. As the gates opened, some 250 passengers streamed up the platform to their assigned cars. Among them was Fred T. MacDonald, a man in late middle age, who had a lower berth waiting for him in the car that at Utica would be switched to the Adirondack Division train. He had mixed feelings as he began the trip. Although he was headed for Saranac Lake, where his wife and daughter were waiting to celebrate the MacDonalds' thirty-fifty wedding anniversary, the event would be clouded by the fact that their daughter was seriously ill in the famous sanatorium there. Several young couples, some with babes in arms, stood out among the majority of middle-aged men of affairs, and there were women traveling alone or with a small child, even little babies, for whose comfort and well-being both Pullman and the Central had long claimed a special solicitousness in their advertising. At the last minute an executive of a big New York dairy, who had already missed an earlier train, hurried through the gate.

No famous personalities made up the passenger list: such people took the *Twentieth Century Limited,* whose departures and arrivals the newspapers covered as religiously as the sailings and arrivals of the great ocean liners. It was a cross-section of plain, ordinary American citizens, by and large, but a study of their occupations and achievements doubtless would have revealed the real authors of the economic and cultural wealth of the nation, and explained why fast, reliable travel was so important. But as the passengers filed down the platform, they glanced in amazement at the very last car on the train. It was an ordinary daycoach, and from its windows stared a sea of expressionless oriental faces. It was a "shipment" of Chinese men whom the Department of Immigration and Naturalization was sending back to Canada, from which they had illegally entered the United States.

By the time the train pulled out of Harmon, with a man of thirty-three years' experience as an engineer at the throttle, many of the passengers who had not fortified themselves with an early dinner in the city were enjoying the very special luxury of dinner in the gleaming diner of a first-class American passenger train. Others were settled in the lounge car, an increasingly important producer of revenue since the repeal of Prohibition, where the clink of glasses and the babble of conversation further reenforced the general feeling of well-being. By now several card games were underway in the private rooms among groups of men who had been total strangers barely an hour before, for the all-night poker games on the Central's elegant passenger runs between New York and Chicago had long since become a tradition.

Traffic on the mainline and especially in the stations and yards along the way was recovering by 1940. Perhaps the *Lake Shore* got behind some slow traffic on the superb four-track mainline up the scenic Hudson River, or perhaps there were more passengers to be taken on than usual at Albany. Whatever the reason, the *Limited* was fifteen minutes behind schedule as it turned its nose westward that night. We shall never really know, but we do know that at 11:23 p.m., as the train approached the Gulf Curve, on the eastern edge of Little Falls, the engineer, James H. Earl, was already twelve minutes overdue in Utica, which was still twenty-one miles up ahead. He would doubtless lose more time there as the pullman for Saranac Lake and Lake Placid was cut out and switched to the Adirondack Division train. The man at the throttle must have chafed at the thought of leaving Utica (next scheduled stop Cleveland) as much as a half-hour late. He had a "clear board" between him and Utica and the temptation was strong to make the most of it. Whether or not he consciously decided to ignore the 45-mile-per-hour speed limit on the Gulf Curve, he hit it at 59, and no one would ever find out why.

A ponderous Hudson-type locomotive (wheel arrangement: ooOOOoo), all 316,000 pounds of it, with fourteen all-steel passenger cars in tow, making sixty miles an hour on a straightaway, has a formidable reluctance to turn sharply. The weight that slams against the rails when it does is monstrous, and on the Gulf Curve a deflection of six degrees to the left, with the Mohawk River on the left and the solid rock walls of a cut immediately to the right, takes a lot of persuasion. The *Lake Shore Limited* refused to take the turn, and in the space of a single human breath the great locomotive shot straight into the rock wall. Right on behind followed the baggage car, two daycoaches, and several Pullmans, all of which telescoped more or less together. Behind them all of the rest of the cars left the tracks except for three Pullmans and the daycoach with the Chinese passengers. The fireman was hurled a hundred feet to his death, but the engineer was crushed beneath the weight of the engine.

Most of Little Falls's citizens had gone to bed by then, for they had to be at work by 8 a.m. in the knitting mills and shoe factories that were their livelihood. (Nearly everybody worked a half day on Saturdays then.) But the explosion of the engine roused them to a scene of horror. Precious minutes went by as they struggled to mount a rescue operation. The scene was almost otherworldly. The proud train, such a warm cocoon of comfort and security a few minutes before, was a pile of grievously smashed pullmans. One, bearing the proud name "Pulaski" on its side, was virtually shorn of its clerestory roof. The walking wounded, some of them out of their minds with shock and mounting grief, tumbled through such doors and shattered windows as were free of debris. Local hospital facilities were quickly swamped, but towns and cities from as far away as fifty miles quickly sent ambulances. Hearses, with their long wicker containers that bespoke disaster, were needed too, for in the wreckage, as would be learned over the next several hours, lay thirty-one dead.

A man who chose not to be identified told reporters that it happened so fast there was virtually no warning. One minute he was playing poker with four other men; the next, he was the only member of the game still among the living. The hoary old anecdote about the sleeping car passenger who refused to disrobe at night, in case there was a wreck, came to life in one seventy-year-old gentleman whose first words on regaining consciousness were, "Give me my pants!" Worst of all were the hysterical shrieks of a young woman whose infant lay dead in the wreckage. She would not budge an inch until the child was removed and placed in her arms. Finally a rescue worker fashioned a sling out of a sheet in which she could cradle the little corpse as she was put into the ambulance. At the very end of the train, the Chinamen still sat in their coach, barely shaken up. Forbidden to get out, they stared stolidly out of the windows at the hubbub, wondering what had caused the delay. New York Central officials blanched at the prospect of breaking the news to Mrs. MacDonald and her daughter that Mr. MacDonald was one of the dead. The dairy executive, who had been headed for his beloved model farm upstate, would never see it again.

Years later, when airline disasters had become more frequent and the death lists larger as planes grew bigger, Captain Eddie Rickenbacker, one of the pioneers of commercial aviation and a founder of Eastern Airlines, would remind Americans testily that there was a price they must pay for speed. They already knew it, for a century of railroad travel had taught them not merely the virtues of speed, but also the risks it entails. There is a special fascination in railroad wrecks, especially big ones. Perhaps it is because there is a principle of compensation at work in the knowledge that the more comfortable and secure and faster a mode of travel, and the more smug a society is about its infallibility, the more like an act of a higher power it is when disaster does strike. Only the lugubrious end of a great transoceanic liner, of which the SS *Titanic* is the classic example, attracted more attention than a major train wreck in the golden age of train travel.

The Little Falls wreck rated a two-column headline on page one of Saturday morning's city edition of the *New York Times,* and the wire services put it on page one across the nation. The Sunday *Times* still had it on page one, as the carnage became known, and ran a huge panoramic photograph of the scene. On the same Friday evening as the Little Falls disaster, in the farming community of Slayton, Minnesota, eleven teenagers had been killed in a head-on collision between two cars as they returned from a dance. The *Times* gave it a small feature head at the bottom of page one. To most Americans, this rather new way of killing themselves wholesale had gone from sensation to banality in a generation.

Safety—The Enduring Quest

The wreck at Little Falls illustrates conveniently many of the factors that contributed to fatalities on the railroads. Excessive speed (as the cab speedometer tape proved) on a notorious curve at a time when the soil underlying the roadbed had been potentially destabilized by ground moisture was the cause, but to say that raises more questions. "Human error," which we still can not compensate for, is what we end up with. Inattention at a critical moment by an engineer who had kept his mind on his business for thirty-three years, rather than a deliberate disregard for the rules, is the inevitable conclusion, for an examination of the locomotive revealed that engineer Earl had slammed on his brakes when he saw the curve dead ahead through the gloom.

Over the previous hundred years, many of the most obvious ways of dispatching passengers had been virtually eliminated. Incineration in wooden cars eventually became all but unknown, and failing structures—like the bridge that gave way under an earlier version of the *Lake Shore Limited* at Ashtabula, Ohio, killing ninety-two in 1878— were far rarer in the age of high-tensile steel materials. Such prosaic occurrences as derailment by articles of cargo that fell from freight cars on adjoining tracks, high speed, and, more frequently than railroad officials liked to admit, vandalism, were still much to be feared, but as on today's high-speed highways, it was probably collisions that were most dreaded. As the national habit of blaming "big business" spread after 1900, it was not surprising that the tendency of relatively brittle Bessemer steel rails to break made a popular issue for politicians and for shallow economic reformers like Louis D. Brandeis, who was profoundly prejudiced against big corporations like United States Steel. It was atomistic competition between a multitude of small operators that, alone, could give people both low prices and quality products, he insisted, ignoring the great bulk of human experience down to that time. (At the very time U.S. Steel was struggling to convert to the vastly superior open-hearth process for making steel, and to make good the promise of stability that it had brought to a deeply troubled American industry, the best rails in the world were being made by the German corporate giant, Krupp.)

The attention that railroad accidents attracted was well deserved until far into the twentieth century, the more so since the spectacular prosperity of the years from 1897 to 1920 placed unheard of burdens, both freight and passenger, upon the railroads. The lines strove to accommodate more frequent and longer trains while at the same time investing record sums in system betterments, notably double-tracking, increasing the number and length of passing tracks, reducing grades and curves, and installing automatic block signals. A traveler in the early twentieth century might have marveled at the frequency with which his train flashed by work crews that had just stepped out of the way minutes before.

The statistical improvement in rail travel safety is impressive. In 1890, about 492 million passengers rode a total of 11.8 billion miles on American railroads, and 286 of them were killed doing so. This came to 24.2 passengers killed for every billion passenger-miles traveled. Such were the fruits of technology and advancing management practice that those numbers steadily declined. In 1906, just ten years later, deaths per billion passenger-miles had been cut to 15.5 persons; by 1920, to 4.8; and by 1943, when wartime travel, virtually impossible by car, rose to an all-time record of 87.9 billion passenger-miles, the rate had further improved to 3.2. Fewer people lost their lives on American wartime passenger trains than in the peaceful year of 1890, even though traffic was eight times as great.

In the closing years of generally available passenger service, the fatality rate approached zero, and in 1970 only eight people among the total who traveled 10.8 billion passenger miles (still almost as many as 1890) were killed. Results may differ from year to year, of course, and in recent years there has been a disturbing tendency for near-tragedies to occur in commuter and rapid-transit service, while Amtrak struggles to maintain safety in a permissive age when the old standards of discipline are sometimes rejected by an entrenched body of railroad labor. Nevertheless, the following statistics demonstrate that the combination of a vigorous development and application of improved technology, experience, and a national policy that always seems to come to its senses when the industry is on the brink, made U.S. rail travel the standard to which all other modes and all other nations ought to repair.

A mass of factors, impossible to weigh individually, lie behind these figures. Railroad men never lost sight of the deadliness of excessive speed, however, and down to the end, few American passenger

Passenger Travel on American Railroads and Fatalities Per
Billion Passenger Miles

	Billions of passenger miles traveled	Number of persons killed	Fatalities per billion passenger miles
1890	11.8	286	24.2
1900	16.0	249	15.5
1910	32.3	324	10.0
1920	47.4	229	4.8
1930	26.9	61	2.3
1939	22.7	40	1.8
1943	87.9	278	3.2
1950	31.8	180	0.6
1970	10.8	8	0.07

Source: Historical Statistics of the U.S.: Colonial Times to 1970, 729–730, 739–740.

trains ever operated at running speeds of more than sixty to sixty-five miles an hour. James J. Hill even kept freight train speeds below twenty miles an hour in the years before World War I and made good his threat to fire any man caught operating a Great Northern freight faster than that. American rail lines were not built for anything like the speeds that locomotives could regularly attain from the late nineteenth century on. Comfort also goes down proportionally as speed goes up, and comfort was an important consideration on crack trains like the *Century*, the *Broadway*, and the many others that catered to an older, more affluent traveler. Only a superb roadbed, lovingly maintained, made average speeds of sixty miles per hour possible on the crack limiteds.

Most trains, moreover, had lots of station stops to make. The Missouri Pacific's *Southerner* in 1929 took five hours to cover the 164-mile daylight run from Little Rock to Fort Smith, Arkansas, with nine intermediate stops (several of them flagstops, to be sure). The 32.8 miles per hour average was not exactly speedy, but it was in line with the 34.0 miles per hour recorded for all American passenger trains in 1936, the first year such data were available. The Wonder State, backward as it was, hardly deserved to be satirized any more than a dozen other states in such popular pulp jokebooks as *Slow Train Through Arkansas*, which candy "butchers," or vendors, hawked all over the country. The national average speed never rose above 41.7 miles per hour (1967), which is about where it stood in 1970. Major reconstruction and renewal expenditures have been required in the few instances that an attempt has been made to speed up schedules in recent years (for example, the Washington-New York-Boston corridor), but really high-speed passenger service will call for specially built and dedicated lines, as the pioneers of high-speed ground transportation, the Japanese, learned long ago. Railroad men know it well and groan audibly whenever yet another inventor appears with a new propulsion or suspension system "guaranteed" to make twenty-first-century speeds possible on nineteenth-century rights of way.

The dramatic reduction in rail travel fatalities was mainly due, naturally, to fewer accidents per billion passenger-miles. Moreover, during the peak travel year of 1943, even though supply and troop trains crowded the mainlines, the average injury was much less serious than in earlier years. Somewhere in this mute statistic is hidden a tribute to major improvements in disaster rescue techniques and medical treatment of the injured. To put it briefly: in 1890 the railroads injured 2711 passengers, of whom 286, or 11.8 percent, died. Fifty-three years later, in 1943, the railroads carried eight times as many passengers yet injured only about twice as many, 5444, of whom 5.1 percent died.

The price of the new technology was not paid by passengers alone, of course. The railroads, by 1900, had become synonymous with danger and tragedy in thousands of households at all levels of the social and economic scale. It was a dangerous occupation: of the 749,000 railroad workers of 1890, 2425 lost their lives and another 22,400 were injured in the line of duty. The years of mushrooming traffic growth (roughly, 1900 to 1915), when virtually every important mile of rail line was undergoing frantic rebuilding to increase the traffic it could carry, were bloody, with 4500 employees—the all-time record—killed in 1907 and 88,000 injured. No industry attacked the problem of employee safety earlier, or with greater energy, or with more dramatic results, than America's railroads. Employee deaths and injuries have shrunk consistently and in recent times have been cut to less than 200 fatalities and about 16,000 injuries a year, notwithstanding the fact that the railroads today carry more freight farther than ever before. In all these dry statistics there is hidden the years of experience and effort that paid off, taming the fierce forces of modern industry that many had despaired of in its early stages.

There were, and still are, victims of the onrush of the iron horse other than passengers and employees. In the early 1920s, when rail mileage and number of trains operated were at or near a maximum, roughly five thousand people who were neither patrons nor employees of the railroads died on the rails; roughly half of these people were trespassing, for example, using the tracks as a convenient path, innocently in most instances perhaps, but illegally and dangerously in any case. The railroads conducted almost continuous campaigns in schools to discourage petty "trespassers," but adventure stories continued to feature the luckless boy or girl who caught a foot in the switch frog or failed to hear the whistle of the *Flyer*. Especially during hard times, the carnage was heavy among hoboes, who were far from being the "kings of the road" encountered in cheap fiction. People who made it their business to know such grim things, such as small-town funeral directors and law officers, knew that leaving a dead or dying victim lying in the path of the next train was a good way to cover up foul play, and many a teenager—"somebody's darling"—ended up mangled beyond identification on an undertaker's slab, dead for the highly prized bowie knife that he had taken with him when he ran away from home. Ironically, it is the further march of technology that has driven many of the hoboes off the trains. Yard employees of the Southern Pacific, who know many of the "regulars" at the Oakland terminal, smile at the story of one tramp who was invited to take a ride between the cars of one of the new seventy-mile-an-hour intermodal freights between San Francisco and Los Angeles. The era of "riding the rods," he proclaimed indignantly at the end of the journey, was finished.

The Romance that Soured:
The Passenger Train and the Automobile

Withal, it has been the continuing struggle by the railroads and cars, trucks, and buses to coexist, that has brought the greatest problems for public transportation policy since the 1920s. The independence, convenience, and lower per-mile cost of the automobile, *per passenger*, has never been seriously challenged in local and short intercity travel, where, even before the advent of the car, the great bulk of traffic has always been concentrated. The price in injuries, property loss, and deaths is high, but Americans have been willing, even eager, to pay it. Automobile accident fatalities per billion vehicle-miles were a lethal 227.3 in 1920, but, contrary to certain reformers' utterances, decades of improvement in roads and vehicles have consistently brought the total down; by 1970, it was 48.7. Since World War II, the number of cars on the road and the average miles driven annually have risen many fold. Nearly 90 percent of all intercity transportation is provided nowadays by private automobile, leaving barely 10 percent to all nonprivate forms, including air and rail. The railroad, which created the heavy industry that created the cheap car, also introduced the modern era, in which the tradeoff between life, convenience, and speed has been considered a fair bargain.

The automobile and the railroad train have had a deep-seated love-and-hate relationship from the beginning. Even before the car, in fact, trains posed a problem for animal-drawn vehicles, and vice versa. Cities like New York, with a rigid grid system of streets, soon discovered that disaster was sure to follow as trains, bound for their terminals, insisted upon their traditional rights of way over vehicular traffic, which was negligible at the time the rails were first laid down. No one remembers today how many drivers of coal wagons, grocery delivery vans, and private carriages in the New York of 1870 had their wits scared out of them as the incessant procession of locomotives up Fourth (now Park) Avenue threatened to cleave them in two every two hundred feet. It was the great-granddaddy of all grade-crossing problems, and required

Figure 4.5 A "rear-ender." Typical of major railroad accidents in the 19th-century era of the wooden passenger car was this rear-end collision between two trains bound in the same direction on the same track at the same time, on the Michigan Central Railroad, halfway between Detroit and Battle Creek, in October 1879.

placing the tracks below grade, at great expense to the New York Central and the city fathers (they shared it equally), but it was only an early example of a nuisance and social call to arms that endures to this day when, if anything, it has been exacerbated by 110-car freight trains.

The grade-crossing problem, troublesome as it was in the towns and cities from the beginning, reached its peak in the countryside. America was a predominantly rural country until well into this century; in the nineteenth century, it was overwhelmingly so, as most people supported themselves in farming. Horse-drawn conveyances, although they were not capable of the excessive speeds that modern cars perpetrate daily, were sometimes hard to control, and animals were often skittish or downright neurotic. Runaway wagons and buggies were common. (Horatio Alger, Jr., might otherwise have been at a loss for a mechanism to move his heroes up the social ladder without the runaway carriage containing the beautiful daughter or pampered young son of the local banker or leading merchant.) But once the country byways became menaces where the snorting locomotive might round a blind curve without adequate warning to the farmer, country doctor, traveling salesman, or courting young people, or poke its nose abruptly out of the tall cornfields, the number of tragedies chronicled in small-town newspapers grew rapidly.

The debut of the practical automobile only made the problem worse. While horses that would balk right on the tracks were not unknown, cars seemed to have a special propensity to do so, and more often than not the reluctance of the driver to abandon his expensive machine to certain destruction by the behemoth bearing down upon it often won out over common sense. Even more foolish was the popular "sport" of racing the train to the grade crossing, which was a long time dying. Henry Ford presented Americans with the Model T, the first car that was designed to be much more (or was it less?) than a plaything, about 1910. Townspeople who could not afford the substantial four-figure price of conventional cars bought it eagerly, but it was the farmer who found it the answer to his dreams. What dreams? His dreams of a practical, convenient, cheap, all-weather means of bridging that last gap between him and civilization: the miles of rutted country roads that were often rivers of mud in the spring and stood between him and the railroad depot. The train and the automobile fitted each other like hand in glove; until mechanical improvements in the car, long-wearing and durable tires, and the national subsidization of thousands of miles of well-engineered, hard-surface roads made the car a practical mode of intercity travel, they flourished together. The founders of the Good Roads Movement early in the new century were the railroads and the bicycle manufacturers. Within a generation, good roads made the one obsolete for local travel and relegated the other to a children's toy.

The new mobility that the railroads brought gave rise to demands for even greater mobility long before Henry Ford came on the scene.

The electric interurban railroad had the shortest and bumpiest career of all modern forms of transportation: technologically impossible before the mid-1880s, it suffered almost sudden death after World War I as the automobile became its obvious successor. But in the critical period of the first two decades of this century, when the railroads were scrounging every dollar of "surplus" income they could to finance system improvements and additions to capacity, the interurbans, which quickly came to parallel the steam railroads between every conceivable pair of modestly populated places in the nation, deprived the loyal servant of a major portion of its passenger revenue, and by far the most profitable portion. Pleas by the railroads to state regulatory commissions to stop this needless duplication of services were ignored. The public demanded the new mobility, for the truth is that the interurbans *were* needed, if only for a tragically short time, to provide both the frequency of service and the multiplicity of boarding points that the steam railroads could not manage. A passenger on the little single-unit "train" trundling across the prairie of central Illinois in 1910 looks up as the car lurches to a stop, and smiles at the barefoot pair standing hopefully on the drying grass alongside the tracks—the grim-faced eleven-year-old girl in the homemade gingham dress who holds her little brother's hand tightly in one hand and their fares in the other as they climb aboard.

In their heyday the interurban lines were excessively popular modes of investment for the proverbial widows and orphans—and colleges and universities, too—but, like little dog Rover, when they died they died all over and so did many a dream along with them. The electric interurban is one of the least edifying chapters in the history of American transportation and finance.

CHAPTER 5

The Passenger Train Exalted, 1900–1990

> . . . races for miles along the Hudson River, flashes briefly past the long red row of tenements above 96th Street, dives with a roar into the mile-and-a-half-long tunnel that burrows beneath the glitter and swank of Park Avenue, and then . . . Grand Central Station! Crossroads of a thousand private lives!
>
> Opening announcement for a network
> radio program of the early 1940s

"Make No Small Plans!"

The onslaught of passengers that descended upon American railroads with the return of prosperity in 1898—a tide that would turn only with the coming of the roadable automobile in the 1920s—can not have come as much of a surprise to railroad leaders, especially in the Northeast. Indeed, although national thriftiness and relatively low disposable incomes tended to confine intercity rail travel largely to business and pressing personal needs in the nineteenth century, city fathers everywhere constantly fretted over the tendency of railroad depots, one after the other, to become clogged with growing traffic before they were ten years old.

When Commodore Vanderbilt opened New York's Grand Central Depot in the early 1870s, it quickly became the city's most popular tourist attraction, largely because of the impressive train shed that had no visible means of support. In barely ten years the depot was inadequate in almost every way. In the days of small locomotives, skimpy wooden passenger cars, and labor costs that were a small factor in operating expenses, the obvious solution was to schedule more trains, to run extra sections of regular schedules, and finally to add cars by double- and triple-heading locomotives, an option that often caused more troubles than it solved. The platforms in Grand Central had been long enough to accommodate any train that the Commodore could imagine, but well before the end of the century trains had to be broken in two and placed on adjoining tracks. Poor ventilation of the shed meant that locomotives could not idle in place at the head of their trains, but rather had to be kept waiting "on point" just outside until the last minute.

There were not enough tracks to begin with, so trains could be placed only minutes before scheduled departure times, and if they were delayed all hell broke loose. A separate arrival building had to be provided to the east of the main building, on what later was the site of the Commodore Hotel, now the Grand Hyatt.

The fact that the harried, conscientious men of the Victorian era kept things running is remarkable. Heads-up timing, and strict discipline, made it possible. Modern railroad men would condemn such a regime as arbitrary, and no doubt it often was, but with primitive facilities it was what made things work. Certainly moderns could not imagine a great, grimy railroad yard, at ground level and filled with several dozen smoky, snorting and whistling locomotives day and night, in the heart of Manhattan. But for a generation it was beloved of New Yorkers, who more than once found in it a warm haven from the elements. During the great blizzard of 1888, no train entered or left the station for several days, but steam was maintained in the locomotives that happened to be in the depot, all of the passenger cars were attached and the steam valves opened, and hundreds of stranded would-be travelers and just folks on the streets were invited to camp out in the cars until things could be dug and thawed out. Grand Central Depot was not a thing of beauty, in its rather undernourished Second Empire, mansard-roofed, red-bricked, cast-iron-quoined dowdiness. No day better marks the beginning of the new architectural era in the world's greatest city than the day they began to tear old Grand Central Depot down.

At the end of the 1890s the old station had been substantially rebuilt. They replaced the side access to the platform gates (a relic of some of the earliest English station designs) with the more modern row of gates at the ends of platforms, added spacious and much more elegant waiting rooms, and gave the growing managerial bureaucracy suites of offices into which they moved their rolltop desks with gusto. Much use was made of marble and other ornamentation; "sody water" may have been just as satisfactory as champagne for the Commodore's dyspepsia, but his posterity raced forward to embrace the monumental age that was so obviously dawning. Boston, a few years before, had raised up the first "union station" in America, largely made possible by the New Haven Railroad's absorption of just about everything that moved in southern New England, and its handsome rounded façade still bespeaks the love of civic beauty that inspired it and has been so grievously abused since.

Sure enough, the "second" Grand Central, opened to the public in 1898, quickly became obsolete. Its fate was sealed one cold January morning in the second year of the new century when a rear-end collision between two commuter trains that were just entering the station killed nearly two dozen people. Steam in the tunnel had reduced visibility, it was said, and the public outcry against steam locomotives operating in tunnels within the city brought instant action from a state leg-

Figure 5.1 The first Grand Central Depot, built in 1871 on an old "wooding-up" yard at 42nd St. and Fourth (later Park) Ave. The location was far "uptown" then, but that changed quickly, a phenomenon effected by the new depot more than anything else.

islature always closely in touch with the will of the voting public. The Central's management, starting with a rather modest plan to electrify its lines as far north as the tip of Manhattan and the Bronx terminal yards, found itself caught up in the expansive outlook of the times (and a shrewd appreciation of the valuable real estate that would be created by placing the whole shebang, terminal yards and all, underground), and the modern Grand Central Station was the result. Widely declared by architectural historians to be the most successful large terminal ever built in North America—and one of the finest two or three in the world—Grand Central has since 1913 brought countless millions of commuters and long-distance travelers into the heart of the great city without a wisp of smoke or a clash of switch engines.

The design of Grand Central Station broke more than one rule, especially the rule of unity of design influence. First there was a competition, a procedure that may strike one as democratic but almost certain to produce an unlovely design. Not entirely liking any of the entries, the railroad executives turned the job over to architects on their payroll. They, in turn, employed an outside firm. The result was a building that has been acclaimed by aesthetes and utilitarian railroad operators alike as one of the most successful terminals in the world, and all we know about its parentage is that it is attributed to the firms of Reed and Stem, and Warren and Wetmore, the former having submitted the original entry. The neighborhood of Grand Central, largely because the station is there, has consistently improved and become more valuable over the years. One would think Grand Central would have long since been torn down for more "practical" structures, and many have tried with might and main to do just that, but the architectural preservationists have resisted with remarkable success.

Perhaps the preservationists exhausted their energies on saving Grand Central, for they failed entirely to do the same for another great old lady of the heroic era of railroad terminal building. If one were to go back to the sidewalk at 33rd and Seventh Avenue, in 1910, about where the Hotel Pennsylvania (as it was originally named) was about to be built, one might encounter a distinguished gentleman occupied in gazing with obvious admiration at the gigantic pile of granite and domineering Doric columns across the street. One might walk up to him and say, "Good morning, Mr. McKim, she's certainly a beauty, isn't she? But what would you say if I told you she will last barely 50 years?" The man who, along with his firm of Mead, McKim and White, was one of the most influential architects in America and responsible for some of our most monumental buildings, would have laughed contemptuously at the prophecy.

Fundamentally, the vast improvement in access to Manhattan from the West, and exit to New England, of which Pennsylvania Station was the only outward sign, has remained, and for that we should be grateful. Far more ambitious than the mere placing of Grand Central and its

Figure 5.2 New York City's Grand Central Station yards as excavation proceeded on the new underground terminal, Oct. 1, 1907. The view is to the southwest from 50th St. The "first bite," on the eastern edge of the site (on the left in the photo), is finished, and a few of the new electric locomotives are barely visible. The two domed towers of the "old" station, as rebuilt in 1898, and the outline of the famous 1870s train shed, are visible through the smoke in the upper left. The pennant-topped, mansard-roofed structure is the Gotham Hotel, which would survive until the end of the 1950s as the uptown offices of the National City Bank. Few photographs show more graphically the transformation of midtown Manhattan in the first quarter of the 20th century. (*New York Public Library*)

yards below grade and under cover, the Hudson River tubes, the sub-way continuation from the station to the East River tubes (that proved much more difficult to build than the longer Hudson tubes!), and the tubes themselves, were a contribution to Manhattan that lifted the city out of the ordinary and made it a machine for urban civilization unap-proached by any other city in the world. The old Jersey City terminal of the Pennsylvania disappeared, and through service, from the tip of Florida to Portland, Maine, became a reality. As a bonus, the trains of the Long Island Railroad, which the Pennsy had bought along the way, were brought into Manhattan.

As a railroad station, however, Pennsylvania Station, notwithstand-ing its memorable interior spaces, one of which, the waiting room, was modeled on the Baths of Caracalla, has achieved neither the respect nor the permanence of Grand Central. There are many reasons for this, one of which may be that Grand Central has served a more affluent and influential commuter region than Pennsylvania Station, which accom-modates the white-collar bedroom communities of New Jersey and Long Island. Location, however, proved the major factor. New York grew at its most vigorous up the spine of Park, Madison, and especially Fifth avenues. By the time Grand Central was completed in 1913, the midtown skyscraper district, which essentially separated the financial and insurance world from the new industrial world's headquarters above 34th Street, was well established, and pedestrians who have to contend for space on the sidewalks today will agree that it has never stopped growing. Pennsylvania Station was an oversize entrance to a subterranean world that has progressively grown less and less pleasant to contemplate. But Grand Central was a building to look at and to savor, and its famous concourse was quickly turned into one of the world's most famous town squares. The late Ogden Nash put it best when he asked, in one of his humorous poems, Why is it that when a movie shows a train leaving Washington, D.C., for New York, it always shows it arriving at Grand Central Station?

The fashion for handsome, even monumental railroad terminals, preferably centralizing all the lines serving a city, in the heart of the office, retail, entertainment, and tourist center, is the most obvious and enduring influence that the railroads had on American urban design. Even where the eager hand on the wrecking crane has brushed the grand old buildings aside, the vestiges of downtown remain. Far more than vestiges remain in Washington, D.C., whose downtown was oth-erwise never much to begin with. But Union Station Plaza grows more impressive, and more beautiful, with each passing year while the archi-tecture being added to the city, by private and public hands alike, grows ever more banal. The Plaza remains perhaps the finest example of the City Beautiful movement, which promised briefly early in this century to make the American city something worth looking at. It is the work, primarily, of one of America's most famous architects, Daniel

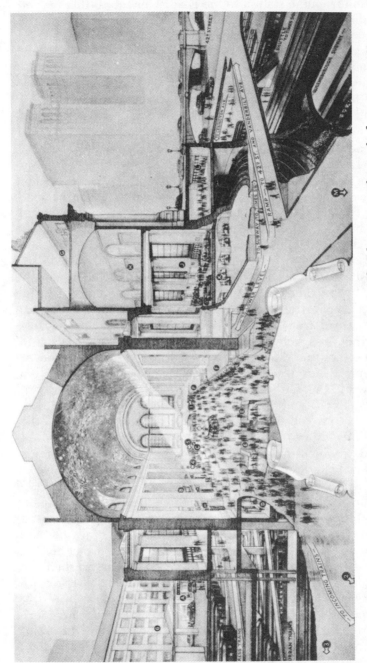

Figure 5.3 The "new" Grand Central Station, completed in 1913. The justly famous Beaux-Arts exterior of this noble structure, often judged one of the most successful railroad stations in the world on both aesthetic and functional grounds, gives little hint of the efficient interior. In this cutaway view, the extensive series of ramps and tunnels linking the station with hotels, subways, and offices is emphasized. They made the terminal a functioning heart of the most highly urbanized area in the world.

Burnham, whose expansive advice to his students—"Make no small plans!"—was followed so well in rendering the big yet dignified station. Up to it the Baltimore & Ohio and the Pennsylvania railroads backed their dozens of trains a day, and through it the southern railroads initiated or ended millions of travelers' journeys to or from Dixie, via a tunnel that spared other millions of visitors the sight of trains on the Capitol grounds. Only the building of the Federal Triangle, in the 1920s and 1930s, starting with "Hoover's Folly" (as the gigantic building with which the then Secretary of Commerce began this big project was called) rivals the rearrangement of Washington's railroads, which had stood in the way of the very concept of a Capitol mall, as an act of intelligent city planning. The guardians of our priceless architectural heritage were napping in the 1970s when the big spenders made a multi-million-dollar effort to turn Washington's Union Station into a "visitors' center" where tourists would see travelogues about the city while the reality stood just outside the front door! We paid for our sins in the 1980s with many more millions spent to reverse the process. The heroic figures of Norse gods and goddesses that line the mezzanine (they are really plaster and fabric on a metal frame, and are repeated every so often as they go around the waiting room, but beloved just the same) now seem safe on their pedestals once more. Washington may do its worst with our future, but at least this bit of our past has been saved.

The "Second City," First in Railroading

"A hog can travel through Chicago without changing trains, but YOU can't!" With these fighting words in the years right after World War II, Robert Young, who was aiming for control of both the New York Central and the Pennsylvania, scorned the backwardness of traditional railroad men. There was no reason, he declared, why people crossing the continent should have to leave their comfortable pullmans upon arriving in Chicago and, dragging their hand luggage along, scramble for a taxi or stand in line for the Parmelee Transfer limousine that hauled the never-ending flood of travelers from their arrival station to their departing station. (This service, by the way, was free to anyone who bought a rail ticket calling for travel through Chicago and a change of stations. The Parmelee coupon was right in the ticket, which sometimes reached hilarious lengths.)

It was Chicago's multiplicity of mostly small railroad stations that the city was famous for, or laughed at for, if you saw it that way. If Young did, however, few transcontinental travelers ever did. The most important eastern trunk lines and western transcontinentals put on through pullmans that were switched in the yards from one station to another, but few Los Angeles- or San Francisco-bound passengers (for example), whose crack trains from the East arrived early in the morning, cared to sit all day in the car until their western connections departed late that afternoon to permit a second-morning arrival on the coast. They preferred to do what their predecessors had done between trains in Chicago for more than a century: get out, stretch their legs, attend a matinee, or just see the sights. Chicago was a popular town with tourists, for what other city in America was like it? The stores were famous: New York had Macy's and Fifth Avenue, but, then, Chicago had Marshall Field's, a far more widely recognized name in retailing, and its Gold Coast, and a not-bad night life, too. Many stretched their pause into a several days' stay.

Chicago had a huge floating population of visitors with less money to spend, perhaps, than Robert Young, but more time and talent to enjoy themselves. To accommodate these crowds, many of whom would not have a chance to "do the big town" again soon, if ever, before heading for their prairie homes, there were some of the most famous hotels in the nation. In the first generation after the Civil War, the Palmer House became a symbol for luxurious service, and it survives today in its 1920s re-creation. Equally famous in the early years, if quite forgotten today, was the Grand Pacific, through whose Romanesque portals passed a steady stream of important people, and in whose parlors many a deal big and small was hatched. The next generation built the famous Auditorium Hotel, by Louis Sullivan, and the Blackstone, still a mecca for popular music lovers in the 1920s and 1930s. In the teens and twenties there came a rush of modern hostelries that emphasized serving the commercial traveler, led by the fabled Morrison, once proclaimed the tallest hotel in the world and ultimately razed for a more profitable office building, and the mammoth Stevens along Michigan Avenue on the lake front, which was the biggest.

Not so large, but infinitely more elegant, was the Ambassador, on Chicago's Gold Coast—the near north side. This luxury hotel was the home of the Pump Room, one of the most famous restaurants in America, and its vaguely oriental motif, with many entrees served flambé, was a byword for high style. It caught on with the Pullman crowd who were between trains as a fine place to meet old Chicago friends. During World War II the dining room was packed with manufacturing and engineering executives relaxing from their wartime labors; officers of the Army, Navy, and Marines pausing on their way to or from the battlefields; a surprising number of enlisted men; and, dressed to the nines, the ladies they were relaxing or pausing with.

Progress, it often seems, means that nothing good ever lasts. Fewer and fewer people remain who can remember that it once took three days to go all the way across the country, and what fun it could be. Today the high-water mark of hospitality has been traded for the dubious advantage of sheer speed. Many of the old hostelries are gone, and in those that are left, as well as in the expensive plastic and glass uglies that have taken the others' place, guests carry their own bags to their rooms. Thousands of convention visitors, who once enlivened "the

Loop" and the Gold Coast of this gusty, gutsy city, never venture off the grounds of the mammoth airport, which has its own hotels.

Only the two newest and most monumental of Chicago's half-dozen railroad stations still handle trains today. Union Station, opened in 1925 in the late afternoon of the rail passenger era, now accommodates all of the Amtrak trains, and thus it can finally live up to its originally misleading name. The North Western station is host twice a day to a horde of commuters who hardly glance at its marble elegance. Chicago's other passenger terminals died a slow death after World War II's record-breaking passenger volume had been dealt with.

Urbanizing America

Without the railroad and its centralizing tendency, it is doubtful that the concept of the city as a *center* of material and cultural activities would have developed so fully. The explosive influence of the automobile strongly supports this conclusion. But downtown has not altogether disappeared, and the automobile is no longer seen as the final or only solution. Downtown had a special appeal to the gregarious human spirit—what better proof than the continuing fascination of "window shopping" in shopping malls—and the American railroad built grandly upon it. It is sorely missed today, as city after city mortgages its future for a new rail rapid transit system, but repairing the damage done by controversial New York City Parks Commissioner Robert Moses and his co-idealists will take a long time.

The new terminals brought to the American city hotels, theaters, office buildings, and department stores whose size and magnificence proclaimed a giant step forward in American sophistication and the standard of living. Downtown was a center of commercial, mercantile, and financial activity during the day. Sinclair Lewis's George Babbitt, having begun his trip to New York at Zenith's big new union station (Zenith being a thin disguise for either Minneapolis or St. Paul, both of which built grand terminals), steps out of New York's much grander Pennsylvania Station onto Seventh Avenue and marvels at the gigantic Pennsylvania Hotel facing him across the street. He whistles softly to himself as, businessman to the last, he calculates the daily "take" of the thousand rooms (every one with its own bathroom!) multiplied by the steep rates of three to five dollars a night.

From such new hostelries however miniaturized, all over America, in the halcyon days between 1913 and the Great Depression, men like George Babbitt and entire families enjoying a vacation in the big city, issued forth each night to patronize the dozens of plays and musical comedies that had only recently been playing to New York audiences, and, increasingly, motion pictures and stage shows in the new movie palaces. Or they indulged, bashfully at first and then with great enthusiasm, in the new American custom of dancing in public places and at night. Hotel ballrooms, night clubs, and cabarets exploited the national craze for dancing that Vernon and Irene Castle had helped create just before World War I, and the musical scores of Broadway shows became part of the "great American songbook" that still lay on the rack of thousands of upright pianos across the country or squawked out of millions of windup phonographs. It was the railroad trains, of course, that brought the performers and their staffs quickly and economically from one engagement to another, while sweating laborers struggled to get their scenery out of the baggage cars and into the waiting vans. That evening a delighted audience would applaud the troupe's clever realism and by midnight it might be on its way to the next city in that world of one-night stands. The trunks of traveling salesmen, actors, and hordes of vaudeville performers crowded station platforms and were heaped high on hand trucks. Summer brought the Big Top to town, and many a boy and his dad rose before dawn to stand on the edge of the meadow where the tents were going up and watch wagon after gaudy wagon roll off the flatcars.

Travel was as frequently damned then as now by gadabouts who quickly came to appreciate the comforts of home, but by comparison with today's travel arrangements, it was all done with remarkable speed, efficiency, and convenience. (At least, one could almost always get a Red Cap porter before World War II put them all in uniform or in munitions plants.) Today's airline passenger begins his journey without really knowing whether he will get to the distant terminal on time (small-towners often travel an hour on a patchwork of rattling conveyances for every hour they spend in the air) and the anxieties at the arrival end are often just as great. The railroad traveler of the golden age had it easy by comparison. The affluent midwestern family whose son was leaving shortly for Yale College phoned the railroad depot the day before and had the expressman call in his van for the lad's trunks and suitcases. Father handed the man the railroad ticket, and he duly punched the square indicating that the traveler's baggage—150 pounds were allowed on a full-fare ticket—had been checked to destination. But he did more than that. He noted on the impedimenta that they were to be delivered to the student's rooms at the college. The business traveler could expect the same kind of service to his hotel, and when his stay was over, unless it was a shabby place indeed, the desk clerk would see to it that the departing guest's baggage was checked and carried to the railroad station. He would also procure tickets, if requested, for this was the age of the agent system, and railroad ticket offices were on every corner downtown, or so it often seemed.

All of these things, which people have long since learned to do without, the railroad passenger train gave Americans, but in the long run its most significant gift to the rise of the "alabaster cities" was itself. Its influence was felt everywhere, down to towns of only a few thousand or a few hundred. The union station idea caught on quickly. (Even Chicago built a handsome Roman temple with such a designation, though it was no such thing, of course; that greatest of the world's railroad centers continued to have half a dozen stations downtown, and any suggestion that the daily thousands of trains that entered and departed from Chicago in every direction could be housed in one building was laughable.)

New or fast-growing cities designed themselves around Union Station. St. Louis is an outstanding example in its very early Union Station, built for the Louisiana Purchase Exposition of 1904, and its elegant plaza. Beloved of trainwatchers for fifty years, the station entertained millions who strolled along a concourse up to which some twenty-three different railroad lines backed their trains. The exuberant display of illuminated end-pieces thrilled them all. Today the old station has been completely "done over" as a kind of shopping and restaurant center. A sixty-five-year-old man who, as a nineteen-year-old, had had a fine thirty-five-cent breakfast in the bustling, steamy, palm-fronded Fred Harvey Restaurant that once occupied the same spot, had a modest steak dinner for twenty-eight dollars, plus tip. There were no trains. Boston's South Station, on the other hand, considered the first "union station" when it was built in the 1890s—although it was no such thing either—is still very much in action as a railroad station, and has been restored accordingly.

On the other side of the state from St. Louis, at the bend in the Missouri River, the much younger and feistier Kansas City built a superb station and plaza in memory of its war dead after World War I. St. Paul replaced a dowdy depot with a handsome granite and limestone terminal, which gave downtown a new lease on life that finally ran out with the automobile. (The long-term result of recent restoration efforts there is yet to be seen.) Cincinnati, on the eve of the 1930s Depression, built a terminal vaguely in the Italian modern style that has been celebrated by architectural historians. Many of the grand terminals from this period, notably the handsome Roman temple in Columbus and New York's champion entrant in the City Beautiful stakes, Pennsylvania station, bowed to the wrecker's ball.

The Golden Age of Train Travel

And what of the trains that Americans rode in such great numbers until the automobile made private transportation possible and the Great Depression made it necessary? It is significant that until the commercial airliner began to be taken seriously and modern highways speeded up vehicular travel, the railroads did not go in heavily for added speed. The blue ribbon, extra-fare trains between the east coast and Chicago revealed what passenger officials thought was most important: comfort, luxury, and safety. Speed was the enemy of all of these, and it is the enemy of track maintenance as well. In fact, railroads that emphasized passenger traffic found that the passenger trains considerably raised the cost of maintenance of way. The heavy coal trains of the Chesapeake & Ohio and the Norfolk & Western, for example, constantly beat down the raised outer rail on curves that permitted the George Washington and Powhatan Arrow to bank comfortably at their higher operating speeds. And who can say how many switch points for sidetracks, factory and warehouse sidings, and wayside depots the *Broadway* or the *Twentieth Century Limited* passed over in their dash between the nation's two greatest cities? Anyone who tried to sleep on either train in their last days knows the answer: too many! Keeping the switches quiet was an expensive responsibility.

Passenger cars, as we have already seen, grew greatly in size and weight, and those on through routes were entirely made of steel by World War I. Statutory specifications for American passenger car construction have been more demanding, in such features as compressive strength, than those of any other nation. At one time, near the end of the old century, it was widely assumed that every mile of important rail route in the nation would soon have to be double-tracked. The rapid development of automatic block signals and, later, centralized traffic control that permits "meets" on single-track lines without either train coming to a halt, made such an undertaking unnecessary, which is just as well, for repressive government regulation made it impossible. Even so, multiple tracking was undertaken where traffic demanded and corporate purses permitted. The ultimate examples were the Union Pacific, the only transcontinental with two mains from one end to the other, and the Pennsylvania and the New York Central, which had *four* mains from seaboard to Lake Michigan. Early in the new century the Pennsylvania built an extra low-gradient freight line paralleling its hilly, scenic original route through the valley of the Juniata. Until the Great Depression put an end to such expansive notions, this "Standard Railroad of the World" was considering electrifying its lines through the Alleghenies.

We shall never know just how much of the spectacular growth in rail passenger travel in the golden age from 1897 to 1920 was due to its various components—business, commuter, and private—although some additional details are available for years after 1920. The job the railroads did, however, was remarkable, at fares that declined for much of the pre-World War I era from an overall average of 2.17 cents per passenger mile in 1890 to a prewar low of 1.93 cents in 1909. But the real story lies in the grand total. In 1890, 492 million people (counting repeats, of course) boarded American trains and rode a total of 11.8 billion passenger-miles. The average length of a journey was only 24 miles, emphasizing the heavy use of the trains for any trip of more than a few miles. (In the wartime year of 1944, for example, the average trip was 104.5 miles, even though by then there were some 5.3 million commuter trips a year.)

From 1890 on, passenger traffic, relatively speaking, rose faster than freight traffic until the early 1920s. By 1910 passenger volume had nearly doubled, to 972 million, but total passenger-miles had tripled, to 32.3 million. The record year for rail passengers in the United States, in war or peace, was 1920, when a billion and a quarter passengers (1,270 million) boarded trains and rode 47.4 million passenger-miles. Total miles traveled, however, were far from a record. By the war years of the 1940s, when the railroads carried virtually all intercity passengers, both the number of passengers and the distance they traveled were far greater, and this in spite of every conceivable discouragement of civilian travel government could think of. The urge to travel is always greater in wartime. Soldiers on furlough (troop train movements are excluded from all of these figures); young wives who refused to be separated from their soldier-husbands for as long as they remained stateside (it was a golden age for the enterprising householder who had a spare room that could be turned into an "apartment" with the addition of a hot plate); parents and other relatives determined to have one more visit before sonny shoved off; glum-faced businessmen who spent millions of sleepless nights on day coaches because Pullman space was rationed and air travel virtually proscribed; and even a substantial number of well-heeled civilians taking a brief vacation from the forty-eight-hour workweek that was general during the war; all these swelled the volume of passenger traffic. How the railroads did it, with a large part of their car fleets dedicated to troop movements and one-third fewer in use than in 1920, is hard to say, but many a wartime traveler remembers at least one wooden coach with stained glass windows, and a hopper in the toilet that was innocent of running water and through which one could see the crossties rushing past. Where such antiques had been stored for the previous thirty years remains a mystery.

By the second decade of the new century the railroads had penetrated deep into the American psyche. "Hear that lonesome whistle, blowin' 'cross the trestle, whooooeeeeee!" ran the song. It was a synthetic, lowdown "beer-hall" song, the 1940s inspiration of some Tin Pan Alley denizen who probably had never been on a train that did not run underground or on elevated tracks, but it summed up three generations of infatuation with the mystique of the passenger train, its coaches and Pullmans full of sleeping passengers on who knew what missions, sliding through the dark night across trestles and bridges, through tunnels and little towns where the sidewalks had been taken in for the night, and heading towards new beginnings. The train trip was the great slatewiper for Americans, and the direction in which salvation lay seemed almost invariably to be westward. When World War II came, millions of boys and quite a few girls found out what lay beyond the vanishing points of the tracks that ran through their little towns. Most of them could not get back home fast enough when their tours of

Rail Passenger Travel in Selected Years, 1890–1970
(excluding commuter)°

Year	Passengers carried (millions)	Passenger miles (billions)	Passenger cars in service (units)	Miles per passenger (units)	Revenue per mile (cents)
1890	492	11.8	26,820	24.0	2.167
1900	577	16.0	34,713	27.7	2.003
1910	972	32.3	47,179	33.2	1.938
1920	1,270	47.4	56,102	37.3	2.755
1930	708	26.9	53,484	38.0	2.719
1933	435	16.4	50,598	37.7	2.015
1940	456	23.8	38,308	52.2	1.755
1944	916	95.7	38,217	104.5	1.875
1950	488	31.8	37,359	65.2	2.563
1960	327	21.3	25,746	65.1	3.014
1970	289	10.8	11,378	37.4	3.924

°Commuter data first appear for 1921. They reached their all-time high of 6.9 billion passenger-miles in 1929 and declined by one-third during the ensuing ten years of depression, to an all-time low of 4.0 billion in 1940, then recovered slowly to about 4.5 billion since the mid-1960s.

Source: Historical Statistics of the United States, vol. 2 (Washington, D.C., 1975), p. 729.

duty were over. It was the trains that took them away, and the trains that brought them back, in one shape or another. It would never be like that again.

Before the automobile and airplane upstaged the railroad in the juvenile imagination, the railroads figured importantly in popular literature, both periodical and hard-cover. Penny-dreadfuls in the Victorian age seized upon the trains as a reliable source of drama and excitement. Dramatists and songwriters did the same. "Do not be afraid," sang the little girl as the train careened through the violent storm, "my daddy's the engineer!" Or, elsewhere and more lugubriously, she sadly intoned, "My daddy's riding in the baggage car up ahead." Even men of the cloth saw the potential: "Life is like a mountain railroad," ran an old revival favorite, and anyone may imagine the Calvinist philosophy it sought to implant. Instructors in vocational and proprietary business schools everywhere held up the railroads as the cream of all employment opportunities, and their executives as paragons of the successful life. Indeed, the new technologies to which American youth are so susceptible have not proved more seductive, at least on one day a year, when a Lionel or Ives or American Flyer electric train, brand new or surviving into the third generation, occupies the place of honor at the base of millions of Christmas trees.

Hear No Lonesome Whistle Blow

Fascination with the American railroad train led to the assumption that it would be around forever, even if all one ever did was watch its empty coaches, parlor cars, and Pullmans slide day in and day out past the depot. The profound obligation to serve the "traveling public," in the popular cliché of the time, proved to be a terrible burden for railroad leaders, even though that "public" was never more than a minority of the population. By 1920 railroad men found themselves faced with the disappearing profitability of more and more passenger runs at a time when a sadly confused public policy was making it ever harder to compensate for deficits in one branch of the service with profits in another. The American passenger train did not die all at once, nor is it likely to if the once-fragile flower of Amtrak continues to grow. Some aspects of the service, however, notably first-class accommodations, had lost their profitability by the time of World War I, as a railroad man told a Senate committee in 1916. Pullman cars, which could comfortably accommodate only about twenty-seven people (two in each of twelve open sections and three in the drawing room, in the standard configuration), had continued to grow in size and weight until just dragging them around had become a burden, especially since many sleepers on less popular routes seldom sold out. The heavy surcharge that the government put on "first-class" tickets (honored in sleeping cars) during World War I turned out, like all forms of artificial stimulation, to be habit-forming, and railroad men pleaded successfully for its continuation after the war. It was notably successful: so much so that first-class travel went into a long-term decline from which it never recovered. The few well-heeled people whom one glimpsed while walking through the quiet, clean, luxurious Pullmans on the way from the daycoach to the dining car, were the first to heed the siren call of the commercial airliner. The richer one is, the greater the hurry one is likely to be in.

The passenger train was a long time dying in anything like the form it had had during its golden age. One can learn a lot about the railroads' many critics just by noting which death-dealing factor they mention first in conversation. It is most likely to be railroad management, in line with the very American tendency to blame all national shortcomings on "somebody who ain't doin' his job," or, what is worse, on sheer corporate malevolence. "The train I ride into the city every morning from Westport is packed," growled the advertising executive to the poor soul from the New York Central account who happened to be sitting at the same table in the executive dining room; "they could damn well make money hauling passengers if they wanted to!" Reminded that after about an hour and a half of intensive service on weekday mornings and evenings, the New Haven Railroad's fleet of expensive commuter cars stood idle in the yard, the indignant one lapsed into silence. But on the very eve of the rush to the private automobile, the New York and Chicago area railroads had been hard pressed to find cars to hold all the people who wanted to ride them into the cities—not just mornings and evenings, but during the day too—and tracks had to accommodate trains that sometimes left the terminals at one-minute intervals. No other line of business, perhaps, ever saw the bottom fall out of its livelihood quite so quickly as the commuter railroads, unless it be the electric interurbans which had begun the process.

Except for New York City, which, with its compact population and efficient, if decaying, rapid transit system, is entirely untypical of the rest of the country, ownership of some kind of "wheels" has proceeded from being highly discretionary to absolutely sociologically and logistically necessary. The most recent development, beginning perhaps in the 1950s, has been the felt need for a car—not just a jalopy—among all age groups. In Florida, where such a large segment of the population is old, surrendering one's driver's license is the last step before dying, and there are a considerable number of stubborn nonagenarians on the roads. Many teenagers demand a car of their own, even if it is only a rusty pickup truck, because in some areas to be without wheels is to be automatically shut out of most after-class school activities, social or otherwise. (Besides, many of them have nearly fulltime jobs after school.) But it was in family vacation travel that the car usurped train travel most completely. Even the most attractive rail excursion rates could not compete with the lure of taking off down the highway in the family car for a hundred or a thousand miles. (Automobile touring was for hardy souls until dependable cars, tough, wear-resistant tires, paved highways, and modern motels, were available—roughly, after 1925 or 1930—but it was a factor in the decline in discretionary rail travel almost from the beginning.) To be sure, the cost per mile of operating the family car, allocating costs the way an accountant would, is very high. But this misses the point. Consumers are not accountants—at least, most of them are not. Original cost, taxes, and most maintenance are automatically charged to the basic function of the car, which is to get the owner to his place of work and haul family members about on a long list of domestic errands, and such costs are unavoidable. Joyriding was "free" (until the 1970s) except for an occasional tankful of that two-bit gas.

The railroads, in contrast, were in a high fixed-cost business. Even in their palmiest days, the railroads noted that only a small decline in freight or passenger volume could mean the total disappearance of net revenues, which was the situation for more and more passenger trains after 1930. The most heavily patronized trains still made money, but the capital they absorbed could have earned more in a savings account. Eventually the railroads faced situations where the economics of passenger service were simply "off the chart"—that is, costs were so high that revenues would not cover expenses even if every seat and every berth on every train were filled every day in the year. Union-boosted wage levels and featherbedding laws were "sticky" and did not decline in the same degree as gross revenues from 1920 on, while state governments, still eager to stick it to the railroads, passed two-cents-a-mile and new-depot bills that kept the cost of rail tickets low and the cost of the service high.

In spite of the eagerness of Americans to impale their society on the hood ornament of the automobile, however, the passenger train remained a necessary service for many people. Like the in-town buses of the postwar era, the last passengers to leave them were the young, the old, and the poor, to whom we may add the residents of thousands of little towns in the hills of Appalachia or on the prairies of the trans-Missouri West which would never have air service—and, as the postwar era was to prove, would not always have even the dumpy old Greyhound or Trailways buses, either. Eventually, they would simply have to do without, and the hardships endured every day of the year by old folks who are unable to get to clinics or pharmacies twenty-five or thirty miles away are ignored. A few grandmas in their wheelchairs, thumbing rides on the interstate highways, might get some action, but what kind of action? The only practical solution in sight is subsidized Yellow Cab service for the boondocks.

It can not be said that the railroad executives, when the roof fell in after 1930, rose very far to meet the challenges of the Depression and the automobile. Their energies were spent largely in trying to pry money out of the Reconstruction Finance Corporation with which to pay the interest on their first mortgage bonds, interest which they were simply not earning. They lost heart. Many, indeed, had never liked passenger trains. James J. Hill did not hide his antipathy towards them, although whether he ever said that the passenger train is like the male tit—neither useful nor ornamental—is doubtful. Still, as the Depression wore on and gave no promise of being replaced by rosier times, some passenger agents, notably on the densely traveled trunk lines and out West, where long, relatively profitable hauls were the rule, saw a way of at least attracting a larger share of what traffic there was, and even increasing the total market in time. The result was one of the brightest ideas the railroads ever had, and it made rail travel enthusiasts out of a new generation of young people who left home for school or to make a living: the deluxe, streamlined, usually diesel-powered, *all-coach* train! When World War II ended, the railroads undertook a massive investment in new trainsets to serve this new market, which would turn out to be all too temporary.

Coach travel on conventional trains, where all the amenities except for the dining car were reserved for first-class passengers, often embittered passengers who were confined to their chair cars despite often being virtually the only travelers on the train. On holidays and weekends, more than one young mother stood in the aisles with her babe-in-arms while the train dragged along a Pullman or parlor car, empty save for the brakeman who lounged there between stops. Sometimes, especially at Christmas, a jolly, bibulous gentleman dragooned coach-bound college students into joining him and his wife in the lounge car, where he entertained them royally and they sang "On, Wisconsin!" or "Going Back to Old Nassau" for him and the train crew smiled, pocketed the tips, and looked the other way.

Train travel could be fun: if you could not put on a lounge and bar car just for coach passengers, why not kick the first-class passengers out altogether and cater to the people who at least were still riding your trains? Never to be forgotten, at least so long as the World War II generation lives, are such celebrated all-coach liners as the Pennsylvania's *Trail Blazer* and the New York Central's *Pacemaker* (New York to Chicago), the Pennsylvania's *Jeffersonian* (New York to St. Louis), the Baltimore & Ohio's *Columbian* (Baltimore to Chicago via Washington, D.C.), the Southern's *Southerner* (New York to New Orleans), the Union Pacific's *City of Los Angeles* (Chicago to Los Angeles), and that alter ego of the famous all-Pullman *Super Chief,* the *El Capitan* (thirty-nine hours Chicago to Los Angeles and San Francisco, which the Union Pacific soon matched). Many of these trains featured enclosed, rounded-end observation cars where young and old could sit for hours and watch the tracks melt away behind them—something they had never expected to be able to afford on a train.

The all-coach trains did just what they were supposed to do for those railroads that had the traffic to justify them and the capital to buy the several trainsets they required. If the course of human affairs had been static, one might have said that a new era in rail travel was at hand. As it was, the airlines, which had gone through hell in the late 1940s trying to get their new DC-4's to fly safely, began to take delivery of newer, bigger, better designed DC-6's and Constellations around 1950. The number of available seat-miles rose explosively and fares responded in the classic manner: they were cut drastically. One day in 1951 the airlines rocked the travel industry with their announcement of "coach-class" fares, which quickly led to all but total extinction of first-class air traffic. The young people of modest means who had been the remaining backbone of rail passenger traffic, noting that the coach section of airplanes arrived at the same time and in the same condition as first class, began to desert the pokey old trains for the air—sometimes with sincere regret. It was a natural development, and nothing has happened since to reverse the basic trend. The trains belong to the days of our youth that are past. As John Steinbeck wrote in *East of Eden,* "Oh, strawberries will never taste so good again, and the thighs of women have lost their clutch!"

'Board!

"On the other hand, *not* so fast," as Finley Peter Dunne's Mr. Dooley would say. The myth lived on that railroad men deliberately neglected the invalid passenger business on its deathbed even when they knew how to make money at it. Experienced businessmen who had never examined a railroad operating statement thought nothing of looking to the railroads for standby transportation—passenger *and* freight— when they knew perfectly well that sooner or later, as James J. Hill had said many years ago, "Every tub must stand on its own bottom." The idea that the railroads were immune to this first truth that any businessman must address himself to daily, lasted until Penn Central, chief victim of the old attitudes, gave up the ghost.

The federal government recognized the hopelessness of the rail passenger system in its old framework in 1970 by creating Amtrak, the National Rail Passenger System. (Canada, with a corporation called Via Rail Canada, has done much the same thing.) The public corporation that was set up to keep a modicum of passenger service alive drew up a severely limited map of routes over which it proposed to maintain service, and the railroads "contributed" to the capital of the new enterprise the passenger rolling stock on their books. Many a city, large and not-so-large, that found itself "demapped" (for example, Cleveland, perhaps the most shocking), set up yelps of civic pride that made for a period of backing and filling, but Amtrak pretty much had its own way. By then American cities, especially Cleveland, had too many other worries that took a higher priority. Today, they are back on track.

The first years of Amtrak were rough, in more ways than one, what with many "flat-wheel" cars rolling on under-maintained roadways. Gradually, as the government's determination to stick with its noble experiment was proved with annual infusions of cash in the high nine figures, things got better. By 1990 Amtrak was operating with a new generation of passenger cars of its own design, hauled by its own modern diesel and (in the northeast corridor) electric locomotives, and to some extent on its own tracks. (The corporation acquired title to the former New Haven and Pennsylvania lines from Boston to New York to Washington, and west from Philadelphia to Harrisburg, part of which—between New York and New Haven—it shares with Metro North, the rejuvenated commuter operation that is besieged by hordes of passengers ten times a week but still does not make money.

The biggest success for Amtrak has been, as one would have predicted, in the northeast corridor, specifically, its frequent, fast service between Washington, New York, and Boston and Metroliner service between Washington and New York. The entire line, all the way to Boston, was extensively rebuilt with welded rail laid on new ties in a reballasted roadbed. Plans that had gathered dust on the shelf for forty years to complete the electrification from New Haven to Boston were dusted off and then, without fanfare, quietly reshelved. There was a reason for this seeming act of betrayal, beyond the lack of enterprise that one finds in so many not-for-profit entities, as we shall see presently.

Meanwhile, Amtrak struggled to make a mark with its long-distance service. Florida, long a big market, got one train out of New York, as did Chicago, St. Louis, and New Orleans; and the west coast, several. The Southwest was served as part of one of the transcontinentals. This is not the sum total of Amtrak schedules, but it suggests the limited nature of the operation. Considering the backbreaking costs, growing ever larger, of operating passenger trains, it could hardly have been otherwise.

It might be said that no other mode competes with Amtrak's long-distance passenger transportation, but, by the same token, Amtrak can't compete with any other mode, either. Amtrak has only two unique functions. It serves to keep alive the idea of rail travel as part of the American heritage, which may make as much sense as collecting fascinating old stuff in the Smithsonian and other museums that are visited daily by thousands, and it provides a novel experience that can be delightful, especially for families with young children (a target of much Amtrak advertising) and on scenic routes. Moreover, it is a logical choice for the few who lack automobiles and are traveling from afar to places that lack air transportation but are, fortuitously, on an Amtrak route. For such places that are not so fortunate, Greyhound Bus Lines (perhaps the only mode to complain about Amtrak) were doing a less and less comprehensive job. Rail travel before Amtrak was strikingly cheaper than air travel before 1951, and it was a lot more dependable than air. Fares, even in coach, however, grew rapidly. Young people who enthusiastically piled aboard the Metroliners when they were new soon found themselves taking the cheaper Washington-New York-Boston trains, which took only an additional half-hour Washington to New York anyway. (Only the exalted fares of the air shuttle services keep them on the ground; they drive if given half a chance, anyway.)

On the long-distance trains, the coach fares were higher than the supersaver fares of the airlines in 1990; as for the severely limited number of sleeper accommodations, the fares came as a shock to the older folk who are not game to sit up two or three nights in a row, so they steel themselves for an annoying, uncomfortable, inconvenient, boring, but blessedly short trip by air. But the biggest problem that Amtrak faced as the old century entered its final decade was dependability. No experienced Amtraker would plan for a quick change of trains or ask busy people to meet him if he has come a long way by Amtrak. It has a deplorable on-time record. In most of the country, it operates on trackage that is operated primarily as a freight railroad by an enterprise that has to compete with trucks and must make money. The question arises whether the railroads did not have to face this problem in the days when they ran many more passenger trains? The answer is, No, because the freights today run on much tighter, faster schedules, are far longer, and consist of much heavier cars, and—most important of all—they are straining to compete for high-rated traffic that demands delivery on time "or else!" In late afternoon of every working day, by 1989, a Roadrailer unit train, consisting entirely of truck trailers running directly on the rails, and packed with automobile subassemblies, was

leaving St. Louis on the old Wabash line of Norfolk Southern Railroad
to arrive in the Detroit yards next morning, where truck power units
would be waiting to haul them to the assembly plants. Auto components
that were coming off subassembly lines in St. Louis the previous day
drive out of the Detroit plant as parts of shiny new automobiles thirty-
six hours later. This is "just-in-time" inventory management. *This* is
productivity. It is based on an intelligent use of a hundred-year-old,
single-track line that bears a maximum speed limit of forty miles an
hour. The secret is continuous movement: railroad men have long
known that schedule speed is achieved not by seeing how far up the
engineer can coax the speedometer needle but by not stopping so damn
much. A single overnight Amtrak train on this route would knock the
entire operation into a cocked hat.

Amtrak, by contrast, operates on slower schedules than the best
trains from the old days. It must, because there are dozens of stops,
whereas there used to be few if any on the crack trains of old. Amtrak,
wielding its authority to operate on any segment of track belonging to
a railroad that is part of the pact, naturally wants its long-distance trains
on the best-maintained routes they can find, which means the best
freight routes. Moreover, the rail routes were surveyed a long time ago,
when avoiding grades was an important *desideratum*. This is still an
advantage to a freight line, where efficiency (meaning how many
loaded cars a given lashup of diesel units can haul on how little fuel for
how long between stops) is paramount. Truly, the long way 'round is
often the best way home, for freight if not for Amtrak.

What Amtrak needs is a new, dedicated high-speed line for its
exclusive use, but it can not hope for such a facility out in the boondocks. There is a strong current of interest running nowadays, however,
in high-speed, high-technology rail lines between pairs of important
cities more than four hundred miles apart. Floridians, reeling from the
most frantic population influx in their history, are desperate for a way
to get their people off the highways, which are expensive to build and
maintain and dangerous to use, besides taking property off the tax rolls.
They seem serious about moving ahead with plans for a state-of-the-art
rail system that may even embody the principle of "maglev" (magnetic
levitation), which the Germans, especially, are itching to have us try.

Many doubt whether any known force will pry Americans out of
the driver's seat. The "family" car in this country, and increasingly in
other countries, is primarily used to get the wage-earners to their place
of work. (As long as thirty-five years ago an observer noted a modest
house in southern California with a total of *eight* cars parked overnight
on the driveway or pulled up on the lawn.) The hard fact is that as part
of a trend that began long ago, but especially since World War II, more
and more Americans have taken up residence in places that can not
conceivably be served economically by any form of public transportation.

The traditional answer has been to provide "satellite" parking lots at commuter railheads, and if gasoline prices ever rise high enough, either through market forces or draconian tax increases, the compromise may be widely resorted to. So far the motivation to give up the feeling of freedom, of being "in charge," even in the midst of an eight-lane traffic jam, has proved too weak. Cost, as in so many things, is becoming a discouraging factor. Some communities served by rail commuter lines from northern New Jersey to Manhattan are now paying close to $250 a month for a commutation ticket. Habit is another factor. San Franciscans, having built a fine new rapid-transit subway system in the 1950s, discovered that it takes a generation to persuade masses of people to use it. (Or, as one who tried their system just once can testify, it may well take the average person that long to learn the fare-collection system!)

Two things seem certain as far as commuter and medium-distance transportation are concerned. One is that the "commuter" airlines have to go, being too dangerous to other airplanes and innocent householders on the ground, and too wasteful of ever more costly terminal facilities. The other is that the enduring dominance of the automobile in both local and medium-distance intercity transportation is going to be seriously challenged. Many mistakes will be made, some very costly, but once more it will be "rails to the rescue."

CHAPTER 6

The First Energy Revolution

> Coal, in truth, stands not beside but entirely above all other com-
> modities. It is the material energy of the country—the universal
> aid—the factor in everything we do. With coal almost any feat
> is possible or easy; without it we are thrown back into the labo-
> rious poverty of early times.
>
> W. Stanley Jevons, *The Coal Question* (1865)

Black Diamonds

When St. John Crèvecoeur saluted "this New Man, this American," in
his *Letters from an American Farmer* (1782), he was thinking most particularly of the farmers of eastern Pennsylvania. Here, among the
gently rolling fields only a day's journey from Philadelphia, industrious
men and women had created an independent society with a standard of
living that would have been the envy of most English squires and the
thriftiest French peasants. Of what lay to the west—rugged hills, near-
mountains really, thickly forested and cut for the most part by rocky
shallow streams that could barely accommodate the hardy trapper's
canoe—Crèvecoeur gave little thought. But by the time the New Man
had erected his own sovereign nation, of which Pennsylvania was the
most affluent state, the pressure of westward movement was already
being felt. The valleys of the Delaware and the Susquehanna rivers
beckoned strongly, but the wilderness created by the first ramparts of
the Appalachian barrier rendered the lands of what would become
Schuylkill, Luzerne, Carbon, Wyoming, and Lackawanna counties useless for agriculture and, the few residents generally believed, anything
else.

Everybody, that is except a few innovative men like the Smith
brothers, John and Abijah, late of Derby, Connecticut, whose rocky
fields offered little future for young men who wanted to amount to
something in the world. They had heard of the "stone coal" that almost
begged to be shoveled out of the hills of the Wyoming valley near the
village of Plymouth, in Pennsylvania. Here they bought land, and in
1807 they built an "ark," a crude river craft that was more than a raft
yet less than a keelboat, loaded it with fifty tons of anthracite, and sent
it down the Susquehanna "on a freshet," when heavy fall rains had
swollen the stream to its fullest. The bustling town of Columbia, just

133

west of Lancaster, like so many older communities, was beginning to feel the pinch of scarce wood fuel and high prices and seemed a good market for the hard coal.

Nothing doing. While blacksmiths had some familiarity with anthracite, sometimes substituting it for charcoal, and ironmasters were experimenting with it in blast furnaces, the householders who represented the potential volume market did not know what to make of these "stones" that the brothers were trying to pass off as coal. John and Abijah dumped their anthracite upon the ground, sold the ark for lumber, and forlornly returned to Plymouth.

But not for long. The brothers were destined for success, after all, as the first marketers of anthracite for domestic heating—eventually a billion-dollar industry—because they had learned that markets do not exist, but must be created. Just a few miles away from their mine, in Wilkes-Barre, Jesse Fell, a judge who also manufactured nails (which involved him in smelting iron) and had an inventive mind, was demonstrating a grate in which householders could burn anthracite successfully. Potential consumers had complained that they often couldn't get the stuff to burn, and, not having the blacksmith's or the ironmaster's bellows, could not keep it burning when they did. A few lazy people, however—a class to whom we owe so many labor-saving devices—tried Fell's grate in their homes and found that they no longer had to get up at 3 a.m. to stoke the fires, for in a proper grate the "black diamonds," as the stone coal would soon come to be called, would burn all night long with a blue, smokeless flame, leaving little ash and no clinkers. That winter the Smith brothers had a blacksmith make up a number of grates to Judge Fell's design, and the following spring took several with them on their second attempt to sell hard coal on the lower Susquehanna. They placed the grates and a supply of the coal in the homes of several influential citizens. The rest, as they say, is history: the history of a succession of efforts to get worthwhile quantities of anthracite to market the year round, at low cost, which frustrated a generation until the steam railroad appeared on the scene. Only then could the first energy revolution take place.

The Economic Inevitability of Coal and the Railroads

Almost no subject in the rise of western "material civilization" is so neglected today as the introduction of coal fuels, their impact upon almost every aspect of human life, and the crucial role of the railroads in bringing to mankind this substance which, if it was not fire, would yet give the modern Prometheus the power to light such a fire as had never been dreamed of in the past. "Out of sight, out of mind," we say, and coal, like the railroads that transport most of it, is out of sight today for we no longer use it to heat our homes and commercial buildings. But coal and its handmaiden, the modern, efficient railroad, are still very much with us, and the future of successor energy forms is not so certain that we can assume that coal will not once more be manifest amongst us.

The industrial revolution, in which coal played a vital role, did not find ready acceptance among the philosophically minded in either England or, a century later, America. For a long time after people had begun to leave the land, work in industry or commerce, and live in cities, they still held to the Arcadian myth that cultivation of the land is a higher calling and the only true source of value. The independent farmer was "nature's true nobleman," but the businessman was a pariah, a "cosmopolitan" of dubious loyalty to his nation, and the industrial worker at best a poor unfortunate who had been deprived of the artisan's independence that was rightfully his. Such attitudes strike us as hopelessly outdated today, but no idea ever entirely dies. "The voice of the Physiocrat is still heard in the land at the county fair," and even Adam Smith, in his landmark *The Wealth of Nations* (1776) did not comprehend that the industrial age was not subservient to agriculture, but marked, in its arrival, as much of a gift of Nature as the fruitful land itself. To Smith, the swelling stream of cheap yet vastly improved goods that were already being turned out by the earliest British factories and workshops were still only "the offspring of agriculture."

A hundred years later much had changed. Another Scotsman, J. R. McCulloch, took strong exception to Smith's views in an edition of Smith's book that McCulloch had published. "The pressure of the atmosphere and the elasticity of steam, which enable us to work the most stupendous engines, are they not the spontaneous gifts of nature?" What has this to do with the impact of coal and its premier transporter, the railroads, on human life? Just that what once was revolutionary has come to be taken for granted, despite the effort that went into establishing the principles at work, which is reason to rejoice that scholars like the English economic historian W. R. Wrigley are pointing these principles out in a fresh and vigorous manner. Of the switch from vegetable fuels (that is, wood, which is replaced only slowly and would not have lasted a generation in the British industrial economy of the mid-nineteenth century) to mineral fuels, he says:

> There is a difference of great importance between mineral production on the one hand, and vegetable and animal production on the other. Production of the former is *punctiform;* of the latter, *areal.* The transport problems involved in moving a million tons of coal from pitheads scattered over an area of only a few square miles are quite different from those involved in grain or timber from an area of several thousands of square miles. The former implies heavy tonnages moving along a small number of routeways, whereas the latter implies the reverse. A heavy capital investment in improved communications is unlikely to give a good return when the raw materials of industry are organic. . . .

In other words, coal made the railroads necessary, and the railroads made the use of coal possible.

The implication of these truths, which were not well understood at the time, is that investment in heavy "social overhead" (public service) facilities for hauling large tonnages long distances would likely never be returned if made in primarily agricultural country. In hauling the output of mines, which, being "punctiform" in character produced a large tonnage within a relatively small area, such investment might be highly profitable. The principle has been demonstrated over and over again in the developed nations of the world.

Enter the railroads? Not yet, not even in Great Britain, where it all began (although, as Wrigley reminds us, Belgium, with conditions similar to those of Britain, was right behind). Necessity had become the mother of invention in Britain early in the eighteenth century, when it came to keeping Britons warm and cooking their food. The "invention" was actually of ancient usage, but no nation before Great Britain had ever built a canal system to match hers. By the late eighteenth century, if not before, Britain's most important cargo in inland trade was coal, carried by water almost to the very point of consumption. No place in England is more than sixty miles from the sea, and the coastal shipping trade, in conjunction with the canals and rivers which brought the coal to and from deep water (usually at ports with names ending in "mouth" for the river that emptied into the sea there) thrived on the coal traffic. Britain's prowess at shipbuilding may have owed as much to crafting prosaic coastal schooners for the coal trade as to first-class ships of the line.

The chain of cause and effect that unlocked Britain's budding industrial market for coal illustrates how, in history, everything depends upon everything else. By the late eighteenth century the great granddaddy of factory industry, textiles, was rapidly being mechanized, but factories required larger amounts of power than the ancient horse-on-treadmill could provide. They soon required more than water-wheels could provide, too, for the rows of spinning frames grew longer and longer. Meanwhile, the coal mines were struggling to keep the pits they were digging in that waterlogged island from filling with water. What would power their pumps? Thomas Newcomen improved Thomas Savery's earlier invention of an atmospheric steam engine that could produce a reciprocating force of great magnitude. All it required was an unlimited supply of coal, which it used prodigously, and that was just what the mines had to offer. From then on the path led directly to the modern steam engine on which most of our present-day mechanical power is ultimately based. (Even electric motors use electricity from steam-turbine-powered generators, whether the steam is produced by combustion or by nuclear energy.)

The vaunted canal system continued to be used for many years in Britain (segments still are) but it has not been a significant factor in her industrial growth at least since the middle of the nineteenth century. Just as it would in America, the steam railroad quickly took over all aspects of transportation in the British Isles, from broad-beamed squires en route to their country estates (which they still fatuously believed to be the true symbol of England's greatness) to "coals," as the British call this precious resource. It was their eventual success in learning how to make full use of coal in both familiar and new processes that opened the gates wide to coal. In the eighteenth century, men had learned how to substitute coke for charcoal in the manufacture of pig and wrought iron, thus saving what was left of England's forests and laying the foundation of its preeminence in industry for over a century. In 1856 Sir Henry Bessemer read a paper entitled "The Manufacture of Iron without Fuel," thus inventing the Bessemer steelmaking process. The new steel became the common ingredient of a thousand processes and thoroughly revolutionized industry. By 1865 men were rolling steel rails in Chicago by the Bessemer process. Other Englishmen developed processes to make illuminating gas from coal, and thus Britons—or at least those who lived in cities where gas mains were practical—were liberated from candles, whale oil, and kerosene, which last was such a boon to their country cousins. Coal was king in Great Britain long before Victoria became its queen.

Not so in America. Virgin forests, particularly of chestnut, which made a charcoal that was superbly adapted to smelting iron, shoved the question of fuel aside throughout the colonial period and into the early years of the Republic. By the 1820s (to pick a decade) the United States had grown in both population and land area, and big changes in the way people went about their daily work were about to take place. By the Civil War farsighted men knew that coal was to be the sovereign fuel of the future, not merely in places a few miles from its source, but *everywhere*, and it would be cheap enough for nearly everybody to use.

What wrought this great change? Eventually, as the price of coal fell (largely because of cheaper transportation), and certainly after the Bessemer process was adopted, the use of charcoal could no longer be justified. It is as dramatic an illustration of the interdependence of events as one can find. Coal and the railroads were inputs to each other, with each benefiting from the output of the other. Of equal importance was the easy success with which new deposits of coal of the finest kind, in easy-to-get-at locations and in great quantity and variety, continued to be found as Americans swept westward after the Revolution. Up to 1880, it has been said, "coal," unless otherwise designated, almost always meant Pennsylvania anthracite, so prominent a commercial product was this premium heating fuel. But well before 1880 bituminous coal, which itself falls into at least half a dozen categories, primarily according to the relative amounts of volatile and nonvolatile elements, was the most important form of coal. It is widely distributed in such vast quantities as to disarm even the most pessimistic futurologists, notably in Pennsylvania (the unchallenged leader of American industry in the "dark, satanic mills" era), Maryland, West Virginia, Virginia, the lower Midwest from Ohio through southern Illinois and into Iowa, and elsewhere, but, remarkably, not a single lump may be dug in the Empire State of New York. The coking coals of the Connellsville area near Pittsburgh are the finest in the world and determined the industrial future of that once-smoky city soon after the Pennsylvania Railroad linked it with the East in 1854. In 1871 the Baltimore & Ohio completed its line down the valley of the Youghiogheny (Yokka-gaynie) River through Connellsville, which gave its name to immense beds of the finest coking coal in the world.

In 1850, which roughly marks the start of the industrial revolution in America, it is estimated that there were 8.5 million horsepower "in place" to do work. Most of it was literally horsepower, as less than one-third came from inanimate sources such as steam engines, water wheels, windmills, and the spindly new railroads. By 1900 it was a new world: there were 64 million horsepower available, and four-fifths of this was inanimate. Not surprisingly, the railroads accounted for more than half of the inanimate power, and nearly 40 percent of all horsepower, notwithstanding the fact that Dobbin was supplying three times as much power as he had in 1850. Electric power was coming along slowly, as the herculean task of wiring America proceeded, along with the construction of the first generation of power stations—mostly small, local, "light plants." But by 1930 electricity provided 43 million horsepower, by which time the railroads had 110 million horsepower in place. (The railroads would never again require so much horsepower to call upon, once passenger trains were virtually extinct.) The diesel locomotive proved far more efficient than steam, when all cost factors are considered, and of course the "internal combustion," as Lucius Beebe called the auto and truck, changed just about everything.

This chapter is not about energy, however, but coal, and how the railroad made it America's overwhelmingly popular form of energy for a century. Together, cheap coal and cheap, dependable, ubiquitous transportation, which could be run right up to and under the tipple of a coal mine, made possible "modern" fuels like oil and gas, and greatly reduced the visibility, but not the importance, of solid fuels in our economy. Petroleum fuels and natural gas and the pipelines that carry most of them to the point of consumption are products of industries that coal and railroads created. As long as it lasts, petroleum (including natural gas) will continue to be the chief fuel whose inherent energy is consumed at the point of use, most notably for transportation and heating residential and commercial buildings, while coal continues to be the most important source of electric power.

The Most Successful of the Canals, but No Final Answer

It remained for the onset of the War of 1812, and the high prices that war brings, to give birth to the anthracite coal industry. In spite of the

Smith brothers' success with Judge Fell's grate, and the general acceptance of the practicality of the stuff in the Wilkes-Barre area, it had not caught on elsewhere. Doubtless the price after delivery to the potential heart of the market, the Harrisburg-Philadelphia region, was why. It bespeaks the isolation that comes from a lack of good, cheap transportation. On the eve of the war, other would-be coal magnates found that there were few takers even at a price that barely covered the cost of transportation. Once the war was under way, however, the market seemed to Jacob Cist, of Wilkes-Barre, as if it might stand a price of fourteen dollars a ton, and he and two partners took some anthracite to the cities. Only by dint of the most aggressive sales tactics, including bribing stubborn blacksmiths who disdained anything but charcoal or the bituminous coal that was trickling in from the West, were they successful. Then the Peace of Christmas Eve ended the war and its attendant high prices, and the infant coal business died in its cradle.

Clearly, if anthracite was to contribute to the economic development of the rugged areas in which it lay, better transportation had to be devised. Whatever method was chosen, it would have to be waterborne, for that was all anybody knew, and since adequate natural waterways did not exist, men would have to dig them. They had been trying to do just that in Pennsylvania since late in the eighteenth century, but even ingenious schemes including lotteries can not raise capital that has not yet been accumulated, and so it was in the anthracite country. By 1821, with the example of the Erie Canal venture to inspire them, Pennsylvanians enacted legislation that saw to completion the canal that had been started years before, connecting the town of Pottsville, tucked in the hills of Schuylkill County, with the potentially huge market at Philadelphia. Prominent among the investors was Stephen Girard, private banker of Philadelphia and reputedly the richest man in America, who knew a good thing when he saw it, and other men who were laying the foundations of the fortunes that would bring so much unhappiness to the characters in John O'Hara's stories about a city very like Pottsville.

When people speak of the "canal mania" that ensued with the brilliant success of the Erie Canal, they are not thinking of the anthracite canals of eastern Pennsylvania. Only the Erie—and only its main trunk—among all the canals that figure in the romanticized story of western expansion, was a financial success. They were all built "ahead of demand," a demand that never really materialized for various reasons such as the coming of the railroad. Indeed, people hardly ever speak of the anthracite canals at all because, in their day, which was a short one, they were eminently successful. No "ahead of demand" nonsense here: the black diamonds had been begging to go to market for a long time before arks could finally navigate from Pottsville to Philadelphia with reasonable confidence that they would complete the voyage.

The western canals, moreover, were built primarily to serve *inland* trade; that is, to connect interior navigable bodies of water such as the

Great Lakes and the Ohio River. The anthracite canals, in contrast, were outlets to tidewater, for when the coal arrived in Philadelphia or Baltimore, or the New York area, much of it was just completing the first leg of its journey. These canals gave a big boost to coastal shipping (just as canals had done in England almost a century before) for the traditionally low cost of waterborne freight meant that the coal from the wilds of Schuylkill County, for example, which had been an oddity in Philadelphia as late as 1815, was becoming a common household commodity by 1830, often many hundreds of miles away from where it had lain for millions of years.

The key to practical transit of the rugged terrain between tidewater and inland points has always been the exploration and exploitation of the river valleys. Here men found not only the easiest gradients, but also plentiful supplies of water of which the canals required a great deal. The canals even ran *across* rivers at a few points: few of man's engineering feats are odder than the great troughs that carried the artificial waterways across the real ones! Why did the steam railroad, when it came, come with such swiftness and displace the canals so thoroughly? The answer seems to be that the canals lacked one great advantage that was unique to railroads: considerable expense was required for wagon transportation from mine to canal, since the canals could not go everywhere, and railroads could. From the earliest times, mines and quarries had struggled to reduce the friction that a horse-drawn vehicle operating on rutted roads encounters, by means of wooden and later iron-sheathed "rails." Some historians consider such intermediate innovations to be the first railways, and it was over such a facility that the first steam locomotive was tested in America—the Delaware & Hudson's British import, the *Stourbridge Lion*, which a prudent management considered too heavy for safe operation over the spindly rails. (The enginemen doubtless agreed, for the thrill of taking the *Lion* across the river trestle that the "railroad" traversed was not something they wished to experience regularly.)

The steam railroad consistently showed itself to be capable of more and heavier work than anticipated, and lines quickly began to occupy the river valleys alongside the canals. The Schuylkill Canal was the first to be jostled by the noisy newcomer, for down its pleasant valleys men built the Reading Railroad. The Lehigh Canal, down the valley of the Lehigh River to the Delaware at Easton, with a connection via the Morris Canal to Newark and Jersey City (across the Hudson from New York) and extensions to Trenton and Philadelphia, was soon host to the Lehigh Valley and Delaware, Lackawanna & Western railroads. And in the extreme northeast corner of Pennsylvania, centering on Honesdale, and admirably situated to supply anthracite to cold Boston and points north that yearned for it desperately, the Delaware & Hudson Company built a line that would be so successful that the next generation of financiers would fight savagely to control it.

Anthracite coal was a growth industry if there ever was one, throughout the nineteenth century. Although the railroads were being operated full tilt by 1850 in carrying anthracite to market (behind wood-burning locomotives!) the canals were busier than ever. In 1840 what contemporaries liked to call the "stream of anthracite" that flowed from the hills to consumers had totaled only two million tons; ten years later it had reached fifty million tons, and what figures we have indicate that the railroads were getting the lion's share of the business. Being open throughout the year, they were able to do a steady business, and thus smaller inventories were required at all points of the distribution system. By the end of the 1850s competition from the railroads had put a fatal dent in canal volume—which did not upset many, since the railroads had virtually taken the canals over by then anyway—and, other than during the Civil War years and for a short time thereafter, canal tonnage began to dwindle. Like most American canals, the anthracite waterways did not die suddenly; they had a long period of desuetude, and by the end of the century almost nothing remained of their once-great volume.

The transition from canals to railroads had been rational, steady, and controlled. The new railroad corporations offered advantages that few could dispute, and being themselves even larger aggregations of capital, and blissfully free from government or labor union interference until the end of the century, they were able to keep their well-oiled transportation machine in first-class order, while offering employment (on the rails and in the mines) that was eagerly sought after, and delivering a vital fuel of high quality at a constantly declining cost to the consumer. After 1900 it would be a different story.

The Lure of Riches Beneath the Ground

Eager to try out the service provided by the relatively new national passenger corporation (Amtrak) over what had been for a century one of the most important routes in the nation, a rail enthusiast boarded the *Broadway Limited* at New York's Pennsylvania Station one warm June evening in 1973. The trip turned out to be both a nightmare and an adventure. He awoke in his roomette bed about 7:30 the next morning, sensing that something was amiss. In the earlier part of the night his sleeper had banged along on the poorly maintained "broadway of steel" of which the Pennsylvania had once been so proud. Since then he had slept soundly, and the reason was easy to see. Raising the blind, he read "Crestline" on the faded name board of the decaying station. The train should have passed that point in central Ohio during the night, for Chicago was still several hundred miles ahead. At that moment the train, which consisted of some eighteen 85-foot cars, began to describe a painfully tight right turn, the wheels squealing in protest against the rails, and a few miles further on, an equally tight turn to the left. Obviously, the engineer had lost his way.

As was happening more and more frequently in those days when the federal government had still not accepted its responsibility for two generations of wrongheaded national transportation policy, there had been a freight derailment up ahead somewhere between Crestline and Lima, Ohio. Nothing to do but turn north to Toledo, where the train could proceed west on the rails of what had been for over a century one of the most well-maintained and profitable stretches of railroad in the world: the Lake Shore division of the New York Central, now the Pennsylvania's companion in the miseries of bankruptcy since the failure of the Penn Central, into which the two once-great enterprises had been merged. To get to Toledo, the errant train had to pass over the tracks of what had once been the independent Toledo, Walhonding Valley & Ohio Railroad until the Pennsylvania leased it back in the 1890s. And to get *there* (which it might have done directly if the conductor had learned of the derailment before clearing Mansfield, a few miles back) the train had to make that hard right turn onto a "foreign road," as the conductor, ignoring such legal niceties as the merger, contemptuously referred to what had once been a part of the New York Central's Big Four subsidiary. (When he had first gone to work for the Pennsy, the mere idea that the *Broadway* would ever detour on New York Central tracks would have been laughable.)

Eleven miles northwest of Mansfield the *Broadway Limited* struck the Walhonding line and turned left onto it. Toledo and the Lake Shore route were 79 miles to the northwest; there was no drinking water left in the tanks of the passenger cars; breakfast was a cold bologna sandwich washed down with lukewarm orange juice; there was to be no lunch at all; and nobody really expected the refill pipestands on the station platform at Toledo to work. (They didn't.) Moreover, the train had to proceed westward all the way to Chicago at about thirty-five miles an hour under manual signals, because the Lake Shore's automatic signal system was out of order. A repair crew in a Penn Central truck, seeking desperately at each signal locker along the track for the source of the trouble, sheepishly followed the train for miles. The *Broadway,* its passengers thoroughly dehydrated, ravenous, and their children crying pathetically for a drink of water, limped into Chicago's Union Station a little after 4:00, some eight hours late.

So much for the ordeal. The adventure lay in the rare opportunity to ride a stretch of track upon which regular passenger service had long since been abandoned. The line had obviously been upgraded some decades before into a very heavy-duty line, and many segments looked as though they had been double-tracked before the American railroad system began to resorb itself. The mileposts were rusty but still readable, made as they were of honest cast iron in a Victorian pattern. The *Broadway*—if you agree that trains are a little bit human—must have been thrilled at the prospect of trundling its mighty length down this segment of line that contained not a single town of any size. The citizens of Gibsonburg, population 2479, about two-thirds of the way to

Toledo, evidently thought so. The station agent had spread the word that "the *Broadway Limited* is coming through here," for by the time it slid past the depot at least three hundred people, many armed with both still and movie cameras, had gathered on the platform to watch it go past. Much vigorous waving between passengers and spectators ensued, and then Gibsonburg, which once had had several first-class trains a day to watch including the *Limited* to Detroit, slipped back into the boredom of the automobile age.

Describing his experience to an elderly lady who had spent most of her life in Ohio, our enthusiast was surprised to hear her say, matter-of-factly, "Oh, that's a coal road." Indeed it still is and may very well be a vital one again someday. The Walhonding line is one of those "coal roads" that were built in the late 1870s, after the depression of that decade ended, for the explicit purpose of taking bituminous coal mined in Pennsylvania, Maryland, West Virginia, and southeastern Ohio north to the flourishing lake ports. By that time the delicate relationship between rail and lake transportation of heavy, bulky commodities like coal, iron ore, and grains, had emerged. Toledo, along with Cleveland, Sandusky, Lorain, Ashtabula, and other lake ports in Ohio and Erie in Pennsylvania, became familiar names in any discussion of the new mid-western industrial economy that was upstaging agriculture as the main occupation of the people.

No lands on the face of the earth had ever beckoned more invitingly to land-hungry Americans in the first half of the nineteenth century, and nearly two hundred years later the Midwest is still feeding millions who could not even point out Ohio on a map. Following the Civil War, however, it was industry, as much as farming, that beat "a thoroughfare for pilgrims' feet" and shifted the center of American population westward. Measured in material terms, an economy based on coal, iron, steel, metals manufacturing, and the railroads that tied it all together, probably produced more wealth than all of the rich farmlands combined. Beneath them lay seemingly unlimited quantities of first-class bituminous coal, suitable for almost every domestic and industrial use, and through these fields men built one of the densest railroad networks in the world. The undue emphasis upon railroads as an agency for populating the trans-Missouri United States has obscured the simple fact that the railroads populated modern America from one ocean to the other.

Those aspects of American economic history that cannot be explained by immigration, population growth, and the longing to own a farm, someone has said, can probably be explained by the Civil War. The old saw has much truth to it where coal is concerned. During the war the demand for fuels for producing the machines of war, which incorporated huge quantities of iron, forced men who would have been perfectly happy to go on cutting down the forests for charcoal until the entire nation was one vast prairie or desert to adopt coal. It was the beginning of the end of the charcoal iron industry. It was the beginning of the transformation of the spindly new railroads into heavy-duty carriers of bulky, low-value-per-ton commodities at low rates that we have already referred to.

While men had learned to use hard coal to raise steam under boilers (thus freeing antebellum mills from having to be located near water power), to smelt iron, and even as a locomotive fuel, it was not really satisfactory in any of these applications. Coal for locomotives, in fact, did not catch on until after the war. As late as the 1850s it still seemed perfectly logical to haul anthracite from Pottsville to Philadelphia behind a diamond-stacked locomotive whose tender was piled high with cordwood! Some success attended the development of fireboxes that could accommodate anthracite, which obviously was cheap for the anthracite railroads, and some railroads continued in the twentieth century to tout the greater cleanliness of travel on an anthracite-burning line. Thus, the Lackawanna's advertising agency had a great success with its mythical character, Phoebe Snow ("my dress stays white though I ride all night, when I take the road of anthracite"). But until electric generating plants outdistanced them, the trains of America were for many years the largest consumers of coal, nearly all of it bituminous.

Bituminous coal was already making a market for itself before the Civil War, as the midwestern canals were opened. Thus the railroads in their turn found a ready market for it, and as the price fell by at least one-third from 1865 to 1880, for example, the industry mushroomed. The great soft coal fields of the eastern United States became the center of the American fuel industry, ranging as far east as Clearfield in Pennsylvania and Cumberland in Maryland; as far south at least as the Pocahontas field in the Kanawha and New River regions of West Virginia; and westward into Kentucky and Ohio and eventually Illinois and even Iowa; but embracing as their sovereign those spectacular beds of near-perfect coking and steam coal around Pittsburgh.* They were the first fruits of the American railroad network after it achieved early maturity, which we may date from the linking of the Pennsylvania, the New York Central, and their allied lines, to Chicago and the Mississippi River in the 1850s, and the completion of the network of these trunk lines, as they came to be called, in the 1870s. As late as the first decade of the twentieth century, the maturing process went on, for the "coal roads" were prosperous in good times and came through in hard times. Even when their business was bad, it was pretty good.

*Historical Statistics of the U.S., Colonial Times to 1970, does not report average prices of bituminous coal for these years, probably because of the great variety of these coals. However, anthracite prices, which were much less competitive than bituminous prices, declined from $7.86 in 1865 to $4.53 in 1880. Therefore, one-third seems if anything conservative as an estimate of the decline in bituminous prices.

The Primacy of Coal in Later Railroad Building

"This country must go through the fire," James J. Hill wrote his old
friend and financial ally, John Murray Forbes of Boston, near the end
of the eventful decade of the 1880s. For over ten years, beginning with
the return of prosperity after the sobering depression of 1873–1877,
the nation had watched awestruck as the most ebullient railroad building spree in history began. In the 1880s the railroads added each year
nearly seven thousand miles of new track, on average, a record never
again approached in the United States or elsewhere. Huge sums of
money had been borrowed on first mortgage bonds, at high *real* rates
of interest judging from the big discounts from par that bond buyers
were demanding. Sooner or later, Hill and most other seasoned railroad
men knew, the chickens had to come home to roost.

Meanwhile, business was good if you looked at the volume of traffic, but rotten if you went by freight profits. Referring to the profits
reported by the Pennsylvania and New York Central railroads for carrying freight, Fletcher W. Hewes commented in 1889, in the pioneering statistical chapter he wrote for *The American Railway:* "The reduction of profits in the history of these roads is from about six mills per
ton per mile in 1870, to about two mills in 1888. . . . The prospect of
the future of freight traffic is not cheerful." After the railroads had,
indeed, "gone through the fire" of reorganization and consolidation
during the watershed depression of 1893–1897, the railroads would
find real prosperity, at least as long as they were free to make their own
basic decisions as to rates. Meanwhile, during the last two decades of
the nineteenth century the struggle for volume continued (any increase
in rates being out of the question), which, among other factors, confirmed the importance of a large, steady coal traffic for most of the railroads east of the Mississippi and north of the Potomac.

The Pennsylvania Railroad became the premier transportation factor in the coal-iron-steel economy of that day, because of its unmatched
location on the industrial "main street" of Pennsylvania, but also
because wise reinvestment of profits in system betterments had
resulted in one of the lowest costs of producing a ton-mile of transportation in the industry. The New York Central and the Erie also carried
large tonnages of coal to the New York area for local use and for water
shipment to New England, which always seemed to be nervously
checking its coal bin from October to May. The anthracite roads that
were intelligently managed, like the Lackawanna and the Lehigh Valley, did superbly, while the Reading suffered from the megalomania
first of Franklin B. Gowen and later of Alexander A. McLeod, and the
Central of New Jersey became a corporate football until finally J. P.
Morgan and Company caught it and made it a winner. The venerable
Baltimore & Ohio, which had started the railroad era in 1828, faltered

in the heavy economic weather and slipped into receivership, as did the Erie. Both were vital factors in the coal-carrying trade.

Competition, especially from new lines like George Gould's Western Maryland Railroad, which paralleled the B. & O. mile after mile through the Cumberland coal fields, and Collis P. Huntington's Chesapeake & Ohio, was the main reason for rail poverty in the coal districts, but low prices for coal also kept rail rates low. Coal mining was still a highly individualistic calling, and the operators were as ornery, in their way, as the brave men who went into the pits each day to dig the coal. It was better, many felt, to run as long as the "no-bills" (for which no buyer was in sight) did not clog your sidings or the railroad refuse to bring you any more cars, than to close down and starve along with the men and their large families.

The railroads, in short, were in the same leaky boat with the coal industry, and they would sink or swim together. The situation called for concerted action, at a time when the shibboleth of "monopoly" was catching on as the chief tool of the political demagogue. Something was going to give, however. Together, the railroads and the coal industry, along with the still-infant steel industry, were in a fair way to create a major industrial depression. Meanwhile, in 1880 a new coal field, about whose rich, thick coal seams amazing things were rumored, was being opened up in West Virginia by a railroad created, or nearly so, for that very purpose. A new day seemed to be dawning to mark a thoroughgoing rationalization of railroads and coal mines as the single industry they had in effect become.

Among the names of railroad entrepreneurs who took the opportunities of the late Victorian era at the flood—Vanderbilt, Cassatt, Garrett, Hill, Huntington, Harriman, and a few others—the name of Frederick J. Kimball (1844–1903) is seldom found. One will look for him in vain in the standard biographical directories. A quiet, colorless man, devoted to business, married but childless, he was a fair, frank advocate for the properties with which he was entrusted and a realist regarding their limitations. He is a major figure in the history of the bituminous coal industry from its coming of age in the late 1870s to the turn of the century, when twenty years of prosperity began. He saw clearly what was needed in the way of further railroad development for the next phase of the story to begin, and he passed the ultimate test of the true entrepreneur: he realized his vision.

Frederick J. Kimball created the modern Norfolk & Western Railroad ("a conveyor belt for coal masquerading as a railroad," someone once said) to open up the Pocahontas coal field nestled in the valley of the Tug Fork of Big Sandy River in extreme southern West Virginia, a few miles west of Bluefield. The coal here was as fine a low-volatile "semi-bituminous" as one could hope for, nearly perfect for steaming, coking, and general use, and it lay in beds as thick as fifteen feet so near the surface, and so easily got at through river banks, that the cost of mining would be ridiculously low. But what to do with it once mined? Eastern markets were much too far for the railroads of the 1870s to carry it overland, and few if any railroads yet existed to carry it across the rugged terrain to the Ohio River on the north.

The answer was a heavy-duty railroad running straight (or as straight as possible) eastward, downgrade most of the way, to tidewater at someplace like Newport News or Norfolk, for water transshipment to east coast cities. Some such line of reasoning had been forming itself into a plan for a classic "venture capital" undertaking, in the mind of Frederick Kimball, who was a practical, experienced railroad man. Before becoming associated with E. W. Clark & Co., investment bankers in Philadelphia, he had gained experience as a motive power and railroad maintenance engineer—not a bad specialty for one who had ideas of hauling great tonnages of freight considerable distances at low cost—and had just come back from two years in England, where an American could still learn a thing or two about the role of the railroad in the coal business.

Kimball studied the possibilities of the Pocahontas field and existing transportation facilities between there and tidewater and realized that something could be done with the Atlantic, Mississippi & Ohio Railroad. This consolidation of railroads dating back to 1837 ran (crawled, rather) 204 miles westward from Norfolk to Bristol, just across the line in Tennessee, where it joined the East Tennessee, Virginia & Georgia Railway. The only towns of any size on this route besides Norfolk were Petersburg, Lynchburg, and Roanoke, and the small volume of short-haul freight that was offered to the railroad did not provide for ordinary maintenance, much less growth. In this, the A.M. & O. was no different from most other southern railroads in this period, and like many of them, when the depression of the 1870s arrived it slipped into receivership.

To reorganize the A.M. & O., Virginians turned to a syndicate of Philadelphia capitalists, among whom the Clarks were dominant. Kimball, of course, was the chief strategist, and the prospectus for the 1881 takeover was mostly his work. It provided for a clear-cut move into the coal business by means of an extension northwestward from Bluefield along the New River to the Pocahontas field. Here, the syndicate would set up mining operations, encouraging others to do likewise—preferably by leasing mining rights from owners of mineral rights, of whom the Norfolk & Western (as the reorganized railroad was called) intended to be by far the largest. The railroad, it hardly needs be added, received exclusive rights to haul the coal. On March 17, 1883, the first shipment reached Norfolk. There, at Lamberts Point, the N. & W. began work on a marine terminal that would grow constantly for the next fifty years into one of the largest facilities for the handling, stockpiling, and trans-shipment of coal in the world. In the intervening years, the N. & W. built hundreds of miles of access branches to mines;

constantly upgraded its right-of-way by reducing curvature, double-tracking, and laying heavier steel rail; bought endless strings of steadily more capacious coal cars and fleets of bigger, more powerful locomotives, and went deeply into debt to extend northwestward to its logical terminals at Cincinnati and Columbus, Ohio. At these last two points, numerous coal roads were eagerly reaching out to take the coal on to the Lakes. Failing to get control of the East Tennessee road, which would have made it a southern trunk line with all the headaches that would entail, the N. & W. dropped expansion plans in that direction. It never went west from Bristol, but right down to the virtual demise of the American rail passenger train, it made money hauling through trains of the Southern Railway over the Lynchburg-Bristol gap in the Southern's through route to Memphis. For this purpose, of course, it used its own locomotives—coal burners to the bitter end. (The N. & W. was the last major U.S. railroad to convert to diesel power.)

Railroads and Coal Mining—A Single Industry

The men who participated in the rebirth of the N. & W. would not have found it worth arguing whether the railroad was an integral part of the coal industry, for they had always intended to pursue a policy of "vertical integration," to use the modern term, backward to the sources, and forward to the customer: "from mine to market," as the historian of the N. & W. subtitled his book. Coal mining began in Tazewell County, near the newly built town of Pocahontas, in January 1882. The arrangement with the mine operators reveals that the N. & W. intended to run the entire show. No tariffs were published stating the rate per ton the shipper was to pay the railroad for hauling his coal. Instead, all agreed to divide whatever price the coal realized at market according to a fixed percentage: 70 percent for the railroad, and 30 percent for the producer. This was a dramatic illustration of the fact that transportation produces value, for the coal could have realized little or nothing at the mine without cheap transportation to market. In fairness to the operator, whose costs were primarily for labor, a minimum realized price was provided for, which would have been just fine if this were a world of fixed relationships, but all over America enterprising men were bringing more and more coal to market at lower and lower prices, contributing significantly to the long-term decline in all prices that characterized the period from 1873 to 1898.

The N. & W.'s control of the industry it had created, in short, was great—it would hardly pass antitrust muster today—but it was not great enough. In any case, fixed ratios were out. Markets would rule, and within that framework the railroad would keep the upper hand—if it could. It organized the Pocahontas Company to sell the coal produced in the field and also led in the establishment of the Seaboard

Figure 6.1 Frederick J. Kimball (1844–1903), in conceiving of a railroad to bring the abundant, BTU-rich bituminous coal of what became the "Pocahontas Region" of western Virginia and West Virginia to eastern consumers, exemplified the classic entrepreneur. *(Virginia Polytechnic Institute & State University)*

Steam Coal Association, described as "a voluntary combination of producers organized to set production quotas and fix prices." Its success depended on the ability of all coal-carrying railroads in the region to adhere to their published tariffs. (The Chesapeake & Ohio was the main competition, but others were on the horizon.) But rebating followed as a matter of course in spite of the new Interstate Commerce Act's pious clause outlawing rebating and pooling. The model for the pool was the series of "gentlemen's agreements" that financial leaders like J. P. Morgan had squeezed out of eastern railroad men with the cooperation of Frederick Kimball in the hectic period 1885–1887; these men also watched closely as the Germans sought to solve similar problems in their burgeoning coal industry with their Reinisch-West-Fälischen coal trust. None of these voluntary arrangements endured in the United States, in the face of an economy that was being thoroughly shaken out by forces whose amplitude few were yet aware of. Coal markets throughout the country were in chaos by 1890, and "markets" had become more like Oriental bazaars. The Association was dead by 1894.

At the same time that the N. & W. had opened the Pocahontas field to the northeastern market, the superb coal of the Clearfield, Pennsylvania, field became more available as trunk line railroads realized the vital importance of the heavy traffic that coal could guarantee. The Pennsylvania and the B. & O. had had Clearfield coal all to themselves via branches from their mainline. In 1883, however, the New York Central built its Beech Creek Railroad from Clearfield to a junction with the Reading Railroad in the improbably named town of Jersey Shore in eastern Pennsylvania. The Erie Railroad, in one of its brief healthy periods, joined in with a branch southward from its mainline to the Reynoldsville field in neighboring Jefferson County.

In 1887 the N. & W. received, net for transportation, an average price of $1.32 a ton for coal hauled to tidewater at Norfolk; by 1898 that figure had shrunk to $1.05, and the price of coal at Pocahontas mines, which had been $1.25 in 1880, was down to 80 cents in 1898. The railroad would soon be unable to cover its interest charges if that trend continued, and Kimball pleaded with the mine operators to accept a lower price for their coal, *but*, notwithstanding the marked decline in the cost of living during the depression, not to cut wages.

Why this compassion for the miners? Kimball knew miner psychology well. A more stubbornly individualistic group never manned American industry, although the mine operators ran a close second. To challenge their right to strike, or even to question the wisdom of a strike, was often enough to produce a work stoppage, while a cut in wages, merely to put in the operators' pockets money that had been going into the pockets of the men who did the hard work, almost certainly would. Kimball knew, furthermore, that a strike of even a few weeks could starve the railroad for traffic and push it into receivership. The operators, most of whom were small businessmen by big business standards and intensely jealous of their prerogatives, cut wages by 20 percent and a four-month strike ensued. The N. & W. petitioned for receivership and, following the sensible procedure established in the previous decade in the case of the Wabash insolvency, had Kimball appointed receiver.

Meanwhile the State of Virginia, anticipating later action by the federal government, passed a law prohibiting railroad companies from buying and selling coal or owning mines the entire output of which was not used for the railroad's own needs. The coal roads now appeared helpless to control affairs, and goodness knows everybody else was. The miners controlled the labor supply (Kimball would doubtless have been amused by the groaning shelf of books that have accumulated since his day insisting upon the helplessness of miners in the face of unbridled capitalism!), and the only course the operators seemed to know was to run full, produce as much coal as possible, and sell it for whatever it could get. In this they were aided and abetted by the landowners, who were eager to lease mining rights and collect the royalties. Only a return to prosperity and a redoubling of the growth rate in coal consumption could save the railroads, and after 1898 they got both. Meanwhile the leaders of the trunk line railroads were planning a course of concerted action in the best tradition of late Victorian America's most successful business enterprise: Standard Oil Company of New Jersey.

The Urge to Combine, and the Forces that Undermined It

"The most successful enterprises have been those which have been so well organized and so efficient that the laborers were paid high wages, the consuming public enjoyed declining prices, and the owners realized large profits." That is the way John D. Rockefeller, Jr., summed up the *raison d'être* for the giant corporation that his father had led into being in the days when the youthful petroleum industry was as chaotic as the coal industry at the turn of the century. Americans' fear of corporate bigness notwithstanding, in all successful business endeavors the participants have been free, first, to agree on what is desirable to be done, what is required to do it, and which industrial leader has the ability to do it, and then to stand aside and allow him to do it. No stewardship is so pervasive nor so powerful that it is not judged by objective results. Perfect examples of these principles, of course, are hard to find in the real world, but perhaps the best—judging by the fact that Americans hesitated a long time before destroying it—was Standard Oil.

The American petroleum industry spent its first seventy-five years supplying an increasingly abundant, cheap, high-quality illuminant in the years before the electric light all but destroyed the market for kerosene. Like coal, oil is an extractive industry, and producers of the raw material, if left to themselves, are likely to want to get out of the ground all the riches that are contained in it as fast as possible and to sell it for whatever it will bring. Inasmuch as all raw materials, even coal, have to undergo some processing and be transported, unbridled production of raw material has dire consequences for profitability in the subsequent stages of the marketing process, for processing, unlike the extractive phase, involves heavy investment and fixed costs in labor, interest charges, and other inputs. Profits, moreover, are not primarily claimed by stockholders or other owners of the equity existing in the enterprise. Frequently, especially in the early years of a new "growth" industry, profits are fully recycled to finance expansion and improvement of plant and innovation in product or service. Unless an industry can find the basis for such a healthy state of affairs, it will sooner or later become a "sick industry." We have had many such in American history—textiles, agriculture, retail merchandising, and, yes, coal—but where corporate combination offered a better way, it was usually seized upon.

The question facing the Standard Oil men was a simple one: at what point in the overall process might one exert a strong, but beneficent hand to grasp the valves controlling the flow and thus adjust inputs and outputs, quantities offered on the market, prices, and profits? Why, at the refining stage, of course. Here was concentrated, under the control of a relatively few men and firms, most of the invested capital in the business. Why not join them together in an agreement to take only just so much oil from the producers as can be refined, transported, and efficiently distributed (that is, with an affordable investment in plant, tank cars, pipelines, and storage facilities), at stable, reasonable prices, and in sufficient quantities to meet the needs of a thrifty, careful populace? Of course, no one believed for a minute that a voluntary pool would be adequate, for pooling agreements were not enforceable in court. Something more formal and more legally binding had to be found. S.C.T. Dodd, perhaps the archetypal corporation lawyer, suggested the common law trust, whereby owners of the stock of as many of the refiners as could be persuaded to join would place their stock "in trust," to be voted by a board of trustees made up of the heads of the larger companies, and all decisions pertaining to the individual refining plants so represented would be made by the board, as if the several enterprises were in fact a single enterprise. Each formerly independent firm would share in the combined net profits of the trust, according to the proportion that the agreed-upon value of the properties it had placed in the trust bore to the total value of all the constituent firms. Each firm would enjoy a return on investment, even if the plant it placed in the trust was shut down for the entire accounting period.

Trust certificates were issued to represent the shares thus deposited with the trustees, and these certificates, being negotiable, traded freely like shares of stock, at prices far above the book or par value of the shares, in mute testimony to the brilliant success of the entire affair. This was "horizontal" integration; there followed "vertical" integration, backwards into crude oil production and forward by making rate deals with the railroads (to whom it supplied the wooden tanks that rode on the railroads' wheels) and building pipelines. Steadily, throughout the rest of Standard Oil's existence, although the trust was replaced by a holding company, the quality and quanity of oil available not only in the United States, but throughout the world, increased and prices declined, as did the price of practically everything else until the end of the century, whether produced by "trustified" industries or sick ones. Inevitably, other firms entered the industry, content to follow Standard's lead.

If the coal industry had found a leader like John D. Rockefeller and his associates, and if it had been allowed to do what they did, perhaps coal would not have acquired its reputation as a sick industry in recent times. For a few years after 1898 something like this was tried and bid fair to succeed, except that popular opinion, politically and bureaucratically crystallized, as is the American way, refused to condone it. The experience tells us much about the futility of trying to promote what is economically ideal in the face of what is politically expedient.

We have no way of knowing whether Alexander Cassatt, who virtually rebuilt the Pennsylvania Railroad in the few years that he headed

it around the turn of the century, or the oligarchy who ran the New
York Central thought of railroad transportation as a stage in the overall
process of bringing coal from where Nature stored it to the user's
bins—analogous, that is, to oil refining as simply one stage in bringing
petroleum from where Nature stored it to the users' jugs, cans, and
tanks. Businessmen are not given to such abstractions, but they *acted*
as though they did. You could look upon the depressed level of rates
they and their few but aggressive competitors received for carrying
coal as merely cutthroat competition, or you could point to the obvious
fact that rates were also related to the price of coal at the mine, which
was subject to cutthroat competition, too. The difference was that the
railroads held the better hand in this game. Voluntary, and thus unen-
forceable, agreements could be replaced by the corporate control of
the other carriers by one or two railroad leaders, and the best mines
with the lowest costs of production could be bought up. The latter
approach had been tried extensively in the last quarter of the old century, notably in the anthracite territory, but the financial and managerial resources required had generally exceeded the resources available.
Buying up competitors' stock required more optimism in the future
than could readily be summoned up during the depression of the mid-
1890s but, as men like Cassatt knew, depressions do not last forever.

By 1903, indeed, much had changed. Mine prices of coal had risen
sharply and were now too high, in the opinion of many. The biggest
shipper of coal on the Pennsylvania Railroad, which was itself far and
away the biggest hauler of coal, was a classic nineteenth-century individualist named E. J. Berwind, operating in the Clearfield district. He
resented the railroads' desire, at this point, for lower coal prices, but
the urban poor were enduring hardship and the first signs of shortages
had begun to appear in the big eastern cities—shortages that would
grow progressively worse for the next fifteen years. When, one day in
1903, S. M. Prevost of the Pennsylvania commented to Berwind that
the price of coal was too high, Berwind, one of the heaviest crosses
Frederick Kimball had had to bear in the defunct Bituminous Steam
Coal Traffic Association, retorted, "What in hell has the railroad company got to do with the price of coal?" He then launched into a dia-
tribe, accusing the Pennsylvania of encouraging a lot of small, cut-price
operators to enter the business and drive down prices, to which Prevost
replied, "But Mr. Berwind, what in hell has the railroad company got
to do with the price of coal?" What, indeed, had happened in the short
five years since the depression ended to force sorehead Berwind to
search so hard for discontents?

Late in 1899, barely a year after the U.S. Supreme Cout had put a
final, formal end to voluntary rate support agreements in the landmark
Joint-Traffic Association case, Wall Street was rocked by the news that
the Pennsylvania and the Central, acting in concert, had bought more
than 40 percent of the stock of the Chesapeake & Ohio Railroad, agree-

ing to hold it for ten years and giving each other the right of first refusal to buy it. The cost was $9.5 million, and it would be a long, long time before C. & O. would sell at such a bargain price again. The big fellows arranged for joint control (how cordial relations can become when times are good!) and, to forestall public censure, announced that their objective was simply to pursue a policy that would "while securing a proper development of its system and the providing from time to time of such facilities as will accommodate its shippers and enable it to properly serve the public, procure the best results for its shareholders."

That was only the beginning, for in 1901 the Pennsylvania invested $65 million (stock prices were on the rise by then) in a 40 percent interest in the B. & O., which had recently been through the receivership wringer and was being extensively rebuilt under the tutelage of James J. Hill of the Great Northern, who applauded the deal. Onto the board of the B. & O. went four Pennsylvania vice presidents, one of whom, L. F. Loree, became president of the B. & O. By the end of 1901 the Pennsylvania had put yet another $17.9 million into 39 percent of the stock of the N. & W. Nothing could have pleased Kimball more, for to him it spelled the new era of mature business practices, and the end of nineteenth century rugged individualism. "It means permanency and . . . a maintenance of rates," he observed.

But the Interstate Commerce Commission, much reinvigorated by growing concern with "monopoly power," frowned long and hard at the railroads' manifest ability to control prices and output in the coal industry (which the government would itself never learn to do years later during the quagmire of the Great Depression), which prompted a general divestment of these stocks by 1906. By then it seemed to everyone that the railroads and the coal industry had learned how to take care of themselves. Besides, all of the rail lines were facing the necessity of substantial improvements and additions to their capacity at that very moment, and by World War I they were hard put to satisfy a demand for fuel in the industrial Northeast that no one could have imagined at the turn of the century. Coal reigned supreme as a locomotive fuel (it was its biggest market), steam-raising fuel for prime movers, heat-producing fuel for hundreds of factories (notably those manufacturing iron and steel) and buildings, while recently laid sidings in thousands of cities and towns were busier each year handling coal for electric generating plants. By 1925 New England alone was consuming some twenty million tons of soft coal a year, of which 64 percent went by rail-and-water routes through New York harbor, Philadelphia, Baltimore, Newport News, and Norfolk, and the rest by all-rail routes.

The Standard Oil model was never seriously tested, therefore, as it applied to the rail-and-coal industry. In the first place, it suffered from a fundamental legal disability: the railroads were common carriers and had to take whatever freight was offered them regardless of its ownership, and they had to charge everybody the same rate. Moreover, as even the Standard Oil model showed in 1911 and the years that followed, the dynamic, ever-changing environment of the American economy would have rendered it obsolete, not so much through judicial application of the Sherman Antitrust law, but in the transformation of both the market and the structure of the industry.

The Reality of Decline and the Promise of Rebirth

For roughly the first two decades of the twentieth century, the sister industries of coal mining and rail transportation were growth industries notwithstanding that the railroads were nearly a hundred years old and coal, much older. In 1913 both industries were at their peak and looked forward to a rosy future, and when that future dissolved quickly after 1920, it was due almost entirely to factors external to coal mining and railroading as practiced during most of their history. The anthracite industry went into a nosedive during the Great Depression and by 1950 was dead. As the number of automobiles and trucks multiplied after 1920, the availability of "middle distillates" (light domestic fuel oils) rose and the price declined. Oil-fired central heat, controlled by automatic thermostats, freed homeowners from shoveling coal and boys in corduroy knickers from carrying out the ashes. Then the expansion of natural gas pipelines did away even with fuel deliveries. Advertisements by the anthracite trade association in the 1930s offered American families greater warmth for the same amount of money they were spending on new fuels, but small-space advertisements in *Collier's* and *Saturday Evening Post* declaring, "You don't have to be cold to be healthy," were but whispers into the wind. Since the end of the coal trade, considerable light industry—much of it employing women—has moved in, but it has been a long time since cities like Scranton, or Wilkes-Barre, or Pottsville, or Hazleton have known the security of being part of a major industry, or the excitement of a miners' payday.

"Anthracite priced itself out of the market after 1901," an old gentlemen told me who had begun in business by "calling on the trade" for the Lehigh Valley Coal Company in 1906. He was referring to President Theodore Roosevelt's solution of the celebrated miners' strike of that year, which amounted to "give the men what they want." The operators never got the upper hand in labor negotiations again, and in later years John L. Lewis, head of the United Mine Workers, bullied them at will. At one point, he even complained that the operators had shown bad faith in selecting their own representatives in negotiations and demanded the right to pick them himself! In 1932, at the bottom of the Depression, when most wages and salaries had been cut by up to one-third and even one-half, anthracite miners—those who were still working, that is—were still being paid at pre-1930 levels.

Lewis showed the same blend of stubborness and arrogance

towards the bituminous industry. Warned in 1947 that continued upward pressure on wages was encouraging the development of marvellous new machines with which a few men could do the work of many, he retorted that no man should have to go down into the bowels of the earth to earn his daily bread! Perhaps he was right, but he must have known that most coal miners neither know nor care about any other way to earn it. The lines of gaunt, unshaven, middle-aged men who queue up every month for their free commodities at welfare offices throughout the coalfields were schoolboys when Lewis made his remark. Such men live in hope, a hope long deferred, even unto the third and fourth generation.

The art of coal mining began to be transformed in 1913 with the introduction of the first mobile, steam-powered excavating equipment (steam shovels and draglines), and strip mining, which had never accounted for more than 1 percent of output before, began to rise consistently from year to year. The new technique today accounts for much more than half of all coal dug. Meanwhile, deep-shaft mining followed suit with high technology (and expensive) underground machinery for digging and loading coal and conveying it to the surface.

The new technology vastly increased labor productivity, while demanding far more capital than the industry, so attractive to the small businessman in the old days, could readily raise. The first long-distance pipeline to convey natural gas from its source to a large urban consuming center opened between the eastern Kansas fields and Kansas City in 1907, and the small mine operators in northwest Arkansas that had lived off this market, to which they shipped what they proudly called "Spadra anthracite," languished. Much coal was dug nearby in geologically unrelated coal fields in both world wars, but it was strip-mined. Today no trace remains of the deep shaft mines that had been sunk, some of them as early as the 1870s. No visitor to the hamlet of Townley, Alabama, some sixty miles west of Birmingham, would guess that it was once a thriving mining center, but gigantic machines will soon roar through, stripping the overburden and grinding the ruins of the hotel, general store, movie theater, ballpark, and jail into final oblivion. The railroad—which began life as the Kansas City, Fort Scott & Memphis, was the Frisco for many years, and is now part of Burlington Northern—still lies only a few yards away from the "center" of town; but the long coal "drags" it stands ready to haul to electric plants will share the rails with sixty-mile-an-hour through freights carrying valuable merchandise such as new autos and shipboard containers with Japanese markings, which roar through almost hourly.

The ghosts of coal mining and coal railroad executives of the early years of this century, seeing all this, probably think that the gratuitous destruction of the American steel industry and a large part of the auto industry—major consumers of steel in the past—presages the end of coal as a fuel. If it were not for the grave question of what people will

Figure 6.2 Two heavily loaded trains of hopper cars of West Virginia coal en route on the Buchanan branch of the Norfolk Southern Railroad, June 15, 1988, to the mainline at Devon. The term "branch line" is relative, inasmuch as this particular branch produces some 30 million gross tons of freight traffic a year for the railroad. (*Norfolk Southern Corporation*)

be content to use to generate their electric power in the future, power for which their appetite seems inexhaustible in the long run, the ghosts might almost be right. But the coal industry, although it was growing weary as the twentieth century neared its close, waiting for the petroleum industry to self-destruct on the rocks of Islamic fundamentalism, is alive and well. The railroads are among the enterprises that have benefited from environmental-improvement laws that mandate the use of low-sulfur fuels in electric generating stations. Supplies of such fuels are inadequate in the populous East, so the railroads have found themselves racking up billions of ton-miles carrying eastward the "brown" (lignite) coals from the prairies of Montana and Wyoming, where Mother Nature has repeated her peculiar joke of hiding fabulous treasures beneath the bleak lands of some of the most inaccessible locations in the world. If and when technology comes forth with a clean way of burning just any old coal, this state of affairs could change almost overnight.

Today's rail-and-coal industry bears little resemblance to that of 1906, or even 1956, for it has come to consist of a few carriers (into which numerous once-familiar corporate names have disappeared) supplying a few customers—mammoth megawatt electric generating plants—under a deregulated system of rates that permits the carriers to make whatever contracts with their customers the competitive situation allows. This has not eliminated the by now familiar custom of running to government to enlist the aid of the sovereign power in beating down rates, but government is very aware that coal today is the railroads' bread and butter, and that power generation, as a high-end application of this ancient fuel, can support a rate that is far more remunerative to the railroads than coal got in the old days. Confirming this is the fact that at many nonunion mines the miners are receiving higher wages than union mines pay, a situation which might have stumped even the great John L., whose United Mine Workers has declined in violence and corruption.

Like democracy as a form of government, coal as fuel is highly undesirable except when compared to the alternatives. Government realizes that the cost of bringing this fuel to a point where it can be used must be paid, and Washington, after its harrowing experience with Penn Central and Conrail, much prefers that the cost be included in the consumer's electric bill rather than in subsidy appropriations for government-owned railroads. Meanwhile the railroads are attacking their main problem, which they assert is the excessive compensation and deficient productivity of railroad labor, with an aggressiveness that bespeaks a new era. The future is full of promise.

CHAPTER 7

Oh, the Farmer and the Townsman Must Be Friends!

> The great cities rest upon our broad and fertile prairies. Burn down your cities and leave our farms, and your cities will spring up again as if by magic; but destroy our farms, and the grass will grow in the streets of every city in the country.
>
> William Jennings Bryan, 1896

> You and I will be rich together, or we will be poor together—and I know what it means to be poor.
>
> James J. Hill, in a speech to farmers, in the 1880s

The First Two Hundred Years

Bryan had history on his side as he addressed the 1896 Democratic convention in Chicago, which eagerly devoured his version of the agrarian myth. Barely a quarter of a century before, the bustling city, well on its way to supremacy in the marketing of agricultural products, had been leveled by just the kind of conflagration that Bryan imagined, yet in a few years it had grown bigger and more prosperous than ever before. As the old century waned, Chicagoans betrayed little of the lingering gloom of the 1890s depression, for most of them had helped their city become one of America's largest. Men like Bryan believed fervently that it was the nation's farms, that primal source of all value and the embodiment of its true wealth, that had done it. The United States in 1896 was still dominated by a rural and small-town population, and at that time and for a long time afterward most Americans probably shared Bryan's belief. The truth was far more complex than even Bryan's famous talent for oversimplification could manage.

The "cities of the plain"—those flourishing urban centers such as Buffalo, Chicago, Milwaukee, Cleveland, St. Louis, Kansas City, Cincinnati, Columbus, Indianapolis, Omaha, and many others that had become the commercial centers and railroad ganglia of trans-Appalachian America—had indeed owed, if not their founding, certainly their subsequent growth to the grim determination of westering farmers to

159

find some outlet for the rich surpluses of grain and its products that they hoped would make their fondest dreams come true: a farm of their own, a more abundant life for their children, and security in their own old age. The inventive genius, capital-husbanding economy, sometimes silly optimism, and always hard, sweaty, grinding physical labor that they applied to the task of getting their bulky, low-value-per-pound produce to eastern markets at a cost that would leave them something for their labors, was downright touching. It was also ultimately discouraging for thousands who had thought to grow rich from the broad, fertile lands that had opened up to settlement after the Peace of Christmas Eve that ended the War of 1812. "We work *hard*, father, and raise a good crop, but somehow it just doesn't seem to pay," explained Daniel Webster's son, Fletcher, in 1850 as he announced that he would not return to Illinois to operate the large acreage of recently virgin prairie that his father had invested in. The problem of the Websters and their fellow pioneers was simple: they were searching for what had not yet been born, a cheap, ubiquitous, year-round system of inland transportation. As Charles Francis Adams, Jr., would put it two generations later, all they would eventually want would be a "double-track, all-steel railroad from the farmer's gate to the point of sale." But until the heady era of rapid industrial growth arrived after the Civil War, they would have to settle for a lot less.

Almost every American history textbook has, somewhere in its early pages, a map of America as it was on the eve of the War of Independence. The populated places hugged the coastline, marking the harbors that it provided, facing earnestly out at the ocean that was their only source of communication with their major trading partner, western Europe, and, very largely, with their sister colonies. The few rivers that emptied into the sea petered out a few miles inland (the Hudson was a notable exception), and they were really only extensions of the harbors leading to the plantations whose landings met the shore. Beyond the foothills of the Appalachians such maps seldom extend. This may be the mapmaker's economy, but it is also a good representation of America as it was then. Still, the urge to fill in the map was strong, and the insouciance with which landless colonists would make a great nation, defying both the Indians and the British, in settling beyond the Proclamation Line of 1763, was a major cause of the War of Independence.

On the other side of the mountains, Nature was not much more provident of highways of commerce. The rivers that drain the eastern half of the great valley of the Mississippi are few in number and puny in depth and length. The Ohio, the Cumberland, and the Tennessee are the only ones on Rand-McNally's list of the 110 longest rivers of the world. Moreover, as any schoolboy should know but probably does not, they mostly flow "the wrong way" to carry produce whose best market is in the East. But it was along these streams, and dozens of smaller ones whose names are generally unfamiliar to Americans who do not live in their vicinity, which flow into the bigger ones or into the Great Lakes, that the first settlements were made. Since these streams saw their first steam-powered vessel only after 1820, navigation upon them in the years of settlement was mostly by luck, for the flatboats that floated down with the current were a risky, dangerous means of getting produce to market. Surely there must have been some causal connection between the antebellum devotion to the little brown jug and the fact that about the only way to transport corn to market economically was as whiskey, at least until the facilities and know-how for pickling pork grew up. A good deal of that cargo was no doubt consumed on the long, tedious voyage.

The farther one was from eastern markets, of course, the harsher the realities of transportation costs, and this was true right down to the emergence of a coordinated railroad network in Indiana, Illinois, Michigan, Wisconsin, and all points west. A block of wood, thrown into most of these rivers, theoretically would end up floating past New Orleans to the Gulf of Mexico. (In truth, it would more likely end up as part of the snags that made life miserable but exciting for steamboat captains.) Willy-nilly, then, early antebellum America (or, to put it more precisely, the Old Northwest), was forced to market its surplus in a southwesterly direction and then from New Orleans, by ocean-going vessel, to east coast ports. This was true even in the case of goods destined for Europe, since backward, fun-loving New Orleans never bothered to develop the extensive financial, insurance, and shipping services that the big business of cotton, for example, demanded, while New York did.

This "counterclockwise" transportation pattern, and the early preeminence of New Orleans in it, is the conventional wisdom imparted to undergraduates, and we are complimented if they remember that much, but the truth, as the poet said, is seldom plain and never simple. There was a major domestic market for the produce of the old Northwest (Ohio, Indiana, Illinois, Michigan, and Wisconsin) in the Old Southwest (Georgia, Alabama, Mississippi, and Louisiana), and as the Civil War loomed it constituted an economic bond between these two new regions of the nation that worried wise northern leaders like Abraham Lincoln sick. The truth was that the South was preoccupied with cotton culture. It was for decades the largest single source of foreign exchange the young nation possessed, and the region could not raise enough food to provide the men and women, white and black, who labored in the fields "from first light to dark," with the high-calorie diet of carbohydrates and proteins such work demanded.

The previous paragraph will seem to some to mark the author as either an antirevisionist or very backward indeed, for this long-held interpretation was savagely attacked by the "new" economic historians when they were riding high in the 1960s and 1970s. Mere historians, with no knowledge of statistical inference, were helpless before the new "evidence" the economists-turned-historians adduced or, more accurately, synthesized, to use the most charitable word at hand. "My god, all those *numbers!*" one prominent historian remarked. But it was the economists' use of deductive reasoning (upon which their own "science" is based) that led them into a field of fatuities. It is a tragedy that only scholars can quite appreciate that economist-historians pay almost no attention to the generation of historians that preceded them or, for that matter, to their contemporaries. Abundant evidence of the dependence of the cotton South upon northern cornmeal, flour, and pork had already been assembled when the new theories were being hatched. John G. Clark, in his superb monograph, *The Grain Trade in the Old Northwest* (1966), provides all the evidence any reasonable person could want (all the *numbers* one could want, and more) that minor cities like Memphis, Natchez, and Vicksburg, for example, intercepted a huge volume of northern produce before it ever had a chance to reach New Orleans. Indeed, from dozens of anonymous landings along the broad Mississippi, Ol' Massa stood beseeching arrogant steamboat captains to drop off part of their cargo there. By the 1840s the proportion of produce going down the Ohio and Mississippi that was reaching New Orleans had dropped to an alarmingly low point. The telegraph, the Atlantic cable, and the railroads would finish the Crescent City off as an entrepôt until our own time.

That is a rudimentary sketch of transportation in the American heartland before the coming of the railroad. Primitive as arrangements were, substantial interests had become vested in them. Throughout the length of the great rivers, port cities from Cincinnati to Prairie du Chien, Dubuque, Cairo, LaCrosse, Dunleith (now East Dubuque) and many others basked in the prosperity of the era before the maturing of the eastern trunk line railroads. The immigrants and the migrants kept coming, although the South's "peculiar institution" of slavery meant that the largest numbers and the most enterprising would settle north of the Ohio and the Missouri. The impact of the railroad upon agriculture, like everything else about this most fundamental innovation in American material life, was not instantaneous. But within a generation thriving towns that had expected to become major American cities languished. They did not go quietly, as the subsequent politicization of the railroad revolution would reveal. As controversial as the railroads were to become in American politics, however, their economic impact was never in doubt. The railroad, in bringing farmers the basis for the profitability they so yearned to achieve, created a host of new urban centers while adding to the good fortune of a few that were in the right place at the right time. The American farm, after the Civil War, looked and behaved less and less like the farms of old. So did the towns and cities. Only the old rhetoric remained. The fact is that the towns and the farms created each other, because, as men like Bryan could not understand—

or, at least, could not admit—human society is a triumph of diverse forces, all highly interdependent, and not a mass of dependent or "parasitic" activities revolving around one source of all real productivity. This chapter is a synthesis of much, but by no means all, of what we have learned about the impact of universal transportation on the long and fascinating marketing process that was involved.

Grain for Our Bread—and Pork Chops, T-Bones, and Mint Juleps

Despite his several years of schooling and competence as a bookkeeper and all-round clerk, the young Englishman from the provinces who roamed London's docks one day in the 1740s had been unable to find work in the great city to support his wife and several young children who awaited his return. In desperation he had accepted a sea captain's offer of a job in the New World as bookkeeper to a Virginia planter and tutor to his children. The ship was about to sail so there was no time even to return home to say goodbye, but he knew that in a year or two he would earn enough to bring his family to America. "I shall miss you and the children dearly," he wrote his wife hastily, "but I promise you that you will eat more wheaten bread in your old age than ever you ate in your youth." That which to us is the staff of life—bread made not from rye but from wheat flour—was a luxury in that day.

In the hierarchy of grains from which a flour suitable for baking bread can be milled, wheat has always occupied top position. Although other field crops, such as rye, potatoes, and soybeans, are more efficient furnishers of nutrition, and rye constituted the chief breadstuff of simple folk in Central and Eastern Europe for centuries, other peoples have been willing to revolt if supplies of wheat failed. Neither the French, whose nation was the richest in Europe before the industrial revolution, nor the poverty-stricken southern Italians would eat anything but wheaten breads and pastas if they could get them. The New World was a land where nobody ever had to make do with less. *"In Amerika es Mann Challa in die Wochen!"* prospective Jewish immigrants from Eastern Europe told each other: "In America, people eat challa [the braided loaf of delicate white bread eaten on special occasions] in the middle of the week!"

A pretty good index of the rise of commercial farming could be had by calculating trends in the percentage of grain grown on the family farm that was not consumed on the farm. A field of wheat was about the first thing farmers everywhere planned for. Millers have existed since ancient times, as more skill and equipment are necessary than the individual farmer can supply, but about all the flour that entered into commerce originated in the share that the miller took for his services. The surplus, in other words, was small on the "self-sufficient" family farm. Another index of the rise of commercial agriculture would be the number of non-farm families that a single farmer could support. In the Middle Ages, it was probably much less than one; today, American farmers produce a surplus that supports much of the food-deficient populations throughout the world, a population far larger than their own numbers.

Wheat was a more complex thing than it seemed, however, and biological forces were at work that were hardly suspected. After wheat has been grown for a protracted period, say twenty years, in a single location in a mild, humid climate, yields begin to fall off alarmingly. The fat farms of New York and Pennsylvania, long the breadbasket of Federalist America, no longer adequately served that end by the 1820s, and the center of wheat growing had begun the steady westward movement that characterized the grain trade well into the twentieth century. By the end of the Civil War, the Old Northwest (Ohio, Indiana, Illinois, Michigan, and Wisconsin) was growing 44 percent of the nation's wheat and over one-third of its corn, and these proportions were rising rapidly. By the turn of the century the trans-Mississippi West was outpacing the old Northwest and by 1910 was producing nearly all of our wheat. Today we associate wheat with the land of Willa Cather, but in the formative decades of the railroad system it was the chief product of the Midwest, as we now call it, the fastest growing region of the nation, and along with corn provided a challenge to conventional transportation routes that they could not meet.

These are the forces behind the "canal mania" that swept the Old Northwest in the 1830s and 1840s, after the Erie Canal had proved a resounding success. By then, the Old Northwest's gigantic output—potential and real—was frantic for a practical outlet to the East. The steamboat had relieved the pressure for a time, and the market to the Southwest was being reasonably well served. (In the old days of the flatboats, very little grain had moved as grain. It went as flour—or as whiskey, pork, and lard—because as a manufactured product it had greater value per unit of weight and volume, even though flour spoils easily and is useless once it gets wet.) But the real volume market was in the Northeast, and the roundabout route via New Orleans was not satisfactory. The rocky, shallow rivers that connected the Ohio Valley with the Great Lakes were not much good for navigation, and the Lakes lay idle, although they eventually would become one of the great trade routes of the world. But these little rivers could serve to provide water for canals, and so the canals were built, and during their short heyday laid the foundation for the Old Northwest's prominence in the grain trade. At Buffalo the Lakes route fed into that manmade wonder, the Erie Canal, and the system could be extended westward, via the Lakes and the short accommodation canals that connected them, all the way to the foot of Lake Michigan and eventually the head of Lake Superior. This canal movement north from the Ohio River region to the Lakes gave early promise to such modest urbanizations as Ashtabula, Sandusky, Oswego, and Erie—as well as to Cleveland, Toledo, and

Detroit, which would eventually find their fortunes as part of the railroad system.

Now flour milling, distilling, and pork-packing establishments of considerable size arose. Flour mills continued to be a familiar sight in most populated places, but Buffalo, the logical place to convert Lakeborne wheat into canal-borne flour, was forging ahead. Cleveland, Toledo, and Detroit became important, while St. Louis, well-served by the Illinois, Missouri, and Mississippi Rivers, sewed up the southern market. But what of Milwaukee, and especially Chicago, which was to become famous for its "wheat pit" in the Board of Trade, and the greatest center for handling agricultural products and everything else, too, for that matter? The two Lake Michigan towns, which grew slowly in their early years only to burst forth with the arrival of the iron horse, were dependent upon the Illinois and Wisconsin hinterland for supplies of grain if they were to become significant entrepôts. (A city can not become an important processing or trans-shipment point just because it has some efficient way of getting rid of the goods; it must also have a dependable, high-volume source of the traffic in the first place.)

Construction of the Michigan & Illinois Canal, joining Lake Michigan at Chicago with the head of navigation on the Illinois River, which emptied into the Mississippi a few miles above St. Louis, did not bring the bulk of grain grown by Illinois farmers to Chicago. It preferred to "swim with the current" down to St. Louis. For a few short years, until the railroads extinguished their hopes for the future, various towns along the Illinois prospered, but who today ever heard of Beardstown, Illinois, one of the most historic places in midwestern history? A century and a half ago it was the major port on the Illinois below Peoria, and a pork-packing center that almost rivaled "Porkopolis" (Cincinnati) itself.

Cincinnati, however, maintained its lead as the premier disassembler of hogs and supplier of pork, pickled in brine in barrels, as well as hams, bacon, a wide variety of sausages and other specialty items, and vast quantities of that keystone of the culinary art before the age of cholesterol: *lard*. The Ohio canals served well the "Queen City," as she preferred to be called. Ohio quickly became the third most populous state in the Union, eventually displacing Virginia as the birthplace of presidents. Farmers who lived near enough to the canals or to a river that would float some kind of craft, at least during a freshet, to the nearest canal, prospered mightily as their hogs went down to the packing plants and then back up to the Lakes. The Erie Canal, on which traffic during its first decade or so had been overwhelmingly westbound, consisting mainly of immigrants and their goods, was now carrying eastward the produce of those very pioneers who had gone out a few years before.

New York was a bigger grain market than New Orleans by 1840. But the transportation situation in the Old Northwest was more unsatisfactory than ever, for into the hinterland were moving subsequent waves of settlers who were no more willing than their predecessors to haul their grain by wagon. This ancient procedure involved tying up a team, a wagon, and a man for five or six days, and it left only a meager profit even when market prices were high and the roads serviceable. Really, it did not pay at all, and it was no basis upon which to build a great nation.

Western Agriculture Surmounts the Eastern Barrier

The first locomotive to turn a wheel in the city of Chicago was the *Pioneer*, a tiny, third-hand "bicycle type" (four pilot wheels but only two drivers: ooO) belonging to the Galena & Chicago Union Railroad, then still under construction. The first section of track, from "downtown" out to Oak Ridge (now Oak Park) had just been finished on that day in 1848 when the little puffer and spindly new road of rails would set in motion events that would change not merely the nation, but the world. Out to the end of track she went, bearing several directors of the railroad and hauling, in addition to their coach, one freight car. After suitable refreshment and speechmaking, the party got back on board and the little train began the return trip to town—in reverse, as there was no wye or turning track at Oak Ridge. One of the directors noticed a farmer in the assembled crowd of onlookers, who was sitting on a wagon loaded with sacks of wheat on its way to town. Why not offer to haul the man's cargo on the train? No sooner said than done and thus the first rail shipment of wheat into Chicago was made. It was the beginning of big things.

In barely a decade, through connections by rail existed all the way from Chicago to the east coast; even more important for the moment, they had continued to send their tendrils west of the city into what shortly became one of the most fruitful farming regions in the world. The produce of these areas between Chicago and the Mississippi made her number one in grain handling and processing as early as the end of the Civil War, but it was only the beginning. The rails had paused only momentarily at the once-formidable barrier of the Father of Waters: the first bridge over the Mississippi was in operation before the war, and by the end of the 1860s the rails had invested the new states of Iowa, Minnesota, Nebraska, and Kansas and, less obviously, begun an era of intensive technological development of rail transportation that has never ended.

In 1848 enterprising grain dealers built the first steam-operated grain elevator on the lakefront, and by 1852 Chicago was receiving more gain by rail than by wagon and canal combined. Acceptance of the new transportation mode was strikingly fast; by 1860 the Illinois Central and Chicago, Burlington & Quincy Railroads had built grain elevators of record-breaking size on the lake, and a growing army of grain dealers were keeping them filled. For a few years, most grain and flour would be trans-shipped to lake vessels at Chicago and to Erie Canal boats at Buffalo, but rail rates declined steeply after 1873, and long before the century was over the railroads had claimed most of the grain movement east. St. Louis was soon "eating Chicago's dust" as a grain entrepôt and would spend the next fifty years attributing its neglect to almost anything save the truth, which was its backwardness in providing handling facilities and a railroad bridge across the Mississippi to make a through rail route to the East.

Flour deserted the water for the rails sooner than grain, because of its greater value per pound. In fact, the railroads made long-distance shipment of flour feasible, and thus flour milling declined east of the Appalachians, although it has never entirely disappeared. Buffalo became the logical point at which to terminate wheat's progress as wheat and to turn it into flour, as reflected in freight rates for wheat inbound by lake to Buffalo that fell from twenty cents per bushel in 1854 to six cents in 1858, quoting end-of-season rates. Of course, once the short, hot summer of the Midwest ended and the lakes and canals froze over, the railroads got it all. By the end of the century they were keeping a large part of it, as grain or as flour, throughout the year. By nineteenth century standards, Buffalo's facilities for producing flour were truly eye-popping. The tall, wooden grain elevators that lined the lakefront gave the city a skyline even before the age of the skyscraper arrived, and on one occasion awed the citizenry with one of the most spectacular conflagrations in memory.

Westward, Ho!

With such vastly improved transportation and handling facilities at their doorstep, the promise of ever-increasing railroad facilities, the end of the Civil War, a suddenly active export market for food grains to damp, chilly Europe, and a resumption of the steady flow of immigrants and migrants, the Old Northwest looked westward with renewed ardor. By 1870 the rails of several emerging "granger" railroads were leaping across the Missouri River onto the flat, fertile, treeless prairies of the Great Plains. A new era in agriculture was being born, the virtues of which were far more apparent than the vices that attended transplanting eastern farming methods into a land of undependable and highly variable rainfall. Settlement—meaning the distribution of the national domain into private hands—became a red-hot political issue, and an expansionist Congress, its Senate no longer frustrated by diehard states-righters, passed measure after measure during the Civil War looking to rapid settlement of the West.

In the years before the onset of federal instrumentalist policies, the young nation had hardly been able to give the prairie lands away. Most notable and hardly believable when one surveys the valuable farmlands of east central Illinois, were the prairie counties almost due south of Chicago. Contrary to popular belief, settling these pancake-flat regions demanded more capital than a typical spread back east. The very flatness was a drawback, for after the spring thaws, and especially in a rainy year, much of the land would lie under water until well past planting time. Many lands had to be drained, giving rise to a new industry, clay drainage pipe, for the young state, and the lack of timber meant that the raw material of barns and homesteads had to be brought in from a distance. There were no streams worthy of even the humblest ancestor of the *African Queen.* Withal, immigrants avoided these lands. The problem, of course, was that the cost of settlement could never be justified until cheap transportation conferred upon these lands a profitability as yet nonexistent.

Just who provided the economic theory behind the idea of granting public land to enterprises that would build a railroad through them is uncertain, but it probably was not Stephen A. Douglas, Illinois' increasingly prominent Democratic politician, nor any of the other men who finally succeeded in getting a land grant bill in aid of construction of the Illinois Central Railroad through Congress in 1850. The idea had been opposed vigorously for at least ten years, but people had finally come round to it, and as the iron horse continued to prove itself, people's natural pragmatism won the idea its approval many years before economic theory explained it. Even Horace Greeley, about whom many a prudent politician might have said that he wished he could be as sure of *anything* as Greeley was about *everything,* was won over. Before that loose cannon, the Credit Mobilier affair, panicked the deck crew of American politics in 1873, thousands of miles of new railroad, encouraged by gifts of millions of acres of "free" land, were undertaken. After that, American railroad builders were on their own—as most of them had been, anyway, for most of the industry's history—and the absence of land grants made little if any difference in the expansion of the railroad network, even in the South.

Looking back, it would seem that almost no continuing American political and economic issue can touch federal land policy for the amount of heat it generated. The outcome, in retrospect, seems never to have been in doubt, as the settlers were not to be denied, regardless of what Washington did. Once the railroads were built, the exploiters of the land were right behind them. Reminiscing in the 1950s about the golden summer days of his boyhood that he had spent on his grandparents' Iowa farm thirty years before, an author recalled that he had been awakened at six o'clock each morning by the whistle of the overnight express from Chicago, which was due in Des Moines in three hours. How fortunate, he had thought then, that his great-grandparents had settled on land across which the Chicago, Rock Island & Pacific Railroad would later decide to build its mainline. It was years later that he learned that the railroad had come *before* his ancestors had homesteaded their farm. What had enticed them there was perhaps what a contemporary had written about neighboring Wisconsin. One could acquire a farm for about one-tenth the cost of a farm in New York State, he wrote, and therefore, "for ten years to come stock of all kinds can be raised for about one-fourth the cost of raising in New York, and grain for about one-half. The transportation will never exceed 20 per cent, rarely 15, and on wool and similar articles will not exceed 3 to 5 per cent."

The railroads' contribution to the emergence of modern America, and especially modern, low-cost, high-surplus agriculture, may have been forgotten or obfuscated by revisionist historians in recent years, but understanding came swiftly to Americans who lived through the process. The 1870s were the decade when the true promise of rail transportation was made manifest. As a technical innovation the railroad was half a century old, or nearly, by 1873, but its time had come, and the realization burst upon Victorian America with the force of a thunderbolt. Congress, or at least its Democratic members, were determined to follow the investigation of alleged excess profits by the Credit Mobilier in building the Union Pacific Railroad with further evidence of their superior grasp of the western farmer's plight. The majority appointed a Select Committee on Transportation Routes to the Seaboard to find out just what was needed to supply the farmer with long-distance, cheap transportation to the only major markets for his produce. The Committee's report to the Forty-Third Congress in 1874, invariably referred to as the Windom Report, in honor of its chairman, Senator William Windom of Minnesota, despaired of the railroads' ability or willingness ever to lower rates to a point where massive volumes of freight could economically move. While recognizing that an all-steel, double-track railroad from the heartland to New York (which by then had become the premier port of the United States) was one possibility, the report plumped for a combination of revival, rebuilding, and new construction of inland waterways—that is, canals. One such ditch, embracing the Kanawha River in the wilds of West Virginia, would have called for a tunnel through the mountains nine miles long with five vertical shafts!

Perhaps no other important report of such a dignified Congressional body was ever so totally outdated within weeks of its appearance. At that moment the Baltimore & Ohio Railroad had finally completed a through line from the seaboard to Chicago, and the Grand Trunk Railway of Canada was cooperating with other railroads between the East and Chicago, thus adding a third and a fourth trunk line almost overnight. The first Bessemer steel rails from the pioneering American steel industry, notably those from Andrew Carnegie's ultra-low-cost mills, had begun to replace the old wrought iron rails as fast as American railroads could get their hands on them (and pay for them with money raised at the beginning of a three-year depression). Longer trains of

heavier cars, pulled by bigger locomotives across steel bridges and trestles that had replaced wooden ones, were soon chugging through the
cornfields. The depression, like all depressions, was meanwhile having
its cathartic effects as American costs of production in all lines of business began a twenty-five-year decline.

New handling facilities, long a demand of western farmers, now
sprang up in terminal cities, making it possible to move crops whose
size no one could have imagined two or three years earlier. New York
became the most important grain-handling port in the country, and
against its skyline were raised ungainly towers that might qualify as
Gotham's first skyscrapers: grain elevators. Even to imagine anything
as prosaic or as rural as grain elevators in chic Manhattan is difficult,
but in 1879 some seventeen stationary and floating wooden structures,
with a total capacity of 16.4 million bushels of grain, dotted Manhattan
and Brooklyn waterfronts.

Meanwhile, in the previous ten years, average rates for all kinds of
goods on the New York Central had declined from 2.7 cents per ton-
mile to 0.9 cents (nine mills!); on the Pennsylvania, from 1.9 to 0.9
cents; and on the Lake Shore & Michigan Southern, the Central's
extension from Buffalo to Chicago, from 2.3 cents to the incredibly low
figure of 0.7 cents, reflecting the remarkable efficiency of that flat,
straight, well-built railroad. Out west, similar trends had been noted:
in the heart of the corn belt, the Chicago, Burlington & Quincy had
lowered its rates from 3.2 to 1.2 cents. (Rates, as any transportation
expert then and now could attest, have a negative correlation with the
volume of traffic.)

In 1879, the real declines had just begun, and uncontrolled competition already was causing even more discontent among shippers,
who needed to know that everybody was paying the same rate and that
it would be reasonably stable. Meanwhile, the Erie Canal had lowered
its rates from 0.9 to 0.4 cents, but when the shipper considered the cost
of insurance for his water-borne cargo, which he did not require on the
common-carrier railroads, and the slowness and the seasonality of canal
transport, its slight cost advantages faded. As it was, the Erie Canal's
income did not pay for even normal maintenance, and its banks were
beginning to fall into the channel.

A Practical Way to Distribute the Public Domain

Whoever nowadays thinks that the railroad land grants represented
nothing less than gigantic "subsidies," or that all the railroads had to
do was open a land office and rake in the settlers' money, has none but
himself to blame for his ignorance. Still, a common retort to even the
mildest assertion that the people have been rather hard on their railroads, is, "And what about the millions of acres of free land that the
railroads got?" Some years ago a badly flawed biography of Alexander

Figure 7.1   View of New York Central's freight yards on the North (Hudson) River in the 1880s, when midtown was still relatively open country. The immense grain elevator bespeaks New York's preeminence as an export port for western grain to a Europe that had lost its self-sufficiency in breadstuffs.

Cassatt, who led the mighty Pennsylvania Railroad into the twentieth century, asserted that the Pennsy had received huge grants of public lands, when all but the village idiot knew at one time that no such grants were made to the Pennsylvania, but to build railroads that lacked any substantial sources of freight or passenger traffic. Few Americans have ever heard of, much less read, Richard Overton's study of the colonization policies of the Chicago, Burlington & Quincy Railroad in Iowa, or Paul Gates's work on the Illinois Central, both of which tell a far different story.

Distribution of the granted lands, beginning in the 1850s and continuing into recent times, despite the determination of the public, in their lust for cheap farms, to build a fire under the railroads, was a wearying, long-drawn-out administrative task. Before any lands could even be put up for sale, the companies had to determine just what they had! Under the preemption law, a sensible and humane statute that gave squatters who had become genuine, well-established settlers the right to buy their lands at low cost, the companies first had to identify such potential claimants and arrange to settle with them. Title to swampy land was retained under the law by the states, thus tempting them to claim swamps where none existed; this led to tiresome wrangling. Speculators were a thorn in the companies' side, as large acreages of both railroad land and the one-half retained by the government were engrossed by people who hoped that scarcity would raise market prices. Much of the land that the railroads were accused of holding off the market in defiance of the law was actually in the hands of owners who had no intention of settling there themselves.

One thing that could really push up the value of land was the selection of the site for a new town. The Illinois Central, indeed, was as much in the business of creating towns as selling farms, or so it seemed for a while. Speculation in town lots was inevitable, no matter how hard the railroad tried to prevent it. Some sites that were supposed to become towns did not, while others that did failed to flourish, all to the disgruntlement of owners of town lots. Many towns that had thrived before the railroads came were ignored by the new, straight-as-an-arrow pair of iron rails, among them such long-forgotten places as Montezuma, Gloster, Moscow, Caledonia, and New Bedford. (At least we can guess where their settlers had come from.)

But location on a railroad was no guarantee of permanent prosperity. Cairo, smug and confident at the confluence of the mightiest two rivers in the nation, the Ohio and the Mississippi, stagnated. Galena, northwest of Chicago, had enjoyed an early heyday as a source of the lead ore that gave it its name, but mines don't last. Dunleith, once the end of the track across the river from Iowa and the place where early travelers changed to a river steamboat, was upstaged by Dubuque when the inevitable bridge was built. Meanwhile, Centralia, Bloomington, Kankakee, and Champaign-Urbana, seat of the new University of Illinois, thrived. Yet the big story, as all of these railroads reached out to gather together the crops and to deliver the endless array of manufactured goods that the settlers suddenly found they could not do without, was Chicago. While the railroads were making of Illinois the classic state of small towns (it contains to this day only one really large city), they were making Chicago into what would be for many years the second-largest city in America. If New York, with its superb seaport and unmatched rail connections, became the crossroads of the world, Chicago could claim that it was the crossroads of America.

The painful task of unraveling the tangled web that government always weaves when it tries to give away the people's goods fell to the railroads in the case of granted lands. They got more than a little help, to be sure, from agents of the states, which had interests to watch out for, but the dozens of problems that arose and the procedure for dealing with them fell to railroad men. The Burlington, with its powerful Boston connections, sought the best man they could find to manage their land matters in Iowa, which was filling up fast. Out from Boston came Charles Russell Lowell, brother of the poet James, still in his early twenties. He brought to the task a combination of a capacity for hard work and a cultivated sense of humor. His description of the proper policy for the railroad in dealing with persons who had squatted, presumably by mistake, on railroad land and had invested much toil and their slender capital in its improvements, is revealing. "Make only a cursory examination," he counseled his agents, "then pat the children on the head, swear they are the image of their father, and leave all in a good humor. However valid our claim, and however valuable the land, I fancy it will always be our policy to charge *bona fide* residents only our minimum rates." Regrettably, such decency and good sense are seldom associated in our history books with railroad land policies. Jesse James is better copy than Charles Russell Lowell.

Administering a land grant was work that demanded attention to incredible detail, and Lowell came close to knowing every landmark, however minor, about more of the seemingly featureless Illinois prairie than anyone else who ever lived. In the end it was all too much, and he resigned to go into an entirely different line of work. Eventually, Americans would tend to tar all their railroad corporations with the same black brush, but the relatively good reputation over the years of the Burlington and the Illinois Central owed much to the good sense of men like Lowell and, of course, to the opportunity to make money, of which there was enough to go around.

Did the proceeds of land-grant land sales pay for the building of the railroads? Hardly, nor were they supposed to. Overton notes that the Burlington disposed of some 2.8 million acres in Iowa and Nebraska (more than 85 percent of it in Nebraska) for a total net profit, after expense, of $15.9 million, which was only a small fraction of the total net worth of these lines by the year 1900. He estimates that the total was slightly more than enough to pay for construction of the mainline from Burlington, Iowa, to Kearney Junction, Nebraska, excluding the Plattsmouth bridge. All of these heavily traveled lines, of course, were constantly rebuilt to accommodate more and heavier trains. Meanwhile, the values of farm lands in the counties fortunate enough to be on the mainline rapidly outstripped those that were not.

Gates paints a picture of social change that the land-grant program wrought in Illinois. From 1854 to 1900, he notes, the Illinois Central made some 40,000 to 45,000 sales of land to dispose of 2.6 million acres. In the 1850s the population of Illinois had been concentrated in the south, reflecting the importance of St. Louis, the nearness of the Ohio River, and the isolation of central Illinois. The majority were Scotch-Irish "southern uplanders," of whom Gates entertained the same poor reputation they had had back in South Carolina, from which many of them had migrated. They were Democrats to a man, but they lost dominance in state politics to frugal, hard-working Germans, Scandinavians, Celts, and Yankees, who joined the new Republican party. The railroad revolution extended right down to grass-roots politics.

Settlement of the semi-arid Great Plains, up to the Canadian border and into the foothills of the Rocky Mountains, is not the same story of virtually unbroken success. At times, it has seemed like a story of unbroken failure. Most of the novels and short stories, the political diatribes, and the efforts at regional history of Kansas, Nebraska, the Dakotas, and Montana, emphasize a bittersweet saga of hardships, triumph over adversity, psychological tragedy, and the stubborn refusal of easterners to recognize the moral superiority of westerners! When times were good, they were bearable and full of hope for the future; and when they were bad, they were horrid. Apart from the lunar aspect of the land, which inspired many a displaced easterner's doleful lament, there was the matter of rainfall.

In the early 1870s, when the legend of the Great American Desert was being verified by explorers, it was dry indeed on the Great Plains. A decade later, new arrivals must have wondered what the complaints were all about, for the wet part of the cycle that people did not yet understand had arrived. The railroad companies, with hundreds of thousands of arid acres on their hands and mile after dusty mile of railroad line to build, were only a little less optimistic than individual promoters, like Paris Gibson, early touter of Montana, who declared to James J. Hill that the danger was rather from too much moisture than too little. (Gibson ended up broke.)

Given half a basis for predicting success, settlers continued to crowd in. There soon were too many people producing too much wheat, on lands that were less and less productive, and getting too low a price for it in world markets. This was the case by the 1880s, despite the fact that Europe had become a steady, good customer for American foodstuffs. Jim Hill tended, as we might expect, to see the problem through Calvin-tinted glasses: "No man can live for 12 months on seven months' work," he declared, but he watched his heroic efforts to encourage diversification of farming on the Great Plains come to naught. Understanding little or nothing of the global economics of the commodities market, the farmer accused the railroads and the speculators on the Board of Trade for taking too large a chunk of what was rightfully his. The price in Liverpool was really all his, the farmer would argue, because he had produced it. "I produce for all," proclaimed the famous poster that the leading farmer uplift society, the Grangers, distributed. Therefore anything that middlemen deducted for their services was not a service, but a "tax," and so went the political rhetoric. Not for the embattled American farmer, nor the politician who coveted his vote, was the abstract idea that transportation creates value.

Meat on the Table

"I pray you, eat without bread," says the Italian peasant who desires to impress the guest at his table. "Beans are the meat of the poor," someone else has said. Both observations underscore how highly meat has been prized by human beings as an item in the diet, and how often it has been missing. Notwithstanding the earnest efforts of reforming vegetarians, however, the vast majority of human beings will probably continue to relish meat, if not at every meal, at least once a day, and would prefer fresh, red meat most of the time, at that. Only in our day, however, and then only in the lands that have attained a very high standard of material well-being, has the majority been able to satisfy this desire.

With few exceptions, Americans, unlike their European cousins, have never lacked for a *source* of fresh meat or the many appetizing (or at least exotic) forms in which people have learned to preserve it. In a land where pigs could gorge themselves on corn surpluses and, in summer, on the big, fat acorns of the forests, while cattle browsed spacious meadows and munched a large portion of the grain harvests, there was plenty of meat to be had—if someone could think of a way to get it to market. It was not much more than a hundred years ago that people living in the flourishing eastern seaboard cities began to enjoy roasts, steaks, chops, and the like that had not arrived in their vicinity still mooing, grunting, or bleating. Pork, pickled in brine or preserved in the forms that it adapts so well to, was acceptable to Americans who could not get the freshly butchered item, but preserved beef emphatically was not. Europeans might settle for it; Americans wanted theirs bright-red fresh. At least by the end of the Civil War they were getting superior western cattle on the hoof for local slaughtering, which was an improvement on the traditional local cattle of pre-railroad times, which so often included a large number of superannuated milch cows and tough old bulls whose harems had deserted them.

Daniel Drew, the prototype of the "robber baron" best loved by American historians and other mythologists, who capped his career in early American finance with a knockdown, drag-out fight with Commodore Vanderbilt for control of the Erie Railroad (Jay Gould won!) invented "watered stock," or so many historians who know so many things that are not so still preach. As a poor boy from upstate New York, he began life as a drover, that extinct functionary who made his living by driving live cattle remarkably long distances (towards the end of the pre-railroad era, from as far away as Ohio) and after whom so many expensive New England restaurants and quaint country inns are named today. "Dan'l," it seems, always gave his tired, thirsty, and probably more than a little emaciated beasts a good, long drink of water before taking them to the local buyer at the livestock yards that once gave elegant residents of New York's Murray Hill a powerful reason to desert the city in the summer. Thus, like his investor-victims later on, unsuspecting livestock buyers would pay good meat prices for pure water. (Anyone who still believes that only Dan'l was sharp enough to think of such a gambit, or that the hardened livestock buyers did not make allowances for it, is naive enough to qualify as a professor of American history anywhere.)

The first intensive use of the new trunk line railroad connections to Chicago was to bring live meat animals to eastern cities, where they would be slaughtered and distributed according to traditional practices. Thus, the joining of Chicago and other midwestern points to the eastern seaboard by rail, or even the advent of dramatically lower rates, did not by itself bring about the rise of large-scale meatpacking establishments. Chicago would remain a "way station" for live cattle on their way from western prairies to eastern markets by rail. The cattle car, an ugly, cruel aspect of railroading, became the symbol of any inhumane conveyance, but it was a vital part of America's food chain until men had a better idea. Meanwhile, Cincinnati, dubbed "Porkopolis," hinted at the grandeur that Chicago would attain as "hog butcher to the world." The reason that Cincinnati became big in pork packing a generation earlier than Chicago is that Porkopolis had good transportation from a well-settled farming territory to the north, first via the valuable (if economically disastrous) Ohio canal system, and by the 1840s by some of the earliest railroads built in America. Thus Cincinnati had a steady, abundant supply of hogs ready for slaughter and an artery near at hand, the Ohio River, to convey her pickled pork, bacon, and hams to the slaveholding states with whom the Old Northwest had such well-cemented economic relations before the coming of the trunk line railroads.

According to Mary Yeager (now Lithgow), the modern authority on the rise of "oligopoly," or competition shared by a handful of large meatpacking companies, Cincinnati was in no wise a prototype of the Chicago that became the giant of the industry. Little attention was paid to product innovation—most Americans knew neither premium quality nor variety in their cuisine in those days—reflecting an industry composed of a large number of concerns (as many as ninety-six), accounting for at most 28 percent of the national pork pack in the 1840s and only 19 percent in the 1850s. Porkopolis was wiped out by Chicago's enterprising spirit, which was determined to change the situation livestock men encountered on the shores of lower Lake Michigan. The Chicago Union Stockyards, which enveloped the city in a fetid smell of success for the ensuing century, rose on the south side's rapidly disappearing vacant land in 1865, by which time Chicago was receiving over fifty-six thousand cattle a year. The railroads contributed most of the capital for the yards and never regretted it for a minute, in view of both the handsome return on their investment and the gigantic source of high-class freight traffic that the yards created. It was a centralized, full-service market, with due attention to the needs legitimate and otherwise of the weary livestock men whose only female companionship for weeks had been a trainload of bawling cows. Banks, hotels, and saloons brought members of the trade together in one place, and, in no time, uniform methods of doing business had developed that had been unknown in the chaotic days of the drovers. Hauling live cattle and other meat animals eastward to market quickly became a highly profitable source of revenue for the railroads serving Chicago. They would not find the next big change in the American meat industry an unmixed blessing, but others soon saw clearly that the railroad revolution had barely begun.

As with most inventions, it is an oversimplification to say that one person—in this case, Gustavus Swift—invented the refrigerator car that made hauling dressed carcasses long distances practical. Swift was not merely an inventor, although he was one of the few who saw that free circulation of chilled air through the cargo was necessary, and that lack of it accounted for the failure of earlier efforts. Swift *was* an inventor, but he was also an entrepreneur, and the two should never be confused; nor are they found in effective combination very often. His vital role was to put a good idea in the way of being realized in practice. Already well established in the meat business, and with excellent connections back East, he put his improved car on the rails in 1878. The railroads, with huge investments in livestock cars, dug in their heels and refused to build "reefers," so Swift had ten cars built on his own account. The impasse was soon resolved by the cutthroat competition between the trunk line railroads that had led to a scramble for volume. No minor factor in the situation was a maverick line, the Grand Trunk Western, a Canadian line that formed a trunk line with various eastern railroads.

The railroads were not, in the end, Swift's biggest problem, for he had his hands full fighting the inevitable resistance that his sides of dressed beef encountered at their destination. Independent meat wholesalers, despite the lower delivered prices at which Swift sold his Chicago-dressed beef, were afraid of rumors that they were carrying moldy beef. What is more, cold storage facilities on the scale needed for stocking and handling the dressed carcasses did not exist, although considerable improvements in mechanical refrigeration had been made, largely because ships used in the export trade of dressed meats had demanded them. In pursuit of his vision of a revolutionized industry, Swift got in deeper and deeper. He bought into wholesale meat concerns at important rail destinations, and he pushed his salesmen hard. Since many dealers did not want entire carcasses, for example, he urged his salesmen to "cut the meat and scatter it out," thus anticipating a much later development in meat distribution.

By not shipping the 45 percent, by weight, of an animal that was not salable as meat, Swift could sell carcasses for as much as 75 cents a hundredweight below the price that a dealer who started with a live animal had to get. As a result, meat prices fell dramatically during the rest of the century. Beef tenderloins at wholesale averaged 27.5 cents in 1883, but only 16.75 cents in 1889, a 40 percent drop. Tallow, a widely used by-product that was rendered in vast quantities in highly centralized locations once Swift's revolution had become general, fell 50 percent in price. Throughout American industry, equally dramatic reductions in the real costs of production were being achieved. It is remarkable how many of them stemmed directly or indirectly from the transportation revolution. As for the meatpacking industry, it would never be the same again. Swift's business had turned highly profitable by 1882, and by 1886 he controlled 31 percent of the cattle slaughtered at Chicago. His closest competitor was Philip D. Armour, who controlled 24 percent, while Cudahy and the firm that became Wilson & Co. were also important factors. All of these companies, taken together, also supplied most of urban America's fresh pork, while more and more small towns came to depend on the new industry as well. The American standard of living rose accordingly.

The structure that the meat industry was to have, with certain modifications as the federal government bore down on the "trusts," had emerged with stunning swiftness, and it endured until the coming of the motor truck in intercity transportation after about 1930. It was part and parcel of a larger trend, which was the emergence of the large, highly integrated manufacturing enterprise, about which we shall have more to say later. The level of technological development—cold storage facilities, intercity transportation, and local methods of doing business—plus greater emphasis upon marketing and advertising as American media were revolutionized, dictated the evolution of a handful of very large firms that controlled the nation's supply of meat from the Great Plains all the way to the local butcher. At its high-water mark, the "meat trust" coalesced into a single giant firm, reflecting the fact that even a few independent giants had not yet mastered the art of price stability under oligopolistic conditions. This was too much for a people bred on an antimonopoly diet, and down to recent times the centralized industry has tended to shrivel.

First the trust was broken up. Later on, the effort of the meatpackers to recoup their disappearing profit margins were rebuffed. (By the 1920s the total wholesale value of the edible cuts of meat in an animal on the hoof came to less than the cost of the animal to the packer, and what profit there was lay in the by-product.) "Your honor, we want to sell at retail," was the plaintive plea of counsel for the packers when the trustbusters, in 1956, attacked their plans to establish their own retail stores and sell a wide variety of products that could increase utilization of their millions of dollars of cold-storage space. Many a middle-aged American today still remembers Swift's Brookfield Brand sausages (including the little links that were a novelty in most Americans' diets) and "creamery butter," which mothers in small towns sneered at in favor of "country butter," churned locally, but upon which they depended more and more heavily. U.S. District Judge Julius J. Hoffman was like stone, however, and the big packers never got to sell in their own retail stores. Meanwhile the perfection of the motor truck, rolling on pneumatic tires on federally financed hard-surface highways, brought about a return to regional packing concerns. It was just what Judge Hoffman and little-business champions like Louis Brandeis could have wanted—but it did not last. Antitrust is a horse which, once you are astride it, may well take you places you had not expected or wanted to go.

At first a host of new brand names appeared on the sides of refrigerator trucks. Developments—retrogression, really—in government regulation of transportation had had much to do with it. Senator Albert B. Cummins, of Iowa, a stalwart Progressive, early in the century had condemned the railroads' low long-distance rates between major terminal cities and relatively high intermediate rates for having put the local and regional packers out of business by 1910. It was one of the few recorded examples of a politician complaining of low railroad rates. By the early 1930s the railroads were forbidden to cut their rates to compete with trucks driven by men desperate for work, and until 1935 truckers could charge any rates they wanted. To this day, truck transportation of *unprocessed* agricultural commodities, including live animals, is free of any rate regulation.

But where did the antitrust horse take us? The latest chapter in this story of technological change complicated by the fatuities of government intervention in economic affairs is a return to centralization. The fifty-year revolution in the retailing of food products has recently accelerated, and any couple who have staggered out the door of a modern supermarket with six big bags of groceries knows why: the drive to save labor costs. Meat cutters today get paid almost as much as steelworkers, and they are doing as efficient a job of destroying their occupation as the steelworkers have done. "Boxed beef" and, more recently, "boxed pork" are the latest thing. A few giant companies process a volume of live animals that would have made even Gustavus Swift sit up and take notice. They go in one end of the plant, and corrugated cartons of steaks, chops, roasts, briskets, hamburger, etc., come out the other. Rushed to market, no longer exclusively by motor truck but also in refrigerated trailers carried on railroad flatcars, or in containers, and often moving directly into the holds of vessels at Oakland, Houston, New Orleans, Port of Newark, and a few other latter-day ports that have replaced New York in preeminence, these ready-to-cook meats have only to be placed neatly in block-long refrigerated display cases and the customer does the rest.

The story of how Americans have found a life and an occupation on the land, and the overriding significance of feed- and foodgrains and the products that are made from it, is one of closed avenues of growth that transportation innovations have repeatedly helped to open. It is very largely a railroad story, and so it remains to this day. An entire book would not be sufficient to exhaust the story.

Done Come to Take de Cotton Away

> Say, darky, hab' you seen Ol' Massa,
>   Wid' de muftash on his face,
> Go along de road so early in de mornin'
>   Lak he gwine to leab de place?

But "Ol' Massa" did not leave the place, or if he did he came right back, whatever the jubilant spirit conveyed in the old Negro minstrel song. Historians who continue to trouble the ghosts of the antebellum South, and the devastated land that struggled to regain its feet in the decades following the Civil War, have produced some bizarre analyses of that unique society, most of which betray the academic scholar's distaste for the most obvious explanations. Like all societies that have been shaken to their foundations, the cotton economy of the South in 1865 faced two problems: how to get the old productive machine back into operation, and then how to adapt to the rapid changes in the cotton trade that had already been on the horizon in 1860. Any other, more idealistic notions of social re-engineering were bound to get a low priority, not merely from southerners but sooner or later from northerners as well.

Not the least bizarre of the pictures that historians have drawn of the cotton South is that of the "feudal society." This conceit goes back to the 1840s, when southern editors, drunk on the overcooked, romantic sentimentality of such authors as Sir Walter Scott, declared that the South was by nature a superior society, in which the most aristocratic men ruled and all other classes, white and black, fell automatically into line. Even then, it was too much for many a plantation owner to stomach who often felt anything but noble after he had disbursed his cotton receipts against his seasonal indebtedness. "Does this mean that we should all go and live in castles?" one of them is said to have grumbled. The feudal claptrap lives on, having been adopted by a certain class of academic historian to fill a gap in the application of Marxist ideology to American economic development (something that Marx himself was too shrewd to try). Since Marxist orthodoxy requires a precapitalist stage, the slaveholding South was elected to fill the bill. Slaves, like serfs, are not paid a wage; therefore, they are not "labor" in the capitalist sense, and the plantation owner does not behave like a capitalist. Or so it goes.

What has all this to do with railroads? Just that the South, like all societies at all times since civilization began, required capital—lots of it—but had it sunk in "human capital," that is, slaves. This capital was destroyed, in a sense, by the Thirteenth Amendment, although the blacks' labor power remained available. Meanwhile the advance of technology offered the South a new transportation regime that demanded great aggregations of capital—something the South had never developed any aptitude for assembling—and promised even greater rewards. The railroads, in short, would be the key to the New

South. They had barely made a start, and the railroad revolution in the South would be a pale echo of what was happening in the North in the last half of the nineteenth century, but slowly it unfolded. The impact upon what had long been the South's main industry, and would remain such until the middle of the twentieth century, was in every way revolutionary. In amazingly short order, a new labor system based on sharecropping got everybody back to work, preserving the supervisory function of Ol' Massa while tapping as much individual enterprise as the uneducated black man could muster. At the same time, old marketing institutions, such as the antebellum cotton factor, declined and the modern system of interior buying replaced it.

As Harold Woodman demonstrates in his *King Cotton and His Retainers* the first seventy-five years or so of the king's reign were the age of the cotton factor. This gentleman, who was absolutely indispensable before about 1870, was a prominent member of that breed of middlemen who wrestled supplies to planters and produce to market and, in the process, produced the characteristically high marketing costs of the prerailroad era. For nearly a century the factor tied the loose ends of a barely visible marketing chain together.

It takes a vivid historical imagination to grasp how isolated were the plantations and small farms on which Americans grew their biggest foreign exchange earner in the antebellum years and, in the more backward areas, for some years thereafter. Transportation and communication, or the lack of it, was at the heart of the problem. Roads were vestigial in the best of times, and little more than well-marked seas of mud in the wet season. It was a world that depended upon its rivers, such as they were, and their names appear prominently in southern literature. The vaunted southern hospitality arose out of the fact that weeks might go by on even the richest of planations without anyone interesting to talk politics or gossip with happening by, and the mail was usually months late. Counties abounded, as did county seat towns, but such towns were rarely more than country villages. The South retained a backwoods image even after the railroad was a common sight in most places. Before the adoption of standard time, a traveling salesman who had penetrated deep into the "boondocks" is said to have inquired whether the clock in the courthouse was set for railroad time or sun time, and received the reply, "Take your choice, mister; you're as far from one as the other." Two counties in Arkansas never had a mile of railroad, and this was not uncommon. But the railroads came close to providing universal mobility until the modern motor truck arrived to supplement them.

The planters depended upon factors to procure for them practically everything that could not be fashioned on the plantation by skilled workers—comprising at best the few black men who had learned simple carpentry and blacksmithing. (Plumbing required no attention, since there was none). Few planters would have known the source of the tools, supplies, and provisions that were called for in quantity by large-scale cotton culture. All they knew how to do was raise cotton. For virtually all of the materials and tools that went into growing it, and for disposition of the crop, they depended upon the factors, businessmen who were generally located at primary shipping points on major rivers or ports on the southeastern Atlantic seaboard. Their chief function, of course, was to accept the planter's cotton on consignment and sell it at his direction or hold it for the best price, all consequent storage costs to be paid by the planter. In practice, the factor was the producer's purchasing agent, banker, and wise counsel about the affairs of a world that grew more perplexing every year.

As the railroads erased the isolation of the communities through which they were built, they destroyed the factor's reason for being. The steamboat on the river in combination with the fleet schooner in coastal service have lived in literature, but they failed to bring the efficiency and dependability of long-distance transportation that the rise of the world cotton textile industry demanded and that American cotton culture so badly needed. As the railroad network matured into the heavy-duty, lost-cost system of hauling goods that it was to become, cotton deserted its traditional routes to market. The transition had barely begun on the eve of the Civil War. By the end of the 1870s it was virtually complete.

We have said that it was the ability of the railroads to go virtually *everywhere* that was their most unique characteristic. Trunk lines stretching across the rapidly industrializing Northeast, and transcontinentals linking ocean with ocean, are more dramatic, but they should not obscure the fact that, especially in the South, the coming of the railroad made even the tiniest hamlet a full-fledged partner in the national system. As the crop was harvested, the local hotel—it was the era of the classic American commercial hotel—blossomed with *buyers* of cotton for the textile mills, not only of New England but of Europe as well. They were working for cotton-buying firms, of course, in most cases, but the point is that they were buying, not seeking to persuade the growers to ship their cotton to them to be sold for whatever it would bring. With the telegraph and the Atlantic cable at hand, even the lowliest cotton buyer knew what he could pay from day to day. Everybody tended to get into the act, until the inevitable thinning out took place and cotton buying became concentrated in a few very large firms. But there was always somebody to buy your cotton, once the railroad had turned an ancient system into a modern business, even if it was only a local merchant whom the railroad had put in the business of supplying the goods that the factor had seen to before.

"The first direct shipment of cotton from Memphis to Liverpool, by the Northern or overland route, was made on Saturday last. The shipment consisted of three hundred bales. It will be taken to Pittsburgh by water, thence to New York via the Pennsylvania Central Rail-

road, and to Liverpool by the usual means of transportation, there to
be sold on account of the Memphis shipper." This brief item, which
appeared in a Memphis newspaper in the spring of 1860, heralded the
new era in the movement of the southern staple to market. A mere
143,000 bales moved east in the 1860–1861 season by this "overland"
route. All-rail transportation would await the development of lines
feeding the eastern trunk lines from the South and the Southwest,
which came swiftly once the Civil War was over. By 1879 shipment by
rail, or "overland from Tennessee" as it was called to distinguish it from
movement by water to Gulf or Atlantic ports, totaled 891,000 bales out
of a crop of 5.8 million bales. Somewhat more than half of this went to
northeastern textile manufacturers, who satisfied 63 percent of their
total requirements in this manner. This cotton headed for the trunk
lines as directly as possible, and this made Louisville and Cincinnati,
which were the northern terminals of the best developed southern railroads, the main points of crossing the Ohio River. But coming up fast
was St. Louis, reflecting the rapid growth of cotton culture in Texas,
the early building of railroads southwesterly from St. Louis, and convenient access to the trunk lines over the impressive new Eads bridge
across the Mississippi.

But what of the 60 percent of the 1879 crop that was exported?
Since this was going to be put on a ship anyway, it did not make economic sense at this point to take it all the way to northeastern ports.
New Orleans, Charleston, and Savannah therefore retained their dominant position in the factorage and handling of cotton, did they not? Not
at all. These ports owed their early eminence in the cotton business to
the fact that they were at the mouths of rivers that served the interior,
but since it was possible to build railroads from interior towns, where
buyers took title to cotton on the spot, to any coastal point that offered
fair harbor facilities, the Galvestons, Port Arthurs, and Wilmingtons
along the Gulf of Mexico and the southeast Atlantic also became important in cotton export shipping.

A fine example of the new enterprises that sprang up to take advantage of the new entrée that the railroad offered to the cotton trade has
been chronicled by the English economic historian, J. R. Killick: the
firm of Alexander Sprunt & Son of Wilmington, North Carolina,
founded in 1866 and liquidated in 1956. For many years the Sprunts
were the largest buyers of American cotton for export, compressing
country bales in their dockside facilities for efficient loading in the
holds of waiting oceangoing steamers. As late as 1922 the Sprunts were
second only to the rising giant, Anderson-Clayton & Co., and sent 6.6
percent of all American cotton abroad. The decline of the older ports
was in part their own fault. New Orleans, for example, never developed
the railroads to serve adequately the interior regions that had
depended in an earlier age upon the Crescent City for moving the cotton and for supplies to the plantations. Once cotton was being bought

in the interior, and the role of the factor was obsolete, the port failed to move with the times. While the casual onlooker might have seen much cotton at New Orleans, most of it was only passing through on export bills of lading.

By the end of the century virtually all of the American-grown cotton that was bought for domestic manufacture moved all the way by rail. It was a natural development, as the input costs of producing rail service fell dramatically and railroad rates shrank extensively and, in the opinion of many, excessively for their financial health. Boxcars grew in size and carrying capacity, while bales grew smaller as a result of constant improvements in the mechanical and hydraulic presses, which could squeeze the big, clumsy bales produced by the puny presses of the country gins into a more manageable size. At the end of the Civil War a boxcar could hold twenty-two bales (about five tons), but by the end of the 1870s up-to-date boxcars held forty-seven bales weighing about twelve tons. Then came the steel-frame and all-steel cars and the general shift to heavier and bulkier loads, although the inherent lightness and bulkiness of cotton made the attainment of hundred-ton loads, as in the case of grains, unlikely. As towns and cities in the cotton belt hailed the coming of the railroads, enterprising cotton buyers saw to the building of warehouse and loading facilities and quickly routinized the entire shipping process from gin to boxcar or ship's hold. Meanwhile generations of little boys (and a few girls) played among the 500-pound bales that tumbled out of the gin doors or jumped up and down on the weighing platform in a vain effort to make their slight weight register on the ponderous scales.

No reasonable person would maintain that the coming of the railroads, or anything else for that matter, reformed or obliterated the many objectionable features that antebellum southern life had manifested. Cotton, the only crop that could readily be converted into the cash that was so desperately needed by a capital-poor economy, was grown to the exclusion of crops that could have assured a more balanced diet and helped conserve the soil's fertility. As the century waned, cotton was grown to excess and the market price sank accordingly. The South remained miserably poor in both spirit and material things. Education, in the long run the only salvation for white and black alike, languished for both races: whites got very little, and that little was of poor quality, while blacks were fortunate to get any at all. In the midst of a people that was slowly and painfully hauling itself up by its own bootstraps, the railroads greatly increased the efficiency of marketing of cotton and such other crops as the South produced; helped attract textile mills, the South's first foray into factory production and later on, an estimable steel industry; lowered the cost of the growing range of goods people bought from distant places; and eased the long-standing social and intellectual isolation. It did nothing to destroy the sharecropping basis for poor southern labor, white and black, but it

Figure 7.2 Receiving cotton from country gins at Alexander Sprunt, Wilmington, North Carolina, ca. 1907. The small size, poor condition, and non-uniformity of the box cars attest to the backwardness of southern railroads well into the 20th century. (*Business History Review*)

made perhaps the major contribution to the slow accumulation of capital that would ultimately make the real New South possible.

Transit to the Greater City: 1865–1930

Paul Leicester Ford was a member of the small American intelligentsia in the 1890s during what Thomas Beer called "the mauve decade." Beer took the title of his book of that name from a remark by John Ruskin that "mauve is just pink trying to be purple." It was a pretentious era, in dress, decor, and decorum, but it was far from being all pretense. It was no "gilded age," as Samuel Clemens jokingly called the 1870s. Ford, in addition to having been the editor of a ten-volume edition of the writings of Thomas Jefferson, was a successful novelist, and it was probably the senseless violence of his death (murdered in cold blood by his insane brother) that put him in Beer's book. Ford's novels are little read today (more than one professor of American literature has never heard of him), although they are in some ways more convincing that the rather mechanical inventions of William Dean Howells, for example. Among Ford's best is *The Honorable Peter Stirling*, which is an incisive commentary upon New York City politics, its consequences, and the rocky road that reformers must travel.

Stirling takes as his cause the deplorable fresh milk industry of the city. New York's chronic tendency was to split its seams in those years, but the furnishing of fresh milk was more than that: it was a public health crime waiting to be exposed. Just as stockyards and slaughterhouses still existed within Manhattan well into the nineteenth century, so did dairies. Since diary farming requires a nearby source of cheap and abundant feed for the cows, one may wonder what a dairy in the heart of a big city could turn to. There was another beverage, even more popular than milk, produced in great quantity in Manhattan: beer. When the mash from which the brew was fermented had yielded up all the nutrients the yeast cells could engorge, what was left was carted down the alley to the nearest dairy and dumped, still steaming, into the poor animals' feed troughs. The cows had to eat huge volumes of spent mash, and this they did, standing in place all day, since they had no place to graze anyway. The milk they gave was pathetic: low in butterfat, sometimes streaked with blood from the beasts' irritated innards, and, as if to add insult to injury, diluted with as much water as the dairyman could get away with. Working-class children got little for their parents' hard-earned money, and the poor got nothing. It was a worthy cause, and the Honorable Peter Stirling heroically set things right.

It was not quite that way in real life, of course. Ford's novel is set in the 1870s, but it was during the Civil War that the vicious system of supplying fresh milk to the city, which was every bit as bad as the above description, began to be replaced with something far better. While

New York's children begged vainly for another glass of milk, there were farms only a few dozen miles to the north, in Westchester, Putnam, and Dutchess counties (then almost entirely rural) on which fine dairy products were produced, from cows fed on the produce of fertile, well-kept farms and grazed on spacious meadows. If only there had been some practical way of getting the fresh milk to the city mass market before it spoiled.

New York City's first railroad, the New York & Harlem, had rapidly become something more than a relatively quick and convenient way of getting from downtown to uptown, as it was extended north into these potential dairy lands. By 1860 farmers were beginning to send fresh milk into the city by early morning passenger train, and soon that fine old American institution, the "milk train," meaning a train whose passengers could expect a stop at every way station, had been born. (In all fairness, the new Erie Railroad may have been the first to bring farmers' milk—from New Jersey—into Manhattan via the Hudson River.)

Without the trains, the development of highly concentrated cities would have stopped long before the end of the nineteenth century. Fresh milk is only a dramatic example of that fact. As we have seen, fresh meat, brought by refrigerator car in the form of dressed carcasses from packing plants a thousand miles away, replaced local abbatoirs and packing plants. And milk and fresh beef, pork, and lamb were still only the beginning. As the natives of the hinterland towns around Boston, New York, and Philadelphia watched with pleasure, the steady stream of young people who had been deserting the Northeast, and especially New England, for a generation, seemed to stop and turn in their tracks. Here at hand was a gigantic market for the produce of their farms, intensively cultivated, just as it was a gigantic milkshed for their dairy products. By the end of the century, truck farming—the raising of vegetables and fruits for city tables—was a thriving industry. Northern New Jersey began to raise prize asparagus, broccoli, tomatoes, blueberries, and the like, almost within the shadow of the glue factories. And what the railroads could do for milk, meat, and spinach, they could also do for poultry and eggs, and they made Long Island the center of potato production for almost a century.

Resort to the hinterland was only an early phase of a widening urban supply area that by this century extended to the Pacific, the Rio Grande, and the Gulf of Mexico. Up to the mid-nineteenth century most cities were located on navigable streams, and the greatest, on seacoasts, but with the coming of a practical, ubiquitous system of cheap inland transportation, the natural advantages of location were minimized. Even New York got its first real chance to transform itself from the dumpy town of antebellum days when rail links with the interior were established. But the truck farms of the urban hinterland, important as they were and have remained, were only the beginning of the story. Many Americans can still remember the eighth-grade geography textbooks from the 1920s and 1930s that seemed to gush with praise for that most amazing example of man's cleverness and resourcefulness: the Florida or California orange that was consumed fresh by the northern or eastern city dweller only a few days after being picked.

Feeding town and city folks in the increasingly luxurious style to which rising standards of living were accustoming them was ultimately a matter of completing the transcontinental railroads and developing railroads in the Deep South and the Southwest. California, which had seemed to beckon so strongly in mid-century, developed slowly until 1900, specializing in growing wheat, whose incredibly low cost of production counterbalanced the long haul to market. But the world of Frank Norris, who immortalized this period of California history in his novel *The Octopus* (1901), with its ultra-conservative railroad president modeled after Collis P. Huntington of the Southern Pacific, vanished after 1900. Edward H. Harriman, who had astounded everyone by reorganizing and rebuilding the Union Pacific Railroad in the late 1890s, and then making it pay 10 percent on the par value of its common stock after 1900, went on to greater things by gaining control of the Southern Pacific and its subsidiary, the Central Pacific, which was the western half of the grand 1860s project that gave us our first transcontinental. Sensible, low through rates to and from the East, Europe, and the Orient were established via the "Overland Route," due west from Omaha across the Great Salt Lake and the High Sierras and into San Francisco or, more accurately, Oakland. Things boomed thereafter. The vast consumer market the railroads opened stimulated everything from irrigation projects in the Imperial Valley that made California a leading cotton-producing state, with yields per acre twice those of Texas, for example; to brilliant research by entomologists who solved the problem of the citrus blight; to the first cadres of motion picture producers looking for a long succession of bright, sunny days; to a growing stream of tourists and retirees; and, of course, to the inevitable real-estate developers.

By 1920 California was a leading supplier of fruits and vegetables, both fresh and preserved by drying or canning, for the rest of the country. The "tin can" faced formidable opposition from the American housewife, jealous of her mastery of domestic science, but by the end of the 1920s she had begun to trade her kitchen garden, bake oven, and canning equipment for a typewriter, retail store counter, or factory bench. The glamour of California, however, should not obscure what was happening simultaneously in the New Southwest (Texas, Arizona, and New Mexico) and in the Deep South. Jay Gould and his heirs turned the chaos of Texas railroads that men of the 1870s like Tom Scott had left behind into a coherent system, greatly strengthening the Missouri Pacific (one must still call it the Texas & Pacific in Texas), whose lines led northeasterly to St. Louis, and improving another, the Cotton Belt. Meanwhile the Deep South, which had been struggling since Reconstruction against the odds of poverty, ignorance, back-woods demagogy and small-minded business philosophies, to rational-ize its railroad system, finally threw in the towel when the depression of the 1890s arrived and turned the job over to J. P. Morgan and his more than capable lieutenants. The galloping prosperity of the first quarter of the new century greased the wheels of entrepreneurship, to be sure, but ahead lay trouble in the agricultural doldrums of the 1920s and the bitter years of the Great Depression. Then came World War II, when suddenly the South and West seemed to have in abundance all the good things—animal, vegetable, and mineral—that the rest of the world needed.

Oh, the Farmer and the Townsman Must Be Friends!

In Rogers and Hammerstein's classic musical comedy, *Oklahoma!*, the cowboys and the farmers celebrate their mixing at a square dance with a rousing number, "Oh the Farmer and the Cowman Must Be Friends." The tensions between those who demanded open ranges on which to graze their herds of beef cattle, and the rapidly multiplying number of farmers who insisted upon fencing in their "spreads," did not last long. Far more long-lived was the agrarian myth, upon which politicians and those small-minded businessmen of whom we just spoke cultivated a self-serving national prejudice. It has almost disappeared now, largely through the continuing industrialization of agriculture, if that is what we may call it.

In the vital years of growth and transformation of material Amer-ica, however, if farmers, railroad men, and indeed all Americans had found the time to step back and consider the intimate bond they had forged between city and country by the 1920s, they would have seen the world's most diversified, productive, and economically efficient machine for bringing the advantages to geographic specialization over an entire continent. No aspect of our material culture illustrated the power of cheap inland transportation—exclusively the steam railroad during the most vital century in our national existence—to achieve these ends more vividly than agriculture. No other people in the world did it, nor have they done it yet, because no other people had a bloom-ing continent at their disposal, a political tool to make "out of many, one," and the gumption to use that tool wisely during the critical years of its history. In this process the great urban centers played a major role.

The city was not dependent upon the farmer, nor the farmer upon the city dweller. Each had shown in earlier years that they could do without the other, and be miserable and frustrated doing it. Neither consented to do it one moment longer than necessary. As a practical matter, the townsman depended more and more upon the ability of the farmer to produce a substantial surplus and get it to him in good condition and at low cost. But equally, the farmer who had pushed into the wilderness—without any idea of how he was to sell the wonderful surplus of his godforsaken acres other than his faith that "God will provide"—depended upon the urban arts that made the steam railroad a reality: the terminals, the shops and forges, the markets and attendant warehouses, and the financial institutions, all little understood and widely abused, but vital, that mysteriously made it all come together. Grass might grow in the streets of every city in America without the farmer, but just as surely would nothing have broken the stillness of the Iowa landscape save the twittering of the birds without the city. The railroads made speculation like Bryan's a waste of time appropriate only for politicians.

Carrying the People's Burden to Market

> The arrangements . . . between connecting railroads for the direct transmission of freights between distant points without . . . any supervision [by] shippers . . . to the point of delivery constitute one of the most important features of our railroad system. The efficiency of railroads is due in a higher degree to such combinations than to any other feature of their existence.
>
> Joseph N. Nimmo, *Report on the Internal Commerce of the United States* (1879)

> These western cities [Chicago, Cincinnati, Cleveland, Columbus, St. Louis, etc.] are full of the life and vigor of early manhood, and their business is conducted by men of unsurpassed energy and sagacity. To suppose their enterprising merchants will be content to *retail* and depend upon New York to import and job for them is what the scriptures call a "vain imagination."
>
> William D. Shipman, railroad attorney, before the Hepburn Committee, 1879

Through a Committee, Darkly

One of the most valuable achievements of the Select Committee on Transportation Routes to the Seaboard in 1874 was the intensive education on the flow of commerce within the United States that it provided an obscure government employee by the name of Joseph N. Nimmo, Jr. Nimmo came to his job well prepared. A graduate civil engineer, he had studied railroads from the viewpoint of an engineer and was now doing so with the simple tools of statistical analysis, which was still in its infancy. In the course of gathering more data on what was going on within the booming post-Civil War economy, Nimmo had reflected long and hard on the patterns of manufacturing and mercantile activity, as well as agriculture, that he discerned. The committee's report, which he appears to have drafted, must have given him pause. During the next several years, as head of the domestic commerce division of the Treasury Department, he would produce a series of reports that are a priceless source of information on the rapid evolution of the American transportation system in its most critical, formative years.

The United States, when the Windom Committee was formed, was preoccupied with political considerations. Reconstruction programs had not yet jelled, and meanwhile the administration of the personally popular Ulysses S. Grant had fallen into disrepute. The presidential election of 1872 had revealed the fault lines between East and West and between Mugwumps and Stalwarts that threatened Republican unity. Other factors were at work that were known, and understood for their effects, only by such specialists as William D. Shipman, who would speak for New York State's railroads during their grilling by the Hepburn Committee. A little noted U.S. statute, passed by Congress in 1870 to achieve a number of objectives, included an obscure section that established inland customhouses for the first time in the United States. Cities of the Midwest that were hundreds of miles from salt water now would be able to collect customs duties on imported goods shipped "in bond" from the traditional east coast ports. Wholesale merchants who had long "broken bulk" in New York, for example, and then reshipped to inland merchants the imported goods upon which the late nineteenth-century American economy so heavily depended, would now lose this business. These factors, political and, on the surface, economic, were bringing about a reformation in American life and the material civilization on which it was based, and raising questions of the nation's transportation system and the policies by which it would be conducted. When the torchlight parades were over, the partisan placards consigned to the dustbin, and the inane slogans they bore forgotten, there remained the hard question of how to get the people's burden efficiently and profitably to market. What the people grew and manufactured, and what they required to maintain a modestly rising standard of living and to equip the economy to scale even greater heights, formed the core of national controversy.

Even before the Civil War, it had become obvious to many that the railroad system was outgrowing its original local or regional role, which had been largely one of linking not-distant interior points, particularly those on navigable rivers, with tidewater or major water avenues to tidewater. Already the "steam cars" were upsetting apple carts, from the wholesalers in grubby districts of New York's lower east side to the self-satisfied bourgeoisie who ground wheat into flour at Rochester, or hammered cowhides into shoes in Utica, or handled grain at such traditional transfer points from local rail to steamboats as Dubuque or LaCrosse or Prairie du Chien, or fermented other grain into beer in dozens of long-established towns and cities throughout the interior. The complaints usually boiled down to the belief that the railroads charged *them* too much, and their *competitors,* especially those much farther from traditional markets, too little to haul their goods. After the war, almost as if nothing had intervened to reestablish "common sense" among railroad men, the sensitivity of the transportation question resumed and was redoubled.

Not the least of the voices raised in protest—indeed, the loudest by far, as politicians saw it, of all the nation's collective voices—were the farmers who had flooded into the Old Northwest in the preceding two decades and were heaping record crops, much of it destined for a new customer—Europe—upon the spindly railroads of that day. Rates, on the average, were very high, often higher than it was worth to the distant shipper to have his goods at a given destination, but at the same time it seemed to shippers located in towns that had enjoyed closeness to the great ports of the Atlantic seaboard that either rates from these distant points should be raised, or their own lowered. To anyone, the linear relationship between distance and cost (and thus the price) of transportation services was obvious in the abstract and, to interested parties, was gospel. Besides, western farmers' costs of production on the fabulous prairie soils were far below those in the older states. If they now received a rate scale per ton per mile below what eastern farmers paid, what would happen to the older regions?

When hard times came in 1873, the shippers' discontent was quickly exacerbated. Something had to be done to rectify the situation, and that was the reason for the appointment of the Windom Committee, which, based upon its superficial study of a situation that was, in fact, in a state of extreme flux, hastily recommended a radically interventionist public policy. We have no way of knowing whether Nimmo agreed with the committee's findings, as he scratched away with his pen far into the night to meet his deadline. If he did, then he learned a great deal about what was going on west of the Potomac River during the next three years. He was, in fact, one of the very first Americans to grasp the seminal role of the railroads in the developing nation, and he never stopped preaching it—a prophet without honor, eventually, in his own land.

The Windom Committee, like most superficial students of the American scene then and since, was doubtless under the spell of Charles Francis Adams, Jr.'s *A Chapter of Erie* (1869), which detailed the unbridled internecine warfare between Commodore Vanderbilt and Jay Gould for control of the Erie, and the barefaced stockjobbing and stock "watering" that had gone on along with it. As far as the senators were concerned, that was the best that could be expected from railroad leaders. The committee saw no illogic in the conviction that the federal government had to compete with the railroads, therefore, in furnishing transportation services, if the principles of classic free enterprise were to be preserved. (This was something mid-Victorians set much store by and politicians find as seductive as ever now.) Misreading, or, more likely, never reading, Adam Smith, the solons averred that railroad men would never cease to collude and that the results could never be anything but bad. The proximate alternative, rate regulation by a governmental body, was explicitly ruled out by a generation of lawmakers who had been appalled by the government's inefficiency during the Civil War.

On the other hand, everybody had been so happy with the non-pooling, nonrebating Erie Canal that a national system of trunk line canals seemed to be the best bet as the backbone of the committee's plan. It covered its bets by noting that an "economically built, double-track, trunkline railroad," say from Council Bluffs, Iowa, the eastern terminus of the new transcontinental railroad in which so much of the national substance was already invested, to New York, might be added to the plan. To use a buzzword that became popular in the next century when municipal ownership of electric utilities was widely supported, the Windom system would provide a "yardstick" by which the reasonableness of rates posted by the privately owned railroads could be established. Nobody can accuse the Windom Committee of lacking vision: it had plenty of vision, and it was turned resolutely towards the past. It was a mighty blinkered vision at that, for not even the bitter experience of the burghers of Philadelphia, who had had to abandon the old Main Line system of canals and inclined planes thirty years before, deflected this resolute committee. The astronomical cost, if anyone had ever gone to the trouble of costing it out, probably would have.

Nimmo had been trained as a civil engineer, but it was not exclusively the practical problems of building canals and railroads through the difficult terrain of the eastern United States that would claim his lifelong attention. As he watched the railroad network grow, his interest in the peculiarities of railroad economics and their implications for both private and public policy grew along with it. Born in Portsmouth, Virginia in 1831, Nimmo had come north to study his profession at New York University, from which he was graduated in 1852, and which would confer upon him the honorary degree of Doctor of Laws forty years later. We have few details of his career beyond his service in the Bureau of Internal Commerce of the U.S. Treasury Department in the 1870s and early 1880s, which he largely created and eventually headed. He lived in Washington, D.C., for fifty years until his death in 1909 and consulted widely for both government and private interests on railroad economic and regulatory problems. He probably would have admitted that, at heart, he thought the American national system of transportation was one of the noblest creations of the human spirit. It is just as well that he died when he did, for its creators were about to be repudiated in the cruelest way.

In 1874, however, all signals were green for America's railroads and the men who would dedicate their lives to creating this great system, while Congress, recognizing the Windom Report for the emergency substitute for action that it so obviously was, laid it quietly to rest. As for Nimmo, he perceived an exceptional opportunity in public service in putting the collection and analysis of internal commerce statistics on a sound footing. While he cleaned out his desk in the Committee's chambers, moreover, developments were occurring in the railroad picture that would relegate the report to the wastebasket almost before the copies were delivered by the Public Printer. For the rest of his life, Nimmo watched closely, consulted frequently, commented passionately, and then passed and was forgotten with the rest.

The Genie in the Bottle

The big change in American economic life after 1865, the change under which most other changes can be subsumed, was the discovery of the railroad as a practical system of cheap, long-distance transportation for goods of low value in relation to their weight and/or bulk. Men's views of railroads before this light dawned were antediluvian. It is not too much to say that railroad men still hardly realized the potential of the railroad freight train in 1865. Like most business enterprises at their inception, the railroads had started operations with very little traffic, fixed investments that were at risk (the British speak of "sunk capital") and consequently had to be recouped as quickly as possible, and a few travelers and shippers who were eager to have themselves and their goods moved. The high cost per passenger or per ton of freight moved one mile (the "ton-mile" and "passenger-mile" units in which transportation services are measured) was not critical, because journeys were short and bulk commodities were moving, if they moved at all, by water, as they always had. The result was that the American railroad during the first generation of its history was a low-volume, high-rate, high-unit-operating-cost business.

Many a businessman, in the early years of a profitable enterprise, has succumbed to the temptation to take all the profits out of the business, then soon found himself left behind in the onrush of economic development. "Today's neat little monopoly is tomorrow's 'cash cow' and the day after's dog." Progressive management combined with research and development are what can build a mighty industry upon what otherwise might turn out to be just a once-in-a-lifetime lucky guess. Businessmen knew this intuitively then, as now, and they recognized that the nation required something more from its business leaders, for the small view that some would take of the potentialities of steam power was no basis upon which to settle a continent—the chief order of business in the nineteenth century. If men's ambitions encouraged the young nation to plunge into the vast unknown of the age of enterprise, the potential of the railroads demanded it. Besides, by the early post-Civil War years the railroad shoe was already pinching badly as the Midwest demanded lower rates to the east coast for their burgeoning crops.

Change, when it comes, always seems abrupt, but in fact the elements behind the remarkable transformation in the economics of railroading after 1870 had been in the making for years. They can be dated at least as far back as the mid-1850s, when the Lake Shore & Michigan Southern Railroad and the Pittsburgh, Fort Wayne & Chicago entered

Chicago, so soon to become the world's greatest railroad center, and quickly formed through routes to the east coast by means of end-to-end traffic agreements with the Vanderbilts' New York Central and J. Edgar Thomson's expansive Pennsylvania Railroad, respectively. These latter roads took control of their western connections in 1869 and the concept of the self-contained trunk line railroad was born. The Vanderbilts soon added the Michigan Central, which further strengthened their control of the seaboard-to-lakes axis, but they failed to wrest the troublesome Erie from Jay Gould's grasp. No two goldmines in the entire history of the human race were ever richer, however, than the Central and the Pennsylvania in their new interregional form, and of course emulation was not long in coming.

The Pennsylvania and the Central competed with each other in a more or less gentlemanly fashion in accepting the fast-growing volume of produce of the Midwest at the Chicago and St. Louis "gateways," hauling it at traditionally high rates to eastern markets, and on the return trip bringing midwesterners the growing list of goods and supplies—much of them imported in those days—that they could no longer do without. This pleasant state of affairs was soon to end. Before the decade of the 1870s was one-third spent, William H. Vanderbilt, eldest son of the Commodore, who was preparing to take control of his father's creation, glumly received the news that the Baltimore & Ohio, under the aggressive John Work Garrett, and even the weak-sister Erie Railroad itself, were pushing their lines westward into Chicago. "Four lines between New York and Chicago, and traffic enough for only two," he is supposed to have growled. The B. & O. made it in 1874, and while another six years would pass before the Erie had its own line, the Grand Trunk, in concert with the Erie and secondary eastern lines such as the Central of Vermont and, later, the Lackawanna and the Lehigh Valley, had quickly made hash of the stately way of doing business along this newest and greatest of the world's trade routes.

Railroad men had not planned for the new era of high-volume, low-rate service. It was still news to many who were attempting to make public railroad policy at least as late as 1879, when W. H. Vanderbilt, from his witness chair in a private meeting room of a hotel in Ogdensburg, New York, patiently explained to members of New York State's hostile Hepburn Committee that competition was the sovereign power in determining railroad rates. "The day of high rates has gone by; got to make money now on the volume of business," he said. Here was the explanation for the Central's remarkable program of quadruple-tracking its mainline from New York to Buffalo. If great increases in volume were to be handled, a pair of tracks (one eastbound and one westbound) had to be provided for freight alone, the more so since passenger train movements had become dangerously frequent for a mere double-track railroad. "Scaling up" the plant is what economists would call increasing the mere size of a railroad—the number of tracks and the number of locomotives and items of rolling stock. What happened was something far more complex, for American economic development has been a supremely dynamic thing, based on factors that do not readily meet the eye and often come, it would seem, "from out of left field." The gain in separating freight and passenger traffic, for example, was actually greater than the sum of its parts, for, with the arrival of automatic and remote signaling and switching, really complex traffic programs could be arranged to meet particular circumstances.

Happily, opportunities for technological breakthroughs were numerous in the nineteenth century. They were almost invariably of the early-payoff, cost-cutting variety, and that was exactly what was needed. No social system, from the authoritarian to the most loosely organized laissez-faire variety, can ignore the fact that in the long run, economic growth can only come from lower production costs per unit of input, and, without material economic growth, there can be no increase in wages, no improvement in standards of living, and ultimately, no political stability.

The Central's four-track main is only a particularly dramatic example of lowering production costs. The struggle to get costs under control went on throughout the railroad system and continues to do so to this day. In the nineteenth century the important railroads of the nation were constantly being rebuilt. As significant, if not as dramatic, as the proliferation of route mileage, mainline tracks, and auxiliary tracks, were the improvements in rail itself. Nothing could be more prosaic, or more vital in understanding how the railroads equipped themselves in less than a decade to carry a vastly increased burden of freight at a fraction of the rates that were being charged as late as 1878, than a study of what the Bessemer process for making steel cheaply had meant to the railroads.

In 1870, barely fourteen years had elapsed since Sir Henry Bessemer stood before an English scientific gathering to read his famous paper, "The Manufacture of Iron without Fuel." The first successful application of the Bessemer process by American licensees was in 1864, and by 1870 old-line wrought iron manufacturers like the Cambria Iron Works in Pennsylvania were turning out the first steel rails rolled in quantity in the nation. It remained for the genius of Alexander L. Holley, entrepreneurially harnessed by Andrew Carnegie, to bring forth truly cheap steel when Holley designed and built the first large-scale, integrated steel mill on the Monongahela River near Pittsburgh in the depths of the 1870s depression. A leading feature of Holley's plan was the provision for ready handling of in- and outbound trains of the three railroads—the Pennsylvania, the Baltimore & Ohio, and the Pittsburgh & Lake Erie. How controlling a factor the new, cheap transportation was, Holley himself has told us:

> As the cheap transportation of supplies of products in process of manufacturing, and of products to market, is a feature of first importance, these works were laid out, not with a view of making the buildings artistically parallel with the existing roads or each other, but of laying down convenient railroads with easy curves; *the buildings were made to fit the transportation*. . . . [italics mine]

The tough, strong, malleable, and cheap material was what American railroad men had been looking for. It almost entirely freed them from European sources of rails (except for very high-quality Krupp rails that found special favor for curves on mountain routes) but that was not the half of it. It may be that most Americans in the 1870s were still perfectly content with their iron pots and pans and storefronts and their wrought iron bridges, but even had there been no other immediate application for cheap Bessemer steel, its superb performance in railroad rails would have guaranteed it a mass market. Making rails was what the American steel industry was all about, or nearly so, in those years. A steel rail would bear up under the pounding of increasingly heavy locomotives and freight cars up to twelve times as long as a wrought iron rail. That meant far fewer occasions when it became necessary to send track crews out, take up rail, ship it to a rerolling mill, and re-lay it somewhere else in the system. The railroads not only made the modern iron and steel industry possible by solving its transportation problems; as a market for the product, they also made it necessary. Their evolutionary histories remain inextricably intertwined.

American railroad men could understand what President Lincoln had meant when he said that he had not sought to control events but was controlled by them. If anyone had a "tiger by the tail" in 1873, it was the men who were presuming at that time to haul the people's growing burden to market at economical rates—that is, rates which would give producers a good profit and leave enough over for continual reinvestment in the "great American bread machine," most notably in the constant augmentation of cheap, universal transportation. On countless technological, financial, legal, and managerial fronts, ways would be found to do the job more effectively, but the search was never finished. In the advancement of the American productive economy during these years, the railroads have been both facilitator and the thing facilitated—as supplier, and as user.

Not a Highway but a Universal Transportation Machine

The archives of the Pennsylvania Railroad contain the 1833–1834 report of E. F. Gay, chief engineer of the Philadelphia & Columbia Railroad, then about to begin operations as the easternmost link in the Main Line works, the new system of canals, inclined planes, and railroads. Gay had been requested to comment on the first question that had to be decided: just how would the public make use of this new method of hauling goods and people? Would the company provide locomotives to haul wagons belonging to shippers? Indeed, would those who had goods to ship simply pay a toll and go upon the railroad at any convenient point with their *own* locomotives and "burden cars?" Silly questions? Not at all. This latter arrangement was the way it had always been, on the famous "king's highway" in England, on the turnpikes of America, and on the common roads everywhere, but of course everyone owned wagons and draft animals or could engage them, with a drover to take them over the route, and if traffic problems arose the parties involved could readily work them out on the spot. Obviously, this was not so with the new mode of transportation. As Gay earnestly pointed out, the company had better provide the transportation services in their entirety, although there was no particular obstacle to patrons' providing their own cars if they met the standards of the road. In other words, this very early steam railroad (to be taken over by the Pennsylvania Railroad a few years later when the Main Line works proved to be a dud) found itself in the business of providing, not a road, but the service of transportation itself. (Such a fundamental distinction is not to be confused with the concept of the "common carrier," but such matters belong in a later chapter.)

The railroad—in England or in America—clearly was not in the tradition of the king's highway, a public way upon which any law-abiding citizen could move himself and his goods by whatever means at his command, with the best wishes of his king, and God have mercy on anyone who would seek to abridge that right. As America's railroads became more and more the center of controversy in the last century, the king's highway idea would not die. Foghorn orators would not give up the resounding phrase, declaring that the railroads were merely America's version of the royal road, which they seem to have confused with the idea of a "public utility." (Ironically, the English never thought that about their own railroads.) We should be grateful that the railroads were left to work out their own operational problems, for it made all the difference in what emerged in the first half-century of railroad history: a national, integrated, coherent, organic system of transportation, in which intense competition, at least between terminal cities, would place a premium on good service at low rates that would cover all the costs of providing the service, including *ad valorem* state real-estate taxes. No king's highway could ever say that.

The question of what the railroads were setting up in business to provide, and what the customers would be paying for, was only the beginning of a host of administrative policy problems that crowded upon the railroads as they were transformed from short lines supplementing water transportation, to long-distance lines connecting regions of the country and integrated, at least at the service level, with other lines. The "theory" of rate-setting, insofar as there was anything that could be called a theory; the rudiments of a philosophy of organization; and a system of analysis of operations had to be established, and their refinement still keeps legions of people employed to this day. A start had to be made, and where else but with rates? Surely, setting equitable rates posed no problem. The farther one's goods were carried, the more one should pay, is that not entirely equitable? Not at all. Early railroad men found out quickly that a per-ton-mile rate that paid them to furnish a freight terminal, boxcars, and locomotives, and haul a shipment of goods from, say, the Baltimore & Ohio's terminal in the city the few miles to Ellicott Mills, might well produce an exorbitant rate if applied to Harper's Ferry, a confiscatory rate to Cumberland, and a bad joke to Wheeling. Such a pro rata policy, once the trunk lines were joined, would have made rail transportation from New York to Chicago more expensive than wagon transport.

When what is not feasible is found also to be less favorable to progressive enterprise than some other solution, it is time to rejoice, and down to the present day the philosophy of low long-distance freight rates has been praised to the skies. In fact, once the goods were aboard and the train made up and manned and underway, early railroad men noted, you could carry the stuff mile after mile with only a slight increment in cost. Still, not everyone was pleased. Merchants in old communities handy to water transportation and close to the seaboard complained that the policy of low rates for long hauls was drawing trade away from these places. "The railroads have no right to break up the jobbing trade of this city and transfer it to the interior," whined a New York wholesale merchant to the Hepburn Committee. Victorian men of affairs had little patience with such crybabies, however, and the prorata tariff movement got nowhere.

Bringing relatively distant communities into the mainstream of American commerce, in fact, was the ultimate promise of the railroads, and it took no longer than the passing of the first generation of innovators for it to be seen clearly. With Americans straining against the reins to move westward in their vast continent, low rates were demanded and received, because they were the key to volume and with volume came profits and growth. Understandably, economists, with their penchant for mechanical formulas in dealing with human problems, have repeatedly brought up the supposed merits of the cost of producing freight service as the basis for rates, but such ideas defy practical application and have been repeatedly judged to be impossible by railroad men and government commissions alike. The philosophy of rate-making that ruled until the day when the railroad's *modal* monopoly disappeared (individual companies seldom had monopolies, and then not for long, on given routes) was that of charging what the traffic would bear. What could be simpler or more reasonable? A shipper will not pay more than it is worth to have his goods at B instead of A. That sets the maximum, but in practice railroad men found they had better leave some net gain to the shipper.

As for the railroad men, they were generally so hungry for volume that they carried much freight below its real totally apportioned costs, a phenomenon that is characteristic of high-fixed-cost enterprises and was the basis of a national market for coal and an international market for agricultural products. A more benign system of making railroad rates could not be imagined: all it required was perfect knowledge of the mental workings of shippers on the part of railroad traffic managers! Lacking that, we got a system that worked, and even reformers were happy once they found they could slyly change "*what* the traffic will bear" to "*all* the traffic will bear," thus implying that the railroads possessed absolute power.

The eastern trunk line railroads were the solid foundation upon which the national transportation system was constructed in the generation after 1870. By the close of the depression of 1873–1879, the general outline of the system, its physical characteristics, essential business practices, and organizational structure, were established. All that followed, until the perfection of the internal combustion engine and the establishment of a national network of government-subsidized all-weather roads, had been set in motion by the 1870s. This is not to suggest that innovation stopped, for on the contrary it was doubled and redoubled in almost every department of railroading.

As the railroad system grew, it brought along with it the creation and maturation of what we have come to call the modern economy. "The generation following the Civil War was mortgaged to the railroads," said Henry Adams, as he surveyed the unbelievable volume of resources that had gone into the orgy of railroad construction that added 114,000 miles to the system by 1900. The railroads made it possible for this land of movers and shakers finally to enter the industrial era, in much the same way as was happening in the new German empire, whose economic development reveals so many interesting parallels with our own. But the railroads also made modern industry necessary, for, as we shall see, they were the first mass markets for the first generation of heavy industry that emerged in the last third of the nineteenth century. Manufacturing and distribution became truly national in scope. Problems of marshaling massive bodies of long-term capital, unprecedented in history, were met and solved, and the result was the creation of new financial institutions centered on investment and commercial bankers. That so much of American property would come to be entrusted to so few by the time the crisis years of the 1890s arrived could not have been dreamed of in 1850. The cliché, "transportation revolution," so beloved of American historians, signifies not merely a revolution of, but more importantly, a revolution by, transportation.

Towards a Vertebrate Nation

We have described the structure of American society on the eve of the coming of the railroad and telegraph as "invertebrate," by which we

Figure 8.1 The four-track mainline of the New York Central Railroad in the 1880s, showing the separation of freight and passenger trains, which was a boon for this busiest of rail routes in the day of frequent, short trains. In 1879, at the very moment that the Hepburn Committee was heaping scorn upon "Billy" Vanderbilt's head, with the eager help of the press, his railroad was making this vital investment in the future economic growth of the nation and, not incidentally, even greater profits for the railroad.

mean that the organizing force by which the people would attain the fullest degree of material, intellectual, and social intercourse between individuals and between regions had not yet emerged. What was the promise that America held out to a people who would move mightily forward? It was the promise of enterprise on a grand scale: the newcomers to the largest land mass on earth, located for the most part in a latitude and at an altitude congenial to human growth, were politically unified against the selfish ambitions of localities that would stifle interregional trade, protected by geography from the constant threat of invasion by other nations, spoke a common language, and prayed more or less, to the same god.

An easygoing *ad hoc* approach prevailed in the 1850s. It could not have been otherwise as long as men were meeting most of their problems for the first time. The old spirit of the commonwealth seems to have guided railroad men, at least at first, for they quickly saw that they were highly dependent upon each other. The discovery that their best business was coming from traffic that they would receive from some other originating line, or would turn over to such at the end of their own line, inspired men to simplify paperwork, especially the execution of bills of lading. Why not a single, through bill of lading for a shipment, complete with all necessary routing instructions? And why not mail this bill of lading ahead, when the goods began their journey, to the consignee, especially when it became apparent that his bank would then advance funds on the loan that made the purchase of goods possible? The bill of lading *became* the shipment, in abstract paper form. Its legal and operational features had been settled by the end of the Civil War, when, in addition, the railroads were learning to master the job of car accounting, since so much of their rolling stock was in others' hands, and vice versa.

Railroad men were so preoccupied with financing and building railroad lines in the 1850s and 1860s that they were not prepared to face up to the problem of adequacy of freight service. Someone who had goods to ship could bring them to the team tracks where the railroads would put them on the cars; when the cars were full, or nearly, they would move out. Switching the cars to the correct connecting line at the end of the originating line was a gamble, which often did not receive the attention that it required. Lost shipments, even lost cars, were common. Cars were not always delivered to shippers who had goods to fill them, and in fact the railroads in these years seldom had enough cars anyway. Andrew Carnegie, who also operated a high-fixed-cost business, could book an order for steel while blandly quoting a 90- or 180-day delivery, and businessmen would understand. That would not do on a railroad.

Very soon the railroad men realized that smart operators were having their own cars built (and painted with names suggesting speed) and in a sense retailing the services that the railroads offered only on a wholesale basis. These were the private-car lines. The railroads caught on to the fact that virtually all of their high-rated freight was going by private-car line, so they quickly moved into the business themselves, forming their own fast-freight lines and buying into others. They were, at bottom, only freight-car pools, with each railroad being compensated for the mileage logged by each car that that road contributed to the total. Meanwhile, that road loaded cars with its own freight without regard to who actually owned a given car. The names of these fast-freight lines—*Merchants Despatch, Red Line, Blue Line*, etc.—can be espied on photographs and woodcut illustrations from the period.

Shippers' ownership of special-purpose cars became customary, but the fast-freight car lines were a transitory arrangement until better financing arrangements under which the railroads could buy cars, such as equipment trusts, were made. The original idea of the proprietary forwarder of the highest class of package freight—that is, express— lived on in the old express companies—Adams Express, United States Express, and those operated by the railroads themselves—until the Parcel Post Act of 1913 killed them off. One way or another, American society got the fast, dependable freight and express service it needed, and was not prepared to do without, and the foundations of the modern economy were laid.

Becoming Masters of Their Fate

What had not yet emerged among railroad men as late as the mid-1870s was a *system* to standardize business practices throughout the productive centers of the country. Everyone was for standardization, but before what more and more people were demanding (even if they did not yet quite realize it) could be achieved, a process was needed that would systematize not only the solicitation, handling, and delivery of freight, but, above all, the rationale behind the pricing of these services that went so far in determining what a merchant had to sell and how much he had to get for it. A system would make the railroads, in companionship with the telegraph, far more valuable than the sum of their parts. Alfred D. Chandler, Jr., who has done more than any other American scholar to take the dusty wraps of time off the complicated, controversial, and wearying process by which the successive stages of industrial form evolved, notes three tasks that railroad men set out to perform: conjoining the lines physically, so that what had generally been envisioned as free-standing routes between stated terminals could become, instead, segments in the grand system; establishing machinery for setting reasonable rates in performing the carrying trade efficiently and equitably; and stamping out destructive competition in the form of rate-cutting and parallel track-laying.

At no time, of course, did railroad men consider that they were laying out, or involved in attaining, any such fixed program. Free enterprise abhors any kind of centralized planning, and wisely so, for it is better to be guided by small errors of judgment, permitting "mid-course corrections," than to make one big, irreversible error. Joseph Nimmo's characterization of the typical railroad executive's motivation is more to the point. In his 1879 report, he declares that the typical railroad man wanted to secure as much traffic as he could, for the longest possible haul, to convey it to towns on whose prosperity that of the railroads mostly depends, for the best rate. "There are certain incompatibles, he warned, "which forbid that the interests of the transporter and of the merchant should be very closely joined together." It was a fair warning of the long, bitter struggle between railroads, shippers ("the public"), and the government that was coming. A smoothly operating national railroad system consisting of vastly reorganized corporate components would indeed evolve by 1900, after years of trial and error and of agonizing reappraisal of the limits of individualism. This new regime, with a booming prosperity that would last a full generation, was the cure for the instability of tariffs that shippers had bemoaned in the 1880s. Even so, there is a bit of the chiseler in all of us, and the centralized corporate power by which the railroads made honest men of rebate seekers was not an unmixed blessing. Meanwhile, the virtues of cooperation, first demonstrated on a grand scale by the railroads and Standard Oil, would not be lost on American industry as it, too, cut loose from the old individualism.

Historian Robert Wiebe stimulated a fresh discussion of the rise of big business in the late nineteenth century in his *The Search for Order.* Wiebe found not simplistic motives of making outlandish profits and amassing great fortunes, but a desire to exploit the wonderful opportunities to advance American material civilization that the new science and technology of the end of the century presented. To achieve these ends, men had to master the forces of competition rather than bend with them. Such a condition of order is what bourgeois society is built upon. Indeed, it is only the most arrogant despots in history who seem to have believed that by just one more war of devastation they could gain hegemony over other potentates with less lofty ambitions to bring order out of chaos. To say that men were searching in the late nineteenth century for a way to control the famous American individualism—"all sheet and no anchor," as Macaulay had described us—would not be saying very much, so Wiebe went on to interpret much of what traditional historians have dismissed as destructive in American economic life in terms of a genuine search for order. The search was more of a desperate struggle, most of the time, yet the outcome was generally constructive until the struggle became one of ideology and political ambition.

American railroads set the pattern for successive industries' search for order, having found earlier and more nearly solved the problems of destructive competition than almost anyone else. One of the greatest

achievements, and certainly one of the most prosaic and least understood, was the general freight tariff classification that emerged within a
decade after 1870. Not that it was set in concrete by 1880. Of course
it was not, for the tariff classification has been virtually a living organ-
ism, forever changing in scope and character in response to infinite
stimuli. Hardly any privilege has been more highly prized by railroad
men than that of absolute flexibility: the right to change (if not as individual carriers at least through voluntary associations of their own
choosing) the class into which a given commodity or manufactured item
fell; the rate for its carriage between basing points; and the differentials
for shorter hauls, rail routes, and east coast terminal ports. The failure
of lawmakers, judges, and shippers to grasp the vital role of flexibility
in any efficient system of establishing and maintaining freight rates has
been a major source of misunderstanding, bad legislation, and decaying
transportation facilities down through the years.

Such an objective demands more than general agreement on a philosophy of railroad rates; it demands an organization, and Victorian railroad men were fortunate indeed that the master builder of such administrative systems was at hand. It was an age in which academically
trained engineers were not only highly literate, but also were, as if by
default, the nation's proto-statisticians and business economists. Albert
Fink, who had already made major contributions to the technique of
railroad revenue and cost analysis and car accounting—the art of knowing where a given piece of rolling stock was at any one time—on top
of a brilliant career in railroad construction, maintenance, and operation, was a key executive on the Louisville & Nashville, the most vigorous of the southern railroads that had crawled out of the devastation
of the Civil War. It was Fink's success in establishing a traffic pool
among southeastern railroads, which had about pauperized themselves
by rate-cutting, that endeared him to the eastern trunk lines that were
beginning to fear the same fate.

The eastern lines had been moving down the scale of voluntarism
consistently from the old end-to-end contracts, by which they had originally attained a measure of stability before everything changed with
such suddenness after 1873. The Pennsylvania had the right idea:
acquire a controlling interest in its connecting roads, like the Fort
Wayne line from Pittsburgh to Chicago, and the "Panhandle" and Vandalia lines that brought the Pennsylvania across the magnificent new
Eads bridge over the Mississippi into St. Louis, and constantly reduce
your operating costs by intelligently reinvesting profits in route
improvements. But these policies took a lot of money, which tightwads
like the Vanderbilts were loath to part with, and shoestring operators
like John W. Garrett and Hugh Jewett, of the B. & O. and the Erie, did
not have. Indeed, Garrett's B. & O., although it made a great noise
about having become a third trunk line in 1874, had only a rather

crooked, patched-together line that would take most of the rest of the century to straighten out.

The Pennsylvania, sensibly eschewing provincialism, had long since realized that its obvious eastern terminal was New York City, not Philadelphia, and it controlled superb freight and passenger facilities in Jersey City, just across the Hudson from the metropolis. Its great barn of a passenger terminal was just about the busiest maritime rail terminal in the world, with hundreds of locomotives steaming in and out of the west end daily, and ferries in and out of the east.

Meanwhile, the New York Central enjoyed the geographically best route, the "water level" of the Mohawk River Valley, with minimum changes in grade and very little curvature, making it the most economical to operate and, as the only railroad that actually entered Manhattan, the most popular for passengers and shippers alike. The Erie had bowed to popular will years before and moved its terminal from the boondocks of Rockland County, a dock at Piermont on the Hudson, from which arriving passengers were expected to float in dignified comfort down to the city. It ended up on the Jersey side, too, just north of the Pennsylvania depot, but its route to Chicago was a difficult one; even though it was the next-to-shortest route (after the Pennsylvania's), its trains barely crept over the same mountains that the Central deftly avoided, and its operating costs were very high. On top of everything else, it was stuck until the late 1870s with that foolish decision to build it to a six-foot gauge, which had long since necessitated laying a third rail for standard-gauge rolling stock from other lines. The B. & O. had no entrée to New York at all except over the tracks of the Reading from Philadelphia to Bound Brook, New Jersey, and the Central of New Jersey across Newark Bay to Jersey City.

The eastern trunk line railroads, in other words, were a mixed bag, varying enormously in their preparation to do business under the increasingly competitive conditions after 1873. Put simply, the railroads that needed revenues most desperately, because of their high costs of operation and hunger for improvement capital, were precisely those that were the least able to attract it. Something had to give, and that was their rates: less desirable service, lower rates, that was only common sense. Besides, chiseling even a slightly lower rate than the published tariff paid off, for hard-pressed shippers knew that their own position in the parade depended upon minimizing their own costs of operation, of which freight in and out was an important component. They would put up with a lot of inconvenience and some delays if the price was right. Such finagling mounted, and soon the Pennsylvania and the Central felt the pinch. Profits in the high-fixed-cost railroad industry are mightily sensitive to small declines in traffic, especially if it is the high-rated merchandise kind. But wouldn't the chiselers go broke cutting rates, and go out of business? Holders of first mortgage bonds might have thought they had effective power to foreclose, but railroad men knew better. Railroads have to run—that has been the decision of the courts in the case of public service enterprises since their beginnings—and insolvent railroads would be placed by the courts under a receiver and excused from paying interest on their bonds until happier times should return.

Even before the old Commodore died, his son, William H., was alive to the problem. His favorite summer vacation resort was Saratoga, whose racecourse offered the ideal place to show off his champion trotters, Maude S. and Aldine, and whose dignified United States Hotel was a fine and private place in which to thresh out matters of great importance. Here, in 1874, he met with the presidents and general managers of the Pennsylvania and the Erie and their western connections, the Lake Shore, the Fort Wayne, and the Atlantic & Great Western. Conspicuously absent was any representative of the B. & O., whose leader was anxious to see where, in the eastern railroad pecking order, his new Chicago connection would leave him if he went his own way. He would soon find out.

Garrett soon was cutting grain rates eastbound out of Chicago, a major class of traffic that was bread and butter for all concerned. Almost simultaneously a fifth trunk line, of sorts, entered the picture, based on the Grand Trunk of Canada (a land whose tiny population could not begin to provide enough domestic traffic to keep its railroads alive), which had connections eastward to Portland and westward over the Michigan Central to Chicago. The Grand Trunk would remain a thorn in the trunk lines' sides for years, even after Vanderbilt acquired control of the Michigan Central in 1878.

Sobered by the growing seriousness of the situation, the trunk lines quite literally fell into line: they agreed upon the percentage shares of westbound traffic that each was entitled to, given the realities of its situation. It was a major concession by these proud businessmen brought up on the principles of rugged individualism. For better or for worse, this long-ago and almost forgotten entente was a real turning point in the conduct of American business, marking acceptance of the concept of "leaders and followers," and it was quick to be copied in many other lines of business during the rest of the century and into the next. It is entirely analogous to what was going on at almost the same time, as the brilliant, prototypical corporate attorney S. C. T. Dodd guided the leading petroleum refiners into the Standard Oil fold. This development, in fact, had been facilitated by an agreement between the Rockefeller interests and the Lake Shore Railroad to cut rates in return for the refiners' agreement to "even out" shipments of oil throughout the year.

The railroad pools, or "cartels" as they are coming to be called fashionably but incorrectly, never covered all the freight traffic of the participating lines. Obviously, purely local, noncompetitive traffic was excluded, which meant generally that the dominant rural population of the nation would be firmly convinced that the pools operated solidly against their interests. It was westbound through traffic on that greatest of history's trade routes, the lines between the seaboard and Chicago, that was giving the most trouble yet had to be depended upon for a disproportionately large share of the lines' profits. Traffic is seldom if ever balanced in both directions on any line of transportation, and the New York-Chicago line was a classic case.

Eastbound traffic on the trunk lines consisted largely of vast quantities of low-rated bulk commodities, of which grains, notably foodstuffs, and petroleum, both crude and refined, were the chief components. They took a lot of railroad cars and produced relatively low ton-mile revenues, but their volume was so great and so steady that it had to be protected at all costs. Westbound traffic was primarily high-rated merchandise traffic, much of it just off the ships from Europe and destined to satisfy a demand among westerners that was growing constantly more sophisticated. It was a prime candidate for rate-cutting, particularly since about half of the boxcars, and sometimes more, rattled westward empty. The famous Trunk Line Pool, therefore, primarily covered westbound freight, but pool agreements came and went in profusion, tailored to meet a given competitive situation wherever and whenever it arose. Of this lucrative westward flow, the New York Central and Erie Railroads were allotted 33 percent each, with the Pennsylvania getting 25 percent and the B. & O., 9 percent. For the moment, Garrett seemed content. It wouldn't last long—merely a couple of years, from 1879 to 1880—but it worked better than anyone had had a reason to expect. The reason was Albert Fink.

Making the pool work was Fink's job, and he went at it with characteristic energy. Before the eyes of the amazed railroad executives, who were still running their offices with only a few clerks, Fink built an organization that at one time employed sixty clerks. In that pre-computer age, the tedious job of collecting and analyzing railroad rates took a lot of manpower, especially as Fink gathered them not merely in trunk line territory but from all over the nation. Solomon himself faced only one seemingly unsolvable problem that we know about, but Fink fielded them all day, every day. That he quickly came up with a plan for a standard freight tariff classification that the participating railroads would accept, and which worked as well as or better than any other before or since, bespeaks years of turning the problems of freight transportation over and over in his mind.

There were, and still are, two kinds of rates: commodity rates, fixed for a given commodity, and class rates, which were the same for all the items in that particular class. Most of the rates related back to the basic, first-class rate between New York and Chicago, which was 75 cents a hundredweight. All other rates for classified freight and for shipments of intermediate distances, were to be based on that 75 cents, which would remain unchanged for the next thirty-five years. By the end of 1878, Chandler notes, Fink had brought into the pool virtually all of the railroads operating east of the Mississippi and north of the Ohio.

Halfway Measures Succeed Halfway

Only a genius could have founded a system that by 1900 would accommodate over ten thousand individual items in six classes; and, as long as merchandise freight remained the railroad's biggest moneymaker, these items represented the backbone of railroad profits, as distinguished from mere volume. From the beginning, however, commodity rates applied to the greater part of railroad traffic by volume. They still do, and while nowadays, with rate-making virtually deregulated, the railroads are regaining much of the quality traffic they lost to trucks, most of it is now "containerized" in containers or truck trailers carried on flat cars, and rates are fixed by contract, "open covenants, openly arrived at."

Commodity rates have always claimed the greater part of traffic executives' time and worry, people being what they are. The principle that "we will be rich together or poor together," as James J. Hill put it to farmers of the upper Midwest, made rates on foodgrains, for example, go down when the market price of the commodity declined. It might not have been by so much, and maybe farmers were netting extremely little during the last quarter of the nineteenth century, but railroad men explicitly recognized that stubbornly keeping rates at a prosperity figure made no sense at all in hard times. If rates were "sticky" on the down side, there was a good reason: when good times came again, nearly everybody with an axe to grind would shout in real or counterfeit indignation when the railroads sought to put rates back on a profitable footing. The historically low rate, in other words, was reflexively asserted to be the proper permanent maximum rate, although there was not a shred of logic in the proposition.

No knottier problem faced Fink and his principals than the question of how to discriminate constructively between roads and terminal ports in their customers' choice of a route to the seaboard. Even if the railroads had arrogantly insisted upon choosing the route by which a pooled shipment would make the nearly thousand-mile-long trip from the seaboard to Chicago or vice versa, as they were frequently accused of doing, the matter of route and port differentials would have had to be faced. This meant that the New York Central, with its superior route leading into the heart of the best port on the east coast, and the Pennsylvania, which, being better managed substantially matched the greater natural advantages of the Vanderbilts' road, ought to charge more per hundredweight for any given shipment into Boston (in the case of the Central) and New York than their weak-sister competitors. The slower, hilly and sinuous routes of the Erie and B. & O., with their

Figure 8.2　Two men sought to bring equity and stability to railroad rates, in quite different ways. Albert Fink (1827–1897), at left, was creator and first head of the Trunk Line Association, a pool that could not stabilize rates in the face of the common law, federal statutes, and temporary excess capacity, but survived in spite of both in the modern rate bureaus that have been found indispensable. Thomas M. Cooley (1824–1897) was a leading Michigan jurist when he accepted the dubious distinction of being the first chairman of a federal regulatory commission (the Interstate Commerce Commission) in 1887, but ill health and an enabling act full of contradictory provisions preordained failure. None of his successors would come any closer to making the Interstate Commerce Commission a constructive economic commission. *(Both pictures courtesy of Library of Congress)*

inferior access to Atlantic harbors, had somehow to charge less. Difference in the quality of the service provided bespoke a differential in rates: nothing seemed simpler or fairer unless one were a New York merchant. These men, who *were* the city fathers in those days, never for a moment accepted the proposition, and their powerful Chamber of Commerce kept the issue alive well into the twentieth century, to no avail. Even today, analysts of the decline of New York Port cite these differentials as having played a major role in the passing of its greatness, as if they had never seen such motion pictures as "On the Waterfront," or visited the superbly efficient new intermodal ports of Newark, New Orleans, and Houston, to name a few.

What could be more remarkable, then, and less in character for a man brought up in the age of individualism under the tutelage of that greatest individualist of them all—the Cornelius Vanderbilt who once remarked, "Cain't I do what I want with my *own?*"—than for William H. Vanderbilt to consent to route and port differentials? That some railroads could charge ten cents less per hundredweight than the Central did on westbound traffic, and three cents less on eastbound? It was mere common sense, because otherwise the B. & O. was sure to shade its rate, regardless of what had been agreed to by Fink's organization, if it wanted any business, and in doing so it would take an inordinate amount from the Central, as people tend to overdo that sort of thing. The Central and the Pennsylvania would have to follow the B. & O. down the rate scale, with the Erie huffing and puffing to keep up. The superiority of New York port a hundred years ago, when freight came by rail and oceangoing vessel to the city's very doorstep, is hard to imagine in these days of decaying piers that have been deserted save by nude sunbathers and members of America's newest social class, the homeless. Far more ships called regularly at New York than at Philadelphia and Baltimore combined; shipments loaded at New York were out on the high seas while those from the other two cities spent a day trudging down Delaware or Chesapeake Bay and another day headed back north before they could gain the great circle route to Liverpool.

New York was not the exclusive scene of action during this period when American railroads made their first concerted grab for the brass ring. In some respects, westerners had gone further and succeeded more nearly, and one of the earliest and most successful pools in the nation was the Iowa Pool. A look at the railroad map of Iowa, with four major mainline railroads heading due west from Chicago in the 1870s, making for the jumping-off point of the first transcontinental railroad at Council Bluffs on the Missouri River, will persuade anyone that a master hand would be required to keep rate-making from assuming the most unpleasant aspects of an Oriental bazaar. That master hand actually belonged to several men, if one may be permitted to distort the metaphor totally, but one man led them all: James F. Joy. His was the most important name in the establishment of modern transportation in what was to become the most fruitful agricultural region on the face of the earth: the Midwest.

Beginning with the Michigan Central, "Democracy's railroad," which the Democracy had made a mess of, Joy brought the Boston capitalists, as they have come to be referred to, whose principal was John Murray Forbes, into the railroad picture from Detroit to the Missouri Valley; and if the Bostonians were not enough backing, he had the strong support of Moses Taylor, a founder of the National City Bank of New York, as well. The Bostonians' line, which was the Chicago, Burlington & Quincy; the Rock Island; the Chicago & North Western; and the Chicago, Milwaukee & St. Paul, managed very well, even in the face of vigorous opposition from Jay Gould's Union Pacific, which would have preferred to make individual deals in dividing through freights with the Pool roads, until continuous building of branches by each of the main lines blurred the picture and the Pool simply outgrew its original function. In the end, events controlled it, not vice versa, as a growing farm population's overproduction of an exportable surplus of foodgrains in this region depressed prices and rates and pretty well demoralized the Pool by the mid-1880s. At that, it had lasted longer and proved stronger than the Trunk Line Pool, where conditions were changing even more rapidly.

Pools sprang up in the far Midwest as well; by the late 1880s there were at least six lines competing for traffic on the busy run between Chicago and the Twin Cities of St. Paul and Minneapolis. Out of these pools operating west of the Mississippi River there evolved the Western Traffic Association, at about the same time that Fink's handiwork came to be referred to as Official Territory for tariff purposes, and the Joint Traffic Association as a rate-making body. The Southwest and the Southeast also established pools, while in the far West C. P. Huntington's Southern Pacific and associated steamship lines, which braved the terrors of Cape Horn to keep the S.P.'s eastern connections reasonable, ruled the roost.

"A doubt justly exists as to whether . . . pooling is finally to become the sovereign and general remedy for all the evils which now afflict the railroad interests," wrote Joseph Nimmo in his 1881 report on internal commerce; "the evolution of the railroad system of the United States has been a constant succession of surprises." Indeed it had, and the surprises had only just begun. The weakness of the pools lay, in practical terms, in the underlying assumption that there was something stable about the percentage shares of revenues that each participating railroad was to receive. The relative position of American railroads was constantly shifting, however, not only because of differential rates of growth, but also because new competition from outside was constantly appearing on the scene.

As to the first, the Pennsylvania Railroad, which was growing phenomenally in these years, was disgruntled to discover at each periodic reckoning of the pool results that it "owed" the pool rather than being owed, because during the year it had carried more freight than the shares allowed for. This situation persisted, despite the fact that as late as 1890 the Pennsylvania was frequently trundling freight over to the B. & O. and Erie's freight yards in Chicago, in direct violation of the Act of 1887 to Regulate Interstate Commerce, and even though some shippers may have chosen the Pennsylvania in the first place. Clearly, the Pennsy would have done all right even if there had been no pool. The new competition appeared primarily in the shape of Jay Gould, who went after a share of the rich profits the trunk lines were making by trying to patch together such lesser lines as the Wabash, the Lackawanna, the Central of New Jersey, and the New York, Boston & Erie (that "scarlet woman," as the poor old financial football was called) into another trunk line. The hard fact, which no one realized better than the realistic Mr. Fink by the early 1880s, was that the railroads were going to have to do some growing up to fill out the ambitious system of rails that they had spun for themselves.

What Remains of the Pools Today

What is the significance of this oft-told story, and why recount it here? Its significance for anyone interested in the permanent impression that the railroads made upon American life is that, at a time when the advantages of voluntary cooperation between corporate members of an industry had not yet been recognized, nor any procedure devised for realizing them, the railroad men achieved a measure of success, at least until the doors of political demagogy slammed in their face with the Act of 1887. One of the most salient points Fink made when called upon, as he frequently was even by railroad men themselves, to defend the idea of pooling is that it was assuredly the only alternative to consolidation of the myriad independent railroad corporations into a few or perhaps even into one giant "corporation of corporations." Later on even that kind of concerted action would run afoul of public opinion, as Americans stretched the old concept of restraint of trade to cover the acquisition of great power, no matter how quiescent or benignly employed, or how efficient in the use of resources. Still later, in our own day, the consolidation of the many into the few has come to seem the most natural development in a new age.

Meanwhile, however, the rate associations became the very prototype of an active, aggressive trade association, a model which the manufacturing giants that were on the horizon by 1880 would find useful. Keeping shippers honest turned out to be almost as big a problem as keeping the constituent railroads in the pool honest, for shippers had learned many ways to get around the classification and weight rules that the railroads laid down. The knotty problem of rate divisions between companies forming parts of a through route also found its first even treatment within Fink's organization.

The traffic associations have proved, in fact, to be as lasting as the problems of uniformity of rates and classifications themselves, and no amount of huffing and puffing by Congress and assorted reformers, Pulitzer-prize-winning "investigative journalists," commisioners of dying commissions, and politicians in search of an issue, has prevailed against them. They are so clearly useful and vital that it hardly seemed necessary to grant the railroads specific immunity from the antitrust laws for agreeing among themselves on the rate schedules they proposed for the Interstate Commerce Commission's approval. But that legislation, bearing the giggly name of the Reed-Bulwinkle Act (1948), had to be passed by a Republican Congress over the veto of that old-fashioned Progressive, Harry S Truman, and still sticks in the craw of his political heirs. This seems to be one aspect of concerted action by businessmen, however, which is in little danger from men "who have learned nothing and forgotten nothing." Informed persons saw the light long ago. Henry Carter Adams, counsel to the U.S. Senate during its hearings on what eventually became the Hepburn Act of 1906, and later a leading thinker early in the new century on the role of big business in society, wrote in his 1905 digest of those hearings:

> Such associations [as the eastern and western rate bureaus] in fact exist now as they did before those decisions [of the Supreme Court in 1897 and 1898 invalidating them] and with the same general effect. . . . In justice to all parties, it is difficult to see how our interstate railways could be operated with due regard to the interest of the shipper and the railway, without concerted action of the kind afforded through these associations.

The brief era of the pools was not without some permanent influence upon American railroad men, having left them with a profound appreciation of the virtues of sweet reasonableness. True, an era of back-scratching deal-making ensued, the likes of which would never be seen again. The pools taught men of the 1880s that, if they had not yet found their salvation, it clearly lay in their own hands. They were right, for neither government laws nor commissions could stem the tide of competition in an era when interest costs were too high, trackage was temporarily excessive, and prices, including freight rates, were too low; and when these conditions would no longer rule, such external controls would be at best redundant and at worst, destructive. How railroad men would solve their problems, and have the good fortune to benefit from the Brave New Century's prosperity, while their enemies multiplied and waxed ever more radical, is a matter for a later chapter.

CHAPTER 9
==

From Mercantile Nation
to Industrial Giant

> The process [of U.S. industrial growth] began well before the
> Civil War, when a few firms espoused a strategy of production
> and sales which rendered middlemen irrelevant. These new
> firms were the . . . direct antecedents of the modern, gigantic,
> integrated iron and steel firms that dominate the industry today.
> The event which called forth these new firms was the coming of
> the railroad—one of the greatest causes of social and economic
> change in the 19th century.
>
> Glenn Porter and Harold Livesay,
> *Merchants and Manufacturers* (1971)

Making Things Becomes Big Business

It was probably no surprise to anyone that when the numerous volumes
of the Industrial Commission's Final Report were released in 1902, the
lion's share of attention had been given to the nation's railroads. The
single, broad question before the group of Congressmen and private-
citizen experts who made up the commission—although it was not
expressed in so many words—was, what are the implications of the
recent consolidations of corporate power in large-scale industry, how
have they come about, and what, if anything can we do, or must we do,
to control the vast access of power over the lives of the citizens that
they imply? The merger movement in manufacturing, as distinguished
from commerce (a distinction that the U.S. Supreme Court had recently
drawn), had only got well underway in the previous decade, under the
stringencies of the 1893–1897 depression, but the railroads had been
combining and recombining corporate properties for decades. And during the depression they had virtually concentrated all of the freight traffic of the nation—if not nearly all of the passenger traffic—in a half
dozen or so "communities of interest," which owed their power to a
little understood alliance of bankers, big shippers, and railroad management executives. Was the same thing now beginning to happen
in the manufacturing sector of the new century's rampant American
economy?

The railroads had created the new industrial giant, which was now flexing his muscles so dramatically. Whereas the railroads, being essentially public service enterprises requiring special state charter considerations and unprecedented amounts of capital, were owned by thousands of persons who had bought stock in them, manufacturing was still mostly privately financed and often very much of a family affair. A prominent railroad president, George R. Blanchard, estimated for the commission that 950,000 people owned stock in American railroads and 300,000 held bonds. Moreover, the railroads were considered such objectively valuable assets (even if rather limited in their physical recoverability) that the greater part of the book value of railroad property had come to be vested in first-mortgage bonds or one of the other grades of debt securities that a highly inventive Wall Street had devised. We have no such turn-of-the-century data on public ownership of shares in American manufacturing industry, but it was obviously small, as revealed by the handful of such concerns for which price quotations on the New York Stock Exchange appear in the daily newspapers of the period.

Anyone with a superficial knowledge of the trials and tribulations of investors in railroad securities since their inception will smile at the statement that manufacturing enterprises, unlike railroads, were essentially risky business. But manufacturing entails routinely shouldering big risks that mean big profits to new enterprises that size up their markets shrewdly, invest prudently in fixed assets, and operate with hard-nosed efficiency. Thence come the profits on which long-term growth is based. Manufacturing innovation is either product-oriented, or process-oriented; usually both. "Build a better mousetrap, my son, and the world will beat a path to your door," went the cliché, but it was only half true. No matter how much better the mousetrap, an enterprise set up to make and sell it has to crawl before it walks, and walk before it runs. It must plow back most—preferably all—of its net profits and perhaps absorb additional capital as well, *if* it can be had. This is risk redoubled. As the virtues of the product become widely known, advertising becomes feasible and our well-managed mousetrap-maker is off to the races. Meanwhile, others are inventing still better mousetraps, preferably bright young men and women on his payroll. Or others may invent better machines for making better mousetraps. Or worse still, improvements in standards of living may vastly reduce the mouse population, especially as better building materials and poisons become available and the population of terriers and housecats grows. For any of these reasons, manufacturing enterprises can quickly become almost worthless drab buildings full of machines and special tools that make the autioneer wonder, "what the h_____l do you suppose *this* was for?"

The emergence of big business, or even not-small business, therefore, was a very delicate process, depending primarily upon the development and the accessibility of a gigantic American market for a manufacturer's goods. As Thomas Cochran has pointed out, this was the vital factor in American economic growth, which was detectable well before the Civil War. As Alfred D. Chandler, Jr., and his many acolytes have demonstrated, the railroad was right at the heart of the forces that produced an America that by 1900 was ready to take its turn as the "workshop of the world." (The 1880s, Chandler feels, are the key to the emergence of big business. It is no coincidence that the 1880s were the golden age of American railroad expansion.)

Not One Industrial Revolution, but Two

The word "mercantile" was a long time dying in the vocabulary of American commerce. For centuries before the American industrial revolution, delayed as it was until almost the middle of the nineteenth century, men who were not members of the learned professions were either farmers, artisans, or merchants and their army of clerks. A mercantile establishment was one that dealt in both selling and buying almost any manner of goods for which the merchant perceived a demand, however fleeting, that would enable him to dispose of them at a profit. The import-export trade, carried on until well into the nineteenth century by "sedentary" merchants, was part and parcel of mercantile business. So was the business of traveling through the countryside to round up supplies or handicrafts for resale in original form or to comprise the few manufactured articles that figured in trade 150 years ago. Most familiar of all was the retail shopkeeper, primarily in the country store, which was the last stop on a circuitous, inefficient, expensive, and time-consuming distribution process before the age of modern transportation. The history of Anglo-American jurisprudence is replete with cases involving relations between buyers and sellers and reveals that in the collection of debts and foreclosure of mortgages the creditor located at a distance often had to resort to the federal court system to protect himself from the provincialism of local judges and juries. The Constitution, many a judge seemed to feel, did not automatically follow the invoice.

Where did manufacturing—strictly speaking, the application of human manual skills to materials to produce useful objects, but later implying the application of machines and artificial power—fit into this scheme of things? The young republic might career westward pell-mell, but somehow men and women would have to get along with only such basic necessities as they could carve out of the forests or raise from the ground until the merchants found a way to bring consumers and producers together. Indeed, most people were both producer and consumer until the latter part of the nineteenth century. The birth of anything resembling an industrial society in the interior, with men and women in workclothes trudging off, dinner pail in hand, to grim factories and ten hours of hard, often dangerous, usually repetitive labor, would have to await the coming of the railroads. So would the higher material standard of living that the new social organization for productive work would bring, most especially for the hordes of peasants, redundant to Europe's economies, who filled the steerages of the first vessels to wallow across the Atlantic at least partially under their own power.

Meanwhile people made do with what they had, while they awaited something better. Natural sources of power, mostly from animals, were made to serve, after a fashion, and, even during the darkening days of the 1770s, when mother England undertook to prohibit colonial manufacture of virtually everything she could supply or that would inflame rambunctious Americans, men surreptitiously practiced an astonishing range of handicrafts. Little of high quality, like fine tools, cutlery, firearms, and clocks, was undertaken, however, and some goods were sternly forbidden to be made for reasons other than economic. (Benjamin Franklin, commenting on the worn condition of printing types in the colonies, which Americans were forbidden to cast for themselves, noted wryly that the best way to keep something a secret was to publish it in America!)

America's backwardness in joining the industrial revolution had two chief causes: the lack of adequate sources of power, and the absence of an effective market for the goods of entrepreneurs limited by the difficulty and the cost of inland transportation to local or regional markets. Adam Smith sagely observed of the factory revolution, which was just beginning in England when he published his *Wealth of Nations* in 1776, that the division of labor is limited by the size of the market. What is true of individual workmen is also true of enterprises: if an entrepreneur was to manufacture clocks, for example, he would have to specialize in clocks, hiring specially trained artisans and investing in special production tools. But the local market would soon have all the clocks it could use. This is all the explanation we need of why American manufacturing remained localized, based on handicrafts and running largely to textiles and wooden and iron pots, pans, and simple tools, and little that was technologically demanding. Withal, there were always the dogged, frequently tragic pioneers, who sought to produce for markets that were not yet there, in the hope that "something will turn up" to carry their goods to market.

Men born after 1800 would face new opportunities because of the precipitous decline in the cost of inland transportation, both of raw materials in, and finished goods out. It is not enough to say that the railroads encouraged the industrial revolution in America, or that they ushered in the big changes that came after about 1830. The railroads, in fact, were *vital* to the emergence of industrial America. Factories were suddenly liberated from the few sites that offered adequate water power. Enthusiasts still study the water wheel in human history, as they study the steam locomotive, but the latter, once it was hauling anthracite coal out of the hills of eastern Pennsylvania, and men had learned to burn it under a boiler to make steam for stationary engines, put the water wheel out of business. It all happened in a remarkably short period of time. It was not unlike raising a curtain on a dramatic tableau called The Modern World.

By the turn of the century, changes were taking place in European and American industry that can not be explained by such simple cause-and-effect relations. After the depression of the 1890s, there seemed to be the most striking outpouring of sophisticated new industries, which promised to revolutionize the lives of all people from the top to the bottom of the social scale and make consumers of us all. The new industries, of which the most important ones were chemicals, electricity (equipment plus generation and distribution of power), automobiles, and radio, or, as it is generalized today, electronics, were based upon fundamental scientific discoveries that were the fruit of a century of near-peace in the western world from 1815 to 1914.

Economic affairs thenceforth were conducted under vastly more complex conditions than before. The railroads, which had pioneered the techniques of marshaling great amounts of capital from myriad sources, now found themselves with the transportation demands of all these new industries heaped upon them. At the same time they had to compete vigorously with them in the capital markets for the always scarce resources with which to march forward into what in every way deserves to be called the second industrial revolution. So different in kind, the second could never have come into being without the great economic strides already made in establishing the basic industries of the first. They deserve a closer examination.

Made in the U.S.A.: The Textile Industry

Anyone who has watched yarn that is to be woven into cloth being spun from staple fiber on an old-fashioned spinning wheel (a sight to be seen at few places in the western world except at fairs and in museums) needs no explanation of why the factory system began with the textile industry. Before the invention of the spinning jenny, from which the modern spinning machine, with its several hundred spindles and perhaps one machine tender for every pair of machines, was developed, a yard of good cloth represented many hours of the most tedious labor. Such labor was often not very skilled, either, and the resulting yarn when woven into cloth often varied considerably in thickness along its length and lacked "hand," or the feel of quality, so that the resulting garment shrieked "yokel" about its wearer. The word "homespun" came to mean amateurish, backward, rooted in the soil.

Once the highly uniform fabrics of the factory era became available, the demand for them from all parts of the world dictated constant additions to mill capacity. Early Marxists seized upon the widespread switch to cheap cotton garments as evidence of the "immiseration" of the working class by capitalists, since presumably the poor could no longer afford wool. It remained for wiser men to point out to Marx and Engels that before the advent of factory-made cotton textiles, the working classes seldom owned more than one outergarment, which they wore until laundering it became a sheer necessity, and, other than a breech-clout, they generally had no undergarments. The featherbed, often the chief item in a bride's dowry, was a necessity in a day when simple folk slept in the nude. The rise of the factory-based textile industry was a social boon second only to advances in food production and the availability of fossil fuels to replace the disappearing forests.

The mechanization of spinning and weaving, in point of fact, did not wait for the coming of the railroad. The industry, like nearly every other economic enterprise, made its first great headway in England, where climate, convenient rivers, and canals gave her a head start on nations that would depend upon railroads. Even in America, however, where good transportation and skilled mechanics were both lacking, the factory system was successfully established by Francis Cabot Lowell and associates early in the nineteenth century on the Charles River falls at Waltham, Massachusetts. The most immediate reason for their optimism was Jefferson's embargo of trade with Europe. But Lowell had traveled in Europe during the earliest years of the century and had somehow got admitted to an English mill where the newly invented power looms were being used. In the face of an English policy that kept such priceless inventions a secret and prevented the emigration of men who could build and maintain them, Lowell brought back to America a mental picture of the looms from which he drew a sketch and, with an exceptionally bright young "mechanic" in his employ, built the first such looms in the United States. Thus his mill was "integrated" with spinning jennies, and the chief obstacle to attaining a volume market— the fact that one spinning machine required up to a dozen skilled, scarce hand-loom operators if its output was to be fully utilized—was overcome. In those days, technological progress made jobs, rather than destroying them, but they were jobs in factories, and they did not require the handicraft skills that weaving always had.

Lowell's factory system featured a personnel policy that supplied it with plenty of vigorous young women who were intent on working just long enough for their dowry (which often went to finance the westward migration of the happy young couple not long after). He saw to their room, board, and moral care (they lived in dormitories under strict supervision), and the new system was a resounding success. The labor system was soon replaced by a much less paternalistic system, but New England, with a growing market at home and abroad and plentiful supplies of cotton arriving by water and soon by rail, remained the center of the American textile industry until well into the twentieth century. The American industry was content until the last third of the old century to leave fine textiles to the English and the Europeans. When the American economy faltered in the depression that began in 1873, it was attributed to high domestic prices and a foreign trade balance that led to excessive imports and a level of consumption that could not be sustained under the heartless gold standard. (The standard was allowed to work the way it was supposed to, but the government would not have known what to do about a depression, anyway, even if it had believed that it had the duty to do anything.)

Until this time America's better-grade cotton fabrics, along with a large volume of ready-made cotton garments, had been imported. With the economy reformed, this was all to change rapidly as the domestic textile industry boomed. In 1870 only 845,000 bales of cotton had been consumed in American mills, while 1.9 million, or more than twice as much, were exported. Twenty years later, in 1890, the American textile industry consumed 5 million bales, slightly more than the 4.9 million bales exported. The number of cotton mills grew, and domestic output grew even faster as productivity soared. Many of the new mills were located in the South after 1900, finally redeeming a promise southerners had made to themselves sixty years before.

The railroads, in company with the telegraph, introduced a new era in the marketing of cotton, vastly reducing the costs of getting the staple from the fields to the mills and export docks. They also revolutionized the marketing of the textiles, as more and more cities, towns, and crossroads stores found the quantity and variety of yard goods greater than ever before, and ready-to-wear garments came into their own. Style became increasingly more important, and by 1900 the American textile and garment industries were but the base upon which retail marketing empires flourished throughout the nation; their goods blossomed forth in thousands of churches each Sunday.

Vulcan Rising

Coal, which was so highly prized for raising steam in boilers and thereby liberating the American factory from sources of water power, must have revolutionized the American iron industry and placed it on the road to modern development too, did it not? Fuel, in such energy-intensive industries as metals, is consumed for two main reasons: to do work, which requires steam power (if only indirectly as electricity to run huge electric motors), and to heat materials so that they can be worked. Since some of the carbon in the solid fuels ends up worked into the finished iron or steel, it is ingredient as well as fuel. Economic historians still wrangle over why Americans stubbornly continued to use wood charcoal fuel to smelt iron from the ubiquitous ore (actually, "bog iron") of eastern locales—as many did right down to the end of the nineteenth century—even though the English, seeing their forests disappear inside the insatiable blast furnaces, had learned to use coal a century before. To be sure, charcoal iron was the finest iron made, and it required less skill to produce a better iron than coal did. (Skilled workmen were the scarcest of resources throughout the old century.) Besides, the chestnut forests that provided the charcoal seemed inexhaustible in America in the eighteenth and early nineteenth centuries.

Both a technological breakthrough and the emergence of a fresh and vastly enlarged market were required to bring American iron and steel producers into the new era. Sir Henry Bessemer supplied the one, and the budding American railroad system, the other. Great Britain had attained costs of production and degrees of quality in producing iron (and, beginning in 1859, Bessemer steel) that no other people could match. Millions of tons—more and more of it in the form of rails for the new railroads—were off-loaded at east coast ports down to the early 1870s. Then Andrew Carnegie, Alexander Lyman Holley, and certain others put America in the way of overtaking Great Britain in iron and steel manufacture after about 1873. Before the depression was over, the virtues of integrating the successive steps of smelting iron, converting it to steel, and rolling or drawing ingots into finished goods,was well recognized and practiced.

No matter how Americans might have longed to adopt the Bessemer process a generation before, if Sir Henry had come along earlier in the history of technology, they would not have been able to do so. The huge amounts of heat energy that were involved required more and cheaper fuel than charcoal could provide. Long before the old century was over, the steel made in one year in the United States, if made from charcoal, would have denuded northeastern forests of chestnut trees. Before the big change, charcoal iron was the only kind there was, and it was employed sparingly. Only the moving parts of textile and woodworking machines, for example, were made of metal until well into the nineteenth century. Wood and leather were used extensively in machine making in those days.

One phenomenon—the railroad revolution—brought both the cheap fuel that made the Bessemer process feasible, and the enlarged market that made it necessary. From the biggest metalworkers to the smallest, coal became the fuel of choice. Henry W. Longfellow's village blacksmith went on clanging away in his little smithy "under the spreading chestnut trees," but it was coal or its refinement, coke, not charcoal, that fired his forge. (Both the smith and the chestnut tree began to disappear after 1900, as the automobile and the chestnut blight spread in America.) Men were soon doing more with iron, and doing it faster, than ever before. The cry for heavier artillery during the Civil War encouraged this infant industry to roll thicker plate and cast and machine larger mortars and cannons than anyone had ever thought possible, and in far less time, while the railroads introduced traffic management procedures that enabled the railroads to do work far more efficiently than ever before. But no wartime stringency could match the remarkable virtues of steel rails when it came to changing the way men did things.

The arrival of the railroads in this rough and ready society, so eager to leap forward and take over from Europe the lucrative job of supplying the needs of what was becoming the largest market in the western world, was like the arrival of Casanova at the French court: affairs multiplied. The entire industry developed, within the first generation of the coal and Bessemer technologies, a marked inclination westward. First to go, naturally, were the old iron establishments of the Northeast, ranging from rural blast furnaces turning out pig and bar iron, like the ones deep in the chestnut forests of Salisbury in northwest Connecticut, to the integrated facilities of such men as Peter Cooper and his son-in-law, Abram Hewitt.

The future of the industry depended upon being able to assemble in one place huge tonnages of iron ore and mountains of coal, in the form of coke, plus sundry other feedstocks. If an abundant supply of coal was handy and it was ideally suited to baking into coke, like that of the Connellsville District in western Pennsylvania; and if the locale was not too far from deep-water navigation, so that the fabulous deposits of hematite (almost pure iron oxide) in Michigan's Upper Peninsula could be brought in cheaply; *and* if vigorous, well-managed railroads like the Pennsylvania and B. & O. were at hand to take the product to market then the result could only be an iron and steel complex second to none in low costs of production. If mid-Victorians had had computers into which to program these criteria, the answer would have come out loud and clear: Pittsburgh! In a few short years, the shoreline of the Great Lakes from Buffalo to Chicago also became a major part of a steel industry that had found the attractions of the Midwest irresistible. If the ferrous metals industry assured the rise of one of the world's most highly industrialized regions barely a century after the last naked Indian had fled the scene, the railroads must bear most of the praise and the blame.

Staff of Life

There was one specialized "manufacturer" that even the tiniest hamlets had accommodated in the preindustrial era: the miller who ground the food grains of the countryside into flour for the people's bread. Indeed, the figures on nineteenth century manufacturing, sketchy as they are, consistently show food products as a major factor in the total, due primarily to the universality of the demand for flour. The demand has remained, despite a steady succession of diet fads in the overfed twentieth century, but not the mills and millers. Save for textiles, no other branch of early manufacturing received more attention from inspired mechanics like Oliver Evans, who designed the first almost totally automated flour mill. Even so, the industry remained on a regional basis until the evolving railroad network, especially west of Buffalo, changed just about everything. As wheat-growing moved westward, less and less wheat went east as grain, and more and more as flour. A rapidly rising population assured a mass market for a flour-milling industry at Buffalo that awed all who observed it. Well into the twentieth century, it ground out flour, while the giant mills of Lackawanna Steel belched clouds of smoke into an Edwardian sky that seemed to promise to dispose of any amount of pollution modern man might send heavenward.

The railroads, with their power to enthrone and dethrone, kept on revolutionizing the flour-milling industry in the nineteenth century. They carried millions of settlers to the virgin prairies of the trans-Missouri West, who set to producing an annual surplus of wheat such as no one had ever imagined. Fortunately for Americans, if not for Europeans, the Old World suffered from a succession of poor harvests in addition to a remarkable obtuseness in the use of their own new railroads. The politically powerful landowners of the Rhineland, for example, made it clear to the bureaucrats of the Prussian State Railways that they would not tolerate the introduction of low through rates on grains and potatoes on the railroad line that the state had built to link distant East Prussia (Germany's "Far West") with the rest of the Wilhelmine Empire. Thus, the low production costs in the eastern lands were not taken advantage of; their new settlers began to wonder what they had come for, some moving on into Czarist Russia; and the Königsberg line operated at a loss because it had little else to carry.

There was a joker in the exceptional fertility of the Great Plains, however, and that is that the winters were much too cold to grow the traditional soft winter wheat from which the western world had long made its fine bread and cake flours. No American housewife, having learned through trial and error—there is no other way—over a period of years to make good bread, would have wasted a minute on the grayish flour that the hard spring wheat of the Plains made. Innovating a little and borrowing a lot from earlier technology, Americans solved the problem with roller mills, operating with finely machined and polished steel rollers in place of millstones, and the "middlings purifier," which separated out the husks of the wheat berry that were the culprit.

On the old theory that wheat should be ground into flour at the closest practical point to its harvest, the milling industry leaned dramatically westward. Lo, there stood the village of St. Anthony, at the falls that marked the northern end of practical steam navigation on the Mississippi River—the only important source of water power in the upper Midwest. By 1870 St. Anthony, renamed Minneapolis, had blossomed forth as the center of the fastest growing segment of the flour-milling industry, and soon the Washburn-Crosby and Pillsbury trademarks had become some of the earliest household names in the new era of branded consumer goods. Meanwhile Minneapolis's Twin City, St.

Paul, was looking to its laurels as the urban center of this fruitful new land. The Twin Cities had been linked by rail with Chicago only in 1867, but rail lines grew rapidly in every direction thereafter, and so did the country.

Delivering the Goods: Growth Phenomenon and Logistical Headache

"The railway situation east of Chicago is rapidly coming to a point where the facilities are taxed to their full capacity. . . . The terminal facilities of five years ago are no longer equal to the service. . . . Many think the only solution will be a decentralization of terminals. . . . It is difficult to bore an inch hole with a half-inch auger." In these comments, made over a period of ten years at the beginning of the twentieth century, James J. Hill described a problem that hung over American railroads like a sagging ceiling. His warning was front-page news, for Hill had become the leading railroad man in the nation in the wake of his and J. P. Morgan's victory over Edward H. Harriman in the struggle to control the railroads of the Northwest. As the North American nations inexorably became a society consisting of densely populated urban centers, separated by thinly peopled agricultural lands and by the considerable distances that made the distinctly American low long-distance transportation rates necessary, their railroads became increasingly aware of the old saying that in any journey, the first and the last few miles are often the hardest.

The railroads, when the century was still new, came to realize that they had created a problem for themselves and society in general that would not be readily nor cheaply solved. The revolution in the production of useful goods and services, which we have sketched earlier in this chapter, amounted to a social revolution as well. For reasons not clearly understood then—or, for that matter, now—Americans seem to have decided almost unanimously that more and more of their productive activities would require them to live cheek by jowl in cities, in closely packed neighborhoods convenient to factories and offices requiring large numbers of intelligent, reasonably well-educated people, who were engaged more and more in abstract ("paper-pushing") activities that seemed to have less and less to do with useful work. With the advent of electric traction after 1885, the central core of cities that was accessible in a reasonable travel time was greatly enlarged, and, of those who prospered in those years in Sam Bass Warner's *Streetcar Suburbs,* more and more were joining the rich folks in the commuter communities, which had long been profitably served by the mainline steam railroads.

Not that small-town America was dead—not by a long shot. America remained the land *par excellence* of thousands of small and medium-size market centers—virtually all of which were calling themselves "cities" in the booster days of the Progressive era—complete with local pride and provincial sneers for the next place of three, five, or ten thousand along the rail line that served them both. Outwardly, even after the basic changes in the structure of American economic society had been completed about 1929, the old independence seemed intact. But by 1910, if you had asked any small-town banker, merchant, or processor of natural resources, he would have told you, with a bitterness that was about to blur political party lines and finally destroy the old standoff between government and big business, that the towns had become mere satellites of the big cities, humbly submitting to powerful bankers their plans for the little enterprises that were closest to local hearts. We are told how much we shall receive for our produce, and we are told what we must pay for the goods we need, and yet no one has given these people the right to decide; such was the cry. Even so, one bond made the picket-fenced white clapboard bungalows of the towns as much a part of the big-city economy as the endless blocks of frame triple-deckers in the old whaling and mercantile cities of the Northeast.

This was the America that the railroads had made, laying a "metropolitan corridor," as John R. Stilgoe has called it, through the hinterland. The force behind its emergence, however, was not the logic of the physical sciences, but of economics. The railroads had not "knitted the country together," as some have said, but on the contrary had differentiated a homogeneous agrarian society into superbly interdependent organic components. They encouraged both people and localities to "do their thing," that is, to concentrate their energies on what they could do best, thus working out insofar as is possible in a highly imperfect world the economist's principle of comparative advantage.

East Liverpool, in extreme eastern Ohio, just across the Ohio River and not far from Pittsburgh, began as a frontier settlement in 1798 in which everybody except a few did just what everybody in Canton, founded in 1806, and Mansfield, laid out in 1808, did until well into the century: farm, practice professions and crafts, run stores, and have babies. When the first trains of what would ultimately be lines of the Pennsylvania began to arrive in the 1840s, a few were doing something else. In East Liverpool, the foundations of a pottery and china business were laid as a few townspeople experimented with the fine clays that abounded in the area, developing a small trade down the Ohio River— in the wrong direction, unfortunately, from the mass market to the east. Meanwhile Canton and Mansfield developed typical small charcoal-fueled iron-smelting furnaces and the beginnings of a superb pool of skilled mechanics.

By the glory days of railroad construction, in the 1880s, all three of these Ohio cities were solidly based communities: East Liverpool made china and earthenware for the millions, and Mansfield prospered in a number of metalworking trades, developed into a substantial factor in "Little Steel," and at the turn of the century welcomed the automobile age with open arms. Canton made roller bearings, vacuum cleaners, and many other metal products, and gave the nation its twenty-fifth president, William McKinley. The products of these and a thousand similar places, larger and smaller, were sold all over the world, and they hardly needed the protective tariff that McKinley championed so successfully. Historians who would explain the decline of small cities like these will have to look farther than liberalization of the tariff or high railroad freight rates. But for a century such cities were proud points along the metropolitan corridor, and their era coincides closely with that of the passenger trains that came through a dozen times a day. Such development of the principle of *e pluribus unum* could not have been achieved, however, even after railroads as well engineered and built as any in the world had linked cities, towns, and countryside, without the remarkable system of marketing institutions that evolved in the nineteenth and twentieth centuries. They were the products of pure pragmatism, for the men and women who created them had been left to their own devices to solve problems as they arose. And that is why they have worked as well as they have.

Who can imagine the delight of the busy farmers and merchants of the area around Worcester, Massachusetts, upon finding out 150 years ago that completion of the Boston & Worcester Railroad had reduced the two-day round trip to "The Hub," which they had to make several times a year, to a single day? Or of Bostonians, who saw the variety and freshness of produce improve just as its price began to decline with the widening of the supply area? Surely it was the millenium, but in truth the changes were just beginning. As we have noted frequently, American railroads remained largely local affairs for their first generation. In terms of their share of total U.S. commerce, they probably did not surpass river transportation until the eve of the Civil War. The wharves of the Ohio at Cincinnati and the Mississippi in the 1840s and 1850s, which were favorite subjects of early artists, teemed with men and goods, and the ungainly steamboats nuzzled each other impatiently for a place to tie up. Change came quickly after 1860, however, and the Civil War proved little more than a ripple in a powerful trend.

The marketing of agricultural commodities, which made up most of commerce at mid-century, responded quickly to the advent of instantaneous communication, which followed the railroad by about fifteen years. In combination with the new all-rail routes from the Mississippi River to seaboard, the long-distance telegraph, which had achieved reasonable reliability by the late 1850s, made trading in commodities for future delivery feasible. Sadly, just as a sophisticated economic control mechanism was emerging, speculators who merely bet on a rise or fall in prices left their gamblers' mark on the system, in the view of the masses—a mark that has proved all but indelible. They upstaged the bona fide traders who sought to insure their purchase of raw materials against price declines. Thus the futures market, though one of the foundation stones of modern commerce, is also one of the most controversial.

By 1870 the foundations of the modern American distribution system had been laid. The process would go from old-style diversified merchants acting as commission wholesalers of the growing stream of mostly imported but increasingly American factory-made goods; to wholesalers who accepted consignments of goods subject to their sale; to merchant wholesalers, largely handling the lines of hundreds of small manufacturers who offered large discounts to wholesalers who would buy outright from them in "job lots" (the entire quantity that it was practical to make in a single factory run) of their specialties. Such wholesalers lived on volume, and in order to get it they had to spread their nets wide, sending men in remarkably large numbers out to "drum up" business. Their appearance at dusty little country crossroads stores, to which they would travel by horse and buggy rented at the nearest railroad town, was often as much social as a matter of business.

Dry goods salesmen—men who spent their lives "in ladies' ready-to-wear," as the burlesque show gag went—carried heavy sample cases, but the touchstone of the merchant wholesaler was that he represented a broad range of small-ticket items that had to be sold by catalogue. Such men inevitably became mere order-takers for goods that required no demonstration or installation. The muscular salesman of anvils who trudged from customer to customer carrying his heavy sample in Meredith Willson's musical comedy "The Music Man," was a humorous fiction. In the days before the automobile and all-weather roads had killed the country store, and eventually the small-town merchant, too, the traveling salesman was the backbone of the rail passenger business. Pullman smoking compartments, thick with cigars' blue haze, were the clearinghouses for the nation's naughtier anecdotes.

The merchant wholesaler never occupied an exclusive role in the distribution process. In certain lines, such as dry goods, including ready-made garments that grew steadily in importance, distribution followed a different pattern, being dominated for a long time by big-city importing and retailing firms whose prestige and knowledge of what the small-town merchant needed formed the basis of some of America's earliest fortunes. The most notable of these institutions—for institutions they were, as much as apple pie and the Fourth of July—were Marshall Field & Co., of Chicago, A. T. Stewart & Co., of New York, and John Wanamaker & Co., of Philadelphia. Their success was based upon the ability of their senior buyers to predict the reaction of customers to specific "nouveautés," as the trend-setting French *magasins*, or department stores, called the style goods in which these famous American "big stores" specialized. These big enterprises were among the earliest volume advertisers in the budding newspapers of the late nineteenth century, demanding front-page placement. They influenced fashions but they did not dictate them, for consumers have always had minds of their own. A. T. Stewart, among the most frugal of men, is supposed to have said—in the closest he ever came to a pungent remark—that one-half of his advertising was wasted but, trouble was, he didn't know which half. It is a witticism that latter-day advertising men have endlessly misinterpreted.

The fastest growing branch of commerce in America in the nineteenth century, however, and well into the twentieth, was industrial goods, as might be expected of a people who were investing every cent they could save and borrow—at home and abroad—in their new cities, mechanized farms, factories, telegraph and telephone systems and, above all, railroads. The merchant wholesaler would not have done at all for the increasingly complex and expensive materials and components that entered the stream of commerce after 1830. A knowledge of the product lines, their strengths and weaknesses, the output capacities of their manufacturers, contact built up over the years with industrial purchasing agents, and last but by no means least, sources of credit for the hard-pressed manufacturers who were typically undercapitalized, was vital. Over the long run, these men made a vital contribution to entrepreneurial innovation by providing their principals with information about new business opportunities and who was deciding the design of components and selecting the supplier.

The manufacturer's agent emerged to supply, primarily, the knowledge of the needs of users and the capacities of suppliers to satisfy them in quality and quantity. Selling has not so completely lost its individualistic touch today that the manufacturer's agent is extinct, for, indeed, these energetic persons still hold the two ends of the industrial chain together. Rapid technological change, so long as it continues, guarantees that agents will remain important. Certain of these agent functions have been assumed by the modern corporate purchasing agent, who systematized the buying procedures of his company, assured himself that supplies would be available in sufficient quantity at such future dates as were anticipated, and worked with technical people of his firm in engineering, maintenance, and other functional departments on specifications for goods and on assessments of performance after the fact.

With these developments, which imply a vastly enlarged economic base as the country grew and industrialized rapidly, the foundation had been laid for the "backward and forward integration" that was a major feature of the coming of "big business," that is, the large, diversified, integrated, and decentralized industrial firm. It was a natural thing for manufacturing enterprises to acquire firms that supplied them (when it was in their interest to do so) especially after the "wheeler-dealers" of the turn-of-the-century merger movement showed how much money could be made in the process. Manufacturers at the same time began to sell direct to buyers, having done so from an early date to their biggest customers.

An immediate result of integration was the disappearance of thousands of jobs for traditional traveling salesmen, and their loud, indignant squawks were prominent among the antitrust voices that were raised as early as the 1880s. What happened, as has so often been repeated in the history of American business, is that their jobs were being replaced by more functional ones, requiring a higher degree of intelligence and a knowledge of the strengths of the competitors' products and the weaknesses of one's own. Graduate engineers—"sales engineers"—came to replace the winers and diners. Usually young men, recently out of college, they learned practical engineering by tackling customers' problems and finding a way to solve them—using one's company's products, of course.

Similar developments were taking place in the marketing of consumer goods, especially in the 1920s, which saw the creation of giant packaged-goods companies embracing such old-line brand names as Maxwell House Coffee, Fleischman's Yeast, Baker's Coconut, Airy-Fairy Cake Flour, and many, many others.

Store detail men appeared, ready to give close, frequent attention to retailers' shelf stock. Their main impact was on the *big* retailers, of course, whose dramatic success in the era of the automobile led directly to the appearance of the supermarket and hastened the advent of self-service merchandising, which replaced the friendly, white-aproned clerk of yore. (TV's Mr. Whipple, who in the 1970s kept an eagle eye out for ladies who could not resist squeezing the oh-so-soft bathroom tissue, was a figment of an advertising copywriter's imagination.) The manufacturer's "detail man," triumph of forward integration in consumer packaged goods, checked the store manager's stock, rearranged the shelves, saw to it that his brand got the facings (shelf exposure) the merchant thought appropriate (and perhaps a bit more), noted the previous period's unit sales by checking invoices of incoming merchandise (of which the manufacturer's headquarters had carefully supplied the detail men with a copy), filled out a suggested order form, and presented it to the store manager, who characteristically hovered near the checkout counters.

The system that big business has brought, if somewhat lacking in the human touch, is efficient and effective and calls for fewer but more intelligent and better trained people at every step along the way. The system was made possible by the automobile and motor truck, which provide the mobility and flexibility that it implies. The railroads seldom play a direct part beyond transporting products to the supermarket warehouse on their way to the consumer, but automotive equipment, the most elaborate of mass produced goods, required the prior development of the world's great complex of heavy industry, of which the railroad is the aorta.

Coming to Terms with the American City

It was the development of railroad transportation, as traditionally conceived, to its peak by 1930 that hastened the big changes, including
the move to the suburbs and greater use of the motor truck and the
automobile as the final links in the distribution process. By then, and
perhaps two decades earlier in the view of farsighted people, the American transportation network's capacity to collect and deliver most of the
vast output of a rich society, including imports and exports, in and to
highly centralized, densely populated urban centers, had reached its
limits. Notwithstanding all the other obstacles, manmade or otherwise,
that stood in the way of further development of rail transportation, it
was this original highly centralized concept of the system that was sure
to be replaced by something better. It seemed a long time dying, but
when the end came, it came faster than anyone had expected.

An elderly resident of St. Paul, Minnesota, where a distribution
ganglia for the commerce of the upper Midwest first developed,
recalled the days of the early 1920s when, as a young man, he walked
to and from his job in "Old Town," as it came to be called, the old
wholesale district where boxy, five-to-seven-storey red brick buildings
marked the farflung distribution activities carried on there by merchant
wholesalers. The level of activity in these old warehouse-offices, built
like fortresses and bearing the ornamentation that was mandatory, it
seems, on even the most utilitarian Victorian commercial buildings, was
already showing signs of decline. Through the fly-specked plate-glass
windows of the high-ceilinged first floor, still bearing in plump, gilded
letters the name of the firm, he could see only a single elderly clerk in
a green eyeshade, bent over a desk piled high with papers under a blue
enamel lamp that gave only a weak yellow light.

The merchant wholesalers were dying, their functions already
reduced to little more than that of warehousemen. They held out longest in the hinterland of deeply agricultural America, particularly in the
South, where the country store still bespoke poor transportation. But
gradually, as the decades after World War II passed, even the southern
country roads were paved, the fords were replaced with bridges, the
farmers all acquired transportation, if only a battered pickup truck, and
their children stared, mystified, when their parents made such folksy
remarks as, "We'll see y'all on Sunday, if the creeks don't rise."

The country stores served for a time in other capacities and then
decayed, save for an occasional example like one built of red brick and
for the ages in the deserted village of McKittrick on the Missouri River
branch of the Katy Railroad, across the river from the old German community of Hermann. The railroad itself is now defunct and will become
a nature trail if the stubborn farmers give up their claim that it must
now revert to them so they can plant more corn to add to the national
surplus. As for the store, it is crammed with farm machinery in the off-

season, but far at the back one can just make out a fine gray mare, immortalized in plaster, on whose broad back and noble head harness was once displayed. Like most of her breed, the small-town wholesale merchants who served these stores, and who raised the most hell about the railroads' long-short-haul rate discrimination, are a fading memory.

But Old Town remained. Almost every city of any size, and especially the oldest and largest cities, has its Old Town. The American railroad system developed, in its first hundred years, on the firm theory that the railroads would control the movement of goods from docks or factories or mines or commodity storage bins, and that most of it would terminate or originate in nuclear cities. The chief features of Old Town, occupying the most land and lying close by the relatively small retail, commercial, and financial district, were the railroad freight yards (usually near the passenger terminal itself), the wholesale warehouses, cold storage facilities, and structures housing a wide range of rough, dirty occupations surrounding the handling of fresh meat, fruits, and vegetables, usually with a produce or farmers' market nearby.

These neighborhoods, so entirely a creation of the railroad era, were well on their way to extinction by one civic or housing project or another, until rising construction costs made people realize the value inherent in these solidly built structures and the latent development possibilities in open spaces requiring little more than the removal of railroad tracks. It is ironic that at this late date much of the spatial opportunity to renew the old central cities is being provided by the departure of that noisome activity which people originally sought to escape from in their flight to the suburbs.

Sooner or later, the freight railroads had to quit the central city, but still the freight had to be delivered to the consignee's door somehow, especially if he was no longer to have "team tracks" or a freight house where he might pick up or dispatch both carload and less-than-carload (LCL) freight. Developments in New York City, as usual, foretold the future for most American cities. This greatest of urban centers had to provide for the daily arrival of all the goods consumed by a huge and fast-growing population and for the dispatch of the myriad goods they produced, and on top of that to handle, at New York's zenith as a port, over one-half of the nation's foreign commerce, in and out. As if that were not enough, the nation's failure to develop adequate alternate rail connections between New England and the interior, west and south, meant that a good portion of this huge flow would make its way somehow through the crowded port. Perhaps it was a blessing that the heart of the city, Manhattan, was an island. The east-west railroads were kept at bay across the Hudson River, and the link was the river itself.

Only the New York Central ever had freight tracks in Manhattan. The Hudson River Railroad which ran up the west side of Manhattan, crossing the Harlem River at Spuyten Duyvil, joined the New York &

Harlem in 1865 in the Vanderbilt railroad empire. Merged with the New York Central running west from Albany, the Hudson River Railroad produced a through line from the southern tip of Manhattan to Buffalo and thence westward on connecting lines. This vastly increased both passenger and freight traffic into and out of the city, and to accommodate it the Commodore got control of a pretty little park at Beach and Laight Streets, on the lower west side. On the site, still surrounded by handsome St. John's Church and row houses in which characters best chronicled by Henry James in *The Heiress* lived, he built in 1867 a behemoth of a freight house. It was commerce defeating aesthetics on a grand scale.

The freight house itself lasted barely a generation, as the northward sweep of Manhattan demanded a higher order of land use, but the site seems unlikely ever to be a park again. For another three-quarters of a century, the New York Central's locomotives, puffing, tooting, and banging as men worked through the long nights to make up freight trains, annoyed residents of the far west side around 69th Street. All freight operations had ended in Manhattan by the 1970s, and the successor to the Central, now the railroad-divested Penn Central, sold its west side freight yards to the real-estate developer Donald Trump for a fraction of what he confidently expected to get for it.

The plight of American cities had been well recognized by the turn of the century, and not only by knowledgeable railroad men. New York had endeavored to increase the effective size of its island by building miles of wharves to which lighters (barges carrying railroad boxcars and shepherded across the Hudson by tugboats) would bring the freight consigned to the city and its environs from the yards of nine different railroads along the Hudson River across from the big city. If San Franciscans think that the sound of the ferryboats on the bay is the symbol of their city, they might consider a ferry route map of New York's harbor at the peak of maritime activity around the first decade of this century.

Traffic on the two rivers never failed to astonish the observant visitor. Passenger ferries made arrival at the Jersey terminals a pleasure, not only for tourists seeing Gotham for the first time, but for commuters as well. All of the Jersey terminals had direct boats to downtown Manhattan and some, to budding midtown. The longest trip was from Weehawken, where Alexander Hamilton had met his death a century before, to downtown. Some went around the tip of Manhattan and up the East River to the Bronx. Others, crowded to the gunwales in summer, went to Coney Island, the Rockaways, and Sandy Hook.

Freight between the west and south, on the one hand, and New England, on the other, depended totally upon lighterage to make the connection between, say, the Erie, B. & O., Pennsylvania, Lackawanna, or Lehigh Valley, on the one hand, and the New York, New Haven & Hartford, on the other. The route was by way of lighter from their respective maritime terminals down the Hudson, around the tip of Manhattan, and up the East River to the maritime terminal of the New Haven's Harlem Division, near the future location of the northern anchorage of the Hell Gate Bridge. Late in the nineteenth century through passenger service from Washington, D.C., to Boston was provided by floating entire trains on this route and resuming the rail portion of the journey at the Harlem or (southbound) Jersey City terminals. Around 1910 the Pennsylvania Railroad, in an outburst of private investment in public service facilities the size of which would never be seen again, put into service a through rail route via tunnels under the Hudson River at 33rd Street, into Pennsylvania Station, underground across the island to tubes under the East River, across the Borough of Queens in a grand sweep, over the Hell Gate Bridge at the notorious whirlpool where the tidal river met Long Island Sound, and on to Boston. These facilities are one of the two main centers of what little passenger rail service remains in the United States, the other being Chicago's Union Station.

The Railroads Create a Great City

If New Yorkers adapted to the railroads, not always with good grace, Chicagoans rejoiced in them. In fact, by far the greater number of Chicagoans who were there by the time of the great fire of 1871 had arrived by rail, for this lusty young city had only been founded in 1833. New York, which had been an important seaport for 150 years before the railroads began to build tracks down its middle, eventually came to ignore even such limited evidence of their presence. Once the smoky, noisy, open wound of the old Grand Central Depot in the middle of Manhattan had been placed underground, Gotham's railroads were all but invisible. But not so in Chicago. Even today, no one can enter "that great big town on the great big lake" without being conscious of railroads everywhere. Driving from east to west on local streets, especially on the south side, a motorist bumps over grade crossing after grade crossing, many of them double-tracked, and he may well wonder how the citizens dodged the hundreds of trains that chuffed daily across street after street or, indeed, how the trains dodged each other at the mazes of switches and crossovers that resulted from the totally unplanned growth of Chicago's creator: the railroads.

Historians will probably continue to insist that it was Chicago's enviable position at the western end of the Great Lakes route to the West that guaranteed her greatness. The argument is pointless, because the role of the Great Lakes in the development of the American West is only a tenth part of the story. To be sure, in 1833 the water route to Chicago, especially in conjunction with the Erie Canal, made such a location especially advantageous, but hardly more so for Chicago than for Milwaukee or, for that matter, Duluth, which Jay Cooke once expected to become an American city of the first magnitude. It was the arrival of the New York Central and Pennsylvania railroads' western extensions (to give them their modern names), thus making Chicago the western terminus of the fabled trunk lines, that made the big difference. While lake traffic has always been and continues to be important in the national transportation system, it was the railroads that called the tune, more and more, after the Civil War. Chicago, it has been said, became the "center hall" of America, and so it remains today.

When the little settlement around Fort Dearborn began to call itself a "place" in 1833, the westward movement of the population was holding up at the western edge of the Old Northwest. Iowa was still a wilderness. St. Paul had yet to be settled, and Minneapolis was undreamed of. The Great Plains were still a poorly charted hunters' paradise, their produce mostly buffalo hides. Commerce, north and south, meant the Mississippi River, reachable via the new canal to the Illinois River, tributary to the Father of Waters. The Father accepted the waters of the Big Muddy—the Missouri—at the old French trading post of St. Louis, which was swelling with a steamboat-based pride that Chicago's railroads would deflate. If one went overland in 1833, however, one went via the Missouri River, a long, slow, tedious and often risky trip on a stream that had more curves than a railroad through the Canadian Rockies.

When the Civil War began, however, the tendrils of the new transportation wonder were being laid westward and southward. The promise of a connection with eastern lines at Chicago spurred on the Burlington, the Milwaukee & St. Paul, the North Western, the Illinois Central, and a dozen other less well-backed railroad enterprises. They took settlers and their goods to new farms in an ever-expanding domain, returning with their produce to the connections that would carry it on east, and then heading west again to deliver to the new republican empire a growing list of eastern and imported goods that farmers and their wives increasingly could not do without. These were the granger roads, as they came to be called, fanning out over the prairies to the foothills of the Rockies, delivering and taking away the essence of American commerce for literally thousands of places small and not quite yet large.

With the selection of Chicago as the eastern terminus of the first transcontinental railroad, any doubts about Chicago's brilliant future as a railroad center vanished. The Great Emporium of the West! Hog butcher to the world! The Chicago Gateway! The sheer exuberance of the world's greatest bourgeois flowering became the subject of countless novels, plays, and motion pictures. The railroads were putting their mark on Chicago in every direction, throwing up some kind of depot for the pressing hordes of passengers that crowded onto their little trains, and grabbing a vacant lot wherever they could, often at prices that would have been exorbitant less than a decade before, to accommodate their freight yards. Such an approach to the problem could not last. While the job the railroads had to do grew by leaps and bounds, the room in which they had to do it closed in around them.

New Yorkers created, or consumed, most of the goods that made their way into their vicinity, or put them onto or took them off of ocean vessels. Not so Chicago. While its growth as a manufacturing center was fast, even frenzied, it was Chicago as entrepôt that quickly set the tone of its transportation role. The railroad buff who tries to identify the railroad that owns a given set of tracks by the markings on the locomotives soon gives up. Chicago became, by the end of the Civil War, the country's premier point of exchange of freight and passengers between railroads terminating there. Congress, late as usual, ratified the practice of exchanging loaded cars of freight between connecting railroads soon after the war, but it had already been accepted as inherent in the railroad business. By the 1870s more than a dozen railroads were delivering freight cars to each other in Chicago. In daylight and dark, rain, snow, or shine, equatorial summer heat or bitter cold of winter, crewmen climbed down from their cabs and exchanged freight manifests that recorded the contents and the destination of the goods packed inside the cars. It took a lot of acreage for which Chicagoans had other uses.

As if on command from some central "boss," the fiercely independent railroads moved their freight yards miles out into the open prairie around Chicago, where they built mammoth classification yards for making up and taking apart freight trains that entered and left the city by the hundreds every day of the year. Steadily, as the years of the old century passed, and then with a rush in the prosperous early decades of the new, the trains grew longer and more numerous; the cars larger and heavier (increasing from a mere net burden of 10 tons in the early 1870s when they were made entirely of wood, to behemoths carrying 100 tons net and made entirely of steel); and the traffic greater than ever. Like the giant airports of a later era, the yards attracted population growth, and towns blossomed around the railroad installations.

Tying all these yards together out in the far environs of the city there emerged a new wrinkle in the fast unfolding railroad industry: the belt-line railroad. The metaphor is apt, and at least one belt line used a stylized man's belt as its symbol. The ideal belt line began northwest of the city, ran more or less straight down the map, and turned east to terminate athwart the busy trunk line railroads whose multiple tracks hugged the south shore of Lake Michigan on their way to and from the East. The belt line intersected as many lines radiating from the center of the city as it could, and back and forth its locomotives chugged ceaselessly, delivering and picking up freight cars. Some of the belt lines were owned by long-distance railroads, and some were important for passenger service as well as freight. John W. Garrett, aggressive president of the Baltimore & Ohio, an unwelcome new face on the Chicago railroad scene if there ever was one, pushed the B. & O.'s tracks to the outskirts of Chicago in 1874, only to find that no railroad wanted to yield it a right-of-way into the downtown terminal it was building. So the B. & O. built its own, the B. & O. Chicago Terminal Railroad, and did a good, profitable business transferring freight cars for other lines on the same tracks that carried its popular east-west trains to and from the depot at Harrison and Wells Streets. Most of the belt lines sought also to serve the succession of giant mills, notably in such heavy industries as steel and petroleum refining, that sprung up along their lines. Other cities made some use of belt lines, but none ever matched Chicago's volume of traffic or its strategic importance in dispatching freight trains; whereas the union station movement that began with Boston's South Station in the 1890s gave rise to terminal railroads that took charge of all movements of passenger cars within the terminal district.

So much for Chicago's mission on the national scene, but what of the rapidly growing population and hordes of visitors that crowded its famous stores around State and Madison streets? What happened to the huge and increasingly burdensome volume of less-than-carload shipments—"package freight"—that the railroads carried for Chicago's famous mail-order houses, name department stores, and wholesalers until the trucks took it over? In downtown Chicago a remarkable system of underground narrow-gauge electric railroads, built on a series of unfinished telephone tunnels, solved the first problem beginning in 1903. The railroads had downtown LCL depots to which merchants sent their drays to pick up incoming merchandise and, as Chicago grew to preeminence as a mail-order center, to dispatch packages. The tunnel system was extended under most of the streets in downtown Chicago, connecting the railroads' package freight depots and the stores and other business enterprises along the way. It worked so well that at the very end of the 1920s the mighty Pennsylvania Railroad built the world's largest LCL freight terminal on the edge of the Chicago River, next to the massive new Union Station.

The freight facilities in the inner city quit during the Depression. It was an inevitable development as the motor truck and new arterial highways, built at public expense, did the job of handling package freight to and from Chicago's mercantile establishments better and, or so it seemed to the untutored observer, more cheaply. Wags said that it was the blasting for the foundations of the new Waldorf Astoria Hotel in New York in the fall of 1929 that caused the stockmarket to tumble, but, to railroad men, it might as well have been the pile drivers pounding in the footings for the Pennsylvania's mammoth LCL freight house. The difference was that after a depression decade swimming in red ink, the Waldorf came back to economic life, but the Pennsy's freight house went dark and was torn down bit by bit. Since the suburban shopping

Figure 9.1   Map of the Elgin Joliet & Eastern Railway, the "Chicago Outer Belt Line," in 1929, showing the complex pattern of railroad entries into the city and how this foremost of beltlines made efficient transfer of through freight from one line to another possible.

centers, largely self-sufficient, spread after 1960, the fate of downtown as a retail center seems to have been sealed. In history, however, nothing is ever final.

Chicago did not keep its dominance in the nation's freight system without a fight. Other gateway cities tried, with little success, to supplant it, and "bridge routes" like the Toledo, Peoria & Western promised to get freight past Chicago with greater dispatch. The Lakes, of course, fought fiercely for east-west traffic, especially in low-rated commodities like grain and lumber. The lake-rail confrontation, so long viewed as a "cap" on rail freight rates, has been accorded more importance than it deserves. Indeed, during the dreary days of the overripe Progressive era, from 1910 to 1917, the cap that government placed on railroad rates neatly reversed the roles of the two modes as far as rate-setting is concerned. Still, anything that takes a single ton of freight away from the railroads was painful to traffic managers who seemed always to need a whipping boy.

The story of the relationship between the lake steamers and the freight trains of the trunk line railroads that paralleled the lakes is far more one of synergy than of tension. Both lakes and rails carried more traffic than either would have without the other. Railroads delivered to the steamers at Buffalo, Cleveland, Sandusky, and other lake ports tonnages that would not have moved at all except at low water rates, and the same was true in reverse. As the old century progressed the rails carried more and more products of the farm and forest to eastern markets that had originally been developed in the generation before the trunk lines matured. In late spring, rail rates on competitive commodities were cut once the lake steamers were no longer icebound, but they were put right back up come fall. As anyone who knows Duluth, a major lake port during the short season, will tell you, the curtain comes down on lake navigation long before all of the year's wheat crop has moved to market. (Mark Twain said the coldest day he ever spent was one Fourth of July in Duluth!)

James J. Hill, who ostentatiously acquired a direct route from the Red River Valley to Duluth and her sister lake port, Superior, Wisconsin, had Mark Hanna's shipbuilding company rush him a number of steel vessels of the latest design. But he did so, as he admitted, as much to break Chicago's monopoly of through freight traffic as to create a direct eastern connection for his Great Northern Railway, and he was not unhappy when his 1900 acquisition of the Burlington gave him his own tracks to Chicago.

Chicago remains the major rail center of the nation, and since rate deregulation the business has grown and changed in scope. The city now receives, transfers, and sends on its way, almost without delay, thousands of flat cars and specialized cars of containerized freight, much of which has not seen the light of day since it was loaded at the factory in Japan, Korea, Taiwan, or Singapore. New automobile carriers that hold up to sixteen vehicles have been prominent since the railroad's victory some years ago in reclaiming that business from truckers, whose clumsy rack trailers, holding only eight autos, terrorized American highways.

More and more, Chicago is the center of the business of hauling the people's burden to market, notwithstanding the continuing rise of St. Louis, Kansas City, New Orleans, and Houston, to name only a few. Back on the horizon, as it was before the Panama Canal confused the issue early in the century, is the "land bridge" that James J. Hill, having reduced his Great Northern's costs to less than a cent per ton-mile over the Rockies and the Cascades, foretold. It is based on the "unit train," which hauls solid trainloads of containers consigned, mostly, by Pacific Rim countries to western Europe, straight across North America between west and east coast ports. Like the Erie Canal after the Civil War, the Panama Canal may soon be crumbling into the ditch.

Saving the Automobile from Itself

A leading authority on railroad terminal design, the late John A. Droege, in a book last revised in 1925, had this to say about the problem of handling freight at destinations, at a time when the consolidation of American railroads was an active possibility:

> The study of the question of consolidation of railroads should be primarily for its effect on the terminal question. . . . This problem is increasing in importance and in difficulty of solution. . . . There is only one serious technical problem in the transportation industry of the United States, and that is the terminal problem.

Droege was revising his authoritative work at a time when fundamental changes had taken place in the matter of leaping across the Hudson. Thinking, no doubt, of the recent opening of the Holland Tunnel, through which motor trucks now had direct access to Manhattan for the first time from the west, he predicted that new terminals would be located at a distance of some miles from the center of the city. But he had little to say about the problem of finding room for the drayage trucks on local streets. In 1925 the automobile had not yet besieged Manhattan and, indeed, no one then would have thought it possible to pack in—much less tolerate—the number of cars that blight the city. But local street congestion had long been a problem in New York and other big cities, even—or especially—in the Age of Dobbin.

The solution that is being resorted to in many cities is the most drastic of all—just abandon downtown, Old Town, and the whole shebang. But New York is still New York, Chicago is still Chicago, and millions of people want to live there. No one knows how many brilliant conversations are interrupted in the new upper east side apartments by the diesel trucks blasting up New York's First Avenue, their mufflers and pollution control devices inoperative or disconnected to achieve greater power and fuel economy, and making both more noise and more smoke than a steam locomotive would doing a hundred times the useful work.

After about 1930, the problem was no longer so much one of making room for delivery vehicles on the streets of the central city, as of what to do with the private automobiles that would cripple public surface transportation of all kinds in another generation. They gave Americans one thing: mobility. And, putting two and two together, Americans accelerated the great move to the suburbs, for which they already had good and sufficient reason, such as the need for affordable houses. The wide open spaces soon produced their own traffic jams, but at least the delivery of the truck trailers and containers, in which goods were being whisked across the country by rail and transferred to trucks at satellite "intermodal" terminals, was unimpeded.

The capacity of these intermodal terminals and their distance from downtown seems to be consistently increasing, as the railroads and trucks continue to divide the world into metropolitan areas and the wide open spaces. The great virtue of the motor truck, it is slowly being appreciated, is not that it gives employment to many thousands of men who do not work well under close supervision, or that it is fast and flexible and—before deregulation and then only if many hidden costs were ignored—cheaper than rail-freight service, but that it is more efficient than rail for distances of under about four hundred miles, when inescapable terminal costs are included.

What is happening to American freight transportation is nothing less than the final rationalization of rail and highway movements, after half a century, by interest groups that placed the cost of carrying the people's burden to market—vital as it obviously is—last. As this is written, another step in the seemingly inexhaustible growth of productivity so characteristic of railroading is the "run-through" freight train. To take one example—and this stems directly from the fact that the Japanese have become major purveyors of high-quality goods to Americans—the Santa Fe Railroad dispatches from its Pacific coast terminals every day as many as a dozen "hot-shot" freight trains, consisting of containers and/or trailers on flatcars, *all* destined for Conrail's terminals in the New York area, which run nonstop except for quick crew changes. Nearly twenty-five hundred miles into its trip, at Streator, on the Kansas City-Chicago "speedway" of the Santa Fe, a lashup of Conrail diesels backs out of the bush through a tight curve, couples onto the train, and hauls it out onto an old single-track line of the Big Four, heavily rebuilt, east and then north to Conrail's own "speedway," and on its way to the east coast. When the Congress of the United States, nervous about the possible reaction of their provincial constituents, reluctantly passed the law back in the 1860s requiring American railroads freely to exchange freight with each other in interstate commerce, they could have had no idea where it would lead. Few acts of Congress have continued to pay off so handsomely for the voters for so long.

The delivery of the trailer or container on flat car to an intermodal terminal far out in the boondocks—Hagerstown, Maryland, no doubt to its great surprise and delight, was selected to be one such location to make up for Norfolk Southern's lack of satisfactory east-coast access of its own—is the outcome of the lengthy process of change that began so many years ago before the astonished eyes of St. John's parishioners.

CHAPTER 10

From Entrepreneurs to Managers: The Founding Years

> I was born in a sawmill . . ., christened in a mill-pond, graduated at a log-school-house, fancied I could do anything I turned my hand to, and that nothing was impossible and ever since . . . I have been trying to prove it, and with some success.
>
> William Butler Ogden, Founder,
> Chicago & North Western Railway

> An engineering education fits a man best for the superintendence no less than the construction of a railway. . . .
>
> John B. Jervis (1795–1885), pioneer railroad engineer

> Any system which might be applicable to the business and extent of a short road, would be found entirely inadequate to the wants of a long one; and I am fully convinced, that in the want of a system perfect in its details, properly adapted and vigilantly enforced, lies the true secret of their failure; and that this disparity of cost per mile in operating long and short roads, is not produced by *a difference in length*, but in proportion to the perfection of the system adopted.
>
> Daniel C. McCallum, Superintendent,
> New York & Erie Railroad, (1856)

The Pattern Established

A railroad is an expensive, complex machine, spread out over vaster distances than one mind can comprehend at a single moment, programmed to do many things in many different places, at the direction of many different people. It either works right, or it hardly works at all, and when it does not it can be disastrous for both human life and property. That railroad leaders worked out the knotty problems of human relations which this proposition implies, however slowly and painfully, and not without some grand failures, is one of the most significant contributions of the railroad to the evolution of American social institutions.

The coming of the railroad placed upon men burdens of care and responsibility that had been virtually unknown even to the most important men in American material affairs up to that time. The brave souls who ventured into this revolutionary mode of moving about had to learn their new "trade" as they were practicing it; the uncertainties were enough to cow the most strong-hearted from the beginning. While some concerns, once paramount, such as basic rules of the road, became routine, others hardly imagined in the pioneer years arose to take their place. By the beginning of the twentieth century, however, the general pattern of management and details of management structure had been established for both manufacturing and railroads, on the basis of three-quarters of a century of experience, advancing human knowledge, and seemingly random sociopolitical twists and turns.

The early twentieth century railroad "manager" (the gradual replacement of "superintendent" with "manager" is evidence of the process we seek to explain) bore all the distinguishing marks of the railroad entrepreneur of the nineteenth century. This chapter and the next seek to demonstrate his development with examples of the wide range of problems encountered by American railroad men and the diversity of human types that attacked these problems in the nineteenth century. Thereafter, we shall proceed to something even more difficult: the elucidation of the efforts of railroad men and government, labor relations, finance, and other social institutions to adapt to each other, as each rapidly grew to its modern form and size in the twentieth century. As late as the great corporate shakeup of the 1890s, railroad men were still the dominant force in railroad affairs. That was to change drastically, so drastically that the nation lost sight, for decades, of its original goal, which was to provide the people with cheap, dependable transportation, while making sure that the power and resources required were in the right hands and achieving a sensible balance between what the railroads owed to the people and what the people owed to their railroads and the managers who had cast their lot with them.

By 1900 American railroads had developed organizations that were based on the "generalist," as we would say nowadays, rather than the specialist. The main organizational problems had been geographical, but they quickly became occupational as well. The Erie, for a time the longest railroad in North America, had been the first to see that splitting the line for operational purposes into divisions was necessary. It soon became equally apparent that, within a division, there could be only one person with the authority to make decisions—from maintenance of way to motive power, rolling stock, rates and other traffic matters, and relations with other railroads—and carry the entire burden of responsibility for the results obtained, in the eyes of *his* superiors at the head office. A headquarters staff of experts in all fields of railroading advised with the division manager and his lieutenants, and if the division manager was wise he gave great weight to the specialist's advice, but there was to be no blaming of headquarters for divisional failures.

Not all of the railroads, or even all of the most powerful of them—

for example, the New York Central—carried this philosophy of organization through. (The Central held to the fading myth of the independence of the various corporations such as the New York Central & Hudson River, the Lake Shore & Michigan Southern, the Michigan Central, and the Big Four, for management purposes.) But the Pennsylvania, by far the most widely emulated railroad in America and the world, had solved just about all of the problems, apparently, that could be solved by clever organization, and in the rising tide of economic optimism that rolled over the United States after 1897, few could imagine any new ones that would escape managers' problem-solving talents.

The railroads, in short, created the prototype of the modern management executive, but no one will ever be able to generalize the specific process by which this much-envied gentleman came into being, for in fact each railroad enterprise, and the problems that its leaders had to solve, differed at least a bit from every other. The great railroads of the nation were begun at various phases of the evolution of the national system. They were led, moreover, by human beings and not some kind of sociological "model," and thus, as the system grew from east to west and from the earliest pioneer days to the final conquest of the far West, each leader placed the mark of his own personality, for better or worse, on the public image of the new man, the professional railroad manager.

The Promoters: New Trade Routes for Old

In the beginning, there were the promoters. They were, almost invariably, what we would call the "big fish in the little ponds" of their localities (for the railroads were almost always local enterprises to begin with), the merchants, bankers, professional men, and "planters," as the well-to-do farmer or "squire," having earned the leisure to take his place among the town fathers in attending to civic affairs, liked to be called. With few exceptions, they were not visionaries. They knew what a risky thing it was to adopt an expensive new technology, of which the practical worth had yet to be fully demonstrated in the 1830s, which would require scarce technical skills to survey, build, and operate, and might well be a total loss if the enterprise proved a failure on any of these points. Most of them expected to profit little directly from the financial returns of the road—and in this they were seldom disappointed, although for their posterity it was often a golden harvest—but most of them hoped for some degree of betterment of their region as well as their trades or professions. Truth to tell, their motives often were no nobler than might be expressed by a weak "everybody else is doing it" (that was far from true, however, in the late 1820s when the "canal mania" was gathering strength), but, even so, it would not do to be remembered as the shortsighted men who led their community into oblivion. A steam railway? It was the least unlikely practical solution for many regions. To build the railroad, and build it *now*, proved to be virtually a categorical imperative to this class of Americans.

We can not do better than to start with Erastus Corning of Albany, New York, merchant, nail manufacturer, bank and insurance company president, railroad iron products manufacturer and importer, and key figure in the 1853 merger that created the New York Central Railroad between Albany and Buffalo. Corning's influence, not to say his persuasiveness, doubtless helped convince his fellow Albanyites that a community that had just witnessed the opening of one of mankind's greatest and most successful enterprises, the Erie Canal, should now build a fifteen-mile steam railway from Albany west to Schenectady. This may sound like selling refrigerators to Eskimos, but in 1831 the Mohawk & Hudson Railroad was opened, operated mostly by horse-power but also by the *De Witt Clinton,* the first steam locomotive in regular scheduled service in the United States; and in 1833 Corning became its vice-president.

Corning as a railroad leader embodied the most important features of the classic entrepreneur: an innovative drive, either original or borrowed from someone else, and concrete ideas of how to go about making that innovation a reality. In Corning's case, it was the spectacle not so much of huge tonnages of produce from the West being trans-shipped from canal barges to river boat at Albany, but rather the hordes of "westering" people who sought to book passage on a canal packet for the long and arduous trip to Lake Erie and the next phase of their seemingly interminable migration to the new Midwest. The first leg, from Albany to Schenectady, would consume ten hours by canal, whereas the Mohawk & Hudson would get them there in one. Soon men were speculating that if a fifteen-mile railroad could save nine-tenths of the time required to complete a short segment of a journey, what might a railroad all the way to Buffalo accomplish? Corning knew, moreover, that although New York State prohibited a parallel railroad from hauling freight in competition with the Canal, whose bonds it had guaranteed, the railroad was free to solicit freight during the months when the Canal was frozen over. In upstate New York, which becomes one giant icebox from November to March, that was more than a foot in the door; it was an arm and a leg, and by 1851 the state had dropped the prohibition entirely.

Westward across New York State, dogging the route of the canal over the ultimately famous water-level route of the Mohawk River, a succession of seven (or was it eleven—it depends upon which authority you read) small railroad enterprises built railroad lines which quickly instituted through service without a change of cars from Albany to Buffalo. Corning was also the power behind the second of these lines, the Utica & Schenectady, and as the idea of fast, through freight and passenger service from the seaboard began to catch fire in the early 1850s, he arranged the merger of all these lines into the New York Central Railroad in 1853. For many years it remained the largest corporate merger in American financial history.

It was all but inevitable that the Central should quickly become part of an all-rail line to New York City, notwithstanding the awesome history of the mighty Hudson River as an artery of commerce. But the inevitable came, not under the aegis of Erastus Corning, but of "Commodore" Cornelius Vanderbilt. This remarkable man, one of the earliest consolidators of what others had begun, made the Central an offer it could not refuse—he offered to stop terminating his passenger trains at the river's edge across from Albany, which had been forcing passengers heading for the Central connection to the west to struggle across on foot in subzero temperatures! And having gained control, he joined it to his Hudson River Railroad. The modern era of transportation was now ready to begin. This exquisitely scenic route up the Hudson, which the Central's advertising agencies promoted with all their might for the next hundred years, was all the more remarkable in the slowness with which New Yorkers had got around to building it. (As their slowness to embrace the cause of independence in 1776 shows, New Yorkers were not a daring lot in those days.) Smug New York City merchants, relaxing in the privileged surroundings of their exclusive Chamber of Commerce and fabled private clubs, and savoring their world-beater of a seaport, a broad river to the interior, and a new canal onward to the Lakes, had seen no need at all for a railroad up the river. But some merchants in Poughkeepsie, a bustling town about a third of the way upstream on the way to Albany, wanted better transportation than was forthcoming from the haughty boatmen on the river, and that meant a railroad. The railroad limped along for over a decade, "smart" New Yorkers never realizing what a sleeping giant of an investment it was. Finally, it began to dawn upon people that railroads were going to take over from water transportation wherever they were available, and that the era of river and canal commerce was coming to a close. It is ironic, but easy to see on reflection, that one of the first to see the light was the nation's most prominent shipowner and sailer of the rivers and the seas: Commodore Vanderbilt.

Corning's entrepreneurial vision had started the avalanche that was railroad expansion, however, and he was well paid for his efforts, especially those in behalf of what became the Central in 1853. He profited from manufacturing iron components, chiefly spikes, for building railroads, and importing English wrought iron rails to a country that had not yet got around to establishing an iron industry worthy of the name. He gave value received: few railroads of that era were so fortunate as to have as an officer a man so well connected in the tripartite world of banking, mercantile trade, and manufacturing. His railroads were well financed, bid successfully for a growing proportion of the commerce to and from the city, and profited from having a secure source of the best English rails at a time when the demand consistently outran the supply. Best of all, he enjoyed a growing reputation and died in the knowledge that he would always be remembered as one of the builders of the Empire State and of the Union. No one could ever call Erastus Corning a "robber baron."

Figure 10.1 Two who exemplify spectacular success and ambitious failure in the development of the trunk-line railroads. Cornelius "Commodore" Vanderbilt (1794–1877), at left, came from his success in the steamship business to the infant industry of railroading when past sixty, and welded several lines into what was the most lucrative of the trunk lines, then and for a generation after he was gone: the New York Central. John W. Garrett (1820–1884) gave his life to the Baltimore & Ohio, the most romantic but also the weakest—except for the Erie—of the trunk lines, but before he died he had lost primacy at both New York and Washington to the Pennsylvania. *(Both pictures courtesy of Smithsonian Institution)*

The New York Central of Corning's day was not a railroad to the interior; it *was* the interior. As for New York City, it was growing so fast and enjoying its many blessings so fully that it woke up one day and found that it had achieved fast, efficient transportation to and from the interior before it ever quite realized how badly it would have fared if it had not. Baltimore, that romantic port of flourishing merchants, shipbuilders, sea captains, and privateers who built up fortunes exploiting the letters of marque and reprisal awarded them by the president during the War of 1812, wisely arranged to channel these pools of liquid capital into a revolutionary facility for maintaining its domination of trade between Chesapeake Bay and the Ohio River. It would not be a turnpike, for any fool could see that the prosperity that the National Road had brought Baltimore's merchants was temporary, and melting under the hot competition of the Erie Canal. A canal of her own? Some poor misguided sods were planning something to be called the Chesapeake & Ohio Canal vaguely in the direction of Cumberland, Maryland, but it followed the valley of the Potomac River to Georgetown, in the

District of Columbia, and thus was too far south to serve Baltimore's interests. The spotlight of history now comes to rest on three well-established men of Baltimore's business community, who pondered these questions long and hard and solved them by putting to work their most valuable possession: their international contacts and influence.

Merchants, bankers, first- and second-generation Americans, mostly Quakers: the backgrounds of the three fall easily into a pattern. Philip E. Thomas had long since parlayed his accumulated profits into the presidency of the Merchants' Bank in Baltimore, and as a commissioner of the C. & O. Canal project he had seen at first hand the fatal flaws of that undertaking. George Brown was the son of Alexander, who had come to America from Ireland in 1800 and made his money importing two of the few luxury items that even the most modest of housewives wanted in those days: Irish linens and eight-day clocks. Now he ran a thriving private banking business under the name of Alexander Brown & Sons. The third man, William Patterson, was a shipowner and importer who had done extremely well in supplying the American army during the War for Independence and continued to flourish as a merchant. His daughter (and no doubt her wealth and social position) had attracted a husband who had skirted history and traded it for the security of life in America. He was Jerome Bonaparte, youngest brother of Napoleon. One of their descendants would serve in Theodore Roosevelt's cabinet as attorney general.

George Brown's eldest brother, William, ran the family's branch in England. He had watched closely the first full-scale experiments or "trials" ever conducted on a steam railway and kept his father fully informed of their outcome. Few human events have electrified more vigorous, visionary men throughout the civilized world than the news that Locomotive No. 1, George Stephenson's newly designed steam locomotive, running on the spindly rails of the Stockton & Darlington Railroad, had won the Rainhill Trials in 1825 by pulling a train of thirty cars on its first try. William's letters were more enthusiastic than ever. Off went Evan, Philip Thomas's brother, to England to inspect the Stockton & Darlington (and no doubt, also, England's first through railroad, the Liverpool and Manchester). In the fall of 1826, at a dinner given by a former governor of Maryland and U.S. senator, Evan presented his findings and conclusions about steam railways. This settled the question as far as Baltimore's most influential citizens were concerned. The steam locomotive was to be the symbol for the new age, as far into the future as human eye could see.

The Promoters: The First Energy Revolution

Railroads like the Mohawk & Hudson and its sisters, the Baltimore & Ohio; the Boston & Worcester, which undertook to do for Boston what the B. & O. was to do for Baltimore; the Erie, at least in its earliest stages when its original mission had been to bring good transportation to the people of the southern tier of New York counties, who were feeling rather left out by the success of the Erie Canal; and, most dramatically, the line from Philadelphia to Pittsburgh that came to be known as the Pennsylvania Railroad, were fairly easily financed by investments of private capital, with a limited amount of state assistance in the form of stock purchases and guarantees of bonds. The myth persists that loans and even gifts of real money were made to these pioneer railroads out of the public purse, and at least one author has granted huge tracts of western lands to the Pennsylvania, which goodness knows the government never did. But capital *was* scarce in America, and would grow even scarcer as opportunities to invest it wisely multiplied. The only pools of liquid assets available for such risky undertakings as a new and relatively untried transportation facility were the accumulated savings of thrifty men. The earliest railroad enterprises still contained a great deal of civic-mindedness (for want of a better term), but once the practicality of the steam railroad had been proved projects quickly began to emerge that brought cheap transportation to mining enterprises that were only then able to carry to market the commodity upon which the industrialization of America would rest: coal.

The promoters of the Philadelphia & Reading were members of Philadelphia's elite, like Edward Biddle, scion of the family that had been in banking for many years, most notably during the period when Nicholas Biddle had headed the Second Bank of the United States; Moncure Robinson, one of the nation's first men to develop a reputation as a civil engineer, who would actually locate and build the road; and such rich citizens as Matthias Pennypacker and George deB. Keim. The road was chartered in 1833, but hard times hit Philadelphia in the 1830s, delaying completion until 1842. The ensuing century was the golden age of anthracite coal, which lay in bountiful beds beneath the rugged topography of eastern Pennsylvania counties in which the now-decaying cities of Allentown, Bethlehem, Scranton, Wilkes-Barre, and Pottsville flourished until the death of anthracite as a fuel. All of the anthracite roads, in fact, or what was left of them that was useful, except the Delaware & Hudson, ended up in the Conrail corral.

Such is the lugubrious epitaph of the Reading, the Delaware, Lackawanna & Western, the Lehigh Valley, and the Delaware & Hudson (rescued by the Canadians) but, oh, the glorious years in between! These railroads were, physically speaking, among the best in the country, prepared as they were to handle long, heavy trains of coal that moved ponderously, majestically around sinuous curves skirting the densely forested hills, across great bridges and viaducts (the Lackawanna built a beauty, once the largest reinforced concrete structure in the world, across the Tunkhannock Valley of Pennsylvania), through smoky tunnels, and into the seamy environs of sprawling railroad yards in big eastern cities.

Like the men who had undertaken the Reading enterprise, the other anthracite railroads were also promoted by men who had long-standing interests in coal lands that needed better transportation than the canals were providing. Starting out as the Morris & Essex Railroad (whose long-term bonds were still in conservative investors' strong-boxes until recent years), to replace the canal of the same name into Newark and Jersey City, the Lackawanna headed northward across difficult country to the Scranton area, at the northernmost limit of the anthracite region. Chief among its promoters were the powerful family for whom the town was named, but the Lackawanna kept very good company, for also deeply interested in its fortunes were Moses Taylor, New York merchant *par excellence* and a founder of the National City Bank, and Samuel Sloan. The Lehigh Valley did likewise. Its chief investor was Stephen Girard, who sat atop the nation's largest private bank and private fortune in the early days of the age of steam.

If anyone doubts the general superiority of the steam railroad over the man-made ditch filled with water (when available), he need only reflect on the abrupt end of the anthracite canals. As internal improvements, they had been strikingly successful. They even made money, or at least the best of them did; in fact, along with the Erie, but not its branches, the anthracite canals were just about the only financially successful canals ever built in the United States, which makes the speed with which the steam railroad replaced them that much more impressive. There is a woodcut from the early years of the Reading that illustrates this point dramatically. A long train of cars, fully loaded with the prized fuel, is eased down the general decline of the ninety-two mile route from Pottsville to Philadelphia. Alongside the railroad runs the canal of the Schuylkill Navigation Company which, in the words of one of the anthracite developers, "are so slow in their movements that we are tired of urging them on." (The locomotive, curiously, is fueled by wood, as were virtually all locomotives in the 1840s, for the market for what the Reading had brought to market was there long before the railroad was built or its operators had learned how to burn anthracite in a locomotive firebox.) The Reading, notwithstanding some benighted management near the end of the old century, was a great success, and until the star of such outstanding regional railroads finally set, its leaders held their own alongside the Pennsylvania Railroad executives in the boardrooms, private clubs, and Mainline estates of Philadelphia.

Every railroad built during the early years was, in many ways, a product of the entrepreneur, the promoters, a "leap into the dark." The kind of men who undertook them deserve, perhaps, to be called "pioneers," rather than promoters. They were not builders of railroads, however, but of a dream which, once demonstrated, called for a new kind of leader who would design, build, develop, consolidate, and in a thousand ways *manage* the ultimate destiny of the few dozen miles of track that had occupied the promoters' dreams. The first step, of course, was to build these pioneer railroads, and in taking it America gave birth to a brand new kind of businessman: the technological expert who undertakes to translate dreams into profitable reality.

The Builders: Emergence of the Engineer

Before the coming of the railroads, there were surveyors, but few who claimed the title of civil engineer. If the few turnpikes and the considerable number of canals had called for something more than a surveyor's skills, however, the railroads called for a great deal more. Notwithstanding the fact that the shortest line was not necessarily the best line, the optimum route would not be any longer than geography dictated. This generalization holds in the face of the obvious fact that previously settled market centers called for some deviation. Such centers were geographic realities, as much as mountains and bodies of water, yet the best lines in the nation seem to have been laid out with more than a casual view to their adaptability to long-distance through freight and passenger service. Americans, at the dawn of the modern transportation era, were if anything painfully aware of the distances to be traversed in such a big country.

The railroad builder's choices of location were greater than those of either the turnpike or the canal builder, but there were serious restraints. One, of course, was grade: the iron horse did not tire, unlike his animal equivalent, but he strained at his drawbars almost as inefficiently as Dobbin at his shafts when more than a gentle rise was encountered. A one-percent grade—involving a rise of about fifty feet to the mile of the road—was the working maximum, but engineers often had to contend with double that, and then some. One could dig cuts through excessive rises and then, brilliantly the first time and obviously thereafter, haul the spoil to the next point that needed filling; or he could weave around the points that posed a gradient steeper than the locomotive with its full complement of cars could negotiate.

A good engineer quickly learned that the expense of cuts and fills was often justified, even in an era when earth was still moved mostly by pick, shovel, and wheelbarrow or wheeled cart. They realized very early that the most cars a locomotive could haul over the steepest grade between two division points, where locomotives could be changed, was the most it could haul over that division *at all*. This was the "ruling grade," and one bad spot could render an otherwise ideal location survey unsatisfactory. Curves, moreover, can be as deadly as a steep grade to the efficiency with which a locomotive, which always seeks to exert its pulling power in a straight line, can haul a string of cars. As much of a knowledge of mathematics and physics as the mid-nineteenth century could supply (and in practice, no doubt, a bit more—call it instinct!) was required to achieve a first-class line. Woe to the promoters, moreover, who did not get the best line to be had, because the penalty was to be stuck playing second fiddle to some competitor who would come along, find the line you missed, and as the low-cost producer dictate rate levels from then on.

The earliest builder of practical railroads in the United States was also one of the greatest. John B. Jervis (1795–1885) was at the heart of American transportation development from the construction of the Erie Canal to the dawn of the age of consolidation and an integrated national system of railroads. He left school at fifteen, as was customary for someone who planned to devote his life to farming. This he did for the next seven years, but upstate New York was in ferment by the end of the second decade of the new century, and working on the canal project, if only as a lowly axeman who cleared the way for the surveying party, had more appeal than farming. Jervis learned everything he knew about civil engineering by observing the experts at work and participating in the hands-on application of their calculations. Benjamin Wright, chief engineer of the canal, was his mentor, and this perceptive man appreciated Jervis's exceptional qualities from the beginning. When Wright was picked to head the building of the Delaware & Hudson Canal, he made Jervis his principal assistant.

It was the inherent shortcoming of the canal idea that put young Jervis in the railroad building business. The D. & H. was to take the coal from the mines around Carbondale, Pennsylvania, to Kingston, New York, on the Hudson River about a hundred miles north of the city, its major market, to which it would be delivered by river barge. But Carbondale, up in the hills, was some sixteen miles from the nearest practical point for starting a canal, which was a place called Honesdale, in honor of New York's celebrated diarist, progressive politician, and investor in the enterprise, Philip Hone. Jervis seems to have had direct responsibility for dealing with this problem. A gravity railroad, with the coal-laden cars coming down a long incline to Honesdale by gravity, and the empty cars hauled back up the slopes to Carbondale by mules, and, in the steepest places, by steam winches, seemed to many the best solution, but Jervis's decision was to use a steam locomotive to furnish the motive power. It was truly a leap into the dark, for in 1827 there was no steam-operated railroad in the country. Jervis, like many others, had observed the gravity railroad that hauled the huge marble monoliths for the Bunker Hill Memorial in Boston from the quarries at Quincy to the docks, however, and he had observed similar facilities in England. He also knew that great progress had been achieved in increasing the pulling power of a steam locomotive, so he ordered one from a firm located in Stourbridge, England.

The *Stourbridge Lion*, as this very first practical locomotive in America was called, worked perfectly—too perfectly, in fact, for the manufacturer had exceeded the maximum weight Jervis had specified. It was too heavy for the tramway, as the men who gingerly drove it over the course on a few trial runs could testify when they saw how the *Lion* had squashed the iron strips into the relatively soft wooden stringers. The *Lion* took its place on the return side of the tramway where it did duty as a stationary engine. A setback for the young engineer-builder? Not at all, for his experience with the *Stourbridge Lion* would soon prove valuable when he undertook to build his first real railroad.

When Erastus Corning and his fellow entrepreneurs shortly went looking for an experienced railroad builder for their Mohawk & Hudson Railroad between Albany and Schenectady, they did not have to look far, for there were few in existence and the best was right at hand. The sixteen-mile railroad was built over level ground, the first link in the water-level route of what became the New York Central Railroad and the newest and busiest of the famous trade routes of the world. It offered no challenge to Jervis. It was in the adoption and design of motive power, rather, that he made his mark on this earliest of American steam railroads. The promoters had ruled out steam power—after all, even horse-drawn wagons, when provided with a well-designed railroad to run upon, were a significant advance over vehicular roads—but Jervis persuaded them that a good steam locomotive could haul as much as a considerable number of horse-drawn wagons. The West Point Foundry, at Cold Spring, New York, about two-thirds of the way down the Hudson toward the city, built for the Mohawk & Hudson one of the first steam locomotives made in America. Mainly because it weighed three tons less than the *Stourbridge Lion*, which it resembled, it worked only moderately well, but it proved Jervis's point. He gave it the rather ironic name of *DeWitt Clinton*, the chief promoter of the Erie Canal, which the road of iron was to render obsolete in less than a generation.

Jervis's most important contribution to locomotive design was what came to be known as the "American type." As any boy (or girl) can appreciate who has despaired of keeping a cheap toy train, with its fixed four wheels, on its track, these early locomotives, with their four driving wheels rigidly mounted in an iron frame, did not conform well to the tight curves that American engineers had to settle for on many routes. Jervis redesigned the chassis so that the first pair of wheels was replaced by two smaller wheels on a swivel, or "bogie," which acted as a pilot to lead the rigidly mounted driving wheels into a turn. The two pilots and drivers quickly became four of each, and the American type 4-4-0 (ooOO) locomotive became the dominant design in America, especially for high-speed passenger trains, well into the twentieth century.

Jervis, unlike the great majority of modern engineers, was an astute businessman as well as a superb technician, at least where judging the practicality of railroads was concerned. He persuaded the men who dreamed of a railroad up the east bank of the Hudson River to Albany that, just as the Mohawk & Hudson had nothing to fear from the Erie Canal, their railroad could compete with the river as a transportation route, and he supervised construction of the most difficult section, between New York City and Poughkeepsie, in 1846. In the intervening years he had built extensions to the Erie Canal and scored a major success in solving New York City's water-supply problems by building the Croton River dam, its aqueduct, and High Bridge, the remarkable 1450-foot-long structure that enables the aqueduct to leap across the valley of the Harlem River, an engineering masterpiece still sound and in regular use after 150 years.

By this time Jervis was in his mid-fifties, but the West beckoned him no less enticingly than it did many another such mover and shaker. In the next fifteen years he made an indelible mark on the railroads that were spreading westward from the temporary terminals of the New York Central and the Pennsylvania railroads. From Jackson, Michigan, down across northern Indiana, he built the Michigan Southern & Northern Indiana, which, in combination with the Lake Shore Railroad, would fill out the most important east-west trunk line railroad, the New York Central. He spent the next seven years extending the Chicago & Rock Island Railroad into Iowa via the first bridge across the Mississippi River, and helped lawyer Abraham Lincoln defend its right to bridge this very navigable stream from the onslaughts, legal and illegal, of the furious steamboatmen.

Hardly less important in the trunk line stakes than the Lake Shore & Michigan Southern was the Pittsburgh, Fort Wayne & Chicago, on which the Pennsylvania Railroad had had its eye ever since an enterprising group of western men promoted its route across America's heartland into Chicago. It was the Pennsy's connection to Chicago by traffic agreement, from the beginning. Until the Pennsy deigned to "make an honest woman" of the "Fort Wayne line," as it was always called in the days when its depot in Chicago was the busiest and smokiest in the city, it was an anemic affair. Jervis, as one authority has put it, completed his transition from engineer to manager of railroads with the Fort Wayne. He had found it in default on its bonds, but Civil War prosperity brought resources that Jervis, with his usual perspicacity, used to improve the operating efficiency of this sleeping gold mine.

Jervis's name is less well known than that of men like Benjamin Latrobe, Jr., of the more public-relations-conscious Baltimore & Ohio, or J. Edgar Thomson of the Pennsylvania, probably because they were associated with famous integrated lines whose corporate names survived so many consolidations. But in the profession he was well known and honored. He traveled to England in 1849 to help celebrate the opening of brilliant, flamboyant inventor-engineer Isambard Kingdom Brunel's famous bridge over Menai Strait in Wales, and was the guest of Robert Stephenson. He helped found one of the earliest professional societies in America, the American Society of Civil Engineers, of which he was an honorary member. He accepted the price that men in his demanding profession had often to pay—loneliness during long service in the field—probably because he realized that never again would men have the chance to pit their energies and talents against such odds on so vast and clean a slate as America. He died at the age of eighty-five, fully occupied with the affairs of an iron works that he had helped found in his hometown of Rome, New York.

Between the seaboard and the gateway cities of the Midwest, three more trunk lines evolved—the Pennsylvania, the B. & O., and the Erie—and all three would have to face the breaching of the Appalachian wall, as the New York Central had not had to do. In many different ways, and with varying degrees of success as far as distance and efficiency are concerned, the engineers managed what a generation before had struck men as impossible. The Commonwealth of Pennsylvania pussyfooted the longest about the best way to do it, before an intrepid group of Philadelphia business and civic leaders took matters in their own hands, raising the initial risk capital themselves in a door-to-door campaign for stock subscriptions. Then they got the best man available for the job of building their line to Pittsburgh and ended up with a mountain railroad that was so well built, so intelligently and prudently improved over the years, and so skillfully managed that it became, in its public relations man's florid words, "the standard railroad of the world."

The Baltimore & Ohio could boast no such affluent parents as a group of well-heeled Quakers, and as an eastern terminal Baltimore was, well, just Baltimore. But the B. & O. did very well in good times and managed to hang on in bad for 130 years, ending up as a second mainline for the coal conveyor-belt masquerading as a railroad, the Chesapeake & Ohio. And as for the Erie, its usefulness as a thorn in the side of Commodore Vanderbilt and son Billy made it a plaything of Jay Gould's. In the next century it made money when the demand for coal on the eastern seaboard was strong and languished when it was not. In modern times millions spent on double-tracking and centralized traffic control could not save the Erie, and now trees are beginning to grow where half-million-pound locomotives once blasted along at the head of mile-long freight trains.

These trunk line railroads sought out the streams that worked their way eastward to tidewater, or westward to the Ohio River, however crooked their courses and narrow the ledges on either side where a railroad might be laid down. The B. & O.'s general counsel, John H. B. Latrobe, had studied at West Point to be an engineer but found solving the line's many legal problems and knotty government relations more to his liking. Fortunately he had a younger brother, Benjamin, Jr., who trained for the law but found engineering problems more interesting. They were the sons of the better known Benjamin H. Latrobe, Sr., a distinguished architect whose designs for the U.S. Capitol were adopted (and who is sometimes taken for his younger son). Benjamin, Jr., spent his entire career with the B. & O., ending as president of the subsidiary that extended the line to Pittsburgh. As assistant to Jonathan

Knight, chief engineer until 1842, Benjamin, Jr., who succeeded Knight, laid out the branch from Baltimore to Washington, D.C., which, in good time, would become the mainline out of Baltimore. It was a better line than the "old mainline" due west from Baltimore, despite the roughness of terrain just south of the city, and its most famous and photogenic feature was, and is, the superb stone arch bridge that Benjamin Latrobe built across the Patapsco River at Relay, Maryland, in 1835, still as good as new 150 years later.

Latrobe and the B. & O. carried an unusual burden in laying out their railroad westward. The only fight on record between a railroad and a canal company for a right of way ensued when the Chesapeake & Ohio Canal, struggling to get itself dug up the course of the Potomac River, attempted to shut the B. & O. out of the extremely tight passes between the forbidding rock walls on either side from Point of Rocks to Harper's Ferry. Eventually the deadlock was settled by a compromise dictated by the Maryland legislature, which by this time was extending financial support to both enterprises through stock purchases. Some very ticklish engineering compromises remained, however, before Latrobe had the track safely tucked into the small space provided, and no doubt he made a mental note of the early betterments of track location, by means of tunnels or cuts, that would await a future and presumably more affluent engineer. Now, before him lay an even greater challenge: getting the railroad across the Potomac River at the point where the Shenandoah flowed into it.

"The view at Harper's Ferry is worth a trip across the Atlantic," Thomas Jefferson is said to have exclaimed, although whether he would have approved of the addition of railroads and bridges to the vista is doubtful. On the Virginia side, when Latrobe's forces arrived, already ran the Shenandoah Valley Railroad, and Latrobe, expecting to use the Shenandoah's tracks for a few miles on the other side, aimed his economy-model wooden covered bridge to align his tracks with them. But the Shenandoah slammed the door in his face, for reasons no one seems to have remembered. Thus the west end of the B. & O.'s bridge sprouted a branch that turned off to the right and hung on via a trestle past the U.S. Arsenal, which was to make Harper's Ferry even more famous in another twenty years as the scene of John Brown's raid. The same arrangement exists to this day, although the bridge has been replaced twice and the approaches vastly improved.

Latrobe was now free to cover some ground, and he lit out for the West with the largest work force ever employed up to that time. Cumberland, Maryland, was to be a major stop on the railroad, with a commodious station and hotel as befitted a place where the Chesapeake & Ohio Canal was to terminate and the National Road began, but it was as far as the B. & O. had progressed when the 1830s depression halted its advance until the late 1840s. If it had not been for the depression, the railroad map of the Middle Atlantic states might have been vastly different, for the Pennsylvania legislature had granted the B. & O. the right to build across the state to any point on the Ohio River, which, had this golden opportunity not been missed, would certainly have been Pittsburgh. It is hard to imagine the mercantile princes of Philadelphia doing business with the raw new emporium on the great western river via Baltimore, but stranger things have happened, and they were fed up with Pennsylvania's great embarrassment, the long, wearying canal and inclined planes of the Main Line works. The legislature's go-ahead expired in 1843, however, and by then the opportunity had passed.

As prosperity returned in the late 1840s, the B. & O. had to decide whether to head for Parkersburg (today in West Virginia), which would have put it in a fair way for the rising cities of Columbus, Cincinnati, and in the far distance, St. Louis, or to stick to its original objective, which had been to reach the Ohio at the earliest possible date. Latrobe chose the latter, which meant Wheeling, now West Virginia, which was gaining prominence in the still-infant American iron industry by specializing in the production of the flat, cut nails with which all American houses built before the Civil War—and many for a long time afterward—were made. Latrobe's skills as a surveyor, bridge builder, tunnel digger, and organizer of great numbers of grading and iron-laying crews, were fully exercised in a burst of activity that culminated in the B. & O.'s arrival in Wheeling on Christmas Eve, 1852. The hardest part of the new mileage had been just west of Cumberland, for in getting the railroad out of the watershed of the Potomac, its bailiwick since Point of Rocks, Latrobe met and mastered the maximum permissible grade of 116 feet to the mile, referred to as a 2.2% grade. The Wheeling line, branching off the main at Grafton, did not have long to bask in the spotlight, for Wheeling soon lay upon a direct line of the B. & O. from Pittsburgh to Columbus, once Latrobe had moved on to play a leading role in bringing the B. & O. into Pittsburgh, thus confirming it as a contender for trunk line status alongside the Pennsylvania Railroad.

It was John Work Garrett, to be sure, who was the key man in the conversion of the Baltimore merchants' modest dream into the interregional railroad it had to become, but Latrobe was essential to his success. When Garrett acquired the Pittsburgh & Connellsville Railroad, it had managed to get no farther than the town of Connellsville, south of Pittsburgh. He renamed it the Pittsburgh, Washington & Baltimore, then made Latrobe its president, with the mission of closing the difficult ninety-five-mile gap between Connellsville and Cumberland on the B. & O.'s mainline, which Latrobe took in stride. His biggest problem may have been in remembering how to pronounce (let alone spell) the name of the sinuous river along which the older segment was built: the Youghiogheny (Yockagaynee). The link was closed in 1871, and Latrobe lived long enough to see it become one of the most valuable segments on the entire railroad. Under the town of Connellsville and for miles around lay, and still lie, massive deposits of some of the finest coking coal in the world. In 1873 Andrew Carnegie, in partnership with a few other farsighted men—including Henry Clay Frick, who had shrewdly bought up mineral leases on thousands of acres of the most promising coal lands in the region—built the first integrated Bessemer steel mill in America near Pittsburgh, and the B. & O.'s reputation as a coal-and-iron railroad was assured.

The Developers: The Aorta

Whoever it was who first advised young people to "be not the first nor yet the last" to grasp new ideas, he probably came as close as anyone to explaining the simple secret behind the successful emergence of the giant industrial corporations. He had in mind General Motors, during the fabulous 'fifties when the automobile was completing its fifty-year impaction of American life, but he might just as well have been referring to the Pennsylvania Railroad, which demonstrated the aphorism so well. By the mid-1840s, the steam railroad had proved its practical worth beyond the capacity of even the most cautious businessman to doubt. The promoters had dreamed the dream, and in the hands of the engineer-builders, their dream was already being realized in many places.

The decade of the 1840s was indeed the time of decision for the city of Philadelphia, with its major port on the Delaware River estuary to the Atlantic, and for the Commonwealth of Pennsylvania, which was growing increasingly aware of the mineral wealth that abounded in its western hills. The merchants of Philadelphia resolved, in 1846, not to miss what was probably the last chance for the city to dominate a direct rail route to the West. Most of the fundamental problems of building a railroad through the mountains had been mastered, or were about to be, by the B. & O. and the Erie, which, being first, had suffered all the pains of trial and error in solving problems of construction, motive power, and rail design. Withal, they would manage to reach their initial goals on the Ohio at Wheeling and Lake Erie at Dunkirk—neither, in the long run, good choices—only a couple of years before the Pennsylvania ran its first train into Pittsburgh.

All of these mountain railroads had their engineering heroes, whose bearded portraits hung on the walls of their boardrooms. The Pennsylvania had J. Edgar Thomson, some say the greatest of them all. Another self-taught engineer, he was a genius of planning, construction, and operation, and possessed of a consuming curiosity about everything new that was being introduced into American railroading. He had, moreover, a remarkable talent for making money on his own and raising it from investors, and, entirely out of character for a Quaker, was a most daring entrepreneur, envisioning a route to Chicago while still struggling to get the first division under construction

Figure 10.2   Two pioneer builders of trunk lines: Benjamin H. Latrobe, Jr. (1806–1878), at left, and J. Edgar Thomson (1808–1874). (Latrobe, Jr.—*Baltimore & Ohio Railroad Museum;* Thomson—*Smithsonian Institution*)

contract to meet the stern terms of the franchise that the legislature had awarded the enterprise.

Thomson's qualifications to extend the existing Philadelphia & Columbia Railroad westward through the mountains lay in his solid experience in having done almost exactly that for the Georgia Railroad. Thomson had undertaken to build this line, beginning in 1834, from Augusta, where it connected with one of the earliest American railroads, the Charleston & Hamburg, to a location yet to be determined in the heart of the upland cotton country. This location was quickly transformed from the tiny crossroads village that was all it had ever expected to be, into an important rail junction that played a major role in the Civil War. It had the distinction of being burned twice—once by General William Tecumseh Sherman and again in 1937—by proxy— on the Hollywood set for the motion picture, *Gone With the Wind.* In the post-World War II era it has been one of America's fastest growing cities. The man who picked it to be the terminus of the Georgia Railroad was J. Edgar Thomson, who also gave it its name: Atlanta.

Thomson enjoyed life in the antebellum South, and it could have put his further service to good use, if its leaders could have raised the capital to continue building a railroad system that still existed mostly on paper. It is just as well they could not, for in returning north and accepting the job of building the Pennsylvania Railroad, Thomson made an incalculable contribution to the economic and social development of the Union, and did much to assure its survival in the conflict that was coming. His personality and superior knowledge of what needed to be done bore heavily on the first two presidents of the road, who were supposed to be his superiors, and he effectively vetoed their constant pleas to proceed more slowly so that income could keep pace with construction costs. Thomson knew that this was no philosophy by which to build a major capital asset like a long-distance railroad, and in the ensuing confrontations he always won the day, for the directors of the road knew that he was probably right and, in any case, irreplaceable. In the last such set-to, Thomson emerged as president, and he hastened to undertake an expensive project that had terrified the old management: a major tunnel under Allegheny Mountain, the last important obstacle between him and Pittsburgh. The first train traveling the distance entirely on the new line entered Pittsburgh in February 1854. Considering what that city and that railroad made of each other and of the nation, 1854 can lay claim as the *annus mirabilis* of American economic history. (In that same year, in fact, the Lake Shore & Michigan Southern completed the seaboard's first link to Chicago).

Completion of the Pennsylvania Railroad into Pittsburgh was only the end of Act One for the railroad and for Thomson, who would spend the rest of his life at its head. After 1854, profits flowed in at a rising rate, and he used them wisely. The State of Pennsylvania, which was holding onto a white elephant in the heavily bonded Main Line system, tried to push the burden onto the railroad by taxing its traffic, so Thomson bought up the entire system for $7.5 million. (It took several years, however, for the political skills of the Pennsylvania's Vice President Tom Scott to get the tax lifted!) According to the Progressive mind-set, which still afflicts many American historians, the Pennsy got an undeserved bargain, for the Main Line had cost a great deal more, but in fact the state got a very good deal, as the system was worthless except for the rather spindly Philadelphia & Columbia Railroad segment.

Just when it was that Thomson began to see that he was, as we would insist, a developer of a railroad *system*, and that a system would have to have, under a single control, a direct connection with the great western emporia of Chicago and St. Louis, is uncertain, although Scott, on his own, had been helping to piece together the eventual route. But we do know that it was Jay Gould, that great catalyst in the swift evolution of the American railroad system after the Civil War, who awakened him to it. By 1870, railroad men just about everywhere had come to take it for granted that freight would be transferred freely from one line to another at the points where they met in a through route transcending any one carrier's corporate boundaries, and that the division of the total through rate as between two or more cooperating railroads would be fair and equitable and would be arrived at by parties of approximately equal bargaining power. After competition began to heat up in the late 1860s, no one could assume that for very long, least of all about Jay Gould; when he seemed to be about to gain control of the Pittsburgh, Fort Wayne & Chicago, the Pennsylvania's end-to-end partner at Pittsburgh, Thomson demanded, and got, from his board of directors a free hand to acquire whatever lines were necessary to preserve the Pennsy's territorial imperative.

Soon the Pennsylvania not only controlled, on long-term lease, the Fort Wayne line, but also the congeries of lines that ran southwest from Pittsburgh to St. Louis, consisting primarily of the "Panhandle" route (Pittsburgh, Cincinnati, Chicago, and St. Louis) and the Vandalia Line from Indianapolis to St. Louis, just when that city was immersed in its great project to build the Eads Bridge across the broad Mississippi at its gates. These routes, but especially the Fort Wayne line, became the veritable aorta of the iron and steel industry that would form the heart of heavy industry about to be born, and the "broadway of steel" that conducted mountains of coal, cornucopias of grain, oceans of petroleum, torrents of mail and express, and hordes of passengers between the centers of the new civilization. Then, with hardly a murmur from the burghers of Philadelphia, Thomson had moved to recognize that the real terminal of the Pennsy was to be New York, by buying the United Canals & Railways of New Jersey, connecting Philadelphia with Jersey City, across the great river from Gotham, and including the old, obsolete pioneer line of the Camden & Amboy Railroad.

Few if any developers of the American railroad system have a better claim than Thomson to the title of first modern railroad executive. A superb technician, he was also a first-class manager, who never hesitated to introduce new practices when called for. As a tactician, he was unmatched, which his unerring rise to leadership of this great new railroad at the beginning of the 1850s confirms. "There is no substitute for being right," a later American, Fiorello H. La Guardia, would declare about his own successes, and Thomson was right, it seemed, about nearly everything. His transformation of the Pennsy into the first great integrated trunk line reveals, moreover, a master strategist. About his only failure was his attempt, in a private alliance with a group of fellow investors, to take control of the Union Pacific Railroad. Here, he was probably luckier than he realized, for as a later generation of transcontinental railroad developers would come to appreciate, the idea of an ocean-to-ocean railroad, ignoring the need to exchange freight at the midwestern gateway cities, was an *ignis fatuis*, an empty dream.

Perhaps more important than any other legacy Thomson could have left his successors, Tom Scott and then George B. Roberts, was the implicit belief that the best investment a thriving railroad can make of its operating profits is in *itself*, and not in large dividends. His appreciation of the quick and substantial payoff of steady investment in system betterments was put fully to work on the Pennsylvania, at a time when the reinvestment of profits seemed a radical step to most businessmen. Even before the line was finished to Pittsburgh, Thomson had begun to double-track segments as they quickly developed a heavy traffic, and there were curves and grades aplenty upon which to exercise the technoeconomic skills that marked the first-class railroad executive. Still famous today are such nineteenth-century engineering wonders as the Horseshoe Curve and Gallitzin Tunnel, but to appreciate the fact that the Pennsylvania is in its entirety the real wonder, one must pore over the volumes of period photographs produced by the Pennsylvania's staff photographers. Thomson knew that a railroad is never finally finished until its useful life is finished. On the Pennsy, with its grades and curves, fast, uninterrupted service was essential if operating costs were to be held competitive with the New York Central. Thomson pushed early for the use of steel rails, the more so since steel was clearly becoming the railroad's number one source of freight. Coal as a fuel was being pressed upon the railroad's superintendents of motive power before they or the builders of their machines may have thought its time had come, but coal, too, made the Pennsy, and vice versa.

How much the nation had accomplished in the generation and a half since the B. & O.'s first halting effort to cross the Appalachians! That it proved possible was something marvelous, but that by the mid-1870s the Pennsylvania Railroad would match the New York Central and its priceless water-level route for efficiency and tonnage was a revelation. All of America's previous expectations had now to be revised, and, while new problems, most of them man-made, would crowd upon America's railroads, living proof of what man could now accomplish lay before them in Thomson's "standard railroad of the world."

The Developers: Dixie

The decade of the 1850s was a time for the South to get going, too. Southerners' views of the nature of the Union and of the rights of its inhabitants were soon to begin a long, painful process of change, especially the view of the states' relationships with each other and within the Union. Imperfect vision would vitiate what could be accomplished with the South's tiny hoard of liquid capital, but some progress was made nevertheless in developing an inland transportation system once the steam railroad had begun to thrive elsewhere. In the potentially rich but sadly isolated "golden crescent" of the North Carolina piedmont, for example, where the broad coastal plain begins to rise towards the mountains and yields fine crops of upland cotton, tobacco, and grains, the hills began to echo with the blasts of the locomotive whistle, which would deliver all that it promised and more.

Nowadays hundred-car trains of trailers or containers on flatcars roar through the yard limits at Greensboro, North Carolina, racing northward or southward with valuable merchandise freight that two or three days before left U.S. factories or was just arriving at Atlantic or Gulf coast ports from foreign shippers. Probably few among the crews or the delighted trainwatchers know that these superb trains are traversing what began its existence over 130 years ago as the North Carolina Railroad. This eighty-four-mile segment between Greensboro and Charlotte of what is today a double-tracked and electronically controlled railroad has been part of a through line from deep in Dixie to Washington, D.C., and, via connections, to New York and New England, for more than a century. It is part of the main stem of what was the Southern Railway and is now the Norfolk Southern Railroad, neither of which ever owned it but merely leased it, in virtual perpetuity, from its stockholders, of whom the largest is the State of North Carolina.

The South was rapidly falling behind in providing itself with railroads, much less a unified system of lines, by 1850. Collectively speaking, southerners could not make up their minds whether they wanted a railroad system that would confirm the supposed self-sufficiency of the South as a region within the Union, funneling its commerce in the direction of its own ports, which were already beginning to lose out to the superior ports of the Northeast and their new rail connections, or a north-south system that would cater to the undeniable tendency of more and more southerners to travel between their plantations and the inviting cities of Boston, New York, Philadelphia, and Baltimore. There were still many Whigs in the South, and their more cosmopolitan interests led them, and not a few Democrats, to speak glowingly of the great advantages that would flow from being able to carry on their commerce directly with the North by rail, instead of by slow, infrequent, and unreliable steamers and schooners out of Charleston, Savannah, and Norfolk.

In the 1840s the classic expression of the provincial policy was the fiery speeches of Robert Y. Hayne, South Carolina's boy-wonder U.S. senator and oratorical foe of the great Daniel Webster, whose own defense of the concept of Union before that august body every schoolboy was once required to memorize. Hayne was the leading promoter of the Charleston & Hamburg Railway, which had been intended to connect the excellent port of Charleston with the bustling Mississippi River port of Memphis, over a thousand miles to the west as the crow flies. Alas, railroads can't fly, and such a project remained an impossible dream for a section of the country that was hard put to find the short-term capital to move its annual cotton crop, much less to sink in a new transportation technology that *might* find a practical way over all those mountains—blue hazes in the distance—that stood between tidewater and the valley of the Mississippi—and might not. Hayne's early death halted a project that would not be carried out for at least another generation.

A public-opinion pollster surveying attitudes towards a railroad-building policy for the South at the beginning of the 1850s would doubtless have found a large majority in favor of self-sufficiency, but pollsters have been false heralds of what was to be many times since.

In North Carolina, there was certainly a yearning for railroads to tide-water, but where? To a real provincial, sending stuff to Norfolk or Petersburg, in Virginia, was just about as bad as shipping overland to the Northeast, if it were possible. There ensued a policy of keeping both options open as long as possible.

It did not take long, or even a Civil War, to prove that North Carolina was not to be a great maritime state in the age of the steamship. The Carolina coast is a fine place for wild horses, whooping cranes, surf fishermen, and summer tourists, but a poor place to bring a ship to harbor. (Cape Hatteras, "the graveyard of the Atlantic," is the main feature of the area.) Not one person in a thousand, probably, ever thinks of the North Carolina cities of Wilmington, New Bern, and Morehead City as ports, but in the 1850s it was worth a try to see if railroad connections to the interior could attract steamships through the Outer Banks.

Meanwhile the railroads of the Old Dominion State, notably the Richmond & Danville, were knocking at the state line of North Carolina and preparing to seduce her little railroads, when they should become reality, into becoming part of a through north-south line. The Whigs and their allies were prepared to build a line from Charlotte, North Carolina, northward to Danville, and to do it, moreover, without any help from the state treasury—in other words, with Yankee money! Thus it was that the machinery of compromise was thrown into high gear. Anxious to move the produce of the interior by a low-cost means that would not absorb all of the gain in market price that the larger market would bring, in January 1849 the legislature chartered the North Carolina Railroad, one of the earliest and most successful in the state's history.

The charter bill got enthusiastic support from Whig members of the legislature, and a substantial minority of the Democrats, passing by sixty votes to fifty-two in the House and twenty-three to twenty-two in the Senate. Members were not unaware that they were authorizing not merely the construction of *somebody's* railroad, but literally *everybody's* railroad, as the state agreed to supply two-thirds of the capital required to build and equip it. Such aid would be forthcoming once the promoters of the road had succeeded in raising the third one-third by subscriptions from the general public.

This proved to be as painful as pulling teeth and to take much longer. Convention after convention and rally after rally, across the east central part of the state, struggled to pry loose what little liquid assets the population possessed. They had very little to begin with: a poor southern farmer had nothing, it has been said, and a rich planter has debts, and what they did have, they held onto tightly. Three former governors of the state headed the fund-raising campaign, among them the man who would serve as first president of the railroad, John Motley Morehead, but it was slow going. Eventually, as always happens in these affairs, the finger of duty pointed to what the fundraisers hoped would be a group of one hundred leading men, each pledging $10,000 to make up the $1,000,000 needed. No one remembers how many hogs and oxen gave their lives in the barbecues that helped attract the crowds to the meetings, but by the end of the year barely $600,000 had been subscribed.

For many years Durham, North Carolina, which became the seat of Duke University, was reachable by through Pullman sleeper from New York over the section of the former N.C.R.R. east of Greensboro. A northerner, traveling in North Carolina for the first time, could get his first good look at the piedmont South from his roomette window as he made his toilet just before arriving in Durham early in the morning. The wayside station of Mebane ("mebbin"), a hamlet on the eastern edge of Alamance County, with its neat sign proclaiming the name of one of the earliest settlers of the area, might slip by unnoticed, but the name of Mebane figures significantly in the touch-and-go struggle to get the railroad built at all. By February 1850, the promoters were almost ready to despair. In newspapers and speeches they had rung all the changes on the economic miracles that railroads were already producing where they had been built, not for just a few, but for everybody. Maybe there just were not a hundred men with ten thousand dollars at their command. Were there ten? At the desperation meeting it was moved that a list of ten men be drawn up to pledge ten thousand dollars each. Beating down motion after motion to adjourn, the tenacious promoters doggedly urged the list all the way up to eight.

Now it seemed that someone was sure to second the motion to adjourn if something did not happen. It did happen: up stood one Giles Mebane, who became number nine. Mebane was proud of his brandnew county of Alamance, which had just been split off from Orange County, for it was at the Battle of Alamance in 1771, when men of the Regulator Movement went down fighting Tory repression, that the southeastern colonies moved another notch toward independence. Thereupon a group quickly formed from Hillsborough, not willing to see Orange County upstaged by upstart Alamance, and pledged the tenth. Some of the Hillsborough men had already pledged subscriptions, and one was in to the tune of eighteen thousand dollars, an enormous sum in those days. He never had cause to regret it, we may assume, but still the episode emphasizes what biography teaches over and over: in the summing up, it is the individual decisions of a small group of rather ordinary human beings, and not vague forces of destiny, that get things done. The promoters of the North Carolina Railroad would have understood Winston Churchill's words in praise of the men of the Royal Air Force: "Never have so many owed so much to so few."

But what of the two-thirds of the initial capital—$2,000,000— that was to be supplied by the State of North Carolina? Surely that represented the savings of the South's multitudes? Not at all. Knowledge-

able men were aware from the beginning, although they understandably did not press the point, that at no time did the South ever possess
the liquid capital necessary to build modern improvements in a backward land. The state financed its share of the total by selling bonds,
virtually all of which were marketed through New York investment
bankers. The roots of northern involvement in southern railroads, notwithstanding what sectional chauvinists would proclaim, obviously
went very deep. The railroad, however, could never have been built
without the applied energies of men who knew what it would do for
the piedmont region of North Carolina, which for the next century
stood out as an island of affluence in a sea of debt-ridden cotton farmers
in most of the Southeast.

During the fund-rising drive, it had been discovered that location
of the line was confusing the issue of building the line at all, and somehow agreement was reached among the promoters to withhold all decisions of location until the project was under way. The railroad as built
served as an east-west line to carry the produce of the state and its
imports between North Carolina ports and the east central counties of
the "golden crescent," which ran roughly northward from Charlotte to
Greensboro, deflecting then northeastward to Raleigh, and then south-
eastward to Goldsboro, where the railroad connected with lines south
to North Carolina ports or north to Norfolk. The nonexistent "Danville
connection," of course, stared from a railroad map like a missing tooth,
but once it was finally filled in the N.C.R.R. would begin to fulfill its
true destiny, which lay overland to the north and not to the forlorn
ports on the Atlantic that looked wistfully across the Outer Banks for
steamships that came only now and then.

What professional management there was on the N.C.R.R. in the
brief decade before the Civil War upset normal operations was practiced under the most adverse conditions, for the N.C.C.R. was a political thing, and the string of mediocre politicians who passed briefly
through the state house made quite a show of voting the state's stock
in the railroad. Without its remarkably faithful bookkeeper, the
N.C.R.R. probably would have had only the vaguest idea of its earnings,
revenues, and expenses. Even so, some semblance of orderly procure-
ment, personnel and labor policies, train scheduling, rate-making, and
other vital functions, developed. Never settled until the N.C.R.R.
became part of a consolidated system was the central question of traffic
policy, which, of course, was the old question of what the railroad had
been built for. The officers, armed with nothing but the scanty traffic
statistics that they kept when they felt like it, recognized that the railroad's passenger traffic was mostly local (that is, originating and/or terminating on the line) but the freight traffic consisted primarily of
through movements. Without the Danville connection, the N.C.R.R.
routed north-south through traffic predominantly over railroads tributary to Norfolk, the best port in the Southeast, to continue its north-

ward journey by steamship. This made sense as long as railroad rates remained at the high levels originally established, but the depression of the 1870s, and the proliferation of rail lines in the decade, changed all that. Of all the changes that the Civil War brought, one of the most striking was that the Confederate Army leaders immediately ordered the construction of the Danville connection, called during its short independent life the Piedmont Railroad.

The prime mover in southeastern railroad consolidation in the 1870s and 1880s was the Richmond & Danville, the main link in the old pre-1893 holding company called the Richmond Terminal. In 1871 the R & D leased the N.C.R.R. on long term as part of its rickety structure, which was chronically weakened by the parochialism of its components. Maury Klein has brilliantly treated the failure of the Richmond Terminal to evolve a strong central leadership or a clear-cut long-term policy of growth, system improvements, and expense reduction. Klein attributes this failure to an atomistic, baronial attitude on the part of large security owners in the various constituent corporations, who recognized no systemwide imperatives requiring the subordination of their individual, short-term profit objectives. Strong, competent leadership would emerge only with the rescue forces that came in after the panic of 1893, and, like the money which the State of North Carolina had secured with its bonds to pay its subscription to the N.C.R.R.'s bonds in the 1850s, first-class managerial talent, too, had to come from the North.

Thirty years and thirty thousand miles of railroad building after the first tentative chugs on the Mohawk & Hudson and the Baltimore & Ohio railroads, the first phase of the evolution of the American railroads had concluded. What we would call professional management, with diverse but well-defined duties, authority, and responsibilities, existed only in fuzzy outline. As we would expect for a phenomenon in its earliest stages of experimentation, this first phase depended upon technically trained men, skilled in on-the-spot innovation in construction of the heaviest kind, to make its decisions. This emphasis upon the engineering type was stronger than ever in 1860, and was further enhanced during the Civil War, to be slowly upstaged by the new commonwealth that had emerged in early modern America by 1900.

The second thirty-year period in nineteenth-century American railroad development substantially completed the long era of *extensive* development. Greater feats of civil engineering, possibly, awaited the engineers as the rails moved inexorably across the Mississippi and headed for the broad Missouri. In attaining them, the thirty years they had already spent in proving and discovering the virtues of the flanged iron wheel running on the steel rail were put to good use, and by 1900 the land was finally ours.

CHAPTER 11

Entrepreneurs to Managers: Across the Broad Missouri

> We cannot expect to combine great skill in the running of the road with great skill and scope in the management of its outside interests. The one is a matter of detail and the other of wide forecast.
>
> John N. A. Griswold, Chairman of the Board,
> the Chicago, Burlington & Quincy Railroad, 1877

> I have long been of the opinion that sooner or later the railroads of the country would group themselves into systems and that each system would be self-sustaining.
>
> Charles E. Perkins, President,
> Chicago, Burlington & Quincy Railroad, 1879

> . . . [T]he complaints of the public are directed against the commercial management of the railroads. . . . We hear of no public complaint against the technical management of the roads; . . . as regards the accommodations and facilities furnished to the American people, the safe and prompt and economical transaction of the passenger and freight traffic, the management of the railroads in this country is superior, or, to say the least, not surpassed in any other country.
>
> Albert Fink, Testimony before the Committee of Commerce
> of the House of Representatives on the Reagan Bill
> for the Regulation of Interstate Commerce, 1880

Those Nerves of Copper

When President William McKinley smilingly held out his left hand to shake the left hand of young Leon Czolgosz at the Pan American Exposition in Buffalo on September 5, 1900, he received from the anarchist's bandaged right hand two bullets, greasy with germs, one of which penetrated deep into and through the president's stomach, ending up somewhere in the back muscle. Eight days later he breathed his last from a massive internal infection. McKinley was lucky. Twenty years before, James A. Garfield had also died at the hand of an assassin's bullet, and his doctors had watched his agonizing decline through month after month of a very hot summer. The state of medical science being what it was in 1881, Garfield need have expected no salvation from any quarter, but hardly an hour before McKinley took his place in the reception line he had toured the scientific wonders of the exposition, and perhaps he had glanced briefly and uncomprehendingly at Wilhelm Roentgen's wonderful new diagnostic tool: the X-ray. Unfortunately, none of the president's doctors, although they knew his condition was hopeless unless they could locate and remove the bullet and apply proper aseptic measures, had the courage to try such a newfangled, untried gadget on the president.

Theories of technological change that gloss over the often dispiriting battles that sometimes raged about new ways of doing things—or even worse, the blasé indifference with which they were usually greeted—miss the best part of the story. Even today, in our technology-happy age, the "smart money" lets the gee-whiz school of management take the lead. Thus it was with the introduction of the telegraph in the operation and general management of American railroads. It may seem strange that railroading, which from the outset involved dealing in new, untried ways of doing things, should have been less than quick to adopt instantaneous communication along the lines of a railroad system by means of the "magnetic telegraph." True, the railroad idea was some fifteen years old before Samuel F. B. Morse demonstrated the first practical telegraph in 1844. As late as the 1860s and even 1870s, moreover, many miles of railroad lines, even high-density ones like the lines radiating out of Boston, were operated "by the book," that is, entirely according to a fixed timetable. Between the ever-present chance of delays along the way, the fact that conductors' pocket watches were seldom the fine twenty-one-jewel Hamiltons or Walthams of a later day, and just plain human error, the opportunity for disaster was great. And disasters occurred—but that is not what assured the universal adoption of the telegraph. Its arrival required a great leap forward in the professional management of the railroads, for the application of technological innovation is, in the end, the job of management—and is the measure of their success in doing not just the difficult, but also the "impossible."

The discrepancy between what was possible and what ruled on American railroads until the professional manager, cost-conscious and ambition-driven to make a name for himself, made our transportation system the most advanced in the world, is easily explained. There is a cost involved in change, no matter how insistently it knocks at the door. People naturally resist change: efficiency in any repetitive task comes with the ability to perform it almost as a conditioned reflex, and change is the enemy of conditioned reflexes, even if it is welcomed by the probing mind. Change costs money in material terms as well as in efficiency, and, in view of the high cost of capital in the Victorian age, the payoff in both cases had to be high.

Finally, there was the usual human mistrust of that which is intangible. Who would entrust his life and the lives of the passengers under his care to a few metallic clicks of a telegraph instrument, interpreted by the operator to mean that the opposing train was running so late that it had not yet entered the next block and it would be held on the siding there while you advanced your train one block? Ah, but ask the question another way. Who would not *hold* his train on the siding because the copper nerves were worrying about a train going in the same direction which had left the station ten or fifteen minutes before but had still not reached the station at the next block? *Fail safe!* Or, as Jim Hill instructed his conductors in one of his very first orders as general manager of a railroad, "When in doubt, take the safe course." And so, as time went by and telegraphic dispatching became more and more routine, its great value in preventing "rearenders," one of the commonest and bloodiest accidents in early railroading, was applied to all phases of train operation.

It came just in time. Or, to put it more realistically, men adopted telegraphic dispatching when there was no near-term alternative to turning away business. The most significant demand that American railroads placed upon the ever-harried superintendents and division managers in the last half of the old century was to do a constantly growing volume of business, including passenger traffic—which was the real moneymaker—with a physical plant that had never been designed for such activity. The telegraph, more than any of the other technological marvels, even the train brake, was more of a godsend to the growing nation than additional hundreds of millions invested in the physical plant and equipment of railroads already built, or thousands of additional skilled employees, when neither the money nor the human capital was available. In the jargon of the economists, railroad managers revolutionized the railroads' "production function" (roughly defined, the output attainable from a given input of labor and capital) by means of the *control* that the telegraph brought. My neighbor fills his swimming pool from a pond, using a new portable pump that is smaller, lighter, and has a bigger output in gallons per minute than the twenty-year-old pump made by the same maker, which took two men to carry and cost just as much, in 1965 dollars, as the new one in 1989 dollars. Like him, the railroad men of mid-century America redesigned their "pump" and thus bought the time they needed to meet the really big leap forward in traffic that was coming at the end of the century.

Control was the key, after all. All of the fancy organization charts in the world would not mean a thing if men had not devised means of control so that the left hand could know what the right hand was doing. The railroads, by the time the big, integrated manufacturing corporations began to appear, had substantially perfected a system of reports and directives, moving upward and downward in the structure, that made the theoretical ideal of the manager or subordinate who knows exactly what is expected of him and what he will have to accomplish it with, and how and by whom his results will be judged, a reality. Such a closed system is possible because the individual is never lost sight of. Hardly a day went by that an employee of a railroad, somewhere, however far down in the order of battle, was not called upon to use his common sense to prevent loss of life or property. It was the stuff of which dozens of railroad novels were made, and to more than one ambitious youngster it was the form in which opportunity came to him.

As the transportation development of the American West proceeded beyond the Mississippi River and especially beyond the Missouri, the railroad builders doubled and redoubled their demands for fresh capital and additional armies of workers. In these thinly settled areas, where the frequency of trains was considerably below that of established eastern lines and passengers and crews were often out of touch with "civilization" for hours and days at a time, lack of a telegraph line would have slowed the advance of the rails drastically. The symbiosis of the railroad and the telegraph was taken for granted from the start, and when the rails began to creep across the Great Plains, the telegraph lines almost flew in advance. The telegraph was like the thin rope that natives of the jungle threw first across chasms they intended to bridge, hauling successively heavier loads behind. They could not conceivably have named the blessing that brought an entire continent to life anything but . . . Western Union!

The Developers: Westward Ho

No better appreciation of the significance of the Midwest and the Great Plains in American transportation history can be had than by running one's hand westward over the surface of a large relief globe of the world, from the Atlantic coast to the Rocky Mountains. The suddenness with which the rough terrain of the Appalachians melts into the flat territory that stretches from eastern Ohio to the foothills of the Rockies says it all. At least as far west as the western edge of Iowa, moreover, this is a fertile, humid land of hot summers, which excels in growing huge marketable surpluses of what it takes to put the bread, meat, and potatoes on the tables of a large part of the rest of the world. It embraces the most valuable farmland in the world, and it is no wonder that men quickly set out, after about 1840, to build the most comprehensive railroad system in the world here, to gather up the produce of these fields, take it to world markets, and then return with the manufactured articles that a budding civilization demanded in increasing volume and variety.

The railroad map of the Midwest when the lines were at their peak, according to a prominent midwestern railroad historian, "looks like a plate of wet spaghetti." Branch lines went almost literally everywhere because, except for horse-drawn wagons, no other means of getting freight to and from the railroad existed. These branch lines seldom paid for themselves directly, for they were short and their traffic light except in harvest time, but they contributed tonnage to the main stem of the railroad which might then carry it for hundreds of miles. It was to replace these branches that the motor truck and its vital concomitant, the hard-surface country road, would make their most rational contribution to American transportation.

The Midwest of the 1840s, when the railroad-building era got under way, meant primarily Ohio, Michigan, Indiana, and Illinois. These states were in about the same shape, as far as the private raising of capital for long-term ventures like railroads were concerned, as the South a decade later. Historians have emphasized the eagerness with which the lawmakers of the raw new states, elected under the ultra-democratic franchise policy of "universal white manhood suffrage," voted state-guaranteed bonds to finance their earliest railroads. The bonds were not generally sold on the market—there was not much of a market for railroad bonds that early—but traded to English and Welsh ironmongers for iron rails. When the states, unable to meet the periodic interest payments during the depression of the 1840s, blandly repudiated them, the supply of British capital stopped flowing for a generation.

Who, then, provided the money thereafter? The fact is that the builders of the eastern trunk lines, running from tidewater to the Great Lakes or the Ohio, had kept an eye on these potential western connections from the beginning and were soon investing heavily in their securities. The balance sheet of almost any important American railroad for the next two generations would include the stocks and bonds of dozens of railroad enterprises in newer parts of the country whose success meant as much to the lending road as to the new line, if not more. The Pennsylvania Railroad was part of the Fort Wayne picture almost from the beginning. Likewise, the Baltimore & Ohio kept company with the Marietta & Cincinnati from Parkersburg, West Virginia, to Cincinnati, and the Ohio & Mississippi from there to St. Louis, a long courtship that finally ended with the B. & O. doing the honorable thing by acquiring full ownership. The Erie did much the same thing with the Atlantic & Great Western westward from Salamanca, New York. Aloof lines like the New York Central, content to stop with the Lake Shore & Michigan Southern, the Big Four, and Michigan Central, found that some seek greatness and others have greatness thrust upon them. Thus the Central reluctantly adopted a second western "extension," the Nickel Plate, which it would have much rather not had.

Farther west, the developers of the railroad system marked the advent of a singular but thenceforth much emulated association between western entrepreneurs and the cautious, conservative guardians of the capital of the northeastern rentier class, who expected and had a good use for a good return on their money. The entrepreneurs were generally rock-solid successful businessmen or professionals who were early figures in the history of states like Michigan, Illinois, and Iowa. The guardians of capital typically were aging stalwarts who might have begun as teenage supercargoes on American clippers to the Orient, and had learned early the art of the trader, the stern lesson that the best trade is one in which everyone comes out ahead, and the vital importance of credit based on absolute trustworthiness. They had first-class minds, were virtual intellectuals by modern standards, were posted on a wide range of subjects dealing with Americans' and Europeans' material concerns, and were cautious to a fault. In them honesty "amounted to a disease," if only because business had come to be based on trust. One of the earliest of these entrepreneur-financier pairings was, in fact, a trio. They came to the rescue of "Democracy's railroad," as historians have labeled Michigan's Democratic regime's efforts to finance, build, and operate a state system of internal improvements based on a railroad from Detroit in the general direction of Chicago. James F. Joy, soon and for most of the rest of the century a name to be reckoned with in midwestern railroading, was a classic example of the bright, educated young Yankee who had everything except expectations when he graduated from Harvard Law School in 1836. He moved immediately to Michigan, which became a state the next year. A highly successful lawyer from the start, Joy benefited especially from having as his senior George F. Porter, who was deep in the affairs of the state's internal improvements. Joy teamed up with John W. Brooks, one of the New York Central's outstanding civil engineers, to take over the Michigan Central, which had managed to build only twelve miles of line and was about to expire.

Joy and Brooks presented their ideas for rebuilding the Central and expanding it by strategic acquisitions of other struggling lines—Joy was fully posted on such possibilities—to a group of Boston capitalists led by John Murray Forbes, and the basis of a long and successful career in midwestern railroad development, eminently profitable to the investors and vital to the settlement and economic growth of Michigan, Illinois, and Iowa (and, later, Missouri, Kansas, and Nebraska), was laid. Forbes was the careful hand on the tiller: his reputation for astuteness and honesty extended all the way back to his late teens, when he went out to China on a cargo, stayed to run the Forbes's import-export business, and became financial advisor to the local mandarin before he was twenty.

The Michigan Central was soon doing all the developers had expected, and more, and was ripe for sale because even greater opportunities lay on the horizon. Out of this association sprouted what became the Chicago, Burlington & Quincy, the most successful of the granger roads, and its subsidiaries: the Burlington & Missouri River, which went straight as the crow flies across Iowa to Council Bluffs, where the first transcontinental began; the Hannibal & St. Joe, which did the same thing, if not quite as straight, across Missouri from Mark Twain's boyhood home to St. Joseph (a slight failure to foresee the future, which was soon corrected by excellent connections to the wide-awake new city of Kansas City); and, finally, the Burlington Railroad in Nebraska. These additions brought the Burlington to the foothills of the Rockies, where it had the good sense to stop and be acquired by James J. Hill as part of his northwestern empire. On a list of the most successful great works in the western world one would have to include this combination of eastern liquid capital, skilled and experienced railroading, and western enterprise, for few ever had so great an impact upon the lives of so many people and upon the history of a great nation.

"All roads lead to Chicago," one might exclaim, upon seeing for the first time a railroad map of the Midwest. "All roads lead *from* Chicago," might be a better way to put it, for Chicago quickly became the center of planning and construction of early railroads leading in three directions, north, south, and west, that would speedily become the nuclei of the greatest of the granger roads. Of all the names that are associated with the rise of Chicago to number two metropolis, a distinction which it enjoyed for many years, names such as Palmer, Field, McCormick, and Pullman, none deserves a prominent place on the list more than William Butler Ogden. Like so many vital elements in a story of development, his origins do not fit the pattern at all. Born in 1805 in Delaware County, New York, just west of the Catskills, he got in on the harvesting of the virgin forests at the beginning of the modern era in American lumbering. In 1835 he was a successful businessman and budding politician, who seemed destined for no particular distinction in the history of New York State, but his election to the state senate placed him in the center of the debate on a proposition to build a railroad across the southern tier of New York counties which marked the beginnings of the Erie Railroad. Ogden spoke expansively at sessions in Albany on the future of railroads, not as isolated lines, but as systems: ". . . continuous railways from New York to Lake Erie, and south through Ohio, Indiana, and Illinois to the waters of the Mississippi, and connecting with railroads running to Cincinnati and Louisville in Kentucky and Nashville in Tennessee, and to New Orleans, will present the most splendid system of internal communications ever yet devised by man." He was soon to have an opportunity to help bring his prophecy to reality when, on the urging of his brother-in-law, who was making a fortune in Chicago's early land boom, he decided to move to the wooden, muddy, overgrown town at the foot of Lake Michigan. Two years later, upon the town's incorporation as a city, its citizens made him their first mayor.

Ogden first attended to the completion of the canal that connected the lake with the Illinois River and via that lazy stream to the Mississippi and the outside world. (As we have already noted elsewhere, the potential this route had been thought to have a generation earlier was never realized, for the railroads fanning out from the city to and beyond the Mississippi quickly provided a better route whereby southern Illinois commerce reversed its traditional flow southward to St. Louis.) The visitor to Chicago several decades ago quickly realized that although Chicago was the terminus of both the great eastern trunk lines and the fabled western transcontinentals, it was the North Western (never, oh never, one word!) that always seemed to come up in railroad talk. That was because the North Western neither ended at Chicago nor began at Chicago; it *was* Chicago, for it bound the rich hinterland of Wisconsin, Minnesota, western Illinois, and Iowa to Chicago so tightly that other would-be metropolises in these areas had to be content with secondary market status. Alongside the Milwaukee Road (the Chicago, Milwaukee, St. Paul & Pacific, long called "the St. Paul" until it was extended to the west coast after 1900), the Chicago, Rock Island & Pacific, and of course the Burlington, the North Western became so intimately a part of the gathering and distribution system of America's bread basket and hog butcher that it could never quite progress to the next logical step in its development by arranging for connections to the West under its own control.

Ogden's involvement in railroads began in the late 1840s when he and several associates took over the Galena & Chicago Union Railroad, which was to connect Chicago with the lead mines in the extreme northwest corner of the state. It never got there, because much superior sources of lead and zinc were discovered in Missouri and elsewhere, but Ogden and friends extended it in 1853 to Freeport, 121 miles up in the boondocks but isolated no longer and ready to carry Abraham Lincoln and Stephen A. Douglas there for one of their historic debates in 1856. In 1855 they completed a second line due west to the Mississippi at Fulton, which for a brief period enjoyed prosperity as the only railroad-equipped landing on the river. The North Western, properly speaking, dates only from Ogden's founding of the Chicago, St. Paul & Fond du Lac to reach the new pineries of a budding lumber state, Wisconsin. In 1859 he reorganized it as the Chicago & North Western, and in 1864 he merged it with the Galena line. By the coming of the Civil War, and largely through the efforts of men like Ogden, the Old Northwest centering on Chicago had cast their lot with the Union despite a large population of southern sympathizers.

Long-Term Entrepreneurial Failure:
The Independent Granger Roads

Except for the Burlington, none of the granger roads heeded Jim Hill's warning, voiced with increasing emphasis from the early 1880s on, that no western railroad would be able to maintain its independence and prosperity unless it managed to control its own connection to the Pacific. By the last decade of the twentieth century two—the Rock

Island and the Milwaukee—had suffered extinction, at least in part because they had ignored Hill's advice, which was part of a larger failure of entrepreneurship from the turn of the century on. The North Western has managed to hang on, although its corporate future as the twentieth century waned was anybody's guess.

"The Rock Island line is a mighty fine line," goes an old American folk song, which may well mystify the young of today, inasmuch as the Rock Island became the first major railroad to murmur a final reproachful word about the insanities of postwar government railroad policy and then, in the mid-1970s, to turn up its toes and die. But the reputation of "the Rock" goes much farther back to a happier day, that day in April 1856 when it reached the Mississippi at Rock Island. The North Western's predecessor, the Galena line, had beaten the Rock Island to what prudent folks in those days considered the logical western terminus of a railroad—the Mississippi River—but the Rock Island went Ogden's road one better: it kept right on going. Across the big river (with the invaluable assistance of the rocky islets which gave the town of Rock Island its name), the Rock Island built the first bridge ever to span the Mississippi. Anyone who doubts the power of such an event to change the course of history must study the bitterness with which the river boatmen fought the bridge project, the stubbornness with which they tried to destroy it in court and, failing, burned it to the water line, and the doggedness with which the railroad built it right back again. The Rock Island bridge case was a milestone in the vast changes in American law and jurisprudence that the railroads were bringing, and a triumph for a Springfield lawyer that would help propel him onto the national scene and to the White House.

The granger roads revolutionized the production and distribution of food and food grains in North America and, very shortly after they reached the great river, western Europe as well. Right behind their construction crews came a hardy generation of settlers, many of whom, in this new American agriculture based on growing large surpluses of storable, shippable commodities, had already made their mark farther east and sold out for a good profit. They would turn the territories of Wisconsin, Minnesota, Iowa, Kansas, and Nebraska into powerful and vociferous states of the Union in record time. The mainlines of these railroads spanned Iowa like strings of a violin and, to complete the simile, they hummed with commerce. They would fight furiously for a growing stream of traffic, putting out their branches aggressively like the streamers of a coral reef to attract what they had been built to carry to market and to distribute what farmers bought with the proceeds.

Somewhere in the far distance rose the Rocky Mountains, and, when a "transcontinental" railroad was finally opened in 1869, they contested bitterly for the right to deliver westbound freight to it at Council Bluffs and Kansas City and to take back east what the Union Pacific brought it. For a generation, that did not amount to much, for the time of Colorado, Wyoming, and the Pacific Slope (much less the playgrounds of Nevada) had not yet come. It was rather the Pacific Northwest that beckoned strongly after 1880, as the Northern Pacific was extended and found a connection to Puget Sound. The real job to be done, for as far into the future as anyone could see in the nineteenth century, was to serve the burgeoning heartland of America. Ignoring the call of the West, the grangers found life simple and sweet where and as it was. Only the Burlington made a feint—an expensive survey westward from Denver to the coast—and the ultraconservative Bostonians who lived on its clockwork dividends no doubt heaved a great sigh of relief when Charles Perkins publicly rejected any transcontinental ambitions for his kind of people. Shortly thereafter this man, who had made the Burlington the mightiest granger of them all, advised his loyal widows and orphans to sell out to Jim Hill's Great Northern (at the amazing price of $200 for each $100 par value share of stock). It was an offer no denizen of the Back Bay could refuse.

Meanwhile the Burlington's closest rival for king of the granger roost, the Milwaukee, was failing utterly to develop a first-class professional management team as two very rich men, John D. Rockefeller's brother, William, and Philip D. Armour, king of the sausage makers, ran the railroad according to their whims. The Milwaukee made all of the classic mistakes that failed entrepreneurship can make. It waited too long to expand to the Pacific, refusing haughtily to take Jim Hill's sage advice to do so in concert with the North Western, which was not winning any prizes for long-range planning, either. When the Milwaukee decided, in 1905, to build its own line, there was no one left to merge with; to make matters worse, it suddenly faced a steeply ascending level of prices and wages after a quarter of a century of steady decline. The Milwaukee's situation, now growing desperate, was also dangerous. It called for the most careful planning, but it did not get it, for the benighted board of directors, eager to get going, authorized the spending of hundreds of millions on the strength of a total figure thrown out by its top hired man at one of their regular meetings. Cost overruns were enormous, rates on long-term bonds were at record levels, and after 1915 the Panama Canal robbed the transcontinentals of much traffic. The outcome was bankruptcy in the prosperous year of 1925, for a railroad that had done so well, down to the mid-1880s, under Alexander Mitchell. Unfortunately, the rich owners who took over as the western railroads were getting ready for the last phase of national railroad expansion did not know any Alexander Mitchells, or if they did, they did not realize how badly they needed one.

The North Western and the Rock Island had had good men, too, in Marvin E. Hughitt and Ransom Cable, but they failed to rise to the occasion. Either might have made a good marriage with any one of the transcontinentals that went west from the Twin Cities, Omaha, Kansas City, or even New Orleans. But the 1880s were not a time for big mergers. Big roads were gobbling up smaller ones right and left, to be sure, but when it came to grand strategy, the granger railroads seemed prepared to sit in their respective corners and glower indefinitely. So fundamental were these enterprises to the economy of the Midwest and the nation that "indefinitely" proved to be a very long time. The North Western, the Rock Island, and the Milwaukee steamed stolidly through the end-of-century depression that brought the nation a massive reorganization of its railroad system, but sooner or later Jim Hill's prediction would be fulfilled.

The Rock Island died, although some of its segments, under other railroads' operations, have been saved and daily prove their fundamental value to the nation. The Milwaukee, corporately speaking, is defunct, as it was acquired by the lowly Soo, which is in reality a subsidiary of the patrician Canadian Pacific, and its line west of a point in South Dakota has been abandoned. The North Western was sold to its employees, and sold and resold to investor groups whose optimism was finally being rewarded as the 1980s ended. Thousands of miles of both main and branch lines that could no longer support record-high union wage scales with their thin traffic have been kept in operation by the expedient of selling them off to newly organized enterprises made feasible by laws passed to relieve these "short lines" of excessive wage scales and unneeded employees. Men and women who would have had to find employment in some other industry have been able to remain in railroading under this arrangement, but their union leaders would just as soon have seen them go, judging by the energy with which they fought and continue to fight the short lines. At the end of our century, the rail facilities of the Midwest, give or take a few thousand miles of rusty branch lines, are proving more valuable to the people of the United States than ever before, and they are having a rebirth in which close attention is being paid to problems long ignored.

Silent Upon a Peak in Darien: The First Transcontinental

Looking back 125 years from today's vantage point it is easy to see what inspired all the romantic shouting about the building of the so-called transcontinental railroads. By now, the mystique of the far West, the vast expanses of rough, uninhabited land (Indians and buffaloes do not count!), the heroics of explorers, surveyors, and builders of thin streaks of iron towards the ever-receding sunset, and perhaps most of all, the American cowboy as the essence of individualism, have long since served to make the building of spindly railroads westward from St. Paul, Chicago, Council Bluffs, or St. Louis (or, to do justice to western entrepreneurs already on the scene, eastward from Portland, San Francisco, or Los Angeles), something special in American railroading. Never mind that it took more than a full generation after the art of railroading had been well developed in the East, to complete the outlines of the rail network west of the Missouri River. Even with massive financial assistance, moreover (all of which would have to be paid back in the depths of a deep depression!), and a large part of the public domain in the form of land grants, the transcontinentals just barely got by in good times, and when the Great Divide of 1893's financial panic struck, three of the biggest and most romantic, the Union Pacific, the Northern Pacific, and the Santa Fe, had to throw themselves on the mercy of judicial receivership.

Perhaps this paradox is not so difficult to unravel. In the first place, the original transcontinental had a dramatically different purpose from any of the railroad ventures up to that time. It was undertaken by the people as a national enterprise. The Union Pacific and the Central Pacific, the eastern and western halves that met near Ogden, Utah (as it turned out), were authorized by Congress as Civil War measures, intended to bind the Pacific coast tier of states, which were entering upon a vigorous statehood, more closely to the Union. It had been impossible for most people to imagine an American republic occupying the entire continent from ocean to ocean before the coming of the steam railroad. Was it any easier to imagine even if one or more railroads were built over trackless wastes, for thousands of miles, through the great American desert which, as far as anyone then knew, would never be worth a single buffalo chip? Americans were not alone in their puzzlement. Our Canadian neighbors, with a population a fraction the size of ours and very little industrial base to support railroads, faced the same problem. Their need, if anything, was even more urgent, but their struggle to traverse the continent with a railroad entirely within the Dominion would not succeed until 1885, and it remained the main issue in Canadian politics for a generation after the Dominion was created in 1867. The peaceful settlement provided by the Oregon Treaty of 1846 was beginning to look shaky as Canada's jewel on the Pacific, British Columbia, was drawn more and more into the commercial and cultural sphere of the empire that had rapidly emerged from Puget Sound to San Francisco. Washington would not have been above welcoming British Columbia into the Union fold, but in fact it was much more worried about the American Confederacy establishing itself all the way to the Pacific.

As a business proposition, moreover, the Pacific railroad projects required far more optimism than most Americans could muster (and it is the optimists who turn out to be right whom we romanticize). Surely no program of great national projects was ever undertaken with more unanswered questions before it than the building of the transcontinentals. They all boiled down to one big question: where were the vast resources of labor and materials required to build even one transcontinental railroad, much less half a dozen, to come from, which is the same as asking, who will pay? The American people would pay, of course, but how? Who would take the lead in marshaling capital? How was it to be done so that the ultimate burden on the people would be made as indirect and thus as easy to take as possible? Not by government, surely. Taxing the populace and waging war are two activities that are exclusively the government's, but the U.S. government was doing a rotten job of both as the 1860s wore on. "Why didn't the government build the transcontinental railroad?" ask American students in their innocence of the past. The answer is, "What government?" The few engineers who were regular army officers would learn far more from brilliant civilians like Herman Haupt than he from them. In any case, the hard-pressed Lincoln administration had little time for western railroads after 1861. With whatever resources he might ultimately be able to scrape up, the good old American entrepreneur was elected.

From the pioneer-promoters who took a breathtaking chance on the practicality of the earliest steam locomotives, to the promoter-pioneers who took an equally breathtaking chance on their learning an entirely new set of rules for building a very long railroad of dubious practical value, we have nearly run the gamut of businessman-types that the railroad created. Many good men, all of them more or less public-spirited, even if in spite of themselves, built the transcontinental railroads, mastering all of the railroad know-how that had been assembled, to which now had to be added the manipulation of the political system in what would otherwise be an impossible venture.

It was in the booming decade of the 1850s, when steam railroading really began to come of age, that they propelled government, and particularly the national government, into their affairs, a move that had profound and enduring effects on American society. Virtually all of the good and the bad that would result from government involvement over the next 125 years now begins. In the first year of his administration, 1853, Franklin Pierce placed his secretary of war, Jefferson Davis, who was to become the only president the Confederacy ever had, in charge of the Pacific Survey. With varying degrees of conscientiousness, some harrowing adventures, and reams of drawings of flora and fauna but only sketchy information about passes through the mountains, the survey reported on six possible routes to the Pacific. (All six, by one expedient or another, became railroads eventually.) To no one's surprise, and with a perfectly straight face at a time when the government seemed to be doing all it could to sweep the institution of slavery under the commonwealth carpet, Davis recommended the selection of the most southerly route.

All this division of polar opposites produced was a decade of stalemate. How, then, was the choice made? The southern route, of course, had been ruled out by the war, while the central route, in view of the well-established port at San Francisco, probably had the edge from the beginning. Stephen A. Douglas, not merely because he owned building lots in Chicago, favored it, and so did the president. There is a tradition that one day Grenville Dodge, an early promoter of a Pacific railroad who would give his entire working life to the Union Pacific, and the one most likely to impress a good judge of men's sincerity, met such a judge. "Dodge, what is the most practical route for a railroad to the Pacific?" asked the president. "The Central route, Mr. Lincoln," answered Dodge without a pause, and that did it. Union Pacific was chartered to build the eastern half, and the Central Pacific, the western, in 1862, and Congress, which had established a Pacific Railroad Committee, was beginning to learn about railroads.

The group of men who seized the ball in 1862 and set out to become the builders of the nation's first transcontinental railroad were as different from the good burghers of Baltimore or Albany who had undertaken the nation's first successful railroads as they could be. The latter placed their faith in true technological innovation, and once the venture was proved in operation, adequate capital and prudent management followed as a matter of course. In the case of the Union Pacific, technology was no problem (although mountain railroading in snow country was still in its infancy). You build a railroad with men and materials, and that takes cash money.

It was a classic promotion: "Trust me!" was what Thomas Durant, the slightly nutty but tenacious cobuilder of the Rock Island's line across Iowa was saying to prospective investors in the nascent Union Pacific. (The fact that the Rock Island was stalled many miles from its goal on the Missouri at Council Bluffs, the scheduled starting point for the Union Pacific, he hoped nobody would notice.) Durant was a terrible manager. He could not or would not make a firm decision, even when his lieutenants were waiting with bated breath for his go-ahead. He spread himself over a dozen chores, chief among which were hammering away at Congress for yet more support, legislative and financial, and sparring with the builder of the North Western, which was also building across Iowa, for the best spot to cross the river. Grenville Dodge, who was proving to be the engineering and construction brains of the outfit, had told him a dozen times that only Council Bluffs would do. After Congress had waited as long as it was willing to wait for Durant to ring up the curtain, it was lucky when all seemed lost to get the blessing, the services, and a great deal of the personal capital of one of the most wrongly judged men in the history of American railroad leadership: Oakes Ames.

Ames was as blue-blooded as they come, a scion of one of Massachusett's oldest families and a descendant of Fisher Ames, the hardest-shell Federalist politician of them all in the early years of the nation. Oakes and his brother Oliver were highly successful businessmen, having taken over the family business of manufacturing shovels at a time when the nation was digging furiously for canals and then railroads, long before excavating machinery had been developed. Together they were worth more than four million dollars. It was logical, perhaps, that

Figure 11.1 Builders of the Union Pacific, conferring in a railroad car on the line in 1867, the year before the link-up with the western half of the first transcontinental, the Central Pacific, are: (seated at table, left to right) Silas Seymour, consulting engineer; Sidney Dillon (1812–1892), pioneer railroad contractor and close associate of Jay Gould; Thomas C. Durant (1820–1885), promoter, first president, and catastrophic administrator; and John Duff, pioneer railroad contractor; and (standing, left to right) Herbert M. Hoxie, holder of first major construction contract; and Sam Read, early survey engineer and construction contractor. *(Union Pacific Railroad Museum)*

the Ameses should invest some money in the transcontinental railroad project, which was bound to be buying a lot of their shovels, but not in the railroad itself.

Meanwhile the construction company that Durant had organized to build the road was expected to yield short-term profits, whereas the railroad's profits from carrying freight and passengers was not expected to equal expenses for the indefinite future. George Train, shipping magnate and a big investor in Union Pacific, suggested to Durant the pretentious name of Credit Mobilier for the construction company, in an effort to borrow some of the prestige of the famous investment banking firm that had marshaled immense amounts of capital to build the French railroad system in the 1850s. Construction companies were used for various reasons, not nearly all of them honest or even honorable, but they were necessary in the case of the Union Pacific because its federal charter did not authorize it to do what had to be done to round up the necessary cash.

Congress had again uncapped the honey pot for the U.P. in 1864, by increasing the size of the land grant and effectively making the U.S. government bonds it was lending to the railroad a second lien on the assets of the road, subordinate to the first mortgage bonds which the railroad was seeking to market on its own. The Credit Mobilier did not expect to be paid for building the road in cash, but in the government bonds. These bonds, although they were guaranteed obligations of the U.S. government, would not come due for thirty years (an almost unheard of maturity for such a debt in those days), were not a first lien on the property, and bore an absurdly low coupon rate of interest. As a result they were selling in the marketplace at about one-half their face value, because the market will have its rational rate of interest no matter what ceiling Congress places on its obligations. The Credit Mobilier was not the first railroad construction company to have to accept the bonds of a government authority, and most certainly did not want to be the next one to lose its shirt if the price collapsed, which was not unimaginable for a nation engaged in a bloody civil war for its very existence. It therefore charged about twice as much per mile for the railroad it built as it actually cost in greenbacks. It was a deal that any practical businessman would understand, but nothing could be easier than making this arrangement appear criminal in the eyes of the electorate, if anyone should find it profitable to do so—and they did.

Oakes Ames gave his attention to the construction company and the building of the railroad, anticipating Jim Hill's philosophy that "it pays to be where the money is being spent." The services he rendered the U.P. were valuable, although he was not as indispensable as some have imagined, according to Maury Klein, who feels the U.P. would have been finished in the decade of the 1860s without his services. The most valuable thing he did was to get rid of Durant, who was becomg part of the problem. He then placed brother Oliver in the presidential

chair, while he turned his attention to building the railroad. The year
was 1867. Within a few weeks he had let contracts to subcontractors
for more than six thousand miles of railroad, totaling forty-seven million
dollars. One of his greatest assets was another important investor who
had come into the U.P. syndicate along wth Ames: Sidney Dillon, one
of the master railroad building contractors of the age of steam. The
U.P.'s great westward surge was by far the biggest project ever undertaken in America up to that time, and the rewards were far from certain, but if it succeeded the stockholders of the Credit Mobilier would
receive handsome dividends representing the profits of the construction company. And succeed it did, for barely two years later, on May
10, 1869, a bevy of eager photographers made some of the most famous
early historical photographs we have as the Union Pacific joined its rails
to those of the Central Pacific at Promontory Summit, Utah, near
Ogden and *pluribus* became truly *unum* at last.

Ames's triumph began to pall not long after he savored it. The
line's future course once the knot had been tied was anything but clear.
Modern historians have argued over whether the U.P. was built "ahead
of demand," but this question is easily answered by pointing out that
development of the West was one of the reasons for building all of the
transcontinentals. Reasons of state also demanded the U.P. Like any
new line, its work of developing a heavy traffic volume was only beginning. Sidney Dillon, who became Jay Gould's chief associate in managing the U.P., answered criticisms of the aggressive rate policy and
branch-line acquisition program by noting that when completed the
U.P. was "an apple tree without a limb," starting in the middle of
nowhere, Council Bluffs, and ending in the middle of another nowhere.
Collis P. Huntington, ruler of the Central Pacific, turned out to have no
intention of sharing a low through rate from the Midwest to San Francisco with the U.P. and busied himself assembling his own transcontinental all the way to New Orleans on the southern route. Until 1882,
when the U.P. built the Oregon Short Line to Puget Sound, and made
iron-clad arrangements for Chicago connections at Council Bluffs, it
remained only a bridge line, for there was not much between western
Nebraska and the High Sierras of California to go there for until non-
ferrous metals mining became important.

Meanwhile Oakes Ames worried constantly about what Congress
might do about the U.P.'s rights under its federal charter, for it was
widely bandied about that millions of dollars of government bonds had
gone into the pockets of the Credit Mobilier people beyond the actual
value of the road as built. Ames proceeded to make the mistake of his
life, by propelling his line into the center of the remarkably nasty politics of the Reconstruction era. All he meant to do was to cement some
friendships with certain members of the Congress who had shown a
special interest in the transcontinentals. He had no favors to ask of
them, other than that they lay off, and he certainly did not offer them

an outright bribe, but he did offer to sell them a few shares of Credit Mobilier stock (very few in any one instance), to be paid for by crediting its dividends as declared. The result was the Credit Mobilier scandal, which politicos of both parties made much of in their respective states and districts. If anything, the operations of the Credit Mobilier were an even greater mystery when Congress finished investigating it than before, and the prosecutorial tone of the proceedings is evident on nearly every page of the committee's report. A future president, James A. Garfield, narrowly escaped with his political life, while the vice president of the United States, Schuyler Colfax, did not, and two congressmen—James Brooks of New York and Oakes Ames of Massachusetts—were subjected to a vote of censure by the House on February 27, 1873. The blow broke Ames, and he died less than three months later.

It also broke the original Union Pacific, in the end, for the destructive fervor that accompanies so many Congressional witch-hunts lasted for the next few years. All plans for future land-grant aid to railroads were abandoned. Union Pacific's stock plunged to new lows as a result of the investigation, and the panic of 1873 ensued, for a variety of reasons of which the Credit Mobilier affair was certainly one. Jay Gould bought control of the railroad and did his best, during the next four years, to make a viable enterprise out of it. The times were not yet propitious for that, perhaps, but the railroad had plenty of other worries. Congress would not let go of the "scandal" of the U.P.'s financing, especially the land grant, which to the uninformed looked like the land grab of all time. Gould's effort to give a sheen of respectability to the U.P. by supporting Charles Francis Adams, Jr., the nation's leading essayist on what had come to be referred to as "the railroad problem," as president, availed nothing but in the long run to make Adams bitter towards all businessmen. Politicians professed to be worried over the safety of the government's "investment," especially the bonds, the principal of which would be due in the mid-1890s. (If they had known in the 1870s what the state of the national economy would be in 1895, they would really have worried!) Nothing less than a sinking fund, taken out of the slender operating profits of the Union Pacific (and the Central Pacific, too, for that matter) and secured by investing the funds in U.S. government securities, would do. Such were the provisions of the Thurman Act of 1878, which was more punishment than prudence.

The U.P. had been a minimal railroad upon completion, to put it charitably, and it would need every dollar of earnings to reinvest in improvements, branches, and extensions if it was to become more than "an apple tree without a limb." The government bonds in which it was required to tie up such earnings instead, were available in the market only at steep premiums and thus paid a bare 2 percent—so completely had national finances changed since the days of poor Tom Durant who had had a railroad to build. The same funds, reinvested in the railroad, could well have earned several times as much as a bond. No one could see this better than Gould, who thus withdrew from the center of the U.P. picture in favor of better opportunities in the Southwest and Midwest. When Adams had done his best to make the U.P. viable, and failed, he departed the scene and the two old hands, Gould and Dillon, took up the reins once more, but their race was almost run and both died before the end of 1892. At least they were spared the disappointment of seeing their creation a financial failure, for the clouds were rolling in fast. The next year the depression of the 1890s struck and almost at the same time the "subsidy" bonds matured. There being not the ghost of a chance of paying them off even with the sinking fund, the U.P. applied to the courts for appointment of receivers.

The Victorian style of management, which amounted to "making bricks without straw," had sufficed to get some kind of railroad built. Now the bricks were crumbling. New, more modern management, innovative leadership, and money—lots of it—were required. All three swept in on the new wave of prosperity. Jacob Schiff, head of Kuhn, Loeb & Co., was one of the leaders of investment banking in its western hemisphere capital, New York, and he commanded sources of continental European capital as only a genteel, upper-class German Jew who had begun his career at age fourteen on a high stool in a Frankfurt countinghouse could. But he could not quite make ends meet when he set out to reorganize the Union Pacific, despite a lengthening record of successful railroad financings. E. H. Harriman, a little-known Wall Street figure with a major interest in Illinois Central, gained control of the U.P., and from that date Harriman's brains and Schiff's prestige, blended with liberal amounts of risk capital that James Stillman, of National City Bank, and the Rockefellers supplied, set a course of action that within barely ten years would see a free and independent U.P., its government bonds paid off and its physical condition transformed into that of an efficient, heavy-duty railroad, reaping the rewards of the Pacific Slope's coming of age, and paying 10 percent dividends on the common stock. Oakes Ames would have been astounded at such a vindication of the faith he had demonstrated in the original idea of building a railroad across the trackless deserts to the Pacific. Brilliant financing was not the sum total of Harriman's contribution, by a long shot, notwithstanding Progressive historians' sneers about his remarkable capacity for making money. He had spent many weeks riding over the line and directing needed improvements. Each man, Ames in his time and Harriman in his, fought off phalanxes of naysayers to give the nation what it had to have.

Meanwhile, on the other side of the Rockies and the Sierras, crafty old Collis P. Huntington had redeemed every promise he made the people of the United States where the Central Pacific from Promontory to Oakland, California, was concerned. Actually, he spent most of the hectic years of the 1890s depression in his spartan office in one of the

New York financial district's dumpy office buildings. When the market balked at the idea of taking Central Pacific bonds to provide funds to pay off its government bond loan, Huntington blandly "went for broke," pledging the full faith and credit of all his other lines, which comprised the booming Southern Pacific, the "octopus" which dominated California and extended over a patchwork of acquired lines to New Orleans: the "Sunset Route."

Huntington now retired to his retreat in the Adirondack Mountains of New York where, his life's work finished, he died not long after. His only heir was a nephew, Henry Huntington, who was soon persuaded by his financial advisers to sell the controlling interest in the Southern Pacific, which also owned the Central Pacific, to a group headed by Harriman. The result was a powerful transcontinental carrier, entirely under one corporate direction from the eastern gateways of Omaha and New Orleans to the Pacific. The idiotic situation that resulted from the government's having split proprietorship of the first transcontinental between the Union Pacific and the Central Pacific was ended. The far West thus entered the new century with transportation facilities far superior to anything it had had any right to expect. It was all too good to be true for, as we shall see, men seldom know when they are well off.

Empire Builders

The other pairing of transcontinental railroad leaders to whom we turn is a different study in contrasts. Oakes Ames was trying to "make bricks without straw," and in accepting help from the only quarter in which it was to be found he ran head on into a swiftly changing system of ethics in national politics. Harriman, who inherited Ames's bitterly won beginnings, had time, money, and priceless experience on his side in creating the modern Union Pacific. In the northern tier of states, however, the contrast was between a man who knew what he was doing, what he wanted, and how to time his campaign on the way to his goals, and other men who did not. Despite the barrier of the glaciers in the Rocky Mountains and the hard winters—more forbidding, even, than those on the central route—men were pushing another transcontinental, also driven by the incentive of enormous land grants.

For the first ten years, men like the Philadelphia banker and financier of the Civil War, Jay Cooke, had spun quite a few wheels getting nowhere with the Northern Pacific. Duluth, on the westernmost reaches of Lake Superior, had been Cooke's choice of the N.P.'s eastern terminus, having as he did the outdated concept of the railroad as a means of connecting navigable bodies of water. Before his financial failure, which ushered in the depression of 1873–1877, a new set of promoters had begun to acquire and finish a line from St. Paul, at the head of navigation on the Mississippi, through the rapidly colonizing

Valley of the Red River of the North. To the promoters of the N.P., it was the thousands of acres of land-grant land that awaited the promoters west of the Red that seemed the main attraction, not the obvious readiness of the Valley to produce an immediate revenue for a railroad. But the new party had a line with a St. Paul terminus, by this time clearly superior to Duluth. The line they took over was Minnesota's very first. It had been aiming for the Red River Valley and the Canadian border, where it would connect with a line to what is now Winnipeg, in the budding prairie province of Manitoba, ever since 1862 when its *William Crooks* had become the first locomotive to turn a wheel in the state. It owned superb acreage on the riverfront in downtown St. Paul, and it had pioneered the best route from St. Paul to St. Anthony, which was about to become the raw new city of Minneapolis. The N.P. easily took over the St. Paul & Pacific, as it was called, but almost immediately lost control when the panic of 1873 brought receivership to both companies.

Meanwhile the Red River country languished for want of good, all-year transportation. The Red froze solid in the winter and by midsummer was so low the steamboatmen jocularly claimed to be navigating on a heavy dew in places. Now the N.P. ran head on into James Hill, one of the most remarkable leaders the railroad era produced, a man who had had virtually nothing to do with railroading during his first forty years other than having watched it closely and with a fine analytical eye as it struggled to be born in his part of the world. He brought to this juncture in the rise of northwestern transportation the powerful combination of entrepreneurial dreaming, firsthand on-the-spot knowledge of the mass of first-class immigrants knocking at the door of the upper midwest and what transportation innovations they required. He knew the Red River country all the way to what became Winnipeg, for he had traversed it in its worst season, and his experience in all phases of transportation up to 1877 was impressive. He was a skilled, no-nonsense businessman who, at the head of a group of Twin Cities coal dealers in the early 1870s, had brought order, structure, stability, and product reliability to the business as coal quickly replaced scarce wood supplies in becoming the basic fuel of Minnesota and the nation: "the first energy revolution."

Hill knew that the Northern Pacific men would go on stumbling at their task of creating a long-distance railroad through undeveloped, even unknown country, as long as they dealt with their minions in the field chiefly from stuffy offices in lower Manhattan. "I find it pays to be where the money is being spent," Hill remarked when he was bursting a gut to complete the St. Paul & Pacific to the international boundary in 1878, but he might have added that there was no substitute for growing up with a country in its infancy to know just what kind of transportation system it needs and can support, not eventually, but *right now*.

He had buttonholed every friend who would hold still for his sermon, punctuated with short jabs of his index finger to his listener's midriff, at their little luncheon club on Seventh Street. It boiled down to this: a railroad, unlike the steamboats, could get an immigrant family to their new home in the valley of the Red River, which usually remains frozen until early April, in plenty of time for the man and his sturdy sons, if he was lucky enough to have them, to begin spring plowing in time to make a crop *that year*. Not having to wait for a crop until next year, the farmer found that the capital required to immigrate was thereby reduced by the cost of their subsistence for a year. Multiplied by the thousands who were surging into Minnesota and beginning to cross the Red into eastern Dakota, the saving of the resources of an individual family became an enormous contribution to the national development and a bulwark against immigrant failure, which could be such a drag on development.

Donald Smith, representative of the Hudson Bay Company in North America and a pioneer resident of Manitoba, was just as aware of these needs and opportunities as Hill, and far better connected back east. Together, with Hill's mastery of the economics and Smith's of the politics and finances, they formed a syndicate with some of the most important men in New York and Canadian finance. Hill, who formed several valuable associations that were vital for his future plans in these years, worked day and night to finish the railroad to the boundary within the terms of its charter. The reborn railroad, under the firm control of Hill and associates, was renamed the St. Paul, Minneapolis & Manitoba. It was a winner from the start and made money, lots of it, for which Hill had endless projects in mind as he swept across the upper Northwest towards the Pacific. Hill's Canadian friends, going their own way, promptly reinvested much of their profits in their great work, the building of Canada's first transcontinental, the Canadian Pacific, all the way from Montreal to Vancouver. Hill meanwhile had to compromise with the N.P. to some extent along the way, but he knew that unless someone rather like him came along it would soon be in trouble again and would pose no obstacle to him as he continued westward.

Soon Henry Villard appeared on the scene, and Hill was sure he was that man. Villard had left behind both his bossy father and the name of Heinrich Hilgard in his native Germany and come to the United States at the age of eighteen. A first-class newspaperman, he made a name for himself as a Civil War battlefield reporter, but, more to the point, he had a superb talent for persuading people, especially thrifty Germans with money to invest, to follow where he led. Up to a point he was as shrewd a railroad strategist as publicity man, for he saw before any of the N.P. men the peculiar value that the Oregon Steam Navigation Company, which was operating steamboats up the Columbia River from a point near Portland, Oregon, would have in a northern transcontinental route. He got the valley of the Columbia River firmly under his control by buildling a railroad, the Oregon Railway & Navigation Company, on its south bank into Portland. It was the natural entrée for the N.P., as it struggled over the Rockies, but N.P. men like Frederick C. Billings seemed determined that the road should build its own, independent line all the way to salt water, the barrier of the Cascade Mountains notwithstanding. Villard then demonstrated his almost magical powers of persuasion by forming his famous "blind pool," in 1881, into which his friends deposited eight million dollars, supposedly without knowing what it was to be used for. All of them, however, could surely guess what Villard had on his mind, which was to use the money to gain stock control of the N.P. and assure its adoption of the O.R. & N. route into Portland—and that is just what he did. He won control of the N.P., pushed it to a junction with his road in 1883, and put on a ridiculously expensive party celebrating the completion of the Nation's second transcontinental, to which, ever mindful of his high-class image, he invited such men as ex-President Grant, Secretary of the Interior Henry M. Teller, and the reformer Carl Schurz. When the treasurer finally caught up with him and read the handwriting on the wall, he agreed to a receivership for the second but not the last time for this benighted national project.

Meanwhile, Jim Hill stayed where the money was being spent and pushed his more modest but infinitely more muscular railroad westward with all prudent speed from Grand Forks, on the Red River, into Dakota Territory. In the decade of the 1880s, which would see the largest mileage ever added to the American system in a ten-year period, Hill extended westward to Montana and eastward on a direct line to Lake Superior, thus giving himself much better bargaining power with the granger and trunk lines that wanted to carry his burgeoning freight traffic east of the Twin Cities. Montana was added, not as part of a clear-cut, hell-for-leather race to the coast, but to develop the mineral riches of the Land of the Big Sky; if anyone besides the political "sons of the wild jackass" belongs in that state's pantheon of heroes, it is its truest hero, Jim Hill. "We do not care enough for Rocky Mountain scenery to spend a large sum of money developing it," Hill liked to point out as that formidable obstacle—through which he still did not know of a suitable pass—loomed up ahead. What he wanted, and he would settle for nothing less, was the lowest-cost line across the top of the northern tier of states. It was not necessary for the railroad, at least at first, to be built to ideal specifications, for one could spend years improving a railroad plant and still it would never be perfect; but it *was* necessary to have the *best* route, or, he said, "some smart fellow" would find it later, build a more efficient railroad, and control the situation thereafter. And control, of course, was everything. Economy was the watchword; anyone who disregarded his stern order that no one connected with the railroad must ever engage in any speculation concerning the part of the country through which he planned to extend the line would be fired summarily. His was the last, and in many ways the best, transcontinental to be finished and by that time—1893—golden spike ceremonies were old hat. The Great Northern, as he named the regional now transformed into a transcontinental, was joined in a desolate spot in the mountains on a cold, snowy day. The foreman of the crew had trouble getting even a corporal's guard to leave the warmth of the cook shack long enough to see the last spike hammered home. As for its builder, he was home in bed with a very bad cold, some fifteen hundred miles away.

Throughout the 1880s he had watched in disgust as the N.P. degenerated into a mediocre line, achieving far less than Hill knew its real potential to be, and allowing myriad corruptions to creep into its operating routine, such as running "light" trains, consisting of only a locomotive and one or two cars, which would keep costs *per train mile* down but play havoc with the cost *per ton* of freight moved one mile. The return of Villard to control of the N.P. further weakened the authority of its few good men, like Thomas F. Oakes, and the day of reckoning came on apace. Villard, ensconced in his pretentious mansion on Madison Avenue and engaged, he thought, in casting the future of the new General Electric Company in his mold, got the news quickly in 1893 that Northern Pacific would be joining the Union Pacific, the Santa Fe, and dozens of other American railroads in receivers' courts. Jim Hill became the man of the hour.

As the new century dawned, Harriman and Hill shared uneasily the highest place in American railroad leadership. Harriman had assembled, with blinding speed, a corporate hegemony south of the Columbia River to the Rio Grande that threatened to become complete. Hill, meanwhile, had solidified his control of the upper Midwest and far Northwest not only by assuming control of the Northern Pacific, as leader of a syndicate of rich men who were determined to bring permanent stability to the western railroad scene, but also by acquiring the Burlington Railroad and thus assuring his two great northern transcontinentals a mighty flow of traffic between the far Northwest and the lower Midwest, and the best freight route from the Twin Cities to Chicago. The administrations of Theodore Roosevelt and William Howard Taft made a great show of applying the axe of antitrust law to these empires, but there is no stopping the power of an idea whose time has come; despite the famous Northern Securities decision against Hill, and the decree ordering Harriman's successors to divest themselves of the Southern Pacific, the assemblages worked out by Harriman and Hill remained in *de facto* existence, professional management found ways to get the substance without the shadow, and the nation profited thereby.

What a vast difference there was in the style, viewpoint, and resources of men like Ames and Villard, on the one hand, and Harriman

Figure 11.2 Four leaders in American railroads' dash to the Pacific, each of whom played a distinctly different entrepreneurial role: (clockwise from upper left) Grenville M. Dodge (1831–1916), Jay Gould (1836–1892), James J. Hill (1838–1916), and Edward H. Harriman (1848–1909). (Dodge, Gould, and Harriman—*Union Pacific Railroad Museum;* Hill—*Burlington Northern Railroad*)

and Hill, on the other! The earlier pair made fatal mistakes, while moving the great work they were engaged in ahead. Ames miscalculated the political potential in the Union Pacific picture and thus subjected the first transcontinental to congressional sodomy of the worst kind that made it a symbol of financial chicanery and blighted its development for a generation. Villard failed to see that a great railroad could not run itself, and that what is today called "hands-on management" is vital to success. Hill and Harriman made no big, fatal mistakes. The most important thing they had learned from their predecessors was the vital importance of controlling all of the forces that go into making one's system complete and viable, and of cooperating to attain stable, rational competition in which the pie is big enough for all, or will be in time, and the failure of even one major enterprise is no longer acceptable in a complete system.

The Professional Manager:
A Creation of the Railroad Era

When the Cunard liner *Britannic* left its Liverpool dock that day in 1879, it was carrying two key men in the evolution of the American system of inland transportation. One of them has been all but forgotten in the shadow of his justly famous and colorful father. William Henry Vanderbilt, eldest son of the Commodore and chief executive of the New York Central Railroad and its subsidiaries since the old man's death two years before, would not have been surprised in later years to learn that even his infamous, ill-advised, and ceaselessly misunderstood exclamation—"the public be damned!"—would be attributed to his father. Now, Billy Vanderbilt, as the newspapers liked to call him in a not-so-gentle reminder of his junior status in their eyes, was a worried man. The mud that had been slung at his railroads and himself, personally, by the Hepburn Committee that summer for the Central's alleged abuses in providing vital transportation for the Empire State's merchants, manufacturers, and farmers had left him on the edge of depression.

A nervous, cautious, choleric man, a true worrier, Vanderbilt had been deeply hurt by the half-truths and injustices that Simon Sterne, the committee's counsel, had allowed a succession of witnesses with the most obvious axes to grind to heap upon him. What had hurt most of all were the devastating newspaper cartoons for which the period was famous, which lampooned him unmercifully. Relatively mild was the color lithograph on the cover of the popular weekly *Puck*, showing Vanderbilt astride the Hudson River, holding all of the railroads serving New York on his leash, and his minions, Jay Gould and Cyrus Field (layer of the Atlantic cable and promoter of New York's elevated railroads) perched on his instep. "The Colossus of Roads," read the caption, in the atrocious punning style of the era. Much harsher in its personal tone was one showing Vanderbilt trying to defend himself against his tormentors with a huge, badly nicked sword labeled "Le Sabre de Mon Papa," which was no longer so sharp in the son's hands.

What did the future hold for private property, of which Billy Vanderbilt had more than any other man in America (largely inherited from his father), especially property represented by investments in giant, powerful concerns that were beginning to be such sitting ducks for every demagogue and airhead reformer that came along? The other man had the answer. He was J. Pierpont Morgan, son of the better known American expatriate banker in London, Junius Spencer Morgan. The younger Morgan was moving from triumph to triumph in his steady rise as a leader in American investment banking and, ultimately, chief symbol of high finance in the age of enterprise. His firm, Drexel, Morgan & Co., which he had formed with the Drexels of Philadelphia at the beginning of the decade, was already a leading factor in railroad finance, which accounted for nearly all securities flotations in the day before American industry began to "go public." Morgan, noting that Vanderbilt's massive 40 percent block of Central stock had to be let out on the market with all due deliberation unless the market price was to break, recommended an orderly secondary offering and proceeded to organize a syndicate that accomplished just that during the next few months. From this event, most historians date the emergence of Wall Street's "control" of America's railroads—a stereotype which became part of American folklore.

Equally significant was the gradual diminishment of Vanderbilt's responsibility for day-to-day management of the Central. Remarkably, however, his New York Central never produced any of the outstanding professional railroad leaders in the golden age of railroading then beginning. His eldest son, Cornelius II, tried to take a primary hand in management, but as the first Vanderbilt to be accepted in New York high society—the gigantic chateau which he built on Fifth Avenue at the entrance to Central Park must have helped—his management was a now-and-then proposition, and he died in his fifties. The Central could almost run itself quite well with the faithful old hands that had worked for the railroad since before they could grow a proper beard, with some help from talented but nearly anonymous outsiders later on as the shoe began to pinch. While the Pennyslvania was producing outstanding railroad men like George Roberts, Alexander Cassatt, and W. W. Atterbury, and a unified, well-thought-out organization chart, the Central remained until 1914 very much a collection of individual railroads: the New York Central & Hudson River; the New York & Harlem; the Lake Shore (whose name, and not that of the Central, was carved on the pediment of Chicago's LaSalle Street Station, western home of the *Twentieth Century Limited*); the Big Four (Cleveland, Cincinnati, Chicago & St. Louis); and many others.

The passing of Billy Vanderbilt may serve to mark the beginning of

Figure 11.3 William H. Vanderbilt, president and far and away the largest stockholder of the New York Central & Hudson River Railroad, which controlled several other railroads, together constituting what was generally called the New York Central. J. Keppler, who drew this 1879 color cartoon in *Puck* magazine, is not as well remembered as Thomas Nast, but was highly effective. The caption, "Colossus of Roads," honored the taste for puns beloved of the Victorians. Cyrus Field, elevated railway magnate, and Jay Gould, are depicted as hangers-on.

the era of the professional manager. Such gentlemen never owed their high position of trust primarily to kinships, much less to ownership of a large block of the company's stock, but to long years of service, if not in every branch of railroading, at least in the most important, which would continue to be engineering and operations for a long time to come. Lack of formal education beyond high school—some didn't complete that—was seldom a handicap. A knowledge of mathematics, surveying, rudimentary physical science, and a full command of the English language in both spoken and written form, were sufficient, and they were available in the most modest of school systems, whereas today even the best high schools fail to impart them. Exemplars of the kind of man we are describing abound in the stories of America's railroads. Three, plus two from recent times, may serve as good examples of the model.

Charles Elliott Perkins (1840–1907) built the Chicago, Burlington & Quincy from its modest form at the end of the Civil War into the leading railroad in the Midwest, a superbly maintained, intelligently planned, and scrupulously operated line that should have been a model for all the other granger railroads. In 1901 he sold the Burlington to James J. Hill, who already controlled the Great Northern and Northern Pacific. The poor son of an old Boston family, Perkins remarked sadly that "of course, it means New York management" but consoled himself with the knowledge that he had got the widows and orphans of the Bay State and the nation a premium of 100 percent over par for their stock. During his career he pushed the Burlington lines west of the Mississippi as far as Billings, Montana, and gradually merged their operation and administration into a single entity. He fought fire with fire in the bitter, cutthroat rate competition that not only Jay Gould but everybody else in the temporarily over-built railroad picture engaged in. He demanded and got from his superiors the nearly absolute powers that characterized nineteenth-century railroad leaders because, as he said, men like Jay Gould moved too fast for anybody who had to submit his decisions to a board of directors.

Perkins conforms as closely as anyone to the model of "rugged individualist," or, in the jargon of modern sociology, the "inner-directed" man; but at the same time he would have agreed with J. P. Morgan that competition was good but cooperation was better. He "shot his Sunday cuffs" at the increase in government intervention in railroad affairs, but only in indignant remarks dictated into his letter-books, because he was in fact a shy person with no taste for the lime-light. His term for Theodore Roosevelt, as the Hepburn Act approached, was "The Boss Lunatic in Washington." Like Alexander Cassatt, of the Pennsylvania, Perkins considered the passage of the Hepburn Act in 1906, giving the Interstate Commerce Commission power to dictate maximum rates to the railroads, a repudiation of what he and his generation had achieved. Both men died not long after. Perkins had retired in 1901 to his beloved estate, "The Apple Trees," in Burlington, Iowa (apparently he never missed Boston), leaving behind a photograph of himself sitting under the trees in the summer sunlight. His role in the evolution of the professional manager was a transitional one during a vital phase in management development.

Daniel Willard (1861–1942) in 1910 became president of the Baltimore & Ohio Railroad, after thirty-one years of railroad experience on the Vermont Central, Lake Shore, Soo, Erie, and Burlington. He guided the B. & O. in some of its most prosperous years; through the disappointments and frustrations of the years when the railroads became a political football of the Progressives; the false good times of the 1920s, when he promoted the B. & O.'s memorable pageant in Baltimore celebrating its one hundredth anniversary; and, finally, the near-receivership of the 1930s Depression. He was an operating man of the first order and over the years acquired an almost Solomon-like power to settle controversies not only on his own line, but for the industry. He had had to leave college after only a few months because of poor eyesight, which never seems to have handicapped him thereafter. He ceaselessly sought the best ways to reinvest the increasingly slender earnings of the B. & O. in the betterment of the system, and to make up for its secondary route by offering good service to both passengers—the B. & O. dining car cuisine beat that of the Pennsylvania and the Central—and shippers. He recognized that the obvious inferiority of the B. & O.'s route over the mountains, compared to the Central's natural water-level route and the Pennsylvania's feats of engineering, need not be fatal.

Today, Willard is best known as the longtime chief spokesman for the railroads, a stewardship of which the high point was his leading role in the 1917 negotiations with the railroad labor unions that settled the eight-hour-day controversy. His portrait shows a stern, bespectacled man who might be a severe clergyman or schoolteacher, but in fact he was the most patient of men, with a talent for seeing not merely both sides but all around a question.

Ralph Budd (1879–1962) was graduated from a small college in Des Moines, Iowa, at the age of nineteen, with a degree in civil engineering, but the record does not indicate that anyone ever held it against him. He entered railroading just as the entire orientation of men who would lead railroads was undergoing a profound change. With the coming loss of the power to decide what services to offer, or what to charge for them, or to bargain on an equal footing with their men, many railroad leaders would fail to adapt. Ralph Budd would not be one of them. He started out in engineering, of course, and did practical rebuilding and maintenance work on the Rock Island. There he met John F. Stevens, who was about to pull Theodore Roosevelt's Panama Canal chestnuts out of the fire for him by showing that a canal at sea level would never be built in their lifetimes, while one with locks would do just as well. Stevens took Budd to Panama with him to rebuild the old Panama Railroad, which had been built across the isthmus in the 1850s; as soon as he could, he left Budd in charge of that project. After Panama, Budd hitched his wagon to the star of James J. Hill, who was building a few more lines in Oregon. Budd's relaxed, gentlemanly, judicious demeanor impressed Hill who, having lost hope that either of his two sons would take hold of the railroad's day-to-day management, put Budd in line for the presidency of the Great Northern, which he attained in 1919.

In the late 1920s Budd carried out one of the biggest engineering projects of that day, an eight-mile-long tunnel—for many years the longest in the western hemisphere—through the Cascade mountain range of Washington. By 1931 the Depression had reduced the income of the Great Northern and the Northern Pacific largely to the dividends on the 50 percent of the common stock of the Burlington Railroad that each owned. Preserving and enhancing such profits as president of the Burlington was to be Budd's job thereafter. Cost reduction remained about the only dimension in which railroad executives were free to operate, and Budd did a superb, if rather painful job of it. He remained in the post until 1949, guiding the railroad through the Depression, the extraordinary demands of World War II, and into the uncertainties of the postwar era. Along with the leaders of the Union Pacific, Budd deserves credit for pressing for the adaptation of the diesel engine to railroad motive power, but historians will give equal weight to his creation of the model of the professional railroad manager in the age of regulation. As "Uncle Dan" Willard aged, Budd became a railroad spokesman himself, especially during the Depression, when he helped keep government policy relating to the financial salvation of the railroads as fully on track as possible. He never really retired until a few years before his death. At one point he was in the Soviet Union, helping the Russians make something less of a mess of their railroads than it then was. He then did the same for the Chicago Transit Authority, which had been trying unsuccessfully to run its new subway system. The late, noted historian of railroads, Professor Richard Overton, who served as public relations assistant to Budd for several years, described him as the most democratic of men, kind, unassuming, eager for the opinions of those whose experience on some matter exceeded his, and fair to all who worked under him.

In the 1970 collapse of the world's largest private enterprise, the Penn Central Railroad, the evolution of both railroad management and national transportation policy reached a watershed. Two men, one the creator of the longest railroad in the world, and the other the leader in the decade of the 1980s of the phoenix that rose from Penn Central's ashes, may represent the new style of management, emphasizing maximum innovation and organizational revolution in a much freer, if not entirely free, environment.

Figure 11.4 Four of the early professional managers were (clockwise from upper left) Charles Elliott Perkins (1840–1906), Alexander J. Cassatt (1839–1906), Ralph Budd (1879–1962), and Daniel Willard (1861–1942). (Perkins and Budd—*Burlington Northern Railroad;* Cassatt and Willard—*Smithsonian Institution*)

Figure 11.5 Two modern professional managers who made a difference are (at left) John M. Budd (1907–1979) and L. Stanley Crane (1915–   ). (Budd—*Burlington Northern Railroad*; Crane—*Conrail*)

John Budd (1907–1979), the son of Ralph Budd, came to the Great Northern in 1926 from Yale University, where he took a degree in electrical engineering and later did graduate work. He served a long apprenticeship, moving through nearly every position in right-of-way engineering and maintenance. Except for a period in the Military Railway Service of the U.S. Army in World War II, and a short postwar stint as president of the Chicago & Eastern Illinois Railroad, he returned to the Great Northern, where he became president in 1951. Thereafter he devoted much of his time to furthering the merger of the three so-called "Hill roads"—Burlington, G.N., and N.P.—which the Supreme Court had in 1904 denied even the right to be held as independently operated lines by the Northern Securities Company. After years of moving through the labyrinth of the Interstate Commerce Commission, which predictably turned the merger down (as it did almost every railroad innovation that came before them) and through every level of the federal courts, the merger was finally approved by the Supreme Court in 1970.

Budd had always aimed at a true functional merger of the three railroads, which would make them far more productive than the sum of their parts, and he remained head of the Burlington Northern, as the new combine was called, long enough to see the transition well under way. Indeed, he and his knowledgeable staff had long since mapped out in detail what they proposed to do. The "mega-merger" became the order of the day in the next few years, largely because Burlington Northern proved that a merger could be a success if its promoters, unlike the men of the Penn Central, knew what they were doing in the first place. Today the letters BN, CSX, NS, CR, and RG (for the combine of the Denver & Rio Grande and Southern Pacific), have replaced initials on rolling stock that were familiar sights for nearly a hundred years. The process is still incomplete, but the functional mega-merger is the most likely form of the industry for the next 100 years. John M. Budd was present at the creation.

L. Stanley Crane (b. 1915) retired from the presidency of the Southern Railway—itself soon to merge with the even more profitable Norfolk & Western—just in time to rescue Conrail, the quasi-government-owned successor to Penn Central's railroad properties, from failure. The Staggers Act, which went a long way towards deregulating the railroads in 1980, was a factor in Crane's acceptance of leadership of Conrail. His story and that of the mostly young men and women who took up the supreme marketing challenge that deregulation implied, are not yet ready to be told. More than one doubting Thomas—nearly everybody in government and academia—was proved wrong in their smug assumption that the railroads, having been regulated for so long, would never rise to the challenge. By 1990 deregulation was a success, not merely on Conrail, but all over the country, and was well established as policy. In history's largest secondary offering of capital stock, the government's stake in Conrail was bought by private investors. It was a powerful victory for freedom of enterprise. Maybe Stanley Crane was just lucky . . . and maybe it was much more than luck.

CHAPTER 12

New Jobs To Do,
New People To Do Them

A man ought to be willing to pay to work for a railroad.

John W. Barriger III

In times like this men go back to primal instincts. Now the public is the carcass and we are all perhaps the vultures . . . The country will pay.

A. B. Garretson, Chairman,
Railway Brotherhood Conference Committee, 1916

Several years ago our labor agreements required engine and train crews consisting of 85 people to operate a train from Chicago to Los Angeles. Today we operate a similar train with about 40 people. Eventually we anticipate that will be reduced to about 30 people, and some of the expedited "just-in-time" trains could make that run with 14 people.

Robert D. Krebs, chief executive officer,
Santa Fe Pacific Corporation, 1990

From the Farms and Artisans' Shops

The late John Barriger, whose startling pronouncement on the pleasures of working for the railroads heads this chapter, was perhaps inordinately fond of the industry in which he made something of a special mark. The dean of American railroad presidents—he claimed to have headed more Class I roads than any other man in history—Barriger spent his long life in or near the seats of power, during the most trying times these great enterprises ever went through, from the era of World War I to their resurgence in World War II, and their postwar public neglect and decline. Yet many men of much humbler station, especially those referred to in the industry as "operating employees" (persons engaged directly in the operation of trains) have shared his love of the calling and said so in their reminiscences. It has been pursued more recently by a few women. "There isn't anything a man can do that I can't," remarked one young lady engineer to the Burlington Northern's publicist, "except go to the bathroom over the side of the locomotive." For abundant good reasons, however, women are scarce in the most exciting jobs—engineer, brakeman, conductor—and railroading remains overwhelmingly a man's world, at least on the head end.

With the passing of the passenger train, which was the average person's only contact with the industry, railroading has become nearly invisible and thus declined in the public's imagination and admiration. So, to all outward signs at least, has the old *esprit de corps* among its practitioners. The old style is mostly gone. Nowadays young men, gaudy in Harry Truman sports shirts and no head-gear of any kind, insouciantly lean out of diesel cab windows. Where are the middle-aged men, smiling gravely and waving at youngsters along the track, who once piloted giant steam locomotives through town? Railroading today is just another job—a damned good one for anyone confirmed in blue-collar American society, in fact—and those to whom it is much more than just a good job are likely to keep the fact under their hats, if any. Sentiment was a nineteenth-century virtue where railroading is concerned.

The need to man our railroads was perhaps the most disruptive force ever to hit workaday America, and at the same time the most creative. Within a generation, and long before the pivotal decades of the 1880s and 1890s which were the founding years of big manufacturing industry, the railroads had created a new class, the wage laborer, who has become a major symbol of the industrial revolution. And when we say "created," we mean that it called forth, and drew into a largely unformed occupation, vast numbers of men of all levels of education and family background who had no idea of the complex and potentially violent forces that would have to be reckoned with in forging a whole new approach to the conditions of work and the relationship between those who pay and those who are paid.

The industrial revolution came late to America. It awaited the railroad, for one thing, without which no true system of regionally specialized factory production could arise. As late as 1830 there were few men and women in the new land who worked for a daily wage under anything like controlled, disciplined conditions. It was still the age of the small shop, whose proprietor, skilled journeymen, and apprentices still recalled the dim outlines of the medieval guild system. Few mercantile establishments had yet grown to the dimensions that would make possible the celebrated paternalism of an A. T. Stewart, whose employees' manual betrayed a desire to regulate the private lives of his clerks according to his chilly views of human nature. The small-town mercantile establishment and, far more important, the country general store, both provided superb laboratories in which young men could practice the arts of the trader and assemble the seed capital that would enable them to set up in business for themselves. But these vital links in the distribution process, although they trained such railroad leaders as Collis P. Huntington and James J. Hill, would not have interested the modern student of what the business schools call "organizational behavior." The professions, if such callings as medicine and the law deserved to be called that in early antebellum days, were entered and abandoned by individuals according to the opportunities they found in their practice, and required, or at least, got, little investment in formal training.

Only the budding textile industry, based on spinning and weaving cotton cloth, and still tied to the limited sources of water power, had been organized along the lines of the factory system, but in their recruitment of workers and their intense paternalism, they bore little resemblance to what American industry was shortly to become. Meanwhile, the great majority of American boys grew up on farms, took up farming in earnest as they became young men and husbands, and perhaps yearned vaguely for something more exciting beyond the hills of home. They were going to find it in astounding numbers in railroading, where they would learn, more or less the hard way, that there were many wrong ways to run a railroad but only one right way. Nearly two generations would pass, more or less noisily, before anything like general agreement would be reached as to which was which.

Walter Licht, in his fine monograph, *Working for the Railroad: The Organization of Work in the Nineteenth Century* (1983) has scraped together probably as much "data"—ranging from authoritative, although almost always incomplete, statistics to the reminiscences of garrulous oldtime railroad men—on the problems of worker-employer relations in the railroad industry during its formative years as we are likely ever to get. His conclusions as to the occupational background of men entering the railroad industry in its early decades (meaning, primarily, the occupation of their fathers, although many men went into railroading after some years in other lines of work) are revealing. Fully 40 percent of them came from farms, and another 28 percent had fathers who were workmen, skilled and unskilled, probably primarily in small shops or self-employed. Only 22 percent of the entering railroad workers came from white-collar backgrounds (18 percent "businessmen" and 4 percent professional) and even in the early years, as many as 16 percent were following in their fathers' footsteps as second-generation railroad men.

How well qualified were these young men for railroad work? Considering how little liability early Victorian enterprises of all kinds shouldered for their employees' welfare, little attention was paid to a candidate's physical condition beyond assuring that he was sound of limb—that is, "had two of everything"—and was not obviously consumptive. If he proved not to be up to the work, the revolving-door principle would dispose of him quickly enough. Their educational attainments, even by the degraded standards of our day, were often atrocious. Many were even illiterate, but Licht maintains that this did not much hinder a man's ability to perform the dangerous and unpleasant work of standing between the cars to drop in the pin when the links of the primitive couplers met, or to run along the tops of boxcars in an icy rain, snow, or sleet storm to set the brake wheels in the days before the air brake. Such men probably began as "navvies," as the British called them: members of maintenance-of-way gangs or trackwalkers, who had the lonely duty of trudging along, mile after mile, looking for broken rails and other hazards. Even so, an illiterate man was a man of limited potential, unable to rise above the job of brakeman, at most, while managers quickly learned the importance of a steady supply of promotable men to a growing enterprise.

It was inevitable, therefore, that the advent of the railroad, with the new emphasis it would place on basic education, became a major impetus to the public-school movement. By the last quarter of the century, the more promising young men entering railroading had at least an eighth-grade education or its equivalent; and if that sounds less than impressive, we should remember that many a railroad foreman of today's high school graduates might wish for an 1890s eighth-grader who had spent the years between ages fourteen and eighteen as railroad waterboy, callboy, messenger, and office boy. Looking away from the operating employees for a moment, we should note that at least a good grammar school education was always required for the army of clerks who were as vital, in their way, as the engineers and their crews. The nineteenth century, moreover, was the age of the autodidact; more than a few young men spent their free hours in independent study, and those fortunate enough to live in cities often attended night school. Correspondence schools ranged from excellent to fraudulent.

The biographies of leading railroad executives until fairly recent times reveal that many had very humble beginnings on the railroad. Even young graduates of the polytechnic schools usually began their engineering-oriented careers as "rodmen," holding the height marker while the surveyor sighted it through his transit. A high order of intelligence, strong moral character (meaning a steely resistance to temptation or just plain otherworldliness), a respect for learning most often revealed in a love of reading, and of course being in the right place at the right time, as well as sheer luck, were the keys to advancement. James J. Hill, when asked for his advice on how to prepare for a business career, advised a young man to study hard, emphasizing mathematics and engineering, but also to read widely in literature and history. "Some opportunity will come to every man in his lifetime," he said. Be ready for it when it comes.

Work on the farm or in the shops and stores went on from day to day and week to week according to a simple, almost unchanging routine, and to a considerable extent the employee on hand could pick his tasks on a given day. Not so on the railroads. If the farmer controlled his job in large measure, the railroader, if he ever reflected on such matters, would have to admit that the railroad itself controlled him. The responsibilities borne by even the lowliest worker were awesome, for

a careless brakeman or maintenance-of-way workman could wreck a
train as readily as a sleepy or bored locomotive engineer. Trains, freight
and passenger, ran on fixed schedules, and, like the modern airline dis-
patcher, the division superintendent often found himself frantically
rounding up a crew on short notice when his best-laid plans went awry.
To the disgust of men who might have had only a few hours of sleep
since their last run, he was often tempted to send the callboy to awaken
them next morning well before they were due. One hour, the men
insisted successfully, was notice enough. That is an obscure detail, but
it illustrates the fact that there is not a single rule or procedure in the
rules book or union contract today that did not have to be worked out
painfully over 150 years of railroad experience, and technological
change assured that there would always be new problems to wrangle
over.

Meanwhile railroading in the early years was almost like the classic
description of the medieval serf's life: "nasty, mean, brutish, and
short." The primitive machines and devices that early railroad men
struggled with were slowly replaced with man-saving and labor-saving
improvements, like the power reversing gear (it was man against
machine to throw the lever as locomotives grew larger); the automatic
coupler; the air-actuated train brake, which was operated throughout
the train by a lever in the cab of the locomotive; and the automatic
stoker. A painfully long time was required to develop the automatic
coupler and the air brake, which were finally adopted towards the end
of the century, mainly because they had to be installed uniformly
throughout the nation as cars moved freely from one railroad to
another. The Master Car Builders Association was not to be hurried,
however, and they did their work well, for these improvements were
appearing on passenger cars early in the 1880s and, by the end of the
century, on a majority of the nation's freight cars, too, although Congress did not require them until 1898. This dramatic demonstration of
the effectiveness of industrywide associations in organizing technological advances with a minimum of wasteful duplication and a maximum
of uniformity, had profound ramifications throughout American industry and, like so many American industrial procedures, it happened first
on the railroads. Professor Licht's casual assumption that the delay in
adopting improvements represented railroad executives' invariable
reluctance to spend the money to install them is yet another example
of an unconscious bias against the American businessman that is so common among American scholars.

Why work for a railroad, then, if it demanded so much of a man's
patience, strength, and eventually his health and maybe even his life?
It gave much, too, not the least of which was reasonably steady work,
especially after one had several years of seniority, at a very good wage
by the standards of the day. Even the humblest navvy could make a
couple of dollars a day in the antebellum era, and the $1.50 a day that

the deflation of the 1880s and 1890s brought it down to in the East was probably a raise in purchasing power. As the years went by, moreover, and the anomalies of pay and working conditions of the early years were worked out and seniority became the sacred rule, a man could better himself, which was more than one could say for jobs of manual labor or in farming, where "acts of God" seemed regularly to wipe out what progress a man might make. If promotion was according to rigid rules—track worker, brakeman, fireman, engineer—at least this amounted to a school in which a green hand could learn a skilled and, in his community, prestigious trade that might well pay five dollars a day someday. After the turn of the century, with the railroad brotherhoods riding constantly higher and the nation's railroads flushed with the prosperity of La Belle Epoque, he found that he could, and thus often did, take his trade from one railroad to another. Indeed, in 1900 the future of both railroad and worker was full of promise.

Study after study of early American labor relations reveals the same factor at the root of much worker discontent: the tyrannical foreman or "straw boss," who seeks always to be just a bit more than "first among equals" and who confuses toughness and harshness with leadership. Management at the officer level on American railroads was very thin before the volume and complexity of railroad operations woke top executives up to the fact that petty despotism was the result of the lack of explicit rules and grievance procedures.

As hard as it is to believe nowadays, railroads began operations without any thought to such obvious (to us) questions as, How many hours in a day constitute a day's work? What extra compensation, if any, does a man get if he works longer than that? How many consecutive, or nearly consecutive, hours of physically hard yet mentally demanding work could be required of him? Is *any* infraction of the rules or commonly accepted procedure, or sin of omission or commission, however slight, sufficient cause for immediate dismissal from employment? Or are there gradations of offenses, and can they be adjudicated by levying fines, and are the offenses additive? What appeal is there from the arbitrary interpretation of vague or misleading rules by one's immediate superior? What responsibility has the company for providing housing for employees, especially where the tracks have outrun civilization? How about comfortable boarding houses or dormitories for men waiting for their return runs, and comfortable reading rooms for men who would just as soon not spend their idle hours in saloons or houses of prostitution? Such questions had hardly ever been thought of when the trains first began to run, and all would generate much heat before the light of reason, fueled by economic success, slowly dawned on railroad leaders. As the budding manufacturing sector faced similar problems after the Civil War, it found similar problems less troublesome as a result of the railroads' early experience.

The despotic foreman always thought he knew what his employers wanted from him: to settle the men's discontents at his level, and not bother them, as they had more than they could handle meeting the payroll, soliciting freight, finding out what rebates their competition was offering their shippers, raising money for further construction and additional equipment, and defending the railroad in court in the damage claim brought by Bill Murphy, who had just tied his ancient cow to the tracks in the path of the *Fast Mail*. (Salting the track was another such racket.) Do not pass your problems up to your superiors; settle them yourself. That is what we pay you for. It was the "doctrine of completed staff work," which the U.S. Army once fatuously drilled into its junior officers. It seldom worked there, and on the railroads it was disastrous. Worst of all was management's insistence that low-level supervisory employees smooth over the men's indignation at "necessary" steps like the general reduction of wages in bad times. The cheerful loyalty of American workers, especially in such exciting jobs as railroading, could be closely matched by their bitter, violent reactions to wrongs real or fancied.

Railroad Men and the Rise of the "Laboristic Society"

Except for top executives and their staffs, the category of railroad workers who had become, by the end of the twentieth century, the most highly compensated were the operating employees who run the trains. In 1987 these workers received average annual wages of $44,275, which were 25 percent above those of the next-highest-paid category outside the executive suite: the yard workers, tower operators, and anyone described as "transportation, other than train engine." The lowest-paid, as one would expect, were maintenance-of-way workers, but at $32,139 for a year's work, they were not much behind the "professionals and administrative," at $34,283. Recognizing that these are broad averages, and that there was a big difference between the pay of an old-timer and a youngster just added to the bottom of the seniority list, or between a day laborer on a maintenance-of-way crew and the civil engineer who was averaged into the same category, these are nevertheless wages that relieve us of the need to cry "exploitation." Indeed, railroad executives were paid, on the average, only $55,561.

It will not escape the careful reader's notice that these broad averages fit nicely with the contours of brotherhood (union) power as it varied from craft to craft, and the nonunionized men clearly received little extra reward for the many years of expensive education that they are sure to have brought to their work. But who is to say what any given craft is "worth," alongside any other? The laborer, according to the old proverb, is worthy of his hire, is he not? No, in the real world of the "laboristic society," the laborer is worthy of what he can get, and the rewards of the operating crafts, when compared to those of the others, reveal clearly that the central thread in American railroad labor policy is the national government's abhorrence of any suspension, however brief, in railroad service to the nation. Such was not always the policy, nor did such a policy always spell submission to the demands of the brotherhoods, or even serious consideration of them, but such it did become as the railroads, at the head of all American industry, which was to tag along behind, revolutionized national policy in industrial strife as they had revolutionized just about everything else.

The railroads were still running and even making money at the time the foregoing figures were published, and one can fairly only compliment the men for their grab at prosperity. Or could one? The railroads are still running, to be sure, but the Class I lines have been aggressively selling off low-density lines that just can't produce what it costs to maintain even minimum freight service (forget passenger trains). These branches have sometimes been acquired by new short-line enterprises that operate with greatly relaxed union obligations or are fully nonunion, and they sometimes succeed in making money and staying in business. But as this is written they can not be looked upon as anything but one more of those fortuitous reprieves that Congress has had over the years as it shrinks from establishing a true national transportation policy. Meanwhile the railroad unions have achieved two goals that are at the top of any labor union's list: they have got handsome compensation for their men who have remained employed on the railroads, and they have managed to hold back the hand of technological progress in many instances to keep men on the payroll who are frankly redundant. Nevertheless, for every two men employed on Class I roads in 1979, barely eight years later there was only one. Total employment plummeted from 482,962 to 248,526 in that short time, and the decline seemed not about to be stemmed as the century neared its end.

We have been describing the working-out of the implications of what the noted Harvard labor economist, the late Sumner Slichter, dubbed the "laboristic society" half a century ago. Slichter was heavily under the influence of the spirit of interventionism that the New Deal had brought, but wise man that he was, he seemed to know that the policy was likely to raise more problems than it solved, in the end. Spelled out, "laboristic society" was one in which the interests of organized labor are identified closely with those of the "general public," and the knottier the issues in a labor dispute, the more likely the government is to resolve it in the direction of *some* net gain, at least, to the union. Just when this policy became manifest, and not to be denied any longer, is a matter of interpretation. Historians of the New Deal are likely to cite the National Industrial Recovery Act of 1933, which, having exempted industry from the terms of the Sherman Antitrust Act in the fatuous hope that its members would thereby collude to keep prices and, presumably employment, up, included its famous Section 7-B giving labor the right to demand collective bargaining, a right which, in the National Labor Relations Act of 1935, survived the death of the NRA's "Blue Eagle." Again, however, the railroads were first. When the new team moved into Washington in 1933 to face a worsening economic crisis, they swept away much of the progress the Hoover administration had made in solving the desperate railroad problem and passed legislation that secured the railroad man's job for him, come what may, affirming, in effect, that "the country will pay."

Confirmation of the "laboristic society" came in 1937. On the last day of 1936, a year that had seemed to signal the return of better times in American industry, workers at a General Motors plant in Detroit staged a sitdown strike on company property. Not only were the men not going to work until their union, the United Auto Workers, was recognized for collective bargaining, but obviously they were not going to let management avail itself of any alternative thereto, short of calling out the National Guard. This, Governor Frank Murphy refused to do, and GM caved in. Such tacit government approval of a clear violation of the rights of private property—there was also some destruction of the premises—removed any doubt as to which way the wind was blowing. Thus, by the time the U.S. Supreme Court got around to declaring sitdown strikes illegal in 1939, the rising industrial unions of the CIO were firmly ensconced in the American automobile industry, and the following year Murphy was elevated to the U.S. Supreme Court.

The origins of the "laboristic society," however, were in the last quarter of the old century and, indeed, its assumptions had been in the wind for some years before that. That there would be limitations to the rights of private property was becoming apparent in repeated efforts of railroad men, from the 1850s on, to join together. Sir William Blackstone, author of the landmark *Commentaries* on English law in the eighteenth century, is said to have been asked why he asserted the absolute rights of private property, and to have replied that such an outrageous principle was sure to be widely assaulted and should, therefore, start out in as vigorous a form as possible.

The first successful railroad labor union was organized along craft lines, and, like virtually all of the earliest successful efforts to form unions, in such occupations as printing and the building trades, it reflected the unique power of the craft, in this case the engineers, to shut down their industry for considerable periods by withholding their services. The Brotherhood of Locomotive Engineers was formed in 1863 by a group of Michigan Central engineers, but its significance dates from 1874 when it ended its adherence to the idealistic notion that strikes hurt everybody. By the end of the century brotherhoods had been formed throughout the industry as the weaker crafts advanced in the protective shadow of the engineers. Data on the penetration of a craft by its brotherhood are sparse and likely to be misleading, inasmuch as the local unions representing men on the nation's most important railroads became all but omnipotent.

Two rather pathetic attempts to organize all railroad workers into industrywide unions—that of the Knights of Labor in the 1880s and Eugene V. Debs's American Railway Union a few years later—came to naught. The Knights, a thoroughly benighted organization, never understood its real opportunity to exploit the economic power of the crafts. It yearned for the good old days of the small shop and the one-to-one relationship of master and journeyman and opposed strikes as immoral and against common sense. The Knights, however, had a stunning success with strikes on the Union Pacific and the Gould roads in the Southwest in 1884 and 1885, when the U.P. was sliding towards insolvency under the leadership of Charles Francis Adams, Jr., and Gould was trying to save himself in the panic of 1884. In 1886 Gould was ready for them and replaced striking Knights with strikebreakers, whereupon the Knights passed into history.

As for Debs, he has been virtually canonized as a saint of the labor movement, but still it must be admitted that he drank too much, was something of a muddle-headed, self-taught socialist, and had a penchant for getting into fights he could not possibly win. The U.S. government, for example, reacted vigorously against the violent boycotts resorted to by the strikers at George Pullman's car-building plant in Chicago in 1894, and President Cleveland firmly backed up with force the refusal of the railroad executives to let the men take out their trains without their normal complement of Pullman sleeping cars. The nation was far from ready to support the men's challenge to the unfettered exploitation of private property, but the event was not without its embarrassment to the nation's leaders. Mark Hanna, a leader of the Republican party who was grooming his man, William McKinley, to return the party triumphantly to the White House in the campaign of 1896, declared about George Pullman that "any man who won't negotiate with his men is a damn fool!" The Pullman strike, however, was the low-water mark of America's traditional favoritism towards the underdog. Theodore Roosevelt's brand of Republican Progressivism burst upon the nation in 1901, notably in the trust-busting movement and his Olympian settlement of the strike in the anthracite coal industry in 1902. And Teddy was one-upped by Woodrow Wilson in the eight-hour-day threats by the railroad brotherhoods in 1916, after which railroad executives must have felt "naked to mine enemies" in future labor disputes. They have seldom had much more than a fig leaf since.

Union labor reached political maturity during the remarkably prosperous years from the late 1890s through World War I, largely as a result of their success at wringing concessions from the railroads, whose man-hour productivity advanced dramatically with major innovations in the physical plant. Railroad labor leaders learned to use the power of government, with its mandate to keep the railroads operating on every last branch line in the country, in their campaigns for higher wages and better operating conditions, the former sometimes disguised as the latter. Railroad executives had been swept up, once the grim depression of 1893–1897 was over, in a great surge of traffic that made nearly redundant the declaratory sections of the Act of 1887 to Regulate Interstate Commerce (ICA) against rebating and pooling. The railroad plant as it existed in 1900 all but broke under the crushing burden of unprecedented traffic levels, nowhere less so than on the proud New York Central, which smarted under the denunciations of thousands of farmers and small businessmen of the Empire State.

A traffic-heavy railroad is likely to be a very profitable one, however, the economics of high fixed-cost enterprises being what they are. With the golden flow of cash and greatly improved credit ratings among the bankers, railroads everywhere undertook expansion and betterment programs that confirmed, once and for all, the railroads' unique superiority as large volume, low-rate haulers of practically everything from ladies' hats to bituminous coal. They did it by reducing curvature and cutting down grades, installing heavier rail, and double-tracking (although not nearly enough), replacing wooden trestles with dirt and rock fill and wooden bridges with steel, expanding freight yards and monumental new passenger stations in major terminal cities (while increasingly quaint wooden Victorian structures would continue to make do in thousands of way stations), and vastly improving automatic switching and signaling equipment. They placed upon these new facilities freight cars that used increasing amounts of steel in their construction and had double and triple the net tonnage capacity of nineteenth-century rolling stock and larger, more comfortable, and safer all-steel passenger cars. Heading up these revolutionized trains were steam locomotives that exceeded in size and pulling power anything theretofore dreamed of, which, to a perceptive few, foretold the eventual replacement of steam power with something better.

With all this new investment, it was never enough. Capital is always scarce among a people who know what to do with it, and so railroad men rationally concentrated their betterments on major lines where most of the nation's burdens were carried. This left plenty of secondary, agricultural, and mining branch lines to form the basis for folksy satires like *Slow Train Through Arkansas*. By the second decade of the brave new century quite a few Class I railroads, particularly in the underdeveloped Southwest, found the shoe pinching uncomfortably. The nation took the golden reward that flowed from the spectacular success of its dominant system of internal transportation—best in the world, more than one foreign observer would admit—in cash, so to speak, in two forms: one, in rates frozen in money terms that consequently declined rapidly in purchasing power as prices and wages continued to rise, and the other in a broad-based liberalization of wage levels and working conditions on the railroads. In following these policies, the public supported the lower rates enthusiastically, never understanding the inflation of the era—which indeed was unprecedented for a nation on the gold standard and in peacetime—and went along with the better deal for railroad workers, since they seemed to have no choice anyway.

Railroads—A Not-Quite-Public-Utility

National labor-management relations policies, as reflected in the statutes, their interpretation by the courts, and, most important, their administration and enforcement by the executive branch and "independent" boards and commissions, had their earliest significant development on the railroads. Nearly everything that has followed, allowing for some detailed differences from industry to industry on the basis of their peculiar needs, was first tried out in the railroad strife that grew increasingly more common after the turn of the century. By 1900 the old idea that strikes were conspiracies to deprive the owners of a business of the basic right of private property to operate their business and profit therefrom was virtually discarded. Otherwise, a substantial majority of Americans, in the prosperous first thirty years of the new century, when anybody was free to "make it," agreed with the doctrine of the sacredness of private property, at least in the abstract.

In general, however, public sentiment was beginning to lean towards the working man, even if the likelihood of serious injury on the job, or of an old age spent in penury, cut remarkably little ice at the governmental level, when one considers the strides forward in social security legislation that otherwise "illiberal" governments like that of the German Empire were making. (To be sure, Bismark had a vigorous Socialist part to worry about, and stealing their thunder was worth quite a few public marks.) When laws making the railroads responsible for compensating workers for work-related injuries and for establishing retirement systems were passed, they were far more burdensome to the railroads and less liberal to the men than such systems enacted subsequently for "everybody else," a fact that railroad men have complained of bitterly for decades without results. Congress has proved to be remarkably reluctant to touch any of the fabric of the railroad labor relations laws, notably the Railway Labor Act of 1926, and railroad leaders take the position that the present law is probably better than anything that might be put in its place. After all, the national policy is that railroad service will not be suspended, and someone will have to pay; railroad executives are not virgins when it comes to subsidies and even national takeover.

Meanwhile the railroad brotherhoods learned early in the new century that the financial ability of the railroads to pay big wages and liberalize working conditions had nothing to do with the case. In 1910 railroad labor learned a lesson it never forgot: if you work in industry that is affected with a vital public interest (for example, hauling coal to northern cities in the winter), you can not tie your demands to the industry's ability to pay them. Array yourself on the railroads' side (and thus, by inference, against the interests of the general public) and you are lost. In that year, so disastrous for the railroads, the brotherhoods supported railroad men's attempt to secure a token general increase in rates under the new legislation that gave the Interstate Commerce Commission the power to suspend any rate increase until proved "reasonable and proper" by the railroad or railroads that applied for it. The commission interpreted (accurately, it would appear) Congress's intentions in passing this legislation (the Mann-Elkins Act of 1910) as an effort to place a "cap" on railroad rates. It acted accordingly and no significant railroad rate relief was forthcoming, in the face of a steadily and steeply rising price level, until the commission had been sidelined in World War I.

In his opinion accompanying the commission's decision to deny an increase to the eastern railroads (the western railroads' application was rejected in a separate decision), crusty Vermonter Charles A. Prouty had declared, "This Commission certainly could not permit the charging of rates for the purpose of enabling railroads to pay their laborers extravagant compensation as measured by the general average compensation paid labor in this country as a whole." If the prose was flatulent, the message for labor was clear: all you have to bargain with is your undisputed power to shut down the nation's lifeline. The country will pay, if the railroad corporations cannot. Once the government, during World War I, showed the men what deep pockets it really had, any philosophical indisposition railroad labor leaders may have had against nationalization of the railroads disappeared, and in the debates over how best to return the war-weary lines to private control the unions came out strongly for the so-called Plumb Plan for government ownership. Ironically, Senator Albert Baird Cummins, a genial Progressive demagogue from Iowa who wanted to be president, and who had never hesitated to frighten railroad leaders with threats of permanent government ownership in the decade before the Great War, completely reversed his position when he saw what kind of proprietor the government would make and that high wages *and* the high rates to sustain them would follow each other like the seasons.

The extinction of railroad management's equal right to hard-nosed bargaining, which might have matched the ICC's and the brotherhoods' toughness, was made manifest in the so-called eight-hour-day crisis. No one, as the spring of 1916 gave way to a blistering summer in Washington, believed for a minute that the railroads could, as a practical matter, arbitrarily limit a railroad operating employee's "trick" to eight hours. Congress had long since recognized that for health and safety reasons, the maximum period on duty could not be left to the discretion of the lowest level of management, and had set it at sixteen hours. What the brotherhoods were after was a law requiring the carriers to pay for eight hours what they were then paying for the standard day of ten hours, and overtime at the rate of time-and-a-half beyond that. The crux of the matter, therefore, was labor's demand for ten hours pay for eight hours work or, put baldly, a grab for a 25 percent wage increase in the guise of humanitarianism. No one fell for the gimmick then, and few knowledgeable people have since, save for a handful of careless historians. The gloves were off, and the brotherhoods were quite prepared to strike, not withstanding President Wilson's Preparedness program to strengthen the national defenses, which was in full swing. Railroad executives saw the occasion as their last stand for freedom to negotiate on the same basis as the men, and the outcome was hardly less devastating than an earlier last stand on the Little Bighorn.

When the railroad leaders explained to the Nervous Nellies in Washington that they were making arrangements to run a few of the most vital systems, east, west, and south, with nonunion employees drawn from the industry at large, President Wilson summoned the leading railroad men who were bargaining for the industry to the White House. During a brief meeting, in which the president apparently did all the talking, he told the men that if there was a strike on the nation's railroads, the people would know whom to blame. He later made certain promises to management as to liberalization of the ICC's frozen stand on rate increases, but the executives knew that in three months Wilson might be a "lame duck" president. Events moved so swiftly thereafter on the world scene that the slow process of correcting the accumulated anomalies in American transportation law was quickly replaced by emergency measures.

It was on the railroads, therefore, that the concept of the "laboristic society" was delivered to the American people. Once the workers had mastered the art of concerted action, it could hardly have been otherwise after the freewheeling economic leadership of the 1920s was replaced by the New Deal. Labor relations in the new era, quite naturally, have become the province of the specialized, highly paid lawyer and the bespectacled economist, and the outcomes of periodic negotiations have repeatedly puzzled onlookers who have been schooled in the virtues of common sense. Two principles, however, are deeply embedded in national transportation policy: a general strike on the railroads will not be tolerated, for even though by the 1980s they were carrying barely one-third of the nation's intercity freight, they were as indispensable as ever; second, what labor wants, it usually gets, at least in big, prosperous industries employing lots of people, and in the sick ones, too, if they happen to be "afflicted with a public interest," as one cynic has put it. The first point has been repeatedly demonstrated, sometimes with much drama and not a little corn, as when, in 1946,

President Harry Truman appeared before a joint session of Congress to ask for power to assume government control of the nation's railroads and thus avoid a strike that seemed inevitable, even after the many stages of mediation that had been ground through. Halfway through an emotional denunciation of both sides, the president was handed a note. Breaking into a broad smile that may well have been genuine, he announced that the warring groups had just reached agreement, and there would be no takeover. Railroad men, after their experiences with government control in World War I, have come to think of nationalization as the "fate worse than death," while labor maintains a remarkable equanimity on the issue. Withal, railroad management continues to uphold the Railway Labor Act of 1926 as the best it is likely to get and considers it more likely to produce palatable results than open warfare would.

The late Senator Tom Connally of Texas once remarked that "The closest thing to immortality on this earth is a government agency." He might have included labor unions in this category, for not even the extinction of a trade or a craft always causes a union to dry up and blow away. The British coal miners doggedly backed up the efforts of their leaders to keep mines open in which not a single lump of coal had been encountered in years, until government finally faced them down. In the same spirit, the Brotherhood of Railroad Firemen and Enginemen had fought to keep a "fireman" in the cab of both freight and passenger diesels while railroad leaders were determined to take them out of the freight engines (passenger engine firemen found that, except for Amtrak's few trains, their steeds have been shot out from under them by the march of the automobile and jet airplane). To the surprise of nearly everybody, and the total confusion of old-time labor reporters like the late A. H. Raskin of the *New York Times*, Congress in 1963 established a compulsory arbitration board and for once knocked the naughty heads together. For the first time and, so far the only but surely not the last time in American labor history, Congress had settled a labor dispute using its power to regulate commerce between the states. It was only temporary, and a few years later the firemen, having "learned nothing and forgotten nothing," like the French Monarchists of the Third Republic, were back demanding that the clock be turned back. Common sense has been a long time winning, but as Fiorello La Guardia said, "There's no substitute for being right!"

The "laboristic society," however, may soon be a thing of the past. Cat-and-dog fighting between management and labor can no longer be confined, for its implications extend far beyond the American economy or, for that matter, the American political system. The world is rapidly becoming one, and even the most mutton-headed theocracy finds itself forced now and then to look at the other side of a question. With power goes responsibility, and all the protestations about the separation of management's and labor's roles mean nothing if one or the other consistently calls the tune. Greater flexibility of wage rates, and freer acceptance of the need for geographic mobility by the rank and file, are on the horizon. Nowhere are they more needed than on the railroads, whose men, regardless of their skills, earn more than 95 percent of all blue-collar workers. Meanwhile both management and labor are looking for some better formula than the Roosevelt-Rosenberg solution, which served to end the supremacy of anthracite coal in 1902 and the long and honorable history of the Studebaker-Packard Company in the mid-1950s: Give the Men What They Want!

CHAPTER 13

Lawyers, Bankers, and "Real" Railroad Men

> Equal Justice Under Law.
> > Inscribed on the U.S. Supreme Court Building

> The law's the true embodiment
> > Of everything that's excellent.
> It has no kind of fault or flaw,
> > And I, my Lords, embody the law.
> > > William S. Gilbert, *Iolanthe*

A Nation Founded by Lawyers Finds a New Use for Them

Americans have no quarrel with the implications of the stern pronouncement that stares down at them from the facade of Washington's most beautiful building: the United States Supreme Court. The implication is that what is declared to be legal, is *just*, of course. The lady with scales depicted on the fly-specked wall of the county courthouse is Justice, is she not? The men who sit in final judgment on the decisions of the inferior courts, the laws of the land, and even the sacred Constitution itself, are themselves called "justices," are they not? Every American believes that what has been duly declared to be legal is just—so long as he agrees with the verdict—and never mind the convoluted reasoning that may lie behind it. Out of this conviction has grown one of America's most basic institutions and, nowadays, with more and more people looking beyond sweet reasoning with each other for justice, one of the fastest growing professions in the country: the practice of law. Not so gently, magnificently bearded Chief Justice Charles Evans Hughes one day reminded an overheated pleader before the Court that it was *not* a court of "justice," but of *law*. In our day another chief justice, Earl Warren, silenced a pleader who had insisted that separate but equal schools for blacks were legal, with the rhetorical question, "Yes, but is it *right?*"

The contours of American jurisprudence might have become even more closely modeled after those of the mother country than they were in the beginning, if the nation had not mastered the problem of cheap, dependable inland transportation and consequently transformed American business into a regionally specialized machine for the production of goods and services. This was a client that scoffed at distances and ignored state boundaries, while thumbing its nose at the provincialism of the people living within them. But that was only the beginning of the transformation that the railroads began and so powerfully advanced. New times require new institutions, and nowhere was the need more pressing than in the matter of the relations between the people and their new servant, which by the last quarter of the old century seemed, to some, about to become their master. Truth to tell, the railroads at that late date were still barely out of their adolescence and had so far failed to master their own relations with each other, and the railroad service provided then satisfied hardly anybody.

In the matter of the railroads' legal place in the American polity, however, great progress had been made by the time the new century began, for the iron horse had not waited to demonstrate the inadequacy of old ways and old convictions. The laws of torts and liability for property loss, of commerce, of insolvency of debtors, of chartering of corporations and their behavior towards each other and the general public and of negotiable instruments, which are only a few of the more obvious examples, were constantly remolded. The concept of a "common carrier" was revolutionized, and steamboating, which had itself been hailed as the creator of empire, was thus hastened to its end. The Constitution, whose full faith and credit clause had bravely declared the right of nonresidents of states to equal treatment with the locals, was put to the test as more and more mercantile trade came to be carried out over long distances. The rights and responsibilities of the federal government in providing internal improvements and otherwise encouraging the great westward movement of the peoples were finally settled, once and for all, by the demands of the railroad. National inventions require a people to think nationally, and the railroads, gradually but with accelerating pace, had come to think and act nationally.

If the coming of modern transportation influenced strongly the evolution of the modern lawyer, it also began the transformation of the lawyer into a general businessman, in charge of an important phase of a big enterprise and, more and more frequently, its chief executive officer. A good lawyer, in fact, was first of all a good solicitor, a quick-study kind of fellow, with a superior ability to set forth in writing as well as orally the many-faceted deals these big corporations made daily, in and out of courtrooms; above all, he had a knowledge of human nature that was indispensable in making mere humans see the advantages in acting like rational, sensible, peaceable creatures. He was, in short, just the kind of fellow the railroads felt an increasing need for after the great engineering battles had been won. The all-purpose executive who left running the trains to others was born. Before the end of the century the American lawyer would be well on his way to becoming the key person

in the conduct of the nation's railroads' business, second only to the
bankers, many of whom had started as lawyers themselves. To conclude, however—as many have—that he had no need of intimate
knowledge of his company's affairs is to miss the point.

A promising young fellow like Abe Lincoln could not get to first
base today in the law business because he did not have nineteen years
of formal education. He would be lost—but only temporarily, if we
know Lincoln—in the strange mixture of jurisprudence, politics, economics, psychology, and half-baked sociology that the modern practice
of law has become. But about all a young man had to have until late in
the old century to study law was reasonably good eyesight and the ability to read, "cipher," and write a fair hand. He had no need of mathematics beyond long division and the computation of interest; a smatter-
ing of land-survey lingo could come later. What he required most of all,
of course, were the good offices of an established lawyer with a good
set of law books, who would let the young man "read law" in his office,
where he could keep his ears and eyes open and his mouth shut, except
when his mentor was free to kick a neat point of law around with him
and whomever else was present, and perhaps empty the cuspidors now
and then.

It may not sound like the best way to learn the philosophical intri-
cacies of the law, but it did teach a young man not to try to pursue a
mere point of law too far beyond the intellect of the judges, the jury,
and the client himself. It was the quickest and probably the only way
to get to know just about everybody who was anybody in the country,
bearing in mind that it was some of these good people whom he would
one day face when he stood up to address a jury, and some of whom
might make good clients. And *that* was just what the railroads required,
for in their comparatively great size and corporate anonymity, they
needed all the local good will they could get. All the Populist hot air of
the 1890s and of the Progressive era in the next century should not
distract us from the realization that the railroads' lawyers were overwhelmingly concerned with the world of the small town and the frontier, not Wall Street, Congress, or even the state legislature. John L.
Larson's fine study of John Murray Forbes, pioneer Boston investor in
midwestern railroads and chief builder of the Chicago, Burlington &
Quincy, and Forbes's relations with local politicians and businessmen
of Iowa who exploited the Burlington in one manner or another, leaves
no doubt that railroad lawyers' problems were chiefly local (*Bonds of
Enterprise*, 1984).

The railroads created a demand for lawyers that had not existed
before, and chances are that the young men who cut their legal teeth
on such exciting causes as Jones's cow that the 8:15 had converted to
hamburger, had arrived in town from the less promising place of their
birth on the same train, not long before. There was not much anyone
could tell an Abe Lincoln, in 1855, or Francis Lynde Stetson, J. P. Mor-

gan's righthand man and legal counsel in the 1890s, or Robert S. Lov-ett, Edward Harriman's chief lieutenant on the Union Pacific and his successor as president of the railroad in 1909, about what the people in the thousands of small towns and cities across the nation thought about the railroads, their problems, and the problems they made for everybody else. Lincoln probably learned these valuable facts easier and faster at his "law school" than others in more impressive surround-ings. It is from the late 1850s, on the eve of the Civil War, that Allan Nevins, in his multivolume history of the Civil War, *Ordeal of the Union* (1947–1960), dates the beginnings of intellectually "vertebrate" America, with its nascent professional organizations. The lawyers would be in the vanguard of movements like that, for they found not only clients but often a career working for the chief creators of a national backbone, or in opposing them in the interests of their users and, in later, less precise times, the "general public."

"There ought to be one uniform law throughout the nation on bills of exchange, promissory notes, insurance policies, and all personal con-tracts." So wrote legal commentator James Sullivan as early as 1801. Already, the binding of thirteen formerly sovereign states into a single nation had stimulated growth in regional trade that was making obso-lete the laws and procedures that had always sufficed locally for settling frictions between local debtors and creditors. The growth of interre-gional trade, however, even under premodern conditions of transpor-tation, had stimulated the expansion of traditional credit instruments that took the place of a hand-to-hand circulating medium (that is, cash) in cementing financial agreements and settling debts. The process of making one out of many was not automatic, and nation-building was not a mere matter of geographic expansion, as contemporaries discovered almost every day.

It was not alone the ever-present "deadbeat" debtor or unfortu-nate merchant against whom creditors sought judgments, or even the fact that creditors had to bring these actions in state courts at consid-erable distances from their places of business, but also the need to decide between debtor and creditor just what the law was, that com-plicated life for the businessman. Such a system worked more badly with each passing year, and in hard times the state courts, sometimes acting under emergency laws of judicial procedure passed by voter-conscious legislators, were more and more likely to shut bona fide cred-itors out altogether. Western states (poverty-stricken Kentucky espe-cially) even undertook to fasten such procedures on federal courts to which cases had been removed!

Such nonsense could not survive two vital influences that brought sanity and order to American commercial law in the critical decades before the Civil War. One was the powerful federalism of Chief Justice John Marshall; the other was the railroad, which expanded the horizons of businessmen all over the nation and dealt the first of many blows to this naive concept of states' rights. By 1842, in the landmark case of *Swift vs. Tyson*, the Supreme Court firmly decided that in cases of diversity of state of residence of the contestants, jurisdiction over which the Constitution gave to the federal courts, the commercial law, and not the law of states, should rule. This was all very well if the party bringing the suit was an individual, and not a corporation. The same states that had tried to make second-class citizens of "foreign" (that is, out-of-state) creditors, now tried to exclude corporations from doing business in the state if they were chartered in some other state. For a while, as long as Congress remained silent on the question of whether a corporation was a "person," the railroads were thus denied access to the federal courts, an insane denial of the railroads' essentially federating nature. It took a while, but in 1844 the Supreme Court under Roger B. Taney made corporations citizens of the state in which chartered; a decade later, it reaffirmed its decision. Both cases involved pioneer American railroads, the Louisville & Nashville and the Baltimore & Ohio. Full-fledged "citizenship" for corporations was delayed until "the bad old days" of the Gilded Age, but by the end of the century the federal courts would be the accustomed haunt of America's railroads.

The new legal problems brought by railroads showed what an excellent ogre self-serving interests could make out of incorporated businesses, especially "foreign" ones. The tradition was a long time dying, if it is dead even yet. As late as the 1930s, when a family from out of town moved in and opened a dry goods store in a certain small town in northwest Arkansas, they were careful to have the sign painter make their store sign read, "Famous Dry Goods Company (Not Inc.)." One of the most curious cases in Supreme Court history arose from the desire of the justices to preserve a role for the state courts in enforcing the Sherman antitrust law of 1890. In the E. C. Knight case of 1895, the court found that manufacturing was not commerce, which the Sherman Act was intended to regulate, and thus Henry O. Havemeyer's sugar trust was not assailable in the federal courts. Counsel for the sugar trust was praised to the sky by trust-minded interests for his legal acumen, and his fortune was made, but Charles W. McCurdy has shown that not Gilded Age conservatism, but rather a clumsy effort to keep antitrust enforcement on the state level, explained such a tortured and short-lived interpretation.

Nineteen-seventy was a bad year for the railroads. In that year they gave the nation the largest bankruptcy case it had ever had, when the Penn-Central, which had merged the equally bad-off former monarchs of railroading, the New York Central and Pennsylvania railroads, declared its insolvency. A picture of some ninety rusting hulks of Cadillac automobiles, brand new when a derailment on the old West Shore Division of the Central flung them down an embankment, was a feature of a *Fortune Magazine* article on the bankruptcy, which dealt mostly with recent efforts—all admittedly bad—of the sick giant to diversify into more promising fields than railroading. In the best tradition of American journalism, the article failed to dig below the obvious factors of neglected "deferred" maintenance that had put the Cadillacs in the ditch, that is, sixty years of destructive government regulation that closed off all the American railroads' opportunities for healthy growth. Railroad and legal historians might have noted, also, that the article virtually took it for granted that the railroad would bear the full liability for the grievous loss of the autos. As a common carrier, the railroad, poverty-stricken though it was, was fully liable for the loss of property.

The origins of the doctrine that some carriers for hire are liable and some are not for anything untoward that may happen to a shipper's goods seem all but lost in legal antiquity, although legal historian Morton Horwitz has obligingly traced them to an 1822 case in the Pennsylvania Supreme Court.* Railroads were almost ten years in the future then, but land carriage was not, for it is as old as horses and wagons, if not older. The question was whether the stern law of England, which made a carrier by any means liable for everything except acts of God, applied to American flatboats, arks, barges, sailboats, and the brand new steamboats on American waters, particularly the wild and wooly waters of western rivers. The placid rivers and ubiquitous canals of England were one thing; on American rivers the snags, sunken logs, sandbars, periods of low water, and uncharted shifts in the channel, and above all the match carelessly dropped by some drunken riverboat gambler onto a cargo of hundreds of valuable bales of cotton, were quite another. If anyone had tried to make steamboat owners, whose captains were responsible for a large passenger list as well as cargoes several times as great as were carried on English river or canal barges, liable for loss due to anything but gross demonstrable negligence, either the nation's burden would not get carried to market or the law would languish unenforced, probably the latter.

Westward the course of empire makes its way, often over the dead letter of law made for another place and another time. As Horwitz notes, *Gordon vs. Little*, 8 Serg. & Rawle 533 (Pa. 1822), was the first American case to question the rule of strict common carrier liability and to acknowledge that the rule was changeable by contract. This obscure case did not so much set in motion the distinction between carriage by rail (once it was to be had), which bore broad liability for loss of cargo, and by water, which did not, as it simply heralded what soon was settled law in America. Railroads, like river boats, were inland transportation but they faced few of the hazards that steamboats did. Being a man-

---

*In a memorandum, May 25, 1971, to Alfred D. Chandler, Jr., in the possession of the author.

made means of transportation, the railroads were fully responsible for any failure in the mode of carriage that they offered the public, always excepting loss due to acts of God.

Insofar as the startling rapidity with which steamboats were replaced by railroads in the burgeoning American carrying trade is concerned, more visible advantages such as speed, ubiquity, and availability in all seasons cold or hot, wet or dry, have probably made more difference than the common carrier factor. Yet the railroads' liability often made the difference in their being chosen over the steamboats. A shipper might do without the railroads' speed, or even their all-year convenience, but if the cost of insurance, on top of what the haughty steamboat captain charged (assuming he would deign to take your cargo when the time came, for he didn't have to under the law) brought water carriage up to the railroad rate, then there was no contest. To be sure, the message had to be brought to the shippers, most of whom were agriculturalists or animal husbandmen out in the bush. A young man in St. Paul in 1865, having just gone into the freight handling and forwarding business for himself, knew this, and he spread the word in little notes industriously penned when business was slow. When you are alone on the frontier you have to be very helpful, and then people will remember your name: James J. Hill.

Lawyers and Railroads:
A Synergistic Relationship

If entrepreneurship is above all else innovation in business enterprise, then lawyers who were concerned with problems of the adolescent American railroad network were indeed entrepreneurs. We have declared that the most sigificant development in the history of railroad transportation was the discovery of its apparently limitless capacity to increase its productivity, and above all, to constitute a practical, low-cost, long-distance hauler of low-value-per-ton freight. The former is primarily the province of the engineers; the latter, which made the American economy such a striking success and world leader by the end of the old century, faced many obstacles of law, custom, and just plain backwardness, which last has never been a stranger to the American system.

Countless laws, judicial decisions, local pride, and the soggy cake of custom lay in the way of the unencumbered through-railroad system. One of the earliest was the indignant wrath of steamboat men, who still ruled the roost in the critical decade of the 1850s. When a pioneer midwestern railroad, the Rock Island, demonstrated that private capital was up to doing something that had never been done before—bridging the Mississippi River—and began to run its trains eastward and westward across the primitive structure that hopscotched across the rocky islands (hence the name) in the great river at Rock Island, Illinois, the

dominant north-south trade flow on the river began to wither alarmingly in favor of east-west movement by rail. The steamboat men
insisted desperately that the bridge was a hazard to navigation and fire,
which they sought to prove by ramming it with the steamer *Effie Afton*
(which would achieve immortality in Lincolniana) and burning it
beyond further use. The railroad's lawyer was one of the best the Midwest ever produced: Abraham Lincoln, so soon to quit the profession
for a wartime presidency, martyrdom, and canonization by the American people.

Lincoln won the case, in the sense that the jury could not agree on
whether the plaintiff, owners of the *Effie Afton*, had deliberately
rammed the bridge and set it afire. But the finger of premeditation
pointed unmistakably towards them. Lincoln, upon taking the case, had
walked out on the bridge to the point of collision, near the center, and
with the help of a twelve-year-old boy had measured the speed of the
current at that point, to later demonstrate in court that mere drift
would not have taken the boat on a collision course. Plaintiffs did not
renew the litigation, but another case, taken to the Supreme Court,
ultimately established once and for all the freedom of commerce to
seek the most direct and economical path to market, while not encum-
bering other modes of transport. Lincoln had destroyed the boatmen's
appeal to precedent, namely the long-standing north-south traffic flow,
by declaring, "But this current of travel has its rights as well as that of
north and south [and thus] this bridge must be treated with respect in
this court and is not to be kicked about with contempt."

The railroads, being "faceless corporations," in the rhetoric of the
times, needed someone like Lincoln to remind courts that they must
take the broad view in weighing equitable rights. In another case a
plaintiff's lawyer was "pounding the table," being unable in this case
to pound the law or the facts, because the man had obviously not suffered the damages he claimed. Corporations, the lawyer is said to have
reminded the court, have "no soul." Lincoln cooly replied that the corporation had more of a soul than the lying witness who had just testified
for the plaintiff and, besides, the corporate name of the railroad was
merely a "conventional name for thousands of widows and orphans"
and for farmers and their wives who had mortgaged their farms and
paid out their butter and egg money to buy stock in it. But Lincoln was
no particular partisan of the railroads. When McLean County decided
that it was going to tax all of the property of the brand new Illinois
Central Railroad within the county's borders, despite the provision in
the I.C.'s charter exempting it from state taxation, Lincoln first offered
his services to the county in the inevitable lawsuit and, receiving no
reply, hired out to the railroad. He lost in the lower court, which shows
how local prejudices could override mere legal principles; but he
argued the case twice more and finally won. He presented the railroad
with a bill for $2000 and was not pleased when their treasurer, pointing

out that no "country lawyer" ever charged any such fees, offered $200. Lincoln sued for $5000 and won. Mrs. Lincoln, with her love of nice things, must have been ecstatic.

As railroads became bigger, presumably richer, definitely more powerful, and certainly more impersonal entities, and as the battle lines between interest groups became more distinct in American political life, Lincolnesque pragmatism fell by the wayside. By 1885, when J. P. Morgan was trying to keep rival eastern interests from building additional trunk line railroads, he could only growl in frustration to his chief counsel, Elbert Gary, "I don't pay you to tell me what I can't do; I pay you to tell me what I *can* do." But after 1887 government took a direct hand in forming national transportation policy, and practice before the original Interstate Commerce Commission in the late nineteenth century became an increasingly fertile field for lawyers in the provinces.

More and more communities hired lawyers to argue their case for a more favorable rate than some competing town's, especially the flourishing railroad terminal points that were destroying the small-town wholesale jobbers' trade. The town of Troy, Alabama, was thirty-two miles closer to eastern shipping points than Montgomery if both places were measured on Troy's only rail line, the Alabama Midland, which formed a highly circuitous route to the east coast in cooperation with several easterly lines. Troy demanded a lower rate than Montgomery under the long-short-haul clause of the Interstate Commerce Act. They did not get it, because Montgomery got its stuff from the East by two or three more direct lines, and the Supreme Court, in the *Alabama Midland* case (1897) interpreted the "substantially similar circumstances and conditions" clause of Section Four of the Act to include rail competition. What Troy wanted, of course, was dirt-cheap rail transportation below Montgomery's rate, which was already determined by strong competition. Distance had nothing to do with it, except that a local lawyer, offering his services to the town fathers, could make a good *prima facie* case for it, until a high-priced railroad lawyer got through with him. Long-short-haul "discrimination" was a very big bone, however, constantly dug up by small-town "boosterism," and men chewed on it for years thereafter.

The railroads that James J. Hill and J. P. Morgan wanted to place under the broad wing of their holding company, Northern Securities, earned the dubious distinction during Theodore Roosevelt's first term (it was all his except for the six months that fate allotted to poor McKinley) of being the case that finally settled the question of whether holding companies (which neither manufactured nor distributed goods) could be subject to the antitrust laws. In a five-to-four decision (Mr. Justice Holmes famously dissenting), the Court decided that the theoretical presence of great economic power was sufficient to require that it be given up. The Hill-Morgan interests quietly resumed their original *ad hoc* method of maintaining control of these properties, which dominated the upper Midwest and the Pacific Northwest—that is, by an informal syndicate—for the next sixty-six years until the Great Northern, the Northern Pacific, the Burlington, and (Hill having built it in the interim) the Spokane Portland & Seattle, too, were united in Burlington Northern, with the full blessing of the Supreme Court in 1970. Everybody got what they obviously had wanted, and Teddy, who desperately wanted to be the first acceding vice president to be elected president in his own right and knew a popular issue when he saw one, got his first. The railroad men, like good businessmen everywhere, demonstrated that with infinite patience, good sense, and expensive lawyers on their side, they would eventually find a way to do what needed to be done. In 1970 Burlington Northern, first of the new breed of "mega-mergers," vindicated these long-dead warriors.

The rise of long-distance rail carriage did not take place automatically, although the Civil War gave it a strong boost. (Congress, as we have seen, even passed a law, after the great virtues of not trans-shipping freights had been demonstrated, requiring all railroads in interstate commerce to exchange freight with each other.) In the 1870s the new western states (the Midwest as we know it today) were demanding low rates to the eastern seaboard, while the commodity dealers in the river towns, who made a good living trans-shipping grain from the short-line railroads that penetrated the hinterland to river boats, wanted through rates to the East kept at par with river rates, plus whatever would reflect the distinctly inferior quality of transport to New Orleans by river and on to the Northeast by ship. We have already discussed the outcome of this critical juncture in American transportation history. Cheap transportation came in with a bang.

The dozens of lawsuits that had been undertaken under the self-contradictory granger laws were settled by Judge Economics and his blue-ribbon jury, the Onrush of Events. The granger laws represent almost as silly an act of public policy as the Windom Committee's recommendation to dig canals furiously across the Appalachians. "Get on board, li'l chillun, get on board," the railroads were saying to Americans, or get left behind. Millions *were* getting on board and leaving the small towns for the cities large and not so large, while those who were left behind didn't like it and were determined to do something about it. They had allies, up to a point, in denizens of the old cities of the eastern seaboard, at least for a while, and clever men in these places pushed for government to exert a stronger hand. The result was the Interstate Commerce Act of 1887, which presaged a change in American law, as applied to railroads, that endured for a century.

No one would be so naive as to suppose that the nineteenth century victories of railroad lawyers in the struggle to harness (or is "muzzle" the better metaphor?) the railroad corporation reflected the simple victory of right over wrong, or, for that matter, good sense over bad. It was more of a damage control effort. As an executive of the Illinois Manufacturers' Association said to the author, "Our important work is done in Springfield, especially when the legislature is in session. Do you have any idea how much harm those guys could do to Illinois business if we weren't there looking over their shoulders every minute?" He was not suggesting mere venality; after all, ignorance can be even more dangerous than dishonesty. But the railroads were very much in politics, right up to their steam domes; and the American legal profession responded with a new kind of lawyer skilled at working behind the scenes, men who might never address a jury in open court. They did what had to be done to enable their principals to do what had to be done to carry the nation's burden to market, including making a profit, because without profit there is no growth and no future. These men had almost these very words from Collis P. Huntington, the most prominent of the Big Four who built the Central Pacific and the Southern Pacific Railroads, as their authority for a policy of *rèal politique* that served the nation well and the railroads' critics in the Progressive era even better. "Standard Oil did just about everything to the Pennsylvania legislature except refine it," wags had been saying since New York State's Hepburn Committee (1879) revealed that the big petroleum combine was receiving rebates—that is, lower rates than competition. (The committee obscured the fact that these concessions were for guaranteeing a steady month-to-month delivery of oil to the railroads and supplying the tanks which, placed on wheel assemblies supplied by the railroad, took the oil to market.)

About bribes, from petty requests for free passes on the railroads' passenger trains to real money, railroad men often remarked that the hand was usually outstretched to demand them before the offer was made. Such remarks fairly infuriated critics who sought to place themselves and everybody who shipped by rail and haggled for the "best" rate on the side of the angels. Considering the obvious opportunities for civic heroism any large traffic in influence would have provided district attorneys, there were few prosecutions for bribery. Soon criticism focused more on favors to valued shippers who simply used their economic muscle, than on factors outside the railroad industry. Perhaps that was safer.

By the late nineteenth century, it was becoming apparent that a young man could not expect to go far in the legal profession without a substantial law-school education. There would never be any substitute for experience and careful observation, to be sure, but the rising complexities of finance and of litigation and legislative relations were making that route to the bar more and more difficult. When the railroads first began to issue stocks and, more importantly, bonds, the law of negotiable instruments was slight, and what there was was very tentative. Sooner or later, changing needs of finance would place a premium on successful innovation of new kinds of securities, with different forms of collateral, if any, and, as sure as anything can be, sooner or later the lawyers would be called upon to dig a struggling railroad out of debt. Corporate reorganizations in the Gilded Age were largely financial in nature, and existing laws and procedure provided little guidance to executives and their counsel. When the consolidation movement got under way in earnest, moreover, lawyers would have to learn a great deal about the law of holding companies, while making new law in the process.

The outstanding example of the innovative role of judges and lawyers in railroad affairs was the case of one of Jay Gould's railroads, the Wabash, in the sharp but brief recession of 1884. American railroads had been financed overwhelmingly by first mortgage bonds, usually bearing a gold clause guaranteeing payment of principal and interest in gold. The fully negotiable bonds had a lien upon the land under the railroad—the *real* estate—and any improvements upon it, such as graded roadbed, rails, bridges, and other structures. This may seem reasonable, but it was not the practice in England, where "debentures," not mortgage bonds, and certainly not stock, were the chief means of financing these long-term projects in a facility to serve the entire body economic. The interest they bore was payable only when earned. The money they raised was "sunk," emphasizing the Englishman's talent for the *mot juste*, because most of the money spent to build a railroad would never be recoverable except by operating it as intended. Otherwise it represented scrap value. American first mortgage bonds, however, gave the owners the right to foreclose, that is, to go into court and seek such emergency arrangements as would protect their rights under the lien, including, theoretically, seizure of the physical assets to do with as they pleased. It must have been obvious to everyone from the start that the extreme course would seldom if every be taken, and in practice the judge's real job was to find someone to take over the running of the railroad and to study recommendations for long-term solution of its problems, usually offered by bondholders' committees. This meant someone new to the management of the road. Or did it?

The only legal mechanism at the judges' command then was the equity receivership, inasmuch as there was no law of bankruptcy on the books. (The Constitution reserves the power to enact such laws to the federal government.) The equity receivership was a very old practice whereby insolvent mercantile concerns with genuine, movable inventories ("clean, merchantable stock," as the auction advertisements say nowadays) could be placed under the wing of a "receiver" (literally someone who would receive temporary control of the assets until an orderly plan could be devised for turning them into cash and distributing it among the creditors). A fundamental principle was that the receiver would not be anyone from the insolvent concern, but an outside, disinterested party. When it came to railroads, however, liquidation was not in order. A plan to get the railroad back on the track, whatever that required, and in a position to start paying its bond coupons as they matured, was what was required, in the view of the bondholders' committee. But such investors, to their initial great surprise, were not the only parties at interest, nor even the most important in the eyes of the judge, for judges are public servants and have responsibilities even beyond widows and orphans. In the Wabash case these realities would call forth legal innovation of the most breathtaking kind, and the exigencies of the railroads would change American law forever in one of its most significant aspects.

On May 28, 1884, the Wabash was not in default on its bonds, although rumor had it that it soon would be. Yet here was one Solon Humphreys, a director of the Wabash Railway and close associate of Jay Gould, standing before Judge Samuel Treat of the U.S. District Court for St. Louis, praying the court to appoint a receiver for the railroad in anticipation of its inability to pay its coupons that were coming due in barely one month, and asking, of all things, that he be that receiver. The indignation over what followed would not be quieted for twenty years, during which you could get a good argument among law professors as to the legal strength of the decision, but Judge Treat, having served thirty-eight years on the federal bench and being deeply conscious of the difference between a judge, a lawyer advocating one side of an issue, and a law professor primly taking both to task, proceeded to do just what Humphreys asked.

Treat had not gone off half-cocked. "I hesitated," he modestly admitted, but only long enough to consult an old friend, Nathaniel Shipman, judge of the U.S. District Court in Connecticut, who probably knew as much about railroad law in application as anyone in the country. The main thing, Treat ruled, was to keep the railroad running, economically and efficiently. Money had to be raised for immediate needs, such as rentals of terminal, bridge, and trackage privileges, and—a surprise to modern scholars—payment of promised rebates (not yet prohibited by statute law) to shippers who were quite prepared to take their business elsewhere. The present management, and no one else, was available to do it. But had they not got the enterprise in its present difficulties? Well, not really. Here was petitioner's lengthy brief, proceeding "with painful minuteness to detail its unavailing struggles with adverse fortunes," like floods and crop failures; disclosing the $3.4 million it had borrowed from a sister railroad on notes cosigned by "persons of high financial standing"; and, as a clincher, noting that "the road owes large sums to a multitude of laborers who have little to live upon other than the fruits of their labor."

From the day of Judge Treat's decision, the hard truth about the so-called mortgage bonds upon which American railroads were largely financed, and would continue to be financed, was increasingly apparent to lawyers and financiers. Debt capital, obviously, would be treated as equity capital when the going got rough. "If you wish that road to be run," concluded Judge Treat, "and there are no funds in the hands of the receivers to run it, who shall pay for the running? It must run at your [the bondholders'] expense. If others choose . . . to deprive people of railroad facilities, the consequence is not with this court." The quasi-public nature of the railroads would become increasingly central to the management of its affairs, even ahead of operational or administrative problems. Public bodies would freely place responsibilities upon the carriers in order to assure continuity of safe, convenient passenger and freight service at thousands of locations—virtually everywhere, in fact—under conditions highly favorable to their employees on active duty and in their retirement years; and, while prosperity endured, without much concern for who would pay for it when and if the cupboard became bare. When the Great Depression struck, however, not only was a thoroughgoing revision of the bankruptcy laws, especially as they related to railroads, in order, but massive loans with which to pay their fixed charges, including interest on their senior securities, were necessary. In the long run the railroads proved to be as good a credit risk as in their best years.

Lawyers, Bankers, and "Real" Railroad Men

It was in the reorganizations that followed the granting of extraordinary powers to receivers under this public welfare philosophy, that lawyers, especially those who were also investment bankers or their legal counsel, came into their own. Indeed, the line between legal and financial counselor became less and less marked as the great period of consolidation, or recasting, of thousands of more or less independent railroad corporations into a few systems, each under a different charismatic leader, proceeded. It was during the great depression of 1893–1897 that activity of this kind reached its most constructive peak. (After 1930 and right down to very recent times, lawyers and financiers became more important than ever, but largely as part of a continuing national effort to save American railroads in the face of an increasingly hostile, indifferent, and just plain idiotic national policy.)

The need to marshall unheard-of amounts of capital into fixed, long-term investments, of which railroads were the chief and for a long time almost the only form, created American investment banking as it existed down to the Great Depression. By the late 1880s American business leaders had come to realize two things: one, that the bankers were here to stay as fundamental forces in the making and carrying out of individual and collective railroad policy; and, two, that the leader among this new class of "railroad men" and chief innovator of methods by which capital could be raised, monitored, protected, and built upon, was the firm of J. P. Morgan & Co. The careers of Morgan; his farseeing father and pioneer merchant banker, Junius S. Morgan (d. 1890); and several of J. P.'s lieutenants—brilliant, hard-working, and in some cases prominent in their own right—have been admirably chronicled in Vincent P. Carosso's magisterial work, *The Morgans, Private International Bankers, 1854–1913* (1987). Well before the end of the century, however, American enterprise had begun to depend also upon such well-established Jewish banking houses as Kuhn, Loeb & Co., headed by the highly respected Jacob Schiff; Jacob Speyer & Co.; and the Rothschilds, to tap the savings of central Europeans, meaning primarily the Germans.

J. P. Morgan & Co. could command the best talent among New York's rising class of merchant bankers, who sometimes had risen from their original positions on the high stools of mercantile establishments. The outstanding example is Charles Henry Coster, who is said to have served on more boards of directors than any other man in history, at least up to the date of his untimely death, at forty-seven, in 1900. From the day that Morgan persuaded William H. Vanderbilt to make a secondary offering of a large block of his stock in the New York Central Railroad, the firm, without taking any special note of the fact, had taken on the responsibility of seeing to it that eagle-eyed bankers "watched that basket" for investors who bought securities floated by J. P. Morgan & Co. The chief instrument of oversight, in the case of railroads that had gone through the "Morganization" process of reorganization, was the voting trust, wherein the owners of the voting stock of a reorganized company would place their shares in a trust on which management would be in the minority, and the bankers would have the final say on all important decisions. This is the origin of the much-maligned "banker control" that would join "Free Silver," "A Tariff for Revenue Only," and "The Money Trust," as shibboleths to put second-rate politicians into office and keep them there. Damnation of bankers would replace all these battle cries among people who knew better, people who should have known better, and people who knew nothing at all, like the tobacco-juice-dribbling philosophers leaning back in their wire-reinforced chairs against the walls of rural courthouses.

But the bankers got the reorganized railroads their money, which took talent that was among the scarcest in America at the turn of the century. The best job of explaining the ins and outs of a major reorganization of a railroad system is Maury Klein's *The Great Richmond Terminal* (1970), in which Morgan, in the person of Charles H. Coster, moneyman, and Samuel Spencer, a "real" railroad man, working with the same spirit of cooperation that built the railroads in even more difficult times, laid about them with an axe to the properties of this insolvent holding company and the balance sheets of several dozen former independent railroads that constituted their assets.

When Coster and Spencer got through they had a well-integrated system, running from New Orleans to Washington, D.C., with other mainlines to important points and lesser branches. This was something the South had never had before. It had a sensible balance sheet on

Figure 13.1 Two men led in recasting the American railroad system after 1890. J. Piepont Morgan (1837–1913), at left, was the unquestioned leader of the American investment banking "industry" in its long formative and growth years before World War I. Charles H. Coster (1852–1900), was J. P. Morgan's "right-hand man," and the guiding hand in most of the firm's railroad financings and reorganizations, especially during the depression of 1893–1897. *(Both pictures courtesy of Morgan Guaranty Trust Co.)*

which realistically issued new securities took the place of the bonds and stocks of the old companies. In the best Victorian tradition, owners of stock, who were promised dividends only when a level of financial performance had been reached, were told to send money by way of an assessment on their stock, or else consider their shares canceled. Thus quick cash was raised to begin a process of virtual rebuilding of the properties that proceeded steadily until the Great Depression. The Southern Railway, as it was aptly called, ultimately formed with the Norfolk & Western the Norfolk Southern, a leading latter-day megasystem and one of the nation's most successful enterprises.

The Morgan team, of course, had specialists and strength in abundance, but this did not keep Morgan's men from developing the regrettable habit of working themselves into early graves. Few made it out of their fifties. An exception was Charles Steele, probably one of the top four or five railroad lawyers in the country down to the time of World War I; but Coster, and next-generation men like George Perkins and

Robert Bacon, who came from opposite ends of the American socioeco-
nomic scale but worked with equal intensity, barely saw the 1920s
come in. The American railroads did not invent the neologism "work-
aholic," but they made good use of an old syndrome.

The banker and the lawyer, working closely with "real" railroad
men, gave us the modern railroad system, or perhaps it was the need
for such a system that gave us the banker and the lawyer in the form in
which they dominated the first quarter of the new century. Edward H.
Harriman, a "broker's boy" in the eyes of some detractors, his legal
counsel, Robert S. Lovett, and their brilliant operating vice-president,
Julius Kruttschnitt, rebuilt the Union Pacific, with much help from
Jacob Schiff and friends, and added the Southern Pacific to this system
after C. P. Huntington died. The entire combine then became unexpectedly profitable as California finally came into its own, with citrus,
tourism, and motion pictures booming in the new century. Harriman
would have added the Burlington, too, backed up as he was by James
Stillman, whose National City Bank was one of the beneficiaries of the
surplus capital that the Rockefellers were accumulating from their
Standard Oil dividends. But James J. Hill beat him to it, and J. P. Morgan, who had rather enjoyed being called the rebuilder of the Northern
Pacific, had to separate the snarling combatants in the Northern Securities holding company, which survived government onslaughts long
enough to get Harriman out of the picture. Stomach cancer would finish this remarkable man's career only a few years later.

Perhaps least well known of all, however, was the born-again
Atchison, Topeka & Santa Fe, which had limped along through the sun-
baked, Bible-thumping Southwest into receivership in 1893. The men
who accomplished this were a "real" railroad man, Edward P. Ripley,
and an unknown who had made one of the most brilliant records at the
Harvard Law School, a cultivated, genial young man of Russian Jewish
ancestry named Victor Morawetz, who published a massive treatise on
corporation law when barely out of school and still in his mid-twenties.
Ripley and Morawetz were good news for American railroads and the
Southwest, if not for the famed Harvey Girls, who had served many
thousands of weary travelers, breaking up their transcontinental
ordeals, at hotel eating houses along the way. The Santa Fe in its post-
reorganization years introduced some of the most popular trains in the
nation, with many comforts even for the poorest travelers, and real luxury for first-class passengers. Fred Harvey transferred his special skills
to the best dining cars in the West (and a few big, warm, comforting
restaurants in the new big-city terminals), and the railroad made great
capital out of the most spectacular sightseeing attraction in the West,
the Grand Canyon, which it served by a branch off the main line at
Williams, Arizona. As the only transcontinental with its own line into
Chicago—which today is nothing less than an aorta of commerce

between the East and the land west of the Missouri—the Santa Fe surged ahead.

Until Ripley became frustrated at trying to get the public and its legislators to listen to reason, he made something of a spokesman for the railroads at the end of the first decade of the new century, when American railroads were finding out how much of an eight-ball they were really behind. Morawetz, meanwhile, had shown an uncanny awareness of the vast power that the federal government was being asked to assume as the nation moved towards rate-setting by commission around 1901: an awareness that neither Congress, nor any of the best legal minds on the railroads' payrolls showed. They would find out the power of the genie once he was out of the bottle. When the time came to return the railroads to private ownership, Morawetz authored a brilliant pamphlet explaining a system that would give the nation the best of both public and private ownership, but railroad leaders showed little stomach for further innovation. They had too many wounds to lick already. Morawetz, by then a rich man, as such wise people who go into business usually become, retired early to the life of a gentleman farmer in Virginia, a man whose time had come and gone with the speed of the Santa Fe's *Super Chief.*

The emphasis any discussion of railroad financing places on investment banking should not make us forget that for the vast majority of Americans, banks and bankers meant the familiar commercial banks. They accepted demand and time deposits, paying interest on the latter and sometimes on the former, too; lent money on short-term promissory notes to local businessmen and farmers to finance their inventories and operations in the coming season, and, very gingerly, on mortgages ungenerous by today's standards, to finance farm, business, and residential real estate; provided checking account facilities for the few businesses or individuals that used them; and, if they were chartered under the National Banking Act, issued National Bank Notes with their name imprinted thereon, the successor to the state-chartered banks' notes that had been eliminated by the National Banking Act during the Civil War.

If only a few of the local citizens had occasion to go into a bank regularly, nearly everybody benefited by the great surge in commercial banking from about 1880 to 1930, and especially in its golden age, about 1898 to 1913. The railroad and telegraph had vastly reduced both time and distance as factors in doing business, as the bank check replaced bank notes, and the percentage of issuing institutions whose paper was accepted "at par" slowly approached 100 percent. The natural result was a resurgence in the state chartering of commercial banks from 7,785 in 1896 to 19,197 in 1913 (the year of the founding of the Federal Reserve System). By the mid-1920s, as the country's banking system became shakier and shakier, there were some 21,500 state-

chartered banks in the nation, of which only about 1,600 were also
members of the Federal Reserve. Since the Great Depression, and
largely because of it, along with changes in American life brought by
the automobile, the total number of banks has declined and their size
has increased. But the real point to make is that fast transportation and
instantaneous communication reduced the time required to clear
checks and drafts, drastically reducing Americans' dependence upon
paper money, and providing the adrenalin for undreamed-of and not
always healthy economic growth.

CHAPTER 14

It's All Politics!

> I have never known much good done by those who affected to trade for the public good.
>
> Adam Smith, *The Wealth of Nations*, bk. IV, ch. 2

> Bryan is a pinchbeck Christ. American civilization and American freshwater colleges are responsible for a lot of them. Halfbakedness is the crying evil of the day.
>
> Charles Francis Adams, Jr.

> I don't disguise my belief that the Sherman Act is a humbug based on economic ignorance and incompetence, and my disbelief that the Interstate Commerce Commission is a body fit to be entrusted with rate-making. . . . I am so sceptical as to our knowledge of the goodness or badness of laws that I have no practical criterion except what the crowd wants. Personally, I bet that the crowd, if it knew more, wouldn't want what it wants.
>
> Mr. Justice Holmes, April 23, 1910

The Search for Order Rewarded

The old century went out with a bang, after all. It really ended in 1897, when the inauguration of William McKinley as president of the United States—after an unpleasant dalliance with the Democrats under Grover Cleveland—resumed the nearly unbroken tradition of Republican presidents that had begun with Abraham Lincoln. A fast-growing America, welcoming each year thousands of sturdy, intelligent, industrious immigrants to her shores, went back to work with gusto, and soon a wave of prosperity and self-renewing optimism swept through the land. William Jennings Bryan spoke Populist cant out of one side of his mouth as he rode the campaign trail in 1896, but a majority preferred the philosophy of McKinley's front-porch campaign, which emphasized more for everybody. The Republican view of human nature won the day. The middle class, which included the skilled workers and affluent farmers (in both cases they were the ones who voted) wanted their youthful industries and expanding farm frontiers protected by the tariff and they wanted "good hard mun," as one Swede put it, in the form of the honest gold dollar. They got both, most notably the Gold Standard Act of 1900, which put the nation, for the first time, on the same mon-

ometallic gold standard with which Great Britain ruled the world of
finance. Industrialists, at first fearing the impact of Teddy Roosevelt's
"splendid little war" in Cuba, soon found that wars did not invariably
dislocate trade and industry. The nation as a whole proudly noted that
North and South had once more fought side by side, and, whatever it
was that we had won, at least we had won. The nation was poised for
greatness in nearly every department of human endeavor, and the people knew it.

McKinleyan prosperity meant good times for everybody, but especially for those enterprises with large fixed costs that don't vary much
with the volume of business done, like the railroads. Indeed they were
inundated with unparalleled volumes of freight and hordes of travelers
who seemed about to jostle each other off obsolete depot platforms.
Profits flowed richly. American railroads had "gone through the fire"
of hard times, as James J. Hill had predicted ten years before and, to
show that sweet are the uses of adversity, had been put through a
wringer of corporate reorganization that did not stop until control of
the important lines that carried most of the traffic was centralized in
some six recognizable systems or "communities of interest." The railroad leaders of this movement had been men like Hill and Harriman,
vigorous competitors for railroad ascendancy in the far West; the aging
Collis P. Huntington of the Southern Pacific; the opportunistic Moore-
Reid interests (who, it would be seen, should have stuck to their cookie,
barbed wire, and tin-plate adventures); and, less well known, Samuel
Spencer, the professional manager who was putting the South back in
the railroad business. Playing a leading role also were the financiers,
who worked smoothly with the railroaders. Among them, J. P. Morgan,
at least, became a household name along with the "barons" of the rails.

How long it would be before railroad leaders would be confident
that their new, highly centralized system had jelled hard enough to
withstand the scrutiny of public opinion, sensitive as Americans had
become to the threat of the "trusts," no one had any idea. But after two
decades of bitter cutthroat rate competition and duplication of rail lines
by individualistically oriented railroad corporations (the *Official-
Railway Guide* in 1890 teems with corporate names you have never
heard of) railroad men had something that worked. No doubt about it.
Listen to the awestruck editor of the *Commercial & Financial Chronicle*,
business bible of Wall Street: "The important systems in the country
are few now, and their security holders . . . exercise a greater influence
in policy than [before]. . . . Freight is abundant . . . the roads are getting all they can carry. . . . All accounts agree that the tariff rates are
being maintained. A Western shipper is quoted in the papers as saying
that he had contracted for the shipment of five million bushels of grain
to the seaboard, and for the first time in years had been obliged to pay
the quoted tariff charges."

For the first time, the railroad *system* began to be run with an eye to efficiency. Very little mileage was abandoned in those days—and a good thing, too, for a branch that was redundant in 1898 very often was vital by 1915. Spite-line building virtually stopped, however, and freight was judiciously routed to take advantage of existing trains rather than increasing train movements unnecessarily. The abundant traffic insured that facilities all along the line would be more fully utilized than ever before. The new locomotives coming on line were put to good use and soon the stylish ten-wheelers that were the pride of the 1890s began to look tiny alongside the fleet Pacifics and powerful Mallets. Railroad workers rejoiced in good steady work for all. If long hours of overtime wore them out, and the number of men who suffered injuries grew, as trains threaded their way over crowded mainlines that were undergoing some kind of repair or rebuilding every few miles, that was all in a day's work.

Then the "basic economic magnitudes," as economists call such measures as interest rates and price levels, took over. While the mindless socialist "thinkers" who multiplied in these good times preached the inability of capitalism to find new investment opportunities for its ungodly profits, events in the real world proved them dead wrong. Railroading was just one of at least a half dozen industries that were entering dramatic growth phases—for example, electric light and power, chemicals, automobiles, and the first generation of domestic appliances—and they all demanded huge volumes of fresh capital. Interest rates went up sharply, and Americans obediently continued the high saving rate of the nineteenth century, especially as the dream of owning one's own home became a reality for many in the course of the biggest building boom up to that time. The market price of bonds that bore 3 percent coupons from the 1880s and 1890s sagged, while investment bankers hired platoons of Princeton and Yale men to sell unheard of volumes of new issues bearing 6 percent.

The thirty-year decline in prices, which has deluded myopic modern economists into calling the hard-working years of the 1870s, 1880s, and 1890s one long depression, came to an abrupt end. Double-digit inflation marked the first several years of the Brave New Century, and the long-term movement continued to 1930. The men, even the sloppy workers among them, had plenty of work, and wages started going up. But prices, which had sometimes seemed to go down faster than wages in the "good old days" (at least in the view of those who paid wages), now seemed to go up faster. Jim Hill could grumble that HCL (High Cost of Living) should be read, "Cost of High Living." Maybe more parlors did have pianos or even one of the new Victrolas in the place of honor, but necessities were what mattered, and up their prices went. What would labor do? Little, for now. The way the wind blew would be determined by the railroad industry, and it was not long in shifting course. In 1902 tongues wagged in Wall Street at the news that the mighty Pennsylvania Railroad had voluntarily, and under no pressure at all from the men, upped wages of its hundred thousand employees by 10 percent. "We have more business than we can handle and can't see our way out of that difficulty unless we keep our men loyal to the company and help them while they help us," said President Alexander J. Cassatt, one of the best operating railroad executives America ever produced. Besides, he might have added, we can certainly afford it!

"The Perils of Prosperity"

Chroniclers of the early years of the twentieth century have emphasized the new problems that an almost runaway prosperity posed for this fast-growing young nation that was about to take its place among the leaders of the western world. It turned out that there were even more opportunities to go wrong, economically and politically, during the flush times than in hard. But this realization came only gradually. The railroads found the last years of the old century and the first of the new to be the best of all possible times. A nationwide system of transportation, claiming virtually all inland passenger and freight movement as its province, and suffering for twenty-five years from excessive and poorly coordinated route mileage, enjoyed a sunburst of profit as the new prosperity flowed onto underutilized tracks.

The men leaped to their posts on the engines and cars, in the roundhouses and yards, and in the great rooms of clerks who kept track of the cars and their waybills. Soon every man with any experience in building and repairing freight cars, passenger coaches, and locomotives was working hard to keep enough rolling stock in good order to carry the loads. Superintendents of maintenance-of-way scoured the flophouses of cities and the general stores of the hinterland for men to work at keeping the thin nineteenth-century rails in condition to carry the burden of more and more train movements, while superintendents of motive power, deep in conference with representatives of the booming locomotive manufacturers, pored over plans for more powerful and much heavier locomotives to haul longer trains of heavier cars that no amount of patching of the old plant would accommodate. Railroad shops were enlarged, and enlarged again, as the lines resourcefully built on their own account more and more of their motive power and cars. By 1901 the high-density mainlines were at capacity, while many a money-losing branch line, built merely to claim territory, fended off bitter complaints about poor service from shippers who plied them with freight. That most regal of railroad corporations, the Vanderbilts' New York Central, found itself unable to meet the demands of thousands of farmers, merchants, and manufacturers throughout the booming Empire State; as a result it caught living hell from critics ranging from Governor Charles Evans Hughes to an army of newspaper cartoonists whose efforts amused and fanned the indignation of millions.

No one who knew the history of American railroading in 1900 believed that the system was complete. A healthy railroad is never finished. The very world of industry and urban areas that the railroads had done more than any other force to create would have ensured that fact, even if the first lines had been built for the ages, which they most certainly had not. Great trunk lines like the Pennsylvania and the New York Central had already been rebuilt a couple of times by 1900 and were about to be rebuilt again. Indeed, virtually every stretch of track in the nation that carried important traffic would be straightened, flattened, tunneled, bridged, embanked, and ultimately double-tracked— or so it seemed at the time. As that was going on, harried financiers could no longer look the other way when knowledgeable operating executives harped on the pitiful inadequacy of terminal facilities. This meant not merely freight yards and passenger depots along the route, but especially maritime terminals at the big east coast ports, where a booming foreign trade had engulfed the skimpy existing facilities.

The heavy, steady flow of expenditures by railroads in new plant and equipment, financed more and more from retained earnings, was keyed to the rate of economic growth enjoyed by America in these early years of the twentieth century. The railroads are the first example of the modern principle of economic growth financed by retained earnings on a large scale. The phenomenon has existed on a small scale since the first bourgeois businessman set up shop in some medieval town, and in fact it is usually the sole basis for success among small merchants facing a growing market for their wares. It was the chief factor in the remarkable growth of Standard Oil, especially in the 1880s, when Rockefeller and associates routinely plowed 40 percent of net profits back into the business in the form of expanded and improved facilities, better transportation, and—most familiar to modern business executives—"research and development," which continually improved the product, made it safer, and lowered its cost. It is the one best source of higher wages and better working conditions, as the petroleum industry and others that have remained effectively masters in their own houses, can attest. Withal, the phenomenon seems to have remained beyond the understanding of historians, politicians, and the general public.

The railroads had discovered early in their history that since stocks amounted to little more than poker chips in the great game of railroads, and bonds could be issued only where some basis in "real" property could be claimed as collateral, something else had to be found to finance such ephemeral magnitudes as present and expected future earning power. Indeed, the very existence of any such values was often cynically dismissed as "blue sky." But no one could quarrel with the retention of "excess" profits above dividend requirements, certainly not Louis Brandeis, who complained that the Louisville & Nashville Railroad was paying out in extra dividends money that should be retained for betterments. (Ironically, Brandeis failed to see that those extra dividends were paid in stock while the money remained in the treasury for improvement of the system.) As long as the railroads were free to make just as much money as good service and a fair rate schedule could produce, they could earn most of the money to keep the system healthy and growing. And at such time as profits were stunted or stinted for any reason, high-cost financing would be resorted to, growth would ultimately stop, and railroad investments would lose value. Beyond that point would lie government ownership, in some form or other, and the bill for the deficit would go to the taxpayer. No one had any idea early in the century that any such outcome could ever conceivably flow from public policy. They would find out, however, if they lived long enough.

The American railroad system was an antique in 1890, but by 1910 it had attained substantially its modern outward form. Improvements over the next thirty years, notably the diesel locomotive, more productive rolling stock, sophisticated signaling and instrumentation, and vastly improved rights of way, continued to be made but that is another story. In the beautiful era, as the French call the first fifteen years of the new century, and on which Americans have fastened the dowdy and misleading label "Progressive," Americans clasped their railroads to their breasts.

As we have already seen, America's "first big business" remained the nation's outstanding growth industry, too, and the dream job of tens of thousands of youngsters. Its trains were the best in the world, as European railroad experts would assure us. Its freight trains were longer, with heavier, better-built cars that were more efficient in handling cargo and were hauled by more powerful locomotives. Its passenger trains were the talk of the nation and of the world where the traffic existed to support them (and hardly worth mentioning where it did not). A nation that occupied great expanses of the earth's surface, and consequently required long train trips, sometimes of several days' duration, and which was young, healthy, and wealthy, could be expected to have great passenger trains. The most fabled of them ran between the great eastern seaboard cities and its burgeoning Second City. Chicago did not mind the term, for when the *Twentieth Century Limited* began its reign as queen of the nation's passenger train fleet in 1901, the big town on the big lake was still thirty-two years short of its centennial.

Consolidation into a few railroad systems speeded up the long-standing practice of assembling through routes between major cities. In the new century full-fledged through service on the eastern seaboard, from Portland, Maine, and Boston in the north to Miami and even Key West (over Henry M. Flagler's "railroad that went to sea") became the wonder of the railroad world. At the end of the 1880s no rails ran down the east coast south of Daytona Beach, and only small villages like Titusville, Cocoa, Rockledge, and Melbourne, dotted the shoreline where today millions live and one of America's most exciting tourist attractions, the Kennedy Space Center at Cape Canaveral, rises incongruously from the beach. By the 1920s, through trains also ran in winter from Chicago to the new playgrounds, and through Pullmans from other midwestern cities. Flagler, who had made it big in Standard Oil as Rockefeller's number two man, had become bored in his Palm Beach palazzo and built the Florida East Coast Railroad, a superbly engineered double-track line with hardly a curve worthy of the name between Jacksonville and Miami, which it reached in 1896.

Other lines built down the Florida peninsula and the state grew, stimulated excessively in the 1920s by real-estate developers until the inevitable grand "bust" left huge concrete slabs and paved streets to weather for twenty years in the salt air. After World War II a more sensible period of development began, and big plush hotels for the millions were built, with air conditioning that made them habitable in the hot, humid summers at greatly reduced off-season rates. In 1935 the causeway that had taken Flagler's pride into Key West was swept away by the great hurricane and converted into a highway. By the 1970s one Amtrak passenger train a day crept down the former Seaboard Airline Railroad's track into Miami, with a branch to Tampa and St. Petersburg. Meanwhile the Florida East Coast Railroad fought an intransigent union to a standstill, took up one of its two mainline tracks, and converted the other into one of the best engineered and signaled freight railroads in the nation. Today it hauls train after train of high-rated merchandise freight, including new automobiles by the thousands, but no passengers. In 1989 the FEC became one of only two American railroads officially to reach the ideal goal of a fair return on its capital investment (as defined by the government), the other being Norfolk Southern.

For speed, scenery, and a fabled land at the end of the tracks, nothing could touch the transcontinental trains that became the epitome of luxury long-distance travel once the installation of air conditioning made travel across the Mojave desert bearable. As the twentieth century neared its end, a large part of the budget of Amtrak, the National Rail Passenger Corporation created to keep America in the business of hauling people by rail, was devoted to four transcontinental services. They were the successors to the *Empire Builder*, on the old Great Northern, now Burlington Northern, from Chicago to Seattle and Portland, Oregon; to the *California Zephyr*, from Chicago to San Francisco over several lines; to the *Chiefs*, between Chicago and Los Angeles over the Santa Fe; and to the *Sunset Limited*, from New Orleans to Los Angeles. The future growth of rail passenger travel in America lies, however, in links between city pairs no more than two or three hundred miles apart. Difficult problems of ultra-high-speed ground transportation remain to be solved, mostly of a technological nature, before long-distance ground travel at speeds well over two hundred miles an hour will be possible. When, and if, these links are built, the traditional routes will be more valuable than ever as they bend, uninterrupted, to their great task of carrying the people's burden to market.

American railroad leaders in the Progressive era were well aware of the perils of prosperity, and they diligently "tread the turning mill" of serving the public, hopefully not into oblivion. They were not inclined to borrow trouble, which after all could come from any one of a number of directions. Whether the great new prosperity would last long enough for the stunning investments that were being made in a dozen industries besides railroads to pay off was not a question to be asked aloud in that optimistic era. Not many railroad executives had the time or the inclination to be public voices for the industry, but there were some. James J. Hill, always good for a quotable quote, spoke darkly of the need for five billion dollars—a huge sum in the early twentieth century—in fresh capital investment beyond what was already going into the system. Samuel Spencer of the Southern, and the public-minded men who succeeded him after his untimely death, and Edward P. Ripley of the reborn Santa Fe worried aloud about the booby traps that lay hidden in seemingly constructive demands for government regulation of railroads. Daniel Willard rose to the top in the hierarchy of the Baltimore & Ohio once it reappeared, fresh from the bath of receivership, refinanced, and rebuilt, as a major factor on the railroad scene, and was the *de facto* spokesman for the industry for the first quarter of the century.

Optimism, indispensable to the entrepreneur, remained nevertheless the order of the day. Much of it stemmed from the new "communities of interests"—something more than traffic agreements but less than formal corporate consolidation—that the industry had instituted, led by Alexander Cassatt, of the Pennsylvania Railroad, who had tucked the eastern coal roads under the mothering wing of the "standard railroad of the world." As long as it was a matter of J. P. and all the little Morgans to the rescue of insolvent roads, fine. But with the knockdown, drag-out fight between Harriman and Hill for control of the Burlington and the two northern transcontinentals that owned it—which had nearly bankrupted half of the brokers on Wall Street—and the formation of the mammoth Northern Securities holding company, these men who symbolized modern railroading may well have blown the fuse of public tolerance. "Monopoly" was always an effective battle cry in American politics. Great power, no matter how greatly used, was somehow inconsistent with the idea that the people rule. Any psychologist knows that the weak feel better in the presence of the weak, at least when skies are clear. Into this situation Teddy Roosevelt, "his accidency," who wanted the presidential nomination in the worst way, seemed about to jump. In that case, the very structure of the railroad industry would be in jeopardy and the Sherman Antitrust Act, heretofore not applied to holding companies, would slip its leash.

The dead hand of government regulation of railroad traffic practices seemed to be stirring again before the befuddled ICC had had an opportunity to demonstrate the virtues of the Hepburn Act of 1906, which had given it the power to set specific maximum rates upon complaint by shippers. The Act had not given the ICC the power to stop discrimination in rate-making as between the short haul and the long haul—truth to tell, the ICC knew the practice was generic to railroading and advised Congress to reject all amendments to provide the power. The old burr under the saddle—personal discrimination between shippers by rebates—had been brought under control easily once railroads had all the business they could handle, but the overwhelming importance of big shippers in the totality of freight business worried traffic men, who knew they had to give the big boys special services like private sidings and freight car shunting on call.

It was nothing but one of the oldest truths in business working itself out, that is, that the bigger the customer, the less he pays per unit or the more service he gets, but Americans were not eager to see it applied to the railroads, which belonged to all the citizens equally. Moreover, politicians were beginning to preach that any blacksmith could grow up to be as big as U.S. Steel as long as he had a level playing field. And then there was small-town America, stuck in the boondocks, originating proportionately less and less freight, and served by a single line. The towns demanded rates proportional to those of the cities farther down the line. It was a situation that could only grow more acute, and for which no easy solution presented itself.

It was not rebating, nor free services to big shippers, nor yet even the plight of small towns feeling the cold wind of economic obsolescence, that would bring matters to a head. It was the inflation of the era, and what to do about the "general level" of railroad rates, which hardly anyone had ever thought in terms of before. More and more railroad men, and especially their bankers, who had to raise the funds, began to speak publicly about the problem. The rising costs of everything the railroads bought and the gathering clouds on the labor horizon emboldened them. Rates by the middle of the first decade of the wonder century were not much above the level they had sunk to by the end of the 1890s depression, and *that* level was far below that of 1873 when the long slide began. Some relief was called for. George Perkins, one of J. P. Morgan's brightest lieutenants, having helped to hold financial fingers in the dike during the short, sharp recession of 1907, explained the situation to his colleagues in the language of the era. The age of financing railroads by means of mortgage bonds secured by a lien on a segment of "real" property was over. The railroads would have to be permitted to *earn* the money they needed.

In modern jargon, extensive development was ending, and intensive development accelerating. The fruits of the entrepreneurial innovations the railroads had been making had to be realized, by allowing them to keep at least some of the very real savings they were achieving in carrying the people and their burdens to market. True, but who would put the bell on the cat? The railroads had never attempted or even considered concerted action to raise railroad rates, apart from periodic efforts to enforce pooling contracts, and they probably would have been severely dealt with if they had. Now, that was what they had to do, and they had a good case. But good cases don't always win in a bad old world, for truth, as Lowell said, is ever on the scaffold and wrong always on the throne. It was not whether it was a good case, but whether what they wanted to do was good politics.

The perilous path of prosperity was visible for only a few yards ahead of railroad men but had to be trod. Forward to meet the experiment perilous they stumbled. At least they were masters in their own house, and a busy, affluent, happily materialistic nation would surely let them run their own show as freely as the rest of the nation ran its own. Why, there were still men and women alive in America who could remember when there were no railroads and had experienced the big difference they had made in American life. The nation was staying young, and so was its most important servant. But the nagging inflation was something new, and few understood what was happening to them, whether businessmen, professionals, or politicians. They knew something had to be done about it, and they thought they knew where to start. The railroads were entering a long, dark tunnel. They would not emerge for seventy years.

Economic Problems Become Political Issues

Long before the brave new world of the twentieth century had dawned, in the stern atmosphere of the early 1880s, the leading financial editor in the country, puzzled as to how the nation might achieve the railroad rate stability that railroad men had failed to supply, was dubious about turning to the sovereign power of government for a practical solution. "The objection to any new government undertakings is understood," he wrote. Indeed it was understood by a generation that still remembered vividly the dismal record of the government in conducting the largest enterprise Americans had seen up to that time—the Civil War effort—and the gross corruption that was the chief outcome of the effort to reconstruct the South on literal civil rights terms.

No doctrinaire belief in "laissez faire" was behind the general attitude, although historians have assumed that nineteenth-century businessmen were ardent adherents of Herbert Spencer's Social Darwinism and Adam Smith's economic liberalism. In fact, few businessmen or other Americans had ever heard of these oft-quoted and seldom read thinkers. The concept of a Washington whose mucky real estate would become the site of block after block of massive government buildings, filled with thousands of specialists on every conceivable aspect of

Figure 14.1 "The Senatorial Round-House" was the title the editor of *Harper's Weekly* gave this cartoon by Thomas Nast in 1886, illustrating what most Americans believed, that politicians were in the pay of the railroad corporations. Railroad men's murmurs that "the hand that took the bribe was generally outstretched before it was offered," elicited only sneers, then and now. The idea that if American politics was rotten it was because it was corrupted by even more rotten businessmen still appeals mightily to writers of textbooks.

human life, and some inconceivable ones as well, was a generation in the future. It was the creation of the so-called Progressive movement, so idealistic in theory and so devastatingly self-serving of politicians and special interests alike in practice. It was the factor that destroyed the wholesome environment in which America's railroads were facing the perils of prosperity. It was on the railroads that these philosophies of government intervention in business were carried farthest in the direction of ultimate disaster.

Theodore Roosevelt's controversialism and devotion to political expediency, so different from McKinley's emphasis on the national consensus, was the reason for it all, some have said. But there was more to it than one portly, macho little man's ambition to be elected president in his own right could explain. Roosevelt was one of the really great politicians and, like that other fine politico, Abraham Lincoln, had an excellent mind that could see the issues as plainly as anyone. The fact is that the Republican party was coming apart at the seams that had been hastily stitched in the 1850s to hold eastern Whigs and western Free Soil Democrats, and thereby the Union, together in the coming conflict. Young western politicians, soon to be praised or damned as "Insurgents" and "sons of the wild jackass," were fretting at the bottom of the congressional seniority ladder. They revolted against the autocratic rule of eastern "stand-patters."

Soon Republican leaders in the Senate, led by Nelson Aldrich of Rhode Island and Stephen B. Elkins of West Virginia, were smarting under the tirades of western politicos like Robert M. La Follette of Wisconsin, Albert Baird Cummins and Jonathan P. Dolliver of Iowa, Benjamin Bristow of Kansas, and William E. Borah of Idaho. T.R. went to work to create a new consensus, built around the concept of an America reaching out to the world, while settling its own domestic differences with sweet reasonableness through the wisdom of well-educated, selfless men serving on commissions and putting to work the new economic knowledge that the booming colleges and universities were imparting. Politicians who caught on to the new approach, which put government in the middle of things as a party at interest, began to call these philosopher-kings "Progressives"; Jim Hill called them "college tack-head philosophers," and a sampling of the effusions from both the storied halls of New England colleges and the raw new academies of the Midwest would seem to bear Hill out. To be sure, T.R. and Progressivism won, but the railroads and, in the end, the nation, lost.

The "railroad problem" was a natural for these men who had searched so frantically for something to replace the tariff and the currency as causes "to go to the country with." Ultimately, the point at issue would be simply, who shall rule in America? Who shall tell consumers how much they must pay for a gallon of kerosene? Who, indeed, shall tell the storekeeper what freight rate he should have to pay to the railroad that brought his drum of kerosene to him regularly? In a republic, or even in a democracy for that matter, the ultimate sovereign power lies in the people, in whose behalf the statesmen are more than happy to act. Somehow, this was coming to mean that final decisions on such prosaic but vital matters as how much transportation to provide, what kind of transportation to offer, and how much to charge for it, could not be left to the railroad men.

Missing entirely from this blizzard of half-truths was any awareness of the moral role of the responsible party—the person or organization of persons who ultimately are judged by the results obtained. In a society that claimed to believe in enlightened self-interest disciplined by free competition, men who "put their money where their mouth is" (or their professional reputations, at any rate), and who must stand or fall by their policies, ought to have a chance to put their policies to the test. T.R., always the good sport, knew this. It was he who had warned the Interstate Commerce Commission, newly invested with rate-setting powers by the Hepburn Act of 1906, that they must act as an economic commission, searching in a professional manner for the unique rate that will best balance the interests of carrier and shipper, and not a sterile judicial body intent on delineating precedents and then passing the buck to a higher bench. But T.R. seems not to have realized that the men he was lecturing perceived their boss to be those people on Capitol Hill, not that man in the White House.

One thing the politicians lacked, as the first years of the new century revealed the need for new issues, was any real basis for believing that the people wanted them to go after the railroads. Now, in the old Progressive interpretation of American history, two propositions were virtually revealed wisdom. One is that at the turn of the century American railroads were still perpetrating on a helpless society the same old "abuses" that had incensed Americans of the late nineteenth century. The other was that by 1905 Americans had joined in a mighty ground swell of public indignation that swept aside the old laissez-faire view of economic society and produced well-conceived and effective regulatory laws, equitably and successfully enforced. The first proposition holds very little water; the second, none at all.

Did the discontent that still showed through the prosperity of these years and the stability which railroads had achieved in rate-making add up to a nationwide ground swell of indignation against the railroads after 1900? Not at all. By this time, in fact, Francis Beattie Thurber, who had led the New York merchants' attack on railroads in the New York State Hepburn Committee hearings twenty-five years earlier, had come to the railroads' side, as had Texan John H. Reagan, who had been one of the staunchest enemies of pooling. Thurber's role as Naderesque reformer had been taken by an opportunist by the name of Edward Bacon, who ran something called the Interstate Commerce Law Convention that was lobbying for a law to give the commission power to set specific maximum rates upon appeal from a discontented shipper. Bacon put his faith in the inflation which was already brandishing the club of antitrust at Standard Oil. (A cartoon of the period showed John D. Rockefeller as a crafty New England country store proprietor, sitting under a sign saying, "Oil has riz; somebody must pay.") It did not work, because everybody was too busy filling orders and raising their own prices or clocking overtime pay on the production line. Until Bacon put his faith in the skill of American political demagogues, he did not make much headway.

Bacon promoted conventions of persons interested in amendments to the ICC Act of 1887, under his direction. He had no trouble attracting the kind of cranks who had been going to such meetings since the days of the old National Labor Union in the 1860s, and farmers, fatally attracted as usual by half-baked philosophies, were much in evidence. The trouble was he could not get shippers to send representatives; when they finally did, he got wind just in time that they intended to vote against giving the ICC the power to set specific maximum rates. Bacon pushed through a resolution requiring a proamendment loyalty oath for admission to the convention and proceeded to pack the hall with proamendment delegates who would register as shippers. Thus was the fight for Progressive railroad regulation launched on the low tide of American democracy.

Bacon was a nobody, but he was noisy and he spoke in terms that made good copy for the booming newspapers and magazines of this remarkable era. The statesmen of the Insurgency, in contrast to Bacon, had what T.R. had called a "bully pulpit" in the halls of Congress. They had had good luck with the antirailroad issue in their home states, and when they saw that its potential appeal was much broader, they adopted it. They were acutely aware that a new class of citizen was growing up in America, better educated in the advancing public schools and raising themselves by means of correspondence courses from the shop to the office. They were grist for the Insurgents' mill wherever they lived, and, soon, following the lead of these men from the land of the alfalfa and the mariposa lily came to be synonymous with being a good citizen. Hardly a quiet Sunday went by without one of the magazines of the period offering them food for thought on the subject of regulating the railroads.

Railroad men's position on regulation, at least in the mild form instituted by the Act of 1906, was largely one of trying to maintain the flexibility of rates. (Very few Americans outside traffic men's offices understood that rates could not be established for all time but had to vary with a host of economic factors.) Railroad men had continued to support, if not very vigorously, others' efforts to regain for them the right to pool freights and to come together to establish uniform tariffs, and they had been willing to submit their joint policies to review and approval by the ICC. They were willing to submit to almost any order of the ICC as long as they were assured of the right to challenge it *de novo* in the courts. That is to say, some of the biggest among them were willing. In the hinterland, a different view prevailed, and a committee of railroad executives was organized under Samuel Spencer. Horrified at the Pennsylvania Railroad's apparently favorable policy towards strengthening the ICC, the committee carried out a sadly misbegotten campaign aimed primarily at country newspaper editors to stop the regulatory movement. In the 1960s, leaders of the short-lived New Left movement in American history were devoted to debunking all earlier economic reform movements in the United States as one kind of capitalistic plot or another. One adherent claimed to have proved that the railroads cultivated a stronger ICC because they intended to "capture" it, and succeeded in doing so. He made an especially good thing for himself of this theory, but even with the help of Theodore Roosevelt he could not prove that the Pennsylvania or any other railroad was willing to forego judicial review. Railroad men in the Progressive era looked to the tough old American federal judiciary as the sole remaining bulwark against the tyranny of bureaucracy.

But they were wrong even on that score. The reason the Act of 1906 does not provide for judicial review of the orders of the commission (except by inference on the questions of constitutionality and due process) is that such a provision would have been repugnant to the Constitution. Congress has the power to regulate interstate commerce, and this most elastic of the economic powers of the Constitution unquestionably covers the setting of maximum railroad rates. Congress has the power to delegate this to a commission established by it for that purpose. The substantive orders of such a commission are beyond the reach of courts or the executive branch. This is what is meant by "independent regulatory commission." The Act of 1906 did so delegate the powers of Congress. The principle, understandably, was not well or widely understood at the time. But the redoubtable Victor Morawetz could have saved the railroad men much time and money in subsequent court tests of the Hepburn Act. In 1905 he had told the Senate Committee on Interstate Commerce, in its hearings on a sheaf of bills seeking to "regulate" the railroads in one way or another, that the commission's mandate to assume the rate-making power would have to be all or nothing. (The Act of 1887 had not delegated any such rate-making power, and in the 1890s the Supreme Court had had no choice but to declare the ICC's rate orders null and void. The almost unanimous view of American historians since then—in countless books, articles, and textbooks—that this is evidence that the Supreme Court had a strong "conservative" bias in the late nineteenth century is insupportable and really ought to be abandoned, or at least modified to this extent.) Victor Morawetz saw clearly that the railroads would not be able to appeal rate orders. "Congress can not vest in the courts power to fix future rates," he said, "or to consider and pass upon the wisdom or policy of the Commission in prescribing a particular rate."

It's all politics. The years from 1903 to 1906 had impressed officeholders and office seekers alike with the great value of an antirailroad stance in American politics. Thus when the railroads, deeply worried by 1908 by inflation's erosion of their earnings, proposed putting into effect a jointly-arrived-at, virtually nominal increase in railroad rates, the politicians came down hard on them. President Roosevelt had been so shaken by the sharp depression of 1907 that he had taken to calling business leaders "malefactors of great wealth," guilty without trial of bringing on the panic, presumably for the chief purpose of derailing his onward-and-upward administration. He convinced George Perkins, J. P. Morgan's righthand man, who had gone to the White House to take the temperature of the political water, that an election year was no time to raise railroad rates, especially when the unspeakable alternative to a Republican victory was William Jennings Bryan, running for the third and last time.

What Americans got in the election of 1908, however, was hardly any better. By 1910, the railroads, despairing like almost everybody else of ascertaining what economic policy President William Howard Taft meant to follow (Jim Hill called him "a plate of mush"), went ahead with their joint 10 percent increase. They were met "at the pass" by the stalwart Insurgents, more and more of whom were calling themselves Progressives and suggesting darkly that perhaps a new party was needed. The railroads never got their general increase, save for a few paltry adjustments, until 1918, when the government, having taken over the railroads for the duration of the war, ignored the ICC. Meanwhile the railroads had spent vast sums on lawyers to make repeated charges against the ICC's impenetrable walls. What they got for their efforts was the Mann-Elkins Act (1910), the first measure ever adopted by the federal government to establish *de facto* price ceilings on a single industry in peacetime and in the midst of a long-term upward trend in prices.

The situation deteriorated rapidly after that. More and more of the railroads' cash flowed out in rising prices and wages, while less and less flowed in in the way of revenue growth. A huge fixed plant, fixed prices received, rising wages and materials prices, and declining volume in the recession that began in 1913 and continued until the end of 1914 was a combination that would have spelled doom for any enterprise. The railroads were sinking into bankruptcy as 1913's recession greeted the presidency of Woodrow Wilson, who had declared war against all forms of bigness in business during the campaign. (He had intended to make the race on the issue of lower tariffs—a dead issue that Democrats were loath to abandon—until a better manipulator of public opinion, Louis D. Brandeis, persuaded him otherwise.) It did not take Wilson long to see that the Mann-Elkins Act was going to wreck American transportation unless something was done, but, political scientist (actually, "professor of jurisprudence") that he was, he shrank from condemning an independent branch of government. To the politicians who admired their handiwork, the Act was anything but a mistake, or a failure of the American political system. It did just what it was supposed to do: slap a lid on railroad rates and keep it there. The men down at the barber shop heartily agreed. The steady rise in prices since 1897 had made everybody feel impotent in the face of the theft of a part of their pay envelopes. "Ya gotta start somewhere," was the thought, and the railroads were the most obvious place.

By 1917 the railroads that were still solvent had few profits to plow back. They were short of equipment, especially locomotives, and the stream of fresh capital for betterments had dried up. With America's entry in the war, eastbound freight swelled to record levels, and the railroads granted their leaders extraordinary powers to apportion freight over the several trunk lines that had any excess capacity left, and to dispatch men and materials bound overseas to alternative ports that were not yet blockaded. For their trouble they were threatened with criminal prosecution by the attorney general under the antitrust laws! This impasse, more than anything else, and the ICC's continuing refusal to grant rate relief, were the reasons the government took control of the railroads, and not any failure on the part of the railroads to perform their tasks. (This episode reveals that sometimes the much-put-upon businessman's best haven from a government agency is another government agency!) The U.S. Railroad Administration provided money for locomotives, pooled and apportioned freight, gave the men, who were leaving in droves to work in war plants, generous wage increases, and raised rates some 60 percent before the war was over. Meanwhile the ICC went into hibernation for the duration. It might well have stayed there, for in its thirty years it had contributed nothing to American transportation save its superb statistics-gathering facility, which was the work of its brilliant statistician, one of the first economic analysts of big business, Henry Carter Adams.

Under the terms of the government's takeover legislation, the railroads continued to be managed by the men who had been running them. ("Thank God," one of their ghosts may murmur.) As in the Civil War, the trains, yards, and dispatch towers were no place for second lieutenants or "bird" colonels, either, for that matter. (During that conflict, railroad engineering genius Henry Haupt had accepted the job of running the military railroads only on condition that the U.S. Army have no jurisdiction over him.) As to railroad economics in World War I, it may be supposed that at least the roads could breathe easily with Uncle Sam meeting all the bills. It did not quite work out that way. To be sure, government paid operating costs (raising rates to do so), acquired new locomotives and rolling stock, and paid a rental. But the carriers had to pay for the equipment later, and they got back a badly deteriorated railroad, which became the subject of long-drawn-out negotiations for damages. The labor market was tight during the war, and maintenance was badly neglected. Government agreed, but the compensation it was willing to pay after long and weary negotiations would not alone have sufficed to put the roads back in shape for the safe, comfortable, high-speed operation that Americans had come to expect. It is the consensus of most observers that America's railroads did not benefit largely from the heavy, but abruptly terminated, increase in traffic volume that the war brought. But at least it had removed the palsied hand of the ICC from the throttle long enough to get rate relief.

A heavy, steady volume of business is precisely what a business like the railroads needs. In this respect they are very much like the electric utilities companies that were growing so fast after 1920. Their physical facilities, too, have to be large enough to meet peak demand yet not so large as to create excess capacity that is such a drag on profitability. Any business needs to keep as large a percentage of its capacity at work, on the average, as it can, for capital is costly even if not used. "Use it or lose it" is the word. The electric companies faced a constantly growing demand, which they were far from meeting, as the government's shouldering of the job of electrifying America's farms proved in the 1930s. But at least they did not want for business, and the franchise system freed them from price-happy competition. Over the years, moreover, a major off-peak load developed in the form of air conditioning.

With the railroads after World War I, it was just the opposite. Congress wrestled for several years with the question of what to "do" with the railroads, but what it came up with, the Transportation Act of 1920 (Esch-Cummins), solved nothing. One thing the railroads did for the nation, however, was to demonstrate the emptiness of past threats of government ownership and operation of the railroads. Senators like Albert B. Cummins and Robert M. La Follette had never hesitated to growl "public ownership," whenever railroad men complained of the steady stream of punitive legislation before the war. The railroad brotherhoods had gone all out for public ownership of the railroads after the war. Their faithful servant, Franklin K. Lane, in charge of government wage policy during the war, had showered largess upon the men. Lane was an affable Washington State politician who had ridden the Progressive bandwagon through a term on the Interstate Commerce Commission onto President Wilson's cabinet as secretary of the interior. He was eased out of this post because he talked too much—a political talent not especially prized in wartime—and when it came to wage policy he learned quickly that there is no point in being stingy when any deficit can be defrayed at the point of a gun. Labor, having discovered in 1910 that to be on the railroads' side in a rate application was disastrous, concluded that it had to break the nexus between profits and wage rates and that the best way to do that would be to make profit extraneous. Such revealed sentiments brought men like Cummins to their senses, and they killed the Plumb plan to nationalize the railroads.

It is like shooting fish in a barrel to poke fun at the fatuities of past railroad regulation from the vantage point of the last decade of the century, but a few words about the valuation project and the recapture clause are unavoidable. One of the more dubious concepts that regulatory economists have advanced over the years is "fair return on fair

Figure 14.2 Three political architects of American railroad policy, constructive and otherwise, were (clockwise from upper left) Francis G. Newlands (1848–1917), U.S. senator from Nevada, about whom President Wilson, upon hearing that Newlands had dropped dead putting the finishing touches to legislation that would free the railroads from regulatory strictures for the duration of World War I, said, "He was not showy; he was useful"; Robert M. La Follette (1855–1925), U.S. senator from Wisconsin, was "showy." He recalls Louis D. Brandeis's remark in a different context: "The greatest dangers to liberty lurk in . . . men of zeal, well-meaning but without understanding"; and Harley O. Staggers, Sr. (1907–), chaired the House of Representatives' Committee on Interstate Commerce that approved the so-called Staggers Act (1981) which after 71 years restored rational decision making to railroad executives. (Newlands and La Follette—*Library of Congress*; Staggers—*West Virginia State Archives*)

replacement value." Find out how much the capitalists invested in the regulated enterprise, and hold rates down to a level that will give them some statutory maximum rate of return. Problems abound when this approach is applied to a franchised monopoly, like a telephone or electric utility. Applied to the railroads, which were always far more competitive than critics have been willing to admit, the system became a costly mistake. In 1913, as a first step in introducing the scientific "fair return" basis for rate-making, Congress passed the Valuation Act, which was to find out just how much the railroads—whose securities were believed to be largely "water"—really had invested in their physical plants, at a depreciated replacement value. It seemed a simple enough task at the time, and a beautifully promising one, so poor old Charles A. Prouty, veteran commissioner, allowed himself to be persuaded into leaving the panel and heading the valuation agency. Fifteen years and several hundred million dollars later, they were still at it. Much of the cost had devolved upon the railroads themselves which, in order to prevent mayhem to their own property figures, felt obliged to employ their own corps of evaluators to work alongside the government men. Adding it all up, the study confirmed the railroads' own 1913 figures as to the worth of the system.

Except to take up incredible amounts of space on library shelves, the reports of the valuation agency never served any visible purpose. It seems to have escaped everybody's notice that rates can not be set for individual railroads when they are in direct competition with each other. All rates for the same service between the same points must be identical. Even those who scream "collusion!" at any sign of cooperation between railroad men have learned that. At any given rate, the New York Central was going to net more return from a ton of freight carried from New York to Chicago than the Erie or the B. & O., or even, for that matter, the Pennsylvania. God himself could not change that; in fact, He was at the bottom of it. What to do? The answer, in the Act of 1920, was to identify the more efficient lines (those with the lowest inherent operating costs), compute their "excess" profits over their statutory maximum rate of return, and then take some of this profit from them periodically to give it to the weak sisters—and Charles Darwin be damned. This was actually done for several years in the 1920s, to loud squawks from the injured parties, but when the Great Depression struck, Congress hastened to lift this latest cross from the back of American railroads.

Adding Rubber-Tired Insult to Political Injury

The Act of 1920 meanwhile gave railroad men powers they had not needed for years; for example, the power to pool freights and the right to consolidate into a few "balanced" systems. There was little interest in consolidation as prosperity continued to offer hope for the future, at least not in some consolidation plan worked out by self-styled "experts." But the Act did nothing to help the industry arm itself against competition from a new, publicly subsidized industry that was just beginning to develop: over-the-road trucking. (Trucking was new in the sense that the heavy-duty pneumatic tire, powerful and dependable gasoline engines, and a national system of all-weather highways, built at public expense, were new; subsidized, in that truckers paid in license fees and taxes for only a small portion of its real cost, a situation that exists to this day; and sweated, in that it is a classic form of self-employment of men ill suited for closely supervised work, who must work illegally long hours and drive at illegal speeds to pay for their or their employers' increasingly expensive rigs.) There is no clean-cut date on which one can say that the motor truck began to be a serious competitor of the railroads, but the opening of the Holland Tunnel, the first vehicular crossing of the Hudson River south of Albany, in the 1920s, is as good as any. This remarkable engineering achievement, made possible by techniques learned slowly over the years, and preceded by the Pennsylvania Railroad's tunnels under the Hudson and East Rivers, opened New York City, and notably Manhattan, to vehicular traffic from the west, thus completing a through route from New England to the South. The city has never been the same since.

The emergence of the over-the-road trucking industry, notwithstanding its antisocial character in some respects down to the present time, could have been an unalloyed blessing to the American transportation system. Trucking was more flexible than railroads, meaning that it could go not only where railroads did not go directly—that is, to the farmer's gate—but where they went only at the cost of perennially money-losing, high-cost branch lines. An intelligent blending of this small-load, short-distance, flexible service haulage with railroad service would have been a great triumph of American transportation leadership. Unfortunately there was little of that remaining in the American railroad industry after 1920, as the railroads were preoccupied with adjusting to their new second-class economic citizenship to which the events of the preceding fifteen years had unmistakably reduced them. "It is not thrift but profit that drives enterprise," John Maynard Keynes has said, and railroad men were simply not free to pursue profit freely by pricing their service intelligently. It makes no sense to look for enterprise in such a situation: mere survival is the goal. Note this 1983 exchange between the author of this book and the late Mr. Donald J. Russell, who retired in 1972 as chief executive of the Southern Pacific Railroad, after some fifty years of service:

THE AUTHOR: Mr. Russell, how was it that American railroads managed to continue to attract first-class executives under repressive government regulation?

MR. RUSSELL: Why, Mr. Martin,—I'm not sure we did.

Neither the railroad men nor the ICC commissioners of 1920 could quite believe that a disorganized horde of carters and draymen could

evolve into serious competition. Three factors proved critically important, however, during the next decade. One was the tariff schedules of
the period, especially for LCL, or less-than-carload freight (the truckers' specialty), which were traditionally based on the economic value
of the railroad's service and usually were far higher than what some
hungry owner of a truck would be delighted to get. Truck transport
would not be regulated at all until 1935.

Another factor was the ICC's determination to prevent a reemerg-
ence of nineteenth-century-style price competition in transportation,
and particularly to prevent the giving of special services to favored
shippers. The commission believed it was carrying out the spirit of the
Act of 1920, which among its redundancies was a clause giving the ICC
the power to set *minimum* rates, thus preventing the railroads from
reducing rates aggressively. During the rate hearings just before the
war, Louis Brandeis, riding high as the commission-appointed (and
paid) representative of "the public interest," had attacked the railroads
for doing special favors for their big customers (like shunting their boxcars and gondolas to where the shipper could get at them). No one had
learned better than the ICC the political power of that particular red
herring. Realizing that they could not cut their rates on LCL freight,
which would have done no more than reflect the inferiority of rail transportation to trucking for small shipments, they tried to combine rail
service with some form of door-to-door delivery service, at a rate equal
to what the truckers were getting, which was more and more likely to
be the railroads' bare terminal-to-terminal rate. In other words, the
railroads wanted to offer the same quality of less-than-carload freight
service to their customers, at no added delivery charge, as the trucks
could offer inherently.

The Pennsylvania Railroad, most notably, devised a locked, metal
container for this high-class freight, several of which could fit onto a
flat car, and they undertook to offload the containers onto a flatbed
truck and deliver it to the consignee's loading dock. The service caught
the fancy of many: the 1931 catalogue of Lionel electric trains proudly
featured a model replica of the flatcar with its green containers. But the
ICC, declaring this to be an extra service, ordered the railroad to
charge extra for it. The idea of the container, and later, piggyback
(truck trailer on flatcar) service, which other railroads were experimenting with, was smothered in its cradle, to be resurrected in happier
and more enlightened times. But LCL traffic, strictly defined, is dead
on the railroads and has been for at least twenty years. Indeed, the railroads, until intermodal service became a reality, had come to depend
almost entirely upon carload freight moving between industrial sidings,
which was all they could expect as long as the ICC continued to run
things.

The third factor that contributed to the truck menace was, ironically, the Great Depression. Carters and draymen, a class who for

eighty years had eked out a living (or, sometimes, made a very good one) handling freight between depots, shippers, and consignees, generally traded their horses and wagons for motor trucks in the 1920s. When the Depression struck, the quantity of freight piling up on the freight depot platforms shrank precipitately. So did the truckers' "variable costs," which is the economist's way of saying that they could take what intercity freight they could handle to wherever the shipper wanted it to go for any rate that would pay for the gas and oil and something for the driver, who was usually the owner. They swiftly became virtual couriers, offering twenty-four hour turnaround service between local mines and mills and cities fifty, one hundred, or more miles away, where mechanics patched up the shippers' worn-out machinery when it broke down and got them back in business. No railroad could do that.

Soon regularly scheduled runs were adopted, over well-defined routes. Shippers in locations with high-cost rail service to junction points and no low through rates meanwhile found they could dispatch their stuff by cheap truck service to nearby cities with cheap competitive railroad rates for the long haul. One young student in Little Rock, Arkansas, earning his room and board in 1939 by banging out motor freight waybills after classes, wondered why the shipments of Tuf-Nut work clothing from the factory just across the street, destined for towns in the Mississippi and Alabama cotton South, were always billed, "Prepaid to Memphis; Gulf, Mobile & Ohio Railroad (e.g.) from Memphis." He knows now. Sure, Tuf-Nut was meeting Memphis manufacturers' shipping costs, but why by truck as far as Memphis and then by rail? The Rock Island and Missouri Pacific Railroads might have tried for a lower rate to Memphis, but the ICC's well-established policy in the matter of intermodal competition made such an expensive game not worth the candle. The motor carrier's rate, of course, had been "grandfathered in" (that is, already existed) in 1935 when truck regulation began.

Industries that required regular supplies of dangerous explosives had always had a problem, since they could ill afford high railroad LCL rates for the small shipments, and sending it by courier on passenger trains was a serious federal offense. A lad who got hold of an adventure pulp magazine in the 1930s never forgot the really moving story of the unemployed man who, for the sake of his starving wife and children, bid low for the privilege of trucking a carboy of nitroglycerine over unpaved roads across the mountain to extinguish a burning oil well. (He made it.) Best of all he remembered the neighborhood girl whose father hauled dynamite through a picket line of angry strikers trying to unionize the pathetic marginal coal mines of northwest Arkansas, where even when the coal business was good, it was pretty bad. This man and his doughty wife made ends meet and raised two daughters by running, with the help of one full-time driver, a small trucking company over a hundred-mile run to Little Rock. Now dynamite is not much good without the blasting caps, which provide the concentrated shock that makes "this dear stuff," as the anarchists called it when it was invented in the nineteenth century, explode. The caps, of course, were never packed with the sticks of dynamite. In this anecdote, the truck, with driver and proprietor in the cab, met fierce resistance, with a fusillade of bullets striking the bed of the truck on which rested the wooden boxes stencilled plainly, "Hercules." "But where are the caps, dear?" cried his wife, who was there to meet the truck. "Right here, dear," replied her husband, as he disgorged them from his swollen cheeks. His mouth had turned out to be the only safe place he had found to hide the caps.

The trucks made steady inroads upon rail freight throughout the deceptively prosperous twenties and the Depression decade. The impact upon the dollar volume and profits of the railroads was an even more serious matter, for the trucks hit their big, clumsy rival right in the bread basket. They took the most lucrative business, which was the valuable merchandise freight that carried a high rate per ton and had not always been treated by the railroads with the respectful handling that it deserved. Meanwhile, the railroads were allowed to continue to carry the coal, iron ore, sand, and gravel that weighed so much and was worth so little per ton that during the heyday of the railroads in the nineteenth century they had often carried it for less than its bare out-of-pocket costs. Who would have carried it, then or later, if the railroads had not?

The railroads made the colossal mistake of demanding and, this time, getting rate increases as the Depression deepened, which only made the trucks look that much more attractive, and in 1935 the railroads successfully demanded that truck transportation be brought under regulation. This proved a boon to the trucks, for whereas they were no longer able to cut rates in a fight with each other for what traffic there was, they also discovered that their flexibility and accommodating service had become so appealing that they could charge the new, higher rates that the railroads posted and make some badly needed profits. That was not the half of it. Truck haulage of *unprocessed* agricultural products was exempted from rate regulation, which meant that they could not only undercut the railroads, but they could charge *more* than the railroads when traffic volume swelled beyond the railroads' capacity, as it did on at least one notable occasion. In the summer of 1973, for example, it was clear that only the golden harvests of the American Midwest and Great Plains stood between Eastern Europe and starvation. In one of those abrupt reversals of traditional traffic flows, a flood of food grains headed due east by rail, making for the lake ports of Duluth and Superior. As the winter that would shut off this cheapest form of transportation approached, the call for rail cars exceeded the supply. In came the trucks, which happily hauled grain east at rates substantially higher than the railroads were able to charge. Thus does politics make flapdoodle of the most beloved economic "laws."

Neither historians nor economists have fully grasped the most valuable lessons to be learned from the story of the selective displacement of rail transportation by motor trucks. The first is that history *is* logical, and every new way of performing the world's work is inevitably the outcome of countless previous human achievements on which the new methods rest. Civilizations grow eclectically. The present does not replace the past, for the past is contained in it. The trucks could not replace the railroads, if only because the heavy industry that made trucks possible and sustains them today depends upon heavy-duty transportation. Second, technology is only a part of the story, and not necessarily the most important part. Hateful as the word "subsidy" may be to the truckers, the fact remains that there are few technological innovations that rode in on such a cushion of implied subsidy as the intercity trucking industry. Just to get into the business without having to build your own right-of-way was boon enough to make truckers happy to pay a "user fee" in the form of licensing fees and fuel taxes, which amounted to much less than one-half of their direct contribution to the cost of building, operating, and maintaining the federal, state, and local highway systems. The succession of government agencies that have administered the U.S. highway program have published report after report attesting to this fact. To be sure, most people who play "wrinkle-fender" with big semitrailer rigs on the highways think that the truckers do indeed pay their way, since all they know is what the panoply of state licenses displayed on the ends of trucks purport to tell them.

When the Interstate highway system was built in the mid-1950s and early 1960s, it instantly conferred upon the truckers the power to run at much higher speeds for longer unbroken stretches. Intercity truck traffic boomed accordingly. The exploits of the "knights of the road" even produced a brief vogue for the romance of the trucker's life until the true human costs began to be apparent. "I sit here at my desk," said a small-town Arizona newspaper editor, "and look out at the Interstate, where the trucks go by day and night without even slowing down or their drivers, hunched over their hemorrhoids, looking right or left." The sweated industries have traditionally subsidized the American standard of living, and trucks are no exception. Self-employed truck drivers may think they are making money, and sometimes they are, but they had better check the declining condition of their equipment before they congratulate themselves. Wage-earning drivers make a fraction of what railroad operating employees get, which should tell us something about which mode has the greater economic productivity. At the same time, there is probably no other occupation than truck driving that better suits the sociological type that abhors "being tied down to a desk job" and so highly prizes at least the illusion of unsupervised work.

This discussion of the essential political nature of transportation laws should teach us, finally, that economics has little to do with the case. "How many divisions does the Pope have?" asked Joseph Stalin when someone told him that His Holiness severely disapproved of his human rights and religious policies. In the same way, economic decisions that have wandered into the maze of the American political process—which means more and more decisions that the American people ought to be making on their own merits—end up being made on the basis of how relatively painless they can be made to the voting public. Economic reality and political policy move along on parallel lines, seldom meeting except when the cure (free enterprise) is no longer considered more hateful than the "command economies." As the case of the railroads shows, that can be a long time indeed. In the fall of 1989, the principle was demonstrated on a much grander and more dramatic scale in Eastern Europe, as the seventy-year-old tyranny of Marxist-Leninist rule, which politicizes *all* economic policy, began to collapse.

To Hell on a Handcar: 1930–1940

The Great Depression confused the issue of national transportation policy badly until this clumsy giant of an economic society began to regain its balance in mid-decade. The extent of the blow was often there for all to see. As 1929 drew to a close, for example, the New Haven Railroad, which had largely recovered from the problems of mismanagement that almost broke it up on the eve of World War I, was carrying the largest passenger load in the world, albeit that many were commuters headed for the booming canyons of New York. The New Haven was the vital link, in addition, that hauled some of the finest trains in the world between New England and dozens of important cities, large and small, to the south and west of New York. When the critical link over the Hell Gate Bridge that took the New Haven through the Bronx, across the inlet to Long Island, then through the borough of Queens and into Manhattan's Pennsylvania Station, was built early in the century, wise heads had provided three main tracks at the northern end of the link to the junction with the New Haven mainline at New Rochelle. The three mains were busy, for this line also carried through freight trains, chiefly at night, when the steady parade of "varnish" (passenger trains) let up. All of the eastern railroads were chronically short of freight cars in those prosperous years, but the collapse of business confidence after the Great Crash "cured" that problem. Soon the third main of the Hell Gate route became the world's longest car-storage yard as unneeded boxcars, gondolas, flats, and cabooses became the symbol of general depression. With the decline in traffic went the railroads' profits, and by 1933 all but the strongest railroads in the country were in bankruptcy or headed for it; and there, until Hitler, Hirohito & Co. rescued them, they would remain for the rest of the decade.

Refusing to confer with President Hoover in the White House after

the November 1932 election, President-elect Roosevelt was determined to build his recovery program from scratch. But Hoover, so routinely criticised then and later for a do-nothing policy, had in fact recognized that the railroads had introduced the nation to yet another
reality of the modern world: the occasional necessity for massive intervention by public money and public power. The solution was the
Reconstruction Finance Corporation (RFC), which pulled more than
just railroad chestnuts out of the fire during the next few years.

Under the redoubtable Jesse Jones, the RFC made loans, huge for
those days, to enterprises that had big fixed charges to meet, such as
interest on bonds, until they could be reorganized, which in the case of
some railroads would not be until the very end of the coming war-
induced prosperity. The spectrum of distress was a wide one: the Pennsylvania and New York Central railroads, along with most of the better
managed railroads in other parts of the country, were bloody but
unbowed and stayed out of bankruptcy, but essentially weak roads like
the Missouri Pacific, which ran through "five-cent cotton and ten-cent
meat" country, did not make it out of the courts until after the war. For
nearly three generations, interest income from railroad bonds had constituted the support of hundreds of thousands of Americans of modest
means. The RFC not only saved big business; it saved American capitalism large and small.

F.D.R. accepted the status quo of providing massive financial help
to the railroads, but much more was needed to solve their basic "sickness," and the railroads did not get it. Stringent laws to protect the jobs
and wages of railroad workers (and the Democrats' near-impregnable
position as the new majority party) blocked any moves to weed out
long-deplored featherbedding practices, and the minimum rate law that
protected truckers from rate competition remained in force. On the
strange assumption that what a nation of people with empty pockets
and no clear way of filling them needed was higher prices, the railroads
were granted stiff rate increases while the NRA, under the increasingly
frustrated General Hugh Johnson (who looked a bit like W. C. Fields),
attempted to do the same thing in manufacturing and trade. The railroads may have had no choice but to raise their rates, since no other
freedom (like reducing employment and wage levels) was open to
them, but manufacturers, small and large, answered the bureaucrats'
plea to raise their prices and maintain output without regard to what
their competition was doing with a resounding "drop dead." And the
"blue eagle" of the NRA did just that.

By 1936 some progress had been made in restoring the railroads
to health, along with the rest of the country, if only because things
could not have got much worse. Indeed, where low prices for agricultural commodities or competition from the booming trucks were a factor, the crisis deepened. In the South, from Texas to the Carolinas, the
railroads settled down to what was beginning to look like permanent

charity. The major coal carriers in the principal mining states of the Northeast had steady business, as electric power consumption continued its steep upward trend, but prices were depressed while freight rates proved "sticky" under regulation. Most marginal coal fields shut down, to be rescued only by Pearl Harbor. In the Northeast, the Pennsylvania made a little money as heavy industry recovered modestly, but the New York Central, once the bluest of the railroad chips and the carrier of fabulous fortunes' worth of merchandise over the world's greatest trade route, headed out of the recession of 1937–1938 with a whopping deficit. Bankruptcies, which in the past had been cleared up with dispatch, hung on like some tropical fever.

Meanwhile, railroads made almost pathetic efforts to regain past glory. Most avenues to improving freight service were closed to them, and had been for years, but where the lines could put on "hotshot" freights, running on passenger train schedules and offering overnight delivery over greater distances than before, they did so. Most improvements, however, were incremental, not revolutionary, and most often made to reduce operating costs. Meanwhile railroad traffic men remained convinced that they simply had to put their best foot forward in their passenger service, as most travelers were businessmen who would not relish shipping via a railroad that was down-at-the-heels. Western railroads plumped for the streamliner craze and found its chief feature, the diesel locomotive, a fine idea that more and more railroads would have liked to emulate. Ice bunkers were added to the bottoms of Pullman cars and day coaches regularly assigned to long-distance trains, which made summer travel a pleasure for the first time in railroad history.

The weary Baltimore & Ohio, almost bankrupt, somewhere found the cash to buy several A and B units of a stylish diesel locomotive, gave a number of its better Pullmans and coaches a facelift, painted them its time-honored royal blue and gray, and presented Washington and Baltimore with their first "streamlined" trains, the *National Limited*, Nos. 1 and 2 between Baltimore and St. Louis, and the *Capital Limited*, Nos. 5 and 6, to Chicago. Coach passengers were favored with their own club car up ahead of the pullmans. In later years passengers remembered the prettied-up old-style twelve-wheel Pullmans as much better riding than the eight-wheel stainless steel cars that began to appear on most later streamliners. To everyone's surprise, the new trains made money, and a remarkable renaissance of passenger service, based on meaningful innovation and real bargains for coach travelers, began. But the hemorrhage of freight to the trucks was not staunched, and only disaster seemed to lie ahead.

What was the Interstate Commerce Commission doing all this time? Just what it had always done: interpreting the Act of 1887, as amended by the Acts of 1903, 1906, 1910, 1920, etc., according to the signals they received from Congress who, after all, were their real masters. That was, simply, to keep everybody in business, as a leading authority on intermodal competition in transportation has put it, make no waves, and do no substantial damage to any of the particular interests involved. At no time did the commission ever measure up to the concept of an economic policy-making body which real Progressives like Theodore Roosevelt had envisioned. The idea of an "independent regulatory commission" had proved to be just one more political vain conceit. If this had been the real purpose behind such commissions, they would have died long since, but sad as it is for a citizen to conclude, they have amounted to little more than insulators between a craven legislative body and its real, if unpleasant and politically costly, duties.

Most of the commissioners had been political hacks, with the exception of a few first-class men like "Judge" Thomas Cooley, the first chairman, whose flat conclusion that cost-of-service can never form a basis for rate-making modern economists would do well to heed; Winthrop M. Daniels, on leave as professor of economics at Princeton, the only commissioner during the rate controversies who spoke for a general increase; Martin A. Knapp, whose "softness" on socking it to the railroads as the Mann-Elkins Act loomed on the horizon got him kicked upstairs to the stillborn Commerce Court in 1911 and then to oblivion as a federal district judge; and colorless bachelor Joseph B. Eastman, who seems to have found some gratification in masterminding transportation policy in World War II.

Railroad regulatory policy, lawmakers and industry leaders were beginning to see, had become national transportation policy—to the extent that we had one—by the end of the 1930s. But it was a hotter political potato than ever. Politicians like La Follette and Cummins, in their day, had browbeaten the commissioners into doing their will. La Follette at one point had seemed almost ready to "put out a contract" on Daniels, who, being from New Jersey, was beyond his reach. Now they were dead and gone and their chickens were coming home to roost. The outbreak of war in Europe in 1939 was forcing Congress to do something, but it proved to be very little. Another Transportation Act (1940) was the answer, and it contained a pallid directive to the commission "to recognize and preserve the inherent advantages of each [mode]," which was subsequently interpreted to mean to take no steps that would unduly upset the apple cart, or put anyone unduly out of business. The same weasel words, more or less, appeared in the Transportation Act of 1958. Open competition between modes would not even be considered for another twenty years.

If Not in Peace, Then in Wartime

The railroads did more to change the art of war than anything since gunpowder, as the Civil War proved. As the third winter of war approached, several officers, tall and mustachioed in their strange uniforms, watched in amazement as train after train—and such *long* trains—passed smoothly onto the B. & O. line to the west from Washington. They were high-ranking Prussian army officers, sent to America to observe engagements in the Civil War, a custom long followed by nations who could not afford to fall behind in the science of warfare. On that hot day in September 1863, they were watching the first long-distance mass movement of troops, their artillery, animals, and forage supplies ever carried out with the speed that only rail transportation seemed to promise. Their ultimate destination, and that of the Prussians, was a point on the Tennessee River in Alabama, opposite the strategic city of Chattanooga, then under siege by General U. S. Grant with limited forces that could not hope, by themselves, to break through the city's defenses and bring the war in the west to a conclusion. The troops heading west were from the Army of the Potomac, then garrisoned near Culpeper, Virginia, on the railroad to Alexandria across the Potomac from Washington. Under the prodding of the daring Secretary of War, Edwin M. Stanton, who was advised by three impressive railroad operating men at his elbow that it could be done in five days, President Lincoln approved the movement west of two army corps, under General Joe Hooker, totaling nearly thirty thousand men with all their battle gear. The president offered to bet the others that that many men with their materiel could not even be got to Washington in five days, but there were no takers.

The railroad men, all of whom knew the embryonic American railroad network (with all its weaknesses that do not show up on maps) like the backs of their hands, were Thomas Scott, second only to J. Edgar Thomson on the Pennsylvania; John W. Garrett of the B. & O.; and S. M. Felton, who ran the Philadelphia, Wilmington & Baltimore. They secured the president's sweeping order that the railroad lines involved were to sidetrack all other traffic until the movement was completed, and that all personnel, high and low, of the participating lines were to ignore any attempt by any officer in the field, however high his rank, to insert his needs ahead of the grand movement. They worked out a route that took the trains northeast to Washington, where they went onto the B. & O. as far as Relay, Maryland; thence westward on the B. & O. to Benwood (now West Virginia) on the Ohio; thence by ferry across the Ohio River to Bellaire, Ohio; thence further westward on the Ohio Central and other connecting lines to Columbus, Ohio, Indianapolis and then Jeffersonville, Indiana; across the Ohio again, southbound, to Louisville; thence over the Louisville & Nashville to Nashville; and finally over the Nashville & Chattanooga to Bridgeport.

The president lost his bet—or would have, if there had been any takers. Indeed, the entire operation, consisting of two army corps totaling twenty-five thousand men, ten batteries of artillery with their horses, and a hundred cars of baggage, was carried out in eleven-and-one-half days, to be followed shortly by a second stream of trains carrying more than a thousand horses and additional guns, wagons, and baggage. They had moved twelve hundred miles over lines that were being furiously repaired by track crews who moved in as Confederate raiding parties moved out, ate cold precooked rations for five days until they gave out, after which they were fed and given additional field rations at the Soldiers' Home near Jeffersonville; struggled to trans-ship their stuff onto a change of cars at Jeffersonville because of a change in track gauge, which took six hours; managed one more ferriage of the Ohio at Louisville; and apparently arrived more or less ready for the fray.

A major role in the creation of modern warfare is the last thing the battered public relations image of America's railroads needs, yet such is their due. *Victory Rode the Rails* (1953) is the title of an entire book on the railroads' role in the Civil War. The new mobility proved a remarkable advantage to those who first recognized and were best able to employ it. The Prussian army did not delay to put the innovation into effect. Only three years later, at the Battle of Sadowa (Könnigratz) the Prussians, to the great discomfiture of the French, defeated the Austrians and cleared the way for the formation of the North German Confederation, the next-to-last stone in the foundation of the emerging German Empire. Just when the Austrians appeared to be winning the battle, the Prussian crown prince and his reserves, rushed to the battlefield by train, came over the hill and won the day. To be sure, their new breech-loading rifles outfired the Austrians' old muzzle loaders, but it was the railroad that got them there, and, while the Austrians raged at this ungentlemanly breach of the time-honored rules of warfare, the sun of the Hapsburgs sank another few degrees towards the horizon. Meanwhile all nations with any capabilities in the iron industry recognized that new iron and steel materials, made possible and affordable by the railroads, would be decisive in the future. During our Civil War, for example, Peter Cooper's New Jersey iron molders had learned that the old limits on the size and casting time of such massive objects as field mortars could be abandoned. The railroads, rushing the still-hot mortars to the siege of New Orleans, stretched the American capacity for both war and peace far beyond old limits.

The record of American railroads in World War I is less clear, but considering the handicaps under which they had to work—not the least of which was having to put up with President Wilson's incompetent son-in-law, William Gibbs McAdoo, as the government's railroad czar—they worked miracles. The war was over so quickly, to be sure, that much of the freight carried for the American offensive became surplus goods; the huge new shipyard near Philadelphia, to which the overworked Pennsylvania and B. & O. Railroads hauled thousands of carloads of material, did not launch a single ship until after the armistice.

World War I was the war to end all wars, we thought, and Americans embraced this shibboleth as if it were a license to forget those bearded foreigners across the ocean and their silly squabbles altogether. If there were any railroad men who objected to the reductions in the physical plant of the railroads, especially after 1930, on the grounds of a possible future war, they did not make much noise. As we saw in an earlier chapter, mileage in place did not shrink much (the Commission rejected case after abandonment case in favor of indignant town fathers), but the rosters of passenger and freight cars and locomotives, and especially the number of men employed, were cut drastically. Fortunately, the railroads were proving that slimmer is often better, for with economy came dramatically improved efficiency in almost every branch of railroading. Freight cars had grown significantly in net tonnage and were approaching a hundred tons. The 1920s were Baldwin Locomotive Works' finest hour (and almost their last) in design and production, and their major competitors managed to survive. Electrification made little headway once railroad profits had been blighted, and not many lines could afford diesels before 1940, after which war production restrictions took hold, but, somehow, the roadways of the more important lines had been maintained and improved, and advances continued in signaling and communication. The railroads of 1940 ran faster, carried heavier loads, and were far safer to work or travel upon than those of a generation before. The nation did not deserve them, but it was soon glad that it had them.

What lover of Americana over the age of sixty can forget the superb campaign of "corporate image" advertising that the well-heeled Pennsylvania Railroad used to bring the message of the railroads at war to America? Full-page, full-color layouts, featuring elegantly detailed paintings of points served by the Pennsy, appeared throughout the war in "leadership" periodicals like *Time, Newsweek, Collier's,* and the *Saturday Evening Post.* Gigantic steel mills, served conspicuously by endless Pennsy freights of iron ore, coal, and finished steel, reared up in the background as a sleek member of the Pennsy's "All-Weather Fleet" raced along the four-track mainline in the foreground, crammed with generals, admirals, lieutenants, sergeants, apprentice seamen, and rosy-cheeked "dogfaces" (privates), all on their way to war but, first, a final short furlough with their families in this greatest of democracies.

The job the railroads did during the war was stupendous. It was a good thing that no one had really thought through what a two-front war, fought to the enemy's utter exhaustion, would be like, and doubtless nearly everybody has forgotten since. The material hauled to dockside on two oceans was as startling in its endless variety as in its quantity. The American soldier went to war supplied, if not always unfailingly, with luxuries that neither our enemies nor many of our allies had enjoyed even in peacetime. America, it has been said, superimposed on a peacetime economy the wartime economy of Rosie the

Riveter. (The percent of women employed full-time outside the home reached new heights from which it would recede only temporarily thereafter.) It would be more accurate, however, to say that we super-imposed a wartime economy upon a magnificent farm and industrial economy that had been loafing along at hardly more than two-thirds of capacity for ten years.

If this sounds too biased in favor of the wartime railroads, it is only because the railroads, so recently forsaken by one shipper and traveler after another, carried it *all*, or nearly. Over one-half of all the puny DC-3's with which the airlines had whittled away some of the first-class rail passenger business were commandeered by the Air Force. The buses, praying that their recapped tires would hold together until the end of a run, did a fine job, especially between isolated army installations and the towns. The railroads carried virtually all of the troop movements, supplementing the entire sleeper fleet with government-supplied troop train sleepers, which looked as though they had been made in a high-school sheet metal class according to a design that one G.I., at least, could never figure out. Even so, many a weary soldier rode a chaircar across the continent in troop trains for which no sleepers could be had on short notice. And withal, do what the government could to discourage civilian travel, wives followed servicemen husbands and warplant executives followed orders from Maine to Washington State, and sometimes the railroads found a spare Pullman berth for them, too.

The trucks were out of it for the duration as far as intercity traffic was concerned, revealing that their services, however deadly for the railroads under the yoke of regulation, had never been more than supplemental. The Japanese had occupied the rubber plantations of Southeast Asia, and in the Northeast gasoline became scarce as German U-boats sank one coastal tanker after another. Tire material was so short gasoline was rationed throughout the country as a means of reducing wear on the nation's dwindling stocks of tires and raw rubber, until workmen could create in full scale the pilot plants in which brilliant chemists had finally succeeded in producing synthetic rubber. "There's a Ford in your future, but the Ford from your past is the Ford you've got now, so you'd better make it last," sang the billboards. Meanwhile freight trains, needing nothing but good old American coal, which they hauled for themselves anyway, carried some 98 percent of all intercity freight during the war, and it was a lot of freight.

We learn from experience, eventually. Thus, one thing the railroads did not have to put up with in World War II was a Railroad Administration, that is, government takeover. There was one brief exception, when government inducted the railroads, if not the men, into the service to avoid a strike. Railroad workers in fact were no more militant during the war than other workers, some of whom, in steel and coal, for instance, were much worse. American labor unions took the golden opportunity to advance their rugged campaign to organize

American factories and mines, but the railroads had already been through all that and there was little more that labor could do to them. Government, bless its heart, had done a fair job of holding down both prices and wages (who needs a white shirt in wartime, anyway?) compared to its performance during the previous war, when it did nothing at all. It was a different war from the succession of "police actions" that soured American society during the 1950s and 1960s. The Japanese had attacked U.S. territory (someday to become a state of the Union) and nearly everybody had a son, perhaps a daughter, in the fight.

Meanwhile the blessed volume of traffic put the railroads resoundingly in the black. Wartime profits, even with excess profits taxes on the books, were lush, and certain industries were being fundamentally advanced, like aircraft, or even created, like organic chemicals, by government support. Savings soared, since big-ticket items like cars, houses, and appliances were unobtainable. The railroads, everybody knew, had been on the way to the poorhouse when war came, and everybody from your daily paper to the *Wall Street Journal* approved heartily when the bankrupt lines paid off their delinquent bond coupons and even began to call in bonds that had years to run. As VJ Day approached, things looked better for the railroads than they had since the first decade of the century. So much had changed. But one thing stayed the same: railroad policy was still good politics. The warmth that railroad men felt at the end of the war was a false spring.

CHAPTER 15

Enterprise Triumphant

If it ain't broke, don't fix it.
Variously attributed

Once More, Dear Friends . . .

"There will be icicles in hell when Erie common pays a dividend," Jay Gould is supposed to have said during his stewardship of that unfortunate railroad. Remembering the old quotation, however apochryphal, a financial editor remarked during the wartime summer of 1942 that they must be having a cool time down below, because the Erie Railroad, for the first time in living memory, had just announced a dividend on its common stock. When the Great Depression struck in 1930 the line had fought hard to stay solvent, but eventually the cruelly long Depression was too much for it and it joined a long procession of railroads, many of them better off in 1929 than the Erie, in the bankruptcy courts. Then the war brought prosperity to the Erie. It was a tough old bird, but we finally managed to kill it. In many ways the Erie's story reflects what was wrong with American transportation policy during its last half-century.

It was the inherently greater productivity (lower real costs per unit of transportation produced) that kept stronger railroads solvent, like the Pennsylvania and the New York Central, the coal roads serving the Pocahontas fields, like the Norfolk & Western and Chesapeake & Ohio, and, out west, the Illinois Central, Great Northern, Burlington, Santa Fe, and Union Pacific. The Pennsy, for example, never knew a dividendless year until its sun began to go down in the 1960s. What saved the Erie and the majority of hard-pressed American railroads that could not even pay their interest charges for much of the 1930s were two truly radical changes in the legal and economic institutions of the nation during the previous half century. With the Reconstruction Finance Corporation (RFC), the federal government had accepted responsibility as the "lender of last resort" to keep these vital enterprises—and quite a few in manufacturing, too—alive. More revolutionary still were the changes in the bankruptcy laws whereby the federal courts would place insolvent railroads under their wing for as long as proved necessary to reorganize and rebuild the enterprises into viable financial

373

establishments, while doing the best they could to preserve the equitable rights of creditors and investors.

Americans, compared to their European forebears, had taken a different view of debtors from the beginning. They were not to be punished, certainly not by debtors' prison, which would profit nobody, but helped. The Founding Fathers, recognizing how subject to corruption any law establishing a balance between debtors' and creditors' interests would be, reserved the making of bankruptcy laws to the federal government. For many years it was an on-again, off-again proposition, for bankruptcy laws were intensely controversial. In the heyday of railroad expansion during the last quarter of the old century, when just about everybody was as far out on the credit limb as they could go, there was no bankruptcy law on the books, but an ingenious adaptation of the old common law of receivership provided a good substitute. Much innovation in the traditional concept was required, however. In the first place, the emergence of the federal courts as sovereign in corporate litigation earlier in the century had ruled out state jurisdiction, although the question of comity between federal district courts sometimes proved embarrassing when one judge ruled differently from another for the same line.

Law professors and disgruntled counsel in specific cases bellowed indignantly at the idea that the executives of a railroad company not yet in default on its obligations could, on their own hook, go into court and successfully pray for the appointment of receivers, and then ask that *they* be recognized as the only ones with adequate knowledge of the railroad's affairs to get it back on track. After the massive reorganizations of the 1890s depression, during which the equity receivership performed beautifully, Congress put a new bankruptcy law on the books incorporating these principles, and there the jurisdiction has remained ever since. The breadth of the courts' powers was enlarged steadily, and with the onset of the Great Depression basic statutes dealing with various kinds of bankruptcies were promulgated. In all of these laws, in the rhetoric of the opposing attorneys who have built profitable practices on an increasingly technical subject, and from the written opinions of the judges themselves, breathes the basic social philosophy of modern bankruptcy law that first developed through the imperatives of the railroad enterprises: the public stake in these institutions is paramount, and the insolvent corporations will continue to operate, so long as a spark of useful life remains, with the protection and overt assistance of the court as needed, until a viably reorganized enterprise is achieved and a reasonably favorable economic climate returns. Now the same view is taken in the cases of enterprises as vastly different, and in trouble for such unconventional reasons, as Johns Manville, Texaco, Federated and Allied Department Stores, Eastern Airlines, and many others. A society built on great enterprises embodying huge amounts of fixed (the British say "sunk") capital and producing vital goods and services while employing many thousands of workers is a vastly different thing from the unfortunate New England merchant whose bank drafts "went to protest." It all began with the railroads.

The first postwar decade featured a run-scared economy that was constantly buoyed up by a consumer demand based on fifteen years of depression and wartime self-denial. Year after year the dreaded post-war recession failed to show up. Two pieces of legislation came out of the brief interlude of Republican domination of the Congress, which seemed to augur well for the future of the railroads. They were the Reed-Bulwinkle law, which relieved regulated transportation companies of prosecution under the antitrust laws for establishing jointly-arrived-at, uniform tariffs. The other was the Taft-Hartley law, which had nothing directly to do with railroads but seemed to reverse in some degree the fifteen-year trend towards the "laboristic society." Both statutes were anathema to the old-time reform Democrat in the White House, Harry Truman, but truth to tell, the Republicans had a lot of help from Democrats in overriding his vetoes.

The railroads gave everything they had, or nearly, to the effort to reestablish themselves as vigorous enterprises with a bright future. They heavily rebuilt and greatly improved their physical plant and added larger and improved rolling stock. The switch from steam to diesel was virtually complete by the mid-1950s, by which time even the prime coal-carrying railroads—like the Norfolk & Western and Chesapeake & Ohio—had given up their stubborn support of coal-fired steam propulsion. The cross of hauling people, without profit but with heavy demands on capital budgets, bore more heavily than ever on the railroads as World War II ended. Air travel began to eat into what the railroads still had of the market for long-distance travel but, more importantly, created the greater part of its ultimate volume on its own merits of speed. The private automobile took virtually all of the short-haul business in a trend that accelerated remarkably, especially after we replaced the dangerous old public highway system, based in large part on two-lane undivided roads on through routes, with the Interstate system.

These developments, of course, did not occur overnight, and for ten years, at least, after the war, public pressure on the railroads to provide better rail passenger service diverted capital funds and management time from intensive development of freight traffic, where it would eventually have done far more good. In what was to be not quite their "last hurrah," the factories of Chicago's Pullman Standard, St. Louis's American Car & Foundry Company, and other rail car builders hummed, filling millions of dollars worth of orders for trainsets to replace the old name trains and to inaugurate new ones. Some of these trains even made money, where there was potential and where they served it well. As Holden Caulfield would have said, it was a "good goodbye."

"It's the Same Old Song They Sing"

Like Amfortas in Wagner's opera *Parsifal*, the major passenger railroads suffered from a wound that would not kill yet was not going to heal itself. But the real problem was with the freight business, which paid the bills and for which real trouble loomed. The Pennsylvania and the New York Central, pacesetters for the industrial Northeast for a century, watched in desperation as their most profitable class of freight traffic, whose profits had been subsidizing the passenger service for years, returned to the trucks with renewed gusto. Few there are who care to admit it, but this development was spurred by a pell-mell rush of thousands of small and medium manufacturing firms to the South, bent on escaping the stubborn policies of the often corrupt unions that ruled their workers. The trucks, cheap and growing constantly cheaper for reasons treated in the preceding chapter, made it possible, for they could go anywhere and were prepared to deal. Furthermore, a plant that had a steady volume of shipments back up north or east did not have to pay high rail *or* regulated truck rates. They could buy and operate their own trucks, lease the equipment, or contract for the services, at unregulated rates hammered out between shipper and hauler "in the good old traditional American way." So attractive was this development that by the mid-1960s, unregulated haulage on the public highways was more important than either regulated trucking or rail for the kinds of traffic everybody coveted.

Architects who had had nearly five years of war-plant expansion during which to practice their art designed one-story, scientifically laid out facilities that persuaded many another company to move, if only out into the hinterland (as long as it was near an exchange with the Interstate). Here is another example of where makers of American transportation policy blamed technology or, worse still, the greed of businessmen. The "technology" was nothing more than the rate umbrella which the ICC had been holding over the entire cast of characters, while burying its head in the sand against the growing evidence that, as always, sins of omission can be just as bad as sins of commission. As for the greed, it has always been a lame excuse. Any manufacturing executive knows that manufacturing is the riskiest form of business, with the possible exception of show business. Profits are not guaranteed and do not last forever. When orders slack off, or expensive innovations in an industry dictate heavy capital investment, you cannot have too much money in the bank. Opportunity must be taken at the flood, as Shakespeare said. (Another Elizabethan, anonymous, said it even better in a bawdy song: "If thou will not when thou may, sir, thou may not when thou will, sir.")

Things were almost as bad in the Midwest. In this rich land, where few had felt that the densely developed railroad network had been "overbuilt" in the pre-World War I era, the old granger roads found the burden of uneconomic, underpatronized passenger trains debilitating. Worse yet were the thousands of miles of branch lines, built so that no farmer could complain to his congressman that he had to haul his corn or wheat or hogs or whatever more than ten miles to the railroad. Frequently the railroads applied to state commissions for permission to abandon the least viable of these lines, and almost invariably they were refused, until the federal government, seeing a bit of light at least, persuaded the state commissions to relent in the worst cases. Meanwhile the trucks ran riot, making a joke of the granger railroads' traditional role as gatherers of farm produce from thousands of individual points and deliverers of merchandise, frequently bearing the address of Sears, Roebuck or Montgomery Ward, to the same places.

The granger railroads that were fading away during the postwar years were precisely those that had failed to heed Jim Hill's warning near the end of the old century that traffic growth would be concentrated on through, long-distance traffic and anybody who failed to control a route, by one means or another, to the Pacific, would fall by the wayside. The transcontinentals, most of whom had nearly died in their efforts to achieve the Pacific coast two generations before, were doing quite well, notably the Union Pacific, the Southern Pacific, the Santa Fe, and the "Hill roads" (Great Northern, Northern Pacific, and the Burlington), which would soon be united in holy merger matrimony after seventy years as *co-vivants*. Men today weep for the Milwaukee Road, which broke every rule known to prudent management by waiting until the low costs of the nineteenth century were a thing of the past and then, without any real planning, lunged westward to build its own line to the coast. It was the most impressive railroad to go bankrupt (for the first time) during the relatively prosperous 1920s, under the weight of interest charges that the system could not earn. By the end of the 1960s it was, so to speak, terminal, as were those two old widows-and-orphans favorites of the nineteenth century, the Chicago & North Western and the Rock Island. The former has not been permitted to die, although if there were any provisions for a "living will" for railroads its owners might have pulled the plug on it long ago. The latter, after waiting thirteen years for the cowardly ICC to make up its mind about the Union Pacific's offer of merger, faded away like the Colorado River which, beset by users who take and give nothing back, dies without a whimper in the desert. Long, useful segments of all of these once-great railroads, much of it once double-tracked, survive as units of other railroads or independent "regionals," but their flags fly no more. (Say it ain't so, Joe.)

The railroads did not lose all their battles. They managed to rid themselves of primary responsibility for the nation's passenger service—what was left of it—in 1970, when the government, rejecting the conventional wisdom that passenger trains, with few exceptions, were extinct in America, turned the remains over to Amtrak, the National Rail Passenger Corporation. The devoted men and women of Amtrak, ignoring opinionated business journalists and hostile congressmen, have worked to make Amtrak a success, meaning that they have constantly reduced the size of Amtrak's annual shortfall subsidy from the government and may yet make it a self-supporting enterprise. The freight railroads, for the most part, still have the job of operating Amtrak's trains under contract over their nineteenth century routes, which in many cases is a real inconvenience to the hundred-car freights that run over these routes—often faster than the Amtrak trains—and pay the bills. In the long run Amtrak will have to build and maintain its own modern routes if the passenger train is to have a *raison d'être* beyond that of a tourist attraction, the part of the market they still dominate. (Anyone who has heard a DC-10 passenger, at thirty-five thousand feet, unwittingly identify the Grand Canyon to his nine-year-old son as a "very bad case of soil erosion" will know what I mean.) Amtrak, with its scarce, expensive sleepers, is to prewar Pullman travel as Seven-Up is to Veuve Cliquot, but with the decline of bus service it is the only way remaining really to see the country.

Some rate relief—the place where the railroad shoe really pinched—was achieved in the postwar shakeout period, but it was not much, and achieving it was hard, expensive, and worst of all, incredibly time-consuming work. The railroads wanted to compete with the trucks on price, and they were convinced they could take back much of the business, and make money, if they could cover variable costs (the costs directly attributable to performing a given service) and have something left over for their huge fixed costs. Nothing doing, said the ICC, thumbing its nose at everything we were told in Economics I about the behavior of firms under competition.

The Southern Railroad was prosperous as railroads go due to the booming postwar economic growth of the Southeast, where both industrial development and a modernizing agriculture, based on livestock and poultry raising, vastly improved fertilizers and insecticides, and cultivation with machines instead of an increasingly redundant black peasantry had produced remarkable results. The Southern decided to fight the issue of rates to a definitive conclusion. Its leaders were confident that at the very least they could embarrass the ICC and show it up for what it was. The resulting Big John case is a landmark in American economic history, and what it teaches about the perils of a politicized decision-making process is one of the railroads' most valuable contributions to the art of self-government.

The Southeast was consuming millions of tons of grain for animal feed, most of which (10.8 million tons) it "imported" from the upper and far Midwest, the South being historically no great producer of grains. Most of this grain arrived in milled and blended form, as a result of "milling in transit" rates offered by carriers. Two-thirds of it came by truck, all unregulated, having come down the Ohio, Tennessee, and Mississippi rivers by barge to appropriate trans-shipment points. The railroads had long since lost most of this business, which they had handled car-by-car in fifty-ton net divided hopper cars or boxcars. The Southern decided to get as much as they could with a rate two-thirds below what the trucks and barges had been charging, which would nevertheless yield a net of two million dollars a year, well above all of the out-of-pocket costs of the service, including amortization of a fleet of newly designed, relatively untried, hundred-ton covered hoppers largely made of aluminum. (The men, true to form, christened the huge conveyance "Big John," and it stuck.) The Southern bought its cars first, then applied to the ICC for the rate. It was time for the pressure to begin to build on the railroads' adversaries, for a change.

Looked at from an economic viewpoint, what the Southern wanted to do was almost, if not quite, equal to inventing the electric light. (Its advantages, at any rate, were more quickly grasped than Edison's invention!) The railroad proposed to carry the grain straight through without milling, in units of five, ten, or twenty cars, constituting 450-, 900-, or 1800-ton shipments. The Southern confidently told the ICC that it expected the innovation in equipment and rates to boost its volume of grain from a paltry 600,000 tons to 3 million tons. Millers in the Southeast were ecstatic, but a lot of other interest groups were horrified. The rate application was filed in the summer of 1961, and nearly two years later, after 15,815 pages of testimony, 766 exhibits, and 150 appearances of witnesses in 139 days of hearings, Division 2 of the ICC (the staff specialists who do the actual work of the commission) made a recommendation to the full commission that the 450-ton rate be approved, as in their opinion its purpose was "to meet unregulated truck competition," and the relevant criterion of reasonableness of a rate in such circumstances was whether it significantly reimburses the carrier for the additional costs it assumes in providing the service. Six months later the full commission rejected the Southern's reduced rates and ordered them canceled.

Division 2, of course, had naively assumed that the purpose of regulation was to secure lower rates for shippers, encourage the growth of economic activity, and secure a better material standard of living for themselves and their posterity. Of course this had to be done without allowing "predatory pricing." This old term, which figured prominently in the antitrust charges against Standard Oil earlier in the century, does not figure in the present instance, but the principle is the same. Predatory pricing meant lowering your price temporarily below your cost of production, with the help of huge fortunes behind you, until your competitors are destroyed, and then raising prices higher than ever. That was not the issue (it was not the truth in the Standard

Oil case, either, for Standard simply had a true cost of production so low that hardly anyone believed it). The issue was simply whether the Southern had the right to take this business away from the northern millers, the northern grain merchants, the truckers, the barge lines, or anyone else who had grown accustomed to cutting himself in on the deal.

The hard fact is that the ICC had not operated primarily in the "consumer interest" for years, but then, folks don't vote (or lobby) primarily as consumers, but as millers, grain dealers, truckers, barge-line operators, and even the Tennessee Valley Authority. The TVA? Although a public body, the TVA pursued its self-interest as narrowly as anyone. The Southern, in figuring its cost of service, said the TVA, should be required to include an amount sufficient to write off the locks and dams built at public expense that would no longer be used by the barge lines the Southern wanted to put out of business—and which paid nothing for the use of these facilities anyway!

Where was the Supreme Court when all this unseemly wrestling was going on? Cowering in its marble temple, hoping that it would not have to bite the bullet and demonstrate that there are limits to congressional power, even when delegated to an "independent" regulatory commission? If that seems harsh, consider what the Court did. In January 1965 the high court ruled on the federal district court's injunction against the commission's order to cancel the rate. That court had said that the commission had exceeded its authority and "was not supported by substantial evidence in the record." The Supreme Court vacated the district court's order, but then remanded the case to the commission to justify its original order. The commissioners were not fools. They had been told to "go back to the drawing board," and they knew what that meant. After a suitable face-saving period (eight months), the commission approved the 450-ton rate and ordered, in effect, that grain to the Southeast would henceforth go by rail in 450-ton lots in Big John cars, which competing railroads could buy if they wanted to stay in the business. It was an outcome in all ways fitting for the Byzantine Empire of old. Surely it could not be anything but the dawn of a new day, a new precedent based upon common sense, fair play, and good government.

Until the ingot mold case. No two industries have been more intimately bound together from their beginnings than railroading and iron and steel. From iron mine to consumer, the railroad has been the handmaiden of the basic metals industry, most notably steel, and for many years its major customer. It is impossible to say which created which: they created each other. By the mid-1960s, however, trucks had eaten away a substantial amount of the freight business originating in the steel industry, principally in hauling finished steel to fabricators and onto the jobs. They had left the heavy hauling to the railroads, but now they were beginning to get into the production chain. A profitable business for the railroads of western Pennsylvania for years had been the hauling of steel ingots, often still hot, in their molds to manufacturers of steel materials and end products who did not make their own steel. A large part of the business consisted in hauling the empty molds back to the steel mills. Under the rates that had prevailed for some years, profits had been adequate for the railroads and promised to be so for the trucks. The railroads applied for a rate considerably lower than the trucks would find attractive, but still well above the railroads' variable costs. Surveys by transportation experts had shown what railroad traffic men knew full well: the commission was grimly sticking to its two chief criteria of relevant costs. These were that traffic should be shared between modes of transportation regardless of the clear-cut superiority of one over the other, and that an applicant who proposed a rate low enough to drive competing modes from the field would have to bear the burden of proof that it would cover *all* of its costs. There had as yet been no full-dress court test of the commission's policy, but the ingot molds promised to supply it.

The Supreme Court's decision in 1968 was a bombshell, or the straw that broke the camel's back, or a declaration of war—take your pick. The Court, after having made clear its low opinion of the commission's criteria for reasonableness of rates in the Big John case, now scuttled back into its shell and slammed the door of legalism tight. The ICC, said the Court, should be the initial determiner of what method of costing should be used in these intermodal cases. The commission should be given "reasonable latitude to decide where it will resolve these complex issues, in addition to how it will resolve them." It was a clear-cut victory for the Interstate Commerce Commission and confirmed a purely political policy—keep everybody in business—as the heart and soul of regulatory policy. But the hour was late, and the decision would prove a Pyrrhic victory at best, for the country could no longer afford such distortion of the economic decision-making process for political ends. The jig was nearly up.

By this time the railroads were as bad off as the Christians in the Coliseum, for whom there was no avenue of escape. If they were going to die, they reasoned, they might as well die together, and they began to merge weakness with weakness, and hopelessness with hopelessness. There were some mergers, to be sure, that made sense, and had for a long time, although they had never been allowed to go forward. John Budd, son of the Great Northern's Ralph Budd, devoted much of his own presidency of that railroad to pressing the ICC for permission to merge the three railroads that had made up the Northern Securities Co. at the turn of the century, plus the line on the north bank of the Columbia that Hill had built when that combine was broken up in 1904. It was to be a unitary, functional railroad, with the best features of each becoming a major virtue of the whole. Finally, in 1970, the cause made its way through the courts, and few have regretted the move since. The merger has worked because of the years of planning and hard work by dedicated operating executives who knew the strengths and weaknesses of the lines like the back of their hands.

The doomed Penn Central, the *Titanic* of the railroad merger era, had no such human resources to make its consolidation of the Pennsylvania and New York Central work. Little sentiment for the merger, or faith in its chances, ever existed outside the respective boardrooms; the top people at the Central, especially, hung onto the old confrontational attitudes that had marked the history of the two great railroads for nearly a century. The sickness unto death of the northeastern lines, however, was the very crystallization of what one railroad leader has called sixty years of "sodomization" by the ICC, Congress, the courts, the labor unions, and a large segment of the public, who naively believed these enterprises to be immortal. It is doubtful if a simple straightforward merger of the two lines could have worked, and by the time Congress got through piling condition upon impossible condition upon the merger, no prudent railroad man could have anticipated success. Still, there was no one at the time to swim against the stream of desperate optimism by denouncing the entire charade. By the end of the negotiations and court ordeals, profound misgivings had multiplied. Now only one force kept the railroads' lawyers from placing their briefs upon the shelf and withdrawing their motion to merge the two railroads. That was the pathetic ambition of Stuart Saunders, lawyer head of the Norfolk & Western, which had none of the problems of the trunk lines, to be chief executive officer of the biggest railroad in the world. But Saunders has been criticized and ridiculed enough. His was an errand in the wilderness.

The first important act of the newly created Penn Central was to give twenty-five million dollars to the New Haven Railroad to pay for diesel fuel oil, the suppliers having placed the deteriorating old line on a C.O.D. basis. *Give,* not lend, for no one would have lent this once-great passenger carrier a red cent. It was now the sole responsibility of the new behemoth, for, although no future existed for the New Haven as a self-supporting carrier, politicians had seized the opportunity to hang it around Penn Central's neck. But that was only the beginning. Millions of onlookers gasped at what came next. Some kind of worker protection had been expected, for the very essence of the merger was to do a better job of transportation with many fewer men, but the guarantees given the redundant employees of the former railroads were overblown, to say the least. No man who had been working for any of these three railroads for more than a nominal length of time was to be laid off without a generous separation payment, and no man who had been with the railroads for ten years or longer was *ever* to be let go, short of the mandatory retirement age, even if his services became grossly unsatisfactory. (Soon after Penn Central had run its course into bankruptcy, the railroad brotherhoods, as if to demonstrate that labor unions are always impelled to seek "more, now," began to demand more from the gallant old wreck. Having been given the moon, they now asked for the stars. No employee of Penn Central, they insisted, should in the future be required, whatever the changing needs of the railroad, to change his place of employment as a condition of retention on active duty.) Other doses of legislative ground glass were scattered throughout the settlement, but these labor provisions were enough to make the merger a farce. No other aspect of this great national charade has received more bitter criticism.

The American *Perestroika*

By late spring of 1970, the American transporation system had reached a critical stage. The immediate jolt to Americans' sense of what was happening was the declaration of the largest bankruptcy in our history up to that time. The Penn Central could not go on as a private, profit-supported enterprise, paying 10 percent for capital that in railroading returned barely 1 percent. Not for a moment, however, did anyone in or out of public or responsible private life suggest that this great railroad should be allowed to follow the normal course of the hopeless bankrupt into liquidation. Even if the railroad had not been absolutely vital to the diversified industry, especially heavy industry, on which the northeastern economy—and thus the economy of the nation and, indeed, the western world—was based, the hard fact that the Penn Central employed thousands of well-organized, articulate workers would have made liquidation unthinkable. The interdependence of America's railroads, moreover, dictated that operations continue. As one example, the Union Pacific Railroad, the nation's first "transcontinental," rich with profits from hauling high-priority freight thousands of miles across the deserts and plains of western America, exchanged millions of tons of through freight with the Penn Central at Chicago and other midwestern points.

The American political character being what it is, a scapegoat had to be found for this crisis, and American journalism showed itself as the pedestrian and hackneyed calling that it so often seems. The postmerger management of the Penn Central was blamed by the press, chiefly on the ground that its program of acquiring nonrelated enterprises diverted funds that should have supported rail operations. It was pure claptrap, but it was what the public had been accustomed to for a century, and few writers knew or cared about the real story. Later it would be different. The fact is that the Penn Central had to find *some* way to pay for the 10 percent capital, and it was not going to be by running a railroad. One of the conditions of the merger was that the Penn Central divest itself of its most prized, and profitable, possession: a huge block of Norfolk & Western Railroad stock. After that it had to thrash around for earning assets to buy with the cash, to earn money to support the railroad in the future. Some of the stuff that business brokers sold these desperate men, like amusement parks, was a disgrace. But the concept of the "conglomerate" corporation was still fashionable; it had not yet dawned on ever-sanguine new business managers that new business grows out of old business. The Penn Central's traditional business was more promising than ever—but first a few changes had to be made. Whatever the shortcomings of management in the last days of these once-great railroads, it was the distortions created in the total American transportation picture by nearly a century of unintelligent, demagogic, and ultimately malevolent railroad regulation that were the heart of the problem.

These distortions, no longer a private matter between railroads automatically viewed as venal and a reformist government, had finally brought on a vast national crisis that was going to claim many hours of reluctant legislators' time, line the pockets of countless Philadelphia lawyers, and, as was becoming obvious, cost the American taxpayer billions of dollars. The "sickness" of the railroads was a wound self-inflicted by the American people upon their material civilization. Would the political system, at this late date, show itself capable of healing itself? Congress, where all bucks stop eventually, including our taxes, had denied the country the sensible leadership it lacked, and now it would have to do the right thing.

Ironically, at this sobering juncture the old drivel about the railroads being dead, technologically and economically, as a basic means of transportation, ceased. The railroad system was not dead—far from it. The railroad is as indispensable to the commerce of the United States as ever. One hundred and fifty years after the B. & O. began the first regularly scheduled railroad service in the nation, the railroad remains the one mode of transportation that we would not part with if we had to get along with just one. One of the most important truths about the railroad train is that it is far and away the most versatile of all modes of land transportation. No mode is superior in all applications, but the railroad is the one mode that can be made to do just about everything. It is also the most efficient, given its vast social investment in a fixed plant, a vigorous management that is master in its own house, and the freedom to evolve methods of doing business based on a sophisticated understanding of the economics of railroading. It has been some eighty years since we first started stripping the railroad system of these indispensable attributes of success. It is a wonder, and a testimonial to the railroads' indispensability, that it took two generations to bring them to their knees.

Taken at face value, government's interposition in the basic decision-making responsibilities of railroad management over the years has looked to historians like a series of earnest actions intended to solve clear and present problems of a myopic capitalism and a "free market" that does not "work." On closer look, the historian may perceive a deathwish on the part of the American people against this indispensable servant that seemed to rule every aspect of their lives. In this they had the enthusiastic cooperation of politicians who were consistently eager to pander to cheap public opinion and short-term expediency. Public policy in transportation matters represents a major failure of the American political economic system, a failure of the sort that James Madison warned against so eloquently in his tenth *Federalist* essay.

Sick as it was, the American railroad system was not dead in 1970. But the Progressive philosophy of government economic regulation was a stinking corpse, and that is one of the most significant developments in American economic history in our time. The idealistic notion of the federal commissioner as philosopher-king, solving tough economic problems that mere businessmen, individually or as members of a group, could not solve for themselves, was dead as a mackerel. Dead also was the tired old concept of "the public interest versus the private interest." It had taken on an archaic sound even to the successors of the shallow legislators and "college tackhead philosophers" who had midwifed the "positive" philosophy of the government's role in economic activity that bears the totally inappropriate name of Progressive. Truly powerful thinkers like John R. Commons and Oliver Wendell Holmes, Jr., had tried to tell their contemporaries how fatuous the philosophy was, but Americans, true to type, preferred to enshrine these men for their liberal-idealist spirit, not their common-sense attitudes about what could be achieved by activist government.

Also stinking, and just as dead, was the infamous "capture" theory of the failure of regulation. At the beginning of the 1960s, the initiative in the rather frayed subject of public policy toward business was seized by the New Left historians, who realized that something had gone seriously wrong with the old Progressive philosophy of regulation. They further sensed that, after a brief, uncomfortable dalliance with the sweet reasonableness of Richard Hofstadter's *Age of Reform* (1955), the American academic was eager for a return to the old robber baron thesis. The New Left put it in a new dress, embodied it in doctoral dissertations handed in to Ivy League history departments that contained not a single person qualified to criticize a dissertation on such a subject, and their work won prizes and national acclaim. Faced with a choice between the invalidity of the Progressive philosophy and "proof" that businessmen themselves had taken over scientific government regulation for their own private benefit, the American intellectual rushed to embrace this "capture theory." This need to accept "revisionist" interpretations of our history, so long as they are congenial, which promptly collapse under the test of mature scholarship, is one of the less attractive features of American intellectualism.

It is a striking paradox of our time that if we wish to point to examples of the loss of freedom in the making of economic decisions—that is, to the *politicization* of economic matters by giving the final say to materially uninvolved statesmen rather than to entrepreneurs at the grass-roots level—we may prefer to cite the history of the American political economy, rather than that of the classic totalitarian states of eastern Europe. What was emerging in the Soviet Union by the end of the 1980s was a national economy that could no longer advance under a grossly misconceived system of rewards and responsibilities and had become so dysfunctional that it could not feed its people or stock the shelves of its state stores with anything much but pitiful little handicrafts from beyond the Urals. The Soviets had been digging their grave for seventy years, and before 1917 had had no real tradition of free, responsible enterprise. Fortunately, the United States was not that bad off, but the bureaucratic shoe was beginning to pinch most uncomfortably by the time men went out to view the smoking ruins of the Penn Central, and others had begun to speak darkly about the "end of the American century."

Leonid Brezhnev's son, Andrei, once remarked to an American, "In you country you struggle so the poor will be rich, and in our country we struggle so the rich will be poor." But westerners have had their Levelers, at least since the seventeenth century, and they sing a siren song, but now and then their song falls on deaf ears, and then the human race takes giant steps forward. Looking backward from the end of the 1980s, we see unmistakable signs that the worm was turning, slowly and clumsily, and most uncertainly, in the Soviet Union, but swiftly, like the release of a long-coiled spring, in the West. Great Britain's program of reversing some of the more outstanding idiocies of its past Labor governments, and, prosaic though it may seem, the partial deregulation of transportation in America, impel us to declare that a kind of Western *perestroika*—a restructuring of economic policy—is well under way. The renaissance of American railroads bespeaks it.

Like almost every aspect of the epic story of American railroads, the history of efforts to replace responsible businessmen's decision-making power with that of a disinterested bureaucracy is fraught with lessons with broad application. They will be most unwelcome in smug schools of government:

The decisions of a commission, although they have profound impact upon the economic health of the regulated industry and its capacity to do what it was created to do, are virtually absolute and without judicial recourse. The Supreme Court settled the matter when the very first case ruled on by the ill-starred Commerce Court (established under the Mann-Elkins Act of 1910, largely at the behest of President Taft) came before the high court on appeal. Basic jurisdiction by the new court to overrule an administrative order of the ICC was denied, and Congress abolished it in 1913. The Commerce Court today is embalmed in the "museum" of historical oddities, unheard of, we dare say, even by most transportation specialists. The real question is one of national policy: what should Congress make subject to a commission's determination? There are many things that can and should be made subject to review and ruling by an administrative commission, the most obvious being safety rules and regulations. In the new environment that has replaced the old Progressive illusions, we have come to see that what is important is that businessmen and women remain free, under the benign eye of a permanent congressional committee's study group, to decide what products to make, what services to offer, and how much to charge for them, and to bear meaningful responsibility therefore.

The existence of a commission with absolute power, short of legislative action, to make decisions regarding equitable relationships as they arise in the normal course of business will not settle issues, but exacerbate them. Once the commission declares, in effect, that the outcome of a dollars-and-cents issue is "up for grabs," the number of suddenly interested parties who come running is truly amazing, as the Big John case revealed. This homely fact has proved a cornucopia for lawyers and bureaucrats. Thus, what for years was considered a contest between the railroads, on the one hand, and the "general public" on the other, quickly became what Mr. Justice Holmes warned in 1904 that antitrust law was becoming: *bellum omnium contra omnes*, "a war of all against all."

Idealists who look to commissions to supply uniquely just and proper solutions to problems as complex as freight rates imagine a vain thing. An administrative body that innovates is a contradiction in terms. It is not created to innovate, but to interpret and otherwise administer the innovations of the legislative branch. The Interstate Commerce Commission has never been more than a clerico-judicial body, and the very style of the body from its beginnings—the deportment of the practitioners, the tone and format of the published and bound decisions—bespeaks the fact. When the commission, in desperation, has attempted to innovate, it has generally been called back by the courts.

In practice, regulatory commissions have demonstrated a very "healthy" awareness of which side their bread is buttered on; that is, who their boss is. Thus, regulatory decisions will be made with an eye single to their political impact, or at least to their impact upon the Congress and especially the members of the committee that oversees them. Commissioners must be at least as good at politics as their masters on Capitol Hill. There is also the role of whipping boy to be assumed, one hopes on very rare occasions. Such an occasion occurred some six months after the Penn Central debacle, as the true consequences of the collapse of that vital economic artery began to be apparent. Senator Mike Mansfield and twenty-nine other members of the Senate released an open letter condemning the ICC for the deplorable state of affairs they had allowed to develop. It had simply ceased to be a regulatory agency, declared the Senators; it should be abolished and its functions transferred to the Department of Transportation (*New York Times*, Dec. 8, 1970).

The view of regulatory agencies is static; life, in or out of the regulated enterprises, is dynamic. Change—subtle, gradual, and, one
hopes, prepared for, is the actuality. Commissions act as though nothing changes until they rule. What is more accurate is that everything
changes while the effective forces in society are chained to the mast,
and, as the poet says, we are left with a sense of loss. This has always
hampered economic growth in America, especially when the vitality of
critical underlying services is concerned. No such manacling of the
effective forces of a material civilization is known among our new competitors in the Far East, and there is detectable a healthy revulsion from
any such hint of totalitarian control in the newly liberated nations of
eastern Europe. A new day has dawned. All the old bets are off.

Corrective measures of public policy, which ought to be the first
act of a thoughtful sovereign, are seldom resorted to when governments wield business decision-making powers. Things have to get so
bad that a crisis, a clear and present danger to the national welfare,
develops. The reason for this is simple. Medicines are often at least as
unpleasant as the maladies for which they are prescribed. Congress,
from which all meaningful changes must flow, must view each change
or reversal in regulatory policy, no matter how heartrendingly pleaded
for, from the standpoint of whom, and how many, will a change please,
and how many will it hurt, in the short run? This is the old legislative
"cost-benefit" calculation that any elected official must constantly
make if he wishes to remain long in office. The railroads were tough,
and they were indispensable, and over the years, if only with the help
of a few gulps of oxygen from the RFC's bottle, they survived. Once
they began to fail, more and more frequently and on a grand scale, croc-
odile tears changed to the real thing on Capitol Hill.

The View from Harper's Ferry

In 1986 the struggle of the Norfolk Southern Railroad to acquire Penn
Central's successor, Conrail, and the attempt by Elizabeth Dole's
Department of Transportation to hand it to them at a bargain price,
were raising choruses of boos across the land. A retired investment
banker with a large investment in Norfolk Southern stoutly condemned
those who would block the deal. "But Conrail has been doing beautifully in recent years and expects to do even better in the future,"
replied his listener. "Oh, that's only because the government put billions into rebuilding it after the Penn Central collapse," was the indignant if irrelevant rejoinder. The banker, like most businessmen, interpreted history—what little he knew of it as it pertained to eastern
railroads—entirely in the light of his own self-interest. But other bankers were aghast at the mere political expediency that would turn the
highly profitable Conrail over to control by only one of the two eastern

mega-mergers, Norfolk Southern and CSX. A consortium quickly formed to underwrite the largest secondary offering of common stock in the history of the New York Stock Exchange. It was oversubscribed, and today the reborn railroad, hale and hearty and a central power in the nation's transportation complex, is owned by the people who had faith in it.

"Conrail"—the Consolidated Rail Corporation—was the reorganized successor to the bankrupt Penn Central Railroad. Its common stock, or most of it, was originally owned by the federal government, whose major financial assistance to the broken railroad had been the salvation of the widows and orphans of America (or at least those who had owned Penn Central's senior securities). The reorganization was a long-drawn-out and frightfully expensive affair. First, the new capital structure had to be worked out. Second, the physical assets of the railroad had to be acquired by the new owner at a fair price that would permit a substantial settlement with creditors and holders of senior debt securities.

The "knockdown" price, after much negotiation, was settled at two billion dollars, and, while this amount, at 1970s prices, would not have come anywhere near duplicating even the old Pennsylvania's tubes under the Hudson and East rivers, the Penn Central corporate shell was delighted to get it. Everybody got something, even if the common stockholders, bringing up the rear, did get only four shares of the new Penn Central for each one hundred shares they had held of the old, and even if those new shares sold on the Exchange for considerably less than old Penn Central had commanded just a short time before the debacle. And, finally, the government invested some three billion dollars in the virtual rebuilding of the important routes of its new railroad, and another three and a half billion dollars to liquidate, once and for all, the generous separation pact with labor that Congress had once thoughtlessly tried to hang on Penn Central. The money for rebuilding was not excessive. Not a penny less would do, and it is generally agreed by people who know the engineering side of railroading that it was used brilliantly; but, after all, the weary executives of the railroad had had a long time to brood on what was wrong with it and what it would take to fix it. Indeed, it had not been fit to accommodate a halfway-modern high-speed passenger train, but, more to the point, it could not accommodate a modern high-speed freight train of a hundred cars at seventy miles an hour either, and *that* was the competition. Three billions sounds like a lot of money, and it is, but it promised to be a very worthwhile investment in that best yardstick of investment, reduced operating costs. Many would term it just another in a dreary series of subsidies the government has given the railroads over the years. Others, better acquainted with regulatory history, may see it as indemnification for the considerably greater amount of profits the Pennsy and the Central *might* have made—and, for the most part, invested in maintenance and betterment of the lines—from about 1908 to 1970. What anyone calls it, however, is beside the point. The entire recovery and rebirth operation was a dramatic success, and if we still had court minstrels it would be told and retold to the young. The government got much of its money back, and the nation got a vigorous, almost new railroad ready to go to work to cut the real costs of transportation.

But money is not everything. If this is all that government had been willing to do for American railroads at this critical juncture, neither Conrail nor its suitor, the haughty Norfolk Southern, would have been riding very high by 1986. For the first several years of its operation the government's baby, Conrail, had turned in ghastly deficits to the U.S. Treasury, and it was beginning to look as though the "whiz kids" who had replaced most of the old management would never get it off the dole (no pun intended). To some extent these hard early years were to be expected. As eastern Europe is finding out, forty years of repression are not to be corrected overnight, much less seventy.

The fact is that another giant step in the American *perestroika* had to be taken before there could be any hope for Conrail: they, and America's railroads in general, were sinking alarmingly by the end of the 1970s, and they had to be set free to find salvation where they could. Now government was in the same boat with the railroads. Rate regulation had to go, except for a few reasonable safeguards that railroad men had never objected to. Railroads, moreover, had to be allowed to engage in other forms of transportation enterprise if Congress's oft-repeated goal of encouraging the best features of all modes was to be realized. It remained for a doughty congressman from, of all places, West Virginia, to lead the way with, in all justice, the help of most of his colleagues and members of the railroad industry. Harley O. Staggers sponsored the bill which in 1980 became the law bearing his name, which gives the railroads the freedom to run the enterprises for which they are responsible.

Perhaps the ghost of another West Virginia politico, Stephen B. Elkins, who had wryly watched his name being fastened to the Mann-Elkins Act of 1910 that he had resolutely opposed, could smile at the thought that finally a legislator from his home state was getting his name on a piece of constructive legislation and, moreover, one that took an optimistic view of human nature and of business for a change. The only cost to the nation was a little Amtrak train bringing daily service over the B. & O. to the rugged interior of Congressman Staggers's beloved state. It carried a few passengers, and more than a few sightseers who wanted to see the scenery at the confluence of the Potomac and Shenandoah rivers, which many declare to be one of the finest landscapes in the world. It was a cost we were more than willing to pay. After all, had not the great Thomas Jefferson himself remarked that the view from Harper's Ferry was worth a trip across the Atlantic? It turned out to be worth a great deal more than that.

Masters in their Own House

"We are not blessed with a lot of coal or bulk commodities along our railroad. To grow we have to reach out for intermodal business." Thus spoke Michael R. Haverty, president of the Santa Fe, as the first decade under the Staggers Act was drawing to its close.

"Railroads just have an inherent cost advantage in long-haul lanes, especially to the west coast. No truckload carrier can compete with a western railroad that has forty-eight hour delivery between the Midwest and west coast and can go seventy miles per hour across the desert." The speaker was Kirk Thompson, president of J. B. Hunt Co., one of the nation's leading premium trucking lines.

Messrs. Haverty and Thompson knew what they were talking about, for they had just concluded a business deal that was typical of the dramatic changes that had taken place in the railroad business—*no, the freight transportation business!*—in the first decade under the Staggers Act. The two carriers were announcing a new door-to-door freight transportation service in which Hunt would handle shipments at the east end of their axis, in eastern Michigan and Ohio, and again at the rail terminal in southern California—shipments which the Santa Fe would haul at seventy miles an hour across the prairies of Illinois and Missouri, the Great Plains of Kansas and Colorado, and then the deserts of New Mexico, Arizona, and California.

Then came the bombshell: the service would cost shippers somewhat more than conventional intermodal ("piggyback") service, but *less* than the best all-truck service available. Hunt's people would do the "marketing" (that is, solicit the business and see that the customers were kept happy) and the railroads would keep the trains moving. Marketing of transportation services by rail—formerly "traffic management"—no longer meant that the shipper would analyze his needs, decide that rail was the best way, and then come, hat in hand, to the railroad to ask for a rate. The smart young men and women who are entering the railroad—no, freight transportation—business now do their best to keep ahead of the customers, to know their needs before they do, and to lay out for them the best way to satisfy them, which they can do because they represent a *system,* not a mode of transportation artificially fenced into what somebody in Washington thought was its proper corner. From now on marketing will be the most dynamic element in transportation management, just as it had become paramount in manufacturing many years before.

The rebirth of America's railroads has meant the long-delayed rationalization of the balance between rail and rubber-tired transportation, a process that is continuing. The conventional wisdom is that rail transportation is never likely to be practical (except for some notable exceptions) for distances under four hundred miles, because of the high ratio of terminal time to running time on short runs. But what the ultimate balance between truck and rail will be is an open question. Other factors than mere cost minimization, such as cargo security, pollution, and safety of the highways, may dictate a shift from truck to rail. There will always be plenty of money to be made in the truck business, quite possibly more than under the old either/or system, once the characteristics of a sweated industry are being removed. The highways are not yet safe from truck misuse, but we have a chance to make them safe. And it should never be forgotten that trucking, a relatively easy business for men to move into and out of, will forever be a better shield against "monopolistic" pricing by railroads than the Interstate Commerce Commission could ever be.

The provisions of the Staggers Act and various minor statutes that also bear on the liberation of the railroads are a subject for dry textbooks on transportation. The important thing was that Staggers did away with the absolute control of the ICC over maximum or minimum freight rates (at first for the railroads and later, as if an afterthought, for the trucks too). The commission was to participate in rate-making only when a careful study of the conditions facing a given shipper or group of shippers in a given locality revealed that competition between carriers did not exist and "monopolistically" determined rates had resulted. The railroads have been careful to avoid offending on such grounds, having learned a long time ago that in such confrontations little business almost always wins over big business, and adducing the "expert" testimony of economists is about as useful as placing opposing psychologists on the witness stand.

Almost of equal importance in the great revolution was the freeing of the railroads to make rate contracts; that is, to agree with a given shipper to haul his goods between stated points for a rate good for the life of the contract. The terms under which a railroad was hauling for a shipper, however, were disclosable to all interested parties, obviously including competitors, and anyone who wished to meet the contract conditions could have the same terms. Such a polished technique of doing business could never have worked in the old days, but by the last half of the twentieth century shippers were, for the most part, large, sophisticated, and eagle-eyed. And thus competition remains "the life of trade."

The boxcar, familiar bearer of the proud corporate name of hundreds of American railroads, is disappearing from our rails. Once a source of entertainment as father and son read off the names in rapid succession while they waited for the train to clear the grade crossing, they are being replaced by "toffsie" and "coffsie"—TOFC, trailer on flat car, and COFC, container on flat car, or just plain "piggyback," to use the old generic term. A gigantic fleet of covered hopper cars also carries much freight that once went in boxcars, for example, grain at harvest time. The truck trailers, of course, originate largely in domestic service, while the containers may have begun their journey tucked efficiently by the hundreds and thousands in the holds of the fleet of *marus* (Japanese for steamship) or other flag vessels, many thousands of miles from the American mainland.

But containers are being used more and more in domestic service, for they are becoming the standard mode of packing, hauling, and delivering merchandise freight. (Thus carriers have taken everything that corrupt or resentful stevedores, pilferers, and vandals could throw at them, and won.) The container, two of which fit neatly on a standard-length flat car, is the reincarnation of the Pennsylvania Railroad's 1920s container, which the ICC stiff-armed to death sixty years ago. But the best was yet to come: by the end of the decade the clear winner in the rolling stock stakes was the double-stack container. Two containers, stacked atop an articulated section of a five-section carrier, place the maintenance-of-way department on its mettle; this is no place for boys. The sight of a hundred or more of these double-stack cars, drawn by a four-, five-, or even six-unit diesel locomotive "lashup" at seventy miles an hour across the Mojave Desert or the Great Plains, around the Pennsylvania Railroad's (now Conrail's) famous Horseshoe Curve, across the long bridge at Harper's Ferry, or through the rolling hills of the Mohawk River Valley water-level route in upstate New York, makes mere words extraneous to an understanding of what has happened to our good and faithful servant, the American freight train.

Now fully established is the "land bridge," which James J. Hill prophesied ninety years ago, in a sea-and-rail route from Asia to the west coast of the United States across the land mass to Gulf or east coast ports and on to Europe. It will eventually make of the vaunted Panama Canal a useless ditch, which, in fact, American railroads were about to make of it at the turn of the century before darkness at noon descended upon them.

Railroad companies, of which there are now only a few, most of which are very large consolidations, have been buying trucking companies and even barge lines, a new freedom for them and in some ways the most revolutionary feature of the Staggers legislation. Wise, enterprising truck lines who know how to operate as modern businesses may find it desirable to remain independent entities, but they know that their lot is now cast with the railroads, and vice versa. User fees are on the way, and the seventy-year free ride of the river carriers will soon be a thing of the past. The sensible idea that users of public roads or waterways should pay their full share of the costs in user fees has been fought tooth and nail by truckers and boatmen, but tooth and nail wear thin, and so does congressional patience with selfish special interests when the members realize where the bill eventually ends up.

Figure 15.1 "If You've Got it, TOFC-COFC Probably Brought It Most of the Way." Not all double-stack container trains are a mile long and streak across thousands of miles of desert and prairie west of the Missouri River. Here, a Norfolk Southern double-stack train from Chicago, with freight that mostly originated on the far side of the Pacific Ocean, arrives at the Welland, Ontario, container terminal after a speedy trip behind a single diesel locomotive with a two-man crew. This fast service has made rail transportation of high-class merchandise fully competitive with highway modes for distances of more than 700 miles, and, more important, has reduced the real costs of such transportation to American society.

From Welland, trucks will take the containers to many Canadian destinations as well as U.S. points in the Niagara Frontier. Under deregulation, these trucks may be operated by certificated trucking companies, private truckers, or even the railroad itself. (*Courtesy of Norfolk Southern Corporation*)

Water carriage, while it has been a thorn in the side of the railroads for a long time, has its own problems. Speed is the key element in service nowadays, not bare cost, and the barges don't have it. Nor are they a truly all-weather mode. The Ohio River, for many years now more a canal than a river, seems increasingly inclined to freeze up in the dead of winter, while at one point in the 1980s a prolonged drought grounded hundreds of millions of dollars' worth of cargo until, after weeks, the rains finally came. The dismal flop of the biggest and most classic pork-barrel caper of them all, the Tombigbee Waterway in Alabama, was a shock to nearly everybody. The railroads that have lined Old Man River for 130 years are fighting back. We will not take up the rails just yet.

As has long been the case, the railroads derive most of their revenues from carload, and even trainload, shipments of relatively few commodities. The old standby has been coal, and today it is booming as environmentalists agonize over which is worse, nuclear disaster or acid rain. The future of the superb and virtually limitless coal deposits in the Pocahontas, southern Ohio, and southern Illinois bituminous fields is at present beclouded by regulations against high-sulfur coals. Eventually we will solve the problem of efficient, clean-burning furnaces, and the future for solid fuels will probably be bright for the next century, at least. Meanwhile, low-sulfur requirements have been a boon to certain western and midwestern railroads. The "brown coal" (lignite) that lies in untold billions of tons in Wyoming and Montana was scorned for many years as long as carbon content and high burning temperatures were cardinal virtues and smoke just another symbol of prosperity. Led primarily by the aggressive new executives of Burlington Northern, which serves these fields most directly, but with the enthusiastic and well-heeled participation of the Union Pacific and a nice cut of the pie to the limping North Western, these fields have been vigorously exploited, and these railroads visibly refreshed. Today trains of previously unheard of length and gross tonnage rack up daily traffic figures over heavily built, beautifully maintained, and carefully signaled single-track mainlines that statistically make America's railroads far and away more important to the nation in absolute terms than ever they were in their so-called heyday.

The story of how the railroads continued to fight for traffic the trucks and barges thought they had locked up is generally disheartening before Staggers, but as we have seen there were isolated victories. A significant one was that the railroads made a clear case for taking the arrogant rack-carriers that were hauling new automobiles to market off the highways, before Jimmy Hoffa's Teamsters Union and the American Trucking Association knew what had hit them. In this case the railroads were able to prove they were offering a fully remunerative rate, which the other carriers could not afford in the long run. Now the railroads pack fifteen shiny new cars on rail rack cars, safely enclosed from the

depredations of vandals, and the truckers have the short haul from dis-
tributors to dealers, and not always that. Airliners, like autos, often go
by rail before they go by their intended mode. Midwestern and eastern
contractors to the Boeing Company build large segments of the fuse-
lage of the big 747 jetliner, and employees of Burlington Northern
grow hoarse answering the same question: "What are those great big
boxes on that freight train?" as they roll across northern Montana.
Meanwhile, modern, automatic, trouble-free refrigeration equipment is
bringing the long-distance haulage of perishables back to the railroads,
including the fresh and frozen citrus from Florida and California that
mean huge tonnages.

It is in the marketing department of the railroads, as it is now
called, that smart young M.B.A.'s start out these days, if they choose to
go to work for a railroad. And while they will take their turn at all
phases of railroad operations, if they can stand the hard work and the
fresh air and the thrill of it all, the marketing department is very likely
where they will find the logical ladder to the top echelons. In the blue-
collar trades, the future is less clear. Only by drastically reducing the
number of workers on the railroads, and resorting to every conceivable
labor-saving device the railroads could dream up and afford, are the
railroads able to compete at all. Obviously, this process must end somewhere, and future growth of traffic may indeed require some small
growth in employment levels. The most unpleasant problem is what to
do about the level of wages, not to mention the brotherhoods' very real
compulsion to ask for more periodically.

The time has come for organized labor to recognize that along with
their considerable power in the affairs of the railroads must go a share
of the managerial responsibility. How to lodge that point right down at
the rank-and-file level? Union executives who counsel no increase this
time around, much less a decrease, don't get reelected to their jobs. A
clear case can be made, however, that a large number of the men who
voted in recent years for constantly more generous wage rates are no
longer railroad men. It is becoming a categorical imperative that wage
structures must be rethought, which is a euphemism for "giveback,"
perhaps, but it often has been found that in the long run, less is more.

Partial deregulation of American railroads has in no way guaranteed their long-term survival. Until the fourteen remaining Class I railroads in the United States have attained a level of return on capital
commensurate with the cost of capital in the free market, and have
squirreled away reserves adequate to carry them through the periodic
net revenue famines that economic downturns bring, they will not be
blue chip investments again, if they ever were. Freedom from the "full
crew" laws and other similar burdens is imperative, but federal incorporation of railroads is not necessary de jure, for it has nearly been
achieved de facto. Freedom to diversify by acquiring other businesses
that are reasonably related to transportation should come next.

One of the most interesting recommendations for a change in national railroad policy has been for the government to acquire title to the rights of way, maintain them, and allow private enterprises to operate their trains upon them at a fee. Such a policy seems neither necessary nor desirable. There never has been any question of whether railroad men could keep their lines in good, efficient, safe condition, but only whether they were going to be allowed to earn enough to do it. Somebody would have to pay, in any event, and the case for adding such a headache to the bloated federal budget at this point is a weak one. Even more to the point is whether railroad executives, even if tempted to seize this opportunity no longer to pay general property taxes on their lines, would really want to operate their superb new freight trains—gigantic convoys of cargo, really—on roadways that might be maintained no better than the Interstate highway system has been in recent years.

Can the railroads continue to produce the miracles of productivity enhancement that they have turned in since World War II? It would be a foolish person who would answer flatly, yes or no, to such a question. "Experience must be our only guide; reason may mislead us." It is marvelous that this oldest of inland transportation technologies should still be the one most fruitful of great gains from modest infusions of fresh capital to raise the amount of transportation a man or woman can produce in a day's work. It will all be needed, and more, for the most conservative projections show intercity freight traffic reaching breathtaking new heights in the new century. Volume today is two-and-one-half times that of 1929, when the railroads carried 75 percent of common carrier intercity freight and the trucks, 3.2 percent. The railroads' share has bottomed out since 1970, amounting to 37 percent in 1988, which represents a cool *trillion* ton-miles, while the shares of other modes seem to have stopped growing. Trains play a leading role in petroleum conservation: in 1988 an average ton of freight was moved 315 miles on a gallon of diesel fuel, which was more than 50 percent farther than in 1955.

What do the railroads need most? Like all worthwhile forms of human endeavor, they need most of all to bid successfully for the best and brightest young people to train for leadership positions in the future. It should not be surprising that there remains a major job of reacquainting American boys and girls with the force that did more than any other material development to create the world they live in. "Why do you spend so much time on railroads, when we don't use them anymore?" asked one young man of his professor not so many years ago. Here is a real job of rehabilitation crying out to be undertaken. But first we must channel both college and high school students back into honest-to-god history courses. At the same time Americans must persuade the teachers and professors who have so much influence upon the young that they must abandon whatever lingering misconceptions they may have about what the late, great French economic historian, Fernand Braudel, called *"civilization matériel."* The work of the people is always their greatest story, and that means from the pick and shovel right up to the executive suite.

Not long after the Staggers Act became law in 1980, a business history professor in one of the nation's oldest and most prestigious universities was pleased to receive a visit from one of his best students. The tall, pleasant, good-looking young man looked like prime material for some future executive suite. He wanted to know what the professor thought about railroading as a career for the likes of him. (He might have asked the school's professor of transportation, but that gentleman was a specialist in truck transportation, not railroads.) The historian gave the young man as objective an evaluation as he could, emphasizing that railroading did not offer the "quiet life" so many of his generation professed to value, and that promotion in the early years was traditionally slow. But much was about to change, he noted. Marketing was coming to the fore, and a premium was on innovation in the services railroads offered. The training he would get in all phases of railroading would qualify him to have good ideas. And good ideas would be in demand.

Whether the young man ever went into railroading, his professor never knew. If he did, he found all the signal lights on the line showing green. As for the professor, he knows well that life almost always looks most worth living to those who do not have all that much of it left to live, but few could deny that a new railroad age was dawning as the much-maligned twentieth century drew to a close. World events presented as favorable an aspect as anyone, young or old, could wish for.

Bliss was it in that dawn to be alive.
But to be young was very heaven.

Comments on the Sources

This is in no sense a "complete" bibliography of documentary or published sources for this book. Such a listing would be impossible, and of little use to the reader. In these notes I have mentioned sources that have significantly influenced my thinking on the broad topic of American inland transportation, and which I think the reader who wants to begin or continue the same process of self-education that I have been going through for at least thirty years, will find fruitful. Readers who wish to suggest vital sources that I have overlooked will, as the Victorians liked to say, "confer a great favor" by letting me know. In this case, to list is not to exclude. Indeed, almost everything that has been written about the rise of material civilization in America during the past century and a half has been, in one way or another, about railroads.

1. Nerves of Copper, Arteries of Iron

There is no comprehensive history of American railroads, and there probably never will be. Such a work would run to several large volumes, lack forward narrative drive because of the need to pay attention to the thousands of individual railroad corporations that were subsequently woven into only fourteen Class I railroads by 1990, and suffer from the weaknesses inherent in joint authorship undertakings. Evidence of this is the *Encyclopedia of American Business History and Biography,* of which the first two volumes deal with railroads. Volume 2, ed. Keith L. Bryant, Jr., *Railroads in the Age of Regulation, 1900–1980* (1988), is a better job than vol. 1., ed. Robert L. Frey, *Railroads in the Nineteenth Century* (1988), which suffered from a change in editorship at midpoint. The *Encyclopedia* in general is weakened by its attempt to be both biographical and institutional/technological in scope and consequently does not do as good a job of either as the resources devoted to it should have permitted, but if used with care it can be very helpful.

John F. Stover, *Iron Road to the West: American Railroads in the 1850s* (1978) is a good first look at the "take-off period" in American railroad development. Stover's *American Railroads* (1961) is a superficial but useful survey, written at a time when the railroads seemed to have little future. Oliver Jensen, *The American Heritage History of Railroads in America* (1975), king of the cocktail table set, is far from adequate as history but does justice to the subject in what has long been one of its most outstanding features: its photogenic qualities. No reader can afford, moreover, to overlook the series of picture books that the irrepressible Lucius Beebe and Charles Clegg turned out, most notably *The Age of Steam* (1957?).

The serious reader will turn quickly from triple-distilled surveys to regional and corporate histories, having doubtless begun to suspect that he is going to have to fashion a personal history of railroads in his own psyche. Moving from east to west, George Pierce Baker, *Formation of the New England Railroad System* (1937), is superb on both the New Haven Railroad and its competitors. Alvin F. Harlow, *Steelways of New England* (1946), is a readable, reliable study by one who made his living with his typewriter by combining a scholarly love of his subject with a felicitous literary style. Another such author was Edward Hungerford, especially his old but still useful work, *The Story of the Baltimore & Ohio Railroad, 1827–1927* (2 vols., 1928). Edward C. Kirkland, *Men, Cities, and Transportation* (2 vols., 1948), magisterial yet very readable, is by a well-respected economic historian who said his main object was "to free New England from the colonial period." Gregg M. Turner and Melancthon W. Jacobus, *Connecticut Railroads: An Illustrated History* (1986), is simply superb. No other attempt to tell the story of railroading in a single state by means of a maximum of period photographs and a minimum of text can match it. Every railroad that ever operated in Connecticut as an independent line is represented.

The Middle Atlantic and the Midwest have not been as well treated as the South and West, although the scholarly literature contains many articles and dissertations on the impact of the railroad upon industrial Pennsylvania and the agricultural Midwest. John Stover, *Railroads of the South* (1955), is invaluable. There are many corporate histories of varying value, most of them now out of date.

Fortunately, there has been a notable improvement in railroad corporate histories in recent years. Such works seem to fall into three categories. One was the company-financed history by a hired author, usually undertaken to celebrate anniversaries. In all justice, they were far better than nothing, and Miles C. Kennedy and George H. Burgess, *Centennial History of the Pennsylvania Railroad Co., 1846–1946* (1947) is still the best we have of this all-important railroad. Apart from the very early history of the New York Central—for example, F. W. Stevens, *The Beginnings of the New York Central Railroad* (1926)—there is no good history of this vital enterprise. More scholarly in their approach, but severely limited by both original documentary sources and the financial resources fully to exploit them, are books like John F. Stover, *Illinois Central* (1975) and *History of the Baltimore & Ohio Railroad* (1987), and Maury Klein, *History of the Louisville & Nashville Railroad* (1972). H. Roger Grant, *History of the Chicago Great Western Railroad* (1984), is an excellent study of one of the smaller Class I railroads, now defunct.

The third phase of railroad corporate history has been marked by professional historians minutely researching railroad archives with the full cooperation and financial support of the company, as well as its patience in waiting to see the results. The late Richard C. Overton, after many a summer and occasional sabbatical year, produced his massive *Burlington Route: A History of the Burlington Lines* (1965), which is crammed with significant information about Boston capitalists and western entrepreneurs and effectively does much to lay earlier notions about the circumstances of western railroad development to rest. Other examples are Ralph W. Hidy, Muriel Hidy and Roy V. Scott, with Don Hofsommer, *The Great Northern Railway: A History* (1988); Hofsommer's *The Southern Pacific, 1901–1985* (1986); and, most impressively, Maury Klein's two massive volumes on the *Union Pacific:* vol. 1, *The Birth of a Railroad, 1862–1893* (1987), and vol. 2, *The Rebirth, 1894–1969* (1989). A neglected region in

American railroad history continues to be the Southwest, despite Ira G. Clark, *Then Came the Railroads: The Century from Steam to Diesel in the Southwest* (1958), which is full of interesting details of railroading in not-the-best "poor man's country." Also useful are several studies of the Santa Fe, the most recent of which is Keith L. Bryant, *History of the Atchison, Topeka & Santa Fe* (1974). A major work on early southern railroad history, which has been badly needed in view of the South's strikingly different social-economic environment, is Allen Trelease, *The North Carolina Railroad, 1849–1871, and the Modernization of North Carolina* (1990).

It would seem a foolish undertaking for anyone to attempt to measure quantitatively the impact of American railroads on American economic growth, in view of the countless factors involved, the paucity of available data, the lack of knowledge of the relationships between these forces, and disagreements on analytical method. The leading evidence of this is Robert W. Fogel, *Railroads and American Economic Growth* (1964), which was at first acclaimed but subsequently refuted on virtually every conceivable point, most notably his faulty application of the marginal analysis that is the basis of modern economic theory. The book today is a curiosity. Its popularity, however short, proved that few historians and almost no economists at that time grasped—or were willing to stand up for—the essentials of proper historical method, which no massive resort to statistics or application of expensive computers can repeal. A similar attempt at measurement by somewhat different methods was published by Albert Fishlow, *American Railroads and the Transformation of the Ante-Bellum Economy* (1966), who at least has not continued to maintain the adequacy of the Fogel-Fishlow technique as stridently as Fogel.

More useful economic analysis is to be found in Harold Barger, *The Transportation Industries, 1889–1946* (1951), and Albert Fishlow, "Productivity and Technological Change in the Railroad Sector," in *Output, Employment, and Productivity in the United States After 1880* (1966), which reveal the stunning advances in output of transportation services per unit of labor and capital input achieved by the railroads in the nineteenth century.

Very little interest has been shown in the telegraph by historians in recent years. Robert L. Thompson, *Wiring a Continent: The History of the Telegraph Industry in the United States, 1832–1866* (1947) needs to be brought down to the present. Richard B. DuBoff, "Business Demand and the Development of the Telegraph in the United States, 1844–1860," 54 *Business History Review* 459–479 (Winter 1980), explains the factors that made the telegraph so much more useful to business in this country than in Europe.

2. A Nation on Wheels: The Formative Years of the American Passenger Train, 1830–1870

3. Mobile, Hard-Working, and Hard-Playing: Rail Travel and the Transformation of American Society, 1870–1900

Travel, especially pre-railroad travel, in America used to be much more popular with historians when they did not mind being considered antiquarians also. Seymour Dunbar, *A History of Travel in America* (4 vols., 1915), especially vol. 2, is very interesting. Many books have appeared over the years on travel from the earliest times, on roads and turnpikes, by steamboats on the rivers, and on canal boats. Among the best I would place Philip B. Jordan, *The National Road* (1947); Francis S. Philbrick, *The Rise of the West* (1965); Wheaton J. Lane, *From Indian Trail to Iron Horse: Travel and Transportation in New Jersey, 1620–1860* (1939); Elise Lathrop, *Early American Inns and Taverns* (1935); Alvin F. Harlow, *Old Towpaths* (1926); Harry Scheiber, *Ohio Canal Era* (1969); and Louis C. Hunter, *Steamboats on the Western Rivers* (1949). There is a biography of President Franklin Pierce by Roy F. Nicholls, *Franklin Pierce, Young Hickory of the Granite Hills* (2nd ed., 1931).

Commentaries by travelers through the United States in the early period are numerous and many have been collected in modern editions. Charles Dickens's opinions of mid-century America, from chewing tobacco to river boats, is noteworthy and figures frequently in Allan Nevins, *American Social History as Recorded by British Travelers* (1934), (1948 edition retitled *America Through British Eyes*), and in Harlow, *op. cit.* The intrepid Harriet Martineau recorded her observations, equally pungent, in *Retrospect of Western Travel* (1838), available on microform. Frederick Law Olmsted did the same for the South in his *Journey in the Seaboard Slave States, 1853–54* (1904). Also see John A. Jakle, *Images of the Ohio Valley: A Historical Geography of Travel, 1740–1860* (1977); Benjamin F. Taylor, *The World on Wheels, and Other Sketches* (1874); Samuel Bowles, *The Pacific Railroad Open—How to Go; What to See; Guide to and Through Western America* (1869); James Fullerton Muirhead, *America, Land of Contrasts* (3rd ed., 1902), earlier editions with somewhat different titles; W. F. Rae, *Westward by Rail: The New Route to the East* (1871, reprinted 1974); Anne Henry Ehrenpreis, ed., *Happy Country, This America: The Travel Diary of Henry Arthur Bright* (1978).

Railroad passenger travel in America developed not merely according to sheer distance but also by the vastly enlarged potential for getting people from one place to another that the steam railroad brought. Through service began to be provided almost from the beginning. George R. Taylor and Irene D. Neu, *The American Railroad Network, 1861–1890* (1956) is the best study of the process by which the bits and pieces of early railroads were physically united. Historians, however, have not given much attention to the development of through passenger schedules involving no change of cars, although such routes began to appear very early, and the perfection of major routes preceded by a generation the recasting of the corporate form of railroads from independents to consolidated systems. The best way to see it happening is in the periodical volumes of timetables that began to appear in the 1840s. Until after the Civil War the leading guides were Appleton's publications, such as *Appleton's Railroad and Steamboat Companion* (1847); *Appleton's Railway and Steam Navigation Guide* (1856); and *Appleton's Companion Handbook of Travel* (1864). There were numerous imitators. All are today considered rare books. One of the best collections of railroad history from all periods is in the Baker Library of the Harvard Graduate School of Business Administration, which also has, for example, a complete run beginning in the 1830s of the authoritative *Railway Gazette* (title varies over the years). In June 1868 the first issue of the monthly *Travelers Official Railway Guide* appeared. It quickly became the station agent's "bible," as it has remained ever since under the title, *Official Guide of the Railways and Steam Navigation Lines of the U.S., Puerto Rico, Canada, Mexico and Cuba.*

Of great and enduring value as a survey of transportation developments in the antebellum period, and the developments in manufacturing and commerce that followed, is George Rogers Taylor's *The Transportation Revolution, 1815–1869* (1951).

4. The Passenger Train Creates Modern America

5. The Passenger Train Exalted, 1900–1990

The technological development of railroad passenger travel has been continuous since the beginning and continues to be so. John H. White, Jr.'s *The American Railroad Passenger Car* (1978), swept all earlier authorities from the field. It is truly magisterial, in its scope and in the detail and precision, and certainly in its physical dimensions. Many of the chapters are in effect short essays on aspects of passenger car design and construction. The one on George Pullman and the rise of the Pullman Company, for example, is better than the book-length studies that have appeared over the years, most of which are concerned primarily with Pullman's admittedly bizarre personnel policies. White's encyclopedic volume identifies and tells something about dozens of suppliers of components of railroad passenger cars who, although long since departed from the scene, were critical in the history of American inland transportation. The vital role of the railroad depot, especially in the small towns that dominated American life before World War I and for some years thereafter, is dealt with in H. Roger Grant and Charles W. Bohi, *The Country Railroad Station in America* (1978), with emphasis upon the architecture. Contemporary with the railroads' development was the enrichment of entertainment in the provinces. The best example is the traveling circus, of which Tom Parkinson and Charles Philip Fox, *The Circus Moves by Rail* (1978), is a delightful pictorial study. The mail and express service as builders of the American town have attracted very little attention from historians, as has the U.S. Post Office since the coming of the railroad. The interurban railroads, however, have fascinated scholars far beyond their actual importance. See George W. Hilton and John F. Due, *The Electric Urban Railways in America* (1960). As sources for appreciating small-town life in that long-ago time, the rich fiction of the period, and the motion pictures that have been based on it since, should not be overlooked.

Safety on the railroads was a hot topic for many years, and one that axe-grinding politicians and reformers have not hesitated to use in a misleading fashion. "A little learning is a dangerous thing," said Alexander Pope, and any set of statistics is a case in point. Direct comparisons of American and European railroad accident figures were repeatedly made and unwarranted conclusions drawn, even as railroad men patiently noted that American practice was to report all accidents requiring treatment, however slight, whereas European railroads reported only those involving the loss of at least two weeks' work. The long-term figures for American railroads in the *Historical Statistics of the United States* and the annual *Statistical Abstract*, both U.S. government publications, permit fair conclusions as to trends. The best work on railroad safety and its occasional, lamentable lapses, is Robert B. Shaw, *History of Railroad Accidents, Safety Precautions, and Operating Practices* (1978).

With the possible exception of the courthouse, the railroad depot was often the most notable building in urban America. In major cities where they have been preserved they are important examples of architectural fashion. Carroll

L. V. Meeks, *The Railroad Station, An Architectural History* (1956), treats the subject admirably and on an international scale. A superb study of America's leading railroad town, Chicago, with valuable photographs and an intelligent text, is George H. Douglas, *Rail City: Chicago, U.S.A.* (1981). John R. Stilgoe, *Metropolitan Corridor: Railroads and the American Scene* (1983), is an interesting effort to describe what the golden age of railroading was like by someone who is too young to be guided by memory and needs to learn a bit more about his subject, especially freight transportation, which he neglects altogether. His efforts at digging up period photographs that show the often grim scenery that the railroads created were highly successful. Equally as impressionistic as Stilgoe is James A. Ward, *Railroads and the Character of America, 1820–1887* (1986), a fascinating look at the earlier period. Ward's literary style, when it works, is worth a thousand pictures in describing the swirling blend of public attitudes that the railroads stimulated and had to deal with.

6. The First Energy Revolution

Coal, someone has said, is "a grubby little product," and the same may be said for its literature, or most of it, judging by the lack of interest in the subject even among economic historians. W. Stanley Jevons, whose early death deprived England of a superb mathematician, elegant theorist, and hardheaded thinker on matters of political economy, would have deplored Americans' tendency to forget their remarkable history of finding new sources of fuel. His little book, *The Coal Question: An Inquiry Concerning the Progress of Our Coal Mines* (1865), tells why. Edward A. Wrigley, *Industrial Growth and Population Change: A Regional Study of the Coalfield Areas of Northeast Europe in the Later Nineteenth Century* (1962), and *People, Cities and Wealth: The Transformation of Traditional Society* (1987), explain why the coming of cheap inland transportation unleashed coal's potential for industrial development. James MacFarlane was a professor of geology at Columbia University in the 1870s. His thick treatise, *The Coal Regions of America* (1873), served as a guidebook to entrepreneurs on the far frontier, one of whom was James J. Hill. The swift puncturing of the surface of the eastern United States with coal mines once rail transportation became general in the 1870s is well treated in a contemporary account, Andrew Roy, *The Coal Mines* (1876). Howard Eavenson, *The First Century and a Quarter of American Coal Industry* (1938, repr. 1942) is perhaps most frequently cited by historians, but its confinement to the period before the mid-1880s and its emphasis upon lengthy extracts from period writings limit it as a history.

The anthracite coal industry, as the higher end of the industry for so many years, has produced many studies. Chester Lloyd Jones, *The Economic History of the Anthracite-Tidewater Canals* (1908) is still valuable, although Julius I. Bogen's *The Anthracite Railroads* (1927) is more frequently cited. (Note that both books focus primarily on the means of getting the coal to market.) The impact of cheap coal, even if it was cantankerous anthracite, on the location of American manufacturing plants, which had formerly been tied to sources of water power, seems obvious, now that Alfred D. Chandler, Jr., has pointed it out in "Anthracite Coal and the Beginnings of the Industrial Revolution in the United States," 46 *Business History Review* 143–81 (Summer 1972).

The bituminous coal industry, which quickly came to dominate the field in both tonnage and value of product, is of greatest interest today. Howard N. Eavenson treated the fabulous coal fields around Pittsburgh, upon which the American steel industry was largely founded, in *The Pittsburgh Coal Bed: Its Early History and Development* (1938). It includes an astounding map of the Monongahela and Youghiogheny River valleys with very small-print lists of mines, by name (apparently for the most part that of somebody's wife or daughter) at various points along the streams. The vital role of transportation is demonstrated even more dramatically by the fact that the incredibly thick seams of fine bituminous coal known to exist in what became the Pocahontas field of western Virginia, West Virginia, and Kentucky, were not exploited until Frederick Kimball led in the takeover of what became the Norfolk & Western at the end of the 1870s. The story is told in one of the best business histories we have, Joseph T. Lambie, *From Mine to Market: The History of Coal Transportation on the Norfolk & Western Railway* (1954). William Jasper Nicholls, *The Story of American Coals* (1908?), in addition to being an excellent analysis of the introduction of coal in America, contains a graphic description of "the largest coal depot in the world," near Perth Amboy, New Jersey.

The period since coal stopped being used as a heating fuel or in locomotives—i.e., since it became invisible to the ordinary person—is concerned largely with "energy," not wood, coal, natural gas, fuel oil, or nuclear power. The death of anthracite, however, is told, rather lugubriously, in *The Story of Anthracite* (no author; sponsored, apparently, by the Hudson Coal Co., 1932), which discusses, rather more in sadness than in anger, the problems of running a dying industry that has been organized by a very much alive John L. Lewis. But see also Richard Ramsay Mead, *An Analysis of the Decline of the Anthracite Industry Since 1921* (1933).

Modern studies of coal and its place in the American economy are generally forbidding to all but specialists. Alexander Mackenzie Thompson, *Technology, Labor, and Industrial Structure of the U.S. Coal Industry—A Historical Perspective* (1979), is perhaps an exception. See also Richard L. Gordon, *Historical Trends in Coal Utilization and Supply* (1976); his *U.S. Coal and the Electric Power Industry* (1975); and, also, his *Coal in the U.S. Energy Market* (1978). Readers who would like to see what the western railroads were doing in the decade of the late 1970s and 1980s to bring the low-sulfur coals of Montana and Wyoming to the rescue of gasping easterners, are referred to the beautifully researched, written, photographed, and cartographed article by Fred W. Frailey and Gary J. Benson, "Powder River Country," 50 *Trains* 40–63 (November 1989).

7. Oh, the Farmer and the Townsman Must Be Friends!

The history of agriculture, once so popular among American scholars and general readers, no longer appeals much to a nearly fully urbanized nation in which the number of farms has declined precipitously since World War I, even if output has continued to set new records. An interesting general history is John T. Schlebecker, *Whereby We Thrive: A History of American Farming, 1607–1972* (1975). Wayne D. Rasmussen, ed., *Agriculture in the United States: A Documentary History* (1975), is obviously far-ranging. The best general works in recent years, however, are Paul W. Gates, *The Farmer's Age, 1815–1860* (1960), dealing largely with the pre-railroad years, and Fred A. Shannon, *The Farmer's Last Frontier, 1860–1897* (1963). Both books are actually general economic histories for their periods, with the focus on agriculture. Shannon's is marred somewhat by a traditional approach which seeks constantly to help the farmer externalize his discontents. For the various interpretations of interregional commerce before the Civil War, see the articles in William N. Parker, ed., *Structure of the Cotton Economy of the Antebellum South* (1970), especially Diane Lindstrom's contribution.

Wheat figures importantly in agricultural history, and its marvels are detailed in John Storck and Walter D. Teague, *Flour for Man's Bread* (1952). Wheat is the leading player in John G. Clark's superb study, *Grain Trade of the Old Northwest* (1966), which chronicles the lengths to which early western Americans had to go to make their farms commercially viable, efforts which were vastly relieved by the coming of the railroads. The history of the rise of produce exchanges, and especially such arcane practices as futures trading, has remained something of a mystery that scholars can not or will not clear up. A practical, nontheoretical book on the evolution of the modern channels of grain marketing from farm to consumer would forestall much fatuous speculation by the "new" economic historians. The social history of efforts to balance supply and demand in rural areas is well told in Thomas D. Clark, *Pills, Petticoats and Plows* (1944), a delightful study of the crossroads country general store.

The disposition of the public domain, and the impact of the railroad upon it, is a perennially popular and confused topic. A basic work is Roy M. Robbins, *Our Landed Heritage: The Public Domain, 1776–1936* (1942). Two outstanding monographs on the administration of major land grants are Paul Gates, *The Illinois Central Railroad and Its Colonization Work* (1934); and Richard C. Overton, *Burlington West: A Colonization History of the Burlington Railroad* (1941). The efforts of economic historians, working in their customary deductive method, to quantify the public and private benefits of land grants have satisfied no one, to some extent because both the facts and the objectives of the grants are unclear.

Mary Yeager (now Lithgow), in *Competition and Regulation: The Development of Oligopoly in the Meat-Packing Industry* (1981), updates much earlier material on the replacement of live cattle in the marketing of fresh meats in the eastern United States with railroad refrigerator car movement of dressed meats. It represents modern business history at its best, as does Harold D. Woodman, *King Cotton and His Retainers: The Cotton Crop of the South, 1800–1925* (1968). On the rise and decline of eastern Atlantic ports in the cotton export trade, see J. R. Killick, "The Transformation of Cotton Marketing in the Late Nineteenth Century: Alexander Sprunt & Son of Wilmington, N.C., 1866–1956," 55 *Business History Review* 143-169 (Summer 1981).

8. Carrying the People's Burden to Market

The literature on the evolution of freight transportation in the United States, even if confined to railroads, is enormous. This chapter is concerned with what was perhaps the railroads' most important single contribution to American economic development: the prompt attainment of a sound freight transportation business in the United States based on through routing on a uniform bill of lading. Even so, the sources cited here could be expanded almost without limit.

Fundamental to the discussion are George Rogers Taylor and Irene D. Neu, *The American Railroad Network, 1861–1890* (1956), and the appropriate chapters in Alfred D. Chandler, Jr., *The Visible Hand* (1977), on "system-building," as he calls it, in the last third of the nineteenth century.

The Windom Committee Report is *Transportation Routes to the Seaboard*, Senate Report 307, 43rd Cong., 1st Sess., vol. 3 (two tomes), serial 1588-89 (1874). The "Hepburn Committee" refers to a select committee of the lower house of the New York State Legislature in 1879 to investigate allegations of abuses by railroads operating in that state. It was chaired by Alonzo Barton Hepburn, who is not to be confused with William Peters Hepburn, a U.S. congressman from Iowa, whose name was given to the Act of 1906 giving the ICC the power to fix specific maximum railroad rates. See *Proceedings of the Special [Hepburn] Committee on Railroads, etc. . . . .* (5 vols., New York, 1879). Only the summary report of the committee members, which is a largely political document, was widely distributed, which was as effective a gag on William H. Vanderbilt and other New York State railroad men as one could want.

While upstate New York politicos were cultivating antirailroad sentiment, an obscure "statistician" (the title was hardly known in the 1870s) was turning out a series of reports that described in detail the transformation the railroads were making in channels of commerce in the United States. He was Joseph Nimmo, of the Treasury Department's Bureau of Internal Commerce. The first report is *First Annual Report on the Internal Commerce of the U.S.*, 44th Cong., 2nd Sess, House Exec. Doc. 46, Pt. 2 (1877); the 1879 report is 45th Cong., 3rd Sess., House Exec. Doc. 32, Pt. 3; and 1881, 46th Cong., 3rd Sess., House Exec. Doc. 7, Pt. 2. Reports for intervening years not cited generally deal with special topics. These reports describe a tidal wave of change, obvious even to the casual contemporary reader, which no force could possibly have turned back or even, it seemed, control.

Much has been published on the theory and practice of railroad freight rate-making, most of it in textbooks by authors with little practical knowledge of the subject. Three early works worth looking into for what they reveal about the change in philosophy between the late-Victorian and Progressive eras are Charles Francis Adams, Jr., *Railroads: Their Origins and Problems* (1878), by the man who knew what was wrong with transportation policy, public and private; Arthur T. Hadley, *Railroad Transportation: Its History and Its Laws* (1886), who thought it was on the way to being corrected; and William Z. Ripley, *Railroads: Rates and Regulation* and *Railroads: Finance and Organization* (both 1915), by the nation's leading "expert" on railroad economics at the time, whose ignorance of the realities of his subject helped him poison the springs of public understanding for two generations. Far more knowledgeable was the economist Henry Carter Adams, chief statistician of the Interstate Commerce Commission, whose treatise on the subject of railroad rates, *Digest of Hearings on Railway Rates . . . ,* 59th Cong., 1st Sess., Senate Doc. 244 (1905) is the best clarification of the subject I have seen. On the problems railroad leaders faced in the formative years, and the evolution of the administrative structure, see especially Thomas C. Cochran, *Railroad Leaders, 1845–1890,The Business Mind in Action* (1953), which is copiously illustrated by excerpts from its subjects' correspondence. Chandler, *op. cit.,* is the leading modern authority on managerial organization.

The matter of railroad "abuses" (a word carelessly applied by critics to any business practice of the railroads to which some interested party objected) has received more mature treatment by historians in recent years. The first myth to go was that farmers were in the vanguard of the Granger movement. That farmers, as usual, followed rather than led—frequently contrary to their own real interests—was demonstrated in George H. Miller, *Railroads and the Granger Laws* (1971). Earlier, Lee Benson, *Merchants, Farmers and Railroads: Railroad Regulation and New York Politics, 1850–1887* (1955), was a milestone, but Benson has never published anything since that promised so much, and he failed to follow up the implications of this highly influential book on the eastern interests motivating the Hepburn Committee. The failure of the ICC Act of 1887 to solve anything led to recantations by once-bitter proponents; see, for example, Gerald Nash, "The Reformer Reformed: John H. Reagan and Railroad Regulation," 29 *Business History Review* 189–96 (Summer 1955). Gabriel Kolko, searching for a "usable history," muddied the waters with his initially praised *Railroads and Regulation, 1877–1916* (1965), and Albro Martin, "The Troubled Subject of Railroad Regulation in the Gilded Age—A Reappraisal," 61 *Journal of American History* 339–71 (September 1974), helped clear them up. For anyone interested in mastering this subject, there is no substitute for browsing through the volumes of the *Commercial and Financial Chronicle,* which began publishing in 1865, for insights into issues that were alive and had not yet been embalmed in textbooks. Ralph L. Dewey, *The Long and Short Haul Principle of Rate Regulation* (1935) ought to be read by historians.

On pools, Julius Grodinsky, *The Iowa Pool* (1950), is the only scholarly monograph on the formation and operation of railroad pools but is very dull reading. The best place to learn about pools and all other "abuses" is the report of the Committee chaired by Senator Shelby M. Cullom in 1886 to investigate the need for a federal law regulating railroads: *Report of the Senate Select Committee on Interstate Commerce,* Senate Report 46, 49th Cong., 1st Sess., Pts. 1 and 2. For a modern summary of the long-short-haul controversy, and especially an answer to the question of why the Interstate Commerce Commission never wanted the power to regulate this "abuse," see Ralph L. Dewey, *The Long and Short Haul Principle of Rate Regulation* (1935). The transitional role of the "private car" lines, now almost forgotten, is told in L.H.D. Weld, *Private Freight Cars* (1908). For light on the highly controversial port differentials (and, by inference, the route differentials), see John Broughton Daish, ed., *The Atlantic Port Differentials: The Important and Official Documents* (1918). Hugo Richard Meyer, *Government Regulation of Railway Rates* (1905), is a classic example of the "prophet without honor in his own land."

9. From Mercantile Nation to Industrial Giant

The Final Report of the Industrial Commission, House Doc. 380, 57th Cong., 1st Sess, serial #4349 (1902), is a grand survey of the changes that were wrought in the American economy in the period since the Civil War and reveals clearly how aware of them Americans were in the new century. Volume 19 covers transportation.

The best study—and a very good one—of marketing in the American industrial economy before the coming of the railroad and in the formative years thereafter is Glenn Porter and Harold Livesay, *Merchants and Manufacturers: Studies in the Changing Structure of 19th Century Marketing* (1973). A brilliant essay on the causes of America's swift rise to world importance as a manufacturing nation is Thomas C. Cochran, *Frontiers of Change: Early Industrialism in America* (1981). Truly magisterial is Edward C. Kirkland's *Industry Comes of Age: Business, Labor, and Public Policy, 1860–1897* (1961), as useful and interesting a book on the great American economic adolescence as has ever been written. American industrialization as an organizational triumph is dealt with in great detail in Alfred D. Chandler, Jr., *The Visible Hand* (1977).

For James J. Hill's summary of the inadequacies of the American railroad system at the beginning of the twentieth century, see Albro Martin, *James J. Hill and the Opening of the Northwest* (1976), 536. The advent of cheap intracity transportation and its impact upon urbanization is well told in Sam Bass Warner, Jr., *Streetcar Suburbs* (1962). Retail trade has never been well served by historians, although men like Marshall Field have sometimes appealed to them. The chapter on marketing in Chandler, *op. cit.*, is a synthesis of the best we have on this subject. The business of distributing goods from factory to retail outlet to consumer has been in such a state of change for so long that one can learn most about it by resorting to a textbook in marketing, of which there are many.

The problem of logistics in large cities is treated in two valuable books by Carl W. Condit: *The Railroad and the City: A Technological and Urbanistic History of Cincinnati* (1977), and *The Port of New York: A History of the Rail and Terminal System from the Beginnings to Pennsylvania Station* (1980), which, as the title suggests, is mostly about the Pennsylvania Railroad's service to New York. The classic source remains John A. Droege, *Freight Terminals and Trains* (rev. ed., 1925). By far the best study of the railroads' natural habitat, Chicago, and one that is well illustrated too, is George H. Douglas, *Rail City—Chicago U.S.A.* (1981). Period pictures of New York in the early days of railroad transportation not easily found elsewhere are in John A. Kouwenhoven, *The Columbia Historical Portrait of New York* (1953).

10. From Entrepreneurs to Managers: The Founding Years

Cochran, *Railroad Leaders*, and Chandler, *Visible Hand*, both previously cited, are outstanding sources for understanding the evolution of managerial organization and procedure as the nineteenth century progressed.

The promoters of the Baltimore & Ohio are portrayed in John F. Stover, *History of the Baltimore & Ohio Railroad* (1987). There is no satisfactory biography of Erastus Corning, but see Irene D. Neu, *Erastus Corning, Merchant and Financier, 1794–1872* (1960), and, especially, Frank W. Stevens, *The Beginnings of the New York Central Railroad* (1926). The question of public assistance to private enterprises has excited much attention in recent years, especially in its application to railroads. The best studies are Carter Goodrich, *Government Promotion of American Canals and Railroads, 1800–1890* (1960); Louis Hartz, *The Liberal Tradition in America: An Interpretation of American Political Thought Since the Revolution;* and, especially, Stephen Salisbury, *The State, the Investor, and the Railroad: Boston & Albany, 1825–1867* (1967). The best example of the transference of capital from one industry to another, the former being in decline and the latter growing, is the move of Cornelius Vanderbilt from shipping to railroads; see Wheaton J. Lane, *Commodore Vanderbilt: An Epic of the Steam Age* (1942). The Reading and other anthracite roads are summarized in Julius I. Bogen, *The Anthracite Roads* (1927), but see also Robert J. Casey and W.A.S. Douglas, *The Lackawanna Story* (1951).

Much has been written about the physical feats of railroad building, but not much of value about the engineers themselves. John Jervis figures importantly in Stevens, *op. cit.*, but his brilliance shines through most clearly in his own work, *A Treatise on the Construction and Management of Railways* (1861), which is virtually unknown. Benjamin H. Latrobe, Jr., who is sometimes confused with his more famous father, the architect of the U.S. Capitol, has been unjustly upstaged by John W. Garrett, who expanded the B. & O., ultimately into bankruptcy after his death. Norbert R. Harwood, Jr.'s *Impossible Challenge: The Baltimore & Ohio Railroad in Maryland* (1979) is excellent on construction and operation on the eastern end of the B. & O. John Stover, *B. & O. (op. cit.)*, and Alfred D. Chandler, Jr., "The Railroads, Pioneers in Modern Corporate Management," 39 *Business History Review* 16–40 (Spring 1965), yield additional information on Latrobe, and Chandler also discusses Daniel McCallum of the Erie, another significant pioneer, as well. James A. Ward, *J. Edgar Thomson, Master of the Pennsylvania* (1980), is a valiant attempt to make bricks without straw, there being few documentary sources extant, but it is interesting for what it does tell us about a man who was more interesting that he probably intended to be. The mercurial Thomas A. Scott, who succeeded Thomson at the P.R.R., has not been popular with historians, probably because he is all but impossible to categorize. He surfaces in the literature from time to time but quickly submerges, as does his successor, no-nonsense George B. Roberts, as unlike Scott as daylight and dark. The early years of the railroads of the South have been poorly treated, but Allen W. Treleaase, *The North Carolina Railroad, 1849–1871, and the Modernization of North Carolina* (1990) is superbly definitive. Also already mentioned are Stover, *Railroads of the South,* and Klein, *The Great Richmond Terminal* (1970). Klein's distinction between two main types of entrepreneurs is provocative. Mark W. Summers, *Railroads, Reconstruction, and the Gospel of Prosperity* (1984) is a remarkable job of research in original sources but only succeeds in telling us what we already knew, that is, that there was so little financial entrepreneurship in the South during Reconstruction that the states had to manage it, and they were not up to it either. Sadly lacking is any indication of what real rate of interest the railroads paid on their politicized bonds, or what the people got in the way of railroads for whatever it cost them.

11. Entrepreneurs to Managers:
Across the Broad Missouri

For the details of McKinley's assassination, see Margaret Leech, *In the Days of McKinley* (1959) and H. Wayne Morgan, *William McKinley and His America* (1963). For the westward extension of the telegraph, see the final chapters in Robert L. Thompson, *Wiring a Continent* (1947). A mildly revisionist view of the early history of the Michigan Central Railroad is Robert Parks, *Democracy's Railroad* (1972). The roles of Joy, Brooks, and Forbes are admirably discussed in Arthur Johnson and Barry E. Supple, *Boston Capitalists and Western Railroads* (1967). The most impressive work of western railroad history, based on full access to documentary material public and private, is Maury Klein's *Union Pacific* (2 vols., 1987, 1989) *(op. cit.)* The outcome of the failure of the Central Pacific to redeem at maturity the U.S. government bonds lent it to build the line in the 1860s has generally been neglected in favor of the more exciting Union Pacific story; but see Stuart Daggett, *Chapters on the Southern Pacific*, which reveals the true stature of much-abused Collis P. Huntington. Albro Martin, *James J. Hill and the Opening of the Northwest* (1976), based on Hill's voluminous papers and the Great Northern archives, is now the standard work. There is no equally complete study of Edward H. Harriman, and probably will never be because his papers were destroyed in a fire; but see Lloyd J. Mercer, *E. H. Harriman—Master Railroader* (1985). James B. Hedges, *Henry Villard and the Railways of the Northwest* (1930), is still valuable but needs bringing up to date for this complicated man, in whom there was both more and less than meets the eye. For a much-needed and fascinating reconsideration of the very real contributions of Jay Gould to the emergence of modern railroad systems, see Maury Klein's *Life and Legend of Jay Gould* (Baltimore 1986).

No one has ever bothered to write a biography of William H. Vanderbilt, but one especially stimulating popular writer on transportation topics in the middle years of this century, Alvin F. Harlow, discusses W. H.'s career in *Road of the Century—The Story of the New York Central* (1947). For J. P. Morgan's role in the Central stock offering, see Vincent P. Carosso, *The Morgans: Private International Bankers, 1854–1913* (1987), pp. 230–34. Both Charles E. Perkins and Ralph Budd are admirably memorialized and analysed in Richard C. Overton, *Perkins/Budd, Railway Statesmen of the Burlington* (1982). Daniel Willard receives copious praise, most of it fully deserved, in *Daniel Willard Rides the Line: The Story of a Great Railroad Man* (1938) by Edward Hungerford, who also wrote a big two-volume anniversary history of the Baltimore & Ohio Railroad; but Stover, *B. & O.*, is more definitive. Both are cited elsewhere herein. Biographies of John Budd and L. Stanley Crane, and many others in public and private life who participated in the deregulation revolution, must await the long-term outcome of this development. By their fruits, we shall know them.

12. New Jobs To Do, New People To Do Them

Two recent books are improvements upon traditional labor history, in that they place the workers more directly in the context of American social and economic development. Walter Licht, *Working for the Railroad: The Organization of Work in the 19th Century* (1983), is especially good on the railroads as one of the first developments that presented the U.S. with the problems associated with large numbers of men working for a wage in a large enterprise. Shelton Stromquist, *A Generation of Boomers: The Pattern of Railroad Labor Conflict in the 19th Century* (1987), is handicapped somewhat by a leading thesis that western railroads had rather different labor problems from their eastern counterparts, but it clarifies what it was in the lives of railroad men that caused such discontent. *The American Railway* (1889, repr. 1988), includes excellent essays on railway labor viewed from the peak years of railroad expansion. *Railroad Facts*, published annually by the Association of American Railroads, is a convenient source of data on wages paid as reported by the carriers to the ICC.

Donald L. McMurray, *The Great Burlington Strike of 1888: A Case History of Industrial Relations* (1956), is the best study of a strike carried to the finish by a major railroad brotherhood against a financially strong railroad; but, like virtually all labor history, it lacks any substantial analysis of the economic merits of the strikers' demands, thus allowing the men to win the moral argument by default. Robert V. Bruce, *1877: Year of Violence* (1959), is a graphic account of the consequences of a grass-roots action that became a general riot. Two books demonstrate what can happen when a born loser and pig-headed industrialist collide: Ray Ginger, *The Bending Cross—A Biography of Eugene V. Debs* (1949) and Almont Lindsey, *The Pullman Strike* (1942). Frank Wilner, "The Railway Labor Act: Why, What, and for How Much Longer," 55 *Transportation Practitioners' Journal* 242–87 (Spring 1988) is the most comprehensive and best informed source on labor relations laws enacted specifically to deal with the railroads. At this writing, Part II, dealing with the shortcomings of the present arrangements for preserving the equitable rights of railroads and their employees, was in press at *Transportation Practitioners' Journal*.

13. Lawyers, Bankers, and "Real" Railroad Men

Historians of American law have not traditionally given much attention to the social, economic, or even political background of the laws and judicial decisions they elucidate. See, for example, Lawrence M. Friedman, *A History of American Law* (rev. ed., 1985). A major breakthrough in legal history came with J. Willard Hurst, *Law and the Conditions of Freedom in the 19th Century* (1956), in which he perceives that the imperatives of human existence are the raw material out of which laws, legal systems, and judicial philosophies are made, and not vice versa. Hurst's influence is clearly seen in younger scholars, for example, Morton Horwitz, *The Transformation of American Law, 1780–1960* (1977). Tony Freyer, *Forums of Order: The Federal Courts and Business in American History* (1979), is an excellent study of the rise of federal court supremacy in cases of "diversity" of state "citizenship" in the litigants. Although Freyer was criticized for not giving more emphasis to the decline of the concept of a "federal common law" in the first half of this century, many are ready to conclude that the iron curtain between state and federal judicial systems is rapidly rusting away. John L. Larson, *Bonds of Enterprise: John Murray Forbes and Western Development in America's Railway Age* (1984), is the best study I have seen of the inevitable entanglements with local and state politics that sapped so much of the energy and resources of nineteenth century railroad builders. The hackneyed view of the U.S. Supreme Court in the late nineteenth century as dominated by a laissez-faire philosophy and a bias in favor of propertied interests no longer serves. Albro Martin showed in "Troubled Subject of Railroad Regulation in the Gilded Age" (cited elsewhere herein) that in the *Maximum Rate Case* the Court was merely refusing to allow the ICC to exercise a power that Congress had not specifically granted it. Charles W. McCurdy, in "The Knight Sugar Decision of 1895 and the Modernization of American Corporate Law, 1869–1903," 53 *Business History Review* 304–42 (Autumn 1979), shows that the court was not motivated by a desire to protect the trusts but, rather, wished to preserve some aspects of antitrust enforcement to the state courts. As Martin further points out in "Troubled Subject," some of the first big antitrust cases decided by the Court went against railroad men's efforts to establish jointly-agreed-upon rate schedules.

Carl Sandburg, *Abraham Lincoln, The Prairie Years* (vol. 2, 1926), 37–38, is good on Lincoln as a railroad lawyer, but, for the *Effie Afton* case and how Lincoln built his case, see William Edward Hayes, *Iron Road to Empire: The History of the Rock Island Lines* (1953), 46–49. For the innovative use of the equity receivership to keep financially troubled railroads in business, see Albro Martin, "Railroads and the Equity Receivership: An Essay on Institutional Change," 34 *Journal of Economic History* 685–709 (September 1974), but also see Charles F. Beach, Jr., *Commentaries on the Law of Receivers* (1887, 2nd ed. 1897), for the contemporary reaction of practicing attorneys to the Wabash case.

There are many examples of important railroad executives, themselves "real railroad men," who worked closely with brilliant lawyers who took the time to learn their clients' business thoroughly, and were frequently involved as coentrepreneurs. Keith L. Bryant, *History of the Atchison, Topeka & Santa Fe Railway* (1974), is especially good on the companion roles of Victor Morawetz and Edward P. Ripley in reorganizing, rebuilding, and managing the growth of this important southwestern transcontinental railroad. Morawetz's remarkable career, which ended once government intervention froze all real discretionary power in the Interstate Commerce Commission, can be glimpsed in his earliest work, a massive two-volume study of corporation law, *The Law of Private Corporations* (1882), and in his valedictory to a much-confused industry, *Solution of the Railway Problem* (1920). Another transcontinental, the Union Pacific, benefited greatly from the close relationship established between the top man and a lawyer. In 1904 Edward H. Harriman took note of Robert S. Lovett, a highly successful Houston, Texas, lawyer, and the two worked together closely to make the U.P. the strongest of the transcontinentals. Unfortunately no satisfactory biographies exist of any of these men. Maury Klein, *Union Pacific*, cited elsewhere herein, discusses Lovett, who took control of the Harriman railroad properties at E. H.'s death.

14. It's all Politics!

Lewis E. Gould, "The Republican Search for a National Majority," in H. Wayne Morgan, ed., *The Gilded Age* (rev. ed., 1970), is not merely the best interpretation of American national politics at the critical juncture of the turn of the century, but just about the only one that cuts through the old image of Republicans as plutocrats. Stuart Daggett, *Railroad Reorganization* (1908), is the best source on the 1890's recasting of the American railroad system. It may be a classic example of old-fashioned institutional economics, but it will be useful long after many an econometric fatuity has been forgotten. The quotation from the *Commercial and Financial Chronicle (CFC)* about the return of prosperity to the railroads at the end of the 1890s depression is in 65 *CFC* 1145 (December 18, 1897). Cassatt's statement about inflation, higher wages, and overweening traffic volume is in the *New York Times*, November 14, 1902. For the views of the *CFC* editor on the need for some stabilizing force in railroad rate levels, see 27 *CFC* 186 (August 24, 1879).

A fascinating and revealing historical essay that for some reason has remained unpublished all these years is Kenneth Templeton's M.A. thesis at the University of Wisconsin (1950), "A Philosophy of American Capitalism," chapter 2 of which treats the activities of Edward Bacon and his Interstate Commerce Law Convention in the agitation for an ICC with powers to fix specific maximum railroad rates. For Theodore Roosevelt's idealistic notion of the ICC as an economic planning commission, and his earnest desire to keep it from becoming merely another federal court in thrall to the principle of *stare decisis,* see Elting E. Morison, ed., *The Letters of Theodore Roosevelt* (8 vols., 1951–1954), vol. 5, 566. Henry Carter Adams's *Digest of Hearings* elsewhere cited herein, is a concise explanation of the system of rate-making established by American railroads in the late nineteenth century, as subsequently modified.

Historians, especially those who face the impossible task of cramming American history into a single volume for the edification of college freshmen who will probably not read another word of history for the rest of their lives— if, indeed, they read the textbook—have generally made the heroic assumption that once "right thinking" was embodied in regulatory statutes, the best of all possible worlds resulted. The question of the *outcome* of regulation has often been avoided, especially when the results are as dubious as those produced by much reform legislation. But see John H. Churchman, "Federal Regulation of Railroad Rates, 1880–1898," unpublished doctoral dissertation at the University of Wisconsin (Madison), (1976); Albro Martin, *Enterprise Denied: Origins of the Decline of American Railroads, 1897–1917* (1971); and, for state regulation, Stanley P. Caine, *The Myth of a Progressive Reform: Railroad Regulation in Wisconsin, 1903–1910* (1970).

The maturing of vehicular freight transportation and the failure of Americans to integrate it intelligently with the older rail mode are highly technical subjects that few attack and almost none fully understand. William R. Childs, *Trucking and the Public Interest: The Emergence of Federal Regulation, 1914–1940* (1985), is something of a disappointment, although one must not criticize a scholar for not writing the book that the reader hoped for. Childs presents long-distance trucking as a fundamentally constructive development and discusses the excessive entry by firms and resulting sweated conditions that led to the inclusion of truckers under regulation, after a painfully long time, in 1935. He assumes that trucking brought "healthy competition"—a term that means all things to all men and women—and views integration of trucking by the railroads as meaning simple entry into the trucking business, which of course is not integration at all. Childs gives no hint of the coming revolution in all forms of transportation. His chapter 2, "Railroads, Truck Terminals, and Gypsies," however, is a chilling confirmation of the inherently sweated nature of trucking— but a "good read." Apparently little has changed in the trucking industry in the last sixty years except the size, weight, and speed of the rigs.

Much more instructive is Ernest Williams, *The Regulation of Rail-Motor Rate Competition* (1958), which demonstrates conclusively that public policy as practiced amounted to little more than "keeping everybody in business." On early efforts at containerization and "piggybacking," John H. White, Jr., "The Magic Box: Genesis of the Container," 158 *Railroad History* 13–93, contains fascinating technological detail, but is inadequate, even dismissive, on socio-economic-political factors that killed early COFC/TOFC and are the heart of the matter.

George Edgar Turner, *Victory Rode the Rails: The Strategic Place of the Railroads in the Civil War* (1953), is excellent on this absorbing subject. No similar study has been produced for World War II, although I suspect that such a rich subject—it was, after all, the last war in which railroads are likely to rule in logistical matters—will not have to wait much longer.

15. Enterprise Triumphant

The late Kent T. Healy, professor emeritus of transportation at Yale University, who was deeply involved in the electrification of the New Haven and Pennsylvania Railroads in the 1920s and 1930s, delivered his valedictory in *Performance of the U.S. Railroads Since World War II* (1985). Although unduly pessimistic, it is an excellent statistical survey of the railroads' efforts to stay alive in the dark days of the 1950s, 1960s, and 1970s and is especially good on the loss, apparently permanent, of less-than-carload freight. Charles F. Phillips, Jr., *The Economics of Regulation* (1969), is head and shoulders above other textbooks on transportation, especially his final chapter. Marver H. Bernstein, *Regulating Business by Independent Commission* (1955) made a hit with his "stages of man" approach to understanding the behavior of commissions over time, but experience has shown that tinkering with our public administration machinery is not the road to a more efficient or equitable society, notwithstanding the huge sums we continue to waste on "schools of government." Learned treatises on how to create, operate, and make suitably repressive various collections of *apparatchiks* seem strangely out of place in the deadly serious game of making America the competitive player in world industry, commerce, and finance that it should be. James M. Landis's aimless speculation on new administrative machinery in *Report on Regulatory Agencies to the President-Elect* (1960), was of little use to John F. Kennedy, who was busy learning that he could not even reorganize and reform the Department of State. The report, however, contains abundant evidence of the approaching crisis in transportation.

There is no good synthesis of American life since 1945, probably because the great controversial issues that grew up with remarkable speed once postwar material wants were largely satisfied are more controversial than ever. The growing activism of the railroads, as specifically demonstrated in the Big John and ingot mold cases, is fully analyzed in Phillips, cited elsewhere herein, pages 375–84. Ann F. Friedlaender, *The Dilemma of Freight Transport Regulation* (1969), is the first solid evidence I have seen that professional specialists were beginning to line up against traditional regulation. Richard Saunders, *The Railroad Mergers and the Coming of Conrail* (1978), is a good narrative of the short-lived merger of the Erie and the Lackawanna Railroads, proving once more that corporate mergers, by themselves, accomplish nothing. A searing account of the progressive demoralization of Penn Central, based on private papers of the chief financial officer and interviews with him, is Stephen Salsbury, *No Way to Run a Railroad—The Untold Story of the Penn Central* (New York, 1982). The National Transportation Policy Study Commission, an arm that the U.S. Congress sprouted, no doubt in a desperate search for common-sense counsel, produced a valuable report, *National Transportation Policies Through the Year 2000* (1979). It is good that the National Policy Study Commission existed, to bring the matter of business regulation back to the legislative branch, where it belongs. This is one commission whose members can say with assurance, "We seen our duty and we done it." It should be revived from time to time in the future. Meanwhile, the best books—and reports—on railroads have yet to be written.

Statistical Note

The United States has the finest transportation statistics of any nation in the world, and we are gradually developing an inclination to live by them in the formation of public policy. Federal and state governments, trade associations, and private sources produce numerous reports on both general operating and financial results and specialized topics, permitting conclusions about national policy that go beyond the boundaries of any one transportation medium. For railroad history, the *Statistics of the Railways of the United States*, published annually by the Interstate Commerce Commission since 1888, is basic. A fascinating statistical look primarily at U.S. railroads on the eve of the era of greatest extensive development is in the U.S. Census of 1880, a huge volume with the impressive title, *Report on the Agencies of Transportation in the United States, Including the Statistics of Railroads, Steam Navigation, Canals, Telegraphs, and Telephones* (Washington, 1883).

Index

Accidents, 88
Adams, Charles F., Jr., 160, 193, 287, 339
Adams, Henry, 78, 201, 215, 355
Adams, John Quincy, 4
Agriculture, 169, 188, 189
Air (train) brake, 20
Air coach fares, 128
Air travel, 375
Alabama Midland case (1897), 328
Aldrich, Nelson W., 350
"All [what] the traffic will bear," 201
Alton Midnight, 63
"American *perestroika*," 390
American Railway Union, 313
American Society of Civil Engineers, 256
American-type locomotive, introduced, 255
Ames, Oakes, 283–87
Ames, Oliver, 283
Amtrak (National Rail Passenger System), 129–31, 141–43, 345, 378
Anderson–Clayton Co., 183
Anthracite (hard) coal: railroads of, 15; region, early, 133; first shipment, 139; limited use in locomotives, 143; strike (1901), 155; decline after 1930, 155–56; and plant location, 219–20
Anthracite railroads, 251–52
Anti-railroad sentiment, growth of, 353–54
Appalachian barrier, 7
Armour, Philip D., 178, 279
Ashtabula (Ohio) train wreck, 56
Atchison, Topeka & Santa Fe RR, 74, 336–37
Atlantic, Mississippi, & Ohio (Norfolk & Western) RR, 147
Atterbury, W. W., 296
Automobile travel, 108, 126–27

Bacon, Edward, 351–53
Bacon, Robert, 335
Baldwin Locomotive Works, 370
Baltimore (City of), 249–50
Baltimore & Ohio (B&O) RR: cornerstone laid, 1; adopts steam, 14; construction

delayed in 1840s, 17; falls behind competitors, 27–28; *Royal Blue* (passenger train) line, 64; East-West through trains, 73; extended to Pa. coking coal fields, 138; completes 3rd trunk line to West, 169; and steel industry, 224; early years under Latrobe, 257–60; reaches Pittsburgh, 259; Baltimore pageant 1928, 299
Bankruptcy laws, 374–75
Barriger, John W., III, 304
Beardstown (Ill.), 165
Beech Creek (New York Central) RR, 150
Beer, Thomas, 186
Belt-line RRs, rise of, 237–38
Berwind, E. J., 183
Bessemer, Sir Henry, 137, 197, 223
Bessemer rails, brittleness of,102–3
"Best Friend of Charleston" (locomotive), 14
Biddle, Edward, 251
Big business, emergence of, 217–18
"Big Four" (Cleveland, Cincinnati, Chicago & St. Louis RR), 69
"Big John" case, 378–80
Bill of lading, through, evolution of, 202
Billings, Frederick C., 292
Bituminous coal, 137–38
Black Pullman travelers in South, 87
Blanchard, George R., 217
"Blind pool," 292
Blizzard of 1888, 111
Bluefield (W.Va.), 146–47
Boosterism, 328
Borah, William E., 350
Boston & Albany RR, 44
Boston & Erie RR, 67
Boston & Lowell RR, 15, 43
Boston & Providence RR, 15
Boston & Worcester RR, 15, 44, 228, 250
Box cars, replaced by containers, 392–93
Branch lines, significance of, 273–74
Brandeis, Louis, 102–3, 343–44, 354, 360
Bribes, 330
Bridges, U.S., early, 37–38, 48
Bright, Henry A., 50
Bristow, Benjamin, 350

417